Service Science and Logistics Informatics:

Innovative Perspectives

ZongWei Luo
The University of Hong Kong, China

A volume in the Advances in Logistics,
Operations, and Management Science
(ALOMS) Book Series

Information Science
REFERENCE
An Imprint of IGI Global

Director of Editorial Content:	Kristin Klinger
Director of Book Publications:	Julia Mosemann
Acquisitions Editor:	Lindsay Johnston
Development Editor:	Joel Gamon
Publishing Assistant:	Deanna Jo Zombro
Typesetter:	Keith Glazewski
Production Editor:	Jamie Snavely
Cover Design:	Lisa Tosheff

Published in the United States of America by
Information Science Reference (an imprint of IGI Global)
701 E. Chocolate Avenue
Hershey PA 17033
Tel: 717-533-8845
Fax: 717-533-8661
E-mail: cust@igi-global.com
Web site: http://www.igi-global.com

Library of Congress Cataloging-in-Publication Data

Service science and logistics informatics : innovative perspectives / Zongwei Luo, editor.
     p. cm.
  Includes bibliographical references and index.
  Summary: "This book provides both business and IT professionals a reference for practices and guidelines to service innovation in logistics and supply chain management"--Provided by publisher.
  ISBN 978-1-61520-603-2 (hbk.) -- ISBN 978-1-61520-604-9 (ebook) 1. Business logistics--Information technology. 2. Service industries--Information technology. I. Luo, Zongwei, 1971-
  HD38.5.S497 2010
  658.500285--dc22
                                    2009047131

This book is published in the IGI Global book series Advances in Logistics, Operations, and Management Science (ALOMS) Book Series (ISSN: 2327-350X; eISSN: 2327-3518).

British Cataloguing in Publication Data
A Cataloguing in Publication record for this book is available from the British Library.

Advances in Logistics, Operations, and Management Science (ALOMS) Book Series

John Wang
Montclair State University, USA

ISSN: 2327-350X
EISSN: 2327-3518

MISSION

Operations research and management science continue to influence business processes, administration, and management information systems, particularly in covering the application methods for decision-making processes. New case studies and applications on management science, operations management, social sciences, and other behavioral sciences have been incorporated into business and organizations real-world objectives.

The **Advances in Logistics, Operations, and Management Science** (ALOMS) Book Series provides a collection of reference publications on the current trends, applications, theories, and practices in the management science field. Providing relevant and current research, this series and its individual publications would be useful for academics, researchers, scholars, and practitioners interested in improving decision making models and business functions.

COVERAGE

- Computing and Information Technologies
- Decision Analysis and Decision Support
- Finance
- Information Management
- Marketing Engineering
- Operations Management
- Organizational Behavior
- Political Science
- Production Management
- Services Management

IGI Global is currently accepting manuscripts for publication within this series. To submit a proposal for a volume in this series, please contact our Acquisition Editors at Acquisitions@igi-global.com or visit: http://www.igi-global.com/publish/.

Titles in this Series

For a list of additional titles in this series, please visit: www.igi-global.com

Outsourcing Management for Supply Chain Operations and Logistics Service
Dimitris Folinas (Department of Logistics, ATEI-Thessaloniki, Greece)
Business Science Reference • copyright 2013 • 596pp • H/C (ISBN: 9781466620087) • US $185.00 (our price)

Operations Management Research and Cellular Manufacturing Systems Innovative Methods and Approaches
Vladimir Modrák (Technical University of Kosice, Slovakia) and R. Sudhakara Pandian (Kalasalingam University, India)
Business Science Reference • copyright 2012 • 368pp • H/C (ISBN: 9781613500477) • US $185.00 (our price)

Fashion Supply Chain Management Industry and Business Analysis
Tsan-Ming Choi (The Hong Kong Polytechnic University, Hong Kong)
Information Science Reference • copyright 2012 • 392pp • H/C (ISBN: 9781609607562) • US $195.00 (our price)

Supply Chain Optimization, Design, and Management Advances and Intelligent Methods
Ioannis Minis (University of the Aegean, Greece) Vasileios Zeimpekis (University of the Aegean, Greece) Georgios Dounias (University of the Aegean, Greece) and Nicholas Ampazis (University of the Aegean, Greece)
Business Science Reference • copyright 2011 • 338pp • H/C (ISBN: 9781615206339) • US $180.00 (our price)

Quality Management for IT Services Perspectives on Business and Process Performance
Claus-Peter Praeg (Fraunhofer Institute for Industrial Engineering, Germany) and Dieter Spath (Fraunhofer Institute for Industrial Engineering, Germany)
Business Science Reference • copyright 2011 • 348pp • H/C (ISBN: 9781616928896) • US $180.00 (our price)

Managing Risk in Virtual Enterprise Networks Implementing Supply Chain Principles
Stavros Ponis (National Technical University of Athens, Greece)
Business Science Reference • copyright 2010 • 408pp • H/C (ISBN: 9781615206070) • US $180.00 (our price)

Service Science and Logistics Informatics Innovative Perspectives
ZongWei Luo (The University of Hong Kong, China)
Information Science Reference • copyright 2010 • 462pp • H/C (ISBN: 9781615206032) • US $180.00 (our price)

www.igi-global.com

701 E. Chocolate Ave., Hershey, PA 17033
Order online at www.igi-global.com or call 717-533-8845 x100
To place a standing order for titles released in this series, contact: cust@igi-global.com
Mon-Fri 8:00 am - 5:00 pm (est) or fax 24 hours a day 717-533-8661

List of Reviewers

Edgar E. Blanco, *Massachusetts Institute of Technology, USA*
Kevin Cullinane, *Edinburgh Napier University, UK*
Henry Fan, *Nanyang Technological University, Singapore*
Hans-Dietrich Hassis, *University of Bremen, Germany*
Frank Straube, *TU Berlin, Germany*
Chelsea C. White III, *Georgia Institute of Technology, USA*
Xiong Youlung, *Huazhong University of Science and Technology, China*
Jose Humberto Ablanedo Rosas, *University of Texas at El Paso, USA*
Evon Abu-Taieh, *Arab Academy for Banking and Financial Sciences, Jordan*
Mohammad M Amini, *The University of Memphis, USA*
Frank Arendt, *ISL Institute of Shipping Economics and Logistics, Germany*
Gildas Avoine, *Universit catholique de Louvain, Belgium*
Indranil Bose, *University of Hong Kong, Hong Kong*
Miguel Gasto Cedillo-Campos, *Supply Chain Research and Development Center, Mexico*
Naoufel Cheikhrouhou, *Ecole Polytechnique Fedrale de Lausanne, Switzerland*
Weiping Chen, *Virginia Tech, USA*
Paul Chou, *IBM Thomas J. Watson Research Center, USA*
Kim Seung Chul, *Hanyang University, Korea*
Christophe Claramunt, *Naval Academy Research Institute, France*
Fragniere Emmanuel, *Haute Ecole de Gestion de Genève, Switzerland*
Yulian Fei, *Zhejiang Gongshang University, China*
Samuel Fosso Wamba, *University of Wollongong, Australia*
GR Gangadharan, *Novay, The Netherlands*
Xin Guo, *University of California - Berkeley, USA*
Byung-In Kim, *Pohang University of Science and Technology (POSTECH), Korea*
Sheung-Kown Kim, *Korea University, Korea*
Danuta Kisperska-Moron, *Karol Adamiecki University of Economics, Poland*
Senthil Kumar, *CMS College of Science and Commerce, India*
Andrew Lim, *City University of Hong Kong, Hong Kong*
Chad Lin, *Curtin University of Technology, Australia*
Miao Lixing, *Tsinghua University, China*
Dubosson Magali, *Haute Ecole de Gestion de Genève, Switzerland*

Table of Contents

Section 1
Innovation Strategies and Mechanisms

> Bikem Turkeli, Marmara University, Turkey
> Alp Ariburnu, Marmara University, Turkey
> Ozalp Vayvay, Marmara University, Turkey

> Zhang Mu, Jinan University, China
> Li Wenli, Jinan University, China
> Luo Jing, Jinan University, China
> Ye Xiang, Jinan University, China
> Ren Congying, Jinan University, China
> Wu Chengjuan, Jinan University, China

Section 2
Logistics and Service Innovation

> Martin R. Fellenz, Trinity College Dublin, Ireland
> Mairead Brady, Trinity College Dublin, Ireland

Section 3
Logistics Informatics and Information Logistics

Section 4
Service Sourcing and Supplier Management

Section 5
Service Management in Industries

Section 6
Industry Service Models, Profession Development and Outlook

Detailed Table of Contents

Section 1
Innovation Strategies and Mechanisms

> *Bikem Turkeli, Marmara University, Turkey*
> *Alp Ariburnu, Marmara University, Turkey*
> *Ozalp Vayvay, Marmara University, Turkey*

In this chapter, innovative strategies for logistics processes that can be used practically in business environment are mentioned. For each innovative strategy title, tools that can be used to innovate operations are presented. By innovating logistics processes, logistics providers can fulfill customer needs rapidly and increase their profit because of having competitive advantage.

> *Zhang Mu, Jinan University, China*
> *Li Wenli, Jinan University, China*
> *Luo Jing, Jinan University, China*
> *Ye Xiang, Jinan University, China*
> *Ren Congying, Jinan University, China*
> *Wu Chengjuan, Jinan University, China*

A real case is selected for Shenzhen China Overseas Logistics Co. LTD (COL) as the empirical objects to analyze its character of the technology and non-technology innovation, and summarize its inner and outer driving force on promoting the service innovation. Thereafter, the typical service innovative model based on innovative driving force has been discussed.

Section 2
Logistics and Service Innovation

Chapter 3

Martin R. Fellenz, Trinity College Dublin, Ireland
Mairead Brady, Trinity College Dublin, Ireland

This chapter reviews the difficulties inherent in using ICTs to manage customer-related information, and identifies the particular challenges for customer-centric deployment of ICTs. It provides a model of different levels of customer centric information use in organizations which helps understand how companies can become more customer centric in their information use. It reviews implications for future research in this emerging area and concludes that the challenges of ICT deployment and use must be addressed with an uncompromising focus on customer value as the central principle of both ICT design and deployment, and of information management in service organizations.

Chapter 4

Gong Li, North Dakota State University, USA
Jing Shi, North Dakota State University, USA

This chapter provides an overview about wireless sensor network technology (WSN), how this technology can be applied to modern industries and especially bring service innovation to supply chain management. The impact of information technologies on supply chain management and service innovation is discussed. Two case studies are provided to illustrate the application of WSN for service innovation in both cold chain management and healthcare settings.

Chapter 5

Han Tao, Shanghai Jiao Tong University, China
Shui Yongan, Shanghai Jiao Tong University, China

It overviews a complementary technology to the integrated circuit based radio frequency identification (RFID) - surface acoustic wave (SAW) based RFID. The fundamental principle and applications of SAW RFID are presented. In order to guarantee the encoding capacity and reliable reading range, the design criteria in coding scheme, tag design and a time domain interrogated reader design are discussed in detail.

Section 3
Logistics Informatics and Information Logistics

     Ulla Tapaninen, Merikotka Research Center, Finland
     Hennariina Pulli, Merikotka Research Center, Finland
     Antti Posti, Merikotka Research Center, Finland

This chapter studies is on logistics service providers (LSPs) that are representatives of typical Finnish supply chains. The purpose of the chapter is to point out the current level of information sharing in supply chains focusing on the information needs of logistics companies, particularly from the LSP's point of view. It revealed that there is a lack of logistics information in the supply chain. The information distribution should be intensified when aiming at achieving a more efficient supply chain.

     Malgorzata Pankowska, University of Economics, Katowice, Poland

It is focused on how information logistics in business organization is supported by standards and best practices of auditing. CobiT, ITIL, ISO/IEC 27002, Val IT as well as the Sarbanes-Oxley Act and ITAF model are analyzed in the aspect of information logistics.

     Roman Gumzej, University of Maribor, Slovenia
     Martin Lipičnik, University of Maribor, Slovenia

In a time, when the "economic crisis" is filling the news, it may seem hard to even think about improvements in terms of research and development, since "there are lacking funds even for the reproduction". However, also the last economic "revolution" was "born" in a crisis. Therefore it is sensible to look at the current situation as an opportunity for the next economic revolution, bringing the economy a new cycle of development.

     Masayuki Ueda, Sapporo University, Japan

The OR/MS decision support is investigated from a new viewpoint of service. It is shown that OR/MS decision support shares characteristics with service and hence can be considered as a kind of service. It turns out that there is surely a problem with communication gap between decision makers and decision supporters. It is effective to utilize "problem specification", which is a decision-maker-friendly description of problems, as one approach to bridge the communication gap.

Section 4
Service Sourcing and Supplier Management

Chapter 10
   Albalicia Martínez Hernández, Universidad Tecnológica de Torreón, Mexico
   Mario Cantú Sifuentes, Corporación Mexicana de Investigación en Materiales, S.A.
      de C.V. Mexico
   Miguel Gastón Cedillo Campos, Tecnológico de Monterrey, Mexico

The quality of service is certainly a complex topic that many companies, although interested in the subject, difficult to address. It is important to define and detect both internal and external suppliers, as well as the cycles and stages of services in which the organization has a close interrelationship with them. In these stages, it is critical to assess the quality of services provided by suppliers.

Chapter 11
   G.R. Gangadharan, Novay, The Netherlands
   Erwin Fielt, Queensland University of Technology, Australia

The sourcing requirements are identified for software based services (SBS) and associate the key characteristics of SBS (with the sourcing requirements introduced). Furthermore, the sourcing of SBS is investigated with the related works in the field of classical procurement, business process outsourcing, and information systems sourcing. Based on the analysis, it is concluded that the direct adoption of these approaches for SBS is not feasible and new approaches are required for sourcing SBS.

Chapter 12
   Tobias Mettler, University of St. Gallen, Switzerland & SAP Research St. Gallen, Switzerland
   Peter Rohner, University of St. Gallen, Switzerland

In this chapter the current findings are adapted on supplier relationship management (SRM) to the health care context. On the basis of a case study a future scenario is developed for drugs supply management and discusses potential performance and quality improvements.

Section 5
Service Management in Industries

Chapter 13
   Joyce M.W Low, National University of Singapore, Singapore
   Loon Ching Tang, National University of Singapore, Singapore
   Xue-Ming Yuan, Singapore Institute of Manufacturing Technology, Singapore

Findings from this chapter show that while conducive economic conditions continue to play a critical role in stimulating demand for cargo service at the airports, the importance of physical architecture has also dramatically risen relative to human factors. Particularly, adequate provisions and utilizations of physical facilities for landside operations appear to be a more significant driving force for demand of an airport's cargo service compared to those of airside operations. Despite the strong emphasis on swift and reliable services, cost savings are found to have regained their importance in the recent years.

Service level agreement (SLA) is becoming an increasingly sought-after topic in recent years, as complex logistics and service chains span across geographical boundaries in the lights of globalization and new technological developments. This chapter introduces the state of the art of the lifecycle management of SLA for service enterprises, which covers stages of terms optimization, contract drafting and compliance tracking. In particular, the deficiencies are identified in the area of term optimization and outline several R&D tracks that would lead to the development of industry-strength SLA optimization capabilities.

Chapter 15

In today's global economy, products and services are provided across international borders. While the big companies have the ICTT resources to source globally at will, small and medium enterprises (SME) are much less prepared to do so, resulting in a large competitive disadvantage. By contrasting SMEs with their more successful "big brothers," the salient ICTT features are highlighted in system architecture as a checklist for any assistance that might be rendered to SMEs and other entities in overcoming their competitive impediment. These findings are the result of numerous international workshops and conferences held in Hong Kong and in Arkansas in the headquarters of Wal-Mart.

Section 6
Industry Service Models, Profession Development and Outlook

This chapter holds the potential to contribute to extending an understanding and management capacity of customer-perceived risks of knowledge-based services. It brings into play a new framework and new risk management process. It also helps with formalizing and making tangible customer added-value.

In this chapter attention is focused on the container terminal optimization problem, given that today most international cargo is transported through seaports and on containerized vessels. In this context, in order to manage a container terminal it is sometimes necessary to develop a Decision Support System (DSS). This chapter investigated the prediction reliability of container terminal simulation models (DSS), through a before and after analysis, taking advantage of some significant investment made by the Salerno Container Terminal (Italy) between 2003 and 2008.

Chapter 18

This chapter argues that an obstacle to business process (re)engineering is the lack of a business process engineer role with an associated professional education, tools, and community. There is an urgent need for a professional business process engineer. In the chapter, it is discussed the skills required of this profession and a first course offered at a university on this subject is briefly described.

Chapter 19

The dynamics of change and the path-dependent evolution of resources and capabilities are central concerns of contemporary strategic management. Companies tend to concentrate scares resources into their core competences. Opportunity, speed, product choices and availability are intangibles that customer value, some times more than the price.

Foreword

"Service Science and Logistics Informatics: Innovative Perspectives" - the title of this book combines the three major challenges in modern logistics and supply chain management; Services, informatics and innovation. These enablers influence mainly the success of business logistics both on a regional level as well as on an international level. They have to be designed and operated having in mind that world trade flows are interconnected and modifiable. Logistics has to ensure distributed production in a dynamic environment on a regional and on a global scale. In line with this, especially the service sector has been playing an increasingly important role in world economy. New businesses, new distributions of tasks and new value added services in international supply chain networks have occurred and will occur in future. Moreover, new innovative control philosophies for logistics operations based on the realization of IT based autonomous decentralized cooperating systems will improve the logistics efficiency in the next years. These developments are confronted with present and future challenges on climate change as well as on international security aspects. Moreover a sustainable trade off between business and living, production and logistics has to be found. The quality of the design and sustainable operation of these relations, and by this, of the innovative design and management of services, can be supported by knowledge management between decision makers as well as common learning.

This book provides updated materials disclosing innovative findings for applied research and development in the interdisciplinary fields between service science and logistics informatics. It covers chapters entitled innovation strategies, service innovation, services sourcing and industry service models. By this, it aims to provide researchers, practitioners, and academicians with insight into selected yet important topics relevant to logistics and supply chain industries. It provides both business and IT professionals a reference for practices and guidelines to service innovation in logistics and supply chain management. As a first of its kind, this book addresses latest applied service science research and industry practices on emerging enabling technologies including RFID, service innovations in logistics and supply chain management, and the transformations of a more efficient economy. The book, built on an excellent portfolio of accepted chapters, including the observations and reports on the world's biggest retailers, world's busiest airports, and world's most dynamic regions, to introduce service innovation in modernizing logistics and supply chain management, serve as a prestigious reference to disseminate the state of the art research, development, and advances of service innovation in logistics and supply chain management.

Hans-Dietrich Haasis
Institute of Shipping Economics and Logistics, Germany

Hans-Dietrich Haasis *studied industrial engineering. He graduated in 1987 and promoted in 1993 to professor at the University of Karlsruhe. Since 1994 he is full professor for Business Administration, Production Management and Industrial Engineering at the University of Bremen. From July 1998 until 2001 he was dean of the department of economics. Moreover, since 2001 he is director of the ISL - Institute of Shipping Economics and Logistics, Bremen. Professor Haasis is author and co-author as well as editor and co-editor of 15 monographs and proceedings. In addition, he has published more than 50 contributions in scientific journals as well as proceedings and collections. He is amongst others member of the Council of Supply Chain Management Professionals, as well as member of the Editorial Board of „Logistics Research", and member of the Editorial Review Board of the „International Journal of Operations and Quantitative Management" and the "International Journal of Applied Logistics".*

Foreword

As world economy gets increasingly integrated, logistics and supply chain management, through the use of advanced information and service technologies, become critically important. This requirement entails tight alignment of business strategy and judicious use of advanced information technologies. It also necessitates infrastructures for streamlining front-end and back-end management and business processes, and resolution of emerging global integration and inter-operability issues. Logistics and SCM services must also address critical needs for a variety of industries in the entire supply chain from manufacturing sites to the retail users everywhere.

The recent emergence of enabling technologies including RFID and other advanced technologies have further aroused interests in people to look into innovative ways to reengineer traditional services in logistics and supply chain management. This book comes at just the right time, providing latest innovative findings for applied research and development in the interdisciplinary fields between service science and logistics informatics. It is a must read for researchers, practitioners, and academicians who are looking for insights in topics relevant to logistics and supply chain industries.

This book is also essential for anyone who desires for references for practices and guidelines to service innovations in logistics and supply chain management. It addresses latest applied service science research and industry practices on emerging enabling technologies to enhance competitiveness towards an efficient and sustainable knowledge-driven economy.

The new interdisciplinary field of service science and logistics informatics yet has a lot more to be discovered. This book also serves as a useful reference for practical applications with coverage on hotspot observations, reports on world biggest retailers and busiest airports. It sure will arouse people's interests and serves as an excellent basis for the development of this new interdisciplinary field of service science and logistics informatics.

Loon Ching Tan
Hon Kong University, Hong Kong

Prof Tan is the Chief Executive Officer of the Hong Kong R&D Center for Logistics and Supply Chain Management Enabling Technologies (LSCM R&D Center). It has the mission to conduct research and develop relevant technical solutions to serve the industries in Hong Kong and the Pearl River Delta region. He is also the founding Director of the E-Business Technology Institute (ETI) of The University of Hong Kong. Current professional interest of Prof Tan concerns mostly with the research and technology transfer of practical solutions in areas such as Logistics and Supply Chain Management, RFID and Wireless Applications, Service Oriented Application Platforms and Internet Infrastructures that are relevant to the Greater China region. Prof Tan serves as Adjunct Professor at Shanghai Jiaotong University, Chongqing University, China Central University of Science and Technology, University of Electronic Science and Technology of China, South China University of Science and Technology, and Harbin Institute of Science and Technology, Guest Professor at Zhejiang University, and holds the positions of Visiting IBM Chair Professorship at the Dept. of Computer Science and the School of Business at the University of Hong Kong. Prof Tan is a Fellow of the Association for Computing Machinery (ACM) and the Hong Kong Academy of Engineering Sciences. He received the BSEE degree from Seattle University in 1963 and his Doctor of Engineering Science degree from Columbia University, New York, in 1969.

Preface

INTRODUCTION

Recent technology advance in service science and logistics informatics has brought major development boost to service and logistics service industries. It enables electronic means of logistics service operations, penetrating various value chains of logistics services. The service science view has been changing participants' behavior in logistics service value chain, making the logistics service and operation more efficient, improving service experiences. With service innovation in the logistics industry continuously increasing, more and more efforts have been directed to value add e-means (i.e. IT means for innovation) for logistics services, With new e-means development, changes have been evident and reflected on the presentation and processes of logistics information, operations, and services.

SOCIAL COMMUNITY FOR INNOVATION

Today's logistics industry also benefits from innovations in social community development. A logistics service community would emphasize on the value of knowledge exchange among locally dispersed community members. In such a community, logistics objects are identified, tracked, and augmented with digital information. However, traditional approaches for recognizing these objects typically rely on either complex pattern recognition techniques or bar code type technologies. Radio Frequency Identification (RFID) technology provides an unobtrusive method of sensing the presence of and identifying tagged logistics objects. With the development of wireless positioning technologies, the position of tagged objects could be determined as well. This interconnection among logistics objects with identification and positioning would supply better quality of information, thus enhance logistics information visibility.

When a wide variety of such sensors are becoming increasingly cheaper, their deployment is becoming increasingly wider. These novel technologies have promised better logistics information visibility for logistics participants. To benefit from enhanced information visibility, logistics information could be used and analyzed to help identify similar logistics service patterns for participants to use. Further, the unique identification provided by RFID tagging enables convenient means to make the service experience better.

With the proliferation of Service science, RFID and other sensing technology, logistics industry would start considering to use these innovative technologies as feasible and strategic business solutions to integrate logistics applications for business processes within the company and across with business partners, forming value chains and communities. In order for the logistics service community to be successful, there are mechanisms required that fit naturally with the way on how the logistics business is conducted. The logistics service community facilitates the packaging of related logistics information, product and service offerings for logistics operations to meet different service needs. It can potentially promote high quality of logistics services and products for service provisioning. It provides a platform of resource visibility and traceability for logistics services implementations, publication, discovery, and consumption. The community is an ideal platform for service innovation to support sharing, access, and managing diverse logistics resources.

CUSTOMER FOCUSED SERVICE INNOVATION

Logistics service community has shown potentials in developing a better eco-system for service innovation in logistics industry. Many case studies have been preformed to reveal technical, business. However, more efforts are needed to drive innovation and adoption to enable a more customer friendly and focused logistics services.

There exists a major gap between the physical and electronic worlds. Thus, there demands technologies to collect data and establish connections between them. Although RFID is one of such promising technologies, there are still many issues.

In the value chain of logistics, diversified population will have various needs. Although RFID would be able to gather and present data for enabling insight generation, there still demands to help participants understand the technology and address their data privacy concerns.

Relevant information to an individual may vary widely under different contexts. Many activities on pervasive information systems focusing on context-aware delivery of application-specific information are only able to operate within narrow application domains and cannot be generalized to handle other heterogeneous types of information. Techniques are needed to extend locales to generalize to support more flexible grouping and broader applications for those location-based services.

Service experience may encounter breakdowns due to functional failures, missing feedback, and inconsistent interaction models. RFID's promise of better information visibility and unique object identification would help establish better information feedback and experience reinforcement. However, technologies still need to help include capacities to enhance service systems to adapt the services to the user's behavior.

SERVICE SCIENCE AND LOGISTICS INFORMATICS

The interdisciplinary field of service science and logistics informatics yet has a lot more to be discovered. Until now, in the market, it is lack of valuable hotspot observations and reports for the interdisciplinary field. Strong demand is there for latest materials disclosing innovative findings for applied research and development in this field between service science and logistics informatics. Those materials would become more valuable if they are experiences and lessons learned on the world biggest retailers, world busiest airports, and world most dynamic regions. World wide researchers, practitioners, and academicians are seeking to focus their attention into the service sector for insights to develop service science discipline. A number of selected yet important topics relevant to logistics and supply chain industries would be of good importance towards those needs.

This book, in which eighteen chapters are selected, is constructed into six sections. It includes enabling technologies, e.g. RFID and other advanced technologies, which have further aroused interests in people to look into innovative ways to reengineer traditional services in logistics and supply chain management. It also includes reports on innovation strategies and mechanisms. Further it includes service innovations in logistics and supply chain management. It also addresses latest applied service science research and industry practices and reports industry experiences in the adoption of the developed and emerging theories and technologies to enhance competitiveness.

Section 1 has two chapters, dedicated for innovation strategies and mechanisms. Chapter 1 reports observations and findings on "Innovative Strategies for Logistics Process". In this chapter, innovative strategies for logistics processes that can be used practically in business environment are mentioned. For each innovative strategy title, tools that can be used to innovate operations are presented. By innovating logistics processes, logistics providers can fulfill customer needs rapidly and increase their profit because of having competitive advantage. Chapter 2 reports observations and findings on "Research on the Innovation Mechanism and Model of Logistics Enterprise: a Chinese Perspective". A real case is selected for Shenzhen China Overseas Logistics Co. LTD (COL) as the empirical objects to analyze its character of the technology and non-technology innovation, and summarize its inner and outer driving force on promoting the service innovation. Thereafter, the typical service innovative model based on innovative driving force has been discussed.

Section 2 has three chapters, dedicated for experiences in logistics and service innovation. Chapter 3 reports observations on "Managing Customer-Centric Information: The challenges of Information and Communication Technology (ICT) Deployment in Service Environments". This chapter reviews the difficulties inherent in using ICTs to manage customer-related information, and identifies the particular challenges for customer-centric deployment of ICTs. It provides a model of different levels of customer centric information use in organizations which helps understand how companies can become more customer centric in their information use. It reviews implications for future research in this emerging area and concludes that the challenges of ICT deployment and use must be addressed with an uncompromising focus on customer value as the central principle of both ICT design and deployment, and of information management in service organizations. Chapter 4 reports observations on "Impact of Wireless Sensor Network Technology on Service Innovation in Supply Chain Management". This chapter provides an overview about wireless sensor network technology (WSN), how this technology can be applied to modern industries and especially bring service innovation to supply chain management. An overview of the history and potential applications of WSN is provided for the necessary background. The architecture, topology, standards, and protocols of WSN are fundamentally important and thus introduced in details. In a general sense, the impact of information technologies on supply chain management and service innovation is then briefly discussed. After that, much emphasis is placed on the possibility, procedures, and critical challenges of implementing WSN in supply chain management. In the end, two case studies are provided to illustrate the application of WSN for service innovation in both cold chain management and healthcare settings. Chapter 5 reports observations on "Application and Design of Surface Acoustic Wave Based Radio Frequency Identification Tags". It overviews a complementary technology to the integrated circuit based radio frequency identification (RFID) - surface acoustic wave (SAW) based RFID. The fundamental principle and applications of SAW RFID are presented. In order to guarantee the encoding capacity and reliable reading range, the design criteria in coding scheme, tag design and a time domain interrogated reader design are discussed in detail. As an example, a low-cost SAW RFID system applied in poultry farming management is introduced.

Section 3 has four chapters, dedicated for new technology and techniques on logistics informatics and information logistics. Chapter 6 reports observations on "Information Needs of Logistics Service Providers". This chapter studies is on logistics service providers (LSPs) that are representatives of typical Finnish supply chains. The purpose of the chapter is to point out the current level of information sharing in supply chains focusing on the information needs of logistics companies, particularly from the LSP's point of view. It revealed that there is a lack of logistics information in the supply chain. The information distribution should be intensified when aiming at achieving a more efficient supply chain. Chapter 7 reports observations on "IT Audit for Information Logistics". It is focused on how information logistics in business organization is supported by standards and best practices of auditing. CobiT, ITIL, ISO/IEC 27002, Val IT as well as the Sarbanes-Oxley Act and ITAF model are analyzed in the aspect of information logistics. Chapter 8 reports observations on "Information and Communication Technology in Logistics as a Comparative Advantage". In a time, when the "economic crisis" is filling the news, it may seem hard to even think about improvements in terms of research and development, since "there are lacking funds even for the reproduction". However, also the last economic "revolution" was "born" in a crisis. Therefore it is sensible to look at the current situation as an opportunity for the next economic revolution, bringing the economy a new cycle of development. This contribution is to lay the foundation for an advanced-research technological platform for logistics applications networks. Chapter 9 reports observations on "How to market OR/MS decision support". The OR/MS decision support is investigated from a new viewpoint of service. Firstly, based on the fact what is provided by OR/MS decision support, it is shown that OR/MS decision support shares characteristics with service and hence can be considered as a kind of service. Next, OR/MS decision support is analyzed from the viewpoint of what are necessary for service of high quality. It turns out that there is surely a problem with communication gap between decision makers and decision supporters. It is effective to utilize "problem specification", which is a decision-maker-friendly description of problems, as one approach to bridge the communication gap.

Section 4 has three chapters, dedicated for a well developed yet important topic, i.e., service sourcing and supplier management. Chapter 10 is on "A Multi-criteria Tool for Evaluating Performance of Service Suppliers - The Case of Met-Mex Peñoles Supply Chain". The quality of service is certainly a complex topic that many companies, although interested in the subject, difficult to address. It is well known that the main reason is due to the intangibility of the service, perishable and heterogeneous. This problem could be helped through a user-friendly tool. It is important to define and detect both internal and external suppliers, as well as the cycles and stages of services in which the organization has a close interrelationship with them. In these stages, it is critical to assess the quality of services provided by suppliers. Chapter 11 is on "Analyzing Requirements and Approaches for Sourcing Software Based Services". The sourcing requirements are identified for software based services (SBS) and associate the key characteristics of SBS (with the sourcing requirements introduced). Furthermore, the sourcing of SBS is investigated with the related works in the field of classical procurement, business process outsourcing, and information systems sourcing. Based on the analysis, it is concluded that the direct adoption of these approaches for SBS is not feasible and new approaches are required for sourcing SBS. Chapter 12 is on "Supplier Relationship Management in Health Care". The structural transformation of modern societies (e.g. aging of population, mobility) as well as continuously increasing market dynamics (e.g. mergers, technological advancement) induce health care organizations to reduce their costs while enhancing service delivery at the same time. However, as the pressure to innovate will increase extensively in the next years, similar developments are becoming relevant for the health care supply chain, too. In this chapter the current findings are adapted on supplier relationship management (SRM) to the health care context. On the basis of a case study a future scenario is developed for drugs supply management and discusses potential performance and quality improvements.

Section 5 has three chapters, dedicated for experiences on service management in industries. Chapter 13 reports observations on "Cargo Service Dynamics and Service-Oriented Architecture in East Asian Airports". Findings from this chapter show that while conducive economic conditions continue to play a critical role in stimulating demand for cargo service at the airports, the importance of physical architecture has also dramatically risen relative to human factors. Particularly, adequate provisions and utilizations of physical facilities for landside operations appear to be a more significant driving force for demand of an airport's cargo service compared to those of airside operations. Despite the strong emphasis on swift and reliable services, cost savings are found to have regained their importance in the recent years. Chapter 14 reports observations on "Lifecycle Management of SLAs for Service Enterprises". Service level agreement (SLA) is becoming an increasingly sought-after topic in recent years, as complex logistics and service chains span across geographical boundaries in the lights of globalization and new technological developments. This chapter introduces the state of the art of the lifecycle management of SLA for service enterprises, which covers stages of terms optimization, contract drafting and compliance tracking. In particular, the deficiencies are identified in the area of term optimization and outline several R&D tracks that would lead to the development of industry-strength SLA optimization capabilities. An initial version of a SLA optimization toolset coded-named SLA-OASIS is reported, in the context of a telecom service, to illustrate such a concept. Chapter 15 reports observations on "Cyber Transportation Logistics: Architecting a Global Value-Chain for Services". In today's global economy, products and services are provided across international borders. The sourcing of these products and services becomes an integral part of international businesses. Information, communication and transportation technologies (ICTT) have made this job significantly more streamlined. However, there is an advantage that big companies, such as Wal-Mart, have over small and medium size ones. While the big companies have the ICTT resources to source globally at will, small and medium enterprises (SME) are much less prepared to do so, resulting in a large competitive disadvantage. By contrasting SMEs with their more successful "big brothers," the salient ICTT features are highlighted in system architecture as a checklist for any assistance that might be rendered to SMEs and other entities in overcoming their competitive impediment. These findings are the result of numerous international workshops and conferences held in Hong Kong and in Arkansas in the headquarters of Wal-Mart.

Section 6 has four chapters, dedicated for industry service models, profession development and outlook. Chapter 16 is on "Perceived Risk Management: Applying the TEID Model to the Traveler Service Chain". This chapter holds the potential to contribute to extending an understanding and management capacity of customer-perceived risks of knowledge-based services. It brings into play a new framework and new risk management process. It also helps with formalizing and making tangible customer added-value. Chapter 17 is on "Prediction Reliability of Container Terminal Simulation Models: a before and after Study". In this chapter attention is focused on the container terminal optimization problem, given that today most international cargo is transported through seaports and on containerized vessels. In this context, in order to manage a container terminal it is sometimes necessary to develop a Decision Support System (DSS). This chapter investigated the prediction reliability of container terminal simulation models (DSS), through a before and after analysis, taking advantage of some significant investment made by the Salerno Container Terminal (Italy) between 2003 and 2008. Chapter 18 is on "New Profession Development: The Case for the Business Process Engineer". This chapter argues that an obstacle to business process (re)engineering is the lack of a business process engineer role with an associated professional education, tools, and community. There is an urgent need for a professional business process engineer. In the chapter, it is discussed the skills required of this profession and a first course offered at a university on this subject is briefly described. Chapter 19 is on "Logistics Services in the 21st Century Supply Chain Integration and Service Architecture". The dynamics of change and the path-dependent evolution of resources and capabilities are central concerns of contemporary strategic management. Companies tend to concentrate scares resources into their core competences. Opportunity, speed, product choices and availability are intangibles that customer value, some times more than the price. This chapter presents general concepts behind the supply chain and logistics industry, as well as a proposal of the general components of the service and organizational arrangements for logistics service providers depending on the complexity of the requirements of the company that hires the service provider.

FURTHER YOUR READING

Interested in continuing your reading? Bear the following, which is summarized to differentiate with others, in mind while you are reading.

As a first of a kind, this book addresses latest applied service science research and industry practices on emerging enabling technologies including RFID, service innovations in logistics and supply chain management, and the transformations of a more efficient economy. It helps the development and advances of this new interdisciplinary field of service science and logistics informatics.

This book, built on an excellent portfolio of accepted chapters, including contributions from three major continentals including Asia, Europe, North/South America, on world biggest retailers, world busiest airports, and world most dynamic regions, to introduce service innovation in modernizing logistics and supply chain management, strives to serve as a prestigious reference to disseminate the state of the art research, development, and advances of service innovation in logistics and supply chain management.

This book helps steer the attention of service innovation exploration in the right directions for logistics and supply chain management. It targets both business and IT professionals for practices and guidelines to service innovation in logistics and supply chain management.

This book is also resulted from a customer focused innovation approach. A story line of this book is set as follows to structure the book, forming a good index for different reading styles, to suite your need.

- Innovation strategies and mechanisms
- Logistics and service innovation
- Logistics informatics and information logistics
- Service sourcing and supplier management
- Service management in industries
- Industry service models, profession development, and outlook.

Section 1
Innovation Strategies and Mechanisms

Chapter 1
Innovative Strategies for Logistics Processes

Bikem Türkeli
Marmara University, Turkey

Alp Ariburnu
Marmara University, Turkey

Özalp Vayvay
Marmara University, Turkey

ABSTRACT

In a time of rapid revolutionary change, today organizations must innovate in ways that allow them to take advantage of change. Competitive business environments force companies to respond to all changes in the market. This response to that change brings innovation in processes. As a basis of all competitive advantages, innovation should be continuous and the only way to maintain this is having the right innovation strategy. In this study innovative strategies for logistics processes, which can be used practically in business environments, are mentioned. For each innovative strategy title tools that can be used to innovate operations are presented. By innovating logistics processes logistics providers can fulfill customer needs rapidly and increase their profit because of having a competitive advantage.

INTRODUCTION

Logistics is defined as a business planning framework for the management of material, service, information and capital flows. It includes the increasingly complex information, communication and control systems required in today's business environment. Logistical processes, those involving sourcing, inbound logistics (receiving, storing, and disseminating incoming goods or material for use), configuration and outbound logistics (movement of material associated with storing, transporting, and distribution a firm's goods to its customers.), and third-party partnerships for inventory management and transportation, are extremely important to successful product delivery (Davenport, 1993). We can collect them into four main clusters and these are purchasing, warehousing (storing), delivery (transportation) and post-delivery.

Recently, many logistics service providers try to improve their operation efficiency by continuous implementation of information or automation

DOI: 10.4018/978-1-61520-603-2.ch001

technologies according to their business characteristics. It is important for logistics service providers, in this age of knowledge-based economy, to accumulate and use their skills and knowledge efficiently and consistently (Lin, & Ho, 2007). Competitive business environment forces companies to respond all changes in market. They can be responsive only if they are open for changes in company.

Innovation is the response to change. And, conversely, change is the consequence of innovation. Globally, we are in a time of rapid revolutionary change. Organizations must anticipate this and innovate in ways that allow them to take advantage of change. In other words, innovation is the basis of all competitive advantage: the means by which organizations anticipate and fill customer needs and the method by which organizations utilize technology. (Prestwood and Schumann, 1997) Innovation should be continuous and the only way to maintain this is having a right innovation strategy.

An innovation strategy guides decisions on how resources are to be used to meet a firm's objectives for innovation and thereby deliver value and build competitive advantage. Its crafting is supported by a number of innovative capabilities that steer the configuration and reconfiguration of a firm's resources. It entails judgment about which kinds of innovation processes are most appropriate for the firm's circumstances and ambitions. (Dodgson et al., 2008)

In this study, innovative strategies for logistics processes that can be used practically in business environment are mentioned. For each innovative strategy title, tools that can be used to innovate operations are presented. By innovating logistics processes, logistics providers can fulfill customer needs rapidly and increase their profit because of having competitive advantage.

INNOVATION IN LOGISTICS SECTOR

The modern logistics industry is a complex network of firms involved in the flow and transformation of goods from the raw materials stage to the end user. Three trends spur innovation in logistics. The first is the increase in the demand for high-tech goods. The global market for high-technology goods is growing at a faster rate than that for other manufactured goods, and high-technology industries are driving economic growth around the world.

The second trend influencing the logistics industry is globalization, the integration of many micro economies into one worldwide, interdependent economy. Top firms in the logistics industry which headquartered all over the world, are not only moving logistics services worldwide but are also creating innovation centers close to the new centers of trade. Reliable, timely accurate data is the keystone of the new global supply chain. Software and hardware innovations that enable greater visibility of product movement to shippers and carriers have become critical to success in the logistics industry.

Innovation in the logistics industry has also been spurred by the growth of the Internet and e-commerce. The Internet and computing Technologies have increased the amount of information available to the buyer and manufacturer about the product and fulfillment process. This causes a rise in expectations relating timely and accurate fulfillment. Innovation in warehouse management software and tracking products support firms' efforts to cope with the demands of the Internet environment.

Future Logistics System must be intelligent and sensible system, sensing, GPS and image processing technology must be used. It must enhance validation functionality, must support global supply chain's visibility for inter-continental business functionality. It must use standard document and exchange protocol and provide interoperability.

Innovation in the logistics sector is created around new or improved:

- Capabilities and processes: This includes improvements in managerial systems, skill development of logistics specialists and supply chain managers as well as the adoption of information technology based systems.
- Products and services: Innovation in this sector ranges from innovations relating to hardware, such as the design of rolling stock and trucks, to the operation of the transporting mechanism, whether it is a train, truck, plane or ship, to the methods and practices used for transporting goods.
- Major infrastructure innovation: This includes involving in a number of initiatives to improve infrastructure and increase capacity. These in turn will promote further innovation in the sector.
- Supply-chain innovation: The rise of supply chains has been an innovation in itself, resulting in freight flowing seamlessly from collecting raw material to delivering goods ready for consumption. (New South Wales Government, Department of State and Regional Development)

The Drivers of Innovation in Logistics Sector

Profit Related Drivers

- Customer demands: Meeting consumer expectations are common drivers of innovation. Companies increasingly need to respond to consumer buying decisions influenced by such factors as fashion, convenience, indulgence, functionality and conscientious consumerism.

- Competition: The need to differentiate one's product or service from the competition often results in process, product, packaging and/or supply chain innovations.
- Research and development: A stable and well-funded base for building knowledge and capabilities, which in turn results in the development of new, more advanced and more profitable services and products. The ability of manufacturers to access research and technological developments is crucial to driving innovation, as is the dissemination of enabling technologies that support production flexibility.
- Enabling and platform technologies: Major advances in enabling and platform technologies have opened up opportunities for new products and services, and operational efficiencies.

Market Related Drivers

- Major projects: The awarding of major projects to companies attracts new investment and drives innovation by suppliers and contractors.
- Investment attraction: Attracting global companies that bring new technologies and innovative labor skills.
- Globalization: Results in increased levels of competition which aims for best practice and brings foreign business to worldwide markets. All of these elements have a flow-through effect on the development of systems, practices and products.
- Industry trends: Trends which occur in a local market or globally, have a significant impact on how business is carried out and how businesses plan for the future.

Legal Drivers

- Regulations: These drivers can take the form of environmental, security and safety regulations, amongst others. For example, across sectors, the regulations associated with occupational health and safety issues have led to innovations which have improved safety in workplaces. (New South Wales Government, Department of State and Regional Development)

INNOVATIVE STRATEGIES

An innovation strategy guides decisions on how resources are to be used to meet a firm's objectives for innovation and thereby deliver value and build competitive advantage. Its crafting is supported by a number of innovative capabilities that steer the configuration and reconfiguration of a firm's resources. It entails judgment about which kinds of innovation processes are most appropriate for the firm's circumstances and ambitions. An innovation strategy identifies the technologies and markets the firm should best develop and exploit to create and capture value. It does so within the limits of the resources available to the firm to support current and future innovation efforts and its evolving corporate strategy, organization, and culture.

The reason why innovation is a strategic management issue is because it is intimately linked to the capacity of the firm to deliver value:

- Creating and appropriating returns from innovations is a key source of competitive advantage for a firm.
- Complex, risky, and expensive activities, such as R & D, product and services innovation design, operations, networking, and collaboration, can hamper a firm's competitive position and may result in piecemeal, short-term focused, and potentially conflicting outcomes unless they are guided by choices that build synergies and grow expertise cumulatively.
- Globalization of technology and markets, with many potential new customers, suppliers, partners, and competitors in different parts of the world, requires companies to take a strategic approach to their innovation activities to provide focus within an ever-expanding set of opportunities and threats.
- Organizational structures and innovation processes that firms adopt to encourage technological innovation need to relate to the corporate strategy pursued by the firm, and vice versa; for example, R & D can be organized according to whether the firm aims to support an innovation leader or follower position.
- Unless firms can articulate their long-term strategic aims for innovation, it is difficult for them to communicate with and benefit from public-sector science and technology policies in areas such as basic science, regulation, and standards creation. They are also less likely to be able to build long-term technological collaborations with partners or to find patient investors
- A firm that identifies innovation as a strategic activity is more likely to attract creative workers in search of exciting opportunities in the 'war over talent'. (Dodgson et al., 2008)

An innovation strategy is only good for a finite amount of time. One of the worst mistakes an organization can make is to assume that because an innovation strategy was successful it will always be successful. The environment shifts, customers' needs change, competition gets smart, technologies improve, and the organization evolves itself. (Prestwood and Schumann, 1994)

INNOVATIVE STRATEGIES FOR LOGISTICS PROCESSES

Companies' efforts to innovate logistical processes involve major uses of information technology and organizational change enablers. These innovations in logistical processes are;

- Electronic data interchange and payment systems
- Configuration systems
- Warehousing technologies and conditions
- Third-party shipment (transportation) and location tracking systems
- Close partnerships with customers and suppliers (Davenport, 1993).

Electronic Data Interchange and Payment Systems

Electronic Data Interchange

According to Clarke (1998), Electronic Data Interchange (EDI) may be most easily understood as the replacement of paper-based purchase orders with electronic equivalents. It is actually much broader in its application than the procurement process, and its impacts are far greater than mere automation. EDI offers the prospect of easy and cheap communication of structured information throughout the corporate community, and is capable of facilitating much closer integration among hitherto remote organizations. A more careful definition of EDI is the exchange of documents in standardized electronic form, between organizations, in an automated manner, directly from a computer application in one organization to an application in another.

The essential elements of EDI are:

- Direct application-to-application communication
- The use of an electronic transmission medium rather than magnetic tapes, disks, or other transmission media
- The use of electronic mail boxes for "store and collect/store and forward" transmission/delivery of documents;

- The use of structured, formatted messages based upon internationally agreed standards (thus enabling messages to be translated, interpreted and checked for compliance to a standard set of rules).

The term EDI therefore does not refer to:

- Electronic mail
- File transfer
- Remote data entry

Increased Effectiveness through Electronic Data Interchange

Electronic data interchange (EDI) is an internationally standardized process that can be used to significantly reduce the number of changes of media in logistics. Despite its many advantages, EDI is not widely used in logistics because of its high implementation costs. Electronic data interchange is a broad term for all electronic processes for the asynchronous and fully automatic transmission of structured information between application systems of various institutions - this can include companies or government agencies, among others. The information is transmitted in several independent steps, and the data are cached several times en route.

EDI reduces the number of human work steps. A fixed structure for the transmitted data is laid down by the system. The prepared data are presented to a human user only after an application system has integrated the information sent by EDI, for instance within the framework of enterprise resource planning (ERP).

The term EDI is used only when at least two different partners are involved in the process - data interchange within an organization is called enterprise application integration (EAI). Once different partners become involved within the framework of EDI, a contractual arrangement becomes necessary. Among other factors, the contract's complexity is related to the number of contract parties such as external IT companies and the different characteristics among the participating companies.

Typical information transmitted by electronic data interchange includes:

- Reporting and planning data such as point-of-sale information warehouse data, forecasts, advertising measures and new product introductions
- Transaction data such as orders, shipping notes and invoices

The Benefits of EDI

EDI and other similar technologies save company money by providing alternative to or replacing information flows that require a great deal of human interaction and materials such as paper documents, meetings, faxes, etc. Even when paper documents are maintained in parallel with EDI exchange, e.g. printed shipping manifests, electronic exchange and the use of data from that exchange reduces the handling costs of sorting, distributing, organizing, and searching paper documents. EDI and similar technologies allow a company to take advantage of the benefits of storing and manipulating data electronically without the cost of manual entry. Another advantage of EDI is reduced errors, such as shipping and billing errors. One very important advantage of EDI over paper documents is the speed in which the trading partner receives and incorporates the information into their system thus greatly reducing cycle times. For this reason, EDI can be an important component of just-in-time production systems.

Data interchange with EDI accelerates reaction times to customer requests. In addition, electronic data transmission creates the possibility of making the latest point-of-sale data from the entire supply chain available at any time. This increases planning and disposition security. Moreover, eliminating manual data entry creates very extensive cost-cutting potential, e.g., by reducing errors and avoiding changes of media as well as multi-entered

data. EDI is very important to logistics companies, whose daily work frequently involves a high share of repetitious business processes. According to the automation of entire business processes, costs can be significantly reduced. For instance, when retail inventories fall below a minimum level, orders can be automatically transmitted to the supplier's production system. The information is sent from there to the logistics service provider who organizes the delivery. This eliminates the need for telephone calls, faxes and e-mails.

Swatman and Swatman (1991) states that EDI's direct impacts include labor-savings in the areas of data transcription, controls, and error investigation and correction; and fewer delays in data-handling. Benefits of Electronic data integration are improved internal operations from a reduction in time, better responsiveness to customers, improved trading partner relationships and increased ability to compete, both domestically and internationally.

The Drawbacks of EDI

Significant costs are associated with implementing and operating EDI systems. This is because solutions available in the market must be adjusted to a company's own needs and employees must be trained. In addition, a pilot phase or an initial parallel operation is frequently necessary. The result is that small and mid-sized companies in particular avoid EDI and rely on traditional forms of data transmission instead. Furthermore, processes in a company must undergo significant changes before EDI can be applied. For instance, a company may normally receive its goods before an invoice is sent in the mail. But if EDI were used, the invoice would arrive before the goods were delivered. Accordingly, processes must be adjusted in such a way that invoices can be processed by the company before the goods have arrived.

EDI and the Internet

In DHL Logbook, EDI and the Internet are expressed. According to DHL logbook, EDI has been available in this form for several decades. The leading data standard at the moment is EDIFACT. It was first developed as a European standard in the middle of the 1980s and was then adapted to American regulations. Since then, EDIFACT has become the central standard for communications between applications systems particularly in Europe as well as increasingly in other regions. One exception is the banking and financial sector. With the help of the Internet, the efficiency of EDI systems has been increased further. For instance, the data format standard XML facilitates the display of hierarchically structured files in the form of text files. "XML" stands for "eXtensible markup language." As a result, graphics in a text format can be exchanged between different applications and processed further. This enables all sorts of business transactions to be displayed. The Internet offers an open, fast, widespread and low-cost environment for managing data traffic, particularly in the areas of transport, retail and administration. In this way, even smaller companies that want to avoid the high investments associated with the development of a "classic" EDI can profit from the benefits of electronic data traffic. One shortcoming of the so-called "Web-EDI" with XML can be the need for encryption mechanisms.

Electronic Payment Systems

Electronic payment systems are becoming central to on-line business transactions nowadays as companies look for various methods to serve customers faster and more cost effectively. Electronic commerce brings a wide range of new worldwide business opportunities. There is no doubt that electronic payment systems are becoming more and more common and will play an important role in the business world.

According to Electronic Payment Systems Handbook of Cyberspace Center, there are four types of electronic payment systems:

- Prepaid cash-like payment systems like Mondex, where a certain amount of money is taken from the payer before purchases are made. The money can be used for payments later.
- Pay-now payment systems like EPS, where the payer's account is debited at the time of payment.
- Pay-later payment systems like Visa, where the payee's bank account is credited the amount of sale before the payer actually pays.
- Cheque-like payment system like E-checking, where a payment is done by sending electronic forms from payer to payee.

Recent Trends in Electronic Payments

Card Payments

Automated Teller Machine (ATM)
An automated teller machine (ATM) is a computerized telecommunications device that provides the customers of a financial institution with access to financial transactions in a public space without the need for a human clerk or bank teller. On most modern ATMs, the customer is identified by inserting a plastic ATM card with a magnetic stripe or a plastic smartcard with a chip that contains a unique card number and some security information, such as an expiration date or CVC (CVV). Security is provided by the customer entering a personal identification number (PIN). Using an ATM, customers can access their bank accounts in order to make cash withdrawals (or credit card cash advances) and check their account balances as well as purchasing mobile cell phone prepaid credit.

Manufactures have demonstrated and have deployed several different technologies on ATMs that have not yet reached worldwide acceptance, such as:

- Biometrics, where authorization of transactions is based on the scanning of a customer's fingerprint, iris, face, etc.
- Cheque/Cash Acceptance, where the ATM accepts and recognizes cheques and/or currency without using envelopes.
- Bar code scanning
- On-demand printing of "items of value" (such as movie tickets, traveler's cheques, etc.)
- Dispensing additional media (such as phone cards)
- Co-ordination of ATMs with mobile phones
- Customer-specific advertising
- Integration with non-banking equipment

Electronic Purses/Wallets

In a general business sense, an electronic wallet (or electronic purse) is a consumer device providing some additional security compared to a mere credit card solution. An electronic wallet could be as simple as an encrypted storage of credit card information that saves consumers to re-enter their credit card data manually each time they make a payment. There is considerable variety of products and services, each called "electronic wallet" or "electronic purse" that turns up in the marketplace and in investors' press conferences, while the technical specifications and the life time of these products and services are left unclear. An electronic wallet is a consumer device which is designed to store and manage electronic funds or electronic cash. In particular, an electronic wallet is used to download funds from a bank account, to store those funds inside the electronic wallet and transfer deliberate amounts to other electronic wallets or point of sale terminals in order to make purchases.

Many firms, particularly those involved in handling large amounts of coinage and bank notes, are finding the costs of handling cash to be increasingly onerous. These costs include expenses related to point-of-sale transactions, accounting, theft, loss

of cash, safekeeping and security, deposits of currency and other services related to the handling of cash provided by financial institutions. Many firms, particularly those involved in handling large amounts of coinage and bank notes, are finding the costs of handling cash to be increasingly onerous. These costs include expenses related to point-of-sale transactions, accounting, theft, loss of cash, safekeeping and security, deposits of currency and other services related to the handling of cash provided by financial institutions.

Electronic Funds Transfer at Point of Sale (EFT/POS)

It is the automatic transfer of funds, using a debit card at a retail point of sale, from a consumer's demand deposit account to the retailer's account. EFT-POS transactions pass through the retailer's back office computer and, if the retailer is part of a chain, may also pass through the data center of the retailer on its way to the EFT processor.

According to Haefner, Web based point of sale (POS) is the best payment system. Its software installation is faster and easier. All software is supported and maintained on the provider's end. Companies should have to pay less money for the system and IT. Because provider owns the hardware and does everything, you need to do on IT. Web-based POS usually eliminates the task of polling. Whether the company have 1 store or 100 stores, up to the second information is available at any time.

Additionally, because it is web-based software, company can access sales numbers, customer information, inventory and much more information from any store. It allows improved inventory management. In a multi-location environment, inventory costs can be significantly reduced because real time tracking can prevent over or under buying and it allows you to have access to on-hand, in-transit, and on-order items. This instant access to information means that companies are able to control inventories for all stores from one location and they can control them much closer. Goods that are ordered by customers can be tracked easily so, customer satisfaction can be improved thanks to this information.

Credit Cards

A credit card is part of a system of payments named after the small plastic card issued to users of the system. It is a card entitling its holder to buy goods and services based on the holder's promise to pay for these goods and services. The issuer of the card grants a line of credit to the consumer (or the user) from which the user can borrow money for payment to a merchant or as a cash advance to the user.

A credit card is different from a charge card, where a charge card requires the balance to be paid in full each month. In contrast, credit cards allow the consumers to 'revolve' their balance, at the cost of having interest charged. Most credit cards are issued by local banks or credit unions, and are the shape and size specified by the ISO 7810 standard.

Debit Cards

A debit card (also known as a bankcard or check card) is a plastic card, which provides an alternative payment method to cash when making purchases. Functionally, it can be called an electronic check, as the funds are withdrawn directly from either the bank account (often referred to as a check card), or from the remaining balance on the card. In some cases, the cards are designed exclusively for use on the Internet, and so there is no physical card.

The use of debit cards has become widespread in many countries and has overtaken the cheque and in some instances cash transactions by volume. Like credit cards, debit cards are used widely for telephone and Internet purchases.

Debit cards can also allow for instant withdrawal of cash, acting as the ATM card for withdrawing cash and as a cheque guarantee card. Merchants can also offer "cash back" / "cash out" facilities to customers, where a customer can withdraw cash along with their purchase.

Smart Cards

A plastic card containing a computer chip and enabling the holder to purchase goods and services, enter restricted areas, access medical, financial, or other records, or perform other operations requiring data stored on the chip. Smart card is a plastic card containing a computer chip for identification, special purpose processing, and data storage. Smart cards have been used more readily in Europe than in the United States. Offsetting their enhanced security features, drawbacks to smart card systems include the capital costs associated with new technology and the wide availability of reliable, on-line, banking systems. Also called chip card or memory card.

Mobile

This uses a mobile device to initiate and confirm electronic payment. In the field of payments, mobile phones opportunity is seen in the embedded SIM (smart) card used to store information of users. This allows customers to do some banking enquires on their mobile phones. Customers do not need to go to their branch to do the following transactions: balance enquiry, transaction enquiry, cheque book request, statement request, and payment of utility bills.

Telephone Banking

Telephone banking or telebanking is a form of virtual banking that deliver financial services through telecommunication devices. Under this mechanism, the customer transacts business by dialing a touch-tone telephone connected to an automated system of the bank. Telebanking has numerous benefits for end users. For the customers, it provides increased convenience, expanded access and significant time saving (Appiah, & Agyemang, 2004).

Personal Computer Banking (Home Banking)

Personal Computer Banking lets customers handle many banking transactions via their personal computer. For instance, personal computer can be used to view account balance, request transfers between accounts, and pay bills electronically.

Online/Internet Payments

The on-line payment systems are e-commerce businesses allowing money transfers to be made only through the Internet. They function as a fast and secure electronic alternative to traditional methods as cheques and money orders. The systems perform payment processing not only for online vendors, auction sites, and other corporate users but between their costumers, for which it charges a fee which is much less than the bank wire transfer equivalent.

Electronic Cheque

Electronic cheques are used in the same way as paper cheque in which the clearing between payer and payee is based on existing and well known banking settlement system. The only difference between paper and electronic cheques are the dematerialization of the payment instrument which is passed on via computer networks like Internet in the later technology (Appiah, & Agyemang, 2004).

Digitized 'E-Cash' Systems

E-cash payment system takes the form of encoded messages and representing the encrypted equivalent of digitized money. One key attraction is that it avoid the time and expense associated with becoming an approved credit card accepting merchant. It does not require the use of intermediary; therefore, anyone can effect payment directly (Appiah, & Agyemang, 2004).

Digital P2P Payments

Bank-based P2P3 system allows users to send money from bank accounts and credit cards electronically. It employs e-mail services to notify recipients of an impending funds transfer. Most bank-based P2P requires the sender to register with the P2P site. Most of the providers allow users to move money a limited amount of money around the world.

Electronic Payment Systems Handbook of Cyberspace Center states that factors such as the accelerating rate of change and complexity in technology, globalization of markets, organizational factors, and increasing demographic diversity, would drive the future of electronic commerce. New technologies would change the current electronic payment systems and would ultimately provide privacy and security, but not anonymity, which magnifies potential risks of electronic commerce.

Configuration Systems

Manual handling of configuration task is becoming a bottle-neck with shorter product life-cycles, increased use of third-party products, and the need to reduce lead times. The possibility to automate the configuration task was recognized in the 1980's, and is now a rapidly growing industry.

Quick and reliable response to customers' needs has been argued to be a key competitive advantage when manufacturing customized products. Increasingly, firms are relying on product configuration in order to promptly meet more and more diverse customers' needs, thus overcoming what has been dubbed as the "customization responsiveness squeeze".

Companies such as Dell Computers and Cisco literally built their business model and success around their product configuration capabilities. Many other companies followed, making product configuration so ubiquitous nowadays that we take for granted the possibility to purchase configured cars, vacation packages, insurance arrangements, and other goods and services.

An Information Processing View of the Product Configuration Task

From an organization design perspective, the more a company customizes its products to its clients' needs, the higher is the uncertainty associated with the task of selling and delivering these products. The front-end of the organization, for example, may have a difficult time estimating the feasibility of a specific customer's request. Likewise, the back-office may experience serious difficulties envisaging technical solutions to comply with this request. Customization, in other words, leads to task uncertainty.

The decision of a company to offer customized products leads, ceteris paribus, to an information processing gap, i.e. the organization does not have all the information it needs to perform its task at the desired performance level, be it time, cost, or any other measure of performance. In the case of customization, the nature of the information processing gap can be thought of in terms of, for example, the lack of information regarding the possibility and profitability of complying with a given customer request.

Traditionally, companies offering customized products have addressed such information processing gaps by using organization design principles, which either reduce the needed information processing capacity or increase the available information processing capacity. Typically, the information processing capacity is increased by establishing lateral relations. This means that customization related problems are solved by cutting across functional boundaries, such that all the individuals and units possessing information relevant to address a customer problem work jointly towards a feasible solution. In practice, this means that often front-end and back-end of the company work together in order to sell and deliver customized solutions.

On the other hand, companies have tried to reduce the information processing requirement needed to sell and deliver customized products. The simplest and easiest way to do this is to rely on *slack resources*, i.e. to simply reduce the level of performance. For example, an organization facing serious information processing constraints in the tendering process may allow itself more time

to come back to the customer with a quotation. Alternatively, organizations may create *self-contained tasks*, meaning that they can reduce the degree of division of labor and place the different actors in charge of the sale and delivery of customized products under the same organizational unit. This is done, for instance, by having salesmen with strong technical background deal with customization, without the need to involve the technical office.

More recently, companies have begun to design configurable product families to reduce the information processing requirements induced by customization, de facto engaging in the organization design strategy known as *environmental management*. This is because, for a configurable product family, product variants are generated by combining sets of *predefined* components, i.e. no new components are designed to address the customers' needs.1 Stated otherwise, addressing the market by means of a configurable product family means constraining the product offer of a company within a pre-determined product space. Evidently, relying on a predetermined product space means drastically cutting uncertainty concerning the sale and delivery of customized products.

By serving the market through a configurable product family, a company does not have to custom-design its product variants. The design task in order acquisition is in this case substituted by a different task – the product configuration task. This task is one for which: (1) no new components are designed during the configuration task; (2) components are connected to other components under a set of pre-defined compatibility constraints; and (3) solutions (configurations) specify not only the components in the configuration but also how they are related.

Companies that serve heterogeneous customers' needs through configurable product families can naturally take advantage of an additional organization design strategy to increase their information processing capability, by establishing *formal information systems*. Such systems would help closing the information processing gap by providing problem-solving information to the appropriate organizational entities. In practice, these systems take the form of product selection and configuration assistants (product catalogues, e-catalogues, product configurators and users toolkits, etc.) (Salvador, Forza, & Claes, 2007).

Warehousing Technologies and Conditions

A warehouse is typically viewed as a place to store inventory but the role of the warehouse is more properly viewed as a switching facility as contrasted to a storage facility. The design of a warehouse management system should address physical facility characteristics and product movement. The warehousing technologies that are commonly used in logistics industry include automated storage and retrieval system (AS/RS), automatic sorting system, computer-aided picking system, and thermostat warehouse (Fagerberk, Movery, & Nelson, 2004).

Due to Naxtor Technologies discussing positive effects of IT on warehouse operations, many of the new warehousing solutions mix the old and the new. The old is technologies such as warehouse management systems, which have been around for a while and the new is software and information technology enhancements. In fact, these innovations are not only giving old technology new efficiencies, but they are also tweaking direct-to-customer distribution and fulfillment activities.

Pick-to-light systems have been given the IT makeover. Newer versions of pick-to-light systems are virtually touch-free. Previously in pick-to-light, the picker had to push a button when he had finished the task. Now newer systems of this long-standing technology have sensors, which detect when the picker's arm is in a pre-designated spot in the picking area.

Warehouse management systems (WMS) have also significantly gained in functionality and now provide solutions to current challenges such as downsizing inventory. Warehouse managers are operating in a buyer's market, with customers demanding quicker delivery with value-added service. In addition, buying patterns have shifted; orders are smaller and more frequent. New warehouse management systems address these issues and trim the supply chain. They are not only more functional, but they can easily interface with other technologies. Many WMS applications enable automation while working with both ordering and shipping systems and logistics routing programmes. These capabilities ensure the smooth flow of merchandise.

Even small warehouses can benefit from IT improvements. Small operations can bring partial automation to their facilities through emerging Internet-based services. Application service providers are driving this phenomenon. They let thousands of small warehouses execute operations, which were previously not possible without complicated and expensive warehousing technologies.

Material handling solutions that are on the IT edge include wireless technologies such as Palm Pilots and Ethernet bridges that can connect several locations to one network. In addition, robotics and automated picking technologies are easier to use, more compact and more efficient.

Automated pallet loaders now use driverless vehicles or embedded platforms that elevate before releasing loads inside a trailer. These robotic advancements significantly increase productivity by eliminating unnecessary strolling.

Voice or speech recognition is also gaining in acknowledgment. Voice recognition frees both hands of the worker, boosting his productivity. Workers no longer have to adjust vocal inflection so that the programme can identify what is being said. Instead, users give speech samples to the system to memorize. In fact, the new versions of this technology can interpret a range of languages and accents.

Speech recognition may even make warehouse radio frequency (RF) technology obsolete, assert many material-handling experts. Radio frequency may avoid becoming outmoded because of its own IT advancements. RF identification tags have successfully tracked trailers, rail cars, marine containers and other costly items. Embedded or attached RFID tags contain data, which can be retrieved by low-wattage radio waves. This can be sent to a computer or saved on other digital devices to be uploaded later. RFID will work even without direct line of sight, and non-metallic objects such as trees will not obstruct radio wave transmissions.

Data warehousing is another IT-driven warehousing solution. Data warehousing notes trends and what SKUs are selling over a period of time. Then utilizing trend analysis and statistical process control, it makes recommendations about where merchandise should be placed in the warehouse. Items in high demand are made more accessible while slower-moving ones are consigned to less-explored places.

Warehouse Technologies

RF

Radio Frequency, more commonly called "RF", refers to reading bar codes to capture data (when picking in a warehouse, to the validation of what is being picked vs. what should be picked). The use of RF increases picking accuracy, and sometimes can increase productivity. Warehouse management system offered by Radio Frequency Barcode Systems is a potent solution for regular warehouses and 3PL operators.

The warehouse management system removes paperwork and streamlines operations by means of its user-friendly interface. Warehouse management system offered by Radio Frequency Barcode Systems assists the manager of the warehouse by

showing a general idea of every awaiting operation in the warehouse including all purchases, pending receipting, pending picking, items nearing their minimum level of stock holding, current activity of all users of warehouse management system and to do list including replenishments of pick locations.

Radio Frequency Identification (RFID)

RFID is a Technology that allows a sensor (reader) to read, from a distance, and without line of sight, a unique electronic product code (EPC) associated with a tag. Applications of RFID are:

- Supply Chain Management: Real time inventory tracking
- Retail: Active shelves monitor product availability
- Access control: Toll collection, credit cards, building access
- Airline luggage management: British airways implemented to reduce lost/misplaced luggage (20 million bags a year)
- Medical: Implant patients with a tag that contains their medical history
- Pet identification: Implant RFID tag with pet owner information

As indicated in Wilding and Delgado (2004), when compared with other automatic identification systems like barcodes, magnetic stripes or manual data entry, RFID offers many potential benefits. Currently the cost of the technology is a barrier but as implementation costs fall this will be less so. The use of RFID technology has many applications in the industrial and warehouse environment such as product handshaking, near real time inventory control and condition monitoring.

Developments in RFID technology continue to yield larger memory capacities, wider reading ranges, and faster processing. Nonetheless, it is highly unlikely that the technology will ultimately replace barcodes, since the integrated circuitry in an RF tag will never be as cost-effective as a barcode label. RFID will continue to grow in its established niches with the greater supply chain already beginning to adopt it but it remains to be seen if warehousing will also provide RFID with such a niche market opportunity.

Voice Directed Picking

Voice picking in warehouses work in a similar fashion as RF devices. Instead of picking tasks displayed on an RF screen, warehouse operators listen to task information on their headsets through a voice systems connected to warehouse management system through a Wi-Fi network. Voice picking also allows task confirmation through spoken commands. Voice picking has numerous advantages in a warehouse such as:

- Voice Picking makes the data entry operation hands free. There is no need to hold an RF device or scan a barcode to confirm a pick task thereby leaving both hands free for physical movement of goods. This significantly boosts operator productivity.
- Picking by voice improves accuracy and importance of accuracy can not be undermined.
- Voice Picking is particularly suitable for environments where punching data on RF devices is not feasible such as freezer section for storing perishables. In such an environment, the plight of the warehouse operators with gloves fumbling and punching data on keyboard can be imagined.

Agarkar (2007) stated that voice picking may not make sense for warehouse area with low volume or pallet picks which can be done equally effectively using traditional RF devices. Voice picking is also most effective for repetitive tasks. If the warehouse operators perform a large number of different transactions, voice picking may not be very effective. A careful cost-benefit analysis is needed to determine what areas of the warehouse can benefit from voice picking.

According to Piasecki (2001) voice technology has come of age in recent years and is now a very viable solution for piece pick, case pick, or pallet pick operations. Miller (Miller, 2004) stated that because operators need only wear a lightweight headset with a microphone and a small, battery powered voice computer on a waist belt, the technology leaves both hands and eyes free for warehouse operators to actually pick product and move easily from location to location.

Pick to Light

According to Piasecki (2001) pick-to light systems consist of lights and LED displays for each pick location. The system uses software to light the next pick and display the quantity to pick. Pick to light systems have the advantage of not only increasing accuracy, but also increasing productivity. Since hardware is required for each pick location, pick to light systems are easier to cost justify where very high picks per stock keeping unit occur. Carton flow rack and horizontal carousels are good applications for pick to light. In batch picking, put to light is also incorporated into the cart or rack that holds the cartons or totes that you are picking in to. The light will designate which order you should be placing the picked items in.

Warehouse Management System

A warehouse management system (WMS) is a key part of the supply chain and primarily aims to control the movement and storage of materials within a warehouse and process the associated transactions, including shipping, receiving, put away and picking. The systems also direct and optimize stock put away based on real-time information about the status of bin utilization.

Warehouse management systems often utilize Auto ID Data Capture technology, such as barcode scanners, mobile computers, wireless LANs and potentially radio-frequency identification to efficiently monitor the flow of products. Once data has been collected, there is either batch synchronization with or a real-time wireless transmission to a central database. The database can then provide useful reports about the status of goods in the warehouse. Warehouse Management monitors the progress of products through the warehouse. It involves the physical warehouse infrastructure, tracking systems, and communication between product stations.

Emerging Technologies

As illustrated in Tompkins Associates, emerging technologies in warehouse management systems are:

- XML Communication: XML, which stands for eXtensible Markup Language, is a communications means where trading partners can define and exchange information in a collaborative format. What XML brings to the warehouse management systems technology is the capability of integration and exchange with other partners, suppliers or customers' systems as well as ERP or other planning systems through the Internet. Combining this communication platform with critical warehouse operations functionality helps in driving inefficiencies and integration costs down in the total supply chain synthesis.
- Web Visibility: This technology allows the users to access information such as receipts status, shipment dates and inventory status remotely through the Internet. This Web enabling capability is also allowing several vendors to host their warehouse management systems without physically implementing the software at a customer site. This approach may lower the overall cost of ownership for some customers.
- Supply Chain Execution (SCE) Integration: Leading Warehouse Management System vendors are integrating their warehouse management systems software to other SCE suites of products. This integration brings

a benefit to the customer by reducing custom interface development with increased functionality. More popular SCE integration offerings are the Integration (Labor Management), Slotting, Transportation Management System (TMS), Yard Management, Order Management, Advance Planning and Scheduling (APS) and Material Handling Integration.

Third-Party Shipment and Location Tracking Systems

Third party shipment is shipping goods to customer on company's behalf. It provides savings and takes workload from shoulder of logistics managers. Third-party firm's profession allows better delivery times and safer transportation.

Tradenet Services mentioned the concept of third party shipping, its advantages and disadvantages as follows:

Concept of Third Party Shipping

Decades ago, it was common practice for a manufacturing or merchandising firm to receive orders, process them, and then ship them to the recipient according to the terms of the agreement. However, in recent years, businesses have realized that managing and maintaining their own delivery vans and shipping departments are costly. Businesses need to repair and keep their delivery trucks in working condition. They need to pay salaries to drivers and staff who are directly involved in delivering the goods. They also need to buy insurance policies to cover for any loss or damage to your goods while they are in transit.

As a result, many suppliers of raw materials and finished goods have been resorting to third party shipping arrangements in order to cut down their overhead. They have discovered many advantages and benefits in using third party providers to handle shipping and delivery on their behalf.

Advantages and Benefits

With a third party shipping arrangement, businesses do not have to maintain their own delivery or shipping department. Everything from trucks to delivery personnel is outsourced. The third party shipping provider will just arrange for the vehicles to come and pick up your goods at your warehouse or factory premises.

Businesses save on costs of gasoline, salaries of delivery employees, insurance, and penalties if the order arrived late at its destination. All these will be the responsibility of the third party shipping agent. Businesses will not have to deal with labor problems, truck breakdowns, or road accidents. In addition, unless contract is long-term in nature, business can always elect other third party logistics companies to handle their deliveries. Alternatively, they can even have non-exclusive contracts with several third party providers.

Disadvantages and Risks

Business is at the mercy of the third party provider if it has an exclusive arrangement. Expect occasional delays as most third party logistics companies also maintain contracts with several other companies. To avoid delays, business should not deal exclusively with just one shipping company, but with several. This will assure that there will always be someone who can be depended on to ship goods promptly.

In addition, business must make sure that someone in the company always keeps track of the status of any deliveries made by these third party providers. Firm must get as much feedback from the customers about the quality of the delivery service. It must be advised that customers that report any problems either with the condition of the goods or the quality of the service accorded by these third party shipping agencies.

The transportation technologies that are commonly used in logistics industry include transportation information system, global positioning system (GPS), geographical information system (GIS), radio-frequency communication system, and transportation data recorder. The transportation information system and geographical information system can help logistics managers planning, managing and controlling transportation issues. The global positioning system, and radio-frequency communication system can track and guide drivers during the transportation of products (Lin, & Ho, 2007).

New technologies in transportation are:

- E-commerce: Using e-commerce tools, the customers of transport and logistics firms can place orders, initiate and track shipments, and even adjust the pace at which orders move through the transport system.
- Vehicle construction: The integration of electronics into truck engines will make them cleaner and more fuel-efficient.
- Embedded systems: The term embedded systems represents a wide palette of new technologies. Some are used to process data needed to manage a logistics operation. Others allow for real-time tracking of a vehicle's technical parameters to optimize fuel efficiency and plot maintenance requirements. Using data streams from on-board computers, logistics specialists can also optimize route management.

According to Sussman (2005), Intelligent Transportation Systems (ITS) apply well-established technologies of communications, controls, electronics and computer hardware and software to the surface transportation system. Intelligent transportation systems have the ability to sense the presence and identity of vehicles or shipments in real-time on the infrastructure through roadside devices or Global Positioning Systems (GPS); the ability to communicate large amounts of information cheaper and more reliably; the ability to process large amounts of information through advanced information technology; and the ability to use this information properly and in real-time in order to achieve better transportation network operations. Algorithms and mathematical methods to develop strategies for network control and optimization are used. In addition to technological and systems issues, there are a variety of institutional issues that must be carefully addressed. The strategic vision for Intelligent Transportation Systems, then, is as the integrator of transportation, communications and intermodalism on a regional scale.

Close Partnerships with Customers and Suppliers

Partnering is a long-term commitment between two or more organizations for the purpose of achieving specific business goals and objectives. The relationship is based upon trust, dedication to common goals and objectives. Benefits of partnering include improved quality, increased efficiency, lower cost, increased opportunity for innovation, continuous improvement of products and services. The three key elements of partnering are long-term commitment, trust and shared vision.

People are key factors in partnering. Companies should build and develop relationships with them. Relationships between customer and supplier need to be collaborative, not necessarily contractual. It should be open and there should be trust, win-win philosophy, and communication between them. Customers and suppliers should be treated as partners in the activity. Therefore, they both should be focused on outcome and share responsibilities.

Wagner and Boutellier (2002) states that because companies can no longer possess all competencies themselves, strategic partnerships between customers and suppliers are becoming more and more essential. In fact, firms rely on strategic partners to achieve and sustain a competitive position. Theory helps explain the choice between arm's length and cooperative relationships, and practice provides some valuable examples. Companies often lack strategic thinking and the necessary supplier management capabilities. Advanced corporations continuously improve internal and external collaboration. Moreover, they allocate their scarce resources and time by selectively managing the full range of relationships across the supplier portfolio.

Ten principles of customer/supplier relations are:

- Customer and supplier are fully responsible for quality control.
- Customer and supplier should respect each other's independence.
- Supplier is entitled to complete information from the customer.
- Non-adversarial contract between customer and supplier is needed for quality, quantity, price, delivery method and payments.
- Supplier should provide quality to meet customers' satisfaction.
- Product quality evaluation methods should be decided by the mutual consent of both the parties.
- Amicable settlement of disputes between customer and supplier should be established in the contract.
- Continuous information exchange improves the product or service quality.
- To maintain an amicable relationship, both the parties should do procurement, production, and inventory planning.
- Best interest of the end user should be considered while doing business transactions.

Development of relationship includes,

- Inspection: The goal is to eliminate or automate the inspection process. It has four phases: 100% inspection, Sampling, Audit, and Identity check.
- Training: All personnel should receive quality awareness, problem solving, technical and safety training.
- Team approach: Customer/supplier teams are established in areas such as product design, process design and quality system.

- Recognition and Award: Incentives/recognition in the form of newsletters, letter of accommodation, ensures that suppliers remain committed to a quality improvement strategy.

For the last 15 years, a lot of purchasing and supply management professionals express interest in establishing "supplier partnerships" as a way of achieving their organizations' goals. However, very few of them understand that true supplier partnerships involve the buying organization helping the supplier achieve its goals, too. These are four common supplier goals and how a company can help its suppliers to achieve them:

- Reduce Payment Cycle: All suppliers want better cash flow (i.e., getting paid more quickly). So, in a supplier partnership, company should try to improve the speed at which its organization pays the supplier. Like any purchasing improvement initiative, understand its baseline, implement improvements, and measure the change against the baseline.
- Increase Sales: To increase sales, suppliers need to have a marketing edge over their competition. Company can help a supplier partner in this regard by offering a testimonial that they can use in their marketing material and/or serving as a reference.
- Reduce Cost & Complexity: Many buying organizations request special treatment from their suppliers. Whether that special treatment comes in the form of customized reports, unique packaging requirements, or something else, "special treatment" has a cost associated with it. If a company can eliminate unnecessary services that its supplier performs for it, it will help supplier achieve cost reductions that can be shared with organization.
- Increase Reliability of Sales Forecasts: One thing that scares executives is having long-term revenue targets without reliable

data to support them. By committing to a multi-year deal, company can increase its supplier's confidence in its future revenue targets.

By knowing suppliers' goals and helping them to achieve those goals, companies will be in a great position to get its supplier partners' wholehearted commitment to helping organization achieve its goals (Dominick, 2008).

SUMMARY

Logistics providers can have competitive advantage by increasing profits and satisfying customer needs only if they respond to changes in business environment. This response to that change brings innovation in processes. Companies should determine strategies for innovation such as other processes, because they should follow the changes in the market continuously and decide what they should do rapidly. Innovative strategies should cover all branches of the company and it is better to manage them with one hand. All of the innovative strategies should be in cooperation for more successful results.

This study has presented some innovative strategies for logistics processes that managers can easily choose and begin to use them practically. Tools that can be used with these strategies are described. As we mentioned before, managers should determine their needs carefully and then select tools that can satisfy their needs. Effectiveness of tool and return of investment should be considered because technological innovations can be expensive and no one wants to waste any money. For the final reminders, innovative strategies should be continuous, from small sized organizations to big players, all of the organizations should seek for innovation and finally, managers should pay required attention to create new innovative strategies to survive in this hardly competitive business environment.

REFERENCES

Agarkar, A. (2007). *Warehouse Voice Picking*. Retrieved May 5, 2007, from http://blogs.oracle.com/logistics/2007/05/warehouse_voice_picking.html

Appiah, A., & Agyemang, F. (2004). Electronic Retail Payment Systems: User Acceptability and Payment Problems in Ghana, School of Management, Business Administration, Blekinge Institute of technology. Blekinge, Sweeden.

Cahnson, S. (1998), Electronic Payment Systems Handbook of Cyberspace Center, *Hong Kong University of Science & Technology,* Retrieved from http://www.cyber.ust.hk/handbook7/hb-7main.html

Clarke, R. (1998). *Electronic Data Interchange (EDI): An Introduction.* Retrievedfrom http://www.rogerclarke.com/EC/EDIIntro.html

Davenport, T. H. (1993). Process Innovation: Reengineering Work Through Information Technology. Cambridge, MA: Harvard Business School Press.

DHL. (n.d.). *Logbook in cooperation with Technische Universtat Darmstadt.*Retrieved from http://www.dhl-discoverlogistics.com/cms/en/course/technologies/connection/edi.jsp

Dodgson, M., Gann, D., & Salter, A. (2008) The Management of Technological Innovation, Strategy and Practice. Oxford, UK: Oxford University Press.

Dominick, C. (2008). *Supplier Partnerships: Your End of the Deal.* Retrieved from http://www.nextlevelpurchasing.com/articles/supplier-partnership.html

Fagerberk, J., Mowery, D., & Nelson, R. (2004). The Oxford Handbook of Innovation, New York: Oxford University Press.

Haefner, J. (n.d.). Web-based POS? *10 Benefits of Web-Based Point of Sale Software.* Retrieved from http://www.merchantos.com/web_based_pos_benefits/

Lin, C., & Ho, Y. (2007). Technological Innovation for China's Logistics Industry . *Journal of Technology Management and Innovation, 2*(4).

Miller, A. (2004). Order Picking for the 21st Century Voice vs. Scanning Technology A White Paper, *Principal Tompkins Associates,* Retrieved from http://www.baxtek.com/products/vocollect/Voice_v_Scan_White_Paper.pdf

Naxtor Technologies. (2008). *Naxtor Technologies discuss positive effects of IT on warehouse operations.*Retrievedfrom http://www.ferret.com.au/c/Naxtor-Technologies/Naxtor-Technologies-discuss-positive-effects-of-IT-on-warehouse-operations-n817737/tags

New South Wales Government. (2009). *Department of State and Regional Development.* Retrieved from http://www.business.nsw.gov.au/innovation/sectors/

New South Wales Government. (2009). *Department of State and Regional Development.* Retrieved from http://www.business.nsw.gov.au/innovation/sectors/logistics.htm

Piasecki, D. (2001). Order Picking: Methods and Equipment for Piece Pick, Case Pick, and Pallet Pick Operations, *Inventory Operations Consulting L.L.C.* Retrieved from http://www.logprojects.lt/uploads/Order_picking_methods.pdf

Prestwood, D. C. L., & Schumann, P. A., Jr. (1994). Innovate! New York:McGraw-Hill.

Prestwood, D. C. L., & Schumann, P. A. Jr. (1997, July 15). *Innovate! Applying Innovation to the Business of Peru* A Summary of the Talk Given at the III Summit on Competitiveness in Lima, Peru.

Salvador, F., Forza, C., & Claes, B. (2007). Effectiveness of the Product Configuration Task: Theory Formalization and Test, *POMS 18th Annual Conference,* Dallas, TX.

Sussman, J. M. (2005). *An Introduction to Intelligent Transportation Systems, SPRING 1.212, Lectures 2, 3.* Retrieved from ocw.mit.edu/NR/rdonlyres/Civil-and-Environmental-Engineering/1-212JSpring-2005/5B253ABF-EC98-4E53-BA43 4F78500628EA/0/lec3.pdf

Swatman, P. M. C., & Swatman, P. A. (1991, February). Electronic data interchange: organizational opportunity, not technical problem. In *Proceedings of the Conference of the DBIS '91 – 2nd Australian Conference on Information Systems and Database* (pp. 290-307). University of New South, Wales, Sydney. Tompkins Associates Monograph Series, (n.d.). *Warehouse Management Systems Technologies, Transforming Customer Satisfaction Through Better Inventory Management.* Retrieved from http://www.idii.com/wp/tompkins_wms.pdf

Tradenet Services srl, (2008). *A Closer Look at Third Party Shipping Arrangements.* Retrieved from http://www.blogsharp.com/news_9626.html

Wagner, S. M., & Boutellier, R. (2002, November-December). Capabilities for managing a portfolio of supplier relationships . *Business Horizons, 45*(6), 79–88. doi:10.1016/S0007-6813(02)00263-X

Wilding, R., & Delgado, T. (2004). RFID – Applications within the Supply Chain . *Supply Chain Practice, 6*(2), 36–49.

Chapter 2
Research on the Innovation Mechanism and Model of Logistics Enterprise:
A Chinese Perspective

Zhang Mu
Jinan University, China

Li Wenli
Jinan University, China

Luo Jing
Jinan University, China

Ye Xiang
Jinan University, China

Ren Congying
Jinan University, China

Wu Chengjuan
Jinan University, China

ABSTRACT

Logistics is a newly developed field in the service industry; it is growing rapidly in the world and is regarded as the fundamental industry and artery in the national economy. The level of its development is an essential measurement for judging a country's modernization level and overall national strength. It works as an accelerator in the economic development. As in the initial stage of transforming traditional logistics service to modern logistics service in China, logistics enterprises have encountered difficulties and problems including the imbalanced supply and demand for logistics service in the market, distempered industrial structure, faultiness of serving process and lagging of logistics technology, since 2005. Compared with the developed countries, there exists great gaps between the Chinese logistics enterprises and the advanced level in the aspects of service concepts, service model, service content and service techniques. So the authors analyze the innovation model integrated logistics, logistics technology and

DOI: 10.4018/978-1-61520-603-2.ch002

logistics network model, value-added service model, based on the service innovation driving force theoretic framework. At last, the authors selected Shenzhen China Overseas Logistics Co. LTD (COL) as the empirical objects to analyze its character of the technology and non-technology innovation, and summarize its inner and outer driving force on promoting the service innovation. Thereafter, the typical service innovative model based on innovative driving force has been discussed.

INTRODUCTION

The focus of current enterprise competition is no more the competition of entity products, but the service competition. So it urges enterprise to take customer and service as the guidance to gain competitiveness by service innovation. Peter F. Drucker (1985) thinks innovation is not a technology term but an economical and social word, and its judgment standard is not science or technology but a reform of the economy and society, a value as well. Therefore, his definition of innovation is to reform output capacity of resource or change the value and satisfaction of clients gained from resource. He also pointed out that innovation is not something happed in organization, but a reform out of the organization. It should be measured by its impact on environment. It is not necessarily to happen, of course, it is not totally accidental, and people should actively seek the chance and try to realize innovation. Therefore, innovation is the cognitive response to outer environment, competitive situation and change of customer demand. It can be the innovation of product and service; it also can be their combination and innovation of process and method which include mentality innovation, technology innovation, organization innovation and market innovation etc.

Logistics service is the important element of customer service, and its value is realized by the utility of time and space, 7R (Right time, place, commodity, quantity, quality, price, condition) is the concrete embodiment of its value realization. With the change of environment, the value based on logistics service features can not describe the nature of logistics service; it needs to extend many value-added activities, such as package, the third party logistics, distribution, circulation processing, barcode and information and so on. In other word, logistics service value refers to traditional time and space value; it also contains service-added value that provides competitive strength in the market. Traditional time and space value is the qualification element of market competition, while value-added logistics service is the dominant element of competition. In fierce market competition, people need to innovate logistics service in order to realize value-added logistics service.

Nowadays, domestic logistics enterprises can barely meet the need of logistics service and competition. The lack of service type, poor service, absence of service mentality seriously impedes the development of logistics enterprise and industry. As the core of logistics industry, service is also the product offered by logistics enterprises. In terms of service, Chinese logistics enterprises should continuously innovate enterprise service model, improve service level and capacity and increase service competitiveness. As for Chinese logistics enterprises transferring from traditional storage, transportation industry, it is full of significance for enterprise development and industry growth to strengthen service innovative mentality and improve innovative competence. This article aims to study the mechanism and model of service innovation in Chinese logistics enterprises based on the analysis of drive element of logistics service innovation.

REVIEW OF THE RESEARCH ON SEIVICE INNOVATION AND LOGISTICS SEIVICE INNOVATION

The main difference between service economy and traditional economy is that service economy focuses more on the dynamic resources, such as process, knowledge and skill, and value creation is regarded as a collaborative process involving both service provider and customers. Some researchers call it as "service dominant logic". The traditional economy, however, focuses more on product manufacturing, emphasizes on static resource (such as natural resource) and take value creation process as the process of transforming the resource to the product and delivering to the customers, which is called "goods dominant logic".

Western academia started systematic research about service innovation in 1980's. Earlier research on service innovation focused on micro-level of enterprise with emphasizing service innovation concept, types and models. The researchers found the universality of service innovation domain and diversity of service innovation type and emphasized the special status of "organization innovation", "unique innovation", and "structural reengineering innovation" in service industry. Thereafter, some scholars described the innovation process of service enterprises with proposing relevant innovation models and had further study human resource and standardization similar to manufacturing innovation. Kandampully (2002) proposed that innovation was the core competency for service enterprises and service innovation relied on three relevant elements including technology, knowledge and relationship network. Ross L Chapman et al. (2002) claimed that network and development, information and exchange technology, human capital, organizational change, intellectual property, competition and rule change are the main elements of service innovation. Based on the research, the service innovation regularities were identified, new impact of the environment on

service innovation was found and the importance of service innovation from industry level perspective was realized. Lin and Wu (2003) introduced the above international research outcomes in the book of "Service Innovation".

From the perspective of research method, the researchers have applied the theory and method system developed in manufacturing industry to service innovation research after the concept of service innovation was proposed and accepted in 1980. The research results found that the innovation theory from manufacturing industry could not completely explain the innovation activities and mechanism. The typical representative research of this stage was named as "reverse product cycle" proposed by Barras (1990) after his study of the typical service industries including financing and insurance industry etc.

Thereafter, the scholars started to study innovation and the related issues from the perspective of service characteristics, which was called "service method" research. This research had found a lot of unique innovative behaviors during service process and revealed a lot of special innovative essence and rules. "Special innovative models" and "service specialty track" are the typical representative theory of this stage. Recently, the development trend of ambiguity and integration of manufacturing and service industry attracts the scholars to look for an "integrated method" to unify the product and service. The typical representative research includes the classification research by Gallouj and Weinstein (1997), and "4-dimension model" of service innovation proposed by Bilderbeek (1998) .The research finds and explains the rules of service innovation from various perspectives, and promotes the research method system of service innovation to be gradually mature.

The initiation for Chinese academia to study logistics innovation is a bit late with a couple of decades. Most of the research was developed regarding supply chain, information technology and value-added services.

Wang and Chen (2007) indicated that the third party logistics enterprises should identify their own resources and core competency, understand the strategic relationships between the upstream and downstream enterprises along the supply chain, and follow the trend of logistics outsourcing and information technology development. Moreover, they should pursue sustainable competitive advantage by providing valuable extended service, integrated service and distinguished service. Peng (2007) found that exploring value-added service was becoming the new trend of logistics development. The third party logistics enterprises needed to strengthen service innovation and extend value-added service, emphasized information construction and hence improved its core competency and logistics service standard. Han (2006) analyzed the importance of providing financial logistics service by the third party logistics enterprises and proposed the financial logistics service model provided by different links along the supply chain. Li et al. (2006) designed a dynamic model for service innovation of logistics enterprise, which described the driving factors for service innovation including external dynamics such as external tracks, doers, and logistics alliances, as well as internal drivers such as strategic management, employee creation and organization innovation. Liu and Wang (2007) discussed the service innovation paths and possible strategies selected by various Chinese logistics enterprises. Liu and Li (2006) argued that the new path to realize service innovation included: building relative systems, effectively managing service innovation, innovating based on customer needs, satisfying customer requirements and striving for the leader of service innovation.

It is concluded that there is not adequate logistics service innovation researches in China and a big gap exists comparing with international research. Hence, the current problem is there is a lack of theoretical guidance for the practical service innovation operation in most of Chinese logistics enterprises.

THE PRESENT SITUATION ANALYSIS OF SERVICE AND INNOVATION FOR LOGISTICS INDUSTRY IN CHINA

With the fast development of China's economy and the uptrend of world's economic globalization, most enterprises hope to increase their profit by decreasing the cost of logistics, which offers a great opportunity for China's logistics enterprises.

Development Trends for Modern Logistics Industry and Service Innovation

Different enterprises have different understanding about logistics service. Generally speaking, it may be regarded as a yardstick to judge their capability to save time and space for certain goods and services which include all the service activities from receiving the orders to the delivering them to customers.

According to the research in 2004, the world's service industry accounts for 63% of the world's GDP. In some developed countries, it makes up 71% in the economy and 32% in China (Liang, Z.P., 2005). It will surely continue to grow rapidly with the development of the economy. Therefore, the service industry has been the pillar for economy development.

Logistics is a newly developed field in service industry; it is growing rapidly in the world and is regarded as the fundamental industry and artery in national economy. The level of its development is an essential measurement for judging a country's modernization level and overall national strength. It works as an accelerator in the economic development. The mission for logistics is to offer first-rate service, to satisfy customers' needs, to develop and create customer value so as to add value in the overall process of logistics.

Modern logistics service bears the characteristics of information technology, socialization and integration with capability of innovation and value-addition. What's more, it provides customer-oriented and first-rate logistics service by improving the efficiency and productivity of supply chain to achieve greater customer satisfaction.

The modern logistics service doesn't simply depend on the upstream or downstream enterprises of the supply chain but relies on the design, integration, E-commerce and information sharing of the logistics system provided by socialized logistics serving firms. It can achieve lower cost and the integration of the enterprises' supply chain by integrating product controlling, transporting, delivering, managing customer service, purchasing, managing storage and information with the integration of the logistics processes of the first party, second party and third party(Chen, F.J., 2005).

The value-added logistics service is based on the completion of basic functions as well as the various extended business activities tailoring to the customers' needs. Relying on the advanced management concepts and the updated information technology, those extended logistics activities realize the added value of supply chain in the process of providing extended logistics service for the customers.

The innovation capability of modern logistics refers to the logistics enterprises' capability of their application of new technology or new production organizing methods to develop new market and new service. It's the economic process of optimum integrating of different kinds of economic factors in which the enterprises achieve the utmost profit as well as the scientific combination of different economic factors and optimum composition of resources(Sun, X.W.& Zhang, Z.M., 2001). It is an innovation that distinguishes modern logistics service from traditional logistics one. In fierce competition of the market, the innovation capability helps the logistics enterprises to improve their competition ability and serves as the driving force for the survival and development.

Bottleneck Problem of Logistics Industry Development in China

As in the initial stage of transforming tradition logistics service to modern logistics service in China, logistics service practice has encountered difficulties and problems since 2005.

The Imbalanced Supply and Demand for Logistics Service in the Market

As both macro policy and sustained development of economy contribute to the increase of total quantity in logistics industry, the market has a significant potential demand for logistics service but the supplying of logistics service is quite limited. However, on one hand, the high cost (The cost of logistics accounts for 10% of GDP in developed countries, while it accounts for 20% in China.) impedes the development of logistics in China; on the other hand, the lack of right understanding of the customer value and customer-oriented concepts makes the logistics firms fail to increase customer value. Therefore, it's impossible for them to provide qualified and standardized logistics service. Their poor service and incapability for creating value for customers has a negative effect on the development of logistics service market.

The Distempered Industrial Structure

Many logistics enterprises still keep the "large and whole" or the "small and whole" management model, and their logistics activities are mainly completed by the self-arrangement of the organization.

According to the investigation, in industrial enterprises, 36% of raw materials are delivered by company themselves and 46% are completed by the material supplying firms. Only 18% of the logistics are completed by the third part enterprises.

In terms of finished goods logistics, 24.1% will be finished by enterprise and 59.8% will be handled by the cooperation of enterprise and third party logistics enterprises, only 16.1% is done by the third logistics enterprises (Lv, G.R., 2005). The self-service-oriented service model will restrain efficient, professional and socialized development of modern logistics service. While in commercial enterprises, 76.5% of logistics service is done by enterprises themselves and 17.6% by suppliers.

From Table 1 it indicates market expectation for the third part logistics enterprises has changed greatly compared with what it expects for the traditional logistics service. The single service of logistics can meet the needs of the market and the third part logistics enterprises must extend their service. From the statistics, there is a great demand for the redesign of logistics network, the construction of logistics information system and bar code scanning system. Meanwhile, people can see a strong demand for product packaging, distribution process, quality control of the raw materials, customer declaration and accounting payment, etc.

The Faultiness of Serving Process

As most of the logistics enterprises are converted from transportation enterprises or storage centre, it's difficult for them to provide integrated logistics service for their weaknesses in small scale and single function. 85% of income comes from the basic service and the rest of 15% is from value-added and information service of logistics service. The basic service handles the market competition with price without any innovation service content which is far more different in developed countries where it enjoys the supply-chain service from organizing production to distribution. Especially, foreign logistics enterprises surging into the Chinese market put greater pressure on the local enterprises, and the price of old logistics service no longer has any advantage and the competition of price doesn't do any good to increasing profit. So the competition among these enterprises changes from price to service gradually. As a result, the present single service with less innovation and value proves less competitive.

Table 1. Market demand for logistics service. Data source: Li, M. & Fan, Z.Q., 2002

Service functions	Expectations of the Content (%)	Existing Functions	
		Production Enterprises (%)	Commercial Enterprises (%)
Warehousing custody	16	20	29
Main line transport	20	48	29
Local delivery	14	28	29
Processing and package	6	4	14
Network reproduction	12	0	0
Barcode Customization	8	0	0
Information system	10	0	0
Materials quality inspection	3	0	0
customs declaration agent	7	0	0
Payment clearing agent	4	0	0

The Lagging of Logistics Technology

Compared with the developed countries, China has to work hard in the aspects of logistics facilities and technology. The scale of transportation infrastructure is rather small, in terms of the transportation network density according to land acreage and population, China is only America's 19.6%, Germany's 9%, India's 25% and Brazil's 71%. China does not only fall behind developed countries, it is also far behind some developing countries like Brazil and India (Zheng, L.P., 2007). The shortage of modern logistics distributing centre and storage infrastructure, the obvious laggard of big integrated delivery centre that can effectively link with different transportation channels and various logistics base and centered constructions what serve original economy and city, the low degree of logistics standardization and disaccording standards among transportation equipment and devices, all these will prevent the harmonious development of all kinds of logistics functions and factors and the improvement of logistics efficiency.

In a word, there exists great gap between the Chinese logistics enterprises and the advanced level in the aspects of service concepts, service model, service content and service techniques which lead to their incapability for innovation and competition, and stop them to create value for the customers and to help enterprises establish a new logistics design, service or products. At the same time, for lack of further study on theories and methods for the innovation of logistics system and structure of the modern business model, it's unable to provide effective guidance for the practical use of logistics service innovation. Therefore, it's quite urgent to make scientific study on the service innovation model, process, technique, and organization management because this will help logistics enterprises to be more competitive with offering higher-quality service.

THE ANALYSIS ON DRIVING FORCE AND MODEL OF LOGISTICS SERVICE INNOVATION

Though lacking of necessary theoretical research, a lot of enterprises are practicing SSME. Therefore, the exploration of logistic service innovation is regarded as the important task in China.

Dynamic Mechanism of Logistics Service Innovation

The Framework of Driving Force for Service Innovation

The basic driving force of service innovation is the foundation to form innovation model, and it is also an important determinant of the innovation process. And combination of the driving force elements would form the system innovation environment for services enterprises. Therefore, to identify and grasp the driving force is the prerequisite for setting innovative strategies, and an important means of service sector in management department to impact the innovation activity as well (Jon Sundbo & Faïz Gallouj, 2000). This service innovation driving force model can be seen detail in Figure 1.

In this model, the driving force of innovation in services is divided into two types as internal and external driving force. Internal power refers to the drive from the internal management, departments, staff and other actors, while the external power of innovation can be analyzed from two dimensions of actors and tracks. Internal power and external power relate to each other. Internal power can not start without external power; while it is difficult for external power to conduct the function of motion-induce and promoting without internal power.

Figure 1. Driving force model of service innovation

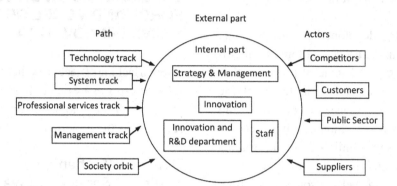

Innovative Consciousness of Logistics Service

Referring to the study method of Tian (Tian, X., 2008), Figure 2 and Figure 3 indicate the change of enterprises business before and after meeting the potential demand of customer enterprise. Figure 2 shows the type of customer enterprises and their demand on logistics services through a two-dimensional matrix, that is, customer enterprises can be divided into two parts: the one who has received logistics services and the one who has not; the demand for logistics services can be grouped as the one that customer enterprise has clearly expressed and the one has not been expressed. The figure indicates no matter how well a logistics company has met the clearly-expressed-need of customer enterprises, if he does not consider the silent and potential demand which is the future development of logistics service, the logistics enterprise may miss a lot of opportunities, even bring him some risks.

Therefore, when the logistics company is attaching great importance to the current needs of customer enterprises, it should also pay attention to the large number of unexploited opportunities to help companies know their own unexpressed but potential demand (See Figure 3) and to meet their satisfaction. This will not only assist the customer enterprises to enhance their competitiveness, to gain success in the field, but it can also help the logistics enterprises to expand the scope of business and profit margins to achieve win-win outcomes.

Figure 2. Logistic enterprises before the provision of potential services requirement

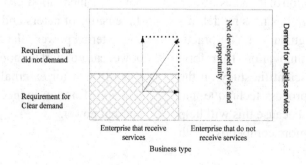

Figure 3. Logistic enterprises after providing of potential services requirement

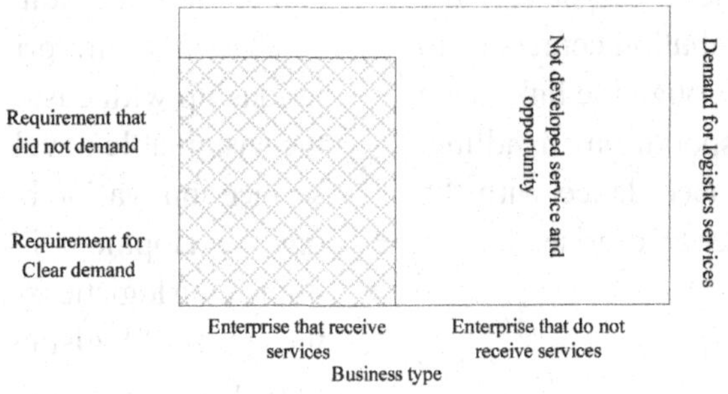

Innovation Model

Integrated Logistics Model Based on the Needs of Customer Enterprises

Integrated logistics is the logistics system that based on a common goal through certain institutional arrangements to integrate all third-party logistics enterprises on the logistics service chain (Li, H.M., 2006). It adopts computer network technology and information technology as the pillar and the global logistics resources as the optional object to manage the internal supply chain in the node enterprises and supply chain among the node enterprises by integrating all kinds of advanced logistics technology and management technology. It makes full use of such sharing resources as personnel, processes, technology and performance standards to achieve the high-quality, low-cost, fast, efficient operational synergies with providing the logistics products or services to meet the market's needs.

The main characteristics of the integrated logistics model are as follows:

- Services integration

The single operation mode of traditional function-based third party logistics enterprises is difficult to meet diversified and personalized demands of the customer enterprises. Integrated logistics, however, can not only provide the basic logistics services such as warehousing, transportation, handling, loading, unloading, packaging, distribution processing and information processing, but also can offer other value-added services such as order processing, logistics program selection and planning, payment recovery and settlement, logistics system design and development program planning, as well as solution design according to the specific business process of the customer enterprises. Then the only thing customer enterprises face is the supplier of integrated logistics services which will have overall responsibility for organization, management, coordination of "one-stop place" of the entire serialized process of logistics services.

- Process seamless

Integrated logistics is a large-span system which organically integrates internal supply chain in the node enterprises and supply chain among the node enterprises by means of the internet technology and information platform with the mechanism elements such as standards, norms, and systems. On the basis of one brand, it conducts integrated, standardized, normalized services with running seamless operation integration. For example, integrated logistics enterprise can design, select the best logistics operation program, and deliver it to the required production location by time, by volume, by species with guaranteeing the quality of service based on the customer company's procurement, production, marketing plans and business process. Meanwhile, it can deliver the off line products to the distribution centers or to every retail outlet directly through the links such as transport, storage, transportation, handling, packaging and labeling in accordance with the requirements of the customer enterprise.

• Organization networking

Integrated logistics carry out planning, designing and practical implementing in accordance with the network in a certain market region through the logistics operation organizations, logistics business organizations, logistics resource organizations and logistics information organizations, and finally form a secondary logistics network system consisting of logistics trunk network, regional feeder network, and urban distribution network in its service market region.

In this secondary logistics network system, the node enterprises connect with the shared information platform and common operational activities. In accordance with the principle of division of labor and cooperation, each of them plays their own core expertise, magnifies the function of each network element so as to achieve the goals of rapid reaction of integrated logistics and total cost optimization for logistics services.

The Model of Logistics Technology and Logistics Network Based on Industry Technology Development

Logistics service is the intangible procedure attached to the tangible operation(such as transportation, storage, portage etc.) which occurs between the customer enterprise and logistics staff, tangible product and logistics service system to solve some substantial problems for the customer enterprises so as to improve their operating effect. In terms of logistics enterprise, its service is the essence of the operation. And the competitive logistics service guarantees its sustainable development. Only the constant perfection of the logistics service content and level will result in the increase satisfaction of customer enterprise to establish long-run relationship with customer enterprises and expand the sustainable development room. The logistics service innovation based upon industry technology development is the significant source for improving logistics service quality which includes the model of logistics technology innovation and logistics network innovation.

The Logistics Technology Innovation Model

The biggest difference between logistics service and general service is that general service mainly relies on the non-technology service of staff. So its innovation can be realized by improving management organization structure and service procedure. While logistics service needs the support from logistics technology and equipment, its innovation contains both technology and non-technology innovation. What's more, the technology innovation of logistics service can improve the operating efficiency of logistics service with creating the time and space utility better and faster. The fact proves that the adoption of advanced logistics technology such as information technology, automatic stereoscopic warehouse and so on can tremendously enhance the service competitive strength of logistics enterprise. Moreover, the biggest advantage of logistics technology innovation is that it is hard to imitate by competitors or the cost of imitation is relatively high.

Modern logistics technology innovation runs through the professional technology and managerial technology of various basic activities in the whole logistics area. According to the source of technological thought and scientific principle, it includes logistics mechanical technology, logistics information technology, logistics electronic technology, logistics automatic control technology, logistics mathematics method and computer technology etc. As for functional activity, it contains transportation technology, storage technology, handling technology, package technology, distribution processing technology and logistics information technology etc. And technological form includes hard technology such as facility, equipment, tool etc, and the soft technology such as information network, logistics project and logistics system. As logistics innovation system presents in various aspects, Table 2 lists the most prominent areas for logistics innovation in real logistics operation, it promotes the development of logistics service with systematization, integrity and cooperativity.

Logistics Network Innovation Model

With the rapid development of economy, the traditional "Vertical integration" can not meet the need of modern enterprise competition. In order to keep its flexibility and improve its essential competitive strength, enterprises outsource its logistics business to the third-party logistics enterprise. Therefore, it has become the basic tendency of logistics development to realize the socialization of logistics service by developing the third-party logistics service and strengthening third-party logistics service innovation. Under this circumstance, innovating logistics network to form the logistics service network based on supply chain becomes the inevitable choice (Li, Y.F. & Pu, G.A., 2003). The innovation model of logistics network mainly includes network innovation, channel network innovation, relationship network innovation and information network innovation etc.

Modern logistics is based on the supply chain, and it is established on the base of strategic cooperation of all members in the chain. Therefore, building close corporative relationship with vendors, distributors, retailers and customers to execute relationship management will basically determine the integrated advantage of supply chain logistics and improve the competitiveness of logistics enterprise (Photis & Panayides, 2005) .

Photis and Meko made the empirical study on the relationship among relationship orientation, organization study, innovation and supply chain performance, and they discovered the relationship orientation didn't directly result in supply chain innovation, but indirectly led to innovation by organization study to get supply chain performance (See Figure 4). The essence of strategic corporative relationship of supply chain is to realize the share of knowledge and information, meet the customer's satisfaction quickly, flexibly and creatively. Innovating relationship network is to rebuild the relationship of supply chain to essentially rebuild value chain to gain the competitive advantage.

The innovation of logistics relationship network objectively needs the innovation of logistics information network. Only realizing the innovation of information network can achieve the real-

Table 2. Technology innovation model in logistic industry

Logistic Hard Technology Innovation	Logistic Soft Technology Innovation
Transport technology(conveyance, facilities)	Prediction technology(Regression analysis, Time series prediction)
Storage technology(Warehouse Construction, Shelf)	Decision-making technology(Analysis of expectations, regret value method in decision making)
Packaging technology (Packaging Materials, machinery)	Standardization technology (Management, operation and technical standards)
Handling technology (Loading and unloading, Handling machinery)	Economic evaluation technology (Target and methods selection)
Distribution processing equipment(Sorting, Processing equipment)	Control technology (Feedback and supervisory control)
Information technology (computer, Communications equipment)	Optimize technology (Operations Research Methods)

Figure 4. Relationship among relationship orientation, organization study, innovation and supply chain performance

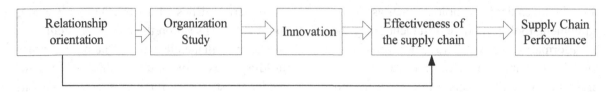

time transfer and share of the information on supply chain member to reduce "bullwhip effect". Hence, the innovation of logistics information network supplies the basic means for service innovation of logistics enterprises.

Logistics Service Model Based on Value-Added Service

Logistics value-added service refers to various stretching business activities under the requirement of customer enterprises on the basis of fulfilling logistics basic function. There are not fixed compounds for logistics value-added function, and the definition for value-added function remains ambiguous. However, it belongs to various stretching services based on basic logistics service with obvious characteristics and creativity.

The difference between logistics value-added service and basic service contains following aspects:

- Logistics value-added service is a deep level of logistics service. It is a special value-added service scheme proposed after getting well known about customer enterprise's logistics needs, it is also the special service scheme faced to specific logistics needs.
- The value-added service of logistics is to increase investment based on the basic logistics service to gain the added value. Therefore, it needs the extra logistics service fee from customer enterprise.

- The value-added service of logistics has the feature of timeliness. With the gradual development of logistics enterprise service, the previous value-added service will evolve to be basic logistics service.

There are two types of models on value-added service offered by logistics enterprise:

- Logistics service model based on integration of supply chain

The first step to realize the diversity of value-added logistics service is to achieve the integration of supply chain. It involves the whole process from the initial vendor procurement, manufacture support for manufacture department, marketing support for marketing department to the products eventually distributed to the customers. The integration of supply chain upgrades channel arrangement to be a corporative power dedicated to improve efficiency and competitiveness from several loose individual enterprises. So it requires all the members of supply chain to corporate with mutual trust to share the basic transaction data and long-term strategic information so that the logistics enterprises can find out the effective means and method to meet logistics need of customer enterprises with easily combining the experience and capacity of supply chain member and then to create sustainable characteristics logistics solution so as to improve the competitiveness of whole supply chain (See Figure 5).

• Customer-enterprise-centered logistics service model

There comes this kind of logistics service model when introducing the Customer-enterprise-centered service to the integration of supply chain (See Figure 6).

In Figure 6, although customer enterprises play a significant role as the service objective of the whole supply chain, it is more than the enterprise on the last node in the supply chain. Meanwhile, it includes the marketing and manufacture departments of manufacture. Logistics enterprises will cooperate with these customer enterprises closely with deeply studying their needs to seek the potential chance of value-added service; customer enterprises also include the vendors who provide products and materials for logistics enterprises, and logistics enterprises will offer value-added service for them as well.

Conclusion of Various Models

The innovation of logistics service is driven by couple of factors which include the development tendency of the whole Chinese logistics industry, the competitive environment of logistics enterprises, the need of logistics enterprises performance improvement, the demand of logistics service in circulation service enterprises, social economy, information technology and fast development of network technology etc. These 5 types of innovation models of logistics service present different strengths, weaknesses and risks (See Table 3).

AN EMPIRICAL STUDY OF THE CHINA OVERSEAS LOGISTICS

The authors selected Shenzhen China Overseas Logistics Co. LTD (COL) as the empirical objects to analyze its character of the technology and non-technology innovation, and summarize its inner and outer driving force on promoting the service innovation. Thereafter, the typical service innovative model based on innovative driving force has been discussed.

The Profile of China Overseas Logistics (COL)

This part will select China Overseas Logistics (COL) as the research object to analyze its operation in technology and non-technology innovation, summarize its inner and outer drive of promoting service enterprise to carry out innovation, recognize the role and change of each drive and explain the typical service innovative model based on innovative drive analysis to study the uniqueness of innovative process of service enterprises.

China Overseas Logistics limited corporation was established on 13th November 1993 as the first

Figure 5. Logistics service model based on integration supply chain

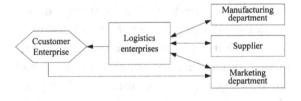

Figure 6. Customer enterprise service-oriented model of logistics services

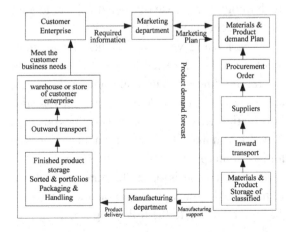

Table 3. Comparison of logistics service innovation models

Innovation Model	Main content	Strengths, weaknesses and risks
Customer's-need-oriented innovation	Innovating logistics service based on customer's need, feedback information, customer knowledge and participation as the innovative source	It could meet customers' current demand and expectation more effectively. However, it is short of strategy with the risks of antinomy between service level and cost.
Logistics technology innovation	Adopting new logistics technology and equipment, improving service efficiency	It enjoys evident competitive strength, but it lacks for flexibility with relatively big investment
Logistics network innovation	Rebuilding relation network, information network, supply network, distribution network, organization network to realize innovation of logistics strategic platform	It is hard to simulate, which helps to share and integrate to achieve integration advantage. However, it may take risking in involving intelligent property, business secret and credibility.
Value-added logistics service innovation	Expanding the content and function of logistics service to create value for customer	The important source of logistics service competitive advantage is based on customer value, but it requires qualified staff
Second-mover competition innovation	Innovating based on simulating competitor's logistics service with setting benchmarking	It is easy to accomplish with posterior strategy and small risk. But it can barely take initiative in competition.

logistics company operating in Shenzhen Futian Free Trade Zone (FFTZ) with registered capital of 50 million HK$. There are four professional subsidiaries as Fuhai division, China Overseas Transportation, China Overseas Information, China Overseas Passenger and Cargo Agent with the total capital amount of 270 million HK$. It is a comprehensive logistics enterprise with electronic products, mechanical manufacture and business etc as client groups integrating with logistics information technology, project consultant, JIT distribution, international cargo agent, multimodal transport, trade agent, custom declaration and inspection, credit settlement.

COL locates in the east and west port area of Shenzhen with taking the Pearl River Delta as the base, it selects key cities such as Shanghai, Chongqing, Xi'an, Tianjin, and big cities in Japan and Korea, the east and west port area in U.S.A. as the logistics nodes to develop the logistics network covering China, south-east Asia, Europe and America etc to make sure customer's goods can arrive in any place of the network anytime.

COL was the first company in logistics industry of China to get the ISO9002 international logistics authentication in 1999. It is also the first enterprise in the logistics industry to develop high-tech electronic product parts distribution and is recognized as "The First Research Base of High-tech Product Parts Distribution" and "The First Demonstrative Enterprise of Electronic Part Distribution" by China Logistics Technology Associate, and it is also ranked as one of the 34 key logistics enterprises of China by China Economy and Trade Committee. The Company always holds the management belief of "Credit First, Customer Supreme." So it strives for offering safe, qualify, fast and accurate whole-course the third party logistics service for customers. With years of unremitting efforts, the company has got the honor of "Top 100 Logistics Enterprises of China", "Experimental Base of Chinese Logistics", "34 Key Logistics Enterprises of China", "The Top Technology Enterprise of Shenzhen" etc to earn the wide acceptance by the society.

Experiencing years of sustainable development, COL has clarified the strategic target for future: Building configuration-optimized logistics entity network, unblocked and perfect logistics information network, reasonable logistics business network to make COL a comprehensive modern logistics enterprise with completed functions, perfect network which is top in China and well-known in the world. Hence, the core business needs to pay full attention to the following areas:

- It will keep a foothold at production logistics to develop port logistics and city distribution, expand service types and extend logistics chain.
- It will keep a foothold at Guangdong, Hong Kong and South of China, develop in Yangtze River Delta, Circum-Bohai-Sea region, middle and east area, south-east of Asia, Europe and America, expand service region and perfect logistics network.
- It will keep a foothold at project management, develop in the direction of network, information, and scale operation to realize corporative management.

Although as the domestic advanced enterprise in service and technology, China Overseas Logistics has some problems need to be solved in recent years:

- Poor flexibility in enterprise operation

What logistics enterprise offers is service rather than product which determines the tightness between logistics enterprise and client market. The staff have to handle with changeable customer's need (the change of order, delivery time and delivery location) and logistics environment. (Such as traffic jam and control, bad weather, natural disaster) They have to react quickly. It requires staff right behavior decision combining with enterprise's and their own experience and lesson. In conclusion, the behavior decision of logistics enterprise staff needs more support from implicit knowledge (experience and judgment). And knowledge management drive can fully cultivate, transfer and use the implicit knowledge in staff's mind.

- the shortage of knowledge mining and management

The management of logistics enterprises differs from that of knowledge-intensive enterprise which objectively results in increase of the dif-

ficulty of "knowledge" management of logistics enterprises. The key of knowledge management is to build the knowledge-shared culture, establish the unblocked and broad knowledge communication passage. Because the management of logistics enterprises emphasizes the strict functional division in regulation (the level of operation, management and decision-making), emphasizes standardization and programmed in thought, and focuses on "goes up and down between different levels" in behavior to operate with obeying the instruction strictly, it is easy to form the shortage of communication among various divisions and management to affect the communication and propagation in the company. For example, there is evident difference of positions, before staff's opinion reaches top management; it has to pass countless levels of middle management. During this process, the middle management will filter the information according to their own understanding so the message to the top may be distorted. Similarly, the instruction from the top may be changed by the middle management's perception. What's more, logistics enterprise excessively pursuing institutionalization does harm to foster knowledge-share-culture. For example, the logistics staff on the level of operation mainly focuses on the repetitive, programmed, and standardized work, so enterprises manage them rigidly with emphasizing the safety and continuity without considering staff's opinion. There is the detailed operation instruction on the setting and operation rules for every position.

Integrated Innovation in COL

COL used to consist of various functional departments. In order to change this situation, they made a series of integration schemes include rebuilding the internal structure of enterprise, improving enterprise's competitiveness which helps COL realize the integration of internal logistics and connect the internal supply chain with the external to implement the integration of supply chain.

- The supply chain of container transportation

COL started with traditional shipping industry and set up five professional shipping companies include container transportation, tanker transportation, bulk cargo transportation, special cargo transportation, and ocean passenger shipping. The container's total number of slots is ranked as No.1 in China and rise to No.5 in the world. The competition of shipping industry is more than the competition of this industry, it will eventually reflect the competition of the whole supply chain. Recent years, the competition of shipping industry brings the maximization and ultra-maximization which on the one hand greatly strengthens marine transport capacity; on the other hand, it indicates the shortage of port infrastructure, wharf operation capacity, storage yard capacity, onshore allocation, port collection and separation which becomes the restrictive factor for the development of shipping industry. Actually, the competition of shipping industry has extended to the onshore from the ocean which includes allocation transportation and logistics service onshore and in the wharf. Therefore, the development of main business of COL requires the cooperation of onshore logistics development; and the development of COL container transportation also needs the cooperation of the development of onshore container transport supply chain. There are many significant factors in COL's success, one of them is "major business centered" strategy.

- Discovering the blue ocean of market

All logistics enterprises especially those with similar background have something in common. The uniqueness of COL strategic option is to have its own choice to select the segment market to establish its development strategy and tactics according to its specific condition. COL chooses the onshore container transportation as the mainline to build the functions of every link in container

transport supply chain. Establishing the service system of container transport supply chain fits COL's development, and it is also the practical choice based on its own resource.

As for the demands of external market, the backward situation of domestic road assemble transport offers the market for COL's development of container transport supply chain. Compared with the fast development of Chinese ocean container transportation, Chinese onshore container transport lags behind seriously which affects the vertical development of container transport supply chain. What's more, according to the routine of transport clause in international trade, people usually adopt Container Yard to Container Yard rather than door-to-door, it breaks container transport supply chain and restrains the development of container transport. Besides that, there are few big companies with big scale of container and goods source. This development blank offers COL the blue sea of market and the opportunity of developing container transport supply chain. This strategic positioning not only suits the need of Chinese logistics market development, but also displays COL's core competitiveness of "valuableness, scarcity and hard to imitate." to enrich the brand of COL with distinctive characteristics.

- Developing the third party logistics

COL provides the professional third party logistics solutions such as bonded storage, import and export distribution, cross-regional transport, customer declaration agent, simple processing, sorting package, freight agent etc to thoughtfully meets customer's personalized need comprehensively with discovering customer's deep demand (See Figure 7).

- Standardized service

COL offers the secure and efficient service such as providing domestic, Hong Kong and Guangdong cross-border trunk and branch transportation,

Figure 7. Information platform of COL

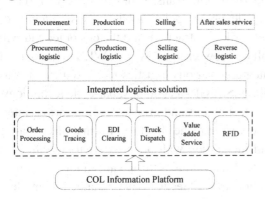

LTL delivery vehicle, GPS/GIS monitoring and dispatching all over the country. COL has more than 120 free vehicles including 1.5T~30T box cars, container tractors etc and it can dispatch more than 500 vehicles with various types. It can not only handle domestic and Hong Kong and Guangdong cross-border etc road transport business,(FTL/Bulk Cargo/ LCL), it also cooperates with the competitive enterprise in the field of waterway, railway, aviation transport to establish a tremendous transport network to offer the omnidirectional transport service for customers. In terms of the personalized service, it provides Milk-run transport model and freight intermodal transport etc to realize "door-to-door" one-stop trunk and branch distribution.

With adopting standardized quality management system and holding regularized market operation mentality, COL provides customer prompt and effective feedback on vehicle information by tracking them with GPS. What's more, it has realized the real time on-line enquiry for cargo transportation and on-line order based on self-researched transport management system.

• Passenger and cargo agent

COL can help clients book domestic and international air ticket and arrange business travel. It can also manage the all-sided agent services including international or domestic cargo shipping, air transport, groupage, export and import clearance. Because it is qualified as the national first-class freight agent, the first-class air passenger transport agent recognized by IATA (International Air Transport Association) etc.

Freight department adopts the integrated operating system including quotation, pickup, custom declaration, document, offering two-way information, cargo track, custom clearance and delivery. There are specific staffs responsible for custom clearance, delivery and onshore transport with the connection with storage, custom, branches and offices. In terms of foreign agent network, company sets up more than 1000 offices in 100 countries and regions all over the world with the support the overseas establishment of China Overseas Holdings Company. The self-researched special software for freight forwarder makes all the documents timely and accurately, the account briefly and clearly. Passenger department establishes long-term and close cooperative and agent relationship with more than 60 home and abroad airlines. And it focuses on the sales of international and domestic air ticket with offering the comprehensive service for customers.

• Storage Distribution

It guarantees accurate and fast operation with modernized logistics management system, standardized quality management system, intelligent warehouse operating equipment and automatic fire safety monitoring system.

According to the different types of business of customer, COL provides the storage distribution model such as transferring and connection, bulk in and bulk out, simple sorting, assembling and packing. Meanwhile, it offers value-added service to meet customer's sale need such as code scanning, simple processing, labeling and the second package etc. As for distribution management, it strictly controls stock with the principle of first in first out to shorten the material time in the warehouse and on the way so as to accelerate the circulation of material. What's more, it tracks the whole process to make sure the accuracy of JIT distribution and promote capital withdrawal. In terms of warehouse system management, COL strives for meeting customer's satisfaction in goods information management with the support of self-researched advanced IT system, EDI technology, wireless network, portable terminal, wireless radio frequency and bar-code recognition technology etc.

Technology Innovation in COL

Integrated Solution of Logistics Information Service

COL takes independent intelligent property of logistics management information system as core, integrates the advanced logistics information technology such as bar-code, RFID, GPS/GIS、EDI etc to implement electronic management on the whole process of order, storage, distribution, transport, custom clearance, settlement and so on. With the help of internet, it offers the service such as on-line order, stock inquiry, expenses inquiry, vehicle and cargo track etc to dynamically assist customer about trade operation. Meanwhile, it realizes the seamless docking with customer information system combining with flexible data exchange way to eventually improve the information share degree of the whole supply chain, the speed of cash flow and logistics operating efficiency.

COL is the professional logistics company that initially starts the third party international logistics service. It has accumulated rich logistics operating experience for years and developed a set of comprehensive logistics management information system fitting for international logistics operation standard and Chinese situation, namely China Overseas Logistics 2000 (COL 2000)

COL 2000 adopts popular Internet/Intranet/ Extranet network structure to work out trade procedure management, data security management and information transmission with browser/ server three levels of applied models. This system uses standard B/S structure, and the customer end will call by browser in the way of WEB. Moreover, it integrates various logistics technologies such as GPS/GSM/GIS technology, bar-code technology, EDI technology and so on to develop various interfaces to secure the effective information exchange and integration with other external system. This system also contains the advanced logistics information applied technology demanded by modern logistics business such as EDI, bar code, intelligent card, GIS, GPS and electronic commerce etc.

COL 2000 is making up of four parts including logistics business management system, logistics enterprise management system, logistics e-Commerce system and customer service system. The business management system consists of storage management system, distribution management system, transport management system, clearance management system, settlement management system, contract management system, customer relation management system and data exchange system; enterprise management system includes finance management system, statistics management system, administration management system and decision support system.

The function of electronic commerce system mainly involves: real time inquiry, bill input, order online, information feedback, on-line quotation, on-line transaction, alliance online, data exchange, information outsourcing and project bidding and so on.

Customer service realized by system contains: procedure inquiry, in-stock inquiry, in-transit inquiry, customization inquiry, bill download, real time track, customization information and consultant service.

With years of practice and improvement, this information system successfully secures the rapid development of COL's business and meets the satisfaction of logistics information integrated management under E-C settings and more than 200 clients' information service. Moreover, it also supports COL's information management such as storage management, transport management, distribution management, freight agent management, declaration management, business management, settlement management, administration management, personnel management, decision management, client management and rebuilding enterprise procedure etc.

Logistics Supply Chain

Under the traditional logistics management model, every link of COL such as transport and storage is isolated, so there is no unified and standard operating procedure in the whole logistics network. While nowadays, because of the rapid development of logistics, it consists of transport, storage, package, handling, distribution processing and logistics information and they are mutually connected, influenced and restrained. The new function by the organic combination and coordinative operation of these links makes logistics function. The harmonious and integrated operation of the whole logistics network needs a set of advanced information system which supports the real time transfer of information in various links.

The overall structure of COL logistics system software is a three-level systematic stereo struc-

Figure 8. The software architecture of COL logistics system

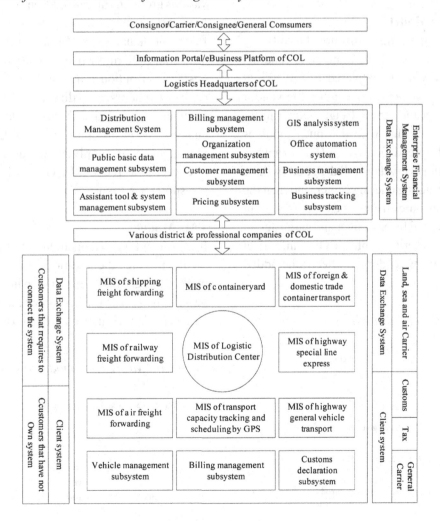

ture and an expanding planar structure. The three levels of structure of the system are: the level of business processing, the level of comprehensive management, and the level of management decision support. Theses three levels represent various applied aspects such as various business management elements and information system. Thus COL successfully executes logistics resource planning management system and multimodal transport logistics management system to provide integrated solution for customer such as JIT production distribution, stock cost control, business procedure reduction, transport route optimization, reverse logistics recovery etc.(See Figure 8).

Operating Model of COL

Cargo Center Model

Freight Gathering Center: this model will firstly gather the goods from large number of vendors, and then they will be delivered to the freight center of COL. Generally speaking, the vendor will subcontract the job of freight gathering to logistics company that will distribute goods as the advanced agreed frequency. (For example, every week, and every day.) All the goods will be delivered to freight gathering center, and then the center will distribute all the goods to the different places of the world by passenger and cargo agent. With freight gathering center, COL can collect all the goods from vendors to offer value-added

service such as storing, setting and assembling, checking, repacking and labeling to realize the docking with overseas sales, stock real-time renewal, the reduction of the cost of overseas operation and human resource to guarantee the due date and the promote repair and return for rejected goods (See Figure 9).

MILK-RUN Model

It is the model of material logistics. Firstly the materials and parts from many vendors will be gathered to a hub, and then they will be assembled and distributed to the manufacture and all the jobs will be operated on their own.

Because the delivery of different vendors is lack of unified and standard management, it brings various problems in information communication, transport security, delivery to increase the difficulty of management. In order to improve this situation, COL runs MILK—RUN model to self-design distribution route, and takes goods from different vendors according to everyday need of receiver, and then distributes to manufacture by chain stores in different places of COL. As the management of supplying goods is unified, it is expected to reduce the cost in bulk logistics transport (See Figure 10).

VMI Model

In the inventory management practice of manufacture product, the traditional inventory control method has gradually shown two inherited weaknesses: the first is the inventory management of enterprise is too simple and extensive with few

Figure 9. Cargo center model of COL

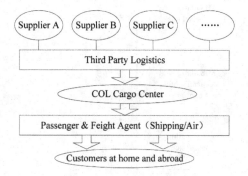

Figure 10. MILK-RUN model of COL

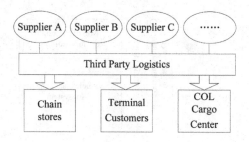

advanced inventory management technologies and methods which results in the high inventory charge. The second is many enterprises manage inventory in their own ways which lead to the serious repetition of inventory facility construction and widespread waste phenomenon.

Nowadays, as many enterprises carry out SCM, the weakness of traditional inventory control method seems more prominent: the enterprise in every node usually enlarges inventory to handle with the sudden change on demand to protect their own benefit. It is understandable, but it actually increases total inventory cost of supply chain and eventually raises the operating cost of supply chain and reduces its integrated competitive strength. Under the circumstance that the competition of enterprises has transferred to the competition of supply chain, it will undoubtedly affect supply chain enterprises to gain dominant advantageous position in competition. Therefore, it is necessary for enterprise to reform traditional inventory control method to seek the new control model to cut the inventory cost. And Vendor Managed Inventory (VMI) can effectively solve the management problem.

VMI is a brand-new inventory management model for the integration of supply chain. And it brings profound influence in supply chain management. It is a strategy of the procedure cooperation between vendor and customer. And it to some extent decreases the inventory level of whole supply chain and reduces the repetitive operation between vendor and customer. Thus it can be regarded as an effective channel to realize inventory optimized control in SCM.

The basic idea of VMI in COL is to integrate the inventory control function of enterprises in each node of supply chain so as to reduce the total inventory charge. As a new model of SCM, it brings the enterprise the advantage of low cost, efficient supply speed and flexible market reacting ability.

General speaking, inventory management is separated. In order to ensure the supply for cli-

ent, the suppliers have his own inventory, and client has his inventory to meet satisfaction as well. This abounds inventories along the whole supply chain and enlarges the demand to greatly raise marketing cost of product. VMI in COL focuses on the integration of supply chain with gathering most of inventory for vendor to manage by integrating business function between vendor and client. During the implementation, vendor will continuously track client's sales statistics and inventory state, and promptly respond the need of market by timely adjusting enterprise production and supply to vendor (See Figure 11).

The idea of VMI in COL is mainly on the integration of SCM. That is, VMI tries to reduce the total inventory charge by integrating inventory control function of enterprise in each node in supply chain. The basic content of VMI is a method that vendor and user have strategic cooperation to adopt the method to minimize the cost for two parties and ask vendor to manage inventory under satisfactory target framework. Compared with traditional control method, VMI has following characteristics: (1) Cooperation: the success of VMI objectively needs enterprises in the supply chain to cooperate closely based on mutual trust. (2) Mutual-beneficial: VMI pursues win-win solution, that is, what VMI concerns is how to reduce two parties' inventory cost, but not how to

Figure 11. Vendor managed inventory model of COL

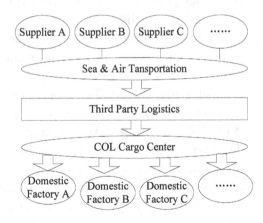

distribute cost load of two parties. (3) Interaction: VMI requires active attitude in cooperation to realize fast reaction and improve the situation of high inventory charge for information blockade. (4)Protocol: VMI needs enterprise share the same objectives to clarify their responsibility and obligation. Specific cooperative issues are clearly ruled with framework agreement to ensure feasibility of operation.

CONCLUSION AND RESEARCH TENDENCY

According to the above empirical study about the COL, the following research conclusions and development tendency could be summarized.

Service Innovation in Chinese logistics Enterprises

There concludes the features of technology innovation of domestic logistics enterprise combining with the research on COL service innovation.

- It establishes comprehensive logistics information system to realize 24 hours logistics network monitoring. For example, COL bases on Internet/Intranet/Extranet network structure and browser/server three levels applied model to use the advanced logistics applied technology such as EDI, bar code, intelligent card, GIS, GPS, electronic commerce to establish COL 2000 system which realizes business procedure management, statistics safety management and information transmission management.

- It runs logistics integrated electronic management with RFID in the link of cargo storage and distribution. As COL takes independent intelligent property of logistics management information system as the core with integrating advanced logistics information technology such as bar code, RFID, GPS/GIS、EDI etc to implement integrated electronic management including order, storage, distribution, transport, declaration, settlement and so on.

- It actively explores the realization of optimal logistics operation with the support of information technology. COL establishes a supply chain to integrate transport, storage, package, handling, circulation processing, logistics information and so on.

- It realizes the strategic option based on enterprise characteristics. For example, COL chooses onshore container transport as the mainline with insisting on the strategy of "main business centered". Centering on this mainline, it establishes the function of each link in supply chain to set up the service system of container transport supply chain.

- It actively explores and develops the third party logistics. For example, COL can offer professional third party logistics solution such as bonded storage, import and export distribution, cross-regional transport, agent declaration, simple processing, sorting and packing, international freight agent and so on. And it has become one of important strategic routes for company development to comprehensively meet customer's personalized need, to cultivate customer's deep need to eventually earn customer's acceptance and trust.

- It expands the value-added service such as transport service, passenger and cargo agent, storage and distribution. For example, according to the different types of business of customer, COL provides the storage distribution model such as transferring and connection, bulk in and bulk out, simple sorting, assembling and packing. Meanwhile, it offers the value-added service to meet customer's sale need. In terms of warehouse system management, COL strives for meeting customer's satisfaction in goods information management with the support of self-researched advanced IT system, EDI technology, wireless network, portable terminal, wireless radio frequency and bar-code recognition technology. Wal-Mart procurement department makes a series of strict procurement standards to guarantee the quality and price of logistics service to meet customer's need more effectively.

Research Tendency in Logistics Service Innovation

According to present home and broad research on logistics innovation service and the empirical analysis in this article, it concludes the following fields need more efforts:

- Foreign advanced logistics service model

People can study logistics service model of foreign household enterprises to propose detailed logistics service innovative model and security system based on the present situation and development tendency of the third party logistics service in Chinese circulation field.

- Combining with supply chain management theory and logistics management theory

Combining with supply chain management theory and logistics management theory, people can have deep and theoretical study on production, sales and logistics service model of Chinese circulation enterprises and put it into practice.

- All-society logistics service innovation model

According to the research on the third party logistics service innovation model in circulation industry, it can be extended to the research of logistics service innovative model of all-society service and manufacture industry to improve the

theoretical research of logistics service innovative model.

- The empirical research on logistics innovation service model and security system

People can have comprehensive empirical research on logistics innovation service model and security system combining specific logistics enterprise with adopting the case of the third party logistics service

- Quantitative analysis

It is expected to have quantitative analysis of Chinese logistics service based on Chinese real situation of social production with empirical statistics.

REFERENCES

Barras, R. (1990). Interactive Innovation in Financial and Business Service: The vanguard of the service revolution. *Research Policy*, *19*, 215–237. doi:10.1016/0048-7333(90)90037-7

Bilderbeek, Hertog, P. D., & Marklund, G. (1998). Service innovation: knowledge intensive business service as cooproducers of innovation. *The Result of SIS Synthesis Paper 3*, 1.

Chapman, R. L., Soosay, C., & Kandampully, J. (2002). Innovation in logistics and the new business model: a conceptual framework. *Managing Service Quality*, *12*(6), 358–371. doi:10.1108/09604520210451849

Chen, F. (2005). Explanation of the new concept of modern logistics services. *Journal of Storage Transportation & Preservation of Commodities*, *1*, 10–12.

Drucker, P. F. (1985). Innovation and entrepreneurship: practice and principles, New York: Harper & Row.

Gallouj, F., & Weinstein, O. (1997). Innovation in Service. *Research Policy, 26*, 537–556. doi:10.1016/S0048-7333(97)00030-9

Haiyin, L., Xiangdang, W., Yunkai, Z., & Yanling, N. (2006). Analysis on the Impetus of 3PL service innovation. *Journal of Logistic Technology, 5*, 15–17.

Han, Q. (2006). Service Innovation of 3PL Company: financial logistics. Beijing, China: University of International Business and Economics.

Huiming, L. (2006). Logistic service and integrated innovation. *China Ocean Shipping Monthly, 6*, 71–73.

Jun, L., & Wang, Y. (2007). How to Select the Way and Strategy of logistics enterprise service iInnovation. *Journal of Logistic Technology, 26*(1), 14–16.

Kandampully, J. (2002). Innovation as the core competency of a service organization: the role of technology, knowledge and networks. *European Journal of Innovation Management, 5*(1), 18–26. doi:10.1108/14601060210415144

Lei, L., & Guisheng, W. (2003). Service innovation. Tsinghua University Press.

Li, Yanfong, & Pu, Guoan. (2003). Research on the value of third-party logistics. *Journal of Commercial Research.* (17), 166-168.

Liu, L., & Li, H. (2006). How to achieve service innovation by logistic enterprise. *Logistics Infor Monthly, 9*, 67–69.

Lu, G. (2005). The analysis of situation and question about the third party logistics in our country. *Journal of Logistic Science Technology, 28*(6), 50–51.

Min, L., & Zhiqi, F. (2002). The logistics model selection. *Outlook Weekly, 32*, 39–40.

Panayides, P. M., & So, M. (2005). Logistics service provider-client relationships . *Transportation Research Part E, Logistics and Transportation Review, 41*(3), 179–200. doi:10.1016/j.tre.2004.05.001

Peng, H. (2007). Research of customer services of third party logistics business. Beijing, China: Beijing Jiaotong University.

Sundbo, J., & Gallouj, F. (2000). Innovation as a loosely coupled system in services. *International Journal of Service Technologies and Management, 1*(1), 15–36. doi:10.1504/IJSTM.2000.001565

Tian, X. (2008). *Research on the innovative model and guarantee system of the third party logistics service in household appliance industry.* Tianjing: Tianjin Polytechnic University.

Wang, X., & Chen, G. 2007). The services innovative research on third-party logistics enterprise. *Journal of Modern management science, 2*, 5-7.

Xianwei, S., & Zhang, Z. (2001). The Service model and development research of modern Logistics. *Science of Science and Management of S. & T, 12*, 46–50.

Zanping, L. (2005). Service science-an emerging science in 21st century. *China Information Review,* 511-13.

Zhen, L. (2007). Study on the logistics industry disparity between China and developed country. *Journal of Fuiian Radio & TV University, 3*, 35–37.

Section 2
Logistics and Service Innovation

Chapter 3

Managing Customer–Centric Information:
The Challenges of Information and Communication Technology (ICT) Deployment in Service Environments

Martin R. Fellenz
Trinity College Dublin, Ireland

Mairead Brady
Trinity College Dublin, Ireland

ABSTRACT

Despite a long history of business-orientated information and communication technology (ICT) deployment, contemporary organizations continue to struggle with customer-centric implementation of new technologies that are profitable and contribute to sustainable service business success. This chapter reviews the difficulties inherent in using ICTs to manage customer-related information, and identifies the particular challenges for customer-centric deployment of ICTs. It provides a model of different levels of customer centric information use in organizations which helps understand how companies can become more customer centric in their information use. It reviews implications for future research in this emerging area and concludes that the challenges of ICT deployment and use must be addressed with an uncompromising focus on customer value as the central principle of both ICT design and deployment, and of information management in service organizations.

INTRODUCTION

In the current strategic environment, business success depends on a company's ability to understand service-based value creation for customers. One core requirement is the ability to transform customer-related data into information and ultimately into

usable knowledge. Winning companies will be those that not only successfully install information and communication technology (ICT), but that also focus on the management of information rather than the management of technology, recognizing information as the strategic asset that can help them gain competitive advantage (Davenport, 2006: Fisher, Raman & McClelland, 2000; Glazer, 1991; Greenyer, 2006; Myburg, 2000).

DOI: 10.4018/978-1-61520-603-2.ch003

Figure 1. The role of customer centric ICT deployment, use and information management for sustained service-based business success

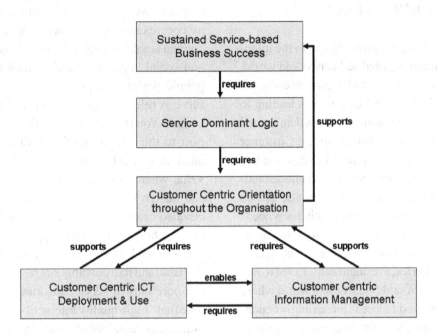

In this chapter we discuss the challenges for companies of adopting customer-centric information management involving ICT. The core premise of this chapter is that to achieve sustainable service-based business success, all firms need to adopt a service-dominant logic (Vargo & Lusch, 2004, 2008) as the basis for organizing and managing their internal and market oriented activities. This in turn necessitates a customer centric orientation throughout the organization, which demands significant changes to the predominant functional organizing principles as well as to predominantly functionally oriented mindsets still found in most service organizations. Such a customer centric orientation in formal (e.g., structural) and informal (e.g., cultural, behavioral) aspects of service organizations requires and – in turn – is supported by customer-centric ICT deployment and use, as well as customer centric information management (see Figure 1).

The reciprocal relationship between such ICT deployment and use on the one hand, and customer centric information management on the other, is the central focus of this chapter. More specifically, we identify and consider challenges involved in deploying and using ICT in service environments to enable customer centric information management.

The chapter is structured as follows: We briefly consider the dynamics of sustained service-based business success by discussing the service dominant logic and customer centricity. In the light of this discussion we then consider in more detail the requirements for ICT deployment and use, and in particular the role of customer centric information management, in service organizations. We present a model of different levels of customer centric information use that highlights the differences between product and customer centric approaches. We then present suggestions for further research to advance understanding of these crucial issues.

THE SERVICE IMPERATIVE AND BUSINESS SUCCESS: THE SERVICE DOMINANT LOGIC

Business challenges are growing due to the intensifying pressure of a globalised networked world, with increased market diversity, intense competition, a major financial and credit crisis leading to global recession, demanding and well informed customers and advances in technology. Customer centricity provides the best means to develop and grow business by staying close to and understanding customer's needs and wants. This also allows service providers to co-create innovative new needs and wants with customers that can prove to be transformational for both customer and company. As Gerard Kleisterlee, President and CEO of Royal Philips Electronics said 'we live in a world where business success and failure is increasingly dependent on a company's ability to align its resources around the customer'. (McClune, 2003). Within these parameters the management and use of customer information becomes crucial. Companies need to ensure that they are 'getting their people to embrace the right behaviors and values for working with information" (Fisher, 2000:70).

Understanding Today's Customers

Part of the requirement for adopting the service dominant logic is to more fully understand today's customers. The customer has become more powerful and expects more from companies especially during an economic downturn. The contemporary customer is co-inventor, co-producer, co-creator, co-promoter, recommender and collaborator – with the result that the barriers between the company and the customer are blurring (Wind, 2008). Many of these developments are driven by technology. Ramaswamy notes that "customers need no longer be mere passive recipients of value propositions offered by firms. They are now informed, connected, networked and empowered on a scale as never before". (2008: 9)

Co-creation or customer creation of value is now a normal activity for many consumers with social networking, gaming and the virtual world as core examples. Wikipedia, a service whose content is solely developed from consumer inputs, and social networking sites which only work if people design and post user generated content serve as relevant examples. From EBay to Wikipedia to YouTube, the information that companies post to the internet battles with user generated amateur content. Similarly, customers co-create value when they log onto the Euro Disney site and design their agenda for their trip. Customers also create value when they purchase from IKEA, choose their pizza toppings or use the self service check-in and seat selection at the airport. Prahalad and Ramaswamy suggest that co-creation is a core part of service business success. They note that "high-quality interactions that enable an individual customer to co-create unique experiences with the company are the key to unlocking new sources of competitive advantage" (2004: 7). Co-creation relates to prosumers, a concept offered by futurist Alan Toffler in 1980 which is a play on the words producer and consumer, and recognizes customers as co-creators of value. Customer participation in the decision-making process offers companies many opportunities to differentiate their offerings, to meet individual and often idiosyncratic needs, to fully align their service offering with customer preferences, and to customize their products and services as well as their marketing operations. It also forces companies to really study and understand the customer experience. "The interaction between the firm and the customer is becoming the locus of value creation and value extraction. As value shifts to experiences, the market is becoming a forum for conversation and interactions between consumers, consumer communities, and firms" (Prahalad & Ramaswamy, 2004: 5). It is the information that can be collected during these unique exchanges that can provide a crucial source of differentiation and future customer value propositions. However, to derive competitive value from such deep customer engagements, companies must understand how to utilize this information.

Understanding the Service Dominant Logic

The orientation in business and academia should be on value, value creation and co- creation for and with customers aligned to a customer centric focus for business. "The focus is shifting away from tangibles and towards intangibles, such as skills, information, and knowledge, and toward interactivity and connectivity and ongoing relationships" (Vargo & Lusch, 2004: 15). Therefore the most appropriate model for understanding the consumer in today's environment may not be one developed to understand the role of tangible products but one which takes a service-centered view not just of marketing, but of all aspects of organizational activities. There has been much discussion of a service dominant logic which moves away from the product centric models of business and the dominant product focus of organizations to a recognition that all businesses are service businesses, and that the fundamental basis of all exchange is service (Vargo & Lusch, 2004, 2008, Gummesson, 2007). Historically, academic business models and practical business strategies have been orientated towards product producing organizations. Yet services and service business increasingly form the core part of the global economy. Service should no longer be viewed as a sub-discipline of the main areas like supply chain, marketing and even production and operation management. Along with the authors reviewed here we argue that the service dominant logic, rather than a product dominant logic, provides a more sustainable and more successful approach in today's market environment.

Sheth and Sisodia (2006) describe this view as customer-centric and market driven. This approach involves collaborating with and learning from customers and being adaptive to their individual and dynamic needs (Vargo & Lush, 2004). It leads to a customer centric, co-creational and relational model of business that requires technology and self services technology deployment to be aligned with the service dominant logic.

DEFINING CUSTOMER CENTRIC ORIENTATION

Peter Drucker noted in 1954 that 'an enterprises purpose begins on the outside with the customer; it is the customer who determines what a business is, what it produces and whether it will prosper' (Drucker, 1954). The concept of customer centricity has been discussed for more than 50 years but businesses are still struggling to become customer centric (Gummesson, 2007; Shah et al., 2006; Wind, 2008) and few are actually truly focused on the customer. For many the focus is internal and operational on what they make or provide, rather than externally on the customer and their needs.

This is often called a production orientation where the product and its improvement is the core focus of the company. This orientation creates products and services that are not determined primarily by customer needs and wants but rather by what the entrepreneur or company wants to produce or provide. Such product or company centricity often coexists with a dominant financial focus. This reflects the Anglo Saxon model of business, characterized by a dominant focus on financial indicators and return on investment (McHugh et al., 1998; Wind 2008). Many of the metrics used to direct activities in these firms are neither customer orientated nor do they truly measure firm activities in ways that help to strategically and operationally keep the business proactively aligned with market realities and customer needs over the long term.

We define customer centricity as a business model that places customer value at the heart of all organizational value creation activities. This means that all parts of the customer centric organizations are aware of how their activities directly and indirectly contribute to (or detract from) the value that customers derive from their interaction with the company, and endeavor to maximize their contribution to the important outcome of customer value creation. Therefore, customer centricity goes beyond simple customer orientation. The term customer orientation is variably used to describe activities (such as customer relationship management) that directly interface with customers, or parts of companies (such as sales departments) that directly interact with customers. Also, it often refers to any activities that attempt to (more) directly respond to customer needs and requirements. What distinguishes these practical operationalizations of customer orientation from real customer centricity is the latter's recognition and acceptance of the primacy of customer value creation over any other organizational activity. What this means is that a customer centric company does not simply build its activities around their customer. Rather, it places the customer – in the form of customer value creation - at the heart of all its activities.

The difference between customer centricity and product or company centricity is more profound than simple differences in sets of key metrics, in management preferences, or in formal structures and processes. It also refers to a fundamentally different understanding regarding the nature and role of the company. This philosophy, ideology or identity revolves around the primacy of customer value, and expresses many of the tenets of the service dominant logic discussed above.

Many companies pay lip service to a customer centric focus and most companies fail to be customer centric (Shah et al, 2005). Again, referring to the words of Peter Drucker, customer centric organizations need to reflect the maxim that

'there is only one valid definition of business purpose: to create a customer. What business thinks it produces is not of first importance-especially not to the future of the business or to its success. What the customer thinks he/she is buying, what he/she considers "value" is decisive - it determines what a business is, what it produces, and whether it will prosper" (1954: 37).

A recent Bain study showed how far most companies diverge from this understanding. Only 8% of customer reported that they felt they received excellent service, while 80% of companies felt that they were providing excellent service. Another survey on Why Customers Quit found that 68% defect because of a company's attitude of indifference towards them in the long term (Nadeem, 2007).

For companies to truly embrace customer centricity there is a large amount of reorientation needed for the strategic move from a product or finance focus. Many companies are not prepared to undertake the challenging changes which would ultimately be rewarding (Shah et al., 2006). Galbraith notes "the product-centric mind-set is an entrenched one and, like the pit bull, does not relinquish dominance easily…with many companies simply putting a cosmetic gloss of customer focus sprinkled around the edges" (2005: 1). Companies need to engage fully with the customer centric concept for it to succeed (Galbraigh, 2005). In a product or finance centric focus the customer is at the end of the value chain and separate from the processes which are all company focused. Within this concept there is an orientation towards lean production with a premium on efficiency and effectiveness of internal operations. What is needed is an orientation towards lean consumption – how all process including the organization's interactions with their customers are designed and managed with a customer centric and services focus (Womack at al., 2005).

Expanding on Shah et al's (2006) work there are four dimensions that a customer centric organization needs to focus on: (1) A pervasive customer-centric ideology or culture, deliberately supported by active leadership towards customer-centric thinking and behavior of all organizational members; (2) structural arrangements that align and continuously realign the formal organization to support service provision and customer value creation; (3) systems and processes that support the customer centric logic, for example through appropriate reward and control systems and through appropriate information availability and use; and (4) revised financial metrics and financial metric use that reflect the primacy of customer value creation and thus guide sustainable service delivery and development. The basic philosophy of a customer centric approach is that the company serves customers and that all decisions start with the customer, with customer knowledge understood as a valuable asset (Shah et al., 2006).

CUSTOMER CENTRIC ICT DEPLOYMENT AND USE

Many companies are struggling to understand from both technological and business perspectives how ICT can be used in service design and delivery (Brethon, MacHulbert & Pitt, 2005; Fellenz & Brady, 2008), let alone to fully understand this from a customer or customer centric perspective. Technology is currently not sufficiently recognized as an important driver of the service development and management process (Agrawal & Berg, 2007). There is a lack of appreciation, often beyond a cost saving imperative as to why, and how, technology is deployed in a service encounter. Much of the technology deployed for services is not reflective of a customer determined or customer centric perspective. In practice many companies are struggling to fully utilize their current ICTs and lack both the appetite and the ability to move into further ICT adoption and more challenging information management issues.

For many companies the design and deployment of ICT is not customer centric and many systems like CRM, decision support systems, internet, extranets and intranets and so on, do not realize real benefits beyond efficiency-based productivity increases because companies lack the requisite customer centricity to realize the full benefits from these systems (Fellenz & Brady, 2008). This has been compounded by the fact that many functional specialists such as marketers and IT specialists lack a deep understanding of how technology and markets interact, as well as how technology influences behavior and cognitions both externally and internally (Berthon et al., 2005; Brady & Fellenz, 2008).

It must be noted that the development and deployment of ICTs has revolutionized the marketplace and in particular the service landscape with companies using technology to improve service operations, increase service efficiency, and provide functional benefits for companies and customers (Lin & Hsieh, 2007; Matthing et al., 2006; Meuter et al., 2003). ICT applications abound in service provision and new customer focused services with a technology orientation have created great new markets and offerings (e.g., Ebay, Google, YouTube, Wikipedia).

From the consumers' perspective, ICTs can enable them to enjoy the services they require with more flexible choice of time and space (Meuter et al., 2003) and provides for increased consumers satisfaction (Lin & Hsieh, 2007; Bitner et al., 2000). The self service technology (SST) literature has also criticized the cost cutting nature of much SST deployment and notes that self service works when the customer has an option to opt in or out and where the customer is at the centre of the design and operation of the technology. SSTs can also create a technology barrier between the customer and the company (Meyronin, 2004) though some customer are more tech savvy and engaged than the companies that serve them (McDonald, 2008). Some SSTs also raise privacy issues and have given rise to dubious business practices which are not customer focused but rather designed to unilaterally benefit the company. Self service technology can be customer centric – like the Eazy pass toll collection RFID tags, but other technologies like automatic telephone answering in customer service environments which are designed for cost savings rather than for customer service often irritates and annoys customers, and can actually destroy rather than create customer value while attempting to increase interaction efficiency.

Due to the rapid growth of ICTs and the many challenges of adoption, marketers and other organizational professionals need to gain an increased understanding of consumer perception and use of these technologies (Venkatesh, 2007; Lin & Hsieh, 2007; Nysveen et. al., 2005). What companies must search for and study is how to make the service more comfortable, distinctive, enjoyable and memorable. To find the optimum balance between human and technology is a marketing and business challenge. As technological innovations continue to be a critical component of customer-firm interactions, technological interfaces that enable companies to produce a service independent of direct service-employee involvement are changing the way consumers interact with firms to create service outcomes (Meuter et al., 2003). "They depend on customers 'opting in' rather than merely acting as passive targets… making marketing a joint, cooperative process" (Mitchell, 2002: 77). These modes of interaction are expected to become key criteria for long-term business success (Lin & Hsieh, 2007).

With heightened interactivity between customer and service provider, often through technological platforms that monitor, scan and record customer engagement with the company, a core challenge is how to manage the huge amount of data flooding into companies. Once companies receive customer information they face the challenge of how to use it in ways that support customer value creation. It remains unclear, however, how the transformation of customer-related data into information and the utilization of the value of this information should be coordinated, and where such coordination should be located. We have argued elsewhere (Fellenz & Brady, 2008) that a facilitation or oversight role may provide ben-

efits. A customer centric perspective throughout the organization also requires structural features that enables the dissemination of customer information and the coordination of customer centric activities throughout all parts of the organization. Typical contemporary ICT deployment models do not appear to support such customer centric information use.

More specifically, it appears that in most service organizations, much of the responsibility for assuring the recognition and use of customer needs and wants is allocated to the marketing function. Pragmatically, however, the role of marketing varies across industries and companies, as does its success in actually delivering added value in this role. Recent studies show that over the last decade marketing is no longer highly regarded within organizations, that there has been a move to focus on tactical rather than strategic aspects within marketing, with an over focus on advertising and promotion rather than real marketing (Gronroos, 2006; Webster, 2005; Wind, 2008). Marketing practices need to change to embrace new mental models of rigor and relevance in this new world and what should be a new world of marketing with new skills and abilities (Wind, 2008). It is questionable, however, if marketers typically have the relevant skill set for this task (Brady, Fellenz & Brookes, 2008; Webster, 2005; Brady and O'Connor, 2007), as well as the ability to challenge the system(s) and other functions to provide them with the information they need for their tasks (Davenport, 2006; Wind, 2008) This is particularly important where new ICTs are considered or deployed because of the danger of them detracting rather than aiding customer centric decision making, for example by "blocking the use of experience, intuition and creativity in handling information" (Piercy, 1981:4; see also Lurie & Mason, 2009).

In addition, even in service organizations most ICT deployment is designed and driven by the IT function who control the IT budget and the relevant technical skills. Business intelligence, analytics and reporting processes as designed from this functional perspective, however, often have a strong or even exclusive technological orientation. Not only does research show that aligning such systems with business needs is problematic according to half the IT executives studied (McAffee, 2006), but IT functions rarely take any direct note of customer preferences and needs. As a result, existing ICT systems and arrangements are neither designed nor suitable for customer centric information use, and while new systems try to achieve more customer information transparency (see Lurie & Mason, 2009), the integration with customer value creation processes lags behind. Customer relationship management systems show a 65% failure rate (Gartner, 2001; Shah et al., 2006), and only a minute proportion of studied companies indicate that their systems provide sufficiently comprehensive and customer centric information (Anderson, 2005: Shah et al., 2006). Given the difficulties and failure rates and the cost involved in deploying modern ICTs (Davenport, 2006; McAffee, 2006), many service companies try to minimize cost and risk of new ICT, and fail to see the central role of ICT for successful customer centric orientations.

Given the costs associated with ICT systems, their design and deployment is often also closely monitored and controlled by the finance function. Thus, cost/benefit analyses and the focus on return on investment primarily through cost reduction often guides design and decision processes. Customer focus is too often an added if not overlooked aspects of such processes that aim at creating and maximizing short-term shareholder value rather than jointly maximizing long-term customer and organizational value (Ambler, 2001; Shah et al., 2006). Most financial measures are unsuitable for measuring or managing customer centric strategies and plans and are "too narrow, too late and too backward looking. They also don't look deeply into drivers and they ignore the real value of intangible assets." Wind (2008:25) "The product-focused metrics most companies rely on

– revenues, growth, and margin – don't reward cross-silo cooperation or customer centricity' (Gulati & Oldroyd, 2005: 6).

Therefore, the challenge of finding and implementing the most appropriate role for ICT must be based on a holistic understanding of the different, competing, but necessary orientations of marketing, IT, and finance. Specifically, (1) the technologists' drive to use what is technologically possible, and (2) the drive of a finance focus on cost cutting and the business logic that requires short-term profitability, must be aligned to the (3) customer centric logic that places customer needs and customer value at the heart of matters and of service companies' efforts to achieve longer-term economic viability and sustainability. (Day, 2006; Fellenz & Brady, 2008). This must happen in the context of a shared customer centric orientation throughout the organization.

INFORMATION MANAGEMENT FROM A CUSTOMER CENTRIC PERSPECTIVE

A customer centric orientation throughout the organization requires customer centric information management. This refers to the collection, processing and use of relevant information about customers in a way that enables all organizational participants to support and directly contribute to customer value creation. This includes not only understanding that they need to harness the customer's provided information in ways that benefit – and delight - the customer, but they must also protect the privacy of that information, and to avoid at all cost to use that information against the customer. Too many companies do this by charging them more fees or bombarding them with unwanted offers (Johnson, 2007).

Information about customer needs and preferences plays an important role in service businesses, and the full utilization of customer-related data and its transformation into usable knowledge is key to competitive success. Such knowledge "represents the currency, as well as the scorecard, of the information age. Only companies with deep knowledge about their customers, competitors and operations will be winners in this age". (Sisodia, 1992:2). Knowledge and knowledge management is a crucial contemporary issue. Too often managers assume that data equals knowledge or competitive intelligence. In fact, from a business perspective data is worthless unless it is given meaning, utilized properly, and deployed to help generate economic value and competitive advantages. (e.g., Myburg, 2000).

Similarly, too often managers believe that more information means better information. Yet in an age of extreme information-overload companies cannot afford to be blinded by the assumption that mere data availability is the answer to any competitive challenge. The notion that more data means more accurate information is logically and empirically unsustainable. Increasingly, service organizations find themselves information starved in a data rich environment. A typical response to this problem is the attempt to increase the availability of customer data, often attempted through the investment in and deployment of more ICT to collect and process this data. Unfortunately, while more data can sometimes lead to more information (although this is not an automatic result), it does not necessarily lead to better information. The challenge for managers and other decision makers in service organizations is to separate ignorance from confusion (Weick, 1995). Ignorance means that these decision makers do not have the relevant information needed to make appropriate choice, while confusion refers to the result of available information that is inconclusive, allows different and equally valid interpretations, and generally fails to provide clear guidance for decision making. According to Weick, "[t]o remove ignorance, more information is required. To remove confusion, a different kind of information is needed" (1995: 99). To deal with these distinct information requirements, different forms of information management are needed.

Aligned to this companies often try to keep every little bit of information they have on their customers when their information management focus should be on data minimization and information availability. This involves moving away from the mindless collection of largely meaningless data by identifying, processing, aggregating, and deploying information where needed (Bradlow & Fader, 2009). Many companies keep excessive information and default to near complete data storage because appropriate data selection processes and information management tools do not exist. Any company can generate basic data or descriptive statistics, but customer centric information management means to move beyond such descriptive information use. (See Figure 2)

The first step in developing more customer centric information management would involve a move towards more analytic information use that focuses on customer relevant information to helps select target customers as well as identify the organizational practices that help maximize the value that the company creates for them. In other words, a focus on relevant data and data minimization, which refers to finding and selecting the gems that matter in the data, is needed as a core requirement (Humby, et al., 2008) However, this step towards analytic information use also involves a reflective element in that it requires the critical evaluation of information with a view to identifying how organizational practices, processes and activities create customer value. Both the customer intelligence function and the value creation analysis function need to be fulfilled for customer centric analytical information use to be achieved.

The next higher level of customer centric information use is the predictive use of information. This includes both the prediction of trends and changes in customer preferences as well as the prediction of customer responses (e.g., to particular interactions, or to new service offerings of the company). As such, predictions require a much more complete and also subjective understanding of customer needs, preferences, and decision crite-

Figure 2. A hierarchical model of customer centric information use

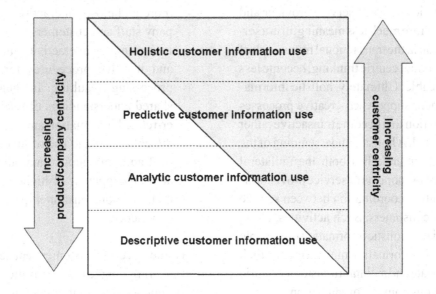

ria. The predictive use of information necessitates the use of richer data that can carry information that can convey rich meanings. A challenge arising from such rich data is that it is frequently open to different and multiple interpretations. As Daft's work has shown (e.g., Daft & Lengel, 1984; Daft, Lengel, & Trevino, 1987; Daft & Macintosh, 1981; Huber & Daft, 1987), the way to deal with such ambiguity (i.e., the degree of uncertainty regarding the actual meaning) and equivocality (i.e., the number of different meanings that available data and information can support) is not to increase the quantity of data but rather to increase the quality of data, and the information derived from it. This can be achieved by increasing media and information richness and using mechanisms that "enable debate, clarification, and enactment more than simply provide large amounts of data" (Daft & Lengel, 1986: 559). Meetings and other direct interactions among organizational members as well as with customers therefore must become an integral part of predictive information use. Thus, just as the difference between descriptive and analytical use of information already discussed is a qualitative rather than simply quantitative difference, the predictive use of information is

not simply the next step in processing information in terms of effort, intensity, or technology deployment. Rather, it requires different data collection and processing mechanisms, including in particular structural and procedural changes in the organization to support more direct human involvement in both customer data collection and information processing.

Finally, in our model of customer centric information management we see the most elaborate, comprehensive and customer centric information use at the level of holistic information use. This level is characterized by information management that enables customer perspectives to be comprehensively identified and understood. Thus, decision makers throughout the organization have the information available that enables them to identify, and -- more importantly -- to identify with relevant customer views. Such a comprehensive understanding requires tacit as well as explicit knowledge of customer views, preferences, and experiences, and by necessity must involve extensive and intensive interactions with customers (Nonaka & Takeuchi, 1995). In some ways, this almost requires that organizational decision makers 'go native' among customers, but a better way to think about this view is that the formal boundaries between service provider and customer, which are much less meaningful in a service context than in the transactional framework of company or product centric thinking, become less and less noticeable. Ultimately, holistic information management supports co-creative processes of value generation that become transactive rather than transactional. A holistic understanding of the service encounter underlies both the unilateral organizational components of service provision as well as the mutual coordination between service providers and consumers. Such activities, along with the associated holistic information use, enable customer centric information management which in turn helps create and maintain a customer centric orientation throughout the organization.

This model does not, as yet, provide a complete, validated model of customer centric information use. It is not based on empirical data of information use, but rather on the analysis of the contributions that different information use can make to customer centricity. Therefore, we do not suggest that customer centric information use necessarily develops along the steps and in the order described by the model. Rather, the model suggests that the degree of customer centricity in information use can be distinguished using these levels. The model may help to assess current organizational information usage, evaluate practices, procedures and systems, and guide considerations for further improvement to achieve more customer centric information management. What appears clear, however, is that the successive levels of customer centric information differ along a number of important dimensions. Higher levels of customer centric information use tend to be, inter alia, associated with

- more human involvement in data collection and customer-related information processing;
- more direct and extensive customer involvement in data provision and information processing;

- richer data collection media;
- more and closer interaction between company staff and customers;
- increasingly interactive, interdependent and iterative procedures for information processing resulting in negotiated and shared understandings of relevant customer-related information among staff; and
- the collection and use of increasing equivocal and ambiguous data, and the associated development of higher quality information about customer perspectives and experiences.

Higher levels of customer centric information use generally suggest a much more integrated, cross-functional way of collecting, sharing, and using information. This is in part necessary to address the higher need for error detection and correction at higher levels of customer centric information use. This can only be achieved through more frequent feedback and through increased and direct customer involvement. To avoid and detect error, different forms of control cycles and feedback loops need to be utilized that short-circuit the often delayed information from traditional external (e.g., market-research) and internal (e.g., revenue, profit or other financial indicators) information sources.

Organizations who wish to employ customer centric ICT will need to change. In theory, by identifying core customers and then appropriately 'slicing and dicing' the relevant data, companies should be able to coordinate the information they have and transform it into customer-relevant knowledge and, ultimately, into customer-oriented action. Reflecting the understanding that this challenge is fundamentally about how information can be used and deployed in ways that enable and steer concerted action by different actors and groups within and across organizational boundaries, Gulati and Oldroyd (2005) frame this 'customer focus journey' as a coordination challenge. They argue that the road to achieving such customer focus in using information involves a number of important steps named communal, serial, symbiotic and integral coordination.

Communal coordination, the first steps, involves the collation of information about the customer. The second step, serial coordination, working with analytic experts and ITC support to study the consumer's past transactions to gain insight into the consumer's wants and needs. The third step, symbiotic coordination, focuses on developing an understanding of likely future purchasing and consumer behavior by implementing relevant information throughout the organization. The final step (integral coordination) revolves around enabling real-time responses to customer needs that are made possible by coordinating all information among employees and the entire organization at corporate level. This perspective highlights again that the challenge of customer-centric ICT deployment transcends purely functional or technological issues. "[G]etting close to customers is not so much a problem the IT or marketing department needs to solve as a journey the whole organization needs to make". (Gulati & Oldroyd, 2005:4).

Companies need to have co-ordination mechanisms to align tasks and information around the customer and ensure that competing silos fully co-operate which could mean time consuming and costly adjustment to internal operations. Staff need to be rewarded for breaking down the silos to deliver customer solutions, and need to be rewarded for sharing what they learn or know about the customer (Gulati, 2007; Gulati & Oldroyd, 2005).

Solutions and Recommendations

The reality of the current global recession is that only companies that can clearly align with customer needs will survive. During the last decade of strong economic growth many businesses succeeded by picking low hanging fruit. During the increased competition in mature and even shrinking markets typical for a recession, only companies that are sufficiently customer centric

will survive. Companies who move away from solely operational and finance focus and engage with understanding the customer will be able to stay in business and continue to produce or provide what is valued by an even more discerning and value conscious consumer or business to business customer.

Deploying ICT in customer-centric ways requires all companies, especially companies with a high service component, to meet four major challenges. These challenges include the (1) acquisition and processing of appropriate customer-relevant data, the (2) management and use of the resulting customer-oriented information, (3) the provision of supportive intra- and interorganizational arrangements, and the (4) development of the relevant understanding and skill-set among those charged with designing and operating the ICT. As suggested by Brady and colleagues (2006), most organizations currently lack the ability to successfully meet these challenges, with many not even aware of the range of skills they need. These skills include but are not limited to:

- ICT knowledge: Understanding of systems and technology (Levy et al., 2001; Ranchhod, 2004).
- Information Management: capturing, analysing and using large amounts of data
- Imagination to envisage how ICT and information can be used in innovation and transformation ways
- Study of interfirm and consumer technology mediated relationships and self service technologies (Schultze & Orlikowski, 2004; Howard & Worboys, (2003).
- Future perspective: Exploiting current and rapidly developing challenging technologies like biometrics, neuromarketing, nano technology etc.

It may be that there is a catalyst needed to change business orientation to customer centricity rather than operational efficiency and short term profit gains which has characterized the last decade of business and ICT implementations. The current global financial crisis and recession suggest that the business models in use for the last years, and particularly the financial service models, are flawed and the whole system needs to be changed (Fellenz, Augustenborg, Brady & Greene, 2009). Now could be the time to hear the customers' voices and for marketing to really engage with customers and business. Unfortunately the marketing department and marketing know-how within organizations may not be strong enough after years of tactical and restricted operations to suddenly have the skills and ability to really advocate the major customer centric changes needed and to operationalized these throughout business (Fellenz & Brady, 2008). Now may be the best time for businesses to re-orientate towards the customers but many functional managers, including marketers, may not ready for the challenge. As we have argued here, the companies that will succeed are those that stay aligned to their customers and who have a strong internal and external focus on customer centricity.

FUTURE RESEARCH DIRECTIONS

The deployment of ICT in service organizations and the customer centric use of information is an emerging research area in need of substantial conceptual, theoretical and empirical attention. A number of fruitful avenues for investigation are highlighted by the discussions of this chapter. Most obviously, the model of customer centric information use would benefit from concerted investigations to provide empirical support for the conceptual distinctions it presents. Such work should initially focus on the operationalization of the different levels and establish their relevant antecedents, consequences, correlates and contingency factors. Ultimately, this work would provide insights into the developmental trajectories of customer centric information use in service organizations which would provide

useful input for practicing managers. Similarly, the overarching framework that links service business success through the service dominant logic to customer centric orientations (see Figure 1) requires further research. Though compelling, much of the conceptual and theoretical work in this area would benefit from further empirical support.

Another important area is the use of ICT in service organizations. The issue of how such ICT can best be used both for orienting internal activities towards customer value, and for managing external interfaces with supply chain partners as well as with consumers, offers important research topics. Regarding the internal arrangements and processes, the way in which ICT can support or at least align with a customer centric orientation in organizations presents a pressing business problem. The external links are already considered by research streams located in supply chain management and marketing, respectively. However, additional research may consider using a broader approach that creates value by crossing such disciplinary boundaries that obscure more comprehensive investigation and a more comprehensive understanding of these matters. Case-studies of successful customer-centric ICT deployment that includes thorough descriptions and assessment of the underlying business case of such ICT use and information use resulting from the technology could generate awareness and interest among companies. Moreover, empirically supported and well-validated prescriptive models that guide the appropriate implementation of such ICT deployment are also necessary.

Finally, we believe that the challenges of product oriented thinking as well as of traditional functional orientations within service organizations would substantially benefit from theoretical and empirical consideration of novel and alternative approaches. Case studies of successful service originations that have achieved success in overcoming such traditional barriers to customer centric service provision promise interesting and useful input into the development of competitive service organizations across many industries. Identifying both best and poor practice would support the development of prescriptive models for how to engage with this challenge. Academic researchers clearly have a role to play in this, as do other stakeholders such as technology and service providers, the companies themselves, and – most centrally – customers.

CONCLUSION

This chapter highlights the challenges for organizations of becoming customer centric which requires them to introduce and manage both their information use and their ICT systems to reflect and support a customer centric orientation. It suggests a framework for customer centric deployment and use of ICT and information management and offers a model of different levels of customer centric information use in service organizations.

The logic of customer-centric ICT deployment requires not simply technologically and organizationally viable ICT solutions, but also a re-orientation of a company's operations and strategic focus in a way that assures that all operations are customer centric and that customer-relevant information is used to generate increased customer value, and thus to provide a sustainable and economically exploitable customer proposition (Fellenz & Brady, 2008; Gulati & Oldroyd, 2005; Shah et al., 2005). It is a unique challenge for functionally oriented decision makers such as operations managers, technologists, marketers, or finance and accounting staff to understand and filter customer-level data to generate the customer oriented information necessary to achieve this. Developing and deploying the necessary skill sets required for such customer centric information use would be a departure in virtually all traditional service organizations where typical approaches focus primarily on functional and operational

needs and efficiencies (Fellenz & Brady, 2008; Humby et al., 2008). What is needed is (a) a strategic fit between the way technology is deployed and the needs of the business to create customer value; (b) developing a fit between staff skills and the customer centric information management task, and (c) assuring a shared customer centric orientation across all business functions to fully align and successfully coordinate all relevant information gathering, managing, analyzing and utilization tasks for consumer benefit.

In the current global recessionary economic environment, the challenges of instilling such an orientation and coordinating complex activities throughout the organization that focus on customer value will include the task of overcoming service organizations falling back on the traditional cost-cutting and efficiency oriented retrenchment responses. Increased competition in mature and contracting service markets requires more focus on customer needs and wants. A customer centric orientation can help achieve this by focusing on the most crucial of propositions for service companies: increasing customer value.

REFERENCES

Agrawal, G. K., & Berg, D. (2007). Technology in the service development process: A missing dimension. *International Journal of Services Technology and Management*, 8(2/3), 107–122. doi:10.1504/IJSTM.2007.012863

Ambler, T., (2004). Why Financial Managers Need To Think About Marketing, *Corporate Finance Review*. Jul/Aug, 9(1), 14-21

Anderson, M., Banker, R., & Ravindran, S. (2006). Value Implications of Investments in Information Technology. *Management Science*, 52(9), 1359–11367. doi:10.1287/mnsc.1060.0542

Angeles, R. (2005). RFID technologies: Supply-chain applications and implementation issues. Information Systems Management, 22(1), 51–61. doi:10.1201/1078/44912.22.1.20051201/85739.7

Ayers, J., (2003, July). Don't get buried in customer data- use it. Harvard Business School Working Knowledge, July 21st.

Bednarz, A. (2001) Gartner: CRM deployment plans holding steady, Computer World, September, http://www.computerworld.com/action/article.do?command=viewArticleBasic&articleId=64179

Berry, L., Shankar, V., Turner Parish, J., Cadwallader, S., & Dotzel, T. (2006). Creating New Markets Through Service Innovation, MIT. Sloan Management Review, 47(2), 56–63.

Bitner, M., J., Brown, S., Meuter, M. (2000). Technology infusion in service encounters. Academy of Marketing Science Journal., 28(1), 138–150. doi:10.1177/0092070300281013

Bitner, M. J. (2001). Self-service technologies: What do customers expect? Marketing Management., 10(1), 10–12.

Brady, M. (2005, September). The role of information technology in marketing: Crucial but overlooked and underexploited. In Proceedings of the Irish Academy of Management Conference, Galway, CD Rom.

Brady, M., & Fellenz, M. R. (2007, August), The Service Paradox: Supporting Service Supply Chains with Product-Orientated ICT', IEEE/Informs Soli International Conference on Service Operations, Logistics and Informatics, Philadelphia.

Brady, M., Fellenz, M. R., & Brookes, R. (2008). The history of Information and Communication Technologies (ICT) with the marketing domain: Reframing the ICT dimension within the CMP framework . Journal of Business and Industrial Marketing, 23(2), 108–114. doi:10.1108/08858620810850227

Brady, M., O'Connor, M., & Saren, M. (2006, July). Marketers for the 21st Century Need ICT Education, In Academy of Marketing Conference, University of Middlesex, Brady, M., Saren, M., & Tzokas, N., (2002). Integrating Information Technology into Marketing Practice: The IT Reality of Contemporary Marketing Practice. Journal of Marketing Management, 18(5-6), 555–578.

Brethon, P., MacHulbert, J., & Pitt, L. (2005). Consuming technology: Why marketers sometimes get it wrong . California Management Review, 48(1), 110–128.

Curran, J., & Meuter, M. (2005). Self-service technology adoption: comparing three technologies . Journal of Services Marketing, 19(2), 103–114. doi:10.1108/08876040510591411

Daft, R. L., & Lengel, R. H. (1984). Information richness: A new approach to managerial behafviour and organization design. In B.M. Staw & L.L. Cummings (eds.), Research in organizational behaviour, 6, 191-233. JAI Press.

Daft, R. L., Lengel, R. H., & Trevino, L. K. (1987, September). Message equivocality, media selection, and manager performance: Implications for information systems. MIS Quarterly, ▪▪▪, 355–366. doi:10.2307/248682

Daft, R. L., & Macintosh, N. B. (1981). A tentative explanation into the amount and equivocality of information processing in organizational work units. Administrative Science Quarterly, 26, 207–224. doi:10.2307/2392469

Davenport, T. (2006). Competing on Analytics . Harvard Business Review, (January): 99–107.

Davenport, T. H., & Harris, J. G. (2005). Automated decision making comes of age. Sloan Management Review, 46(4), 83–89.

Day, G. S. (2006). Aligning the organization with the market. Sloan Management Review, 48(1), 41–49.

Drucker, P. (1954). The Practice of Management, New York and Evanston: Harper & Row

Fellenz, M., & Brady, M. (2008). Managing the Innovative Deployment of Information and Communication Technologies (ICTs) for Global Service Organizations. International Journal of Technology Marketing, 3(1), 39–55. doi:10.1504/IJTMKT.2008.017339

Fellenz, M. R., Augustenborg, C., Brady, M., & Greene, J. (2009). Requirements for an evolving model of supply chain finance: A technology and service providers perspective. In K.S. Soliman (ed.), Proceedings of the International Business Information Management Conference: 1171-1179. Cairo, Egypt.

Fisher, M., Raman, A., & McClelland, A. (2000). Rocket science retailing is almost here - are you ready? Harvard Business Review, 78(4), 115–124.

Galbraith, J., R (2005) "Designing the Customer-Centric Organization: A Guide to Strategy, Structure, and Process, Jossey Bass Business and Management Series

Glazer, R. (1991). Marketing in an information-intensive environment: Strategic implications of knowledge as an asset. Journal of Marketing, 55(4), 1–19. doi:10.2307/1251953

Greenyer, A. (2006). Back from the grave: The return of modelled consumer information . International Journal of Retail & Distribution Management, 34(3), 212–219. doi:10.1108/09590550610654375

Gronroos, C. (2006). On defining marketing: Finding a new roadmap for marketing. Marketing Theory, 6, 395–417. doi:10.1177/1470593106069930

Gulati, R. (2007). Silo busting: How to execute on the promise of customer focus. Harvard Business Review, 85(5), 98–106.

Gulati, R., & Oldroyd, J. B. (2005). The quest for customer focus. Harvard Business Review, 83(4), 92–101.

Gummesson, E. (2007). Exit services marketing – enter service marketing . Journal of Consumer Behaviour, 6(2), 113–142.

Holland, C. P., & Naude, P. (2004). The metamorphosis of marketing into an information-handling problem . Journal of Business and Industrial Marketing, 19(3), 167–177. doi:10.1108/08858620410531306

Howard, M., & Worboys, C. (2003). Self-service - a contradiction in terms or customer-led choice? Journal of Consumer Behaviour, 2(4), 382–392. doi:10.1002/cb.115

Huber, G. P., & Daft, R. L. (1987). The information environment of organizations. In F. M. Jablin, L. L. Putnam, K. H. Roberts, & L. W. Porter (eds.), Handbook of organizational communication (pp. 130-164). Newbury Park, CA: Sage.

Humby, C., Hunt, T., & Philips, T. (2008). Scoring points: How Tesco continues to win customer loyalty (2nd ed.). London, Kogan Page.

Jones, P., Clarke-Hill, C., Shears, P., Comfort, D., & Hillier, D. (2004). 'Radio frequency identification in the UK: Opportunities and challenges. International Journal of Retail & Distribution Management, 32(3), 164–171. doi:10.1108/09590550410524957

Kotler, P., Wong, S., & Armstrong, G. (2007). Principles of Marketing, 12th International Edition, London: Pearson.

Levinson, M., (2003, December 1-12). The RFID Imperative. CIO Magazine.

Levy, M., Powell, P., & Tetton, P. (2001). SMEs: Aligning IS and the strategic context. Journal of Information Technology, 16, 133–144. doi:10.1080/02683960110063672

Lin, J. S., & Hsieh, P. (2006). The role of technology readiness in customers' perception and adoption of self-service technologies . International Journal of Service Industry Management, 17(5), 497. doi:10.1108/09564230610689795

Lurie, N., & Mason, C. (2007). Visual Representation: Implications for Decision Making . Journal of Marketing, 71, 160–177. doi:10.1509/jmkg.71.1.160

Marchand, D. A., Kettinger, W. J., & Rollins, J. D. (2000). Information orientation: People, technology and the bottom line. Sloan Management Review, (Summer): 69–79.

Matthing, J., Kristensson, P., Gustafsson, A., & Parasuraman, A. (2006). Developing successful technology-based services: the issue of identifying and involving innovative users . Journal of Services Marketing, 20(5), 288–297. doi:10.1108/08876040610679909

McAfee, A. (2006). Mastering the Three Worlds of Information Technology. Harvard Business Review, 84(11), 141–149.

McClune, J. (2003) Contentious Debate? It Works at Philips: A technology powerhouse masters the "strategic conversation", Interview Series, Mercer Management Journal, 16. Retrieved from http://www.oliverwyman.com/ow/pdf_files/MMJ16_Interview_Contentious_Debate.pdf

McDonald, M., & Wilson, H. (1999). Improving marketing effectiveness through IT. Cranfield Management Research Series - working paper, (pp. 30-45).

McGovern, G. (2000). Managing information in the digital age: How the reader is king. Irish Marketing Review, 13(2), 55–61.

McGovern, G., & Moon, Y.,(2007, June 2-7). Companies and the Customers Who Hate Them, Harvard Business Review.

McHugh, G., Fahy, J., & Butler, P. (1998). Accountant behaving badly: A marketing perspective . Irish Marketing Review, 11(1), 19–26.

Meuter, M., Ostrom, A., Roundtree, R., & Bitner, M. J. (2000). Self-service technologies: Understanding customer satisfaction with technology-based service encounters . Journal of Marketing, 64(3), 50–65. doi:10.1509/jmkg.64.3.50.18024

Meyronin, B. (2004). ICT: the creation of value and differentiation in services. Managing Service Quality, 14(2/3), 216–225. doi:10.1108/09604520410528635

Mitchell, A. (2001). Radical Innovation. BT Technology Journal, 19(4), 60–64. doi:10.1023/A:1013730529933

Myburgh, S. (2000). The convergence of information technology and information management. Information Management Journal, 34(2), 4–16.

Nadeem, M. (2007). Emergence of Customer-Centric Branding: From Boardroom Leadership to Self-Broadcasting . Journal of American Academy of Business, 12(1), 44–49.

Nolan, R. (1973). Computer data bases: The future is now. Harvard Business Review, 51(5), 98–114.

Nolan, R. (1998, July-August 3-14). Connectivity and control in the year 2000 and beyond. Harvard Business Review.

Nonaka, I., & Takeuchi, H. (1995). The knowledge-creating company: How Japanese companies create the dynamics of innovation. New York: Oxford University Press.

Nysveen, H., Pedersen, P., & Thorbjørnsen, H. (2005). Explaining intention to use mobile chat services: moderating effects of gender . Journal of Consumer Marketing, 22(5), 247–257. doi:10.1108/07363760510611671

O'Connor, M., & Brady, M. (2006, September). The Hotel Sector In Ireland–Technology-Based Marketing Enterprises? Irish Academy of Management Conference, University of Cork, Ireland.

Piercy, N., (1981) Marketing Information bridging the quicksand between technology and decision-making, The Quarterly Review of Marketing, Fall,1-15.

Prahalad, C. K., & Ramaswamy, V. (2003). The new frontier of experience innovation, MIT. Sloan Management Review, 44(4), 12–18.

Prahalad, C. K., & Ramaswamy, V. (2004). Co-creation experiences: The next practice in value creation. Journal of Interactive Marketing, 18(3), 5–14. doi:10.1002/dir.20015

Ramaswamy, V. (2008). Co-creating value through customers' experiences: The Nike case. Strategy and Leadership, 36(5), 9–14. doi:10.1108/10878570810902068

Ramirez, R. (1999). Value co-production: Intellectual origins and implications for practice and research. Strategic Management Journal, 20(1), 49–65. doi:10.1002/(SICI)1097-0266(199901)20:1<49::AID-SMJ20>3.0.CO;2-2

Ranchhod, A. (2004). The changing nature of cyber-marketing strategies. Business Process Management Journal, 10(3), 262–276. doi:10.1108/14637150410539678

Reichheld, F. F., & Schefter, P. (2000). E-loyalty. Harvard Business Review, 78(4), 105–113.

Schultze, U., & Orlikowski, W. J. (2004). A Practice Perspective on Technology-Mediated Network Relations: The Use of Internet-Based Self-Serve Technologies. Information Systems Research, 15(1), 87–106. doi:10.1287/isre.1030.0016

Schweidel, D. A., Fader, P. S., & Bradlow, E. T. (2008). Understanding Service Retention Within and Across Cohorts Using Limited Information. Journal of Marketing, 72(1), 82–94. doi:10.1509/jmkg.72.1.82

Shah, D., Rust, R., Parasumam, A., Stalin, R., & Day, G. (2006). The path to customer centricity. Journal of Service Research, 9(2), 113–124. doi:10.1177/1094670506294666

Sisodia, R. S. (1992). Marketing information and decision support systems for services. Journal of Services Marketing, 6(1), 51–64. doi:10.1108/08876049210035773

Spekman, R., & Sweeney, P. (2006). RFID: From concept to implementation. International Journal of Physical Distribution and Logistics Management, 36(10), 736–754. doi:10.1108/09600030610714571

Srivastava, L. (2005, July). RFID and the internet of things. Presented at ICT Trends and Challenges in the Global Era. International Telecommunication Union, Twist, D. C., (2005). The impact of radio frequency identification on supply chain facilities. Journal of Facilities Management, 3(3), 226–236. doi:10.1108/14725960510808491

Vargo, S. L., & Lusch, R. F. (2004). Evolving to a new dominant logic for marketing . Journal of Marketing, 68(1), 1–17. doi:10.1509/jmkg.68.1.1.24036

Vargo, S. L., & Lusch, R. F. (2008). Services Dominant Logic, Continuing the evolution . Journal of the Academy of Marketing Science, 36(1), 1–10. doi:10.1007/s11747-007-0069-6

Venkatesh, V., Davis, F., & Morris, M. (2007). Dead Or Alive? The Development, Trajectory And Future Of Technology Adoption Research. Journal of the Association for Information Systems., 8(4), 267–287.

Webster, F., & Malter, A., & Shankar Ganesan. (2005). The Decline and Dispersion of the Marketing Competence, MIT . Sloan Management Review, 46(4), 35–43.

Weick, K. E. (1995). Sensemaking in organizations. Thousand Oaks, CA, Sage.

White, A. (2005). RFID: Why reusable asset tracking is the best place to start. San Jose, CA: BEA White Paper, BEA Systems Inc.

Wind, Y. (2008). A plan to invent the Marketing we need today . MIT Sloan Management Review, 49(4), 21–28.

Womack, J. P., & Jones, D. T. (2005, March). Lean Consumption . Harvard Business Review, 58–68.

ADDITIONAL READING

Andal-Ancion, A., Cartwright, P. A., & Yip, G. S. (2003). The digital transformation of traditional businesses. Sloan Management Review, (Summer): 34–41.

Cohen, W. M., & Levinthal, D. A. (1990). Absorptive Capacity: A New Perspective on Learning and Innovation. Administrative Science Quarterly, 35(1), 128–152. doi:10.2307/2393553

Davenport, T. H., & Grover, V. (2001). 'Special issue; Knowledge management. Journal of Management Information Systems, 18(1), 3–4.

Davenport, T. H., Harris, J. G., & Kohli, A. K. (2001). 'How do they know their customers so well? Sloan Management Review, (Winter): 63–73.

Fenn, J., & Linden, A. (2005). Gartner's Hype Cycle Special Report for 2005. Stamfort, CT: Gartner, Inc. Retrieved February 14, 2008, from http://www.gartner.com/resources/130100/130115/gartners_hype_c.pdf

Friend, S. C., & Walker, P. H. (2001). Welcome to the new world of merchandising. Harvard Business Review, 79(11), 5–11.

Frohlich, M. (2002). E-integration in the supply chain: Barriers and performance. Decision Sciences, 33(4), 537–557. doi:10.1111/j.1540-5915.2002.tb01655.x

Loveman, G. (2003). Diamonds in the data mine. Harvard Business Review, 81(5), 109–113.

O'Brien, T. V., Schoenbachler, D. D., & Gordon, G. L. (1995). Marketing information systems for consumer products companies: A management overview. Journal of Consumer Marketing, 12(5), 16–36. doi:10.1108/07363769510147777

Payne, A. (2006) Handbook of CRM, Oxford, UK: Butterworth-Heinemann

KEY TERMS AND DEFINITIONS

Customer Centric Orientation: We define customer centricity as reflecting a business model that places customer value at the heart of all organizational value creation activities. This means that all parts of the customer centric organizations are aware of how their activities directly and indirectly contribute to (or detract from) the value that customers derive from their interaction with the company, and endeavor to maximize their contribution to the important outcome of customer value creation. Therefore, customer centricity goes beyond simple customer orientation.

Data Ambiguity: The degree of uncertainty regarding the actual meaning of data.

Data Equivocality: The number of different meanings that available data and information can validly support.

Chapter 4
Impact of Wireless Sensor Network Technology on Service Innovation in Supply Chain Management

Gong Li
North Dakota State University, USA

Jing Shi
North Dakota State University, USA

ABSTRACT

Driven by the rapid development of information and communication technologies (ICT) as well as today's globally competitive environment for enterprises, service innovation has drawn considerable attention in such fields as supply chain management (SCM). Wireless sensor network (WSN) technology, which can provide a mobile, scalable, and reliable monitoring solution, has gone through rapid development in recent years. The objective of this chapter is to provide an overview about wireless sensor network technology and a discussion on how this technology can be applied to modern industries and especially bring service innovation to supply chain management. An overview of the history and potential applications of WSN is provided for the necessary background. The architecture, topology, standards, and protocols of WSN are fundamentally important and thus introduced in details. In a general sense, the impact of information technologies on supply chain management and service innovation is then briefly discussed. After that, much emphasis is placed on the possibility, procedures, and critical challenges of implementing WSN in supply chain management. In the end, two case studies are provided to illustrate the application of WSN for service innovation in both cold chain management and healthcare settings.

INTRODUCTION

Wireless sensor network (WSN), also known as Ubiquitous Sensor Networks (USN), is identified as one of the 21 most important technologies for the 21st century by Business Week (1999) and one of 10 emerging technologies that will change the world by MIT Technology Review (2003). Basically, a WSN is a wireless network consisting of spatially distributed small autonomous devices using many scattered sensors to cooperatively monitor environmental or physical conditions such as temperature,

DOI: 10.4018/978-1-61520-603-2.ch004

vibration, pressure, location or motion, at different sites (Römer & Mattern, 2004, Haenselmann, 2006). Low-cost and smart devices with multiple microsensors deployed in large numbers over wide areas and networked through wireless links and the Internet can provide an unprecedented feasible tool for automatically monitoring, tracking, and controlling the entities of interest.

It has been well recognized that supply chain management and its service innovation are strategically vital to corporate competitiveness and profitability in today's operating environment (Burgess, 1998). Supply Chain Management (SCM) offers a firm greater insights into potential opportunities and threats that its supply chain may carry by integrating supply and demand management within and across all supply chain organizations. The successful coordination, integration and management of key business processes across the entire supply chain determine the ultimate success of all supply chain members. The main goal of service innovation in SCM is to achieve information sharing in SCM and reduction of total cost, thus improving operation efficiency and enhancing competitive advantage. It is generally true that newer IT technologies can offer better services in managing the entire supply chain. With the recent development of WSN technology, WSN has shown its great potentials in different areas such as military sensing, environment monitoring, traffic surveillance, object tracking, nuclear reactor control, fire/flood detection, etc. Therefore, it is necessary to evaluate how this state-of-art technology can be applied for service innovation to reshape supply chain management.

Development of Wireless Sensor Networks

As its name may imply, the development of wireless sensor networks is closely related to the advancements of sensing, wireless communication, and computing technologies. The research in sensor networks originated from the defense applications in sensor networks. During the Cold War, the networks of air defense radars as well as a system of acoustic sensors on the ocean bottom called the Sound Surveillance System (SOSUS) were developed and deployed. From then on, many more sophisticated sensor networks have been developed. Note that these sensor networks generally adopt a hierarchical processing structure. In other words, information is processed at consecutive levels until it reaches the user (Chong & Kumar, 2003). Modern research on sensor networks started in 1980s with the development of Distributed Sensor Networks (DSN). The technology components for a DSN were identified in 1978, which include acoustic sensors, communication under high-level protocols, processing techniques and algorithms, and distributed software (Habermann, 1978). Later, military systems soon utilized the benefits of sensor networks to network-centric warfare (Alberts, Garska, & Stein, 1999). In network-centric warfare, the mounted sensors and weapons are controlled by separate platforms that operate independently but share information with each other over a communication network. Sensor networks can provide multiple observations, extended detection range, faster response time, and the necessary redundancy for high reliability, and thus the detection and tracking of objects can be improved. It is well recognized that the development cost can be effectively lowered if the commercial network technology and common network interfaces can be exploited.

Wireless communication networks have a long history (Callaway, 2004). In 1920s, for example, the U.S. Army Signal Corps established the War Department Radio Net, a nationwide radiotelegraphic network that was called the largest and most comprehensive radio net of its kind in the world (Raines, 1996). Later, the Transcontinental Corps (TCC), a peer-to-peer network, was built to facilitate communication among different area nets in the United States, and this has become a basis for the architecture of wireless sensor network due to its low power ad hoc design and longevity

(Callaway, Hsu, & Shankar, 2002). The ALOHA system (Abramson, 1970) was developed by adopting a random channel access protocol, which is generally recognized as the first successful wireless data communication network. Meanwhile, the amateur packet radio communications were also developed, and this advanced the development of the Multiple Access with Collision Avoidance (MACA) channel access protocol that employs a binary exponential random backoff mechanism (Karn, 1990). In 1990, the 802.11 Working Group was established by the Institute of Electrical and Electronics Engineers (IEEE) 802 LAN/MAN Standards Committee (LMSC). The first WLAN standard was released in 1997, which enables the data rates of 1 and 2 Mb/s. The 802.11 standard specifies the carrier sense multiple access with collision avoidance (CSMA/CA) channel access method, which is a refinement of the MACA protocol (O'Hara & Petrick, 1999). In 1997, the Home RF Working Group was formed, followed by the formation of the Bluetooth Special Interest Group in 1998 (Haartsen, 2000). Revision 1.0 of both specifications was released in 1999, representing the development of Wireless Personal Area Networks (WPANs).

Recent advances in wireless communication and computing techniques have resulted in a significant development in wireless sensor networks. However, it is urgently needed to find new networking techniques suitable for highly dynamic ad hoc environments and information processing methods for extracting useful, reliable, and timely information from the deployed sensor network. Low-cost sensors based on Micro-electro-mechanical system (MEMS) and nano-scale electromechanical systems (NEMS) start to appear. Advances in IEEE 802.11a/b/g-based wireless networking and other wireless systems such as Bluetooth, ZigBee, and WiMax are now facilitating reliable and ubiquitous connectivity. The SensIT project launched by the *Defense Advanced Research Projects Agency* (*DARPA*) in 1998 has been focusing on wireless, ad hoc networks for large distributed military sensor systems (http://www.darpa.mil/). A network of SensIT nodes can support detection, identification, and tracking of threats, as well as targeting and communication, both within and outside the network.

WSN is attracting intensive research efforts due to easy deployment and a large variety of application scenarios. Typical state-of-art efforts on the prominent development of wireless sensor networks include the Wireless Integrated Network Sensors (WINS) project (www.janet.ucla.edu), the PicoRadio program (bwrc.eecs.berkeley.edu) the μAMPS (ww-mtl.mit.edu), the Terminodes project (Hubaux et al., 2001), the Mobile Ad Hoc Networks (MANET) (www.ietf.org), system-level aspects of wireless sensing such as localization (Yun, Lee, Chung, Kim, & Kim, 2008), energy-efficiency (Ye, Heidemann, & Estrin, 2001; Anastasi, Conti, Francesco, & Passarella, 2009), novel and secure routing paradigms (Rao, Papadimitriou, Shenker, & Stoica, 2003; Karlof, & Wagner, 2003), Sensing coverage and network connectivity (Ghosh & Das, 2008), and data processing modules (Govindan, 2004; Cao, Chen, Zhang, & Sun, 2008).

Existing and Future Applications

The earliest proposed uses of wireless sensor networks were for military applications in which a variety of sensors, such as acoustic, vibration, magnetic, and ultra wideband radar sensors, can be equipped (Horton et al., 2002). Inexpensive low-power processors, and inexpensive sensors based upon MEMS and NEMS enable various applications of wireless sensor networks. Current applications for wireless sensor networks include, but are not limited to, military sensing and security control, environmental sensing, industrial monitoring, asset tracking and supply chain management, health monitoring. Some examples of these typical applications are listed as follows.

- Military applications: Monitoring inimical or friendly forces and equipment, monitoring military-threat or battlefield surveillance, targeting, battle damage assessment, attack detection, etc.
- Environmental applications: Monitoring microclimates, forest fire detection, flood detection, etc.
- Health applications: Remote monitoring of physiological data, tracking and monitoring doctors and patients inside a hospital, drug administration, elderly assistance, etc.
- Home applications: home automation, instrumented environment, automated meter reading, etc.
- Commercial applications: Environmental control in industrial and office buildings, inventory control, vehicle tracking and detection, traffic flow surveillance, etc.

An important application of wireless sensor networks is object tracking, e.g., in supply chain management. The use of wireless sensor networks for the tracking of nuclear materials was already realized in the Authenticated Tracking and Monitoring System (ATMS) (Schoeneman & Sorokowski, 1998). In a large distribution chain, one of the most vexing problems facing the distributor is to track the flow of products quickly and accurately. Real-time monitoring the product flow and even the condition of distribution in the entire supply chain can help a business operate more efficiently and effectively. The deployment of wireless sensor network technology can bring such benefits in this regard. Another example of object tracking is to track the shipping containers in a large port, which may have tens of thousands of containers, some being empty and in storage while others being bound for many different destinations. The containers are stacked, both on land and on ship. By placing sensors on each container, its location can be determined. Also, it is often difficult to locate items in a large warehouse due to lack of record or misplacement, and this might lead to the loss of sales and wrong inventory decision. Wireless sensor networks can be used to avoid this situation.

Another market for wireless sensor networks that is expected to grow quickly is in the field of health monitoring (Lee & Chung, 2009). Health monitoring is usually defined as "monitoring of non-life-critical health information," to differentiate it from medical telemetry. Two general classes of health monitoring applications are available for wireless sensor networks. One is athletic performance monitoring, for example, tracking one person's pulse and respiration rate via wearable sensors and sending the information to a personal computer for later analysis (Berkowitz, 2001). The other class is at-home health monitoring, for example, personal weight management (Pärkkä et al., 2002), daily blood sugar monitoring and remote monitoring of patients with chronic disorders (Lubecke & Lubecke, 2002), wearable personal health monitoring systems (Milenkovic, Otto, & Jovanov, 2006), etc.

WIRELESS SENSOR NETWORK TECHNOLOGY

Wireless sensor networks are usually composed of many small low-complexity nodes that can sense local environment, communicate information with neighboring nodes through wireless links, and in many cases, perform basic computations on the data collected. The nodes themselves can be stationary or dynamic, homogeneous or heterogeneous (Chong et al., 2003). Although the wireless sensor networks for various applications may be significantly different, they usually share common technical issues such as general physical network structure, networking technologies, and communication protocols, etc.

Physical Structure of Wireless Sensor Network

Topology of Wireless Sensor Networks

A vast amount of R&D efforts on networking architecture in recent years generate many concepts and classification methods regarding the topology of wireless sensor networks. A fundamental classification method is introduced in this section. The basic elements of a WSN are the sensor nodes, sinks, and gateways. According to the complexity, WSN can be divided into two broad types: single-sink WSN and multi-sink WSN.

Figure 1 (a) illustrates the schematic of a traditional single-sink WSN. Note that this type receives more exposure in the majority of scientific literature because of its lower complexity. Its disadvantage is the lack of scalability. Although the amount of data sensed by the sink can increase by adding more nodes, once its capacity is reached, the network size cannot be expanded. Besides, the performance of such WSNs are usually independent of the network size considering the medium access control (MAC) and routing issues (Verdone et al., 2008).

A more general category of WSN contains multiple sinks in the network, as shown in Figure. 1 (b). With a given level of node density, the utilization of a large number of sinks can decrease the probability of the isolated clusters of nodes that cannot deliver the data due to poor signal propagation conditions. It must be noted that a multi-sink WSN does not represent a trivial extension of a single-sink network. All sinks in the network can be either unconnected or connected through a separate network. If the sinks are not connected with one another, the utilization of multiple sinks can just partition the monitored field into smaller areas, which has no significant difference in discovery mechanisms from simple sink, especially from the viewpoint of communication protocols. However, if the sinks are connected with one another, the data collected by a node can be forwarded to any other element in the set of sinks, which means that a selection can be done based on such a suitable criterion such as minimum delay, maximum throughput, or minimum number of hops. It thus demonstrates better performance compared with both the unconnected multi-sink case and the single-sink case, but the communication protocols are more complex and should be designed according to proper criteria.

Both types of WSN do not contain actuators which are devices capable of manipulating or changing the surrounding environment. Recently, the wireless sensor and actuator networks (WSANs) have also been studied in literature. Because a WSAN contains both sensing nodes and actuators, as shown in Figure 1(c), the information flow in a WSAN is expected to be reversible. In this case, the protocols are generally more complex than those of common WSNs since they should be able to manage many-to-one, one-to-many, or even

Figure 1. Types of WSN: (a) single-sink; (b) multi-sink; (c) WSAN

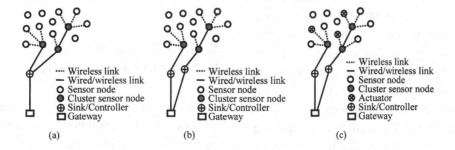

point-to-point communications when a specific actuator has to be reached. These communication protocols should also allow an easy deployment of nodes and the network must be self-organizing and self-healing when some local failures are encountered (Verdone et al., 2008).

Architecture of Sensor Nodes

The sensor nodes, also called wireless nodes, smart dusts, motes, or COTS (commercial off-the-shelf) motes, are the fundamental devices in a wireless sensor network. In general, they need to be small, cheap, or energy efficient. In the same time, they should be equipped with the right sensors, necessary computation and memory resources, as well as adequate communication capability. Besides, to achieve the desired good performance of a WSN such as sufficient network lifetime, the battery-powered devices used in most applications must be capable of working for a sufficiently long period using the battery energy. This indicates that the energy efficiency of the nodes is important for the WSN as well.

In general, the key components of a senor node include a power unit (batteries and/or solar cells), a sensing unit (sensors and analog-to-digital converters), a processing unit (along with storage), a transceiver unit (that connects the node to the network), and a memory/storage unit (that stores data and application codes). The connection between the components is illustrated by the general architecture of a sensor node in Figure 2. The optional components include a location-finding system, a power generator, a control actuator, and other application-dependent elements. The environmentally-intrinsic analog signals measured by the sensors are converted to digital signals by analog-to-digital converters and then are supplied to the processing unit. Since one or more sensors are used to obtain data from their local environment, and all these devices are powered by a battery, it is desirable that all data processing tasks are normally distributed over the

Figure 2. General architecture of a sensor node

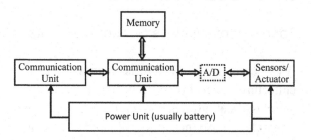

network to achieve high energy-efficiency for a WSN. Correspondingly, the nodes cooperate to provide the data to the sinks.

Based on the hardware components of the sensor nodes, there are five basic software subsystems correspondingly, namely, (1) Operating system (OS) microcode, the board common microcode used by all high-level node-resident software modules to support various functions. TinyOS is one such example of commonly used OS; (2) Sensor drivers, the software modules that manage the basic functions of the sensor transceivers; (3) Communication processors, which manage the communication functions, including routing, packet buffering and forwarding, topology maintenance, medium access control, encryption, and FEC; (4) Communication drivers (encoding and the physical layer), which manage the minutia of the radio channel transmission link, including clocking and synchronization, signal encoding, bit recovery, bit counting, signal levels, and modulation; (5) Data processing mini-apps such as numerical, data-processing, signal-value storage and manipulations, or other basic applications that are supported at the node level for in-network processing.

Sensor Nodes and Networking Technologies

According to the complexity of hardware/software components and functionality, sensor nodes can be classified in different ways. For instance, there exist four categories in terms of size, namely, large, small, microscopic, and nanoscopic; and two categories in terms of mobility, namely, mobile, and static (Sohraby, Minoli, & Znati, 2007). Sensor nodes can be configured in various hardware formats. They can either connect with a LAN and permanent power sources or communicate via wireless multihop radio frequency (RF) radio powered by small batteries (Cornell Database Group, 2009). The trend is moving toward very large scale integration (VLSI), integrated opto-electronics, and nanotechnology.

The value of wireless sensor networks lies in their low cost and distribution capability in large numbers. To enable the widespread and cost-effective deployment of WSN, certain features of WSN should be standardized to make the products from different vendors compatible. For instance, the communication protocols should be standardized for the various layers of wireless sensor networks. Incompatible protocols, even they might be optimal individually, will limit the size of the overall wireless sensor market. Meanwhile, it is better to make use of existing and/or emerging commercial off-the-shelf (COTS) wireless communications and infrastructures rather than designing entirely new ones.

A number of wireless COTS technologies are available for WSNs, such as Bluetooth (IEEE 802.15.1), ZigBee (IEEE 802.15.4 and UWB IEEE 802.15.4a), wireless LANs (WLAN, IEEE 802.11a/b/g/n series), broadband wireless access (BWA)/WiMax (MAN-scope IEEE 802.16), radio-frequency identification (RFID) tagging, and 3G. Each standard possesses different characteristics, as summarized in Table 1.

ZigBee wireless technology is a short-range communication system for applications in wireless personal area networks. Mainly adopted in the implementation of WSNs, ZigBee wireless technology is characterized by its low complexity, low cost, low power consumption, low data transmission rate, and compatibility with cheap fixed or mobile devices. The IEEE 802.15.4 standard only supports the data transmission rate ranging from 20 kbps to 250 kbps. However, it has the lowest power requirement among the above-mentioned technologies. Most ZigBee devices can run several years on a single set of batteries. Bluetooth is a short-range communication protocol widely used in mobile phones and PDAs. It usually operates in the 2.4-GHz ISM band with a bandwidth of approximately 1~3 Mbps. WLAN is a collection of related 802.11 technologies that can operate

Table 1. Comparison of wireless protocol technologies

Standards	WLAN (IEEE)					WPAN (IEEE)		WMAN (IEEE)
	802.11 Legacy	802.11a	802.11b	802.11g	802.11n	802.15.1/ Bluetooth	802.15.4/ ZigBee	802.16/ WiMax
Release Year	1997	1999	1999	2003	2008	2002	2003,2006	2004,2005
Frequency Band (GHz)	2.4	5.8	2.4	2.4	2.4-5.8	2.4	0.868 0.915 2.4	2-66
Maximum Range (m)	~70	~100	~100	~110	~160	~10	~100	~50,000
Max data rate (Mbps)	2	54	11	54	248	3	250	134
Number of users	Dozens	Dozens	Dozens	Dozens	Dozens	Dozens	Dozens	Thousands

in the 2.4-GHz ISM band, the 5-GHz ISM band, or the 5-GHz UNII bands. It is well-known to have the longest range of the common unlicensed wireless technologies, and as rapid as a 54 Mbps data transmission rate.

Recently, along with the successful deployment of IEEE 802.11b/11g-based hotspot services (Wi-Fi) to support the Internet access and VoIP applications (Minoli, 2002), the metro-wide Internet/VoIP services using the newer WiMax connectivity have also been delivered, where WiMax is the marketing name of the IEEE 802.16 standard. IEEE 802.16 protocol can provide very high capacity links on both the uplink and downlink. Applications of WiMax include point-to-point communication between stations, point-to-multipoint communication between the base station and clients, backhaul services for Wi-Fi (802.11) hotspots, broadband Internet services to home users, private-line services for users in remote locations, and metro-wide WSN applications.

Radio frequency identification (RFID) is a special form of wireless network technology. Passive RFID tags (with no on-board battery) are powered by query RF signals from a reading device and send back the ID information to the reading device. Self-powered (active) tags can be read from a greater distance. Most RFID tags have integrated circuits (ICs), microelectronic semiconductor devices with a large number of interconnected transistors and other components. RFID can operate in low frequency (less than 100 MHz), high frequency (more than 100 MHz), and UHF (868 to 954 MHz). Presently, RFID is mainly used for labeling and tracking, and thus low cost is the dominant factor for RFID tag design and manufacture. As a result, most RFID tags carry no sensing capability and the tags can only communicate with the RFID readers and this makes this technology simpler than the general-purpose WSN.

Communication Protocols for WSNs

Communication in wireless networks is performed via the electromagnetic signal transmission in the air, where the transmission medium is always expected to be fairly shared by all sensor network nodes. A medium access control (MAC) protocol must be properly utilized in order to achieve this goal. Meanwhile, energy efficiency is one of the most important goals in designing protocols for wireless sensor networks. To do that, the protocols should address the major sources of energy waste on MAC and routing levels.

Medium Access Control Protocols

In a WSN system, the physical layer typically includes a specification of the transmission medium and the topology of the network. Generally, the physical layer typically provides such services as the encoding and decoding of signals, preamble generation and removal to achieve synchronization, and the transmission and reception of bits, while the MAC layer must manage the communication channels available for the node thereby reducing energy waste caused by collisions, idle listening, overhearing, and excessive overhead. The MAC protocol is designed to regulate the access to the shared wireless medium such that the performance requirements of the underlying application are satisfied (van Dam & Langendoen, 2003). This objective of the MAC protocol is provided by the lower sublayer of the data link layer (DLL). The data link layer is necessary to accommodate the logic required to manage the access to a shared access communications medium.

Although many novel MAC protocols are still being developed (Ceken, 2008; Liao, & Wang, 2008; Kim, & Park, 2009), currently available protocols can generally be categorized into two broad groups: schedule-based and contention-based MAC protocols. The schedule-based protocols are a class of deterministic MAC layer protocols in which the access to channel is based on a schedule and limited to one sensor node at a time. This is achieved by pre-allocating the resources to individual sensor nodes. While with the contention-based MAC-layer protocols, a single radio channel is shared by all nodes and allocated on demand. The contention-based MAC layer protocols can only minimize, rather than completely avoid, the occurrence of collisions. To reduce energy consumption, these protocols differ in the mechanisms which reduce the likelihood of a collision while minimizing overhearing and control traffic overhead.

Routing Protocols

Routing realizes the process of sending a data packet from source to destination, during which intermediate nodes are often used before reaching the final receiver. In WSNs, data communication might be achieved from the sensor nodes to a monitoring node, among neighbor nodes, or from a monitoring node to the sensor nodes. Data communication from the sensor nodes to a monitoring node is the most common application. On the other hand, information will be forwarded from a monitoring node to a set of sensor nodes if the information is needed to be sent to those nodes, e.g., queries to the network.

Many different routing strategies for WSNs have been proposed, as surveyed by Akkaya & Younis (2005). These routing protocols can be divided into three broad types: flat-based routing, hierarchical-based routing, and adaptive-based routing. Flat-based routing assumes that all sensor nodes perform the same role, while nodes in hierarchical-based routing have different roles in the network, static or dynamic. Adaptive routing is characterized by automatically changing its behavior according to the specific application and network conditions. These routing protocols can be further classified into multipath-based, query-based, or negotiation-based routing techniques depending on the protocol operation (Boukerche, 2008).

In WSNs, routing protocols are closely related to information fusion because it addresses the problem of delivering the sensed information to the sink node. It is natural to think of performing the fusion while the pieces of data become available. However, the way information is fused depends on the network organization, which directly affects how the role can be assigned. Hierarchical networks are organized into clusters where each node responds only to its respective cluster-head, which might perform special operations such as data fusion/aggregation. In flat networks, communication is performed hop-by-hop and every node may be functionally equivalent. Proper routing can also overcome the limited processing, storage, data transmission capabilities resulting from cost-effectiveness and sensor miniaturization. Although the sensor nodes and communication links are likely to fail due to these limitations and hostile operational environments, networking a large number of sensors together to form a distributed sensor network can overcome this weakness.

SERVICE INOVATION IN SCM AND IT TECHNOLOGIES

This section focuses on the impacts of modern Information technology (IT) including wireless sensor networks on the service innovation in supply chain management. The discussion starts with the relationship of IT adoption, service innovation, and competitive advantages in an organization. An introduction is then provided on the general role and importance of information technology in supply chain management innovation. Also, the typical information technologies available presently for SCM innovation are summarized. Finally, the possible benefits of applying WSN in modern industries are briefly analyzed.

Relationship of IT Adoption, Service Innovation, and Competitive Advantages

Nowadays, information technologies have been widely adopted by organizations in managing such key activities as procurement, manufacturing, distribution, customer relationship, and the supply chain, etc. (Agarwal & Sambamurthy, 2002; Liao, Chem, Liu, & Liao, 2004; Lai, Wong, & Cheng, 2006) to enable their products and services innovation (Xu, Sharma, & Hackney, 2005), and thus their competitive advantages are enhanced (Sambamurthy, Bharadwaj, & Grover, 2003; Berry, Shankar, Parish, Cadwallader, & Dotzel, 2006).

According to the Information Technology Association of America (ITAA), **Information technology (IT)** can be defined as "the study, design, development, implementation, support or management of computer-based information systems, particularly software applications and computer hardware." Generally, **IT adoption** refers to the use of hardware and software to capture, convert, store, protect, process, transmit, and securely retrieve useful information. At the organizational level, current IT adoption usually focuses on *IT infrastructure, strategic alignment, organizational structure*, and *individual learning*. *IT infrastructure* includes management and provisioning of large-scale computing, electronic data interchange (EDI) and shared databases, networks, and R&D in identifying new technologies (Davenport, Hammer, & Metsisto, 1989; Fink, & Neumann, 2009). *Strategic alignment* involves the development and reconfiguration of information technology (IT) to support business strategies (Chen, Sun, Helms, & Kennyjih, 2008). Strategic alignment of information technology and business strategies is critical for successful IT adoption since the possible performance improvement from IT adoption mainly depends on whether and how well the IT strategy and corporate strategy coincide (Palmer & Markus, 2000). *Organizational structure* usu-

ally needs to be modified while adopting new IT technology to improve performance (Currie, 1996). *Individual learning* is necessary for end-users and practitioners to acquire new IT-related knowledge and skills, which greatly influences the final success of IT adoption (Grover, Fiedler, & Teng, 1999; Ruizmercader, Meronocerdan, & Sabatersanchez, 2006).

Innovation can be defined as the initiation, adoption and implementation of ideas or activity that are new to the adopting organization (Fichman, 2001). **Service Innovation** can be comprehensively defined as a new or considerably changed service concept, client interaction channel, service delivery system or technological concept that individually, but most likely in combination, leads to one or more new service functions that change the service/goods offered on the market and require structurally new technological, human or organizational capabilities of the service organization (Van Ark, Broersma, & Den Hertog, 2003). Service innovation, which is becoming more and more important for modern firms, usually includes service product innovation, service process innovation, and innovation in service organizations. **Service process innovation** suggests the adoption of new methods, e.g., a novel way of handling a commodity commercially, that can be applied to the entire value chain process of manufacturing, distribution and service. **Service product innovation** refers to the introduction of new goods or improved quality of existing goods to the market and the development of new consumer and capital goods and services. **Innovation in service organizations** refers to organizational innovations and the management of innovation processes within service organizations.

IT adoption has significant impacts on the innovation of service processes – both internal operational processes and external cross-enterprise processes. For example, IT adoptions can improve the company's delivery efficiency, enable progress visibility, and facilitate the design of new service processes. It may also enhance service administration efficiency, shorten service product design period, etc. On the other hand, adopting information technology provides a means for production and marketing staff to create numerous opportunities for service product innovation. For example, IT adoption can enable practitioners to access past service innovation projects, allowing them to learn from previous experiences. In doing so, firms can develop new services better fitful for market demand and offer better post-selling services to meet customer needs (Demirhan, Jacob, & Raghunathan, 2006). Therefore, it can be concluded that the higher the level of IT adoption, the greater the level of service innovation (Chen et al, 2007).

Competitive advantages, viewed internally as organizational capabilities and externally as outcome performance, can be achieved and enhanced by successful service innovation practices (Bhatt & Grover, 2005). Usually, a company's competitive advantages can be greatly improved by increasing the degree of service innovation practices. Internal competitive advantages, reflected by employee job satisfaction, domain knowledge and level of creativity after new services are launched (Van Riel, Lemmink, & Ouwersloot, 2004), depend on internal resources and capabilities. It highly values a corporate working environment for employees to plan, develop and launch innovative services since employees in such environments tend to become more satisfied, creative, and motivated to acquire new knowledge (Rubery, Earnshaw, Marchington, Cooke, & Vincent, 2002). External competitive advantages, usually reflected by customer satisfaction, can be achieved via providing high-quality products and services to meet customer anticipations and timely keeping the pace of market changes, trends and competitors' current situation, thus improving the firm's competitive advantage and leading to the sustainable success in business operations.

Importance of IT Adoption in SCM Innovation

Today's enterprises often cooperate with global suppliers, partners and a multitude of stakeholders to deliver service and/or product packages into the market via the complex supply chain (McLaughlin, Paton, & Macbeth, 2006). Service innovation must come from within the supply chain or network. By understanding how the supply chain manages the transfer of knowledge/information (innovation commodity) and subsequently engages with the knowledge/information, we can better stimulate meaningful innovation and general value adds (Paton & Mclaughlin, 2008).

A **supply chain** is comprised of facilities and activities in network form, which performs the functions of product development, procurement of materials, materials handling, manufacturing of goods, distribution of finished goods, and aftermarket services to customers (Mabert, 1998). The successful coordination, integration and management of key business processes across the entire supply chain determine the ultimate success of all supply chain members. As a source of competitive advantage, SCM offers the firm greater insights into potential opportunities and threats that its supply chain may carry. Supply Chain Management integrates supply and demand management within and across all supply chain organizations, linking their major business functions and business processes into a cohesive and high performing business model.

Figure 3 illustrates the schematic of a simple supply chain. It can be seen that the supply chain is closely related to the flow of products and information between the supply chain organizations. Especially, serving as the driver to create a coordinated supply chain, information provides the basis for supply chain management decisions at all phases (strategic, planning, operational). The information is required to be accurate, real-time, and enabling supply chain visibility, and such information allows performance to be optimized for the entire supply chain, not just for one stage. **Supply chain management (SCM)** has become a strategic tool vital to corporate competitiveness and profitability in today's global operating environment (Burgess, 1998). The key concept of SCM is to effectively manage the interconnection of organizations through upstream and downstream linkages between different processes that produce value in the form of products and services to the ultimate consumer (Slack, Chambers, & Johnston, 2001). During the past decades, along with the increasing trend of globalization, companies around the world have been driven to increasingly integrate the supply chain and improve their supply chain operations via the adoption of advanced information technology.

The effective adoption of IT technology in supply chain management can have a significant impact on supply chain performance. The applications of IT technologies, e.g., the development of inter-organizational information system for the supply chain, can bring many distinct benefits such as cost reduction, productivity improvement, and product/market strategy optimization. IT infrastructure capabilities provide a competitive positioning of business initiatives such as reducing the production cycle time or inventory level, implementing the redesigned cross-functional processes. Companies must realize the power of IT in collaborating with their supply chain partners. It is generally true that the newer IT technologies can offer better services in managing the entire supply chain. However, it should be noted that, while selecting an IT system for a company's SCM innovation practice, the level of sophistication should be aligned with the needs and its key success factors.

Current IT Adoptions in SCM Innovation

Supply chain management innovation is recognized as an important area for IT adoption and investment (Bowersox & Daugherty, 1995; Smirnov & Chandra, 2001; Lai et al, 2006). The main goal is to achieve the information sharing in SCM and reduction of total cost, thus improving operation efficiency and enhancing competitive advantage. Indeed, a study report by Radjou (2003) indicates that U.S. manufacturers are increasingly dependent on the benefits brought about by IT to improve supply chain agility, reduce cycle time, achieve higher efficiency, and deliver products to customers in a timely manner.

With the progress in circuit miniaturization and affordability, the general IT technology has been gradually accepted in SCM applications. Numerous IT technologies have been successfully applied for innovation to improve SCM performance such as bar code, data warehouse, Electronic Data Interchange (EDI), Radio Frequency Identification Technology (RFID), wireless, the Internet and World Wide Web (WWW), and Information Systems (IS) such as Electronic Commerce (E-Commerce) systems and Enterprise Resource Planning (ERP) systems. For the purpose of brevity, a few representative IT technologies are introduced as follows (Mishra, 2006).

- **Bar codes and Scanners**: A bar code is usually used to identify a specific kind of product and/or its manufacturer. Bar code scanners can be seen widely used, e.g., in super markets.

Figure 3. Schematic of a simple supply chain

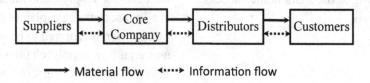

Material flow ⬅···➤ Information flow

- **Data warehouse**: Data warehouse is a consolidated database maintained separately from an organization's production system database. It organizes the time dependent informational subjects rather than specific business processes.

- **Electronic Data Interchange (EDI)**: EDI refers to the computer-to-computer exchange of business documents in a standard format. EDI describes both the capability and practice of sharing information between organizations electronically. EDI is characterized by quicker process to information, better customer service, reduced paper work, increased productivity, improved tracing and expediting, better cost efficiency, competitive advantage, and improved billing. EDI enables the supply chain partners to overcome the information distortions and exaggeration by improving technologies to facilitate the real time sharing of actual demand and supply information.

- **Enterprise Resource Planning (ERP)**: ERP system (e.g. SAP) has been viewed as the core of a company's IT infrastructure. It has become an enterprise wide transaction processing tool which captures the data, and reduce the manual activities and tasks associated with processing financial, inventory and customer order information. ERP system achieves a high level of integration by utilizing a single data model and establishing a set of rules for accessing data.

- **Electronic Commerce**: Electronic commerce represents various IT tools and techniques utilized to conduct business in a paperless environment, including EDI, e-mail, electronic fund transfers, electronic publishing, electronic bulletin boards, shared databases and magnetic/optical data capture, etc.

As a well known fact, another popular IT technology being adopted in SCM innovation is RFID technology. Due to its decreasing cost, RFID has recently been introduced into the logistics industry to enhance the operational efficiency of supply chain management. An RFID system combines various information technologies, such as database management system and computer network, to provide an automatic, secure, and convenient real-time control system. The accuracy and timeliness are two main concerns in the operation process control of supply chain management. RFID technology can support real-time control of goods in the supply chain including raw material, work in process (WIP), and finished product. It can enhance the degree of automation, reduce the probability of error, and greatly improve the visibility of supply chain. Thus, the RFID systems can be used in the receiving and dispatching of goods, stock management, theft prevention, product assembly, and personnel control.

The range of applications of RFID technology is far reaching, including logistics, retail, transportation industries, and health care. To name a few, Angeles (2005) proposed an application process of RFID system, which included five steps: estimate the ROI for RFID system, choose the right RFID technology, anticipate RFID technical problems, manage the IT infrastructure issues, and initiate a pilot project for learning experiences. Ngai, Cheng, Au, & Lai (2007) suggested that a system architecture integrating mobile commerce and RFID applications in a container depot could keep track of the location of containers, provide greater visibility of the operation data, and improve the process control. Bose & Pal (2005) discussed three-levels of Auto-ID technology application in the supply chain management, namely, the strategic level, the tactical level, and the operational level. Sabogal & Tholke (2004) provided a guideline on the integration of RFID technology with the SAP ERP system for manufacture of pharmaceutical products. Adams &

Burke (2007) discussed about how RFID system might be incorporated in the filtration phase of the pharmaceutical product manufacturing.

Advantages of Adopting WSN in Industries

The WSN technology has many advantages, such as mobility, extendibility and ease of installation, reliability and flexibility, improved monitoring capabilities and information quality, etc (Ilyas & Mahgoub, 2005). Note that the architecture of a distributed wireless sensor network is dependent on its specific application in some fields.

A dynamic or moving sensor can improve system monitoring capabilities and achieve effective communication. In many cases, sensors need to be deployed randomly rather than located precisely, especially when the entity of interest cannot be well monitored based on the spatially fixed sensors. Although currently most existing work focuses on the networks of fixed nodes, mobility has been introduced into the sensor networks recently. Compared with traditional ad hoc network or a wired sensor network, a WSN may provide much larger overall coverage. The overall coverage area of a WSN is the union of many small coverage areas of low-cost sensors, so the coverage is more flexible and can be conveniently adjusted or expanded by moving nodes or adding new nodes, respectively. Wireless sensor networks are also characterized by their adaptability and flexibility in monitoring and control applications. The capability and reliability of a single sensor node are restricted, but multiple sensors will provide fault tolerance, thus making the whole system robust and flexible. A WSN is adaptable to the changes in the configuration of equipment as well as in the layout of the network itself. When a sensor dies, its neighbor nodes can provide the same or similar information. If some monitoring devices are taken away or break down, the network should reconfigure itself automatically. The self-organization feature of sensor networks provides the adaptive agility

to various environments and dynamic changes. The flexibility of WSN is obvious in view that its sensing coverage can be adjusted by moving or expanding nodes, that trade-off between delay and information accuracy can be made via collaboration among sensors, and that balance of power consumption between nodes can also be achieved by cooperation. Improved monitoring capabilities and information quality can be attained by a WSN via the simple aggregation of data from plenty of nodes.

As wireless networking technology advances, it is also becoming more cost effective. The size of sensor and the production costs are both decreasing. Recent advanced hardware technologies result in more powerful sensors as small as a few millimeters volume. Current wireless sensor networks are designed to ease development and integration with other systems. No customization, integration, or development is required, and there are no wiring or installation costs. Battery-powered motes do not require AC power, which can make wireless networks suitable for locations where power distribution is not designed for additional monitoring equipment.

Along with the increasing importance of services in logistics and supply chain management, the performance and efficiency of information collection and data transmission become very critical. For example, companies in the food, chemical, or pharmaceutical industries depend on the monitoring of environmental conditions such as temperature and humidity throughout the supply chain in order to prevent losses. A small, low-power WSN can monitor the physical environment at high resolution and will lead to a vast increase in the quantity and quality of information available to organizations.

Wireless sensor networks can be used for process control and verification in transport and logistics processes. They can play an important role in improving operational efficiency of supply chain management as well. It can be foreseen that the WSN technology will be applied in more service industries. Real time location system (RTLS) will eventually be affordable and technically appropriate for use in major supply chains where it will locate things from a distance in real time but, unlike WSN, they will not comprehensively monitor conditions or have the other advantages that attributed to WSN. Progress is now rapid and the much smaller size of the latest WSN devices is one indication. While the original concept is for billions or even trillions of tags the size of dust, the first ten years of development of WSN has more often seen expensive tags – some of earlier products are close to the size of a videotape. Further miniaturization and cost reduction are now imminent.

APPLICATIONS OF WSN IN SCM INNOVATION

General Deployment Procedure for WSN

The deployment procedure is sometimes regarded as the most important issue in the applications of wireless sensor network (Karl et al 2000) since most applications need certain infrastructure to achieve the data sensing, processing and communication tasks with low power consumption. The traditional way in the deployment of WSN is mostly placing sensor nodes in a random or ad hoc method which is convenient and suitable for outdoor applications (Heinzelman, Chandrakasan, & Balakrishnan, 2000, Younis, Youssef, & Arisha, 2002). In such cases, the sensor nodes are capable of self-configuration and self-discovery. In many cases, however, to reduce power consumption, a reliable communication channel should be considered and constructed before putting any application-oriented devices into action (Àlvarez et al., 2004).

Although the deployment of WSN is quite different from the wired network and different applications of WSN have their specific limita-

tions and requirements, the general procedure is similar, usually including deployment planning, device configuration, performance validation, and deployment completion (Huang, Lai, & Ku, 2006).

Deployment Planning

An Internet backbone is made up of a large collection of interconnected high-capacity data routes and core routers that carry data across the world. In the step of deployment planning, it should be determined first of all whether an Internet backbone is necessary to be constructed for the specific WSN application. After that, some fundamental issues should be checked such as the network connectivity, the signal coverage in the area, and the number of necessary devices, the layout of devices, etc. For example, the network connectivity determines whether the information packages can be successfully sent to their destination via the network. All the devices in the backbone network should be interconnected to construct a reliable network.

Device Configuration

The partitioning decisions to be made at the beginning of WSN construction are complex. In addition to the components of the communication transceiver itself, the decision-maker must consider the presence of any host processor that affects hardware/software trade-offs, the type of power source(s) available, and the type of interface(s) needed to communicate with sensors and actuators. One important but often overlooked factor in the design of wireless sensor network nodes is the effect of the finite stability of the node time base on the minimum attainable duty cycle, and therefore, the minimum attainable average power consumption of the network node. The resulting trade-off between the cost of the node time base and the attainable life of the battery (or other power source) must be decided properly to achieve success.

Node implementation is of primary importance in the design and deployment of a successful wireless sensor network. To a large degree, the practicality of a wireless sensor network node rests on its ability to meet the low power consumption goals typically set by the specific application. Low system power consumption depends on a good match between the power source and the load itself, so that significant amounts of power are not lost in conversion processes. The selection of the power source itself is often the key to a successful implementation; the use of energy scavenging is possible only with the low power consumption. Meanwhile, antenna selection is another design decision often overlooked. It is critical to the overall performance of the wireless sensor network node in that the antenna greatly affects the product cost, market flexibility, and range of the node. The antenna design and selection can also affect the external appearance of the node, and certainly has a major influence on the internal circuit board layout. In addition, since wireless sensor network nodes are typically small, often exposed to the environment, employ small geometry CMOS integrated circuits, and may have plastic housings to enable the use of internal antennas, the design consideration on electrostatic discharge (ESD) protection is important. For the products in nonconductive housings, ESD protection can be largely mechanical engineering task, with the goal of eliminating any holes or gaps in the housing that may present a pathway for the discharge to reach the sensitive circuits.

Finally, much of the success of the wireless sensor network application depends on standards, so that nodes from multiple vendors can be interoperable. This will rescue the industry from its present state of very successful but incompatible proprietary communication protocols existing in a number of niche markets, with their combined volume too low to reach economies of scale needed for significant growth. The developers of WSN systems now need to determine which off-the-shelf wireless systems already defined by various standards bodies (e.g., Wi-Fi, Bluetooth, ZigBee, WiMax) can be used by way of employing and/or integrating preconfigured chipsets and integrated circuits, antennas, drivers, and protocol machinery.

Performance Validation

After the WSN system is constructed, the developers will need to verify and validate the functionality and performance of the system such as interconnectivity, network coverage, and device coverage, etc. The network topology is formed as a tree, so by ensuring that each edge connection in the tree is valid, one can be sure that the network interconnection is valid. It means that if all the devices are connected to their parents, they are connected to all the devices in the network. The purpose of parent connectivity testing is to retrieve the connection status between a device and its parent. Network coverage is used to verify the coverage of the network in the target region. The purpose of the network coverage test is to make sure that all packets from the target region can be successfully sent to their destination. Device coverage test aims to check the connection quality from a specific network device to some locations of interest.

Deployment Completion

If the wireless sensor network constructed according to the planning result does not meet the requirement, it might indicate that the network connectivity or the coverage of the network is not valid to the applications to be applied upon the network structure. There are many reasons that could cause the incapability, such as incapable space model, invalid antenna modal, theoretic and realistic mismatch, and inaccurate device planting location. Such problems must be fixed via certain tools or methods, for example, by inserting additional devices to help detect the problem. If the test result obtained from network verification procedure reveals that the network is too far from being capable, the users should reverse back to the planning procedure, modify some constraints or the space model, and repeat previous procedures.

Challenges in WSN Applications

WSN has become a most prospective IT technology for service innovation of SCM in the near future. To enable high performance of a WSN, however, there still exist a number of challenging issues in both research and practice. As mentioned before, wireless sensor networks are featured by self-organizing capabilities, short-range wireless communication and multihop routing, as well as limitations in energy, transmit power, memory, and computing power. Therefore, before wireless sensor networks see their truly ubiquitous applications, a number of hardware limitations and software constraints need to be overcome, which include, but are not limited to, power efficiency, node costs, limited functional capabilities, transmission channels, topology management complexity and node distribution, standards, scalability concerns, etc. (Callaway, 2004, Sohraby et al., 2007, Boukerche, 2008, Verdone et al., 2008).

Power Efficiency

Although it is possible to obtain energy from external power supply sources, e.g., solar cells (Want, Farkas, & Narayanaswami, 2005), a battery is still necessary to be used since the supply of such external power sources are often discontinuous or unsteady. That is, sensors are normally powered by a battery which only has very limited power. Therefore, energy conservation is one of the most crucial design issues in energy-constrained wireless sensor networks since the network lifetime directly relies on the efficient management of sensing node energy both the behavior of the power source and the power consumption of the system must be considered in the process of ap-

plications as early as at the WSN design stage. Since the main functions of a sensor node are event detection, local data processing, and data transmission, power consumption should be focused on the three functional domains. Various power conservation mechanisms proposed in the literature (Liu, Zhao, Cheung, & Guibas, 2004; Pantazis & Vergados, 2007; Anastasi et al, 2009) are either active or passive. Active power conservation mechanisms achieve the energy conservation by utilizing energy-efficient network protocols, while passive power conservation mechanisms save a node's power by turning-off the transceiver module whenever no data is to be received or transmitted (Pantazis, Vergados, Vergados, & Douligeris, 2009).

While designing or constructing a WSN, a critical behavior of batteries should be considered is that a battery undergoing pulsed discharge generally has a greater capacity than an identical battery undergoing a constant discharge. Usually, the lower the duty cycles of the pulsed discharge, the greater the battery capacity. The use of this charge recovery effect has been proposed as a method of extending the battery life of portable communication devices (Chiasserini & Rao, 2000). In practice, taking advantage of the charge recovery effect means that the protocol should activate high-power dissipation components (e.g., the sensor) in infrequent bursts, resulting in a low duty cycle of operation. Also, the bursts should be separated from each other by the maximum extent possible, thereby giving the cell the maximum possible time to recover before the next discharge pulse. Besides, because the active power consumption of the transceiver in a WSN node is much greater than its standby power consumption, the node must operate its transceiver in a low duty cycle mode to obtain low average power consumption.

Cost Issues

The cost of hardware such as chips and external parts in the physical layer is significant in the total cost structure of WSN. A WSN usually consists of a large number of sensor nodes, indicating that the cost of an individual node is critical to the total cost of the wireless sensor network. Obviously, the cost of each sensor node is expected to be as low as possible while meeting the functionality requirements. Currently, sensors based on Bluetooth technology (with limited bandwidth and distance) cost as low as $10/unit, and the price keeps dropping. However, the cost of a sensor node for massive deployment is generally targeted to be less than $1, and this is still beyond the reach of the current state-of-the-art technology (Sohraby et al, 2007). To reduce the cost, hardware integration should be pursued in the design process. Certainly, a concurrent measure is to maximize market size, thus achieving cost reductions via volume production (Callaway, 2004).

Security Issues

The sensor network consists of numerous mobile sensor nodes organized in a flat or hierarchical structure, making the sensor networks susceptible to more attacks than ordinary networks. Most of the services in WSNs are designed to be distributed, thus, security in WSNs should focus on dealing with various attacks, protecting confidentiality, integrity, and availability of the communications and computations. Threat analysis is needed based on multiple forms of active and passive attacks which could happen in both routing and packet forwarding. Routing attacks refer to advertising routing updates that do not follow the specifications of the routing protocol, whereas packet forwarding attacks cause the data packets to be delivered in a way that is intentionally inconsistent with the routing states. For passive attacks, illegitimate stealing and disclosure of information could easily take place since an attacker can eavesdrop on the wireless communications.

Main security threats in WSN are related to radio links and sensor nodes. WSN security is closer to computer security than the Internet security. WSN nodes are typically easily accessed because they are out there in the "field". Exchanges of location information might cause attackers to identify the node locations. An attacker could then disable the sensor node by draining the battery or physically destructing the device. Furthermore, a node can be compromised when the attacker subverts the sensor node to disrupt the network. Denial-of-service (DoS) attacks, which could diminish sensor network functionality, are analyzed in details by Wood & Stankovic (2002). Meanwhile, Karlof et al (2003) discussed various attacks and countermeasures on WSN routing which include bogus routing information, selective forwarding, sinkholes, Sybil, wormholes and hello floods. All these attacks are non-trivial to fix, especially when the routing protocols are designed without any regard to security. Thus, a multi-fence security solution should be in place which could be embedded into every component of the network. Table 2 summarizes these threats, the respective requirements and possible solutions.

In brief, wireless sensor networks have promising potential for many applications. In the absence of adequate security, however, deployment of sensor networks is vulnerable to a variety of attacks. A sensor node's limitations and nature of wireless communication pose unique security challenges. Numerous on-going research works cover many different aspects of WSN security such as group key management, key revocation, link layer security, network layer security, secure localization, secure time synchronization, secure data aggregation, secure communication channels (Husain et al, 2008). However, research toward a complete secure sensor network is still in its infancy stage. For instance, a number of key management schemes have been proposed in both distributed and hierarchical sensor networks (Lorincz et al., 2004; Liu, Ning, & Du, 2005, Du et al., 2005), but the performance of those schemes under various mobile scenarios has not been assessed. A fast, scalable, flexible and resilient key management scheme for mobile sensor networks is urgently needed.

Table 2. Typical security threats and the possible countermeasures

Security Threats	Security Requirements	Possible Countermeasures
Unauthorized access	Key protection; Trust setup	Random key distribution; Public key cryptography.
Message disclosure/jamming	Privacy; Confidentiality	Link/network layer encryption; Access control.
Message falsification	Integrity; Authenticity	Keyed secure hash function; Digital signature.
Denial-of-Service (DoS) attack; Node capture; Radio jamming	Availability; Adaptively	Intrusion detection; Adaptive antennas; Redundancy; Spread spectrum.
Subversion; Compromised nodes; Malicious nodes	Resilience to node compromise	Inconsistency detection; Malicious node detection & isolation; Tamper-proofing
Routing attacks (wormholes, sinkholes, routing loops)	Secure routing	Secure routing protocols; Key management.
Intrusion; High-level attacks	Intrusion protection; Secure data aggregation.	Secure group communication; Intrusion detection

Other Issues

In addition to the major issues related to WSN applications, there are other concerns that should be looked into before the design and deployment. Some of those concerns are summarized as follows.

- *Environment*: Sensor networks often are expected to operate in an unattended fashion in dispersed and/or remote geographic locations. Nodes may be deployed in harsh, hostile, or widely scattered environments. Such environments call for challenging management mechanisms.

- *Transmission*: Sensor networks often operate in a bandwidth- and performance-constrained multihop wireless communications medium. These communications links operate in the radio, infrared, or optical range. As indicated by Table 1, different communication standards may use different frequencies. Typically, in-door WSNs now tend to look to use ZigBee/IEEE802.15.4; out-door WSNs may find other technologies useful, in particular,

the IEEE-based wireless LAN standards. To facilitate global operation of these networks, the transmission channel selected should be available on a worldwide basis.

- *Connectivity and Topology*: Deploying and managing a high number of nodes in a relatively bounded environment requires special techniques. Hundreds to thousands of sensors in close proximity may be deployed in a sensor field. Although many protocols and algorithms have been proposed for traditional wireless ad hoc networks, they are not well suited to the unique features and application requirements of sensor networks (Akyildiz, Su, Sankarasubramaniam, & Cayirci, 2002, Su et al., 2004). Nodes could be deployed en mass or be injected in the sensor field individually. Any time after deployment, topology changes may take place due to changes in sensor node position, power availability, malfunctioning, reachability impairments, etc.

CASE STUDIES

Two application cases are discussed in this section, for cold chain logistics and healthcare systems, respectively. The application of wireless sensors coupled with RFID technology demonstrates great potentials for tracking the flow of products in the cold chain logistics. Also, WSN systems illustrate their abilities in real-time collecting, transmitting, sharing, and securely storing the patient data, thus significantly improving the quality, accuracy and efficiency of the healthcare services. Considering the aforementioned advantages and application challenges, it should be noted that only the general adoption framework and procedures are presented here although they are to be or being implemented in practice.

Cold Chain Logistics for Food and Pharmaceutical Products

Both food and pharmaceutical industries are gigantic. The worldwide sales of processed food reached $3.2 trillion in 2004, and the total sales in the United States alone was $1.16 trillion in 2007. Also, it is reported that the global sales volume of the pharmaceutical industry reached $602 billion in 2005. The quality of food and pharmaceutical products is of vital importance to human health, and it has a great deal to do with the conditions of distribution chain. The distribution chain is often called "cold chain" when temperature control is needed. Improper temperature control can lead to the growth of microorganisms in foods and many pharmaceutical products. Due to the pressing need, regulations are established to protect the safety of cold chain. For instance, the U.S. Food and Drug Administration (FDA) demands the establishment and maintenance of records, which must identify the previous source and subsequent recipient of foods in the U.S. supply chain. This is also called the "one up and one down" rule.

Sensor and RFID technologies are regarded as the most promising IT technologies in cold chain logistics to combat the threats of unsafe foods and pharmaceutical products by monitoring the distribution conditions and increasing the visibility of cold chain. Studman (2001) surveyed the applications of sensor technology for post-harvest applications. To date, a variety of sensors are used in monitoring the conditions of products, inventory controls, sorting and weighing, transportation, and further handling at the distributor and/or the stores. Furthermore, wireless sensor technology has shown the potential in cold chain logistics because of its distinct advantages over conventional wired sensors in terms of deployment flexibility. For instance, Wang, Zhang, & Wang (2006) investigated the effects of wireless sensor technology in agriculture and food industry. It is estimated that once the sector reaches critical mass, wireless sensor networks expects to grow by 200% per year till the market is saturated. Meanwhile, the decreasing cost of RFID products has driven the application of this technology in cold chain for labeling and tracking purposes. In terms of item-level or even pallet-level tagging, passive RFID tags are preferred because of their lower cost compared with active tags. Currently, sub-10 cents tags are widely available on the market thanks for the miniaturization of circuit and the improved manufacturing and packaging processes. The price is projected to drop below 5 cents soon. For cold chain distribution, cost is always the dominant factor. Wireless sensor nodes can carry all the functions of RFID devices and many more, but they are still prohibitively expensive for item-level tracking and monitoring. As a result, currently the integration of wireless sensors coupled with RFID technology has the most potential for this application. The products can be tracked and traced, and, at the same time, important parameters during the processing and distribution of the products can be closely monitored, stored and evaluated.

The complete visibility of product flow and quality information from "farm-to-fork" can be realized by accomplishing (1) real-time tracking the products; (2) real-time monitoring environment parameters; and (3) effective management of the pedigree information. Being real-time is important in that prompt response can be taken to prevent the quality deterioration of products as well as the spread of potential threats. For a general distribution chain, the stationary link points (stakeholders), which include manufacturers, distribution centers, and retailers, are connected by transportation to achieve the flow of products. As shown in Figure 4, product monitoring is relatively straightforward at these stationary stages. The inventory can be counted with the help of identification technologies, and the measurement of environment parameters is feasible. Actions could also be taken immediately if environment conditions become out of control or any quality problems are detected.

Nevertheless, the complete visibility of the cold chain also relies on the monitoring of foods in transportation, in which the product information and environmental parameters also need to be collected. This is critical because the potential threats can grow with poor environment control on carrier vehicles, and they could be spread geographically. As a result, on carrier vehicles, wireless sensors and GPS receivers need to be installed. The GPS receiver collects the location information and can be interfaced with an onboard

controller wirelessly. Environmental parameters are constantly collected by the wireless sensors and sent to the controller. As shown in Figure 5, the controller also sends and receives information via the cellular modem and cellular network infrastructure, and thus establishes the connection with a remote data server.

To automatically identify each product that is loaded into or unloaded from the truck container, we employ the inexpensive passive UHF RFID technology. The product IDs will not be read during transportation for system operation efficiency. Meanwhile, each wireless sensor node has the capability of "sense and send", as well as a unique ID, which acts as the liaison to connect with the product IDs during transportation. Depending on the number of sensor nodes and their reading ranges, the sensor nodes can be configured as a centralized structure so that all the data are directly transmitted to the on-board controller; or as a decentralized structure so that the information can go through a route of multiple sensor nodes before it reaches the controller.

In brief, the devices used within the proposed solution to this application provide the following key capabilities:

- Wireless Communication – real-time reporting via global GSM cellular network.
- Identification and tracking – RFID systems are incorporated for both item- and pallet-level tracking.
- Temperature/Humidity Reporting – integration of wireless sensor nodes in the carrier container to report environment parameters.
- Door Security Monitoring – wireless or wired door sensors that can detect proximity, light to determine if a door has been opened.
- Location Reporting – integrated GPS receiver provides longitude/latitude coordinates of the device.

Figure 4. Schematic of cold chain management

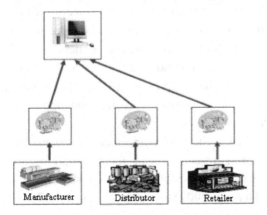

Figure 5. Quality monitoring during transportation

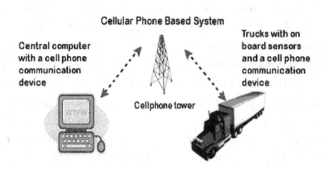

In the e-pedigree building process, either central or distributed repository concepts can be used. For a large scale cold chain, the latter concept is more suitable in that the information explosion can be more effectively handled. However, the former is simpler to construct. Building the e-pedigree begins from the manufacturer's raw material supplier (e.g. farm). To simplify the situation, we will start the process from the manufacturer.

1. After packing the products and attaching RFID tags, RFID readers capture all the tag information and send it to the manufacturer's server and pass to the central server.
2. Carrier vehicles leave the manufacturer for the distribution center, during which product ID information is collected and environment conditions from wireless sensor nodes are transmitted to the central server via cellular network at constant time interval. Alarm will be issued if the control parameters are above a threshold value.
3. Once the carrier vehicles arrive at the distribution center, the validity of the goods needs to be checked first. After verifying the pedigree, the distribution center adds the data (shipping, ownership, dispatching and etc) to its own server, then pass it to the central sever.
4. Carrier vehicles leave the distribution center for the retailer, during which similar operations as Step 2 are performed.

5. Once the carrier vehicles arrive at the retailer, the pedigree information for the products needs to be verified. If valid, this pedigree is certified and indicates the authenticity. More importantly, the data retrieved will include the entire temperature history, as well as the estimated shelf life. Retailer can therefore make decision such as pricing.

Tracking, Positioning, and Condition Monitoring in Healthcare Industry

Real-time collection and transmission and sharing as well as secure storage of patient data can significantly improve the quality, accuracy, and efficiency of the entire healthcare industry. Wireless sensor network technology is a viable solution for sensing and transmitting the data collected from the physical entity and the environment, and thus a proper integration of wireless sensor networks with existing consumer electronic infrastructures can assist in the tracking, positioning, and condition monitoring of patients and the relative areas of health care industry. As a result, healthcare has become one of the most important and rapidly growing research and application areas for WSNs.

During the past years, many advances from research projects have been reported in this area. To name a few, MobiHealth (Konstantas, Jones, & Herzog, 2002) is a system based on 2.5~3G technologies, integrating the sensors and actuators into a wireless body area network. The sensors and actuators can continuously sense and transmit vital data to health service providers. Ubiquitous monitoring environment for wearable and implantable sensors (UbiMon) (Ng et al., 2004) is a system architecture composed of five major components, namely, the body sensor network nodes, the local processing unit, the central server, the patient database, and the workstation. The data measured by independent nodes on a patient measure are transmitted to the local processing unit (such as a PDA) and then forwarded to the central server via Bluetooth/Wi-Fi or cellular networks. Scalable medical alert response technology (SMART) (Waterman et al., 2005) is a system for patient tracking and monitoring during the entire process of transporting the patient from their previous location to the healthcare facilities. The system is based on a scalable location-aware monitoring architecture, with remote transmission from medical sensors and display of information on PDAs. Patients, medical equipment, healthcare providers are located by SMART on demand. CodeBlue (Lorincz et al., 2004) is a wireless infrastructure integrating low-power, wireless vital sign sensors, personal digital assistants (PDAs), and PC-class systems, which aims to enhance the first responders' ability of assessing patients where they are found, ensure a seamless transfer of data among healthcare personnel, and facilitate efficient allocation of hospital resources. Similarly, PPMIM (Jea & Srivastava, 2006) represents remote medical monitoring three-tier architecture with a GSM/GPRS peer-to-peer channel. In the MobiCare project (Chakravorty, 2006), short-range Bluetooth technology is adopted for the wireless communication between a body sensor network (BSN) and BSN managers, and GPRS/UMTS cellular networks between BSN Managers and health-care providers. Besides, Baker et al. (2007) introduced several prototypes for home health monitoring systems and analyzed the enabling technologies for automated home health monitoring. Dağtaş, Pekhteryev, Şahinoğlu, Çam, & Challa (2008) present a ZigBee-based wireless communication system for real-time health monitoring with secure transmission capability. A comprehensive system architecture for sensor networks in various healthcare settings is proposed in (Ng, Sim, & Tan, 2006), and it is shown in Figure 6.

In addition, Hao & Foster (2008) provided a good review on the wireless body sensor networks for health-monitoring applications. The

Figure 6. System architecture of wireless sensor networks in healthcare industry (Ng et al., 2006)

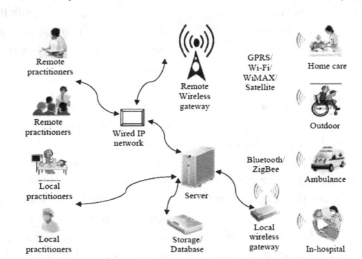

system employs various wireless sensor nodes to measure the patient's physiological data and wirelessly communicate with the network base unit, e.g., a wireless network coordinator connected to a monitoring and control terminal where the physiological data can be stored, analyzed, and displayed at demand. The base unit can also function as a gateway to other networks such as GPRS, WLAN, or the Internet, thus enabling remote real-time processing or storage of the physiological data.

The potential benefits which will stimulate the research advancement and accelerate the deployment of WSNs in healthcare applications are summarized as follows (Ng et al., 2006, Hao et al., 2008).

- Faster, lower cost of care delivery,
- Convenient access to the latest patient data with high accuracy,
- Enabled individual health monitoring systems to shift the healthcare expenditure,
- Reduced risk of infection and/or failure,
- Enhanced mobility and usability.

However, since the information regarding the health of an individual is private and highly sensitive, it is of paramount importance to defend the network against any illegal access and malicious attacks to the entire system. It can he foreseen that, in the near future, such systems will be further improved and see a widely deployment in the healthcare industry.

SUMMARY AND PROSPECTIVE

Supply chain management (SCM) has become a strategic tool vital to corporate competitiveness and profitability. Along with globalization and increasing competition, the performance and efficiency of information collection, storage, processing and sharing have become critical for SCM as well as other key activities of an orga-

nization. Service innovation in SCM is urgently needed by adopting the rapid development of information and communication technologies (ICTs) since ICT adoptions have significant impacts on the entire service processes of the supply chain. Supply chain management innovation is recognized as an important area for ICT adoption and investment. Integrating the supply chain via adoption of advanced information technology can achieve information sharing and reduction of total cost, thus improving operation efficiency and enhancing competitive advantage. The use of information technology in managing the supply chain process has thus drawn increasing attention in the corporate world.

With many innovative IT technologies putting into SCM application practices recently, increasing research attentions have been directed toward wireless sensor networks. Identified as one of key technologies for the 21st century, wireless sensor network has many advantages, such as mobility, extendibility, reliability and ease of installation. Wireless sensor networks provide adaptive monitoring systems with the flexibility and adaptability needed in an organization's monitoring and control strategy. Wireless motes are placed where needed without the need of specialized RF skills or site surveys, while the network handles the rest such as wireless connectivity, routing redundancy, and frequency agility. Additionally, these networks are adaptable to changes in both the configuration of equipment on the plant floor and in the layout of the network itself. If monitoring devices are added or removed, the network simply reconfigures itself automatically.

As wireless networking technology advances, it is also becoming more cost effective. The size of sensors and the production costs are both decreasing. Current wireless sensor networks are designed to ease development and integration with other systems. No customization, integration, or development is required, and there are no wiring or installation costs. Battery-powered motes make wireless networks suitable for locations where power distribution is not designed for additional monitoring equipment. It can be foreseen that the WSN technology will be applied in more service industries. However, the WSN technology is just emerging from academic research into commercial application, many areas or aspects need further investigation, such as MAC protocols in the Industrial, Scientific, and Medical (ISM) bands, safer routing algorithms, security and privacy issues as well as the hardware.

REFERENCES

Abramson, N. (1970). The ALOHA System - Another alternative for computer communications. In *Proceedings of AFIPS Fall Joint Computation Conference*, 37, 281-285. Retrieved from http://doi.acm.org/10.1145/1478462.1478502

Adams, G. (2007). Pharmaceutical manufacturing: RFID-reducing errors and effort. *Filtration & Separation, 44*(6), 17–19. doi:10.1016/S0015-1882(07)70179-9

Agarwal, R., & Sambamurthy, V. (2002). Principles and models for organizing the information technology function. *MIS Quarterly Executive, 1*(1), 1–16.

Akkaya, K., & Younis, M. (2005). A survey on routing protocols for wireless sensor networks. *Ad Hoc Networks, 3*(3), 325–349. doi:10.1016/j.adhoc.2003.09.010

Akyildiz, I. F., Su, W., Sankarasubramaniam, Y., & Cayirci, E. (2002). A survey on sensor networks. *Communications Magazine, IEEE, 40*(8), 102–114. doi:10.1109/MCOM.2002.1024422

Alberts, D. S., Garska, J. J., & Stein, F. P. (1999). Network Centric Warfare: Developing and Leveraging Information Superiority. Retrieved April 2, 2009, from http://www.nps.edu/Academics/Centers/CEP/docs/Alberts_NCW.pdf

Àlvarez, C., et al. (2004). Efficient and reliable high level communication in randomly deployed wireless sensor networks. In *Proceedings of the second international workshop on Mobility management & wireless access protocols* (pp. 10information and communication technologies (ICTs)Information technologyOperating system (OS)6-110).

Anastasi, G., Conti, M., Francesco, M., & Passarella, A. (2009). Energy conservation in wireless sensor networks: A survey. *Ad Hoc Networks, 7*(3), 537–568. doi:10.1016/j.adhoc.2008.06.003

Angeles, R. (2005). RFID technologies: supply-chain applications and implementation issues. *Information Systems Management, 22*(1), 51–65. doi:10.1201/1078/44912.22.1.20051201/85739.7

Anonymous, . (2003). 10 emerging technologies that will change the world. *MIT's Technology Review, 106*(1), 33–49.

Baker, C. R., et al. (2007). Wireless sensor networks for home health care. In *Proceedings of the 21st International Conference on Advanced Information Networking and Applications Workshops*, 2, 832-837.

Berkowitz, B. (2001, April 20). Technology catches up to runners. *Washington Post, sec. E*, pg.1.

Berry, L. L., Shankar, V., Parish, J. T., Cadwallader, S., & Dotzel, T. (2006). Creating new markets through service innovation. *Sloan Management Review, 47*(2), 56–63.

Bhatt, G., & Grover, V. (2005). Types of information technology capabilities and their role in competitive advantage: an empirical study. *Journal of Management Information Systems, 22*(2), 253–277.

Bose, I., & Pal, R. (2005). Auto-id: managing anything, anywhere, anytime in the supply chain. *Communications of the ACM, 48*(8), 100–106. doi:10.1145/1076211.1076212

Boukerche, A. (2008). Algorithms and protocols for wireless sensor networks. New York: John Wiley & Sons.

Bowersox, D. J., & Daugherty, P. J. (1995). Logistics paradigms: the impact of information technology. *Journal of Business Logistics*, *16*(1), 65–80.

Burgess, R. (1998). Avoiding supply chain management failure: lessons from business process re-engineering. *International Journal of Logistics Management*, *9*(1), 15–23. doi:10.1108/09574099810805717

Business Week. (1999, August 30). 21 ideas for the 21st century. Retrieved April 1, from http://www.businessweek.com/1999/99_35/2121_content.htm

Callaway, E., Hsu, S., & Shankar, R. (2002). JAN: A communications model for wireless sensor networks, Technical Report, TR-CSE-02-12, Boca Raton, FL: Department of Computer Science and Engineering, Florida Atlantic University.

Callaway, E. H. (2004). Wireless sensor networks: architectures and protocols. New York: CRC Press.

Cao, X., Chen, J., Zhang, Y., & Sun, Y. (2008). Development of an integrated wireless sensor network micro-environmental monitoring system. *ISA Transactions*, *47*(3), 247–255. doi:10.1016/j.isatra.2008.02.001

Ceken, C. (2008). An energy efficient and delay sensitive centralized Mac protocol for wireless sensor networks. *Computer Standards & Interfaces*, *30*(1-2), 20–31. doi:10.1016/j.csi.2007.06.001

Chakravorty, R. (2006). A programmable service architecture for mobile medical care. In *Proceedings of the 4th Annual IEEE International Conference on Pervasive Computing and Communications Workshops (PerCom '06)*, pages 532-536.

Chen, J. S., & Tsou, H. T. (2007). Information technology adoption for service innovation practices and competitive advantage: the case of financial firms. *Information research: an international electronic journal*, *12(*3), 314. Retrieved April 3, 2009, from http://InformationR.net/ir/12-3/paper314.html

Chen, R., Sun, C., Helms, M., & Kennyjih, W. (2008). Aligning information technology and business strategy with a dynamic capabilities perspective: A longitudinal study of a Taiwanese semiconductor company. *International Journal of Information Management*, *28*(5), 366–378. doi:10.1016/j.ijinfomgt.2008.01.015

Chiasserini, C. F., & Rao, R. R. (2000). Routing protocols to maximize battery efficiency. In *Proceedings of MILCOM: 21st Century Military Communications Conference*, 1, 496-500.

Chong, C. Y., & Kumar, S. P. (2003). Sensor Networks: Evolution, Opportunities, and Challenges. *Proceedings of the IEEE*, *91*(8), 1247–1256. doi:10.1109/JPROC.2003.814918

Chris, K., Naveen, S., & David, W. (2004). TinySec: a link layer security architecture for wireless sensor networks. In *Proceedings of the 2nd International Conference on Embedded Networked Sensor Systems*, New York: ACM Press.

Cornell Database Group. (2009). *Cougar: The Network Is the Database*. Retrieved April 2, 2009, from http://www.cs.cornell.edu/bigreddata/cougar/index.php

Currie, W. (1996). Organizational structure and the use of information technology: Preliminary findings of a survey in the private and public sector. *International Journal of Information Management*, *16*(1), 51–64. doi:10.1016/0268-4012(95)00061-5

Dağtaş, S., Pekhteryev, G., Şahinoğlu, Z., Çam, H., & Challa, N. (2008). Real-Time and Secure Wireless Health Monitoring. International Journal of Telemedicine and Applications, 2008, Article ID 135808, 10 pages

Davenport, T., Hammer, M., & Metsisto, T. (1989). How executives can shape their companies' information systems. *Harvard Business Review*, *67*(5), 130–134.

Demirhan, D., Jacob, V., & Raghunathan, S. (2006). Information technology investment strategies under declining technology cost. *Journal of Management Information Systems*, *22*(3), 321–350. doi:10.2753/MIS0742-1222220311

Du, W. (2005). A pairwise key predistribution scheme for wireless sensor networks. *ACM Transactions on Information and System Security*, *8*(2), 228–258. doi:10.1145/1065545.1065548

Dutertre, B., Cheung, S., & Levy, J. (2004). Lightweight key management in wireless sensor networks by leveraging initial trust. *Technical Report SRI-SDL-04-02*. Retrieved April 3, 2009, from http://www.csl.sri.com/users/bruno/publis/sri-sdl-04-02.pdf

Elson, J., Girod, L., & Estrin, D. (2002). Fine-grained network time synchronization using reference broadcasts. ACM SIGOPS Operating Systems Review, 36(SI), 147-163.

Fichman, R. G. (2001). The role of aggregation in the measurement of information technology-related organizational innovation. *MIS Quarterly*, *25*(4), 427–455. doi:10.2307/3250990

Fink, L., & Neumann, S. (2009). Exploring the perceived business value of the flexibility enabled by information technology infrastructure. *Information & Management*, *46*(2), 90–99. doi:10.1016/j.im.2008.11.007

Gaynor, M., Moulton, S., Welsh, M., Rowan, A., LaCombe, E., & Wynne, J. (2004). Integrating Wireless Sensor Networks with the Grid. *IEEE Internet Computing*, *8*(4), 32–39. doi:10.1109/MIC.2004.18

Ghosh, A., & Das, S. (2008). Coverage and connectivity issues in wireless sensor networks: A survey. *Pervasive and Mobile Computing*, *4*(3), 303–334. doi:10.1016/j.pmcj.2008.02.001

Govindan, R. (2004). Datacentric routing and storage in sensor networks. In Znati, T., Sivalingam, K., & Raghavendra, C.S. (eds.), Wireless sensor networks (pp.185-205). Boston: Kluwer Academic Publishers.

Grover, V., Fiedler, K. D., & Teng, J. T. C. (1999). The role of organizational and information technology antecedents in reengineering initiation behavior. *Decision Sciences*, *30*(3), 749–781. doi:10.1111/j.1540-5915.1999.tb00905.x

Haartsen, J. C. (2000). The Bluetooth radio system. *IEEE Personal Communications*, *7*(1), 28–36. doi:10.1109/98.824570

Habermann, A. W. (1978). Dynamically Modifiable Distributed Systems. In *Proceedings of a Workshop on Distributed Sensor Nets* (pp. 111-114). Pittsburgh, PA: Carnegie Mellon University.

Haenselmann, T. (2006). Sensornetworks. *GFDL Wireless Sensor Network textbook*. Retrieved April 2, 2009, from http://www.informatik.uni-mannheim.de/~haensel/sn_book

Hao, Y., & Foster, R. (2008). Wireless body sensor networks for health-monitoring applications. *Physiological Measurement*, *29*, 27–56. doi:10.1088/0967-3334/29/11/R01

Harrop, P., & Das, R. (2009). *Wireless Sensor Networks 2009-2019: The new market for ubiquitous sensor networks (USN)*. Retrieved April 3, 2009, from ID http://www.idtechex.com/research/reports/wireless_sensor_networks_2009_2019_000212.asp

Heinzelman, W., Chandrakasan, A., & Balakrishnan, H. (2000). Energy-efficient communication protocol for wireless sensor networks. In *Proceeding of the 33rd Hawaii International Conference on System Science, 8*, 8020.

Hill, J. (2000). System architecture directions for networked sensors. *SIGOPS Operating Systems Review, 34*(5), 93–104. doi:10.1145/384264.379006

Horton, M. A. (2002). Deployment ready multimode micropower wireless sensor networks for intrusion detection, classification, and tracking. *Proceedings of the Society for Photo-Instrumentation Engineers, 4708*, 290–295.

Huang, T. C., Lai, H. R., & Ku, C. H. (2006). A deployment procedure for wireless sensor networks. Retrieved April 5, 2009, from: http://acnlab.csie.ncu.edu.tw/wasn06/CR2/p19.pdf

Hubaux, J. P. (2001). Toward self-organized mobile ad hoc networks: the Terminodes project . *IEEE Communications, 39*(1), 118–124. doi:10.1109/35.894385

ITAA. (n.d.). *Information technology definition aggregation*. Retrieved April 3, 2009, from itaa Web site: http://www.itaa.org/es/docs/Information%20Technology%20Definitions.pdf

Iyengar, S. S., & Brooks, R. R. (2004). Distributed sensor networks. Boca Raton, FL: Chapman & HalVCRC.

Jea, D., & Srivastava, M. B. (2006). A remote medical monitoring and interaction system. In *Proceedings of the 4th International Conference on Mobile Systems, Applications, and Services (MobiSys '06)*, Uppsala, Sweden.

Karl, H., & Willig, A. (2003). A short survey of wireless sensor networks, TKN technical report TKN-03-018. Retrieved April 3, 2009, from http://www.tkn.tu-berlin.de/publications/papers/TechReport_03_018.pdf

Karlof, C., & Wagner, D. (2003). Secure routing in wireless sensor networks: attacks and countermeasures. In *Sensor Network Protocols and Applications, 2003. Proceedings of the First IEEE. 2003 IEEE International Workshop on*, (pp. 113-127).

Karn, P. (1990). MACA - A new channel access method for packet radio. *ARRL/CRRL Amateur Radio 9th Computer Networking Conference appears in* (pp. 134-140). London: ARRL.

Kim, J., & Park, K. H. (2009). An energy-efficient, transport-controlled Mac protocol for wireless sensor networks. *Computer Networks, 53*(11), 1879–1902. doi:10.1016/j.comnet.2009.03.002

Konstantas, D., Jones, V., & Herzog, R. (2002). Mobihealth - innovative 2.5 / 3g mobile services and applications for healthcare. Retrieved April 5, 2009, from http://aps.ewi.utwente.nl/public/bibliografie/Thessaloniki.pdf

Lacoss, R., & Walton, R. (1978). Strawman design for a DSN to detect and track low flying aircraft. In *Proceedings of 1978 Distributed Sensor Nets Conference on*, (pp. 41-52).

LaFollette, R. M. (1995). Design and performance of high specific power, pulsed discharge, bipolar lead acid batteries. In *Proceedings of the 10th Annual Battery Conference on Applications and Advances*, 43-47.

Lai, K.-H., Wong, C. W., & Cheng, E. T. C. (2006). Institutional isomorphism and the adoption of information technology for supply chain management. *Computers in Industry, 57*(1), 93–98. doi:10.1016/j.compind.2005.05.002

Lansford, J., & Bahl, P. (2000). The design and implementation of HomeRF: a radio frequency wireless networking standard for the connected home . *Proceedings of the IEEE, 88*(10), 1662–1676. doi:10.1109/5.889006

Lee, Y.-D., & Chung, W.-Y. (2009). Wireless sensor network based wearable smart shirt for ubiquitous health and activity monitoring. *Sensors and Actuators. B, Chemical, 140*(2), 390–395. doi:10.1016/j.snb.2009.04.040

Liao, S., Chem, Y., Liu, F., & Liao, W. (2004). Information technology and relationship management: a case study of Taiwan's small manufacturing firm. *Technovation, 24*(2), 97–108. doi:10.1016/S0166-4972(02)00037-8

Liao, W., & Wang, H. (2008). An asynchronous Mac protocol for wireless sensor networks. *Journal of Network and Computer Applications, 31*(4), 807–820. doi:10.1016/j.jnca.2007.07.001

Lin, L. C. (2009). An integrated framework for the development of radio frequency identification technology in the logistics and supply chain management. *Computers & Industrial Engineering, 57*(3), 832–842. doi:10.1016/j.cie.2009.02.010

Liu, D., Ning, P., & Du, W. (2005). Group-based key pre-distribution in wireless sensor networks. *ACM Transactions on Sensor Networks, 4*(2), 11.

Liu, J., Zhao, F., Cheung, P., & Guibas, L. (2004). Apply geometric duality to energy-efficient non-local phenomenon awareness using sensor networks. *Wireless Communications, IEEE, 11*(6), 62–68. doi:10.1109/MWC.2004.1368898

Lorincz, K. (2004). Sensor networks for emergency response: challenges and opportunities. *Pervasive Computing, IEEE, 3*(4), 16–23. doi:10.1109/MPRV.2004.18

Lubecke, O. B., & Lubecke, V. M. (2002). Wireless house calls: using communications technology for health care monitoring . *IEEE Micro, 3*(3), 43–48. doi:10.1109/MMW.2002.1028361

Mabert, V. A., & Venkataramanan, M. A. (1998). Special research focus on supply chain linkages: Challenges for design and management in the 21st century. *Decision Sciences, 29*(3), 537–552. doi:10.1111/j.1540-5915.1998.tb01353.x

McLaughlin, S., Paton, R. A., & Macbeth, D. K. (2006). Managing change within IBM's complex supply chain . *Management Decision, 44*(8), 1002–1019. doi:10.1108/00251740610690586

Milenkovic, A., Otto, C., & Jovanov, E. (2006). Wireless sensor networks for personal health monitoring: Issues and an implementation. *Computer Communications, 29*(13-14), 2521–2533. doi:10.1016/j.comcom.2006.02.011

Minoli, D. (2002). Hotspot networks: Wi-Fi for public access locations. New York: McGraw-Hill.

Mishra, R. K. (2006). Role of information technology in supply chain management. Retrieved April 1, 2009, from www.indianmba.com/Faculty_Column/FC461/fc461.html.

Ng, H. S., Sim, M. L., & Tan, C. M. (2006). Security issues of wireless sensor networks in healthcare applications. *BT Technology Journal, 24*(2), 138–144. doi:10.1007/s10550-006-0051-8

Ng, J. W. P., et al. (2004). Ubiquitous monitoring environment for wearable and implantable sensors (UbiMon). In *Proceedings of the 6th International Conference on Ubiquitous Computing (UBICOMP '04)*, Nottingham, UK.

Ngai, E. W. T., Cheng, T. C. E., Au, S., & Lai, K. (2007). Mobile commerce integrated with RFID technology in a container depot. *Decision Support Systems, 43*(1), 62–76. doi:10.1016/j.dss.2005.05.006

O'Hara, B., & Petrick, A. (1999). The IEEE 802.11 Handbook: A Designer's Companion. New York: IEEE Press.

Palmer, J. W., & Markus, L. M. (2000). The performance impacts of quick response and strategic alignment in specialty retailing. *Information Systems Research, 11*(3), 241–259. doi:10.1287/ isre.11.3.241.12203

Pantazis, N. A., & Vergados, D. D. (2007). A survey on power control issues in wireless sensor networks. *Communications Surveys & Tutorials, IEEE, 9*(4), 86–107. doi:10.1109/COMST.2007.4444752

Pantazis, N. A., Vergados, D. J., Vergados, D. D., & Douligeris, C. (2009). Energy efficiency in wireless sensor networks using sleep mode TDMA scheduling. *Ad Hoc Networks, 7*(2), 322–343. doi:10.1016/j.adhoc.2008.03.006

Pärkkä, J., et al. (2002). A wireless wellness monitor for personal weight management. In *Proceedings of IEEE EMBS International Conference on Information Technology Applications on,* (pp. 83-88).

Paton, R. A., & Mclaughlin, S. (2008). Services innovation: Knowledge transfer and the supply chain. *European Management Journal, 26,* 77–83. doi:10.1016/j.emj.2008.01.004

Perkins, C. E. (2001). Ad hoc networking, Reading, MA: Addison-Wesley.

Perrig, A., Szewczyk, R., Tygar, J. D., Wen, V., & Culler, D. E. (2002). Spins: security protocols for sensor networks. *Wireless Networks, 8*(5), 521–534. doi:10.1023/A:1016598314198

Radjou, N. (2003). U.S. manufacturers' *supply chain* mandate. *World Trade, 16*(12), 42–46.

Raines, R. R. (1996). Getting the Message Through: A Branch History of the U.S. Army Signal Corps, CMH Pub 30-17. (pp. 224). Washington, DC: Center of Military History, United States Army.

Rao, A., Papadimitriou, C., Shenker, S., & Stoica, I. (2003). Geographic routing without location information. In *Proceedings of the 9th Annual International Conference on Mobile Computing and Networking on,* (pp.96-108).

Römer, K., & Mattern, F. (2004). The design space of wireless sensor networks. *IEEE Wireless Communications, 11*(6), 54–61. doi:10.1109/ MWC.2004.1368897

Rubery, J., Earnshaw, J., Marchington, M., Cooke, F. L., & Vincent, S. (2002). Changing organizational forms and the employment relationship. *Journal of Management Studies, 39*(5), 645–672. doi:10.1111/1467-6486.00306

Ruizmercader, J., Meronocerdan, A., & Sabatersanchez, R. (2006). Information technology and learning: Their relationship and impact on organizational performance in small businesses. *International Journal of Information Management, 26*(1), 16–29. doi:10.1016/j.ijinfomgt.2005.10.003

Sabogal, J., & Tholke, J. (2004). Compliant manufacturing with SAP in the pharmaceutical industry. *Die Pharmazeutische Industrie, 66*(11), 1405–1412.

Sambamurthy, V., Bharadwaj, A., & Grover, V. (2003). Shaping agility through digital options: reconceptualizing the role of information technology in contemporary firms. *MIS Quarterly, 27*(2), 237–263.

Schoeneman, J. L., & Sorokowski, D. (1998). Authenticated tracking and monitoring system (ATMS) tracking shipments from an Australian uranium mine. In *Proceedings of the 31st Annual 1997 International Carnahan Conference on Security Technology on,* (pp. 231-240).

Shih, E., et al. (2001). Physical layer driven protocol and algorithm design for energy-efficient wireless sensor networks. In *MobiCom '01: Proceedings of the 7th annual international conference on Mobile computing and networking,* (pp. 272-287). New York: ACM.

Slack, N., Chambers, S., & Johnston, R. (2001). Operation Management. Essex, UK: Pearson Education Limited.

Smirnov, A., & Chandra, C. (2001). *Information Technologies for Supply Chain Management*, (pp. 437-460)

Sohraby, K., Minoli, D., & Znati, T. (2007). Wireless sensor networks: Technology, protocols, and application. New York: John Wiley & Sons, Inc.

Studman, C. J. (2001). Computers and electronics in postharvest technology – A review. *Computers and Electronics in Agriculture, 30*(1-3), 109–124. doi:10.1016/S0168-1699(00)00160-5

Su, W., et al. (2004). Communication Protocols for Sensor Networks. In Raghavendra, C.S., Sivalingam, K., & Znati, T. (Eds.). Wireless Sensor Networks, New York: Kluwer Academic.

Van Ark, B., Broersma, L., & Den Hertog, P. (2003). Services innovation, performance and policy: a review. Retrieved April 30, 2009, from http://www.ez.nl/dsresource?objectid=143412&type=PDF

van Dam, T., & Langendoen, K. (2003). An adaptive energy-efficient Mac protocol for wireless sensor networks. In *SenSys '03: Proceedings of the 1st international conference on Embedded networked sensor systems,* (pp. 171-180). New York: ACM Press.

Van Riel, A. C. R., Lemmink, J., & Ouwersloot, H. (2004). High-technology service innovation success: a decision-making perspective. *Journal of Product Innovation Management, 21*(5), 348–359. doi:10.1111/j.0737-6782.2004.00087.x

Verdone, R., Dardari, D., Mazzini, G., et al. (2008). Wireless sensor and actuator networks Technologies. London: Academic Press.

Wang, N., Zhang, N., & Wang, M. (2006). Wireless sensors in agriculture and food industry - Recent developments and future perspective. *Computers and Electronics in Agriculture, 50*(1), 1–14. doi:10.1016/j.compag.2005.09.003

Want, R., Farkas, K. I., & Narayanaswami, C. (2005). Guest editors' introduction: Energy harvesting and conservation. *Pervasive Computing, IEEE, 4*(1), 14–17. doi:10.1109/MPRV.2005.12

Waterman, J., et al. (2005). Demonstration of SMART (Scalable Medical Alert Response Technology). *Proceedings of AMIA 2005 Annual Symposium,* pages 1182-1183.

Woo, A., & Culler, D. E. (2001). A transmission control scheme for media access in sensor networks. In *MobiCom '01: Proceedings of the 7th annual international conference on Mobile computing and networking,* (pp. 221-235). New York: ACM Press.

Wood, A. D., & Stankovic, J. A. (2002). Denial of service in sensor networks. *Computer, 35*(10), 54–62. doi:10.1109/MC.2002.1039518

Xu, H., Sharma, S. K., & Hackney, R. (2005). Web services innovation research: towards a dual-core model. *International Journal of Information Management, 25*(4), 321–334. doi:10.1016/j.ijinfomgt.2005.04.004

Ye, W., Heidemann, J., & Estrin, D. (2001). An energy-efficient MAC protocol for wireless sensor networks. *Proceedings of Twenty-First Annual Joint Conference of the IEEE Computer and Communications Societies, 3,* 1567-1576.

Younis, M., Youssef, M., & Arisha, K. (2002). Energy-aware routing in cluster-based sensor networks. *Proceedings of the 10th IEEE/ACM International Symposium on Modeling, Analysis and Simulation of Computer and Telecommunications Systems on,* (p.129).

Yun, S., Lee, J., Chung, W., Kim, E., & Kim, S. (2008). A soft computing approach to localization in wireless sensor networks. *Expert Systems with Applications, 36*(4), 7552–7561. doi:10.1016/j. eswa.2008.09.064

Chapter 5
Application and Design of Surface Acoustic Wave Based Radio Frequency Identification Tags

Han Tao
Shanghai Jiaotong University, China

Shui Yongan
Institute of Acoustics, China

ABSTRACT

This chapter overviews a complementary technology to the integrated circuit based radio frequency identification (RFID)—Surface Acoustic Wave (SAW) based RFID. The fundamental principle and applications of SAW RFID are presented. In order to guarantee the encoding capacity and reliable reading range, the design criteria in coding scheme, tag design and a time domain interrogated reader design are discussed in detail. As an example, a low-cost SAW RFID system applied in poultry farming management is introduced.

INTRODUCTION

Radio frequency identification (RFID) tags have created growing applications for tracking, sensing and identifying various targets in wide-ranging areas. However, the RFID market is currently dominated by integrated circuit (IC) based RFID. SAW RFID first appeared in non-stop road tolling in California(USA) and Oslo(Norway). In recent years, SAW RFID provides some solutions to identify in harsh environments or where long read ranges are

required, where ordinary semiconductor based RFID technologies have been unsuccessfully deployed. And it turns out to be fairly complementary to IC RFID in different applications. As a matter of fact, SAW devices have been mainly used as the radio frequency filters in signal processing devices in military and the radio frequency filters in applications, such as mobile phones and televisions since the invention of the interdigital transducer (IDT) by R.White and F.Voltmer in 1965[1]. In this chapter, a comprehensive comparison between these two technologies is presented. The state-of-the-art of SAW tags system design is also discussed.

DOI: 10.4018/978-1-61520-603-2.ch005

FUNDAMENTAL PRINCIPLE AND STRUCTURE

The operating principle of SAW RFID is shown in Figure 1. An interdigital transducer, reflectors and piezoelectric crystalline material as substrate compose of a SAW tag. As soon as a SAW RFID tag enters the interrogation range of the reader, a RF pulse from reader antenna is received by the tag with an antenna, and then the signal is conversed into a surface acoustic wave through the IDT by the inverse piezoelectric effect. The excited SAW propagates with a relatively low velocity compared to the speed of electromagnetic wave (in a factor of 10-5). Several coding reflectors are located at the SAW propagating path on the tag surface, and each reflector gives rise to a partial reflection of the interrogating pulse. After a certain delay, which is proportional to the distance between the reflectors and the IDT, the reflected SAW is reconverted into an electrical signal by the IDT and is retransmitted by the tag's antenna as a pulse train to the reader. This signal implicates the information about the number and location of reflectors as well as the propagation and reflection properties of the SAW and can be used for extraction of identification code and/or certain sensing parameters.

Because the IDT and reflectors are built on the surface of piezoelectric crystalline materials rather than silicon, the physical mechanism of operation is based on the acoustic wave propagation and reflection rather than semiconductor. Therefore, SAW RFID is a chipless and passive device (no need for power supply).

COMPARISON BETWEEN TWO KINDS OF RFID

According to the operating principle, there are fundamental differences between SAW tags and IC based RFID. Some specific applications of SAW RFID are introduced.

Merits of SAW RFID

SAW RFID tags are truly passive. By contrast, silicon RFID tags need a very strong powering signal which is rectified to the DC power to operate the IC chip. The unique physics of SAW chips can solve major RFID issues and achieves:

1. The reading signal of SAW tags is about 100 times smaller than IC's[2], and thus, it has stronger capability of a longer reading range, better signal penetration, and tagging on containing cases of metal or liquid. In many applications, the read range of SAW tags is sufficiently large so that passive tags

Figure 1. Fundamental principle of SAW RFID

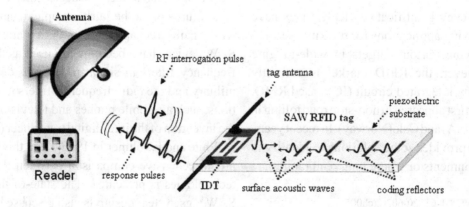

can replace high-cost battery-powered active tags. It is reported by RFSAW Inc. that 100% of all 104 palletized cases with shampoos inside can be successfully identified by using SAW RFID tags. In addition, SAW tags have also been used to the International Space Station for asset tracking because of the above advantages [3].

2. Because the substrate materials of SAW tags are piezoelectric crystal, SAW tags can work from cryogenic temperatures up to several hundred degrees and can withstand high energy x-rays, or gamma ray that will make semiconductor devices out of work. Correspondingly, SAW RFID is ideal for applications where very low/high temperature and/or sterilization of the tagged items are required, such as surgical instruments in hospital, circulation boxes for supermarkets, molten metal containers, and so forth.

The commonly used material for SAW tags is LiNbO3, which begins to decompose at 300°C. If special package techniques and crystals are utilized, which includes electrode materials of IDT (such as Au, Pt, W, Mo and et al.), adhesives, boding wires, housing material of packaging, and substrate of antenna, the operating temperature range can be extended to a higher temperature. Available but limit supplied crystal substrates such as La3Ga5SiO14 and GaPO4 are known to be high temperature resistive up to 1000°C. Some of them have been used successfully in wireless SAW sensor systems for high temperature applications [4].

SAW tags from AirGATE Technologies Inc. have been used for monitoring drill pipe and other down hole tool in the oil and gas fields because they have been developed and packaged specifically to withstand temperatures up to 300°C and pressures up to 20,000 psi with a large reading range [5].

3. SAW tags can identify the objects with high moving speed.

Because a readout procedure requires only a few microseconds, a hundred thousand interrogations can be performed per second, thus permitting reliable identification of particularly fast moving objects. In comparison, the standard regulations limit the silicon tag reader to a low rate. The SOFIS SAW RFIDs made by Siemens were used in Munich's subway system in the early 1990s. The maximum velocity of a train passing by can be 350km/h [6,7].

4. SAW tags are capable of being multifunctional devices, such as simultaneous identification, sensing and/or real-time location. Surface acoustic waves are sensitive to many different parameters that affect the phase velocity of acoustic, each of which possesses a potential sensor response. Currently, there are some commercialized wireless and passive SAW sensors, such as temperature sensors, pressure sensors, torque sensors, humidity sensors, vibration sensors and so forth[7,8]. With the legislation in logistics operations, there is a key requirement of RFID tags with integrated sensors (e.g. temperature, humidity, acceleration or shock) for recording how the transported items in applications, such as pharmaceuticals, hospital transfusions, clinical trials, foods are treated. Another promising application for SAW sensing RFID is the intelligent tyres system, which need identify the tyres for anti-counterfeiting and measure the pressure, temperature insides the tyres and the friction in driving processing[7,8]. All the functions can be implemented by SAW devices.

Moreover, evaluation of a SAW tag response incorporates precise time delay measurements leading to an accurate distance determination of tags relative to the reader. Therefore, SAW systems offer significant benefits for two-dimensional localization systems. Other systems can typically only determine the tag's location within a 10-foot radius, SAW technology enables it to be identified within 2 feet of its exact location [9,10]. These more precise location identification features are now enabling SAW tags use in wireless sensor network.

Drawbacks of SAW RFID

1. SAW RFID is read-only. The encoding of SAW RFID is dependent on the positions and number of reflectors, which is predetermined in the photolithography processing of a tag. This limits its applications.

2. Code capacity of SAW RFID is restricted by the dimension of the substrate. Some commercialized SAW RFID systems at 2.45 GHz have 32-bit of code capacity [6,7,11]. In order to be compatible with EPC-96 and EPC-128 RFID specifications, it is an important task in SAW RFID research and development to implement an encoding scheme within limited substrate area.

3. There has been no completed anti-collision solution yet. Since the responses of SAW tags are not orthogonal and individual tags can not be switched on and off, according to the reader's instruction, neither the ALOHA method in ISO15693 nor the Binary-Tree Search algorithm in ISO18000 standards is suitable for SAW-RFID directly. A method for enhancing the orthogonality of the SAW tag response signal would be helpful. However, a single multiple access technique in modern communication technology still can not resolve the anti-collision completely. For example, the time separation has restricted use in practical applications because the number of non-overlapping time segments is rather limited and such tags require SAW devices that have longer delay times. This leads to devices with extra

cost and tag losses. For the code division multiple access (CDMA) applied in SAW RFID, it suffers from the near/far effect and the coding capacity [12].

However, numerous recent efforts have demonstrated the feasibility of anticollision capability of SAW RFID, especially in the cases that not a high volume of ID is required[13-16]. It may be implemented by compound approaches. RFSAW presents its anti-collision method, which includes: a hierarchical interrogation, signal strength discrimination, time division or time separation, spatial discrimination based on selective antenna patterns to limit the physical region being interrogated, code division separation and matching correlation[15]. However, the directional antennas is suitable for 2.4 GHz or higher frequencies tags, as highly directional antennas at 900 MHz are quite large and unlikely to be practical for indoor use.

SYSTEM DESIGN OF SAW RFID

Although many considerations in reader and antenna design can be shared by SAW and other types of RFID, there are some exclusive requirements in system design of SAW RFID, including the coding scheme, tag design as well as reader design. The specification in a practical SAW RFID system include: encoding capacity, reliable reading range, anti-collision, tag size, antenna gain and polarization, useable temperature range, as well as the price. One has to implement a tradeoff among various applications, the governmental mandated emission requirements and the cost.

Reading Range

The reading range is probably the most obvious characteristics of RFID, and of most interest to the system user. However, it is also the most difficult parameter to specify. The maximum "open field" reading range of the RFID tag r with regard to the electromagnetic wavelength λ0 can be estimated by the following radar equation [7,8],

$$\frac{r}{\lambda_0} = \frac{1}{4\pi}\left(\frac{P_t \cdot G_r^2 \cdot G_t^2}{kT_0 BW \cdot N_F \cdot I_r \cdot SNR}\right)^{\frac{1}{4}} \quad \text{(Eq.1)}$$

Where Pt is the transmitter power, which is limited by the regulations for ISM bands or short range devices. Some spectrum regulations for UHF RFID readers in the 860-960 MHz band are presented in Table1. Gr and Gt are the antenna gains of the reader and the tag, respectively. Ir is the insertion losses of the SAW tag, which is in the order magnitude of 30-50 dB depending on the operating frequency, the substrate material, the configuration of IDT and the reflectivity of reflectors. kT0BW represents the background noise level from the read antenna (where k, T0 and BW are the Boltzmann's constant, temperature and system bandwidth, respectively.). NF stands for the noise figure of the reader, and SNR is the minimum signal-to-noise ratio required to safely demodulate the received signal. It is dependent on the coding scheme of tags. Obviously, the reading range is dependent on the sensitivity of reader, the insertion losses of tags and the antenna gain.

Coding Scheme

Any of the amplitude, time delay, and carrier phase of each pulse in the impulse response of tags or their combination can be used for encoding. For example, the simplest coding scheme--on/off pulse amplitude modulation is implemented by a reflector presence ("on") or absence ("off") at each predetermined time slot, as illustrated in Figure 2. Other commonly used coding schemes including pulse position modulation (PPM) and phase shift keying (PSK) are also illustrated in Figure 3 and Figure 4. The later two coding schemes achieve a higher code-density with less number of reflectors.

The time spacing between two adjacent slots can be much smaller than the pulse width. The reference pulse is used for data synchronization.

As a matter of fact, the code capacity is restricted by the dimension of the piezoelectric substrate. And a minimum allowed spacing of

Figure 2. Principle of on/off pulse modulation

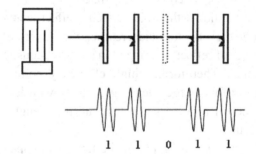

Table 1.

Countries / regions	Spectrum regulation
USA/Canada	902-928MHz erip≤4W
Europe	865.6-867.6 MHz erp ≤2W 865-868MHz erp≤100mW
China	920.50-924.5 MHz erp≤2W 920-925MHz erp≤100mW
Japan	952-954 MHz eirp≤ 4W
Australia	920-926 MHz eirp≤4W

(erip: equivalent isotropic radiated power, erp: equivalent radiated power and erp×1.64 (2.15 dB)= eirp)

Figure 3. Principle of pulse position modulation

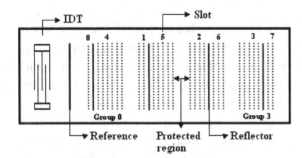

Figure 4. Principle of phase shift keying modulation

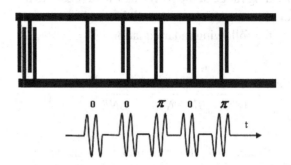

two adjacent pulses should be enforced in order to avoid the inter-pulse interference. This minimum interval in time Δt is limited by the interrogation pulse bandwidth BW (which is restricted by the industrial, scientific and medical (ISM) bandwidth for RFID), and the excess delay spread τm of the radio channel properties in a specific application [8], see Eq.2

$$\Delta t \approx 2\tau_m + \frac{2}{BW} \qquad (Eq.2)$$

A BPSK coded tag is illustrated.

In additional, the multi-reflection effect occurs among the reflectors and it restricts the maximum number of reflector arranged in a single acoustic channel. Therefore, a high efficiency coding scheme for a large encoding capacity with less number of reflectors (i.e. less substrate length) is required.

As shown in Figure 5, the time overlapped pulse position with simultaneous phase offset modulation(TOPPS) proposed by C.S. Hartmann[17] is a more efficient scheme, which can enlarge the code capacity greatly under the same number of reflectors. It bases on PPM but has more than two pulses in a data group. In PPM coding scheme, the resolution of pulse position can not be high by only using the delays of the pulse envelops which is limited by the RF bandwidth. In case of TOPPS, the phases of the carrier wave in reflective pulses are utilized for pulse position

determination, which is equivalent to evaluating the location of the reflector to within a fraction of a carrier wave cycle, the resolution of the pulse time delay can be greatly enhanced. Two neighboring pulse can be partially overlapped but a minimum number of slots must be exist between two pulses to satisfy the Nyquist criteria. Then two partially overlapped pulses in a data group can be inerrantly detected by their prominent difference in carrier wave phases.

In the following, we define the bit density, the pulse efficiency and the quality factor Q as the measures of overall performance of each coding scheme[18].

$$D = \frac{R}{BW \cdot T}, \quad R = \text{int}(\log_2 C) \qquad (Eq.3)$$

$$E = \frac{R}{n} \qquad (Eq.4)$$

$$Q = D \times E \qquad (Eq.5)$$

where BW represents the RF pulse bandwidth, T is time span length of a code, and C is the code capacity encoded by n pulses.

There are 2 data groups, 75 time slots in each group and 4 pulses in a group. The minimum

Figure 5. Schematics of multiple pulse position modulation combined with phase offset (source from: RF SAW, Inc)

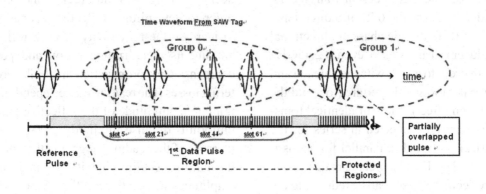

number of empty slots between pulses is 12. The reference pulse is used for data synchronization, phase reference and temperature compensation.

In Table.2, we list the comparison results of the above coding schemes of SAW RFID. Here, MPSK stands for M-ary phase modulation. When M=2, it is equivalent to BPSK modulation as shown in Figure 4. In case of TOPPS, we suppose the number of data group is m; the number of time slot in a group is i; and the number of pulse in a group is n. k is the minimum number of slots between two pulses.

And the minimum time span of a data group $m\dfrac{\tau}{k}$ in Eq.4 can further be reduced by increasing the time delay resolution. One of good solutions is a time overlapped pulse position modulation combined with phase offset, which distinguishes two adjacent pulses by their phases of the carrier wave within the pulse. For example, when i=75, k=12 and n=4, six data groups will be compatible with EPC-96 RFID specifications. Some redundant codes can be used for anti-collision and error checking. However, the required signal-to-noise ratio SNR mentioned in Eq.1 has to be higher than those of the OOK and the common PPM coding scheme.

In summary, the efficiency of scheme with phase information can be high enough and be compatible with EPC requirement. However, it puts high demands on tags design of locating the reflectors exactly with the desired phase in design. And all disturbing factors which change the delay of a bit, e.g., variations in the SAW velocity and the accuracy of the fabrication process, must be controlled within a small fraction of a SAW wavelength to meet the requirement of high phase accuracy[7]. According to the authors' experience, some design criterion will be discussed in the following part.

Tags Design

According to the given specifications and the chosen coding scheme, the positions and number of reflectors in line and their reflectivity are determined in design. There are some principles should be obeyed in this process.

1. According to Eq.(1), reducing the tags insertion loss to the minimum is important for reliable read range capability. The main loss mechanism in SAW tags includes[19]: the bidirectional losses of IDT, the channel mismatch losses, the impedance mismatching losses between IDT and the antenna, the reflection losses, SAW propagation attenuation as well as the bulk wave scattering

produced when the incident Rayleigh waves pass through a reflector, and resistivity of the busbar and electrodes in transducers. In order to reduce the 6dB of bidirectional losses of IDT, a single phase unidirectional transducer is usually used, even at 2.45GHz [20]. In order to match with the antenna and to have not too small aperture (to avoid the diffraction effect), a few of identical transducers may be connected in series for the electrical ports and in parallel for acoustical ports[21]. The channel mismatch losses and reflectivity losses can be reduced to the minimum by arranging all the reflectors in line with reflectivity as high as possible. However, number of reflectors and the maximum reflectivity are limited by the multi-reflection between reflectors.

2. Suppose that N of reflectors are arranged in line. The reflection coefficient and transmission coefficient are Pi and Ti (i=1,2,...,N), respectively. Because of the bulk wave scattering produced when the incident Rayleigh waves pass through a reflector, $P_i^2 + T_i^2 < 1$. Neglecting the propagation losses, the reflected energy from the ith reflector is

$$E_i = E_0 \cdot P_i^2 \left(\prod_{m=1}^{i-1} T_m^4 \right) \qquad \text{(Eq.6)}$$

where E0 is the incident energy. It can be seen that the amplitude of reflective echoes gradually decrease along with the order of the echoes. In order to get uniform reflective echoes, on has to increase the reflectivity of each reflector by varying its metallization ration and period to compensate the propagation and bulk wave scattering losses. The reading range depends upon the minimum amplitude of the reflective pulse. The uniformity of pulse amplitudes in fact means the increase of the reading range. On the other hand, the multi-reflection is inevitable and the uniform amplitudes means the multi-reflection effect is reduced to the minimum.

Many reflector configurations (open-circuit, short-circuit, interdigital transducer, positive-negative electrodes reflectors, et al) can be used to obtain a given value of reflectivity, as illustrated in Figure 6. The best choice is to use a structure with minimum scattering losses. However, the phenomenological models, such as the coupling of modes (COM), are not suitable for modeling and analysis of the above reflectors with few electrodes. A more accurate and fast method, called source regeneration method[22] is proposed based on Green's function combined with finite element analysis to obtain the reflection, transmission and scattering of reflector with a few electrodes, which are the basic knowledge for a good SAW tags design. In the tags with relative bandwidth over 1%, the open circuit reflector on 128°YXLiNbO3

Figure 6. Configuration of typical reflectors

(a) (b) (c) (d)

(a) open circuit reflector ; (b) short-circuit reflector ; (c) a transducer as reflector (d) substrate is usually chosen [23] because of less scattering losses and electrode resistivity losses than short-circuit reflector. In case of uniform amplitude compensation of reflective pulses, the reflectivity of last reflector is not too high. It helps to obtain more reflectors inline under the limitation of multi-reflection effect. In Figure 7, the measured frequency-domain(Tr3) and time response (Tr2) of a SAW RFID using Agilent E5070B vector network analyzer are presented. It can be seen that fast oscillations occur in the frequency-domain response. They are contributions of the ten reflected echoes and the multi-reflection among reflectors. Additionally, Due to the increasing reflectivity of each reflector to compensate for the energy losses, the amplitude uniformity of pulse is within a range of ±1dB according to the Tr2.

3. If the tags with phase modulation are designed, the reflector must be appropriately located to obtain the defined phase in carrier wave of reflective echo, in addition to a proper location of the envelop of the wave pulse [24]. To achieve this, one has to know not only the reflection phase and transmission phase of all the reflectors so as to compensate the phase changes when the wave propagates through the reflector and/or reflected by the reflector. A good design also needs to know the phase accuracy in the system, including the case that the temperature is different from the designing one. Without the information of phase errors, one has to design his encoding scheme with much fewer code capacity for the sake of reliability[21].

Reader Design

There are the air interface standards, ISO18000 series, for UHF IC based RFID readers, where signals are defined without reference to either

Figure 7. The measured frequency and time responses of a SAW tag. Tr2 is the logarithmic magnitude of the time response with 1dB/grid. Tr3 is the frequency response from 885MHz to 945MHz

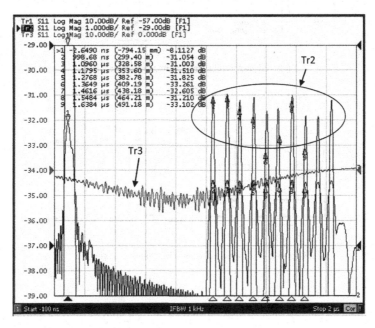

the interrogation or response devices. These air interfaces are logical if both such devices are active. However, they inefficiently over-specify the essential requirements being used for SAW RFID readers because SAW tags are passive and only respond to signal stimulus. Identifying SAW RFID tags can be done through the theories in fields of pattern recognition and system identification. The commonly used method is calculating the impulse response functions of tags. Variety of approaches in designing SAW tag readers to obtain the impulse response functions are permitted because there is no limitation on type of interrogation signal apart from the governmental mandated emission requirements. The reader architectures operated in time domain or in frequency domain are shown in Figure 8(a) and Figure 8(b), respectively.

In a time domain reader, a tone burst pulse simulating the Dirac signal$\delta(t)$, which covers the total system bandwidth at once is interrogated, then the reflected signals from tags are the impulse response functions. This reader architecture is suitable for identifying the fast moving objects[7,25]. In addition, the interrogation signal could also be an amplitude weighted burst to shape the signal in frequency domain and to keep the allowed bandwidth.

A sufficient isolation between transmitter and receiver (Tx/Rx) is additionally critical because the direct coupling of the transmit signal to the receive path leads to DC signal at the output of quadrature demodulation and hence a reduced dynamic range. The isolation of the antenna switch is superior to a circulator because of the non-continuous wave mode. It is also feasible that the power amplifier can be disabled during the receiver begins to work.

The minimum signal power applied to the reader input that gives the required output signal

Figure 8. SAW RFID transceiver architectures operated in time domain or in frequency domain

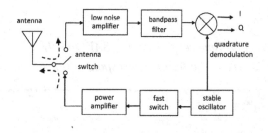

(a) Block diagram of a burst interrogation reader

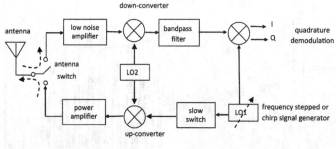

(b) Block diagram of frequency-domain interrogation reader

to noise ratio can be expressed as follows[26]:

$$(P_{\min})_{dBm} = -174dBm + (N_F)_{dB} + (10\log BW)_{dB} + (SNR)_{dB}$$
(Eq.7)

Here, (NF)dB is the overall noise figure of the reader. The cascaded noise figure of a chain of devices is primarily dominated by the first and the second stages, i.e., the noise figure of the low noise amplifier(LNA), the insertion losses of the RF bandpass filter and the antenna switch. The bandwidth BW shows the importance of the narrow bandwidth in attaining high sensitivity. In the superheterodyne receiver, the bandwidth is mainly dominated by the bandwidth of the intermediate frequency bandpass filter(not present in Figure 8(a)). In a time-domain reader, a tone burst pulse covers the total system bandwidth at once is interrogated, therefore the bandwidth is

high. Otherwise, an inter-pulse interference or a reduced code capacity will occur. The last term in Eq.7, which has also mentioned in Eq.1, is the signal-to-noise ratio required at the decoder input to achieve a defined code error rate. In case of the same decoding error rate, the (SNR) dB is dependent on the tag coding scheme as presented in Table2. A coherent demodulation is usually used for all the encoded tags. In this case, the theoretical sensitivity of a RFID reader with 5MHz bandwidth and the noise figure of 6dB can be approximate -90dBm.

Assuming that one of the echo signal from tags can be expressed as $A\cos(\omega_0 t + \theta_r)$, it can be decoded by coherent quadrature demodulation. The outputs of the inphase I and quadrature Q signals are

Table 2. Comparison of OOK,MPSK and TOPPS coding scheme

coding scheme	OOK	MPSK	TOPPS
Code capacity C	2^n	M^n	$\left(\dfrac{(i-(n-1)\cdot(k-1))!}{n!(i-(n-1)\cdot(k-1)-n)!}\right)^m$
Time span length of a code T	$\dfrac{n}{B}$	$\dfrac{n}{B}$	$(\dfrac{1}{kB}\cdot(i-1)+\dfrac{1}{B})\cdot m$
Bit density D (bit/second)	1	$\log_2 M$	$\dfrac{m\cdot\log_2\left(\dfrac{(i-(n-1)\cdot(k-1))!}{n!(i-(n-1)\cdot(k-1)-n)!}\right)}{B\cdot(\dfrac{1}{kB}\cdot(i-1)+\dfrac{1}{B})\cdot m}$
Bit efficiency E	1	$\log_2 M$	$\dfrac{m\cdot\log_2\left(\dfrac{(i-(n-1)\cdot(k-1))!}{n!(i-(n-1)\cdot(k-1)-n)!}\right)}{nm}$
Quality factor Q	1	$(\log_2 M)$	$\dfrac{k\cdot\left(\log_2\left(\dfrac{(i-(n-1)\cdot(k-1))!}{n!(i-(n-1)\cdot(k-1)-n)!}\right)\right)^2}{(i+k-1)\cdot n}$
Required signal-to-noise ratio SNR in demodulation	high	depend on M	close to OOK

$$I = \frac{1}{2} AB \cos \theta_r \qquad \text{(Eq.8)}$$

$$Q = \frac{1}{2} AB \sin \theta_r \qquad \text{(Eq.9)}$$

where A and B are the amplitude of the echoes and the local oscillator output. θr is the phase of the echo carrier wave and it implicates the encoding information in TOPPS or MPSK tags. As an example, the inphase I and quadrature Q signals for a pulse position modulation tag with 4 reflectors are shown in Figure 9. Then the amplitude and the phase of the echoes can be obtained by

$$A = \sqrt{I^2 + Q^2} \qquad \text{(Eq.10)}$$

$$\theta_r = \arctan \frac{Q}{I} \qquad \text{(Eq.11)}$$

After A/D converter, the signal processing algorithm in reader include: pulse accumulation, digital filtering, auto gain control, optimal threshold determination, interpolation and correlation.

A low cost burst SAW RFID reader at 920MHz is developed as shown in Figure 10. The main specifications of reader are listed in Table 3.

The system is applying to the chicken management to replace the existing bar codes. As show in Figure 11(a), the tags are installed in the non-essential meat area of the chickens with a one-inch polypropylene fastener. The chickens in a same farmer, birth date and laying period have a same code. This kind of tags can be implemented by SAW RFID at low costs. In Figure 11(b), a tag prototype with the antenna dimension (in millimeter) are demonstrated.

Figure 10. A low cost burst SAW RFID prototype

Figure 9. Coherent demodulation outputs, inphase I (Channel 1) and quadrature Q (Channel 2) signals for a pulse position modulation tag measured by TDS3052 oscilloscope

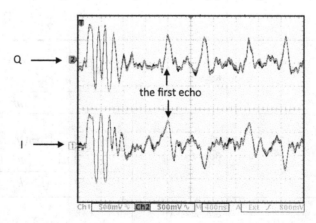

Table 3. Main specification of burst SAW RFID reader

Frequency	920MHz
Coding capacity	typical 2,000,000 (up to 64bit coding)
Transmitter max power	10mW-1W (adjustable)
Bandwidth	3-5MHz
Reading distance	up to 8m
Anti-collision	read 10 tags simultaneously
Antenna ports	One or two separate antenna
Output interface	COM & USB
Dimension of tag	6.5×13.5mm or less (not including the antenna)
Antenna of the tag	depends on the applications

The SAW RFID reader can also be operated in frequency domain[27-29]. One reader architecture is presented in Figure 8(b). Another one proposed by Stelzer et al is similar to the dechirping scheme in high resolution range radar[26]. As shown in Figure 8(b), the interrogation signal can be either the stepped frequency signals or the frequency-modulated continuous waves (chirp signal) generated by the local oscillator(LO1). If the stepped frequency signals is used, the frequency response can be achieved by multi-scanning and recording the inphase I and quadrature Q signals. Then the impulse response can be obtained by fast Inverter Fourier Transform. Therefore, this reader architecture is only suitable for the slow-moving or the quiescent object identification. The isolation between Tx/Rx and the implementation of the sweep oscillator with high frequency resolution and low phase noise are the kernel of the reader. The reader operated in frequency domain suffers from the identification speed, but owns the advantages of high time delay resolution and high sensitivity of reader. The processing gain available is limited by the maximum length of the interrogation pulse and the bandwidth of the tag.

CONCLUSION

SAW RFID provides some solutions to identify in harsh environments or where long read ranges are required. And it can be fairly complementary to IC RFID in different applications. A coding scheme with high efficiency, especially utilizing the carrier phase of each pulse in the impulse response of tags can greatly improve coding capacity of SAW RFID. The design criterion for tags and reader are discussed.

Figure 11. Application of SAW RFID in poultry farming management (a) and the antenna of SAW RFID (b)

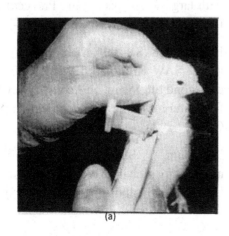

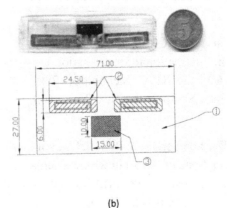

(a)

(b)

ACKNOWLEDGMENT

This chapter is supported by Natural Science Foundation of China under grant 60774052 and Shanghai Rising-Star Program 08QA14037.

REFERENCE

Arumugam, D., & Ambravaneswaran, V. (2008). 2D localization using SAW-based RFID systems: a single antenna approach . Int. J. RFID Technology and Applications., 1(4), 417–438.

Bazuin, B. J., Atashbar, M. Z., & Kirishnamurthy, S. (2004, January 4-7). A prototype burst transceiver for SAW sensors interrogation, International Conference on Intelligent Sensing and Information Processing (pp. 190-195), Chennai, India.

Bechteler, T. F., & Yenigün, H. (2003). 2-D Localization and Identification Based on SAW ID-Tags at 2.5 GHz . IEEE Trans, MTT, 51(5), 1584–1590. doi:10.1109/TMTT.2003.810142

Bensky, A. (2004), Short-range wireless Communication: Fundamentals of RF system design and application (second edition), New York: Elsevier

Brandl, M., Schuster, S., Scheiblhofer, S., & Stelzer, A. A new Anti-Collision Method for SAW tags using Linear Block Codes, 2008 IEEE International Frequency Control Symposium, 284-289

Brown, P., Hartmann, C., et al. (2007). Asset Tracking on the International Space Station Using Global SAW Tag RFID Technology, 2007 IEEE Ultrasonics Symposium, New York, (pp. 72 – 75).

Bulst, W.-E., Fischerauer, G., & Reindl, L., choll, G., et al. (2001). State of the art in wireless sensing with surface acoustic waves . IEEE Transactions on Industrial Electronics, 48(2), 265–271. doi:10.1109/41.915404

Edmonson P. J., & Campbell C. K. (2004). Encoded SAW RFID tags and sensors for multi-user detection using IDT finger phase modulation US6827281

Fachberger, R., & Bruckner, G. (2004). Applicability of LiNbO3, Langasite and GaPO4 in high temperature SAW sensors operating at radio frequencies, IEEE . Trans. UFFC, 51(11), 1427–1431.

Han, T., Lin, W., Lin, J. M., Wang, W. B., Wu, H. D., Shui, Y. A., et al. (2008).Errors of Phase and Group Delays in SAW RFID with Phase Modulation. IEEE Ultrasonics Symposium.

Han, T., Shi, W., & Lu, W. (2003). Reflection of impedance-loaded SAW IDT and its application in wireless information . Chin. J. Electron., 12(2), 185–188.

Han, T., Wang, W. B., Lin, J. M., Wu, H. D., Wang, H., & Shui, Y. (2007). Phases of Carrier Wave in a SAW Identification Tags. IEEE Ultrasonics Symposium,(pp. 1669-1672)

Han, T., Wang, W. B., Wu, H. D., & Shui, Y. A. (2008). Reflection and Scattering Characteristics of Reflectors in SAW Tags . IEEE Transactions on Ultrasonics, Ferroelectrics, and Frequency Control, 55(6), 1387–1390. doi:10.1109/TUFFC.2008.802

Hartmann, C. S. (2002). A global SAW ID tag with large data capacity. In . Proceedings of the IEEE Ultrasonics Symposium, 1, 65–69.

Hartmann, C. S. (2004, March 15-19). Design of global SAW RFID tag devices. In Proceedings of Second Int. Symp. on Acoustic Wave Devices for Future Mobile Communication Systems., Chiba.

Hartmann, C. S., et al. (2004). Anti-collision methods for global SAW RFID tag systems, IEEE Ultrasonics Symposium,(pp. 805-808).

Hartmann, C. S., & Claiborne, L. T. (March 26-28). Fundamental Limitations on Reading Range of Passive IC-Based RFID and SAW-Based RFID, 2007. In Proceedings of IEEE International Conference on RFID, (pp.41 – 48).

Kuypers, J. H., Reindl, L. M., Tanaka, S., & Esashi, M. (2008). Maximum Accuracy Evaluation Scheme for Wireless SAW Delay-Lin Sensors . IEEE Transactions on Ultrasonics Perforlctrics, and Frequency Control, 55(7), 1640–1651. doi:10.1109/TUFFC.2008.840

Lehtonen, S., & Plessky, V. (2000). Unidirectional SAW Transducer for Gigahertz Frequencies. IEEE Trans. UFFC, 50(11), 1404–1406.

Li, Q., Ji., X., Shi, W. & Han.- T. (2009). Walsh Matched-Threshold Filtering in SAW Tag Applications to Provide Multiple-Access Capability . Journal of Shanghai Jiaotong University, 14(6), 681–685. doi:10.1007/s12204-009-0681-3

Ostermayer, G., Pohl, A., Hausleitner, C., Reindl, L., & Seifert, F. (1996). CDMA for wireless SAW sensor applications. In Proc. IEEE Int. Spread-Spectrum Tech. Applicat. Symp., (pp. 795–799).

Pohl, A. (2000). Review of wireless SAW sensors. IEEE Trans. UFFC, 47(2), 317–332.

Retrieved from http://www.baumer.se/rfid.htm#OIS-W

Scholl, G. (2003). SAW-based radio sensor systems for short-range applications . IEEE Microwave Magazine, 4(4), 68–76. doi:10.1109/MMW.2003.1266068

Stelzer, A. (2004). Identification of SAW ID-Tags Using an FSCW Interrogation Unit and Model-Based Evaluation. IEEE Trans. UFFC, 51(11), 1412–142.

Stelzer, A., Schuster, S., & Scheiblhofer, S. (2004). Readout Unit for Wireless SAW Sensors and ID-Tags, in 2nd International Symposium on Acoustic Wave Devices for Future Mobile Communications (pp. 37–44), Chiba, Japan.

Wang, W. B., Han, T., Zhang, X. D., Wu, H. D., & Shui, Y. A. (2007). Rayleigh wave reflection and scattering calculation by source regeneration method. IEEE Transactions on Ultrasonics, Ferroelectrics, and Frequency Control, 54(7), 1445–1453. doi:10.1109/TUFFC.2007.405

White, R. M., & Voltmer, F. W. (1965). (n.d.). "Direct piezoelectric coupling to surface elastic waves . Applied Physics Letters, 7, 314–316. doi:10.1063/1.1754276

X-Change Corporation Delivers Surface Acoustic Wave (SAW) Tag Technology for the Oil and Gas Industry. Retrieved from http://www.thefreelibrary.com/X-Change+Corporation+Delivers+Surface+Acoustic+ Wave+(SAW)+Tag...-a0176649458

Section 3
Logistics Informatics and Information Logistics

Chapter 6
Information Needs of Logistics Service Providers

Ulla Tapaninen
Merikotka Research Center, Finland

Hennariina Pulli
Merikotka Research Center, Finland

Antti Posti
Merikotka Research Center, Finland

ABSTRACT

This chapter explores supply chains, all the way from the manufacturing point to the customer site. The concentration is on logistics service providers (LSPs). In terms of overall quality, the information infrastructure in Finland has constantly ranked among top 10 positions in international comparisons regarding information society development (e.g. WEF 2008). The purpose of the chapter is to point out the current level of information sharing in supply chains focusing on the information needs of logistics companies, particularly from the LSP's point of view. A study conducted by the University of Turku revealed that there is a lack of logistics information in the supply chain (Pulli & al. 2008). The information distribution should be intensified when aiming at achieving a more efficient supply chain.

INTRODUCTION

A broad definition of supply chain management (SCM) states that SCM is an integrative philosophy to manage the total flows of a distribution channel from supplier level to production, to distribution and, ultimately, to the end customer (Helo & Szekely 2005). However, the fact is that there are always points where the stability of the supply chain is disturbed. One example of these points is ports, where shipments are unloaded and reloaded. The handling points of transported goods along the supply chain can sometimes turn out to be bottlenecks. These points can be controlled if the information sharing between the supply chain partners is well organized. Logistics service providers (LSP) manage, co-ordinate and deliver logistics activities on behalf of a shipper (Choy et al. 2006). This task requires integration between the LSP and the other parties in the logistic chain. Virtual integration can help the actors of a supply chain to achieve more flexible and transparent chain, and to share informa-

DOI: 10.4018/978-1-61520-603-2.ch006

tion more easily. As an example, Internet can be utilized to serve the needs of an integrated supply chain. Through Internet the actors of a supply chain can interact with each others, for example by sharing information of their stock levels. In order to quickly respond to the customer's needs, it is necessary for the companies in the chain to collaborate and integrate as a whole (Zhang et al. 2006). Naturally, the integration can not necessarily be achieved with every member of the chain. The objective of this chapter is to point out the information elements the LSPs need to share to reach an efficient supply chain.

BACKGROUND

Logistics can be described as the management of the flow of goods, information and other resources. This chapter focuses on the transportation side of logistics. Logistics companies face a great challenge in their every day operations. They should deliver the transported goods to the customer as fast and as reliably as possible. Ideally, efficient supply chain management is based on information flow and full visibility over the chain. The goal is to provide detailed visibility into the entire chain; from the availability of raw materials to the time the customer receives the goods (Kalakota & Robinson 2000, Singh 1996). The full supply chain visibility enables the planning and controlling in each stage of the supply chain. Through visibility, it is possible to optimize the use of resources, to speed up the chain and to react more effectively to unexpected deviations in the process. Without this visibility, the uncertainty in the chain needs to be compensated by creating buffers (inventories, time buffers or production capacity). In logistics, this could mean reserving for example extra transportation units or vehicles.

Logistics service providers co-operate with many branches of industry, which fundamentally limits their possibility to focus on certain ICT standards. It is probable that also in the future, LSPs

need to cope with several standards, which increases their operational complexity (Kekäläinen 2006). Another challenge can be the culture change that is required to gain open information sharing in the supply chain. The benefits of transparency should be made clear to the actors of supply chains. That should encourage them, when trying to overcome the difficulties that can emerge when reaching a transparent supply chain.

IMPORTANCE OF INFORMATION IN SUPPLY CHAIN MANAGEMENT

Information is an essential part of logistics and supply chains. In other words, without information sharing the flow of products could decelerate. The flow of information consists of data that is needed to launch the flows of material and capital and to steer them. The achieving of an efficient supply chain requires sharing of adequate amount of information between all possible partners at the right time. If logistics information is at the right time shared between the actors of the supply chain, it produces smooth flow of material. Smooth flow means that products move steadily in the chain and with as few and short stops as possible.

The significance of information in logistics can be seen as twofold. Without a well-utilized information system the managers of the company cannot make well-rationalized decisions. This point of view stresses the strategic role that information possesses. In addition to this strategic role of information, precise and real-time information is needed to steer all the logistic activities on the operative level (Reinikainen et al. 1997). Logistics processes require for example data concerning forecasts, so that a company is able to reserve enough capacity (vehicles, employees etc.) and material for different processes. Also information about orders and location of materials and products is needed to complete the logistics processes. It is essential that actors of a supply chain immediately or with just a short delay receive all the information that could affect the forecasts. Rapid reaction to possible changes in a supply chain requires rapid sharing of information. That in turn requires proper information channels. Well-organized sharing of information can also reduce the need for warehousing (Singh 1996).

When actors of a supply chain want to achieve more efficient supply chain, the key is optimization of the entire chain. This refers to the fact that supply chains should be considered as a whole and also treated as a whole. It is not very rational to only optimize a single process of a chain, but rather the whole chain. This is not a very simple task, so managing one order from its starting point to the delivery point can be considered as a great challenge in supply chains. It is common that the supplier controls the information about the production and quality of the products and also information about when the products are leaving the production plant. Transport companies know the products they are carrying and also where these products are located. Supply chains consist of many different actors working together, which may lead to situations that are difficult to handle. Especially when some changes, like, for example, damages and weather conditions occur; it can result to huge extra manual work (Laaksonen et al. 2004). If information is handled more automatically, and actors of a chain know where certain products are and where they are needed, it is possible that products can move ideally Just-In-Time (JIT) and the need for warehousing is at its smallest. The reaching of a situation where transported products can be precisely traced requires integration of logistics processes of different actors and tracing of products with advanced IT systems.

Information can be generated in three ways: current information, forecasts and historical information. First, some logistics models are based on current information. As an example, vehicle dispatching models need information about today's orders, vehicles available and driver status. Other models are based on forecasts. Historical data is then used to predict future demand, avail-

able production capacity, and so on. Third, some models use actual historical data to calibrate model accuracy. This means that model outputs can be compared to what actually happened to ensure the model is valid (Ratliff & Nulty 1997).

Supply Chain Integration

The main principle behind the concept of supply chain management is to integrate all the activities in a chain into a well-functioning entity. It is not reasonable to separately optimize the different activities. The various functions and groups in organizations work for goals that are set together. The goals can be, for example, to reduce production costs, to improve the quality of products / services or to develop new products / services. Working for goals set together can be described as integration. SCM is primarily concerned with managing relationships with supplier and customers in order to deliver the best possible customer value at the lowest cost. SCM emphasizes effective and efficient flows of both information and also physical items to meet customer requirements, starting from the source of raw materials to the consumption of the product. Also recycling of the consumed goods is part of supply chain management. The management of these processes requires close collaboration among the different parties in the supply chain, including raw material suppliers, manufacturers, distributors and retailers. IT can able real-time integration of supply chain actors, by making it possible to share large amounts of information along the supply chain (Li et al. 2009). Integration of supply chain is considered to be of strategic as well as operational importance. It has been claimed that supply chain integration impacts first on chain performance, which, in turn, impacts on overall performance (Fabbe-Costes & Jahre 2008).

A common challenge that many organizations face is the fact that the time it takes to acquire the raw material, to manufacture the products and to deliver the products for customers, is usually longer than the customer desires (Christopher 1992). Traditionally, the solution for this problem has been forecasting the consumption and thereby keeping stock. Forecasting is often thought to be the case of manufacturing companies, but also other branches have to plan their activities for a long time ahead into the future. Because customer demand is not often perfectly stable, logistics companies must forecast demand to be able to reserve enough resources. Forecasts are based on statistics, and they are rarely perfectly accurate. Because of this uncertainty, companies often create additional stocks that can be called as inventory buffers. When moving up the supply chain from end-customer to the suppliers, each actor in the supply chain has greater observed variation in demand and thus greater need for safety stock. The variations are amplified as one moves upstream in the supply chain. This is often called the Bull-whip effect. Errors easily occur if the companies in the supply chain do not co-operate and share essential information needed for forecasts. Making of forecasts that are satisfyingly accurate is rather difficult if the actors of a certain chain do not achieve long-term collaboration (Lysons & Farrington 2006).

As stated above, an integrated supply chain can be the answer for lead-time gap, forecast inaccuracy and transparency of the chain. The basic idea behind the concept of integration is that the performance level of a company or a supply chain can be improved through the better sharing of information and through the planning of the activities and their interfaces together. Through the co-operation between the supply chain partners, it is possible to optimize the performance level of the entire chain and to satisfy the customers' needs better than before. It is easier to meet the needs of the customers and to reach overall customer satisfaction if the movement of the goods and related information is well-managed. The information shared in the supply chain has to be accurate, right-time and transparent. Information itself is not the answer but rather the right kind of

use of it. It is essential for a company's employees to know *when* and *what kind of* information to use (Singh 1996).

Supply Chain Transparency

Often the only piece of information that a company receives concerning the market demand is the actual customer orders. Christopher (1992) describes this as the tip of an iceberg. If the supplier could see "underneath the surface", for example, receive real-time information about the actualized consumption, the supplier could have more time and knowledge to prepare to the customers' needs and the activities could be more effectively timetabled. In other words, the company would have more time to plan what to do and when. If the supplier has no information on the future material flow, stock levels and demand, it usually has to compensate the uncertainty with stocks. For logistics companies the compensation could for example mean reservation of extra containers or vehicles. Naturally, this brings some extra costs for the companies.

Transparency of a supply chain refers to the fact that partners of a chain are able to track the delivery (location of products, deviations in delivery timetables etc.) and costs of the transport. With a full view of the chain, it is possible for all partners to gather and receive the information concerning the deliveries and products. This information should be easily reached and employed. When the supply chain is transparent, it is easier to manage it: to direct, plan and track the deliveries in every phase of the chain. With better management, it is possible to speed up the deliveries. If the supply chain has become more transparent, it is also possible to manage appearing deviations better than before. Transparency allows the actors of the chain to see the possible bottlenecks and thus remove them. One major challenge for transparency is globalization and the continually accelerating pace of world trade. It offers more possibilities and new markets for companies, but can also create complexity in the information sharing and visibility (Mäkinen et al. 2005).

There are some preconditions for the gaining of a transparent supply chain. It requires that actors of a chain freely share information with each others. This is essential if the actors want to meet their customers' needs in time. To achieve this open information sharing, actors of a chain should have reliable enough relationships with each other. And the achieving of trust requires some level of transparency (Kauniskangas 2007). All this leads to the fact that companies should have close and reliable enough relationships with their suppliers and customers. Well-functioning collaboration enables companies to integrate their activities (Spekman et al. 1998). Integration in turn forces companies to consider their processes and to minimise possible bottlenecks.

Even if a company recognises the importance of right-time information, it is not self-evident that the company automatically makes its processes more effective and transparent and starts to share more information with its partners. There have to happen changes in the culture of the management level before a company begins to distribute more information more openly than before. Traditionally companies have shared information mainly inside their own departments. Sometimes companies do not necessarily see the possible advantages that could be achieved through better sharing of information. For example, one fear is that competitors gain delicate data and exploit it on the markets. In some cases it can even be the technology used that restrains the achievement of transparency. For example with an ERP (Enterprise Resource Planning) system it may be difficult to reach a complete view over the chain, because these rather old systems do not necessarily offer information in such forms that could be utilized in effective ways (Salmela et al. 2006). If a company cannot see the advantages of the sharing of information, it is not very highly motivated to share information. Thus, the goal should be to make all the actors of

a chain understand the importance of each piece of information in the chain.

Real-Time or Right-Time Information

Information in a supply chain can be shared real-time or right-time, for example. Real-time information can be utilized without delays, but right-time information is available when it is most useful. Real-time information makes it possible to react quickly, especially when some changes occur. Immediately received information concerning, for example, ETA (Estimated Time of Arrival) that has changed, gives a company the opportunity to reorganize its resources. However, real-time information is not always necessary. It should be considered in every process whether it would be reasonable to use information with a short delay. In this case, it is a question of right-time information. In some cases, real-time information can even decrease flexibility in a dynamic environment. Also generating real-time information may cause great costs, for example, as a result of system integration. Right-time information also brings challenges for information systems. The most important issue is to find the processes in which real-time information is truly useful. The survey, which consisted of six cases (Kone, Nokia, Metso Automation, Fujitsu Invia, ABB and Outokumpu), revealed that real-time information is not always a prerequisite for business. Real-time information is most useful in the situations in which a quick reaction to the emerged deviations is required (Salmela & Jahnukainen 2003).

3 LOGISTICS AND IT

Information technology is one of the key factors in integrated supply chains. It is not even possible to implement or control integrated chains without information technology. The efficient use of IT in a supply chain requires sharing of information between different operations. Technology, infrastructure and information are combined in information technology. All these three fields should be managed properly so the benefits of information technology can be maximized (Gopal & Cypress 1993).

Information Systems in Logistics

Information systems that are utilized in the controlling of supply chains can be divided, for example, to a) internal systems operating inside the company and b) external systems operating between different companies. A system based on open information helps to share information both inside the company and outside the company. Such an open model can include, for example, the key suppliers, manufacturers and end customers of the company. The sharing of information can be based on different kinds of database systems or data warehouses located in various locations or companies. When sharing information in the chain between different actors, the actors have the possibility to improve the marketing time of their products and to cut costs. In general, better access to information helps actors to allocate their resources for the future. SCM systems include, for example, warehouse management systems, which provide real-time information on the material flows of the warehouse and the movements of the products. With this information storage space, labor and the use of tools and vehicles can be optimized (Helo & Szekely 2005).

Development of IT has had and will have a significant role in logistics and supply chain management. IT enables for example real-time information and transparency. These two concepts bring more efficiency to logistics management (Punakivi et al. 2001). Telecommunications will be more continuous and multilevel in future. The different levels can be actors, locations, means of transport, containers/cases and consumer packages. The amount of data will grow because more and more information and communication will be handled automatically between vehicles and storages. Real-time communication is based on wireless connections between these different spots. The versatility of technologies brings its own challenges to logistics (Laaksonen et al. 2004). One word to describe logistics as a business is diversity. Logistics is not dependent on just one branch of industry or business but consists of many different businesses and actors. This is the main reason why logistics actors cannot focus on just one standard. Logistics service providers must cope with many different standards which can really complicate their processes (Kekäläinen 2006). A company has to do business with many other actors and this also brings along many different interfaces. This is probably the situation also in future because it is not very probable to reach a situation of just one standard.

ERP (Enterprise Resource Planning) systems are worth noticing in the field of logistics. They can have a great impact on the intensification of activities in a company. With ERP systems, it is possible to reach better quality of information and for example utilize real-time information. They also help to intensify the activities in a company and diminish the lead time of products. The basic version of the ERP system has been developed to serve the needs of a manufacturing company. With this in mind, it is easy to understand that standardized ERP systems do not necessarily fit into the processes of logistics companies. Standardized software does not usually well support some new SCM models, like VMI (Vendor Managed Inventory) or utilization of sales forecasts. Elcoteq Inc. has solved this challenge so that it uses many separate standardized software packages to manage its processes, and has executed the integration of these systems by itself. Outside Elcoteq it looks like these different systems are just one entity (Kauremaa & Auramo 2004). The basic idea behind VMI is managing inventory by the vendor on the behalf of the buyer. By doing this, the customer can focus on its core business.

In addition to ERP, also EDI (Electronic Data Interchange) is a commonly used technique in logistics companies. EDI stands for standardized automated transmission of data between two information systems. As an example of the use of EDI is transmission of different documents, such as orders, invoices and customs documents. With EDI these are automatically transmitted from the sender company's IT system to the receiving company's information system. The using of EDI is very reasonable when there are large flows of goods and the company's partners are being settled on. The building of EDI connections is expensive and there has to be quite a large amount of transactions for the system to pay itself back. These facts make it unprofitable for SMEs (small and medium sized companies) to use EDI (Kauremaa & Auramo 2004).

The versatility of standards can also be considered as a downside of EDI. It is possible that a company is forced to use different kinds of EDI messages with different customers because of the customers' demands. Some logistics companies have begun to use the open standard XML (Extensible Markup Language) aside EDI. XML is an extensible language, because the user can define the mark-up elements. The purpose of XML is to help information systems share structured data, especially through Internet, to encode documents, and to serialize data. XML makes it possible to define the content of documents separately from the formatting, which makes it easy to reuse that content in other applications. The most important note is that XML provides a basic syntax that can be used to share information between different kinds of applications and different organizations without needing to pass through many layers of conversion. It has been forecasted that the use of XML will rise beside of EDI, thanks to the flexibility of it. One benefit of XML, when comparing it to EDI, is that it does not take so great investments to build the connections between different actors. Most of the companies today have connection to the internet, and it can be used as a base for XML related data transmission. On the other hand, besides the flexibility and profitableness

of XML, it possesses more standards than EDI (Kauremaa & Auramo 2004). The main difference with these two is that EDI is designed to serve the needs of business, and is a process, when XML is a language (Lysons & Farrington 2006).

Different kinds of web-based solutions can be considered as modern technologies in logistics. The great benefit of web-based solutions is that a company does not need to build heavy point-to-point connections when using web-based solutions. Companies can, for example, begin to receive their orders through Internet or extranet. Kauremaa & Auramo's (2004) research concerning advanced Finnish logistics companies revealed that the focal features of web-based solutions are the receiving of orders and the sharing of information about the state of deliveries to customers. One benefit in the handling of orders through the web is that customers have to obtain all information (in comprehensive format) related to the ordered products before the order is accomplished. Otherwise the order is not accepted in the system. By using the web, a phone call related to the order is not required; at the same time a company can avoid making later additional questions, because the customer has to provide more comprehensive information than in the telephone order. Making orders through the web may be beneficial also to the customer, because he does not need to queue on the phone. Also tracking services are often provided on the web (Kauremaa & Auramo 2004).

Kauremaa & Auramo (2004) noticed that only 19% of advanced manufacturing and trade companies in Finland use these modern tracking services within their purchases. Among sales about a third (31%) of these companies uses tracking services. It was stated that companies are not very interested in the following of the location and condition of their deliveries but are interested if some changes occur. The most essential part of tracking services in the moment is in-vehicle terminals. Quite a lot of emphasis is being put on them by IT companies that are developing techniques related to these terminals. The in-vehicle terminals provide the opportunity to have a better view of the transactions that occur during transportation. When a driver acknowledges the status of a delivery at predefined points, the haulage organizer knows where any certain vehicle is, and is able to plan the schedule for the next transportation tasks. One notable asset of these in-vehicle systems is that they offer information both for the company's own operation planning, and also provide the customers with the same tracking information (Kauremaa & Auramo 2004). Often tracking services are provided on the web, which is easier for the customer because he can check the status and location of the delivery at any time. At the same time, the logistics company's customer service saves time as the number of enquiries decreases.

Product Tracking and Tracing

The exact location of transported products is not necessarily essential information for companies. Instead of precise location data, a company is often interested to know the points the delivery is situated between. This information can be provided if the carrier of the delivery acknowledges the predefined points with certain status information. The management of product tracking is usually well controlled as long as the delivery is handled with just one logistics company. Then the tracking information can be found in just one information system and is quite easily reachable. As the networking between companies increases and supply chains become more global, there is an increasing amount of companies in one chain. Nowadays, supply chains should be called networks rather than chains. This is because the bunch of activities a delivery requires, reminds more a net than a chain, thanks to the concept of outsourcing, which leads to the diversity of logistics companies in a chain. Great challenges can occur when the companies of a supply chain are trying to communicate with each others. Integration of IT systems is not a simple task to perform (Främling 2002). This chapter presents

two systems that can be considered to be the most suitable for tracking the location of transported goods: RFID (Radio Frequency Identification) and GPS (Global Positioning System).

When there is a need to follow delivered products world-wide, every tracked product should have a tag (e.g. bar code) that globally individualizes it. This is not a very simple task to manage, since there are several parallel identification systems and some of them provide global individualization and some do not (Främling 2002). RFID (Radio Frequency Identification) has come to the markets to "compete" with bar code. Radio identification systems that use short-range radio technique are a rapidly growing area of interest. The system consists of a) RFID tags that are identified with their unique serial number or with some other certain data, and of b) one or more RFID readers. The whole system is controlled by RFID IT-system and the company's other IT-systems. Within RFID systems, many different radio technical solutions and different frequency ranges can be used. RFID technology does not provide real-time data but rather status information. The information is created every time the tag is read and then the status of the delivery is updated. The very first RFID tags were made for to mark domestic animals. Today RFID can be used at many different lines of business, such as trade, manufacturing, logistics and health care, to enhance efficiency. RFID can also be used to protect product safety and to fight against counterfeiting (e.g. medicines) (Talvela 2006).

An enquiry conducted by VTT Technical Research Centre of Finland showed that company representatives believe that RFID related applications will be widely used by the year 2015. It is expected that with RFID, it is possible to bring more efficiency to logistics. The most important benefits of RFID concern tracking of products and transport means, and also the transparency of the supply chain. One successful introduction of RFID technology was at ABB's factory at Helsinki. There the packages of raw material are identified with UHF (Ultra High Frequency) RFID. This was the first solution of this kind in Finland (Rytsy 2007).

Although the technique for RFID has been ready for use for a few years now, there are some factors that decelerate the adopting of it. One of the possible hindrances is the relatively high price of the RFID system. On the other hand, when a large amount of companies begin to use RFID, the price will come down. Not very many companies use RFID, and it is possible that other companies are still waiting to see if the use of RFID will increase. In innovation adoption, there are always pioneers that quickly adopt the innovation, and followers that monitor the innovation diffusion before they have the courage to adopt it too. One of the challenges of RFID systems concerns the tags. The selection of tags is wide, so finding the right kind of tag can take some time and effort. It also requires resources to find the right spot in the product where the tag can be attached. For example, if the tag is inside a paper roll, the antenna cannot read it, because there are 1.5 metres of paper between the tag and the antenna. If the tag is attached on the top of the roll, the tag can break (Siltala 2007). Also metal and different fluids can be challenging product groups for RFID (Rytsy 2007).

The Global Positioning System (GPS) can be utilized, when the supply chain actors desire real-time data about the location of the transported goods. GPS is a global navigation satellite system that is developed by the United States Department of Defence. It operates globally and is available 24 hours a day. With GPS the user can determine his location and velocity and also the current time. GPS became fully operational on 1995 and it has become a widely used aid to navigation worldwide. A GPS receiver calculates its position by timing the signals sent by four or more GPS satellites. GPS has proved to be reliable and accurate navigation system. The navigation accuracy of GPS is depended on conditions of environment and on the technique of the GPS system. The typical

accuracy of GPS ranges from few metres to tens of metres. With different extensions of GPS it is possible to achieve accuracy of less than one meter. There are also other satellite navigation systems (GLONASS, Galileo and Beidou) but GPS is the most common and is the only system that operates fully. Satellite navigation systems has been utilized, for example, in map-making, land surveying, commerce, scientific uses and tracking. In logistics, it is possible to track vehicles and transportation units with GPS in real-time (Airos et al. 2007).

INFORMATION NEEDS OF CAPACITY PLANNING OF LOGISTICS COMPANIES

Traditionally, production planning has been seen as a matter of manufacturing companies. But just like manufacturers, also logistics companies have to plan the use of their resources, for example to reserve enough labour or transport capacity for each day. The companies in a supply chain need information about forecasts, changes, ETA, the location of products and the condition of product and so on. Ratliff & Nulty (1997) have defined the information that companies in a supply chain require. Figure 1 presents their view. One can see that this definition lacks the transportation companies' site.

The previous figure illustrated, on a fairly rough level, information that companies are exchanging with each another. In this report, however, the emphasis is on the capacity planning side. The chapter 4.1 presents the information elements that companies in a typical supply chain need for their operations. Basic transportations consist at least of the loading of goods in the transport unit, the transportation of goods to the destination and the unloading of goods at the destination. The transportation process also includes various planning, procurement and other preparation and ancillary activities, which can have a notable part

Figure 1. Information needs of companies in the supply chain (Ratliff & Nulty 1997)

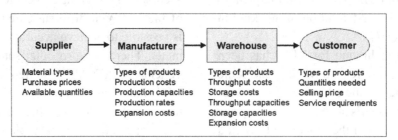

in the whole process. Importance of planning is emphasized in the cases where the transportation task is new to the company. The development of information technology has made it possible to control transportations nearly real-time. Products and services are produced, supplied and consumed more and more through an (electronic) information network. Transport planning and control systems can be integrated into the company's ERP or SCM system. The most typical information elements, which are exchanged between various parties, are information concerning the customer, the product and the order. In order to achieve a supply chain that is as efficient as possible, each party must commit itself to the interactive collaboration and information reporting.

Information Elements Essential for Capacity Planning

The following text presents five different information elements which are considered important for the logistics company's capacity planning.

Forecasting can be seen as the main ground for planning and decision-making in a company. Forecasts are based on presumptions and they can prove to be wrong or they can be affected by factors that cannot be seen beforehand. The longer the time scale of the forecast, the bigger the uncertainty (Lysons & Farrington 2006). Lysons & Farrington have defined six questions that a company should consider before making forecasts. First, the purpose of the forecast should be decided. Answering

this question helps a company to determine, for example, the accuracy of the forecast. Secondly, the time scale for the forecast has to be formed. The time scale for forecasts can be long, mid or short. One challenge is to find the most suitable forecasting technique. Fourth, a company needs to decide on the information the forecast is based on; it depends on the purpose of the forecast, the accuracy level required, and the resources that have been reserved for forecasting. Finally, the form of the forecast presentation and the accuracy of forecast have to be solved.

Logistics companies need forecast information of their partners' planned deliveries, so they can reserve an adequate amount of resources (vehicles, labour) for each time period.

ETA (Estimated Time of Arrival) is important information for logistics companies. It is used to indicate the estimated arrival time to the destination. ETA illustrates, for example, the arrival time when the control of the transport vehicle or transport unit transfers to the logistics company. Without this information, it is very difficult for a logistics company to reserve enough resources (such as labour) for actions that are needed for the handling of the arriving products.

Information concerning *changes* is also essential for the capacity planning of logistics companies. Changes can be, for example, related to the schedule or the route in use. Information concerning changes received as early as possible helps companies re-measure their resources and make other necessary rearrangements related to companies' activities.

Information concerning the *location of the transported goods* can also help logistics companies to plan their operations. With the help of the location information, companies can monitor the progress of the deliveries and plan their schedule and capacity. When a company has real-time information about the location of the transportations, it is easy to optimize the transport schedule, when new transportation tasks occur. In that way, the company is able to react efficiently to changing situations. The most important position systems are the systems based on satellite navigation (GPS) and mobile communication technologies (GSM, Global System for Mobile Communications and UMTS, Universal Mobile Telecommunications System). In addition, particularly the largest transport companies can nowadays offer their customers a service that makes it possible to track their deliveries through Internet. So far, this information is not based on real-time location, but the bar code/RFID tag of the shipment is read at various stages of the transportation. This status-information is updated to the database, and the customer can see, for example, whether the delivery is in the terminal or truck (Logistiikka 2001).

Condition of the transported goods is information that companies may need, mainly when some changes occur. Particularly customers need information concerning the condition of their products. There are a lot of possibilities for damages, because products, transport routes, transport modes and transport conditions may vary in each case. For example, when transporting cold products, it is essential to maintain an unbroken cold chain. The most common reason for the damage to goods is denting or dropping of products during the transfer phase, which may occur either in the terminal or during loading and unloading. If the information concerning the possibly altered condition of the products is shared in real-time or with just short delay, the companies can take some corrective actions in time and make sure that the transportation survives with so few harms as possible.

Case Study: LSPs in Finland

The previous chapter presented the information the companies in a supply chain need in order to control their deliveries through the supply chain. A study concerning the logistics service providers in Southeast Finland was accomplished to clear out the current level of information change in port-related supply chains. The purpose of the study was to find out if the studied companies share the previously mentioned data elements (forecasts, ETA, changes, location and condition) with each others. Altogether 14 companies were interviewed in 2008. The studied branches of industry were shipping, transporting, forwarding, port operating and port authority. The persons that were interviewed were responsible for logistics and information management in their companies. The interviewed companies represent the typical supply chain actors in Finland. Table 1 illustrates the results of the study.

The studied companies are engaged in port-related supply chains of Finnish foreign trade. The companies were asked what kind of information they receive and, on the other hand, deliver to their partners. Interviews are based on the information

Table 1. Information needs in port-related logistics chains

	Shipper	Transportation company	Port operator, Forwarding agency, Port authority
Information received	- ETA - forecasts - location - condition - changes	- ETA - changes - location - condition	- ETA - forecasts - location - condition
More information needed		- forecasts - location - changes - loading instructions - customer's volume increase	- forecasts - location - changes

elements that were previously presented. The study revealed that the typical supply chain in Finland is not very transparent. The table indicates that the shipper receives information well but the other actors in the chain do not. There is a lack of information concerning forecasts, location and changes. Two of the interviewed companies also told that they would like to receive information about their customers' possible volume increase. One company told that it does not have the loading instructions. The most desirable information concerned the changes. All of the interviewed companies would like to have information when some changes emerge and they wish that this information would be available earlier than it is today. Forecasts were also seen as important although many of the companies did say they were satisfied with the amount of information today. The desired time scale of forecasts varied from one to 20 days. Usually forecasts were wanted for 1–2 weeks ahead.

Many of the studied companies were rather satisfied with the current information sharing. This is quite bizarre because for example only a few received information about their customers' needs, other than the actual order. It is possible that many of the companies are not fully aware of the benefits the increased transparency would bring to the supply chain.

Companies were also asked if there is some information they would like to receive in the future. One topic was raised above others and it was the need for more accurate information. Too often the information received was not as accurate as it should have been. Another important point was that information should be received earlier than it is today. At this moment, some essential information is received only few hours before. Naturally, this causes problems to the production planning of the companies.

The IT level of the companies varied quite a lot but also the size of the companies varied. Some companies controlled almost all of their processes electronically when some companies rely just on

e-mail. The primary notion was that most of the companies use many different applications to run their businesses. Because of the differences in the IT levels of the studied companies, it is not possible yet to turn all the information in the chain electronic. It is rather usual that even if some data is sent electronically, it can become a paper version at some point of the chain. The objective should be to keep the information flow electronic all the way in the chain. Then also the manual processes would diminish as would the potential for mistakes.

During the last 20 years, the principle of detailed visibility in the logistic chain has been successfully applied in numerous industrial companies. Similarly like manufacturing companies also LSPs have to plan the use of their capacity, for example, to allocate enough employees or transportation capacity for each day. According to the case study conducted in Finland, there is evidence that the information sharing in supply chains could be improved. The influences of better collaboration and more effective information transfer could be further studied by case studies. Perhaps the starting level of information sharing at some chain could be first evaluated. Then the processes in the chain could be studied closely and the information distributed could be increased or intensified other ways. At the end, the effectiveness of the starting level and the end level could be compared.

The greatest challenge concerning the logistics information is the culture of information sharing in the company. This could be avoided by close, reliable relationships and by highlighting the benefits of information sharing (Hoyt & Huq 2000).

CONCLUSION

Companies within a supply chain need information about forecasts, changes, the estimated time when the cargo is arriving, location and condition of the items. Forecasts are the base of all planning and decision-making. Forecasts are composed of assumptions so they can prove to be wrong and they can be affected by such things that cannot be foreseen (Lysons & Farrington 2006).

The case study presented in chapter 4.2 revealed the lack of information sharing. ETA is very important for logistics service providers, offering the information about when the transported items arrive in their destination. The study points out that information concerning ETA is quite well shared. Information about the changes in plans is essential for the capacity planning of companies. Many of the companies in this case study did not receive enough information of changes and this information element turned out to be the most desired data for the companies. The information regarding the location of the transported items is also important for the companies in a supply chain. Real-time information about the location makes it possible to optimize the transportations, especially when new transport tasks occur. Additionally, the information about the condition of the transported items is needed when there are changes in plans. Forecasts were also seen as important although many of the companies did say they were satisfied with the amount of information today. Finally, almost all of the companies wished that they would receive the information earlier than they do today.

Logistics service providers co-operate with many branches of industry, which fundamentally limits their possibility to focus on certain ICT standards. It is probable that LSPs need to cope with several standards also in the future, which increases their operational complexity (Kekäläinen 2006). Based on statistics, EDI was used by only 13 per cent of all companies in Finland in 2006 (Statistics Finland, 2008). An interesting observation is that the use increases steadily according to the size of the company in terms of employed personnel. Companies employing over 100 professionals use EDI in almost 50% of their operations. Furthermore, statistics show that the transport sector is on the lower end of the industry branch if technology adoption figures are concerned (Statistics Finland 2008). Interestingly, the EDI adoption level in the transport sector is lower than national average even though transport operations require a considerable amount of documentation and information transfer.

The main conclusion of this chapter is that logistics service providers need more information in order to manage their operations more efficiently. Practically every company that was presented in the case study lacks information it would need. By adding just the amount of information shared, is not enough. The information shared should also be truly beneficial; unnecessary information may slow down the operations in the supply chain. Also information accuracy and timeliness are important attributes for information that is shared in supply chain.

REFERENCES

Airos, E., Korhonen, R., & Pulkkinen, T. (2007). *Satelliittipaikannusjärjestelmät (Satellite navigation systems)*. The Finnish Defence Forces. Riihimäki. Retrieved June 5, 2009 from http://www.mil.fi/laitokset/pvtt/satelliittipaikannus.pdf

Choy, K. L., So, S. C. K., Lau, H. C. W., Kwok, S. K., & Chan, F. T. S. (2006). Development of an integrated logistics information system for third party logistics facilitators. *International Journal of Business Performance Management*, 8(2/3), 170–193. doi:10.1504/IJBPM.2006.009035

Christopher, M. (1992). Logistics and supply chain management: Strategies for reducing costs and improving services. London: Pitman Publishing

Fabbe-Costes, N., & Jahre, M. (2008). Supply chain integration and performance: a review of the evidence. *The International Journal of Logistics Management*, 19(2), 130–154. doi:10.1108/09574090810895933

Främling, K. (2002). *Tavaravirran seuranta osana Internet-pohjaista tuotetiedon hallintaa. (Tracking of deliveries as a part of Internet based product data management).* Retrieved April 15, 2009 from http://dialog.hut.fi/publications/ TiekeArtikkeli.pdf

Gopal, C., & Cypress, H. (1993). Integrated Distribution Management: Competing on customer service, time and cost. The Business One Irwin.

Helo, P., & Szekely, B. (2005). Logistics information systems – An analysis of software solutions for supply chain co-ordination. *Industrial Management & Data Systems, 105*(1), 5–18. doi:10.1108/02635570510575153

Hoyt, J., & Huq, F. (2000). From arms-length to collaborative relationships in the supply chain: an evolutionary process. *International Journal of Physical Distribution & Logistics Management, 30*(9), 750–764. doi:10.1108/09600030010351453

Kalakota, R., & Robinson, M. (2000). E-Business 2.0 Roadmap for Success. Reading, MA: Addison-Wesley.

Kauniskangas, M. (2007). *Asiakkaasta partneri (From customer to partner).* Logistiikka – The magazine of Finnish Association of Purchasing and Logistics, Iss. 5.

Kauremaa, J., & Auramo, J. (2004). Logistiikan sähköisten tieto- ja viestintäteknologioiden hyödyntäminen – Kokemuksia suomalaisista yrityksistä (Utilization of electronic information and communication technologies in logistics – Experiences from Finnish companies). Technology Review 154/2004. Tekes.

Kekäläinen, H. (2006). Logistics technology roadmap for e-business. Technology Review 189/2006. Tekes.

Laaksonen, P., Nelimarkka, P., & Nyman, M. (2004). *Logistiikan tulevaisuus Itämeren alueella. Yhteenveto asiantuntijoiden kirjoituksista ja keskustelutilaisuudesta 16.8.2004 (The future of logistics in the Baltic Sea area. The summary of the articles and discussion by experts Aug 16, 2004).* Retrieved May 4, 2009, from http://www. tedim.com/default.asp?file=819

Li, G., Yang, H., Sun, L., & Sohal, A. S. (2009). The impact of IT implementation on supply chain integration and performance. *International Journal of Production Economics, 120*(1), 125–138. doi:10.1016/j.ijpe.2008.07.017

Logistiikka (2001). Paikannuksen merkitys tavaraliikenteessä (The meaning of positioning in cargo transport). *Logistiikka – The Magazine of Finnish Association of Purchasing and Logistic, 6,* 36–38.

Lysons, K., & Farrington, B. (2006). Purchasing and supply chain management. Pearson Education Limited.

Mäkinen, T., Mäntynen, J., & Vanhatalo, J. (2005). *Logistiikka ja kuljetusjärjestelmät (Logistics and transport systems* (Tech Report 38.) The Tampere University of Technology, Faculty for transport technologies.

Nevalainen, E. (2006). *Kuljetusriskien hallinta (Management of transportation risks).* Pohjola Insurance Ltd. Retrieved January 7, 2009 from http://www.finva.fi/eoppiminen/materiaalit/Materiaali2006/Nevalainen_luento_2006.pdf

Pohto, P., Sihvola, I., & Kallio, J. (2005). Logistiikan sähköisten tieto- ja viestintäteknologioiden hyödyntäminen – Kokemuksia Euroopasta (Utilization of electronic information and communication technologies in logistics – Experiences from Europe). Technology review 173/2005. Tekes.

Pulli, H., Kajander, S., & Tapaninen, U. (2007). Satamasidonnaisten yritysten tietotarpeet. (Information needs of port related companies). Research report of University of Turku, Centre of Maritime Studies, B:149, Turku

Punakivi, M., Aminoff, A., Auramo, J., Pajunen-Muhonen, H., Lehtinen, J., & Yrjölä, H. (2001). *Karkelo – Kartoitus elektronisen liiketoiminnan logistiikasta (Survey of the logistics of electronic business)*. Retrieved February 3, 2009, from http://www.tuta.hut.fi/logistics/publications/Karkelo.pdf

Ratliff, H. D., & Nulty, W. G. (1997). Logistics composite modelling, In The planning and scheduling of production systems–Edited by Artiba, A. & Elmaghraby, S.E. Chapman & Hall (eds.), Methodologies and applications.

Reinikainen, P., Mäntynen, J., & Rantala, J. (1997). *Logistiikan perusteet (The basics of logistics)*. Tampere, Finland: Tampere University of Technology, The Faculty for Transport Technologies. *RE:view*, 27.

Rytsy, A. (2007). *RFID veti väkeä Logistics 2007 -tapahtumassa (RFID raised interest in Logistics 2007 event)*. Logistiikka – The Magazine of Finnish Association of Purchasing and Logistics, *5*, 38–39.

Salmela, E., Nieminen, L., & Lukka, A. (2006). *Prosessien kehitys ja ICT:n hyödyntäminen hankintatoiminnassa, logistiikassa ja toimitus-ja kysyntäketjun hallinnassa (Development of processes and utilization of ICT in purchasing, logistics and supply chain management.)*. Retrieved February 17, 2009, from http://partnet.vtt.fi/serviisi/tiedostot/serviisi_loppuraportti.pdf

Salmela, H., & Jahnukainen, M. (2003). IT enabled global customer service: findings and conclusions from six case studies, In Reponen, T, (ed.), Information Technology-Enabled Global Customer Service. Hershey, PA:Idea Group Publishing.

Siltala, T. (2007). *RFID ei vielä tartu (RFID does not spread yet)*. Retrieved December 20, 2009, from http://www.tietoviikko.fi/taustat/kaikki_jutut/article136836.ece

Singh, J. (1996). The importance of information flow within the supply chain. *Logistics Information Management*, *9*(4), 28–30. doi:10.1108/09576059610123132

Spekman, R. E., Kamauff, J. W., & Myhr, N. (1998). An empirical investigation into supply chain management: a perspective on partnership. *International Journal of Physical Distribution & Logistics Management*, *28*(8), 630–650. doi:10.1108/09600039810247542

Statistics Finland. (2008). Use of information technology in enterprises 2008. Statistics Finland, Helsinki.

Talvela, J. (2006). Lyhyen kantaman langattomat tekniikat (Short range wireless techniques). Kotka, Finland: Kymenlaakso University of Applied Sciences. (Research Article 2007).

WEF. (2008). *The Global Competitiveness Report 2008–2009*. London: Palgrave Macmillan.

Zhang, Z., Cheng, T., & Yan, B. (2006). A Portal of Logistics Service Provider to Integrate Supply Chain. In *Proceedings of the 2006 IEEE Asia-Pacific conference on Services Computing (APSCC'06)*.

Chapter 7
IT Audit for Information Logistics

Malgorzata Pankowska
University of Economics, Katowice, Poland

ABSTRACT

The main goal of the chapter is to consider how information logistics in business organization is supported by standards and best practices of auditing. The first part of the chapter covers the discussion of what information logistics is and how it is developed within and supported by business organizations. The second part comprises considerations on Information Systems Audit and Control Association (ISACA) information technology audit standards and practices that support information logistics development and realization. Particularly, CobiT, ITIL, ISO/IEC 27002, Val IT as well as the Sarbanes-Oxley Act and ITAF model are analyzed in the aspect of information logistics. The third, and last part covers presentation of information logistics development in data warehousing and data warehouse management and auditing problems.

INTRODUCTION

Control and audit of information systems are becoming increasingly important due to the competitive impact of information technology (IT). In fact, information systems are critical for the general functioning of our society and information is confirmed as the business organization's most valuable

asset. Another important aspect to be taken into account is the amount of IT resources expended by business organization departments. Business units have difficulties with appropriate management of information. Nowadays they do not lack it, but quite opposite, the information overload seems to create the challenge of information logistics. Therefore, it is assumed to support the information governance and organizational decision making.

DOI: 10.4018/978-1-61520-603-2.ch007

BACKGROUND - INFORMATION LOGISTICS

Logistics

Logistics encompasses the integral control of material flow and the integration of all decision making concerning the flow of materials. The goal is to optimize the behavior of the total systems instead of optimizing parts of the system logistics (Gerrits, 1995). Logistics is concerned with the organization, movement and storage of materials and people. The term logistics was first used by the military to describe the activities associated with maintaining and fighting force in the field and describing the housing of troops (Ghiani et al., 2004). Over the years the meaning of the term was gradually generalized to cover business and service activities. A fundamental characteristic of logistics is its holistic integrated view of all the activities that is encompasses. Logistics mission is to get the right materials to the right place at the right time, while optimizing a given performance measure (e.g. minimizing total operating costs) and satisfying a given set of constraints (e.g. a budget constraint). In this context, the information logistics must concern information provision to the appropriate recipients at the right time. Information must be actual, complete, readable, protected and verifiable. The key issue is to decide how and when raw data, semi-processed data and information should be acquired, moved and stored.

Logistics is responsible for the flow of materials through a supply chain. It is the time-related positioning of resources there. The supply chain is a sequence of events intended to satisfy a customer. The information logistics managers feel to be responsible for the achievement of two goals. The first is to move information through and out of the organization as efficiently as possible. The second aim is to contribute to an efficient flow through the whole supply chain. There are several measures of efficiency, including fast deliveries, low costs, little wastage, quick response, high productivity, low stocks, no damage, few mistakes, high staff morale, and protection of integrity of information, applications and IT infrastructure. They are all indicators rather than the real aims, because the real aim is the satisfaction of the information consumer i.e. end user.

Information supply chain is a complex logistics system, in which raw materials (i.e. data) are converted into information products (e.g. decisions) and then distributed to the final users (Waters, 2003, Sadler, 2007). It includes data supplies from different sources, data centers, data warehouses and decision support systems. In the information processing systems, data is cleaned and ordered to be put into the data marts and data warehouses. The distribution system consists of the data distribution centers and final terminals for end users. The core logistics issues are the design and operations of data centers and transferring points.

Traditionally, in products' logistics products flow through the supply chain from raw material sources to customers, information follows a reverse path. It traverses the supply chain backward from customer to raw material suppliers. However, not always it is true. Rather, it is noticed, that production and information flows cannot move instantaneously and be transferred simultaneously through the channels. First, freight transportation between raw material sources, production plants and consumption sites is usually time consuming. Second, manufacturing can take a long time, not only because of processing itself, but also because of the limited plant capacity. Finally, information can flow slowly because order collection, transmission and processing take time. Although people would like to have the processing of information and products simultaneously done, in practice there is a certain dispersion among these activities, lack of synchronization of them, weaknesses in scheduling, but because of the development of virtual organizations there is a strong pressure to implement asynchronic processing of information and material goods. Therefore, information production and transfer is aimed to be realized independently from goods' generating and assembling. As it is in the classical science of management, an information supply chain is said to be vertically integrated if its components (i.e. information sources, databases and information systems) belong to a single firm. Nowadays, more frequently, the supply chain is operated by several autonomous, but interdependent companies. There, interdependent information producers receive information from different sources, process information at different data centers and eventually receive or subscribe at the data warehouses to assemble it in the reports or to generate decisions. Cross-organizational logistical management systems are supported by implemented workflow system. Masters suggests that a primary issue to a workflow management system is resource allocation. The whole concept of users and roles exists to map people to the operations that they are capable of performing to advance a business objective. The Workflow's Management Coalition's glossary defines workflow as "the automation of a business process, in whole or part, during which documents, information of tasks are passed from one participant to another for action, according to a set of procedural rules". From a workflow perspective, a participant can be a human, an application, a machine or another process or workflow engine.

The workflow process is traditionally defined in office terms – moving the paper, processing the order, issuing the invoice. But the same principles and tools apply to filling the order from the warehouse, assembling documents, parts, tools and people. Workflow management software is a proactive computer system, which manages the flow of work among participants, according to a defined procedure, consisting of a number of tasks. It coordinates users and system participants together with the appropriate data resources, which may be accessible directly by the system or offline, to achieve defined objectives by set deadlines (Jablonski & Bussler, 1998). The co-ordination involves passing tasks from participant to participant in a correct sequence, ensuring that all fulfill their required contributions, taking default actions when necessary. A workflow management system is an active system that manages the flow of business processes performed by multiple persons. It gets the right data to the right people with the right tools at the right time. The description of selected workflow systems according the following scheme covers:

- modeling elements (e.g. workflow, roles, applications, data), they determine the expressiveness of a workflow management system,
- tools, languages and application programming interfaces (APIs). Workflow modelers as well as workflow management system users have to interact with a system through user interfaces,
- system architecture and implementation. Workflow types are instantiated during run time by workflow management system (more specifically by so-called workflow engines) in order to execute business processes. Issues like distribution, scalability and reliability of computer systems are discussed here as well as openness and interoperability of business processes,
- application area specifics. In this part of the description, the functionality for specific application semantics is reported (Jablonski & Bussler, 1998).

Summarizing, the workflow process benefits are following:

- simplification of business processes and making information processing operations simpler and less bureaucratic,
- integration – cross-functional and interorganizational information flow, interoperability ensurance,
- standardization – using standard procedures, information formats, semantics, interoperability implementation,

- concurrency of operations – moving away from serial operations of information processing towards parallel working,
- variance control – ensuring high quality and avoiding waste information garbages,
- automation – to improve effectiveness and efficiency,
- resource planning – to remove bottlenecks in information channels and to ensure a smooth flow of information.

The capacity of workflow process sets the maximum volume of information products that can be delivered to the final consumer in a given time.

Information as an Asset

Information as a valuable resource in economical system is included under the following processes; creation, registration, storing and delivering to recipients in time in appropriate forms under reasonable costs. The types of assets that ISO/IEC 17799 identifies as needing to be inventoried include:

- information assets: databases and data files, other files and copies of plans, system documentation, original user manuals, original training material, operational or other support procedures, continuity plans and other fall-back arrangements, archived information, financial and accounting information,
- software assets: application software, system software, development tools and utilities, e-learning assets, network tools and utilities,
- physical assets: computer equipment (including workstations, notebooks, PDAs, monitors, modems, scanning machines, printers), communications equipment (routers, cell phones, fax machines, voice conferencing units), magnetic media, other technical equipment (power supplies, air-conditioning units), furniture, lighting, other equipment,

- services: groups of assets which act together to provide a particular function such as computing and communications services, general utilities, e.g. heating, lighting, power, air-conditioning,
- people: their qualifications, skills and experience – the knowledge and skill capital of the organization. This is a particularly complex process for which external consultancy help might be sought,
- intangible assets such as reputation and brand (Calder & Watkins, 2006).

As ISO/IEC 17799 points out that, the procedures need to cover all formats of information assets, both physical and electronic. There should be procedures for the following types of information processing activities:

- acquisition of information,
- copying (electronically, by hand and through reading and memorizing),
- storage, both electronic and in hard copy,
- transmission by fax, post, e-mail,
- transmission by spoken word, including mobile phone, voicemail and answering machines,
- chain of custody and logging of security events, particularly important when dealing with computer-related crime,
- destruction, when no longer required (Calder & Watkins, 2006).

The term information is a static stock concept. It suggests inventories of different kinds of knowledge as valuable assets. The term communication is a dynamic flow; it is associated with flow of messages and exchanges of information, knowledge and values. The value of information cannot be a priori estimated, however, there are certain characteristics of information that must be present if the information is to be useful. In the model of recipient and provider of information:

- from the point of view of the provider: the information is flowing to the intended recipient and the confidentiality, integrity and availability of the information have not been compromised, the information provider is interested in ensuring the generation, validation and propagation of information,
- from the point of view of the recipient: the information has not been compromised and the source of information should be validated and known as reliable, the information should be selected, integrated and acquired.

In information production, particularly, when the effect of production is a decision, the main capacity bottlenecks are the employees. Employees play a different role in information production than in material production. They are both on the capacity oriented side as well as on the material oriented side. Flow of information is included in the implemented business process. The material product life cycle consists of the following stages: engineering, fabrication, assembling, delivery, installation and maintaining. Information system life cycle covers conceptualization, analysis and design, implementation and evaluation as a base for further reconstruction. According to Singleton (2009) information life cycle management includes more than data, it comprises compliance, information security, tools, business continuity, disaster recovery, appropriate policies and procedures. To effectively manage information, all of it must be identified, relevantly collected, properly classified and effectively controlled (Singleton, 2009).

Information production processes are particularly well developed for bureaucratic, administrative decision making. Administrative decision process covers information intake, data gathering, judgment for completeness, processing and informing about the decision, and edition of a paper document. The analysis allows distinguishing five types of processes in information production concerning their flow time characteristics:

- information order processing, where the customer asks the information producer to deliver a certain product (the flow time performance is measured as the interval between the moment the customer expressed demand and the moment the product is delivered),
- reporting process based on data that the organization has gathered, either from the customer or other sources,
- customer's reaction process to the reporting process,
- collecting process, in which data is gathered to be used in order to report processes,
- dissemination process, in which gathered information is distributed to known and anonymous recipients, authorized or for free.

Information production processes are initiated by customers i.e. information consumers. Economic situation causes a certain demand for the particular information; people are able to collect more and more information and to pay more for it. Government legislation concerning a certain financial information product will influence the changes in this demand as well as promotion actions and information product adevertising websites. The information product demand can be controlled by the business organization itself. For example, the controlled demand is formulated among the reporting processes and reaction processes, so the capacity management should be aware of the relationship and plan the shipment of reports in such a way that demand is flattened. However, actions undertaken by any certain departments may increase the demand. Generally, the information demand side is driven by access to advanced infrastructure, ability to consume i.e. utilize the information for the decision making, competitive pricing, content driven by user requirements, convenience of IT usage, culture to accept IT in information economy (Turner, 2000). According to Turner, the information supply side is driven by strong existing supply base, having strong telecommunications, access to capital to create and meet new demands and skills of information economy professionals as well as IT people (2000). Information logistics forces the general managers to understand how information enables their company to achieve superior performance today and compete in existing or new markets in the future. Information within the company is utilized to manage the business and financial risks, reduce the costs of business processes, add the value to products and service, profile customer behavior, create new business opportunities covering innovations and product inventions (Marchand, 2000).

Information Logistics

Information logistics, as a section of information management, deals with the flow of information within an organizational unit or between any number of organizations that, in turn, form a value creating network. Information logistics is business- and process-driven, focused on the creation, acquisition, procurement, delivering and storing, further processing and dissemination of information. The primary goal is the optimization of the availability and cycle time of information. In other words, information logistics is about providing the correct information, at the accurate point of time, in the correct format and quality, for the intended recipient at the right location . Methods for achieving the goal include the analysis of the information demand, the optimization of the flow of information, securing technical and organizational flexibility. The set of activities on information resources (to ensure effectiveness, efficiency, and successfulness) should be rationally integrated. The integration of flows of information in systems is a logistical activities domain. It is to rationalize the provisioning the information

in enterprise, so the utilization of concepts, tools and techniques for coordination of the flow of resources can be utilized. The analysis of functioning information for information provision for companies through the aspect of client service allows to formulate some basic assumptions:

- contemporary, integrated information systems, constructed on the basis of a wide system of analytical and synthetical accounts do not ensure objective provision of information in the enterprise for managerial purposes,
- system approach to redefining quantitative and qualitative scope of information from the point of view of supply as well as demand is necessary,
- contemporary information systems should eliminate in enterprise the organizational structures of which basic function is to consolidate the date from lower levels and their transmission to a selected point in organizational hierarchy. These functions should be realized by computer systems, reengineering the business processes, and decentralization of management system,
- management information systems should allow the enabling of application of controlling and audit systems.

In materials' logistics, flows of information are analyzed, but as supplementary to basic flows of materials. In information logistics, the basic concept is the flow of information which is not it necessarily accompanied by flow of materials, rather flow in itself is for the special purpose of making decisions on time, for the right person in the language known by him. Agility in information logistics means the ability to deliver actual information successfully in a short time. Generally, agility is the successful exploration of competitive bases (speed, flexibility, innovation proactivity, quality and profitability) through the integration of reconfigurable resources and best practices in a knowledge-rich environment to provide customer-driven products and services in a fast changing market environment (Schelp & Winter, 2007). Agility requires the ability of not only detecting, but also quickly responding to changes in conditions that require the formulation of alternative objectives. Agility is an ability to detect opportunities for innovation and seize the competitive market opportunities by assembling required assets, knowledge and relationships with speed and surprise. Therefore, an agile information system is the necessary enabler of organizational agility. Agile information system is to enable the firm to identify needed changes in the information processing (Lui & Piccoli, 2007). Information logistics agility is the ability to cost-effectively receive and deliver information products although sources of supply and recipients change (recipient location change, globalization, postponement). Goals of information logistics are as follows:

- agility and adaptability of business processes and systems based on reusable patterns of information, alignment of business processes and information systems, fast development of computer systems to support new information products and distribution channels, acceleration of the processes and business integration,
- information integration and coordination across supply chains, enterprises and databases,
- acceleration of information requirements and process models based on the prefabricated reusable patterns,
- creation of automated tools for aligning of information systems with business facilitation of the development of an integrated Computer Aided Process Engineering (CAPE) and Computer Aided Software Engineering (CASE) tools.

IT AUDIT FOR INFORMATION LOGISTICS

Information Systems Audit and Control Association as well as Information Technology Governance Institute develop methods and standards that could support information logistics. IT Governance Institute focus area covers:

- strategic alignment that focuses on ensuring the linkage of business and IT plans: defining, maintaining and validating the IT value proposition, and aligning IT operations with enterprise operations,
- value delivery, which is also executing the value proposition throughout the delivery cycle, ensuring that IT delivers the promised benefits against the strategy, concentrating on optimizing costs and proving the intrinsic value of IT.
- resource management that is about the optimal investments and the proper management of critical IT resources, applications, information, infrastructure and people,
- risk management requires risk awareness by senior corporate officers, a clear understanding of the enterprise's appetite for risk, understanding of compliance requirements, transparency about the significant risk to the enterprise and embedding of risk management responsibilities into the organization,
- performance measurement that tracks and monitors strategy implementation, project completion, resource usage, process performance and service delivery, using for example balanced scorecards that translate strategy into action to achieve goals measurable beyond conventional accounting. Processes should be in place to track and monitor strategy implementation,

project completions, resource usage, process performance and service delivery. IT governance mechanisms should translate implementation strategies into actions and measurements to achieve these goals (Moeller, 2008).

In the document "IT Control Objectives for Sarbanes-Oxley" the IT Governance Institute discusses the IT control objectives that might be considered by business organizations. International standards and good practices such as ISO 17799, ITIL, the Sarbanes-Oxley Act play a vital role in ensuring the appropriate governance.

Sarbanes-Oxley Act

The Sarbanes-Oxley Act (SOX) is a large complex piece of legislation covering many areas. Section 404 of SOX covering reviews of internal accounting controls has received perhaps the most attention and compliance activity. Section 404 covers processes where an enterprise is responsible for reviewing, documenting and testing its own internal accounting controls. Section 404 Compliance Review Work Breakdown Structure includes purchase order management, inventory management, warehouse management, demand planning, order processing, shipping and receiving, logistics management, billing and invoicing, accounting systems, information systems, human resources, and internal audit (Moeller, 2008). According to SOX information access management covers information filtering, timely submission of information, formal and informal information channels, information framework development and regular briefing sessions realization. Managers to operate effectively must have access to accurate and timely information to support proper analysis and decision making. In order to achieve it, it is necessary to ensure existence of an effective information framework throughout the organization. Top managers should take responsibility for ensuring that they have the right amount of information. Information will arrive

through formal and informal channels and they need to be structured and organized so that the management knows exactly what information is to be provided. Information will arrive through formal channels including formal meetings, management reports, financial reports, proposals, management information systems, regular briefings, structured presentations and board meeting paper and other documents. Information will arrive through informal channel including telephone, emails, informal discussions, informal meetings with management, information gathering. In SOX it is important to set up a structured process for handling information throughout the organization and ensuring that information that needs to be communicated to the board members is provided in an effective manner.

ITIL

Information Technology Infrastructue Library (ITIL) is a detailed framework or description of a number of significant IT practices, with comprehensive checklists, tasks, procedures and responsibilities that are designed to be tailored to any IT organization (Moeller, 2008). The use of ITIL best practices should help an enterprise to better manage and operate all aspects of its IT resources and ensure stronger SOX internal control compliance. ITIL best practices are based on the widely recognized concept that information is the most important strategic resource that any enterprise must manage (Aligning…, 2008). The quality of an enterprise's IT systems and services is the key to the collection, analysis, production and distribution of the information on the operational and strategic level. ITIL supports those activities. ITIL elements concern:

- planning and delivery of high quality IT services,
- service support and maintenance,
- IT infrastructure management including the testing, installation and deployment of IT components and services,

- service management implementation planning and strategy development
- IT application management,
- Business perspective for support of IT people,
- Security management.

ITIL is oriented towards IT deployment, therefore the information management and information logistics are treated as secondary problems.

ITAF

The Information Technology Assurance Framework (ITAF) is a comprehensive and good-practice-setting model that:

- provides guidance on the design, conduct and reporting of IT audit and assurance assignments,
- defines terms and concepts specific to IT assurance,
- establishes standards that address IT audit and assurance, professional roles and responsibilities, knowledge and skills, diligence, conduct and reporting requirements (ITAF.., 2008).

ITAF sections mostly concern IT assurance, however Section 3425 IT Information Strategy concludes that organizations require a strategy under which information they collect, use, disclose and share can be efficiently managed. The role has traditionally fallen to the IT department, but the role should include all information with which the organization deals. The Section 3427 IT Information Management provides guidance on the management of information entrusted to the IT department. It addresses the issues concerning the integrity of information, provision of access and ownership. Custodianship, retention, archiving and destruction are the main important problems, also from the information logistics point of view. Anyway, it is a certain weakness of the model that

ITAF focuses on IT department information, and not on the total enterprise volume. According to Section 3427, information management includes the classification of information so that appropriate level of security, access etc. can be developed and managed. The ITAF Section 3450 IT Processes ensures discussions on the various operational activities, in which the IT organization is involved. It provides the reader with an introduction to the organization of an IT department and based on its size, indicates the activities and the separation of duties and responsibilities issues.

Val IT

Val IT focuses on the investment decision (are we doing the right things?) and the realization of benefits (are we getting the benefits?), while CobiT focuses on the execution (are we doing them the right way, and are we getting them done well?) (Enterprise…, 2008). Val IT supports the leadership by providing a comprehensive framework, with a full complement of supporting processes and other guidance materials, developed to assist the board and executive management in understanding and carrying out their roles related to IT-enabled business investments. In Val IT model the strategic question demands the managers' answer if the investment is in line with the business vision, consistent with business principles, contributing to strategic objectives and providing optimal value, at affordable cost and at an acceptable level of risk. The architecture question requires answer if the investment is in line with enterprise architecture, consistent with architectural principles, and in line with other initiatives. The value question concerns an answer if the managers have a clear and shared understanding of the expected benefits, a clear accountability for realizing the benefits, relevant metrics, and an effective benefits realization process. For the delivery question, the managers are asked to provide answer is they have an effective and disciplined people, delivery and change management process, competent and available technical and business resources to deliver the required capabilities.

Val IT model IT–enabled investments are managed as a portfolio of investments. They are considered as a certain scope of activities that are required to achieve business value, therefore value delivery practices are assumed to be evaluated and managed as different categories of investments. Value delivery practices are required to engage all stakeholders and assign appropriate accountability and measurement for the delivery of capabilities and the realization of business benefits. The goal of value governance in Val IT model is to optimize the value of an organization's IT-enabled investments by establishing the governance, monitoring and control framework, by providing strategic direction for the investments and by defining the investment portfolio characteristics. In Val IT model, the value is perceived as a result of IT investments. Proponents of this approach focus on IT implementation and they do not see business information as a source of value as well as they do not consider information management and information logistics for value creation. This weakness of such an approach can cause the IT investment to be perceived as a goal in itself.

CobiT

CobiT is a globally accepted framework for IT governance based on industry standards and best practices. Once implemented, it is aligned effectively with business goals and better directs of the use of IT for business advantage (Cascarino, 2007). CobiT provides a common language for business executives to communicate goals, objectives and results with audit, IT and other professionals. CobiT model assumes that the enterprise strategy should be translated by business into objectives related to IT-enabled initiatives (the business goals of IT). These objectives should lead to a clear definition of IT objectives, which in turn define the IT resources and capabilities as well as the enterprise architecture for IT. Once the aligned

have been defined, they need to be monitored to ensure that actual delivery matches expectations (CobiT ..., 2007). Within the CobiT framework the responsibility domains of plan, build, run and monitor are specified. So, the business people are responsible for properly defining functional and control requirements and using automated services, and IT people are responsible for automating and implementing business functional and control requirements and establishing controls over the integrity of computer software applications. The strong point of CobiT model is the including of the enterprise strategy development and the business requirements which require information services that imply the information criteria and influence the governance requirements.

ISO/IEC 27002

The guiding principles in ISO/IEC 27002: 2005 are the initial point for implementing information security. They rely on either legal requirements or generally accepted best practices. The international standard was published by ISO (www.iso.org/iso/home.htm) and the IEC, which established a joint technical committee, ISO/IEC JTC 1. The historic source for the standard was BS 7799-1, of which essential parts were taken in the development of ISO/IEC 17799:2005 Information Technology – Code of Practice for Information Security Management. It was developed and published by the British Standards Institution (BSI), labeled as BS 7799:1: 1999. The goal of ISO/IEC 27002-2005 is to provide information to parties responsible for implementing information security within an organization. It can be seen as a best practice for developing and maintaining security standards and management practices within an organization to improve reliability on information security in interorganizational relationships. Measures included in ISO/IEC 27002 comprise protection and non-disclosure of personal data, protection of internal information and intellectual property rights. Best practices mentioned in the standard include information security policy, assignment of responsibility for information security, problem escalation and business continuity management. Although the standard focuses on information security management, several critical success factors should be considered. First and the most important is that the security policy, its objectives and activities should reflect the business objectives and cultural aspects of the organization. Other factors are connected with the operational management for security assurance, therefore senior management engagement, risk management, marketing of security and users trainings, security control contracting and performance measurement are considered. The standard does not clearly specify the need of information logistics development for information assurance for business. The issues are only mentioned in the business objectives specification and business continuity management.

DATA WAREHOUSE AUDIT AND FURTHER RESEARCH OF INFO LOGISTICS

Data Warehouse

Large businesses often suffer from a common problem: data is stored everywhere, some in locations known only to a few selected users – and it is associated with many different types of applications and kept in a variety of formats. In some cases, information is locked away in legacy systems to be accessed only when the data processing department is willing to write special programs to extract it. Data may also be stored for use with transactional systems (e.g. billing, inventory, and order entry) and is not organized in a manner that is useful to the user. As a result, it is impossible to consolidate data across applications or to compare data between systems; no one has a reliable picture of the business as a whole. A data warehouse resolves these issues by delivering

improved information access and higher-quality decision support (Moeller, 2001).

Data warehouse assemble data from all over an organization – from legacy systems, desktop databases, spreadsheets, credit reports, sales calls and more. This collective data structure makes a larger amount of summarized data available to a wider group of users that would be possible with any of the underlying systems. It can be mined and queried in ways that are useful for decision making through a common, centralized database or through distributed databases and easy-to-use query software. The data warehouse is a combination of operational and historical data, repackaged to accommodate knowledge workers who want to report, analyze, or drill down without having to access operational files directly. Data warehouse has four major architectural components:

- data extraction and transformation facilities,
- data movement and triggering facilities
- database management systems
- decision-support and analysis tools (Figure 1).

Most of the effort in building a data warehouse evolves around data integration – making sure that the data has the quality and the structure necessary for inclusion in the data warehouse. Several steps are involved in this process: extracting data from the source systems, transforming data, matching and consolidating data, eliminating data redundancies, validating and cleansing data, loading the data structures, managing the metadata.

Architecture is a high-level description of the organization of functional responsibilities within a system. It is not a prescription that cures a specific problem or a road map for successful design. The goal of architecture is to convey information about the general structure of systems; it defines the relationships among system components. The architecture of every data warehouse consists of the fundamental components, which may comprise

Figure 1.Data Warehouse architecture

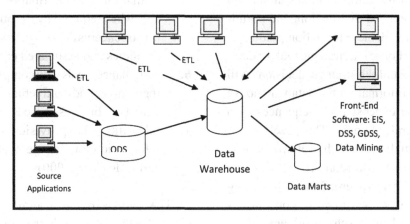

operational systems, source applications, dimensional data warehouses, ETL (Extract Transform Load) software, front-end software (Inmon, 2002, Inmon, 2005). Taking into account Michael Porter's value chain (1985), the operational systems are the inbound logistics systems and the sources applications that support the execution of a business process, recording business activity and serving as the system of records. Operational systems may be packaged or custom-built applications. Their databases may reside on a variety of platforms, including relational database systems, mainframe-based systems, or proprietary data stores. For some data, such as budgeting information, the system of record may be as simple as a user spreadsheet. The most important part of the value chain model of M.Porter is the operation. In data warehousing operation means transformation of entrance information and archiving temporarily in the Operational Data Store (ODS) or for a long time in the data warehouse. Sometimes data are transferred to the dimensional data warehouse, which is a database that supports the measurement of enterprise business processes. It stores a copy of operational data that has been organized for analytic purposes, according to the principles of dimensional modeling. Information is organized around a set of conformed dimensions, supporting enterprise-wide cross-process analysis. A subject area within the data warehouse is referred to as

a data mart. The dimensional data warehouse is usually implemented on a relational database management system.

Extract Transform Load (ETL) software is used to move data into data warehouse tables. This process involves fetching data from source system (extract), recognizing it as required by the star schema design (transform) and inserting it into warehouse tables (load). ETL may be accomplished using specialized, packaged software, or by writing custom code. The ETL process may rely on a number of additional utilities and databases for staging data, cleansing it, automating the process, and so forth.

Front-end software is utilized to support the outbound logistics of information. Front-end software means any tool that consumes information from the data warehouse, typically by issuing an SQL query to the data warehouse and presenting results in a number of different formats. Most architectures incorporate more than one front-end product. Common front-end tools include business intelligence software, enterprise reporting software, ad hoc query tools, data mining tools, decision support systems (DSS) and group decision support systems (GDSS) and basic SQL execution tools. These services may be provided by commercial off-the-shelf software packages or custom developed. Front-end software often ensures additional services, such as user- and group-based security administration, automation of report execution and distribution, and portal-based access to available information products.

The data warehouse is a strategic tool for decision making. Most of the strategic decisions will be based on the information the data warehouse delivers, and the expensive consequences of a failure are generally known. The development investment is usually very high. Data warehouse are high risk systems, with a contrasted failure rate reaching about 50% (Rodero, 2000). Regarding management, one of their main responsibilities is to safeguard all the assets of the enterprise, especially those which give more value to the organization, so at the data warehouse it is the same also. From the data warehouse users' point of view, there must be some guarantees about the filling of minimum quality requirements regarding supplied data. For this purpose, independent accreditation processes, which provide the guarantee, are needed. The definition of the control objectives will be approached from two different perspectives i.e. the life cycle for data warehouses and the framework or architecture of the data warehouse.

Data Warehouse Audit

The audit process is to control information that satisfies the business requirements. The goal is achieved through seven criteria:

1. effectiveness: the information has to be relevant and pertinent to the business process, as well as delivered in a timely, correct, consistent and usable manner,
2. efficiency: the provision of information through the optimal use of resources,
3. confidentiality: the protection of sensitive information from unauthorized disclosure,
4. integrity; relates to the accuracy and completeness of information, as well as to its validity in accordance with business expectations,

5. availability: the information has to be available when required by the business process, it also concerns the safeguarding of necessary resources and associated capabilities,
6. compliance: deals with complying with laws, regulations, and contractual arrangements to which the business process is subject,
7. reliability: the provision of appropriate information for management to operate the entity (Rodero, 2000).

The data warehouse audit process should start from the data warehouse construction point of view. So, it is necessary to consider project framework covering project proposal and approval, subprojects definition, architecture and infrastructure, subproject iterations, the ending the project. The feasibility study should be expressed so it is needed to state what functionality will be given to the data warehouse system, how much it will cost (time, personal resources, users' participation, hardware, software etc.), what benefits it will report. The decision on whether building the data warehouse both makes sense and is cost-justified, should be taken on the basis of the feasibility study.

From the information logistics point of view the phase of Extracting, Transforming and Loading Data is important. The objective of this phase is to move data from source systems to the warehouse, making all the transformations and calculations established in the data mapping stage. This phase includes:

*   developing extraction and load procedures,
*   developing programs or configuring tools to make the data transformation, as well as calculate aggregates,
*   automating and scheduling the processes of extraction, transformation and load according to the required frequency of actualization,

- setting the backup and recovery procedures and update the security plan consequently.

Problems of quality lack in data should be reported to those responsible for the legacy system from which they come. Specifications to transform data from the source systems to the warehouse should be documented, including the way, order and other conditions to execute each of them. When the warehouse is updated from several sources, the information should be previously synchronized in order to maintain the data coherence. Decomposing the data warehouse architecture results in three kinds of units:

- storage elements, intended to house system implementation
- data handling procedures, also known as handling services
- human factor, consisting of final users and technical staff involved in the project.

The data warehouse should take into account the diverse types of information available (text, images, fax, video, sounds) as well as information coming from external sources. Source data, both of internal and external origin, must be completely documented, including the data model on which they are based. If the models do not exist, they must be obtained, either manually or automatically, by means of specific reverse engineering tools. This will be necessary to carry out the data-mapping phase in the life-cycle.

The process of the data acquisition can be broken down into data source identification and data extraction. As soon as the location of necessary data has been identified, data must be read and unloaded, using for this purpose the systems that store them. If the destination for extracted information is a system different from the original, consideration can be made about compressing at the same time as extracting, in order to reduce

interchange with the destination system. Filtering consists of selecting, according to specific criteria, only a part of the information from the source system. Among the most usual criteria are temporal interval, geographic area etc. The process can be performed simultaneously with extraction. Cleaning processes are intended to eliminate inaccurate or inconsistent information by means of a number of checking and correcting operations.

The data exploration from the warehouse is seldom a direct copy of the data found in the data warehouse. Instead, the exploration warehouse starts with a subset of the data found in the data warehouse. The primary purpose for an exploration warehouse is the creation of assertions, hypotheses and observations. A data mining warehouse has the purpose of proving the strength of the truth of the hypotheses. The exploration warehouse is optimized on breadth while the data mining warehouse is optimized on depth. The purpose of an exploration warehouse is to provide a foundation for heavy statistical analysis. Once the exploration warehouse has been built, there will be no more contention problems with the data warehouse. Statistical analyses can be run all day long and there will be no contention issues because the processing that is occurring is happening on separate machines. The data warehouse can be compared to the huge factory of information, so as such it demands appropriate inbound and outbound logistics. Therefore, Information Technology and Information Systems auditors should focus on the development of methods and standards to ensure control over the processes of information acquisition, processing, storing and transferring. Particular attention is required for the entrance processes, on the selecting, filtering and cleaning the information, because otherwise the prophetic utterance Garbage-In-Garbage-Out (GIGO) will be fulfilled.

CONCLUSION

Generally, the information logistics approach is underdeveloped in comparison with material logistics and military logistics. Practitioners as well as academicians prefer the treatment of information and IT systems as media to enable successful (i.e. effective and efficient) development of logistics of material products. It is visible in the supply chain management methods and software tools. However, to deal with the information overload, because of the huge IT progress, the information logistics methods would be demanded, to teach information user careful analysis and relevant governance of available information.

Information Systems Audit and Controls Association (ISACA) standards are rather IT investment- and IT implementation-oriented. Concluding, according to ISACA and IT Governance Institute information is not the most important value in itself and information logistics approach is not developed for information assets management. At IT Governance Institute and ISACA the attention is focused on Information Technology implementation.

REFERENCES

Aligning CoBiT 4.1. (2008). *Aligning CoBiT 4.1., ITIL V3 and ISO/IEC 27002 for Business Benefit, A Management Briefing From ITGI and OGC*. Rolling Meadows, IL: IT Governance Institute. Retrieved March 8, 2009, from http://www.isaca.org

Calder, A., & Watkins, S. (2006). International IT Governance [London: Kogan Page.]. *An Executive Guide to ISO, 17799*(I), SO27001.

Cascarino, R. E. (2007). Auditor's Guide to Information Systems Auditing, Hoboken, NJ: J.Wiley & Sons.

Cobi, T. 4.1. Executive Summary Framework (2007) *ISACA*. Rolling Meadows, IL. Retrieved March from http://www.isaca.org

Enterprise Value. *Governance of IT Investments*. (2006). *Enterprise Value: Governance of IT Investments, The Val IT Framework*. Rolling Meadows, IL: IT Governance Institute. Retrieved March 8, 2009, from http://www.isaca.org

Gerrits, J. W. M. (1995). Towards Information Logistics, An Exploratory Study of Logistics in Information Production. Amsterdam, The Netherlands: Vrije University.

Ghiani, G., Laporte, G., & Musmanno, R. (2004) Introduction to Logistics Systems Planning and Control.Chichester: J.Wiley & Sons.

Inmon, W. H. (2002). Building the Data Warehouse. New York: Wiley Computer Publishing.

Inmon, W. H. (2005). Building the Data Warehouse. New York: Wiley Publishing.

ITAF. *A Professional Practices Framework for IT Assurance* (2008) *ISACA*, Rolling Meadows, IL, Retrieved March 8, 2009, from http://www.isaca.org

Jablonski, S., & Bussler, C. (1998). Workflow Management, Modeling Concepts, Architecture and Implementation. London: International Thompson Computer Press, ITP.

Lui, T.-W., & Piccoli, G. (2007). Degrees of Agility: Implications for Information Systems Design and Firm Strategy. In Desouza K.C. (Ed.) Agile Information Systems (pp.112-134), Amsterdam: Elsevier, Butterworth-Heinemann.

Marchand, D. (2000). Why information is the responsibility of every managers? In Marchand D. (Ed.) Competing with Information (pp. 3-17), Chichester, UK: John Wiley and Sons, Ltd.

Moeller, R. A. (2001) Distributed data warehousing using Web technology, how to build a more cost-effective and flexible warehouse, New York: Amacom.

Moeller, R. R. (2008) Sarbanes-Oxley Internal Controls, Effective Auditing with AS5, CobitT, and ITIL. Hoboken, NJ: J.Wiley & Sons.

Porter, M. E. (1985). Competitive Advantage. New York: Free Press.

Rodero, J. A., & Piattini, M. (2000). Auditing Data Warehouses. In Piattini M.(Ed.) Auditing Information Systems (pp.109-148), Hershey, PA: Idea Group Publishing.

Sadler, I. (2007). Logistics and Supply Chain Integration, Los Angeles: Sage Publications.

Schelp, J., & Winter, R. (2007) Integration Management for Heterogeneous Information Systems. In Desouza K. C. (Ed.) Agile Information Systems (pp.134-150), Amsterdam: Elsevier, Butterworth-Heinemann.

Singleton, T. W. (2009). What Every IT Auditor Should Know About IT audits and data. *ISACA Journal, 2*, 12–13.

Turner, C. (2000). The information e-conomy, Business strategies for competing in the digital age. London: Kogan Page.

Waters, D. (2003). *Logistics An Introduction to Supply Chain Management*. London: Palgrave Macmillan.

KEY TERMS AND DEFINITIONS

Information: The quality of a message from a sender to one or more receivers.

Audit: An evaluation of a person, organization, system, process, project or product. Audits are performed to ascertain the validity and reliability of information and activities within processes.

Logistics: The management of the flow of goods, information and other resources (e.g. finance, energy, people) between the point of origin and the point of consumption in order to meet the requirements of consumers.

Information Logistics: The management of the flow of information from the point of its creation to the destination i.e. to the information consumer. Information logistics is developed to ensure the right information at the right time to the right decision maker.

Standard: An established norm or requirement, practice recommended for application

Data: Pieces of information or description of facts usually collected as the result of experience, observation or experiment.

Data Warehouse: A repository of an organization's electronically stored data.

Chapter 8
Information and Communication Technology in Logistics as a Comparative Advantage

Roman Gumzej
University of Maribor, Slovenia

Martin Lipičnik
University of Maribor, Slovenia

ABSTRACT

In a time, when the economic crisis is filling the news, it may seem hard to even think about improvements in terms of research and development, since there are lacking funds even for the reproduction. However, the last economic revolution was born in a crisis. Therefore it is sensible to look at the current situation as an opportunity for the next economic revolution,. bringing the economy a new cycle of development. The potentials for growth with the globalization have been mainly exploited so far, bringing considerable negative consequences into our lives and our environment that have triggered anti-globalist and ecological movements around the world. Now it's time to think how to make things better and more humane. The main goal of this chapter is to lay the foundation for an advanced-research technological platform for logistics applications networks.

INTRODUCTION

In times of big economic growth the need for ecologically aware and logistically perfected production was small. Now economy is seeking savings on each step and the benefits of good logistics come to front – companies with good logistics were able to adapt to new circumstances more quickly and have been more successful in redesigning their production to suit the needs of the market. Hence, we see the future of a logistically well supported business in both ways – technologically and organizationally advanced and interoperable, to lower the costs of production and transport, and ecological, where companies would integrate the ecological criteria with their quality standards to provide for a healthy environment in the long run (Pfohl H.Chr., 2004).

DOI: 10.4018/978-1-61520-603-2.ch008

Improving the existing logistics support especially in production and transport has proven possible by integrating Information and Communication Technology (ICT) with a well developed infrastructure in the developed world (Ballou R.H., 2004). In other application areas appropriate partial solutions are also gaining importance. In developing regions of the world (e.g. China, northern Africa) the logistics infrastructure is being built intensively (Bartens S., 2008). Hence, we might say that the next economic "(r)evolution" is probably going to be a logistic one and will be founded on the use of modern ICT technology (Straubhaar T., 2008).

The European Union (EU), being a heterogeneous and strongly connected market, has invested largely into building transport nodes and connections for different kinds of transport. The time has come for improvements of the existing infrastructure and establishing/improving interfaces with the global world. Since the European economy is largely oriented at services and production – the import of raw materials and product components and export of products – the efficient use of its storage and transport infrastructures is of utmost importance. On the other side flexibility in production through the achieved higher levels in factory automation is gaining importance due to quick market changes and demand on lowering production expenses while maintaining the con-

stant high quality of products. In this chapter some of the guidelines for using the ICT technology as infrastructure in modern production and transport systems of the future are outlined.

The goal of this contribution is to encourage the systematic integration of modern ICT technology into contemporary logistics systems in production, transport and services. Due to great diversity of the application areas first the technologies and their impact on the quality of service in their application areas are explored and categorized to determine the critical factors, which must be observed for their successful integration. After that the layouts of future integrated solutions are defined for the application areas under observation. Finally, based on an example of good practice, a foundation for reference technology platforms for logistics applications that would enable systematic modular integration of ICT technology into modern businesses by application area is laid out.

ICT Technology as Infrastructure

In Figure 1 the schematic representation of the ICT infrastructure and its application areas are presented:

1. systems/devices with their services and data processing capabilities; here, on one side, a very broad spectrum of embedded computing

Figure 1. ICT components and applications (schematically)

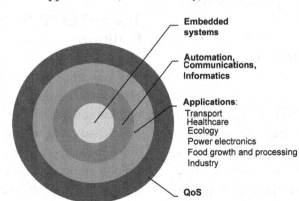

devices are being used, ranging from GSM transmitters and factory automation sensors and controllers to computing nodes for production control, and computing systems for enterprise resource planning on the other,

2. networks interconnecting computing systems/devices; here special emphasis is put on WANs (Wide Area Networks) and VANs (Virtual Area Networks), connecting heterogeneous networks among themselves,

3. applications of the mentioned infrastructure in diverse areas of everyday life. The most integral and diverse applications thereof are summed up with their logistics information systems for transportation, healthcare, power electronics, food processing and industrial production (e.g. automotive industry),

4. quality of service (QoS) is improved by the use of ICT technologies – among them especially dependability, availability and JIT (Just in Time, i.e. Real-Time operation) are being given top priorities.

Since logistics is present in all the listed applications (c.p. Figure 1) it is considered a complex system and may hence benefit from the use of ICT technology. Being the driver of the supply chain, it has some well defined limitations that are being upgraded by new services, partly being introduced by market changes and in part by the advanced use of the ICT technology that can help improve the quality of the production system, the products, and finally – quality of service (QoS) to the customer.

Strategic Goals of Logistics Management

According to (BMBF, 2007), main European strategic areas of logistics management improvement include transport, (waste) water management, power electronics, food growth/processing systems and industrial production systems. They represent the majority of EU economy and are

subject to long-term improvement processes through modern technology (BMVBS, 2009). In particular the individual areas and their supporting technologies are presented in the sequel.

The listed key ICT technologies provide solutions for improvements that are possible / necessary to improve the efficiency and QoS in the mentioned key fields of EU economy. Since they share several key technologies and affect the majority of the population as well, a unified solution is sought for improving the overall logistics of the EU economy. As an example, below a scientifically-founded approach to the assessment of the listed goals for embedded intelligence and systems is briefly presented – the ARTEMIS platform (Artemis, 2008). It is a public-private partnership led by the European industry with the goal to establish and implement a coherent and integrated European research and development strategy for Embedded Systems.

According to (ZVEI, 2007), the main goals to be achieved by the advanced use of the ICT technology for improved logistics support and QoS in logistics systems are the same as the desired properties of ARTEMIS reference architectures, namely their composability, networking & security, robustness, diagnostics & maintenance, integrated resource management, upgradeability and self-organization. Since computing systems found in logistics applications are predominantly embedded, the ARTEMIS guidelines are largely applicable to logistics systems.

The ARTEMIS Technological Platform

The concept of the ARTEMIS technological platform (see *Table 1*) is to combine the technology and science into a method for supporting the mentioned areas with state of the art ICT technological support. The goal of the platform is to support minimal effort engineering by creating a generic library of abstract components, which are being combined, based on common properties,

Table 1. ARTEMIS overview

Development methods and tools
o architecture-based design by composition,
o model-based approach,
o interoperability & integration,
o verification of all embedded systems' properties,
o certification,
o security planning,
o traceability,
o ARTEMIS meta-model for modeling embedded systems,
o system environment modeling.
Reference designs and architectures
o architectures research (generic architectures) supported by target application areas,
Communication
o on physical (network), logical (data) and semantic (information) levels.
Middleware
o support for reliable and safe self-organization of the system during operation in various working conditions.
Security
o security assurance on user, application as well as transaction levels.

with modules defined for specific applications. Containerization / modularization of production process are considered important factors of ensuring its manageability, flexibility and to provide for its optimization.

The scientific basis of the platform is composed of generic and advanced technologies as well as the rigorous foundation of the reference models, architectures, middleware and communication technology, joined in the *method*. The architectures are attributed the following properties: modularity, hard real-time, heterogeneity, compatibility, self-organization, adjustability, reliability and safety. The crucial design concepts supported by using them are "correct-by-construction" and "pre-validated components". The desired properties of the designs to be achieved by the properties of the architectures are: composability / interoperability, reliability / safety, performance & scalability, and

economical operation. Interoperability is achieved by open interface standards defining innovative interfaces among systems. Other design properties are achieved by the systematic use of development tools supported by verification & validation methods in simulation and testing tools, as well as traceability of system components throughout the production lines for embedded systems.

The approach to building the ARTEMIS (Advanced Research & Technology for EMbedded Intelligence and Systems) platform consists of:

1. collection of concrete requirements and constraints that were considered relevant from the point of view of different application domains,
2. classification of the collected requirements and constraints in order to find communalities and differences among the different application domains and to establish a limited number of categories of appropriate abstract requirements and constraints,
3. evaluation of the state of the art in meeting these requirements and constraints, and
4. identification of research priorities and their importance by time and relevance.

TRANSPORT

According to (ZVEI, 2007) guidelines on traffic improvement and (European Commission, 2006), one wants to ensure mobility on one hand and avoid traffic jams on the other. This can be achieved by the balanced use of traffic paths. ICT technology supports this feature by managing and providing up-to-date traffic information. This way traffic density can be predicted and jams avoided by e.g. regulating the speed of travel and diverting the travelers to less densely populated transport paths. In public transport ICT provides for higher quality of service by managing timetables and informing passengers about possible delays and connection possibilities. Herewith, also an assessment of energy consumption is possible.

Of course all these require building appropriate infrastructure for gathering traffic information and information dissemination. Since all these involve diverse sensors, actuators, proprietary computing devices as well as computing nodes of different kinds, complexities, and sizes, to achieve their interoperability, standardization is necessary.

In general one may say that the balanced use of traffic paths is best achieved by planning the transports and building itineraries for the most effective transport, considering cost, time and energy consumption. With the aid of the provided traffic information this goal can be achieved, provided planning is done on-time. Because of limited resources real-time constraints on transport play a big role in ensuring timely traffic.

In road-traffic the supporting ICT infrastructure comprises intelligent sensors and actuators for remote traffic monitoring and appropriate signalization for traffic-flow regulation. The information on traffic events and density, accumulated by the mentioned sensors, goes to traffic control centers as well as traffic information centers (e.g. government agencies, auto-clubs). In case of extraordinary situations (e.g. accidents, jams, etc.) traffic control centers may take immediate regulative actions by triggering activities through appropriate actuators. Simultaneously they can emit additional traffic-information messages that may inform the travelers about the event to traffic-monitoring agencies (e.g. auto-clubs). By running traffic-simulation/prediction models, they can undertake additional measures and inform travelers about possible bypass routes or reduced recommended speed of travel to avoid jams. The traffic-information messages are emitted through (digital) radio broadcast technology by the RDS (Radio Data System) (prEN 50067: 1997) and TMC Traffic Messaging Channels (ENV 12313: 1997). TMC information can be used by in-vehicle GPS (Global Positioning System) satellite navigation systems for (re-)calculating a (new) route based on the current position of the vehicle as well as the information of traffic events on the

foreseen track. For tracking purposes the GPS information on the current position is often used by transport companies to follow their vehicles. Usually, this tracking information is transmitted through the GPRS (General Packet Radio Service) data transmission protocol on the GSM (Global System for Mobile communications) network, since it is wireless and the transferred information does not require a broadband connection.

As opposed to road traffic, travel routes and traffic densities in the air and on water are termed very differently, although the goals of traffic management are similar. Here, remote radar tracking systems, sensors and radio transmission play a key role to ensure traffic safety. To assure safe and stable communication lines among vessels and ground stations, besides VHF (high frequency) radio transmission here satellite communications (e.g. ATS-I, ATS-III, Inmarsat (Moe R.L., 1988) and Iridium) are used. Since security of the transferred information is also an issue here, the datagrams at both ends are often encrypted. Besides voice messages, data transfers among ground stations and vessels in the air or on water are transferred. They contain meaningful information about the identification of the vessel, its route and velocity, type and quantity of its freight, etc. In order to prevent electronic (and actual) hijacking of the vessels, these data need to be uniquely signed and their contents protected by encryption. The freight units are uniquely identified by their tags preferably implemented using RFID (Radio-Frequency IDentification) technology because of greater data-capacity and easier scanning.

Table 2 sums up the main goals in transport. For each of the goals the appropriate means are listed, categorized into methods, devices, and information management together with the pertaining standardization efforts required. The main goal of transport management is to obtain sustainable transport models that would provide for transport predictability on the one side and improve its dependability also through enhanced integrity and maintainability of transport infrastructure on the other.

Table 2. Traffic improvement measures and their effect on critical QoS parameters

Means & Goals	Methods	Devices	Information management	Standardization
Timeliness	route planning & tracking	desktop computers, PDA[1]s, PNA[2]s with GPS technology	timetables, itineraries, maps	timetable and map data
Availability	traffic simulation	computing systems	traffic density	traffic density data
Reliability	traffic information management	networked computing & control systems	incident information acquisition	traffic information data
Safety	traffic information dissemination	RDS, TMC transmitters	incident information dissemination	traffic information data
Security	vehicle tracing	GPS, GPRS terminals	tracking information acquisition	vehicle data and security
Integrity	traffic planning	networked computing & control systems	route information management	traffic route data
Maintainability	infrastructure maintenance	networked computing, control sensor and system	route information management	traffic information data
Ecology	energy consumption management	CO^3, noise, etc. sensors	pollution sensor information management	traffic maps and route data
Interoperability	transport planning	Inter-transport relocation platforms	ticket, bill of material information management	ticket, CARGO unit & bill of material standardization

[1] Personal Data Assistant

[2] Personal Navigation Assistant

[3] Carbon (Mon-)Oxide

The mentioned means assuring dependability and timeliness of transport are considered in transport quality management. Transport energy management, on the other side, is optimized with respect to timetables, efficiency and comfort during travel. Another noteworthy issue, which is gaining importance as an optimization criterion, is the quantity of harmful emissions and noise produced by vehicles with respect to the demand on the increasing quality of life and cleaner environment.

Standardization efforts in traffic include tagging, security, freight units, application programs used, open interfaces of networked systems, etc. With all kinds of passenger transportation the information on timetables, ticketing and connections are customary. To accommodate multimodal travel, the ticketing information should be standardized in order to enable easy transport-switching. In freight transportation these standardization efforts have already been undertaken (e.g. transport unit tagging) and provide benefits to Warehouse Management Systems (WMS). With improved QoS in transportation, however, it should also facilitate Just-In-Time (JIT) production.

(Waste) Water Management

Water is becoming more and more valuable and with it the concern about waste-water management is growing. Since the earth's water system is cyclic and because of extensive use of water in households, production systems and the agriculture, one wishes to take part in the recycling process and support the natural regeneration as source of clean water also for future generations. Since only clean water is useful for the above purposes, and there are limited supplies thereof on earth, waste water treatment systems have been devised in order to (1) clean waste water and reuse it or (2) detoxicate polluted water from industrial plants, so it does not reach the environment. *Table 3* shows an overview of the goals and means one strives for with (waste) water management. These goals also correspond with guidelines of (ZVEI, 2007).

Because of the complexity of waste water treatment systems, here in the planning process as well as during operation of wastewater treatment plants and their sewer systems ICT technology is utilized (e.g. Simba (Alex J. and Jumar U., 2005)). On one hand one needs autonomous systems on plants to monitor and control their operation, and on the other one needs communication technology (preferably wireless) to be able to coordinate the

network of plants and the sewer system between them.

In *Table 3* most of the crucial infrastructure and technologies associated with waste water treatment are listed. Part of them mainly concerns planning and optimization of the plant and sewer systems by providing support for simulation-/assistance-/autonomous-systems (e.g. Simba). These aim at the economical use of pipelines and sewers in order to reduce extensive use of expensive procedures and bio-chemical substances (e.g. in agriculture automated watering-systems analysis can cut on cost and water consumption and provide for a well balanced water-supply). Another part of them deals with the diagnosis and maintenance of the plant / sewer system.

Table 3. (Waste) water management improvement measures and their effect on critical QoS parameters

Means & Goals	Methods	Devices	Information management	Standardization
Availability	simulation systems	assistance/ autonomous computing systems, aux. power sources	sewer system / plant information management	sewer system / plant data
Reliability	integrated system monitoring applications	assistance/ autonomous computing systems	weather and flow information acquisition	meteorological, sewer system / plant data
Safety	treatment procedures, remote diagnosis	diagnostic and leakage sensors, mobile terminals	diagnostic and leakage information dissemination	sewer system / plant data
Security	remote diagnosis and billing	assistance/ autonomous computing systems	plant / consumer data	data transfer security
Integrity	simulation systems, integrated system monitoring applications	assistance/ autonomous computing systems, radio transmission	sewer system / plant information management	sewer system / plant data
Maintainability	treatment procedures, integrated system monitoring applications	assistance/ autonomous computing systems, radio transmission	sewer system / plant information management	sewer system / plant data
Ecology	treatment procedures, remote diagnosis	diagnostic and leakage sensors	pollution sensor information management	throughput, max. pollutant data
Interoperability	standardization	control systems, communication devices	sewer system / plant information management	weather, sewer system / plant data

Economical sensors for quick diagnostics provide automated water treatment and sewer management systems the ability for quick response to incoming polluted water. On one side they are reducing the amount of bacteria-cultures needed to normally reproduce clean water by waste-water treatment and on the other they are preventing them to die out by taking preventive measures in case the amount of the incoming polluted water is too extensive. The self-regulative function is especially important in smaller water-treatment plants, which have been designed for lower throughputs, but occasionally have to survive "shocks" like floods, conventions, trade fairs, sports events, etc.

Sensors and systems for leakage control in combination with autonomous robots are used for pipeline- and sewer- inspection. Supported by a robust industrial network technology they should aid the water and pipeline management companies with sustaining their sewers and pipelines by providing them feedback on the state of their systems. In combination with mobile terminals with integrated SW-applications for system monitoring and water consumption billing they should enable them a transparent water and pipeline management. Here novel technologies (e.g. short range radio transmission), auxiliary power sources, new treatment procedures, as well as new security concepts (against break-down/sabotage), should all contribute to improve (waste) water management.

Standardization in the field of water management, offering communities and water management companies regulative power to ensure reasonable and sustainable usage of their systems and resources as well as proper (standard compliant) use of certified components and their interoperability, should further improve the QoS of these systems.

Power Electronics

Being the most important energy source, electrical power generation and distribution is crucial for ensuring and sustaining the quality of life. In the future taking the following measures shall improve the QoS in electrical energy production and distribution management through (ZVEI, 2007):

- preventive maintenance with appropriate diagnostic tools and optimization of maintenance intervals,
- remote utilization sensors enabling the tracking of malfunctions and break-downs as well as cost optimization,
- containerization of energy devices by providing them with some basic resource functionality for uniform treatment,
- control systems for running small decentralized as well as big power plants (through e.g. virtual power plant programs),
- optimization of the energy production based on energy supply by contract ("spot-market"),
- network stabilization with the aid of control technology enabling targeted overloads (besides channeling superfluous energy these are also useful for targeted ice-melting on power-lines in winter) and improved battery technology,
- automatically documenting the output of malicious exhausts (in thermal power plants using fossil-fuel) for revisions,
- automated alert-system for monitoring and signaling critical conditions, and
- tools for operators - (mobile) terminals enabling transparent and meaningful overview of the network status.

As with (waste) water management systems the crucial infrastructure and technologies associated with power electronics also comprise intelligent sensor technology. Sensors attached to control / communication devices at different spots of the network provide us with information about its status and possible exception conditions (e.g.: broken lines, overheating, plant outages, etc.). These context-sensitive information should be joined by the network-management control systems combining the possibility of devices / plants monitoring with the possibility to take corrective actions through interconnected actuators.

The control software should be upgraded by self-learning expert systems for preventive maintenance, which would also provide the operator with the ability to make informed decisions more quickly in case alert conditions require regulatory action. The command input could be supplemented by voice-control systems in order to additionally shorten response times and provide a more natural man-machine interface.

Appropriate for network maintenance, control technology should support the different control actions issued by control centers and enable decentralized power-plant integration through their containerization. Regardless of the size some general data on a plant's properties and status can be unified. As with wind power plants, based on these data, one may manage the plant system as a whole and develop plans for maintenance and regulatory actions in cases of emergencies, requiring shutting down / cutting off individual plants / lines without unwanted energy supply outages.

Standardization should provide for the interoperability of sensors/actuators and control devices as well as plants. It should also include energy consumption billing. Like with water management systems, the sensors on the network should enable remote billing where short range radio transmission can be used to transfer these data safely and securely while cutting on the cost of billing at the same time.

Table 4 sums up the main goals in power electronics. For each of the goals the appropriate measures are listed, categorized into methods, devices, information management and standardization efforts required.

Food Growth/Processing

Being the next most important energy source, food growth and distribution is crucial for ensuring and sustaining the quality of life. In the future the following measures shall improve the QoS in food growth (ZVEI, 2007):

- system-level optimization in production (ensuring performance and safety in food processing with respect to the basic "quality at low price" criterion),
- automation-applications for food processing procedures (e.g.: mixing, pre-prepared frozen food,…),
  - data preparation for intelligent system guidance (based on information gathered from the current production processes),
- man/machine interfaces (as in previous areas here also voice-command systems are expected to improve response-times and operator efficiency),
- sensor-systems for "inline" quality control in correspondence with the pertaining standards, and
- machine hygiene ("cleaning in place").

The crucial infrastructure and technologies associated with food growth and processing are collected in *Table 5*. It sums up the main goals in food growth. For each of the goals the appropriate measures are listed, categorized into methods, devices, information management and standardization efforts required.

The goals in food growth mainly pertain to automated internal logistics (acceptance and incoming goods control, storing goods), automated packaging, filling and commissioning by employing robots for manipulating soft and fragile food (e.g.: pastry, fruits and vegetables, drinks, etc.),

Table 4. Power electronics improvement measures and their effect on critical QoS parameters

Means & Goals	Methods	Devices	Information management	Standardization
Availability	simulation systems	control systems, battery technology	electrical power- plant information management	power-line / plant data
Reliability	integrated system monitoring applications	control systems	utilization information acquisition	power-line / plant data
Safety	expert systems, remote diagnosis	remote diagnostic sensors, mobile terminals	diagnostic information dissemination	power-line / plant data
Security	remote diagnosis and billing	control systems	plant / consumer data	data transfer security
Integrity	simulation systems, integrated system monitoring applications	control systems, radio transmission	power-line system / plant information management	power-line / plant data
Maintainability	containerization, spot-market operation, expert alert system	control systems, radio transmission	power-line system / plant information management	power-line / plant data
Ecology	malicious exhaust control	remote diagnostic sensors	pollution sensor information management	power consumption, max. pollutant data
Interoperability	containerization, standardization	control systems, communication devices	electrical power- plant information management	power-line / plant data

Table 5. Food growth improvement measures and their effect on critical QoS parameters

Means & Goals	Methods	Devices	Information management	Standardization
Availability	system-level control	assistance/ autonomous computing systems	growth and production information management	plant data
Reliability	intelligent system guidance, automation-applications	assistance/ autonomous computing systems	quality-control information acquisition	meteorological, product, plant data
Safety	diagnostic and control systems	inline quality control sensors	inline quality-control information dissemination	product, plant data
Security	diagnostic systems	assistance/ autonomous computing systems	plant / consumer data	data transfer security
Integrity	simulation systems	assistance/ autonomous computing systems	production system information management	product, plant data
Maintainability	automation-applications	assistance/ autonomous computing systems	production system information management	product, plant data
Ecology	inline quality control, cleaning in place	machine hygiene and inline quality control systems,	inline quality-control information management	quality control data
Interoperability	Standardization	control systems, communication devices	plant system	weather, product, production data

RFID technology for tracking among production departments and tracking information standardization, "Manufacturing Execution Systems" offering system optimization on production level (e.g. SAP ERP[1] system for planning purchases, production and cost calculation), temperature-controlled logistics (uninterrupted cool-chain), etc.

Industrial Production Systems

Being the next most important social component, production systems are crucial for producing added value and ensuring and sustaining the quality of life through it. In the future the following measures shall improve the QoS in production systems (ZVEI, 2007):

- cooperating robot-systems (ensuring quick response to market changes by reconfigurations in the production process),

- operator-robot interaction (control systems networking, visualization as well as voice control of the robots for easier handling),
  - precise, intelligent sensor systems with picture processing capability,
- diagnostic tools for heterogeneous system components as well as the production process as a whole, and
- virtual production process (production process start as a "digital factory" to determine critical factors and accommodate JIT production).

The crucial infrastructure and technologies associated with production systems are joined in *Table 6*. Future applications of ICT technology especially address:

- unique identification of products/parts,
  - utilization of "intelligent" SW-agents

Table 6. Production systems improvement measures and their effect on critical QoS parameters

Means & Goals	Methods	Devices	Information management	Standardization
Timeliness	virtual production planning	computing systems	production database	production timetable
Availability	virtual production process, production reconfiguration	assistance / autonomous control systems	growth and production system planning	plant data
Reliability	co-operating robot-systems, self-organization, visualization, voice-control	assistance / autonomous control systems, mobile terminals	inline quality-control information acquisition	product, plant data
Safety	diagnostic tools	intelligent sensor systems	inline quality-control information dissemination	product, plant data
Security	diagnostic systems	intelligent sensor systems	plant / consumer data	data transfer security
Integrity	simulation systems	assistance / autonomous control systems	production system information management	product, plant data
Maintainability	centrally optimized planning and optimization	assistance / autonomous control systems	production system information management	product, plant data
Ecology	inline quality control	inline quality control systems	inline quality-control information management	quality-control data
Interoperability	vertical integration and standardization	assistance / autonomous control systems	plant system	product, plant data

for reactions on imprecise context dependent formulations, especially in combination with voice controlled robot systems,

- ○ "Plug & Play" functionality and functional safety,
- self-organization, vertical integration and standardization of production "islands" on ERP level,
- centrally optimized planning and documentation of the production process for JIT/JIS production,
- product tracing for quality control and de-commissioning, as well as
- modularization and networking through mobile communication technology, wired and wireless on- demand connections (e.g. Industrial Ethernet).

OUTLOOK

Corresponding with our efforts on defining a common technological platform for logistics applications and networks mainly the goals and means with their impact on QoS needed to be explored for every application area. In particular, the methods and devices used depending on the application area, and the information flow and data security issues according to application area were emphasized, since they represent the key areas where ICT technology comes into play.

Since the primary focus of this contribution remains on the ICT technological support for the individual application areas, key technologies are identified as well as methods and standards supporting improved QoS in these key areas are stated and their interrelations further explored. Here especially modern mobile computing and communication devices are expected to be the driving technologies of future logistics applications. On the other hand, for improved planning, the logistics operations and sites are being considered in a modular fashion by their containerization. Besides classifying logistics sites for uniform handling and optimizing the individual logistics processes, standardization efforts have to be undertaken in order to make these systems and their components inter-operable for joined logistics.

Based on the idea of the ARTEMIS platform the foundation of an Advanced-Research Technological Platform for Logistics Applications' Networks (ARTPLAN) platform shall be defined based on:

- reference architectures and components
- methods and tools,
- communication interfaces, and
- standards.

In order to achieve this goal, best practices and sound architectures shall be collected and explored for JIT/JIS logistics processes optimization using ICT technology. Key components shall be identified and their standard properties assembled and joined in a knowledge-base. The methods and tools will be collected from logistics applications and will build the technological platform's logic. Key communication interfaces and appropriate technologies will be identified and assembled in the mentioned base of knowledge. And finally, standards will be explored, to assure QoS on one hand and provide for interoperability of networked components, systems and plants on the other.

As in the case of ARTEMIS, the platform should build on best practices from the industry and sound research from the academia, hence joining the two in logistics applications' networks research. The industry shall provide standard components, technology standards and best practices, while the academia shall provide methods for supply chain optimization and research on new methods, tools as well as solutions for interoperability among components, systems and plants.

CONCLUSION

QoS properties of logistics applications are supported mainly by diagnostics, traceability, ease of maintenance and standardization. Efficient support for logistics applications is available from contemporary ICT technologies especially in terms of simulation, monitoring and control systems, self-organization, wireless open standard communications (used in VAN and WAN networks) and the supporting applications. The applications, which are targeted especially at logistics support, are networking of control systems as well as their safety and security. All these features, which are addressed by the ARTEMIS platform for embedded control systems, can be transferred to system / plant levels. Hence, it is given here as an example of an all-encompassing technological as well as technically advanced solution, based on which a similar technological platform for logistics applications' networks shall be devised – the ARTPLAN, representing a technological platform for logistics applications networks, focused on the QoS.

REFERENCES

Alex, J., & Jumar, U. (2005). Simulation zum integrierten Prozessentwurf von Abwassersystemen, *GWF Wasser/Abwasser, 145*(2005), Nr.10. http://simba.ifak.eu/simba/

Artemis (2008). *European Technology Platform, Embedded Intelligence and Systems*, Retrieved fromhttp://www.artemis.eu/

Ballou, R. H. (2004). Business Logistics/Supply Chain Management – Planning, Organizing, and Controlling the Supply Chain. Upper Saddle River, New Jersey: Prentice Hall.

Bartens, S. (2008). *China setzt auf Ausbau*, Logistik auf den Punkt, Heft 6.

BMBF - Bundesministerium für Bildung und Forschung. (2007). *IKT2020 - Forschung für Innovationen.* Retrieved fromhttp://www.bmbf.de/de/9069.php

BMVBS - Bundesministerium für Verkehr. Bau und Stadtentwicklung (2009). *Masterplan - Güterverkehr und Logistik.* Retrieved from http://www.bmvbs.de/Verkehr/Gueterverkehr-Logistik-,2829/Masterplan.htm

Chr, P. H. (2004). Logistiksysteme – Betriebswirtschaftliche Grundlagen. Berlin Heidelberg: Springer-Verlag

ENV 12313 Traffic and Traveller Information (TTI). (May 1996-June 1997). *TTI Messages via Traffic Message.*

European Commission (2006*). Sustainable Surface Transport – Research Technological Development and Integration*, Luxemburg: Office for Official Publications of the European Communities.

Moe, R. L. (1988). Networking and Ship-To-Shore Ship-To-Ship Communication, CH2585-8/88/00005-3, IEEE. http://ieeexplore.ieee.org/iel5/738/906/00023558.pdf?arnumber=23558

prEN 50067: (1997, July) *Specification of the radio data system* (RDS).

Straubhaar T. (2008). *Drei Vorteile der Krise*, Logistik auf den Punkt, Heft 6.

ZVEI - Institut für Zukunftsstudien und Technologiebewertung. (2007). *Integrierte Technologie-Roadmap.* Retrieved from http://www.ttn-hessen.de/npkpublish/filestore/77/zvei.pdf

ENDNOTE

[1] Enterprise Resource Planning

Chapter 9
How to Market OR/ MS Decision Support

Masayuki Ueda
Sapporo University, Japan

ABSTRACT

This research examines what to do to have decision makers more utilize OR/MS decision support. We investigate OR/MS decision support from a new viewpoint of service. Firstly, based on the fact that what is provided by OR/MS decision support is information to aid in decision making, we show that OR/ MS decision support shares characteristics with service, hence can be considered as a kind of service. Next, we analyze OR/MS decision support from the viewpoint of what is necessary for service of high quality, and we clarify the issue of communication gaps. If we investigate preceding research in OR/ MS (Operations Research/Management Science), it turns out that there is surely a problem with communication gap between decision makers and decision supporters. Finally, we show that it is effective to utilize problem specification, which is a decision-maker-friendly description of problems proposed by research groups including the author, as one approach to bridge the communication gap.

INTRODUCTION

Interest in the service science (Services Sciences, Management and Engineering: SSME) has been rising since the idea of service science was proposed at Almaden research institute of the U.S. IBM (Refer to Hidaka, 2006, for education and research activities of the service science in Japan and abroad). Behind this, there are the facts: the share of the service industry in many developed nations accounts for 70% of GDP, and over recent years the profit from service-based businesses has been rising dramatically even in the manufacturing industry. These facts have required deeper understanding of service more than ever.

In many cases, service are mostly conducted by a seat-of-the-pants approach, and as a result low productivity of service has been pointed out. Contrarily, service science transforms service into an object for scientific analysis. In Hidaka (2006),

DOI: 10.4018/978-1-61520-603-2.ch009

one purpose of service science is stated as "to solve problems arising from the characteristics of services" (p.39).

In OR/MS, mathematical techniques are applied to decision maker's problems. The activity of offering information for a decision maker's problem by using such mathematical techniques (OR/MS decision support, hereafter) can be considered as a service. Taking advantage of rising interest in service science, it is meaningful to investigate OR/MS decision support from a new viewpoint of service.

Service quality has two dimensions: technical quality and functional quality (Grönroos, 1994; Parasuraman, Zeithaml, & Berry, 1985). Technical quality focuses on what is delivered (i.e. outcome). Functional quality focuses on how the service is delivered (i.e. process). In this research, we analyze OR/MS decision support not from the viewpoint of what kind of information is offered, but from the viewpoint of how the information is offered to decision makers (i.e. functional quality).

In this research, we will show (1) that OR/MS decision support is a kind of service addressable by service science, (2) that a communication gap exists between decision makers and decision supporters, and (3) that a new approach that utilizes problem specification is effective to bridge the communication gap.

This chapter consists of 6 sections. Section 2 is background. In Section 3, we analyze the characteristics of service and OR/MS decision support, and show that the activity to support decision making with mathematical techniques is a service. In Section 4, we analyze OR/MS decision support from the viewpoint of what are necessary for service of high quality, and clarify the issue of communication gap between decision makers and decision supporters. In Section 5, we show a case exemplifying the effectiveness of utilizing problem specification, which is a decision-maker-friendly description of problems, to improve the issue. Section 6 provides concluding remarks.

BACKGROUND

Service science requires multidisciplinary approach that integrates elements of computer science, operations research, industrial engineering, business strategy, management sciences, social and cognitive sciences, legal sciences, and so on (Council on Competitiveness, 2004; IBM Research). OR/MS is commonly thought to play an important role in service science where service are scientifically analyzed. However, as Hidaka (2006) pointed out, service usually include many components that cannot be properly expressed as mathematical models and thus cannot be solved by OR/MS in isolation. It may be caused by human factor or social practice and regulation. For such problems, it is necessary for OR/MS to collaborate with other fields of research.

As mentioned above, OR/MS is in general regarded as one of the tools of service science. Compared with this, this research regards OR/MS (more properly, OR/MS decision support) as one of the objects of research in service science. There are some bodies of research that discuss the necessity of applying OR/MS to service or the expectation to such studies. However, there is little research that explicitly analyzes OR/MS as a service.

If we investigate some preceding research in OR/MS, we notice situations where OR/MS is not fully utilized. Little (2004) pointed out that "the big problem with management science models is that managers practically never use them" (p.1841). Little (2004) concluded that "a model that is to be used by a manager should be simple, robust, easy to control, adaptive, as complete as possible and easy to communicate with" (p.1841). This article was selected as one of the most influential in the first 50 years of *Management Science*. This indicates the importance of the problem that Little (2004) pointed out. Levasseur (2007) focused on how to promote the benefit of OR/MS more effectively to prospective customers. Levasseur (2007) pointed out that the approach in promoting OR/

MS depends on whether we judge most customers as having a high level of OR/MS knowledge or not. Murphy (2005) pointed out that "the main unsolved issue for OR practitioners is developing ways of communicating and marketing solution that is intangible to managers [i.e. prospective customers] when most managers do not understand the mathematics involved" (p.155).

For the problem mentioned above, this research examines what to do to have decision makers more utilize OR/MS decision support from a viewpoint of service.

OR/MS DECISION SUPPORT IS A SERVICE

Common Characteristics of Service

Service is a commonly used term. However, despite that many researchers have attempted to define what meant by service, we have not yet reached a consensus on the definition. For example, service is defined as activities offering what is useful for a person, supporting activities needed for a person or an organization to achieve its purpose, and an activity or series of activities provided as a solution to customer problems (Hidaka, 2006; Kameoka, 2006). According to the definitions of service, OR/MS decision support can be intuitively said to be a service. The following shows that OR/MS decision support shares characteristics of service.

Because service are activities, intangibility, simultaneity, and heterogeneity are commonly cited characteristics that differentiate service from product (Berry & Parasuraman, 1991; Hidaka, 2006). Intangibility implies that the things to be provided by service are effects through a series of activity, and are unable to be physically handled. That is, service is not a thing (or things) that is born as a result of activity, but activity itself. By this intangibility, the quality of service becomes ambiguous for users. Simultaneity implies that

service is activity where production by service-providers and consumption by users are done interactively and concurrently. That is, service is over if the activity is concluded. Heterogeneity implies that the value of service cannot be determined in itself, but it depends on the user's mental state and environment. That is, service is offered to users who might have different demands and values from that of service-providers (or what service-providers provide). Therefore, the adjustment of the views between service-providers and users, or in other words, communication is indispensable. The value of service must be improved by interaction between service-providers and users.

OR/MS Decision Support

Figure 1 shows a standard problem-solving process of OR (Ackoff & Sasieni, 1968). Generally, when a problem is first found (or posed), the scope of the problem is ambiguous and what is meant by solution of the problem is not clear. Therefore, one needs to formulate the problem into a well-defined form that should be solved in a proper way (Step1). After formulating the problem, one needs to construct a mathematical model for the problem and clarify the structure of the problem: the objective function and constraints (Step2). In Step3, one needs to derive a solution of the mathematical model. Note that a solution derived here is a solution for the mathematical model constructed by step2, but it is not a solution for the problem itself. Therefore, one needs to test whether the mathematical model is realistic, and to evaluate the solution in the real world (Step4). If the result of the evaluation is satisfactory, the solution is carried out without changes. If the result of the evaluation is unsatisfactory, one needs to return Step1 and restart by reformulating the problem, or Step2 to improve the model.

In what follows, we assume that OR/MS decision support is performed by following the steps of Figure 1 between decision makers and decision supporters. If decision makers have sufficient

Figure 1. The standard problem-solving process of OR

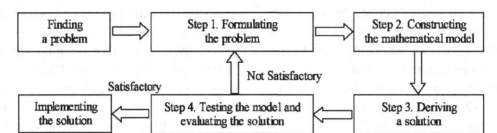

OR/MS knowledge, especially mathematical knowledge that is required in OR/MS, wide communication gaps do not occur because they can perform most steps alone or they can understand what is carried out through the whole process. However, it is something else whether decision makers actually choose to independently perform the concerned problem-solving process. It will be judged depending on their roles in the management. On the other hand, if decision makers have insufficient OR/MS knowledge, communication between decision makers and decision supporters becomes difficult because the steps in which decision makers can participate independently and autonomously are limited (discussed later). Here we assume that decision makers have insufficient OR/MS knowledge unless otherwise stated.

What is Provided by OR/ MS Decision Support

OR/MS decision support provides information that contributes to the problem-solving process of decision makers through the aforementioned process. That is, what is provided by OR/MS decision support cannot be handled physically. This characteristic corresponds with intangibility of service.

The information provided by OR/MS decision support is obtained from analyzing a mathematical model. Good mathematical models are often characterized as those that simplify the decision problem and express its essential structure in a

skillful manner. That is, a mathematical model is not a faithful description of a decision problem. It becomes difficult for decision makers to judge the quality of the provided information since they need to judge whether the process of simplification and abstraction are appropriate.

A purpose of OR/MS decision support is not to derive a solution of a mathematical model, but to provide information that contributes to the problem-solving process of decision makers. Under such purpose, interaction or exchange of information between decision makers and decision supporters becomes essential to conduct Step1 and Step4. That is, the decision maker's use of decision support and supporting activity by decision supporters must be performed simultaneously. This corresponds with simultaneity of service.

OR/MS decision support is performed through information acquired in Step2 and Step3. The value of the decision support is recognized only when decision makers predict the effect of the information in the real world. No matter how mathematically sound information that decision supporters provide is, the value of the information cannot be recognized when decision makers judge that it is unsuitable for implementation. In other words, the value of OR/MS decision support is evaluated depending not only on the information itself that decision supporters provide, but also on the situation of decision makers who examine the administration of the information. This corresponds with heterogeneity of service.

The above-mentioned analysis shows that OR/MS decision support has three characteristics of service: intangibility, simultaneity, and heterogeneity. From this discussion, we theoretically conclude that OR/MS decision support is a service.

ANALYZING OR/MS DECISION SUPPORT AS A SERVICE

Mental Intangibility

Figure 2 is one of the schemes for classifying service proposed by Lovelock (1983). Service are divided into an upper and a lower half depending on whether the nature of the service act is tangible or intangible. Service are also divided into a left and a right half depending on whether the direct recipient of the service act is people or things. By these questions, service can be classified into four broad categories: (1) services directed at people's bodies, (2) services directed at goods and other physical possessions, (3) services directed at people's minds, (4) services directed at intangible assets. In services directed at people's bodies, the users need to be physically present throughout service delivery. In services classified as services directed at goods and other physical possessions, there are service where the users need to be present only when initiating and terminating the service. There are also service where the users do not necessarily have to be physically present by utilizing information technology: such as services directed at people's minds or services directed at intangible assets.

In OR/MS decision support, the data that describes the problem situation of decision makers is processed through an intangible action. Therefore, if we follow the taxonomy of Lovelock (1983), OR/MS decision support is classified as services directed at intangible assets. As referred to hereinafter, when decision makers have insufficient mathematical knowledge, the steps in which decision makers can independently and autonomously participate are limited. In OR/MS decision support, decision makers do not necessarily have to be physically present throughout service delivery. Lovelock (1983) pointed out that in the case where the users can get the service even if they do not enter the service factory (i.e. a physical place where service operation is performed), "the outcome of the service act remains very important,

Figure 2. The scheme for classifying service (Adapted from Lovelock, 1983, p.12)

What is the nature of the service act?	Who or what is the direct recipient of the service?	
	People	Things
Tangible actions	Services directed at people's bodies: • Passenger services • Hairdressing • Medical services • Restaurants/cafeterias	Services directed at goods and other physical possessions: • Freight transportation • Auto and other repair services • Laundry services • Cleaning services
Intangible actions	Services directed at people's minds: • Education • Broadcasting • Entertainment services • Religious activities	Services directed at intangible assets: • Legal services • Banking • Accounting • Insurance

but the process of service delivery may be of little interest" (p.13). However, this does not apply to the case of OR/MS decision support.

Intangibility is composed of two dimensions: physical intangibility and mental intangibility (Laroche, McDougall, Bergeron, & Yang, 2004; McDougall & Snetsinger, 1990). Physical intangibility implies that what is provided cannot be touched physically. Mental intangibility implies that one cannot evaluate what is provided if one lacks the experience (or knowledge) with it. In the case of OR/MS decision support, which is the activity using mathematical techniques, it is necessary to recognize not only merely that what is provided is information (i.e. physical intangibility), but also that decision makers having insufficient mathematical knowledge cannot appreciate what is provided (i.e. mental intangibility). Given this perspective, we can realize that, though OR/MS decision support is classified as services directed at intangible assets, it is also necessary to analyze it from the dimension of services directed at people's minds (Figure 2). Lovelock (1994) pointed out that (even when the users do not necessarily have to be physically present) unless the users are mentally present, they cannot enjoy the benefit of the service in services directed at people's minds [1].

Then what does that users are mentally present mean in the context of OR/MS decision support? Walker (2000) pointed out that one of the major reasons why the results of policy analysis (i.e. information to aid in decision making) do not get used is that the policymakers (i.e. decision makers) do not understand how the results are obtained. This implies that, in OR/MS decision support, it is necessary for decision makers to understand how the provided information is produced (e.g. how a problem is formulated or how a mathematical model is constructed) so that the information is made use of by them (Figure 1). However, as referred to hereinafter, some preceding research point out that decision makers do not understand the mathematical models or that decision makers

do not fully understand the relation between their problems and the mathematical models. In the situation where it is difficult for decision makers to understand the mathematical models used for producing the provided information, it becomes important to enable decision makers to be convinced that their problem is solved through the whole process so that they can enjoy the benefit of OR/MS decision support. In Parasuraman, Zeithaml, & Berry (1985), communication is cited as one of the determinants of service quality. This communication involves assuring the customer that a problem will be handled properly. From this, "decision makers are mentally present" can be understood that decision makers can be convinced that a mathematical model analyzed properly expresses their problem; in other words, that a problem is shared between decision makers and decision supporters through the whole process.

In the following, we investigate the issue of communication gap that is linked to the sharing of a problem between decision makers and decision supporters.

Necessity of Improving Communication Gap

What OR/MS decision support provides is information to aid in decision making. For such information to be made use of by decision makers, sufficient understanding of the process through which the information is produced is necessary. So, participation of decision makers in the process becomes important.

However, when decision makers have insufficient mathematical knowledge, the steps in which decision makers can independently and autonomously participate are limited: the step to formulate the problem of their own (Step1) and the step to evaluate the feasibility and effectiveness of the solution provided by decision supporters in the real world (a part of Step4). When the steps that decision makers can participate in are limited as mentioned above, it is difficult for them to judge whether a mathematical model analyzed properly expresses their problem, that is, whether a problem is shared between decision makers and decision supporters. In the situation where it cannot be said that decision makers are mentally present, it is difficult for decision makers to evaluate the provided information.

Under such a situation, decision makers might estimate the value of OR/MS decision support to be low because the way in which the information is provided is wrong with decision makers. It is necessary to recognize that service is evaluated depending not only on what is delivered (i.e. technical quality) but also on how the service is delivered (i.e. functional quality). The value of service is created by interaction between service-providers and users. We cannot expect high value from a service that is provided without proper communication with the users. In order to provide service of high value, it is important to pay careful attention to users' perception of the service. From that viewpoint, the current state of OR/MS decision support, where it cannot be said that decision makers are mentally present, is considered to be insufficient as a mechanism to improve the value of service from the users side.

Morimoto & Sawatani (2005) pointed out that in a collaboration across domains such as occupational capability, area of industry, domain identity and area of study, it is important for the participants to understand the differences of sense of purpose, sense of values and vernacular, and to come to a mutual compromise. At the same time, Morimoto & Sawatani (2005) insisted that in such collaboration, mediators who can understand the participants' opinions and ways of thinking become indispensable. This can be considered as pointing out the difficulty of communication performed across domains. Indeed, Morimoto & Sawatani (2005) asserted that "improvement of communication gap between participants performing collaboration is one of the issues to be addressed by the service science" (p.124).

In OR/MS decision support, communication across different domains is required: one is the real world where decision makers recognize a problem, and the other is the mathematical world where decision supporters analyze a mathematical model for the problem. There is great difference between decision makers and decision supporters in terms of occupational capability, intellectual background and vernacular for describing problems. This is the reason why we need to examine how to improve the communication gap between them.

As mentioned above, if we analyze OR/MS decision support from a viewpoint of service, the issue of communication gap between decision makers and decision supporters becomes clear. In the next section, some preceding research in OR/MS are investigated and are discussed in relation to the communication gap.

Preceding Research Related to Communication Gap in OR/MS

The importance of making clear the relationship between problems that decision makers have and mathematical models for their problems is pointed out in Little (2004), Banerjee & Basu (1993). Little (2004) asserted that the reason why OR/MS models tend not to be used by managers (i.e. decision makers) lies in the interface between manager and model. Little (2004) also claimed that managers do not understand OR/MS models and they tend to reject what they do not understand. Little (2004) considered this as one of the reasons that managers do not use OR/MS models more widely. Banerjee & Basu (1993) pointed out that "managers may not be aware of the fact that the problem at hand can be solved by the solution procedures [including OR/MS techniques] that are available to them" (p.76). This can be considered as asserting that it frequently happens that managers do not fully understand the relation between their problems and mathematical models for these problems.

What can be said from their research is that the reason why OR/MS models tend not to be widely used does not always lie in the information itself produced from these models. A real reason might be that decision makers cannot appreciate the information produced from OR/MS models because they do not understand OR/MS models. Furthermore, it is pointed out that cases frequently occur where OR techniques tend not to be used for the reasons that are not directly related to the validity of solutions (Yamada, 1984). This is recognized as the background of the OR implementation problem.

The discussions above make clear that in order to realize more effective OR/MS decision support, it is important not only to construct a better mathematical model and develop a more efficient solution, but also to examine how to provide information through the whole process so that decision makers can appreciate the provided information. Banerjee & Basu (1993) insisted that "in order to use model based DSS [i.e. OR/MS decision support] effectively in a decision making paradigm we need to get the decision makers involved in different problem solving phases" (p.76). However, as mentioned previously, when decision makers have insufficient mathematical knowledge, the steps in which decision makers can independently and autonomously participate are limited. From this, it can be understood that Banerjee & Basu (1993) asserted the necessity of

communication to confirm that a problem is shared between decision makers and decision supporters through the whole process.

As mentioned above, if we investigate preceding research in OR/MS, it turns out that there is surely a problem with communication gap between decision makers and decision supporters.

IMPROVEMENT OF THE COMMUNICATION GAP

Existing Methods for Improvement

The left of Figure 3 illustrates the situation of OR/MS decision support pointed out by preceding research. For decision makers, it is difficult to judge whether a mathematical model, which is analyzed to produce the provided information, properly expresses their problem. This situation is expressed with arrows of dotted lines connecting decision problems and mathematical models in the figure. On the other hand, as Ackoff (1974) pointed out that "we fail more often because we solve the wrong problem than because we get the wrong solution to the right problem" (p.8), it is difficult for decision supporters to precisely grasp decision maker's problems (This may also apply to decision makers). This situation is expressed with ellipses of dotted lines that surround decision problems in the figure.

Figure 3. The introduction of problem specification

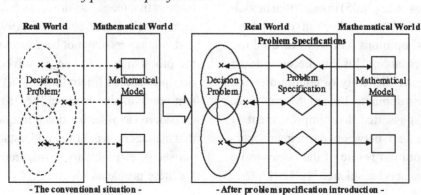

Miyazaki (1990) examined interactive OR from the standpoint of SSM (Soft Systems Methodology). Miyazaki (1990) pointed out that one purpose of interactive OR is, through model-based interaction, to promote improvement of the model, understanding of the target system, and consensus-building between participants in an integrated way. This accords with SSM where a conceptual model and interaction are regarded to be important as a method of the mutual understanding between participants. However, if we apply this in case of OR/MS decision support, we need to facilitate interaction based on mathematical models. It is required for participants (i.e. decision makers) to have sufficient mathematical knowledge so that such interaction can be effectively performed. This situation does not change basically even if we introduce high operability and various graphic expression of model by utilization of information technology that is one of the characteristics of interactive OR. That is, as far as mathematical model-mediated communication is concerned, it is insufficient to bridge the communication gap between decision makers and decision supporters.

Another method proposed for bridging the communication gap between decision makers and decision supporters are to use Structured Modeling Language (SML, hereafter) suggested by Geoffrion (1987) and Entity-Relationship with Linear Mathematical Programming (ERLMP, hereafter) suggested by Choobineh (1991). SML and ERLMP are examples of problem description methods. One of their purposes is to increase the understandability of mathematical models. However, information described by them is substantively limited. They explain clearly what kind of problem the concerned mathematical model describes. However, they do not directly describe the problem in the real world modeled into a mathematical model. When decision makers judge whether the concerned mathematical model properly expresses their problem, they are requested to translate these mathematical descrip-

tions into the real world situations. Therefore, it cannot be said that improvement of the communication gap between decision makers and decision supporters with these problem description methods is large.

Problem Specification Approach

The author of this paper suggested another method elsewhere. The method is one that utilizes a problem specification (See the right of Figure 3). Problem specification is a description of a problem by the vernacular of decision makers in the real world [2]. More specifically, the proposal is that by preparing a description of a real world problem to be modeled into a mathematical model, the burden to judge whether a problem is shared between decision makers and decision supporters might be reduced.

Preparation of a problem specification is carried out independently with construction of a mathematical model. That is, a decision problem is described as recognized by decision makers. In the case of problem specification, unlike mathematical model, judgment on simplification and abstraction is not concerned. Decision supporters may communicate with decision makers naturally about mathematical modeling in mind, and help decision makers to articulate their problems. However, they must do it by the vernacular of decision makers. So, problem specification is convenient to communicate between decision makers and decision supporters about what kind of problem is to be modeled into a mathematical model and what kind of problem the concerned mathematical model describes.

Decision makers and decision supporters share a problem specification as decision maker's problem. Decision supporters guarantee that a mathematical model properly expresses the problem specification shared. Thus, when decision makers place credence in decision supporters, decision makers can be sure that the concerned mathematical model properly expresses their problem.

Miyazaki (1990) pointed out two problems that have principal influence on problem solving in the modeling process. One is the problem with regard to understanding and agreement of the problem situation: how one understands a decision problem. The other is the problem with regard to precision of a model: whether the understood problem is properly expressed as a mathematical model. Problem specification is a description of what decision supporters, who are builders of a mathematical model, shared with decision makers regarding the problem situation in terms or vocabulary that decision makers can understand autonomously. So, it corresponds to the former problem. That a problem specification properly expresses decision maker's problem must be guaranteed on the decision maker's responsibility. This situation is expressed with arrows connecting decision problems and problem specifications in the figure 3. On the other hand, that a mathematical model properly expresses this shared problem must be guaranteed on the decision supporter's responsibility. This situation is expressed with arrows connecting problem specifications and mathematical models in the figure 3.

Even if we introduce problem specification, the steps in which decision makers can participate independently and autonomously through the whole process are unchanged. However, by sharing problem specification, decision makers can be convinced that their problem is solved through the whole process. That is, decision makers can be mentally present during OR/MS decision support process. If decision supporters try to improve the information provided to decision makers, decision supporters must not perform it only in the mathematical world. Decision supporters firstly need to change the problem specification in the real world (shared with decision makers), and then let the result appropriately reflected in the mathematical world.

As for a method of problem specification, the author adopts Generic Entity-Relationship Model (GERM, hereafter) proposed by Mukohara &

Sekiguchi (2002), Mukohara, Sekiguchi, & Bao (2005). GERM is a method to describe decision problems in the real world with the style of an extended Entity-Relationship Model. GERM problem specification consists of description of object types and their relationships that constitute world of discourse. An object type is a set of similar objects. Object type is described by a set of attributes and their values. GERM describes qualitative attributes as well as quantitative attributes. Most of the qualitative attributes concern structure of mathematical model, and they are not explicitly described by the existing problem description methods such as SML and ERLMP. Figure 4 presents object types and their relationships appearing in a GERM problem specification of a scheduling problem (that are used in the case illustrated in the next section) [3]. Double squares are object types and double diamonds are relationships. Three relationships at the rightmost position are relationships of two operations (but lines to show the second operation are omitted). Instantiation (i.e., determining values of all attributes) of a GERM problem specification generates a problem type. A problem type is what is described by existing problem description methods, and instantiation (i.e., determining value of all attributes for all related objects) of a problem type generates a numerical instance of a problem type [4].

Mentioned above, GERM regards, as things to be described, object types and their relationships that are natural objects of recognition in the real world. Because GERM problem specification describes qualitative attributes, it can describe a wide range of information about decision maker's problems in the real world. Therefore, GERM problem specification would enable decision makers to recognize how decision supporters understand decision maker's problem more easily than the existing problem description methods do. This will help to bridge the communication gap between decision makers and decision supporters.

Figure 4. GERM problem specification in the style of Entity-Relationship diagram

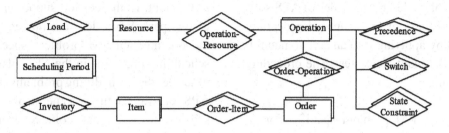

A Case Study of Problem Specification for Bridging Communication Gap

The author of this paper proposed a procedure for APS software selection problem that utilizes GERM problem specification to bridge communication gap (refer to Figure 5) [5].

To use APS software, its users must describe the problem type of their scheduling problems following the rule prescribed by the APS software (problem description rule, hereafter). Once the problem type is described, by feeding data that generate an instance of the scheduling problem, the APS software generates a feasible and fairly good schedule. This means that users must adequately select an APS software whose problem description rule allows to describe their problem type. The problem description rules are largely explained in a user-friendly manner. However, terminology used there includes many jargons (i.e., mathematically

rigorous terms) developed in theoretical scheduling research. And, the information obtained from the specification (or user's manual) of APS software is one regarding how to describe the scheduling problem. Conventionally, a problem type of scheduling problems that can be solved by APS software is not explicitly described. Thus, it is often difficult for plant workers/engineers to determine which APS software fits to the problem type of their scheduling problems.

On the other hand, suppliers (or vendors) have rich knowledge of APS software, but do not have precise knowledge of problem types of their customers. This is the reason why decision support is necessary in selecting APS software. In this case, problem description rule of APS software corresponds to mathematical model in the preceding argument.

Ueda & Sekiguchi (2005) proposed a procedure to support selection of APS software. The procedure utilizes GERM problem specification

Figure 5. The utilization of problem specification in APS software selection

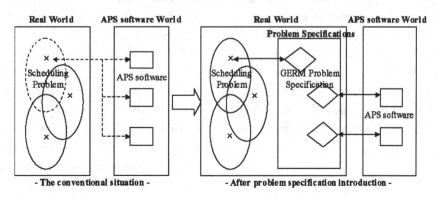

in describing scheduling problem types of both users and problem description rules of APS software. Effectiveness of the proposed procedure was verified by applying it to an actual machining plant (ABC plant, hereafter). The procedure is the following.

1. Prepare GERM problem specification to each APS software that seems fit to the target plant. This step is done by organizing problem description rules as object types, their attributes and attribute values.

2. Prepare GERM problem specification to the problem type of scheduling problems that can emerge in the target plant. For doing this, interview managers and workers of the target plant and identify object types, their attributes and possible attribute values. Because it is often the case that the plant workers/engineers know their scheduling problem well, but have never articulated it in a rigorous form that can be read by others, decision supporters must explain how each objects and relationships in the target plant can be described by utilizing terminology used in GERM problem specification of APS software. Moreover, ask the customers if there are phenomena or properties in their plant that are observed but not described by the explained terminology.

3. Compare the GERM problem specification developed in step (2) to each one developed in step (1), and identify APS software whose GERM problem specification contains all object types, all attributes of each object type, and all attribute values of each attribute included in the GERM problem specification of the target plant. If there is one or more such APS software, anyone of them is feasible choice. If none, none of the candidate APS software is adequate to the plant as it is.

The above procedure was applied to the ABC plant. Both decision supporter (the author of this paper) and decision makers agreed that the obtained GERM problem specification of scheduling problems in the ABC plant precisely describes their scheduling problems. The selected APS software actually generated a satisfactory schedule to a set of data collected from the plant. The procedure performed by only four meetings of two hour long, which is far short compared to average cases of conventional APS software selection (according to an expert consultant of APS software deployment).

From above-mentioned experiment, we confirmed (1) that by preparing problem specification, a problem is shared between decision makers and decision supporters, and (2) that decision makers become able to check the appropriateness of the selected APS software by receiving an explanation of the process where the problem specifications were compared. From this, we found that it is effective to use problem specifications for bridging the communication gap between decision makers and decision supporters.

CONCLUSION

In this research, we examine what to do to have decision makers more utilize OR/MS decision support from a viewpoint of service. We analyze OR/MS decision support not from the viewpoint of what kind of information is offered (i.e. technical quality), but from the viewpoint of how the information is offered to decision makers (i.e. functional quality).

What is provided by OR/MS decision support is information that contributes to the problem-solving process of decision makers (i.e. intangibility). Intangibility is composed of two dimensions: physical intangibility and mental intangibility. In the case of OR/MS decision support, which is the activity using mathematical techniques, it is necessary to recognize not only merely that what is provided is information (i.e. physical intangibility), but also that decision makers having insufficient mathematical knowledge cannot appreciate what is provided (i.e. mental intangibility). It is necessary for decision makers who have insufficient mathematical knowledge to be mentally present so that they can enjoy the benefit of OR/MS decision support. That is, it is important to enable decision makers to be convinced that their problem is solved through the whole process.

If we analyze OR/MS decision support from the viewpoint of what are necessary for service of high quality, we understand that communication between decision makers and decision supporters becomes important. However, there is a great difference between them in terms of occupational capability, intellectual background and vernacular to describe problems. This is the reason why we need to examine how to improve the communication gap between them.

If we investigate preceding research in OR/MS, it turns out that there is surely a problem with communication gap between decision makers and decision supporters. In this research, we show that it is effective to utilize problem specification as one approach to bridge the communication gap.

As a result of analyzing OR/MS decision support from a viewpoint of service, it leads to the conclusion that communication between decision makers and decision supporters is critically important. This is nothing but the improvement of communication gap between participants performing collaboration that was pointed out as one of the problem of service science to be settled at the very beginning in Morimoto & Sawatani (2005). If we take recognition that OR/MS decision support is service, it is hoped that we take further suggestions for improving OR/MS decision support from the research results of service science.

REFERENCES

Ackoff, R. L. (1974). Redesigning the Future: a systems approach to societal problems. New York: John Wiley & Sons.

Ackoff, R. L., & Sasieni, M. W. (1968). Fundamentals of Operations Research. New York: John Wiley & Sons.

Banerjee, S., & Basu, A. (1993). Model type selection in an integrated DSS environment. *Decision Support Systems*, *9*(1), 75–89. doi:10.1016/0167-9236(93)90024-W

Berry, L. L., & Parasuraman, A. (1991). Marketing Services: Competing through Quality. New York: Free Press.

Choobineh, J. (1991). A diagramming technique for representation of linear models. *OMEGA International Journal of Management Science*, *19*(1), 43–51. doi:10.1016/0305-0483(91)90033-P

Council on Competitiveness. (2004, December). *Innovate America: thriving in a world of challenge and change*. Presented at Global Innvation Ecosystem 2007 Symposium.

Geoffrion, A. M. (1987). An Introduction to Structured Modeling. *Management Science*, *33*(5), 547–588. doi:10.1287/mnsc.33.5.547

Grönroos, C. (1994). From Marketing Mix to Relationship Marketing: Towards a Paradigm Shift in Marketing. *Management Decision*, *32*(2), 4–20. doi:10.1108/00251749410054774

Hidaka, K. (2006, April). Trends in Services Sciences in Japan and Abroad. *Science & Technology Trends Quarterly Review*, *19*, 35–47.

IBM. (n.d.). *IBM Research*. Retrieved from http://www.research.ibm.com/ssme/

Kameoka, A. (2006). Saabisu, seihin, gijyutu inobesyon wo yuugou, sousyutu, hukan suru tougougata senryaku roodo mappingu [An integrated strategic road mapping that fuses, creates and surveys service, product and technical]. *Operations research as a management science research, 51*(9), 573-578.

Laroche, M., McDougall, G. H. G., Bergeron, J., & Yang, Z. (2004). Exploring How Intangibility Affects Perceived Risk. *Journal of Service Research, 6*(4), 373–389. doi:10.1177/1094670503262955

Levasseur, R. E. (2007). People Skill: Marketing OR/MS - A People Problem. *Interfaces, 37*(4), 383–384. doi:10.1287/inte.1060.0254

Little, J. D. C. (2004). Model and Managers: The Concept of a Decision Calculus. *Management Science, 50*(12), 1841-1853 (a reprint of a paper originally published in *Management Science*, 1970, *16*(8), 75-89).

Lovelock, C. H. (1983). Classifying Services to Gain Strategic Marketing Insights. *Journal of Marketing, 47*(3), 9–20. doi:10.2307/1251193

Lovelock, C. H. (1994). Product Plus: How Product + Service = Competitive Advantage. New York: McGraw-Hill.

McDougall, G. H. G., & Snetsinger, D. W. (1990). The Intangibility of Services: Measurement and Competitive Perspectives. *Journal of Services Marketing, 4*(4), 27–40. doi:10.1108/EUM0000000002523

Miyazaki, M. (1990). Atarasii sisutemuzu apuroochi to taiwagata OR: taiwagata OR no houhouronteki haikei wo nagamete [New Systems Approach and Interactive OR: Looking at methodological background of interactive OR]. *Operations research as a management science research, 35*(8), 454-456.

Morimoto, N., & Sawatani, Y. (2005, November). Saabisu saiensu no kanousei [The Potential of Service Science]. *Diamond Harvard Business Review*, 109-124.

Mukohara, T., & Sekiguchi, Y. (2002). The DSS architecture based on problems specification and model/solver independence. In E. Kozan, & A. Ohuch (Ed.), Operations Research/Management Science at work: Applying Theory in the Area Pacific Region (pp.281-298). The Netherlands: Kluwer Academic Publishers.

Mukohara, T., Sekiguchi, Y., & Bao, J. (2005). Jittai-kanren gainen no kakutyou niyoru sukejyuuring mondai kijyutu no tokutyou to ouyou [Scheduling Problems Specification by Extending Entity-Relationship Concept: Characteristics and Applications]. *Transactions of the Operations Research Society of Japan, 48*, 66–84.

Murphy, F. H. (2005). ASP, The Art and Science of Practice; Elements of a Theory of the Practice of Operations Research: A Framework. *Interfaces, 35*(2), 154–163. doi:10.1287/inte.1050.0126

Parasuraman, P., Zeithaml, V. A., & Berry, L. L. (1985). A Conceptual Model of Service Quality and Its Implications for Future Research. *Journal of Marketing, 49*(4), 41–50. doi:10.2307/1251430

Ueda, M., & Sekiguchi, Y. (2005). Mondaiteigi wo katuyou suru APS sofutouea sentaku tejyun no yuukousei nikansuru kenkyuu [Effectiveness of a Procedure for ASP Software Selection Based on Problem Specification]. *Journal of the Japan Society for Production Management, 11*(2), 57–66.

Walker, W. E. (2000). Policy Analysis: A Systematic Approach to Supporting Policymaking in the Public Sector. *Journal of Multi-criteria Decision Analysis, 9*(1-3), 11–27. doi:10.1002/1099-1360(200001/05)9:1/3<11::AID-MCDA264>3.0.CO;2-3

Yamada, Y. (1984). Manegiment sisutemu to OR: tokushuu ni attate [Management system and OR: In planning for this special topic]. *Operations research as a management science research, 29*(11), 632.

ENDNOTES

[1] Lovelock (1994) cited that "sleeping in class will not normally leave students much wiser at the end than they were at the beginning" (p.14) as an explanation for addressing if users are mentally present or not.

[2] There are several bodies of preceding research that propose methods for describing problems to be modeled into mathematical models (i.e. problem description method). However, the information described by the proposed methods is limited to explanation of the concerned mathematical model. Therefore, in this research, we use a term problem specification and make a distinction between problem specification and problem description method.

[3] A figure like Figure 4 is often used to make it easy to understand the interrelationship among object types (or objects). However, it is not an essential element in GERM problem specification. Refer to Ueda & Sekiguchi (2005) for what Figure 4 implies and the content of GERM problem specification corresponding to this figure.

[4] Refer to Mukohara & Sekiguchi (2002), Mukohara, Sekiguchi, & Bao (2005) for more details on GERM problem specification.

[5] APS (Advanced Planning and Scheduling) software, such as Scheduling Komei (Toyo Engineering Corp.), ASPROVA (Asprova Corp.), and Joy Scheduler (JT Engineering Inc.), is one for dealing with production planning and scheduling problems in an integrated way.

Section 4
Service Sourcing and Supplier Management

Chapter 10
A Multicriteria Tool for Evaluating Performance of Service Suppliers:
The Case of Met–Mex Peñoles Supply Chain

Albalicia Martínez Hernández
Universidad Tecnológica de Torreón, Mexico

Mario Cantú Sifuentes
Corporación Mexicana de Investigación en Materiales, S.A. de C.V. Mexico

Miguel Gastón Cedillo Campos
Tecnológico de Monterrey, Mexico

ABSTRACT

The purpose of this document is to expose an applied methodology for improving performance of service supply chains mainly focusing on performance of service suppliers running operations in emerging market context. In fact, this solution (methodology and informatics tool) was conceived as a standardized instrument for suppliers of the metallurgical sector. Whereas some researches analyze the service supplier selection, the originality of this work is its continuous improvement approach, based on a standard instrument to measure and improve the quality of service in a metallurgical supply chain. From a logistics standpoint, this applied approach was helpful to the practitioners who were faced with complex evaluating supplier tasks. Comparing with other approaches, the main advantages of the solution proposed is its hybrid methodology founded on a strong systemic point of view and, continuous improvement purpose, as well as its easiness of utilization by service suppliers themselves.

DOI: 10.4018/978-1-61520-603-2.ch010

INTRODUCTION

Although most of the studies aimed at analyzing the performance of the supply chains only involve the management of suppliers of tangible items (Beamon, 1998, 1999, Mabert, V. 1998), and the measurement of their performance within a value network becomes crucial for the competitiveness of the company. Since the primary objective of a supply chain is the satisfaction of its customer profitability, effectiveness, and efficiency. The cooperation of all the companies that are involved in a supply chain determines the competitiveness of the companies (Terzi and Cavalieri, 2004, Flores A., 2004). In fact, Beesley (1996), Duclos et al. (2003), and Cedillo et al. (2006) agree that competitiveness systematically involves all the supply chain, not only isolated entities.

As for the service suppliers, since the relationship between suppliers and buyers of the service includes many points of contact (Albrecht 1998), it is imperative to establish reasonable ways to measure the performance and the process monitoring (Franceschini, 1998, Hossein, 2002, Bellido, 2004, Vandaele 2007, Khurrum S., 2002).However, due to the intervention of human factors as the characteristics of intangibility, heterogeneity, and simultaneity of the production process and service consumption (Fernández, 1996; Zeithaml, Berry and Parasuraman, 2004), measuring the performance of service suppliers is a complex task.

Three major groups of organizations can be seen in any supply chain: 1) users (organization); 2) suppliers; and 3) customers (distributors, dealers). Each of these actors requires suppliers to provide them with everything they need for their activities. Because of this close dependence and the intense current competition, all members are obliged to accomplish the requirements and improve the ones perceived as added value by the customer. One of these specifications is the quality of service which requires organizations to have performance measures that provide information on the operation of processes.

Although most studies have been directed towards the measurement of tangible goods, service suppliers are a special case where the measurement of performance is a complex task. Nowadays, due to globalization, we can obtain required supplies for any kind of process from anywhere in the world. Consequently, the service is a dominant factor to be a difference backing up the competitive advantage of an organization.

Consequently, the increased integration of service suppliers to the operations of companies, force organizations to establish better control of supplier performance, especially in services that impact on time and therefore on costs of production processes.

This is particularly true of Met Mex Peñoles, which is oriented to the metallurgical sector, where our research was conducted. It requires provision of services such as: a) maintenance of equipment, machinery and facilities throughout the organization, b) fixed asset projects such as the expansion of areas, installation of machinery and equipment, c) major repairs to equipment, machinery and plant facilities. It should be noted that these services are essential to the proper functioning of the process, and therefore, are as important as the flow of supply of tangible products (Martinez et al., 2006).

Based on this interesting research area representing the service operations, the objectives of this document are to highlight the importance of quality service in the metallurgical sector, and show a tool for evaluating performance of service suppliers simple to implement and use in an emerging market context. In fact, this solution (methodology and informatics tool) was conceived as a standard instrument for suppliers in the Mexican metallurgical sector. Whereas an important quantity of researches analyzes the service supplier selection, the originality of this work is its continuous improvement approach based on a standard instrument to measure quality of service in a metallurgical supply chain. Actually, it was conceived as a support for improvement performance more than a supplier selection tool. The main advantages of the proposed method is its easiness of utilization by service suppliers themselves, and reliability founded on well established tools as SWOT (Strengths, Weaknesses, Opportunities, and Threats), moments of the truth, SERVQUAL, and AHP (Analytic Hierarchy Process).

After an important literature review it was visible that, as Seth et al. (2006a) argue, "The buyer-supplier relationship and management is a well-explored area but fewer studies are seen on the applicability of service quality concepts on the supplier side". At the same time, even if there are many information about dimensions of service quality, "there is no universal set of dimensions for measurement of service quality" (Seth et al., 2006b). At the same time, because in emerging markets there are substantially more operational risks due to factors like market and financial volatility; quality fade; supply disruptions; infrastructural challenges; lack of transparency and performance measurement problems; ad hoc solutions taking into account the impact of external environment factors on quality of service and easy to implement by all members of supply chain have to be found. In fact, when in a research context where there is complexity and lack of well-supported definitions and metrics a case study approach is favored (Yin, 1989; Stuart et al. 2002). Thus, this research was developed based on the particular case of the Met-Mex Peñoles the methodological design and implementation through a software tool has shown their high relevance. This analysis provides a method of performance evaluation in three stages.

In the balance of this document, the next section shows the background to the study, showing the characteristics of service suppliers and context of operation where the implementation was carried out. Section three exposes a literature review seeking to both the particularities of performance measurement of service suppliers, and aspects of the measurement of the concept of quality in service delivery. Section four discusses the proposed methodology and the informatics tool developed for its implementation. Finally, some conclusions about the process and future work are exposed.

BACKGROUND

Met Mex Peñoles is a mining group founded in 1887 with integrated operations in smelting and refining non-ferrous metals, and producing chemicals. Called just "Peñoles", it is the world's top producer of refined silver, metallic bismuth and sodium sulfate. It is also the leading Latin American producer of refined gold, lead and zinc. Currently, it is one of the largest net exporters in Mexico's private sector. The company has 12 production sites and is organized around four divisions: 1) Exploration, engineering and construction Division; 2) Mining; 3) Metals-Chemicals; 4) Infrastructure.

The exploration, engineering and construction division is engaged in locating, studying, analyzing and developing valuable deposits of non-ferrous metals in Mexico and Latin America, in order to build up the Group's current reserves. This division is also responsible for developing engineering projects and construction for the Group's operating divisions.

The mining division is focused on the exploration of minerals with metallic contents of gold, silver, lead, zinc and copper, to produce lead, zinc and copper concentrates, gold-silver precipitates, and doré. It operates the world's richest underground silver mine (Fresnillo), the richest underground gold mine (La Ciénega), the largest open-cut gold mine (La Herradura) and the largest under ground zinc mine (Francisco I. Madero) in Mexico.

The Metals-Chemicals division operates two businesses: Metals and Chemicals. The Metals business operates the largest non-ferrous metallurgical complex (Met-Mex Peñoles) in Latin

America, and the fourth largest in the world in terms of production value. Its facilities include a lead foundry, a lead-silver refinery and an electrolytic zinc refinery; it also operates plants that make sulfuric acid, cadmium, bismuth, ammonium sulfate, and liquid sulfur dioxide. The Chemicals business is engaged in the production and sale of sodium sulfate, magnesium oxide, magnesium sulfate, and ammonium sulfate (fertilizer). It has the largest sodium sulfate plant (Química del Rey) in the world.

The infrastructure division is focused on seeking and managing projects to guarantee the supply and control the costs of the logistical and electrical energy needs of Peñoles. It also seeks out opportunities that can contribute to growth and diversification of the company in keeping with its overall vision. It has an international marine terminal (Termimar) for shipping chemical products in bulk, a railway line (Coahuila-Durango) for carrying raw materials and finished products, two companies (TECSA and IACMEX) engaged in the administration of municipal drinking water service in Mexico City, an integral concession (Desarrollos Hidráulicos de Cancún) that manages and cleans water in the municipalities of Cancun and Isla Mujeres and is responsible for assigning energy from the company's thermoelectric plant (Termoeléctrica Peñoles) to group operations.

Service Suppliers in the Met Mex Peñoles Supply Chain

Service suppliers, as a central element of the supply chain, are no longer viewed as isolated entities. The current trend is to create customer-supplier alliances in order to generate mutual benefits in terms of time and cost. In Met Mex Peñoles there are two types of suppliers:

a. Internal suppliers: they are staff within the organization that provide either tangible property (which leads to offer a service) or an intangible asset (service).

b. External suppliers: These are individuals or corporations who do not belong to the organization and provide a tangible good or an intangible asset.

In its relationship with the company, a supplier goes at least through two steps: the entry and stay in the supply chain. At the stage of admission, the supplier is selected from a group of other vendors who do the kind of work required by the company. On the other hand, once the supplier has been selected, before the continuous improvement approach is implemented, the organization assesses its performance so as to determine its permanence within their supply chain.

In the company, the evaluation occurs in two ways to suppliers of tangible assets: 1) evaluating the quality of the product, 2) evaluation of service delivery that is involved. For service suppliers, the evaluation is performed only in the perception of quality service. Assessing the quality of the product is relatively simple, because it is tangible to measure weight, height, thickness, etc. However, to evaluate a service, the task is more complex because the main feature of the service is perception.

In the latter case, it should also be noted that any service is intangible, heterogeneous and momentary. It is intangible because the service cannot be measured, weigh, and so on. It is heterogeneous since the services provided by different vendors are different, and momentary as the customer-supplier interaction in the process of service (hereinafter such interaction will be referred to as servuction[1]) is given in a short period of time (Fernández, 1996).

Development of Service Suppliers and Maintenance System

For the development of applied research, the study was developed in four plants of Met Mex Peñoles: 1) Zinc 2) Foundry, 3) Refinery and 4) Unit Bermejillo. The company requires three types of outsourcing in these plants: a) maintenance of equipment, machinery and facilities throughout the organization, b) fixed asset projects such as the expansion of areas, installation of machinery and equipment, c) major repairs for equipment, machinery and plant facilities.

To support the development of its suppliers, the company has a management of suppliers called "Development and maintenance of service suppliers". The steps for this system are:

1. **Selection of the supplier:** administrative procedures for the recruitment of the supplier are carried out in this phase. At this point, the supplier must be selected with the following requirements: a) knowledge of the operational processes of the plant Peñoles, b) security measures, i.e. PPE (Personal Protective Equipment), and implemented elements of ecology, c) equipment and work tool of last generation, d) communication systems, at least, radios and cell phones, e) administrative computer systems; network and internet, f) qualified staff for the type of work to do, g) minimum staff turnover, h) quality systems in place, i) economic solvency.

2. **Training supplier:** Training provided for suppliers is focused in two ways: i) quality systems and ii) security systems. This emphasizes the prevention of accidents.

3. **Evaluation of the supplier:** The company has a portfolio of suppliers that is divided into two groups:

    a) **Supplier Development Group:** It is formed by 34 suppliers. These are the most frequently performed works representing 80% of the work.

    b) **Suppliers of retail group:** This group of suppliers is performing minor and infrequent works, representing 20% of the work.

The vendor evaluation is conducted in two phases:

*   **Assessment of quality of service (or daily assessment)** is done each time you receive a service without regard to the group to which the supplier belongs. It is restricted to evaluate the services that have a cost over $ 3000.00 dollars.

*   **Evaluation of supplier's quality system:** the evaluation process is as follows: it forms a team of three people: a client (the person who requested the service), an engineering supervisor (who contracted the service) and an engineer of service area (whether health and safety, quality or engineering). The team visits the plant of the supplier, the assessment and the data obtained through an analysis of strengths and weaknesses are unified criteria. It develops a final report, which is delivered to the supplier. The supplier outlines a strategic plan to deliver improvements in a month, after receiving the report; He has a term of six months to improve his weaknesses. It is necessary to mention that this evaluation phase is not involved in our case study, however, it is important to show the way in which it is conducted. With regard to the processing of information it is relevant to stress that 125 evaluations are performed a month. The assessment consists of averaging the points earned by the supplier in each reagent. The capture of data is performed by a single person in Microsoft Excel. The final qualification of the supplier is formed by the weight of 70% -30%, corresponding to the first assessment of the quality of service, and 30% for evaluating the supplier's quality system.

4. **Development:** Development to suppliers is focused exclusively on the updated concepts of quality, health,

hygiene and safety, technical training is the responsibility of the supplier.

5. **Acknowledgment:** If the supplier obtains a score higher than 90 in their evaluation, he is recognized as "reliable", and can evaluate Met-Mex Peñoles as his client. Similarly, he accesses to sign annual agreements, between $ 10,000.00 and $ 200,000.00 U.S. dollars. The supplier evaluation system described above is, like all systems, possible to improve. With this in mind, the following analysis was conducted on strengths and weaknesses.

Strengths and Weaknesses of the System

This is an approach that was created at the beginning of the seventies and produced a revolution in the field of corporate strategy. The analysis of strengths and weaknesses is part of the SWOT analysis (Strength, Weaknesses, Opportunities, Threats), which is a methodology for studying the competitive situation of a company within its market and its internal characteristics. For the analysis of the weaknesses and strengths, we tried to identify the internal factors that create or destroy value in the company's operations (See Table 1):

1. Selection of the supplier.
   a. **Strengths:** an administrative procedure for suppliers has been established, and the company has established a portfolio of suppliers.
   b. **Weaknesses:** The firm only considers the hiring of a new supplier if the service required cannot supplied by one of its suppliers. This policy limits the consideration of potentially reliable suppliers.
   c. **Opportunities:** the process generation that helps the supplier evaluation once they belong to the organization.

   d. **Threats:** rejection to change could be strengthened, and the improvement of the process or supplier evaluation performance could be neglected.
2. Supplier training.
   a. **Strengths:** one of the company policies is to provide an induction seminar for staff of suppliers entering the plant for the first time.
   b. **Weaknesses:** the induction training is essential to prevent any situation, for example: the company procedures, safety and hygiene, and to complete the organization's needs, so as not to show weaknesses at this stage.
   c. **Opportunities:** based on the organization needs, suggest the suppliers what kina of technical training is required in order to get a better specialization of the offered services.
   d. **Threats:** lack of a training system on the side of the supplier, so as to identify training needs and development, as well as lack of commitment to invest on training.
3. Assessment to the Supplier.
   a. **Strengths:** the company attaches importance to the evaluation of suppliers this is why a system which has evolved over time was designed ten years ago.
   b. **Weaknesses:** when assessing a service, the form will not be immediately delivered to the administrator. The suppliers fall into two categories: trusted or not trusted.

This classification is not optimal because the means of the observations tend to take the value of the average population, and the point cloud formed by the middle of suppliers will be dense.

The focus of the criteria is given in three areas: quality, quantity and timeliness; these terms, in the tangible environment, may be easier to implement, especially the term of quantity, because the supplier must meet a number of pieces to deliver.

c. **Opportunities**: to define a tool that helps evaluate the supplier performance, taking

into account that one of the main service characteristics is perception, contributing to a supplier classification in which three aspects are possible to distinguish: accepted (which means that the offered services go

Table 1. Summary of strengths and weaknesses of the system development and maintenance of suppliers

#	STAGE	STRENGTHS	WEAKNESSES	OPPORTUNITIES	THREATS
1.	SUPPLIER SE-LECTION	It has established an administrative procedure for suppliers. The company has a portfolio of established suppliers.	This policy limits the consideration of potentially reliable suppliers.	Generation of an evaluation process to current suppliers.	Enhancing the resistance to change
2.	THE SUPPLIER TRAINING	The company has a training plan for suppliers.	No weaknesses were identified at this stage	Suggestion to improve technical training in the specialization of suppliers	Lack of commitment to investment in training. Lack of a training area
3.	ASSESSMENT TO THE SUPPLIER	There is a procedure for evaluating the supplier. Instruments are designed to carry out the assessment. Quality criteria are applied to the structure of the instrument.	The assessment of the supplier is given by averaging the points obtained in the reagents considered. The information system gathering and processing the data is slow. The assessment tool contains 13 criteria, of which only 8 are caught. The criteria are focused on three concepts: quality (as such, is a comprehensive approach), quantity (with a focus on the service) and opportunity (taking only the availability of the supplier for the service). Deliveries of the assessments are late. No respect in the valuation range provided in the instrument. Service is over-evaluated.	Definition of a tool to consider levying the assessment of suppliers and that classify them. Integrate a tool that contains the assessment, improving the administration in terms of time and cost evaluations.	High resistance to system change of suppliers.
4.	SUPPLIER DE-VELOPMENT	An induction training supplier is given. Whenever there is a new concept with respect to "Quality" is given to the supplier for upgrade.	Lack of application of statistical tools by suppliers in order to improve control their processes, which agree with the requirements of the assessment of the quality system applied by Met-Mex.	Achieve matching requirements of the organization with the interests of suppliers.	Resistance to growth as an organization.
5.	RECOGNITION TO THE SUPPLIER	For the company, it is important to recognize suppliers who meet the specifications.	No weaknesses were identified at this stage	Establish a greater emphasis on the growth of both organizations	Due to the resistance to growth, suppliers are not attracted to acknowledgments.

on fulfilling the specifications), conditioned (warning for the supplier about the fulfillment of the corporation requirements), rejected (it is defined as the last indicator which once conditioned did not show improvement, then the reposition is carried on). With the use of a system to administrate the evaluations, which will help on time and cost of used material, and generates specific reports about the suppliers.

d. **Threats:** high rejection to the management change of the supplier evaluation process.

4. Development of the supplier.

    a. **Strengths:** training to suppliers of group development is focused on keeping them updated on the new concepts that emerge around quality.

    b. **Weaknesses:** Met-Mex Peñoles requests the use of statistical tools for suppliers in the evaluation system of quality, for which it is necessary to provide training focused on the requirements of the assessment.

    c. **Opportunities:** make both the requirements of the organization and the suppliers' interests agree with each other .

    d. **Threats:** There is a resistance on the part of suppliers to have a growing company.

5. Recognition to the supplier.

    a. **Strengths:** The Company believes it is important to reward the suppliers that meet the specifications, giving them both moral stimuli (with a diploma where the suppliers are called "reliable") and incentives in kind. The latter are granted through signing of agreements with a specified amount, creating stability for a year, working with the supplier.

b. **Weaknesses:** The combination of recognition and moral generate stability in the staff of any organization, therefore, there are no weaknesses at this stage.

c. **Opportunities:** in addition to the recognition that the company currently provides, it is vital to emphasize the need to achieve the quality required by both organizations.

d. **Threats:** Due to the difficulty of growth, suppliers won't be attracted to achieve this kind of recognition.

LITERATURE REVIEW

Moments of Truth

For our research work, it was understood that the service consists of the set of processes which aim is the satisfaction of needs, presented in the form of an intangible asset. According to Evans and Lindsay (2001), the service "... it is a social act that occurs in direct contact with users and representatives of the service organization ...." As such, during the interaction between users and representatives there is a moment in which the client live an experience, which may be said to be good or bad (Gronroos, C.,1982, Juran J., 2001)

Carlzon (1987) who was head of Scandinavian Airlines Systems (SAS), popularized such moments as the moments of truth, making SAS more than business-oriented operations, a customer oriented one.

Richard Normann (1991), who took a metaphor referring to the bullfights explained: "We can say that quality is perceived in the moment of truth when the service supplier and the client confront one another on the ring. At that time, they depend largely on themselves ... These are the skills, motivation and the tools used by the company representative and the customer's expectations of behavior that create the process of service. "

Under this scheme, two moments are defined: a) Stellar (when according to the customer, the service met his expectations); b) Bitter (otherwise). It should be noted that the moments of truth may also result from interaction with the infrastructure (anywhere the service cycle is carried out).

For the identification of the moments of the servuction, it is important to understand the factors involved in the service and which are the bases for the identification of processes are. Karl Albrecht (1984) presents a triangle of the service, which shows those factors: a) staff, which provides customer service oriented, b) systems, i.e. how to process the service organization; c) strategies to effectively enable the system to satisfy customer expectations. Having identified the factors of the service, another important concept was the service cycle, which is the sequence of activities in stages that allow observing servuction, and it is where the moments of truth are strongly identified.

Defining the service cycle is a principle of the establishment of the moments of truth, as it has been said; they represent the bitter or stellar situations trough which the customer goes during the service. The advantages of structuring the moments of truth are classified as follows (Albrecht, 1984):

a. Establishing and knowing how the service cycle is carry out.
b. Identifying the key activities of strong interaction between the customer-supplier.
c. Identifying persons involved in each moment of truth.
d. Knowing the situations faced by people involved in the service cycle, through which it might be relevant to evaluate the service.
e. Knowing all strengths and weaknesses of the system in conjunction with the client.

Once the service cycle is established, and relevant activities identified in the client-supplier relationship, the customers involved in the transaction service are identified with the aim of researching "moments" experienced in servuction (stellar or bitter) on the field. As a result, it is possible to define strategies on the one hand to support and enhance the great moments and on the other hand, the search for improvements to the bitter moments.

SERVQUAL (Service Quality)

One of the models representing the real level of quality achieved in an organization from the standpoint of their clients is that of Parasuraman, Zeithaml and Berry (Ruiz, 2001, Cronin, J. J. and Taylor, S., 1992, 1999), through a questionnaire. According to Heung et al. (2000) SERVQUAL is a simple, inexpensive, and easy model to implement that considers two factors in providing a service: a) the expectation, a customer creates an expectation which is given as a service, b) the perception, when after the service; the customer gets a perception and then makes a distinction between what is expected to eventually obtain.

As the numeric indicator shows:

$$SERVQUAL = \sum \left(P_i - E_i \right) \qquad (1)$$

Where:

P_i = Perceptions
E_i = Expectations

With the information obtained from questionnaires were calculated perceptions (P_i) minus expectations (E_i) for each pair of statements.

Actually, the conceptual model of quality of SERVQUAL is divided into two parts, which are related to one another: 1) Client: refers to the manner in which they form an opinion of the quality of services received, 2) Enterprise: the deficiencies that may occur in the organization and leads to a decline in the quality of supplies to customers

(See figure 1). Although a number of critiques on a range of issues of SERVQUAL, it is one of the most accepted tools in the field of service quality (Seth et al., 2005). In fact, most of the studies in the service quality area are based on the work of Parasuraman et al. (1985, 1988).

It can be seen, there are "gaps" in the model, which are defined as discrepancies between expectation and perception. These discrepancies are attributed to the clients or the organizations providing services. The "gaps" are defined as follows:

- **Gap1:** Indicates the discrepancy between customer expectations on service and the perceptions that managers have about what the consumer of that service must expect.
- **Gap 2:** Is the difference between the perceptions of managers and specifications or quality standards.
- **Gap 3:** Is the difference between the specifications or standards of service quality and delivery of it.
- **Gap 4:** Is the discrepancy between service delivery and external communication.
- **Gap 5:** Is the discrepancy between service delivery and perceived performance.

- **Gap 6:** Is the difference between expected and perceived performance, identifying with this the level of quality achieved.

Another important aspect of the model is the establishment of attributes called dimensions, which must develop and maintain any organization focused on service, which deal with general aspects that must be evaluated in a service and are summarized in five:

1. Tangible elements: it refers to the physical appearance of facilities, equipment, personal and communication materials.
2. Reliability: it indicates the ability of the organization to run the service promised in a reliable and careful way.
3. Response capacity: it refers to the willingness to assist clients to provide prompt service.
4. Safety: it is the knowledge and care shown by staff and ability to inspire confidence and credibility.
5. Empathy: individualized attention offered by companies to their customers. The implementation of the dimensions of service is general, i.e., any service can be assessed.

Figure 1. A model of satisfaction (Zeithaml, 2004)

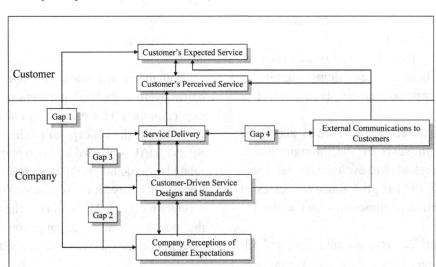

Methods of Multi-Criteria Decision

Process for Decision Making

Decision making is a process of selection among alternative courses of action based on a set of criteria to achieve one or more targets, and is a term generally associated with the first five stages of the process for problem solving (Simon, 1960).

The decision making has three aspects: a) a problem, for which one should obtain a solution, b) a decision-maker, who is the person or persons that must make the decision, b) alternatives, representing the different options to choose for the solution of the problem, taken by the decision-maker.

The way in which a decision is made, begins at the time a problem appears, with different alternatives for its solution, which must be looked for. Then, one of the alternatives is chosen and fixed.

Simon (1960), mentions that decision making can take two forms: qualitative and quantitative. The quality is involved when the reasoning and experience are taken into account, and even the perception of the decision maker, while the qualitative data involves the facts associated with the problem, and can develop mathematical expressions that reflect the problem, its restrictions, and existing relationships.

The problems that have a single decision criterion for their solution are called single decision criterion, while those with more than one is called multi-criteria decision problems.

Analysis of Multicriteria Decision

Once described the process for decision making, it appears that the measurement of performance of service suppliers is undoubtedly a multi-issue, because there are at least two conflicting approaches in their assessment, after they have been selected. Multi-criteria decision making has developed a personality that uses a specific terminology, including new concepts such as: a)

approaches, which are the possible solutions or actions taken by the decision-maker; b) attributes, characteristics used to describe each of the alternatives available (quantitative or qualitative), and each alternative can be characterized by a number of attributes (chosen by the decision-maker); c) objectives, which are the aspirations that suggest directions for improving the selected attributes and are associated with the wishes and preferences of decision; d) goals, which are the aspirations that specify levels of attribute wishes; e) criteria, which are the parameters, guidelines and benchmarks that will allow assessment of the options or alternatives presented in the decision process (Chen, S.J. and Hwang, C.L., 1991, Triantaphyllou, 2000, Wang G. 2004, Wei-Ning 2005).

Assessment Methods and Discrete Multi-Criteria Decision.

Evaluation methods and multi-criteria decision making include the choice between a set of feasible alternatives, optimization with multiple objective functions simultaneously, a decision-maker and agent evaluation procedures and consistent sound (Martínez and Escudey, 1998).

These methods help the decision-making process, including decision-maker preferences, in order to obtain an ordering (ranking) of the alternatives selected, the latter being a finite number. In the 80's, Saaty proposed the analytical method of ranking (Analytic Hierarchy Process, AHP), which becomes ever more popular, among others (Belton, V., and Gear, T., 1983, Brady, M. K. and Cronin, J.J. 2001). AHP is a method of selection of alternatives, depending on a number of criteria or variables, which are often in conflict, such as the criteria to be evaluated in a supplier.

AHP both ponders the criteria and the various alternatives using the paired comparison matrices and the fundamental scale for peer comparisons. Within the method, Saaty proposes a measurement scale, which is shown in Table 2.

Table 2. Scale of relative importance (Saaty, 1980)

Importance intensity (numerical assessment)	Definition	Meaning of the assessment
1	Equally important	Criterion *A* is as important as criterion *B*
3	Weak importance of one over another.	Experience and trial slightly favor *A* over *B*.
5	Essential or strong importance	Experience and trial strongly favor *A* on *B*
7	Very high importance	Criterion *A* is much more important than *B*.
9	Extreme importance	Most important criterion
2,4,6 and 8	Intermediate values between two adjacent judgments	When it is necessary to qualify
Reciprocal of the above	If the criterion *A* is significant compared to criterion *B* the notations would be the following: criterion *A* versus criterion *B* 5/1, and criterion *B* versus criterion *A* 1/5.	

With such an assessment a matrix $A_{n \times n}$ is constructed, where a_{ij} is the comparison between the *j* item and the *i* item. And it must meet certain characteristics. The aim is to find the eigenvector showing the weights of the ratings given to the alternatives and criteria so that the method is based on the principles of principal components, thus helping to classify the performance of service suppliers.

Even if there are other existing multi-criteria techniques that can be used, AHP is proposed as a suitable technique because it may be helpful to practitioners who are faced with processes where service suppliers are involved.

METHODOLOGICAL DESIGN AND IMPLEMENTATION

Basis for the Methodological Design

According to Jankowicz (1991), the methods and techniques appropriate depend on the problem and goals. The main objective of our study was to develop a methodology to respond to the competitive needs of a specific business operation (Crosby P. 1984, Chase, Aquilano and Jacobs 1998, Cantú, H. 2001). After analyzing the various tools related to quality of service, the need for appropriate methodology for measuring and support service

suppliers in the metallurgical sector in Mexico to continuously improve its performance was identified. The methodology has three stages: a) Definition a set of indicators, concepts and dimensions to provide quality service through the tool moments of truth, in combination with the dimensions SERVQUAL (defined as the base platform), b) Analyze of the relevance of methods such as multi-criteria decision support tools for measurement, c) Development of an informatics tool as support for continuous improving process of services suppliers (see Figure 2).

Using the Moments of Truth

The purpose of the application of the moments of truth was to obtain information on the criteria that impact customer who maintains a strong interaction with suppliers. The application of the moment of truth was divided into two stages described below:

- **Stage 1:** Defining the service cycle in which the client-supplier interaction.

Today the organization has set diagrams of processes, which reflect the service cycles for facilitating the identification of the activities in which customers are strongly linked with suppliers and staff to accomplish this task.

The review of the process diagrams identify two processes in which customers interact with service suppliers: a) work orders, b) service requests. Note that each process has its own internal policies established by the organization. Within each of the process, the stages where there is a stronger interface between customer-supplier are highlighted, giving way to concrete steps. In our case study, the *supervisors*[2] act strongly with both the supplier that is *advisers*[3] and the *contractor*[4], because the supervisors evaluate the two types of suppliers.

The way that defines the application process and work order[5] is summarized as follows:

1. **Client:** delivers work order or request from the domestic supplier for the recruitment of the outside vendor providing the service. The client maintains feedback during the execution of the work with both the external and the internal supplier.

2. **Internal supplier:** receives the order or request for work, the advisers select and hire external suppliers within the pattern of the organization, to carry out the work. The adviser supervises during the performance of the external service supplier.

3. **External supplier:** any contract that belongs to the pattern of suppliers of the organization

Figure 2. Methodology for measuring the performance of service suppliers

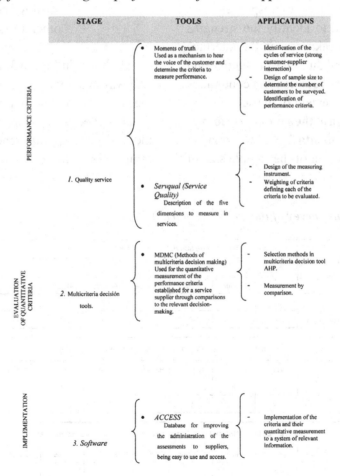

is available to contest for the work that the organization needs to make, and the selection is realized according to the established criteria.

- **Stage 2:** Collecting and analyzing data.
    1. **Development of format for data collection:** The format for data collection plan was established, which took into account only the phases of strong interrelationship between customer-supplier. In the format, there are no response options provided to respondents, in order not to bias their responses since what was sought was that both the stellar and bitter moments were expressed. The significance of responses later helped to identify the strengths and weaknesses in the interface set, and thus take preventive and corrective actions for continuous improvement of the service.
    2. **Design of the sample size for the implementation of the survey:** the design of the sample size of

the staff survey was done through a stratified sampling, which was relevant considering that the population of the different plants that use the services of internal and external suppliers of study is divided into strata. This took into account within the population (who are appointed applicants), those with a greater percentage for all services provided in a year, received more services (higher percentage of applicants). In the Figure 3 shown by columns, plants that make up the organization in the region such as the zinc plant, smelting, refining, fertirey, bermejillo, alezin and other areas.

As shown in Figure 3, a comparative sample size was made with respect to all applicants vs. the higher percentage of requests made to service suppliers, because the population size is very small, there is not a big difference between it and the sample size. The survey was conducted with an

Figure 3. Results of the survey of the moments of truth

Concept	SAMPLE SIZE FOR THE SURVEY OF THE MOMENTS OF TRUTH							Staff total number
	Zinc	Foundry	Refinery	Bermejillo	Fertirey	Aleazin	Others	
Demand of service	20	16	16	3	4	4	6	69
Major demand percentage	12	11	11	2	2	2	3	43

Percentage error	SAMPLE SIZE INCLUDING ALL THE DEMAND OF SERVICES							Staff total number
	Zinc	Foundry	Refinery	Bermejillo	Fertirey	Aleazin	Others	
3	19	15	15	3	4	4	6	66
5	17	14	14	3	3	3	5	59

Percentage error	SAMPLE SIZE INCLUDING ONLY THE MAJOR PERCENTAGE OF REALIZED REQUEST							Staff total number
	Zinc	Foundry	Refinery	Bermejillo	Fertirey	Aleazin	Others	
3	11	10	10	2	2	2	3	40
5	11	10	10	2	2	2	3	40

3. **Application:** pre-explanation on the methodology, the importance and impact on the improvement of the assessment instrument, the survey applies to specific groups of people.

4. **Combination of information criteria:** once the data format was filled by supervisors, each of the criteria defined by plant and per cycle was collected. Similarly, both the stellar moments of truth, and the bitterness were captured.

5. **Determination of the frequencies on the basis of experience embodied by the supervisors:** the frequencies were determined with the criteria that were common to supervisors for every step of the service cycle rated.

6. **Diagram Frequency:** once certain frequencies were concentrated, we obtained concepts in common. Finally global concepts were established, which in turn contain all the provided by the supervisors. The weighting was determined by the individual criteria.

7. **Final results:** criteria that the supervisors provided, reflect the need to evaluate both the expectation (i.e. what they expect the service will provide) and perceptions (what has finally be obtained from all their experiences suppliers).

SERVQUAL as a Platform for Evaluation

The design of the instrument performance was given after obtaining the general criteria together with their weights. However, SERVQUAL provides the five dimensions to evaluate any service, as well as the analysis of the criteria provided by the supervisors, involving the need to evaluate both the perception and expectation, and these are the two main features of the model.

Global benchmarks belonging to each defined service level are intertwined with the dimensionality of SERVQUAL, obtaining a final assessment with the following characteristics: a) assesses levels of service previously identified, b) assesses the stages where there is a strong customer-supplier relationship, c) contains the general criteria where the perceptions and expectations of customers are integrated with the dimensionality of the service.

Measurement and Evaluation of Classification Criteria

Since the service is measured mostly by qualitative attributes, how to measure these attributes is a sequential series of services, it is necessary to find the preferences of those who were involved during the service process (Nelly, 1995). The standard way of classification means of numerical averages. In this sense, they are averaged for each criterion along successive assessments, i.e. whether $c_i=(c_{i1},c_{i2},\ldots,c_{ip})'$ represents the vector of average values of the criteria of the attributes for the supplier, $i=1,\ldots,n$ and being $a=(1/p,\ldots,1/p)$ where a is a vector of weights, then the overall average m_i for the $i'th$ supplier is given by the following expression:

$$m_i = c_i'a, \qquad i = 1, 2, \ldots, n \qquad (2)$$

However, the classification using this approach can become complex because, speaking freely, the averages tend to be "very close" since the media has a minimal variance.

Another reasonable approach is to use a linear combination, $r_i = c_i'\gamma$, of the average values of the criteria that has maximal variance. Principal component analysis (Mardia et al. 1979) provides the vector $\gamma=(\gamma_1,\ldots\gamma_p)'$.

In fact the vector that maximizes the variance of linear combinations is the eigenvector associated with the largest eigenvalue of the covariance matrix whose components are the global averages of the ratings of the performance criteria of suppliers.

Another possibility is to use multi-criteria optimization tools, such as Analytic Hierarchy Process (AHP) (Satty, 2000), because they incorporate, by weight, customer preferences for performance criteria, thus taking into account his or her opinion in the decision making. The weights can be obtained from information contained in the survey. Indeed, preferences for the criteria are the relative frequencies of global benchmarks.

Following the steps (Aznar, J. 2006) to implement the AHP model, the process was performed for the classification of service suppliers:

1.   It starts with the interest of the decision-maker to select the most attractive among all of them (strategies, investments, assets, etc).

The need to make decisions on suppliers who have entered the organization is relevant to any organization, since it can prevent re-work which are of high cost and the time of replenishment from suppliers.

2.   Define what criteria will be used to determine the selection, i.e. what characteristics that can make a more desirable alternative over another.

These criteria were provided by the supervisors, with whom he designed the assessment tool.

3.   Once the alternatives are known and the criteria defined, we must first order and balance the different interests of each of the criteria in the selection of alternatives through the evaluation of the criteria in pairs.

The weight, just as was stipulated in the assessment instrument, is contained in each of the criteria.

4.   Once the weighting of criteria is known, we need to weigh the different alternatives according to each criterion.

At this point the matrix was constructed, making assessments, with the valuation range of the tool itself. This is an $m \times m$ matrix which is denoted as $A=\{a_{ij}\}$, and is such that if $a_{ii}=1$ and if $a_{ij}=x$, then $a_{ji}=1/x$. A matrix is often called reciprocal. See Figure 4.

5.   With the two previous processes c and d two matrices are obtained, a column matrix $n \times 1$ with the weighting of criteria (with n the number of criteria) and a matrix $m \times n$ of weights of the alternatives for each criterion (where m is the number of alternatives).

Then Figure 5 is made up as follows:

*   **First column:** Displays the scale representing each of the criteria overall.
*   **Second column:** Indicates the number of items to evaluate. Rows shaded in red represent the first evaluation cycle service identified, the blue of the second cycle and so on.
*   **Third column:** Criteria to assess.
*   **Fourth column:** Shows the response options, consistent with the valuation range of the tool itself.
*   **Fifth column:** Shows the value of each criterion according to the response option selected, which build the first matrix that indicates the valuation of the criteria.

With matrix A, an eigenvector close approach is obtained as follows: is $1=(1,...,1)'$ a column vector m X 1; being

$$ev(n) \leftarrow \frac{A^n \underline{1}}{\underline{1}' A^n \underline{1}}$$

A common formula, evaluate it until you find the value of n, lets say n, so that $|ev(n_o)-ev(n_o-1)| \leq \varepsilon \underline{1}$,

Figure 4. Valuation matrix

ITEMS		1	2	3	4	5	6	7	8	9	10	11	12	13	14	15	16	17	18	19	20	21	22
		1	5	3	5	1	3	9	9	3	3	5	3	9	9	9	3	7	9	3	9	9	9
1	1		5	3	5	1	3	9	9	3	3	5	3	9	9	9	3	7	9	3	9	9	9
2	5	1/5		3/5	1	1/5	3/5	1 4/5	1 4/5	3/5	3/5	1	3/5	1 4/5	1 4/5	1 4/5	3/5	1 2/5	1 4/5	3/5	1 4/5	1 4/5	1 4/5
3	3	1/3	1 2/3		1 2/3	1/3	1	3	3	1	1	1 2/3	1	3	3	3	1	2 1/3	3	1	3	3	3
4	5	1/5	1	3/5		1/5	3/5	1 4/5	1 4/5	3/5	3/5	1	3/5	1 4/5	1 4/5	1 4/5	3/5	1 2/5	1 4/5	3/5	1 4/5	1 4/5	1 4/5
5	1	1	5	3	5		3	9	9	3	3	5	3	9	9	9	3	7	9	3	9	9	9
6	3	1/3	1 2/3	1	1 2/3	1/3		3	3	1	1	1 2/3	1	3	3	3	1	2 1/3	3	1	3	3	3
7	9	1/9	5/9	1/3	5/9	1/9	1/3		1	1/3	1/3	5/9	1/3	1	1	1	1/3	7/9	1	1/3	1	1	1
8	9	1/9	5/9	1/3	5/9	1/9	1/3	1		1/3	1/3	5/9	1/3	1	1	1	1/3	7/9	1	1/3	1	1	1
9	3	1/3	1 2/3	1	1 2/3	1/3	1	3	3		1	1 2/3	1	3	3	3	1	2 1/3	3	1	3	3	3
10	3	1/3	1 2/3	1	1 2/3	1/3	1	3	3	1		1 2/3	1	3	3	3	1	2 1/3	3	1	3	3	3
11	5	1/5	1	3/5	1	1/5	3/5	1 4/5	1 4/5	3/5	3/5		3/5	1 4/5	1 4/5	1 4/5	3/5	1 2/5	1 4/5	3/5	1 4/5	1 4/5	1 4/5
12	3	1/3	1 2/3	1	1 2/3	1/3	1	3	3	1	1	1 2/3		3	3	3	1	2 1/3	3	1	3	3	3
13	9	1/9	5/9	1/3	5/9	1/9	1/3	1	1	1/3	1/3	5/9	1/3		1	1	1/3	7/9	1	1/3	1	1	1
14	9	1/9	5/9	1/3	5/9	1/9	1/3	1	1	1/3	1/3	5/9	1/3	1		1	1/3	7/9	1	1/3	1	1	1
15	9	1/9	5/9	1/3	5/9	1/9	1/3	1	1	1/3	1/3	5/9	1/3	1	1		1/3	7/9	1	1/3	1	1	1
16	3	1/3	1 2/3	1	1 2/3	1/3	1	3	3	1	1	1 2/3	1	3	3	3		2 1/3	3	1	3	3	3
17	7	1/7	5/7	3/7	5/7	1/7	3/7	1 2/7	1 2/7	3/7	3/7	5/7	3/7	1 2/7	1 2/7	1 2/7	3/7		1 2/7	3/7	1 2/7	1 2/7	1 2/7
18	9	1/9	5/9	1/3	5/9	1/9	1/3	1	1	1/3	1/3	5/9	1/3	1	1	1	1/3	7/9		1/3	1	1	1
19	3	1/3	1 2/3	1	1 2/3	1/3	1	3	3	1	1	1 2/3	1	3	3	3	1	2 1/3	3		3	3	3
20	9	1/9	5/9	1/3	5/9	1/9	1/3	1	1	1/3	1/3	5/9	1/3	1	1	1	1/3	7/9	1	1/3		1	1
21	9	1/9	5/9	1/3	5/9	1/9	1/3	1	1	1/3	1/3	5/9	1/3	1	1	1	1/3	7/9	1	1/3	1		1
22	9	1/9	5/9	1/3	5/9	1/9	1/3	1	1	1/3	1/3	5/9	1/3	1	1	1	1/3	7/9	1	1/3	1	1	

Figure 5. Screen of valuation of the criteria

DIMENSIONALITY	No.	QUESTIONING	RESPONSE OPTIONS	VALUATION
SECURITY	1	Were the requirements for the service understood?	Neutral ▼	1
EMPATHY	2	Was there kindness and courtesy during the provision of service		5
RELIABILITY	3	Did you trust that the recruitment would be done correctly for yo...	Neutral / Weakly understood / Understanding / Absolutely understood / Extremely understood	3
RELIABILITY	4	The final document of the budget was		5
RESPONSE. CAPA.	5	Were you handed the budget in?		1
RESPONSE. CAPA.	6	The reaction to process changes of the requested service was	moderate reaction	3
TANGIBLE	7	The use of the media during the service was	Extremely used	9
SECURITY	8	The compliance of the rules was	Extremely satisfied	9
EMPATHY	9	The warmth during the performance of the service was	Displayed moderately	3
RELIABILITY	10	Order during and after the execution of the service was	Moderately satisfied	3
RELIABILITY	11	Cleaning during and after the execution of the service was	Highly satisfied	5
RELIABILITY	12	The specification compliance of the requested service was	Moderately satisfied	3
RELIABILITY	13	The monitoring carried out during the execution of the service wa...	Extreme supervision	9
RESPONSE. CAPA.	14	The performance of the service was	Extremely time	9
TANGIBLE	15	The equipment and tools used in the service was	comprehensive and extremely goo...	9
TANGIBLE	16	The number of staff used for the implementation of the service w...	Moderately suitable	3
TANGIBLE	17	Personnel who performed the service was	...ained and experienced very stro...	7
SECURITY	18	The service adviser counted on	Knowledge ends	9
RELIABILITY	19	Supervision during the execution of the service was	...e beginning, during and after the s...	3
RELIABILITY	20	The coordination of the requested service was	Extremely suitable	9
RESPONSE. CAPA.	21	The problem solution was	Extremely suitable	9
RESPONSE. CAPA.	22	The use of the media during the service was	Extremely used	9

with $\varepsilon>0$ an arbitrary but fix number, $|z|$ represents the vector of the absolute values of vector $\underline{z}$ y $\underline{y} \leq \underline{z}$ it means that each element of vector $\underline{y}$ is, minor or equal to its corresponding element of vector $\underline{z}$. $ev(n_o)$ will be the wished eigenvector, ε is the approximation, and n_o the number of iterations. This process may be implemented in some programming language. In this study case the procedure was developed in S-Plus v. 8.0; where $\varepsilon=0.0001$, resulting $n_o=5$ and $ev(n_o)$ the eigenvector shown on Figure 6. The normalized principal eigenvector is also called **priority vector.**

The next stage in to calculate λ_{max}, the maximum eigenvalue, so as to lead to the Consistence Index, *CI*, defined as

$$CI = \frac{\lambda_{max} - m}{m-1}$$

Figure 6. Shows the eigenvector of the assessment tool, using MMULT

No.	DIMENSIONALITY	EIGENVECTOR
1	SECURITY	0.16458
2	EMPATHY	0.03292
3	RELIABILITY	0.05486
4	RELIABILITY	0.03292
5	RESPONSE. CAPA.	0.16458
6	RESPONSE. CAPA.	0.05486
7	TANGIBLE	0.01829
8	SECURITY	0.01829
9	EMPATHY	0.05486
10	RELIABILITY	0.05486
11	RELIABILITY	0.03292
12	RELIABILITY	0.05486
13	RELIABILITY	0.01829
14	RESPONSE. CAPA.	0.01829
15	TANGIBLE	0.01829
16	TANGIBLE	0.05486
17	TANGIBLE	0.02351
18	SECURITY	0.01829
19	RELIABILITY	0.05486
20	RELIABILITY	0.01829
21	RESPONSE. CAPA.	0.01829
22	RESPONSE. CAPA.	0.01829

m is, as before, the size of the square reciprocal matrix A. In order to calculate λ_{max}, the AHP theory (Saaty, 1980) says that A $ev(n_o)=\lambda max\,ev(n_o)$, so twenty four estimates of λmax can be get by the simple expedient of dividing each component of $Aev(n_o)$ by the corresponding eigenvector element. The mean of these values will be taken as λmax. In this case of study $\lambda max = 24$, and in consequence $CI= 0$.

The final step is to calculate the Consistency Ratio, CR, for the set of judgments defined to be:

$$CR = \frac{CI}{CIs},$$

where $CI_{s,}$ is the corresponding CI value from large samples of matrices of purely random judgments. This number was derived from Saaty in his book (Saaty, 1980), he argues that a CR < 0.1 indicates that the judgments are consistent. In this case of study $CI= 0$; which indicate a perfect consistency.

This way the company can observe and identify the aspects and/or the criteria that the staff prefers from this supplier, and other aspects that need to be better because of their weight, to be considered a supplier of high quality.

This way the company can observe and identify the aspects and/or the criteria that the staff prefers from this supplier, and other aspects that need to be better because of their weight, to be considered a supplier of high quality.

Software Tool for Evaluating Performance

The software tool applied to the model for improvement performance measurement service suppliers in this study case shows the advantages and competitiveness that have resulted in improvements in the supply chain of the company.

The suggested model could be integrated into a database for easy use and access for any user. The platform selected for the development of the system was selected ACCESS because it is a system included in MS-OFFICE, and therefore the cost of accessibility is reduced (Cassel P., Eddy C., Price, J., 2002). In this system, we have included the following modules:

1. **Suppliers:** In this module, we have all relevant information to the general data of the suppliers, which belongs to the detail of the quality committee.
2. **Evaluations:** the essence of the system is the evaluation module. It includes the evaluation set, and it is the part where the inclusion of the combo box for selecting the valuation of the criteria is. The math to find the eigenvector is currently being finalized to be integrated.
3. **Services:** it contains the definition of services to assess, containing the general data for it.

4.   **Advisers:** includes the general data of the consultants, who supervise external suppliers for the execution of the service, besides they are also evaluated by the customer.

5.   **Reports:** Through the report module is the monitoring and the classification of suppliers, as joint assessments by the supplier, as well as the overall assessment. Compared with other software packages available on the market, the system selected had the following advantages:

   a.   Improves the administration of assessments, due to the filling directly into the system, updating of the database faster.

   b.   Ease in monitoring the daily performance of suppliers.

   c.   Easy to use, due to MS-Office environment.

   d.   Updated information.

   e.   Includes the appropriate evaluation criteria to the provided services.

   f.   The inclusion of a statistical measurement for the classification of suppliers, it and being able to make decisions on their performance.

CONCLUSION

The quality of service is certainly a complex topic that many companies, although interested in the subject, find it difficult to address. It is well known that the main reason of this is due to the intangibility of the service, it is perishable and it is heterogeneous, but this work has shown that through a user-friendly tool, important results in the short term may result.

In this study, we found it important to define and detect both internal and external suppliers, as well as the cycles and stages of services in which the organization has a close interrelationship with them. In these stages is the critical time to assess the quality of services provided by suppliers.

Listening to the customer's voice has always been of great importance in any of the methods provided for measuring the quality of service. However, the method proposed above is remarkable because of the direct collection of clients, focusing on the critical stages of client-supplier interaction. Another key part of the methodology was the detection of the moments of truth.

With the input provided in the study by customers, it was feasible to structure an assessment tool that includes their preferences, such as the variables defined in the literature review and mentioned by prominent authors on the issue of service quality using SERVQUAL.

Furthermore, another important contribution of the work is related to the measurement criteria. This is the difference between the use of averages or percentages and measurement using a specific vector considering the preferences of assessment. This type of assessment leads to a process of continuous improvement and focuses on specific aspects that the organization wants to improve.

The use of the tool Analytic Hierarchy Process (AHP) in the selection, demonstrates its potential for making decisions, but it is clear that the selection is just the first step in a process of outsourcing, along the supply chain, because once the supplier is within the organization, the aim is to have a robust supplier and be responsible for its development. Similarly, another important contribution is the visibility and transparency for all members of the supply chain by providing preventive monitoring to the performance of suppliers, which helps lower the costs of replacement of the suppliers with poor performance.

Likewise, the use of technology facilitated the implementation processes in the organization's supply chain. The ease of use and effectiveness in the evaluation were the two main added values of the system developed. Thus, the combination of methodological development and ease of use through the computer showed its significant potential to use them together.

It is a fact that the use of these tools must be considered by any entity that provides services and/or wants to start a project to improve the quality of services rendered to them. However, in preliminary experiments where the implementation to the supply chain of tangible products was sought, excellent results have been achieved, that is why it is considered that it is feasible to use in product supply chains. A future line of research, involves the application to supply chain products and services, which involves the adequacy of the methodology and tool in this hybrid form of operation.

REFERENCES

Albrecht, K. (1998). *La Revolución del servicio.* 3R Editores LTDA.

Albrecht, K., & Zemke, R. (1985). Service America. New York:Mc.Graw Hill.

Aznar, J. (2006) Jerónimo Aznar Bellver-Dialnet, [en línea], Retrieved July 30, 2066, http://dialnet.uniroja.es/servlet/extaut?codigo=336[07.30.2006]

Beamon, B. (1998). Supply Chain Design and Analysis: Models and Methods. *International Journal of Production Economics, 55*(3), 281–294. doi:10.1016/S0925-5273(98)00079-6

Beamon, B. (1999). Measuring supply Chain Performance. *International Journal of Operations & Production Management, 19*(3), 275–292. doi:10.1108/01443579910249714

Beesley, A. (1996). Time compression in supply chain. *Industrial Management & Data Systems, 96*(2), 12–16. doi:10.1108/02635579610112606

Bellido, L. (2004). Metodología para la Evaluación de Servicios de Telecomunicaciones desde la perspectiva del usuario. Dpto. de Ingeniería de Sistemas Telemáticos, Universidad Politécnica de Madrid.

Belton, V., & Gear, T. (1983). On a Short-Coming of Saaty's Method of Analytic Hierarchies. *Omega, 11*(3), 228–230. doi:10.1016/0305-0483(83)90047-6

Benedetto, J., & Ferreira, P. (2000). Modern Sampling Theory: Mathematics and Applications. Boston: Birkhauser.

Brady, M. K., & Cronin, J. J. (2001). Some New Thougths on Conceptualizing Perceived Service Quality: A Hierarchical Approach. *Journal of Marketing, 65*(3), 34–49. doi:10.1509/jmkg.65.3.34.18334

Cantú, H. (2001). Desarrollo de una Cultura de Calidad. New York: McGraw Hill.

Carlzon, J. (1987). Moments of Truth. Cambridge, MA: Ballinger Publishing Co.

Cassel, P., Eddy, C., & Price, J. (2002). Aprendiendo Microsoft Access. Pearson Educación.

Cedillo, M., Sanchez, J., & Sanchez, C. (2006). The new relational schemas of inter-firms cooperation: the case of the Coahuila automobile cluster in Mexico. *International Journal of Automotive Technology and Management, 6*(4), 406–418. doi:10.1504/IJATM.2006.012233

Chase, A. Jacobs. (1998). Production and Operations Management. Eighth edition, New York: McGraw Hill.

Chen, S. J., & Hwang, C. L. (1991) Fuzzy Multiple Atribute Decision Making: Methods and Applications. Lecture Notes in Economics and Mathematical Systems, No. 375. Berlin, Germany.

Cronin, J. J., & Taylor, S. (1992). Measuring Service Quality: A Reexamination and Extension. *Journal of Marketing, 56*(July), 55–68. doi:10.2307/1252296

Cronin, J. J., & Taylor, S. a. (1994). SERVPERF versus SERVQUAL: Reconciling performance based and perceptions-minus-excpectations measurement of service quality. *Journal of Marketing, 58*, 125. doi:10.2307/1252256

Crosby, P. (1984). Quality Without Tears. New York: McGraw Hill.

Duclos, L., Vokurka, R., & Lummus, R. (2003). Conceptual Model of Supply Chain Flexibility. Industrial Management Data Systems, 103(6), 446-456.Eiglier, P. & Langeard, E. (1991). El marketing de servicios. New York: McGraw Hill.

Evans, J., & Lindsay, W. (2001). The management and control of quality. Quinta edición, South-Western College Pub.

Fernández, M. (1996). Como medir la calidad en los servicios. Información Comercial Española ICE: *Revista de economía, 755*,113-125.

Flores, A. (2004), Medición de la efectividad de la cadena de suministro. Primera edición, Panorama Editorial.

Franceschini, F., & Cignetti, M. (1998). Comparing tools for service quality evaluation. *International Journal of Quality, 3*(4).

Gronroos, C. (1982). *Strategic Management and Marketing in the Service Sector.* Helsingfors: Swedish School of Economics and Racine.

Gronroos, C. (1984). *Strategic Management and Marketing in the Services Sector.* Helsingfors: Swedish School of Economics and Business Administration.

Heung, V., Wong, M., & Qu, H. (2000). Airport-restaurant service quality in Hong Kong. *The Cornell Hotel and Restaurant Administration Quarterly, 41*(3), 86–96.

Hossein, M. (2002). Supply Chain: Crisp and Fuzzy Aspects. *International Journal Appl. Math. Computer Science, 12*(3), 423–435.

Jankowicz, A. (1991). Business Research Projects. London: Chapman and Hall.

Juran, J. (2001). Manual de Calidad. New York: McGraw Hill.

Khurrum, S., & Bhutta y Faizul, H. (2002). Supplier selection problem: a comparison of the total cost of ownership and analytic hierarchy process approaches. *Supply Chain Management: An International Journal, 7*(3), 126–135. doi:10.1108/13598540210436586

Mardia, K. V., Kent, J. T., & Bibby, J. M. (1979). Multivariate Analysis. New York: Academic Press.

Martínez, A., Cantú, M., Cedillo, G., & Arriaga, J. (2006) *Medición del desempeño de proveedores de servicio y su importancia en la cadena de suministro.* XXVIII Congreso Internacional Calzatecnia, León Guanajuato.

Martínez, E., & Escudey, M. (1998). Evaluación y decisión multicriterio. UNESCO-Editorial Universidad de Santiago, Chile.

Nelly, A., Gregory, M., & Platts, K. (1995). Performance Measurement System Design. *International Journal of Operations & Production Management, 16*(4), 19–34.

Normann, R. (1991). Service Management: Strategy and Leadership in Service Business. Second Edition, pp. 16-17. New York: John Wiley & Sons Ltd.

Parasuraman, A., & Zeithaml., V. A. (2004). *Service Quality.* Marketing Science Institute.

Parasuraman, A., Berry, L. L., & Zeithaml, V. A. (1991). Understanding customer expetations of service. Sloan Management Review. Cambridge, MA: Harvard Business Press.

Parasuraman, A., Zeithaml, V. A., & Berry, L. L. (1985). A Conceptual Model of Service Quality and Its Implications for Future Research. *Journal of Marketing, 49*(Fall), 41–50. doi:10.2307/1251430

Parasuraman, A., Zeithaml, V. A., & Berry, L. L. (1988). SERVQUAL: A Multiple Item Scale for Measuring Consumer Perceptions of Service Quality. *Journal of Retailing, 64*(1), 12–40.

Ruiz-Olalla, C. (2001). Gestión de la calidad del servicio, [en línea] *5campus.com, Control de Gestión.* Retrieved May 24, 2009, from http://www.5campus.com/leccion/calidadserv

Saaty, T. (1980). The Analytic Hierarchy Process. New York: McGraw Hill International.

Satty, T. (2000). Fundamentals Of Decision Making and Priority Theory. Pittsburgh, PA: RWS Publications.

Seth, N., Deshmukh, G., & Vrat, P. (2005). Service quality models: a review. *International Journal of Quality & Reliability Management, 22*(9), 913–949. doi:10.1108/02656710510625211

Seth, N., Deshmukh, G., & Vrat, P. (2006a). A framework for measurement of quality of service in supply chains. *Supply Chain Management: An International Journal, 11*(1), 82–94. doi:10.1108/13598540610642501

Seth, N., Deshmukh, G., & Vrat, P. (2006b). SSQSC: a tool to mesure supplier service quality in supply chain. *Production Planning and Control, 17*(5), 448–463. doi:10.1080/09537280600741764

Stuart, I., McCutcheon, D., Handfield, R., McLachlin, R., & Samson, D. (2002). Effective case research in operations management: a process perspective. *Journal of Operations Management, 20*(5), 419–433. doi:10.1016/S0272-6963(02)00022-0

Terzi, S., & Cavalieri, S. (2004). Simulation in the supply chain context: a survey. *Computers in Industry, 53,* 3–16. doi:10.1016/S0166-3615(03)00104-0

Triantaphyllou, E. (2000). Multi-criteria decision making methods: a comparative study. The Netherlands: Kluwer Academic Publishers.

Vandaele, D., & Gemmel, P. (2007). Purchased business services influence downstream supply chain members. *International Journal of Service Industry Management, 18,* 307–321. doi:10.1108/09564230710751505

Venkataramanan, M. V. (1998). Special Research Focus on Supply Chain Linkages: Challenges for Design and Management in the 21st Century. *Decision Sciences, 29*(3).

Wang, G. (2004). Manufacturing Supply Chain Design and Evaluation. *International Journal of Advanced Manufacturing Technology, 25,* 93–100. doi:10.1007/s00170-003-1791-y

Wei-Ning, P., & Chinyao, L. (2005). Supplier evaluation and selection via Taguchi loss functions and an AHP. *International Journal of Advanced Manufacturing Technology, 27*(5-6).

Yin, R. (1989). Case Study Research: Design and Methods. 2nd Edition, Newbury Park, CA: Sage

Zeithaml, V., Berry, L., & Parasuraman, A. (1988). Communication and control processes in the delivery of service quality. *Journal of Marketing, 52,* 35–48. doi:10.2307/1251263

Zeithaml, V., Berry, L., & Parasuraman, A. (2004). Service Quality. Marketing Science Institute.

ENDNOTES

[1] Elaboration process of a service, i.e. all the organization of the physical human elements in the client-company relationship, necessary to the realization of a service (Eiglier P., and Langeard E.,1991)

[2] Plant staff

[3] Engineering department, internal suppliers

[4] External suppliers

[5] The difference between the application process and the work order is the cost

Chapter 11
Analyzing Requirements and Approaches for Sourcing Software Based Services

G.R. Gangadharan
Novay, The Netherlands

Erwin Fielt
Queensland University of Technology, Australia

ABSTRACT

Increasingly, software is no longer developed as a single system, but rather as a smart combination of so-called software services. Each of these provides an independent, specific and relatively small piece of functionality, which is typically accessible through the Internet from internal or external service providers. To the best of our knowledge, there are no standards or models that describe the sourcing process of these software based services (SBS). We identify the sourcing requirements for SBS and associate the key characteristics of SBS (with the sourcing requirements introduced). Furthermore, we investigate the sourcing of SBS with the related works in the field of classical procurement, business process outsourcing, and information systems sourcing. Based on the analysis, we conclude that the direct adoption of these approaches for SBS is not feasible and new approaches are required for sourcing SBS.

INTRODUCTION

Services dominate well-developed economies such as the EU and US. The sheer size of the services sector in the overall economy and their potential in creating economic growth and welfare (through considerable opportunities for productivity gains) motivate a growing interest in understanding and developing services. Information Technology (IT) is one of the major drivers for improving traditional

services and introducing new ones. IT moved from a back-end to a front-end role and business and technology become more and more integrated. Moreover, the increasing role of IT in business processes also acts as a driver and enabler of other developments like more demanding customers and organizations specializing and partnering in globally operating networks. All of this entails that we need new ways of thinking about and working with IT. The traditional approach to IT, with large monolithic systems, has been very successful in achieving a high degree of efficiency in case of high-volume,

DOI: 10.4018/978-1-61520-603-2.ch011

standardized products and services in a stable environment. However, the abovementioned developments are much more difficult to accommodate with traditional IT systems.

A flexible and integrated approach to the development of business services and their supporting software, will contribute to more agility and a better alignment between business and IT. The business perspective – business processes, functional specifications, information models, and service level agreements – can be taken as the starting point. This is combined with a different approach to software: "thinking in services". For example, think of on-line services for checking creditworthiness of customers, processing credit card payments, or computing exchange rates. These are just small examples of a much more profound development. Next to that, we also see entire software packages delivered as an online service, as witnessed by the success of companies such as Salesforce.com.

Increasingly, business software is no longer developed as a single system, but rather as a smart combination of so-called software services. Each of these provides an independent, specific and relatively small piece of functionality, which is typically accessible through the Internet from internal or external service providers. This raises the issue of sourcing these software based services (SBS). Sourcing of SBS presents a considerable challenge because it should align a number of organizational processes on strategic, tactical, and operational levels. To the best of our knowledge, there are no standards or models for dealing with the sourcing process of services completely.

In this paper we will address the *what* of sourcing of SBS (sourcing requirements) and the *how* of sourcing SBS (sourcing approaches). The salient contributions of our paper are as follows.

- We identify certain service requirements for sourcing SBS and we associate the key characteristics of SBS with these sourcing requirements.

- The sourcing approaches in the field of classical purchasing, business process outsourcing, and information systems sourcing can guide the sourcing process of SBS to a certain extent.

- As the sourcing requirements of SBS have a close knit relationship with the key characteristics of SBS, the direct adoption of these approaches for SBS cannot be feasible. New approaches are required for sourcing SBS.

As the concept of SBS is gaining more and more prominence, sourcing of SBS emerges as a promising area of research, requiring the interdisciplinary convergence of supply chain management and information technology.

SOFTWARE BASED SERVICES

Thinking in Terms of Services

Service is a widely used term, with different meanings in different disciplines. In economics, a service is claimed to be a process that creates benefits by facilitating either a change in customers, a change in their physical possessions, or a change in their intangible assets (Hill, 1977). Service provision has been defined as an economic activity that does not result in ownership, and this is what differentiates it from providing physical goods.

In marketing, a service is a process that relates to the performance of an activity executed in co-operation with the customer (Grönroos, 2007). Four basic characteristics of (consumer) services are often emphasized in defining services (Zeithaml, Parasuraman, & Berry, 1985): Intangibility or non-material, inseparability of production and consumption, heterogeneity (nonstandardization) of service outcome and processes, and perishability (cannot be stored). However, this is mostly directed at services involving a significant amount of human processing and this may, therefore, be different for SBS. Moreover, the dichotomy between physical goods and intangible services is not discrete and should be viewed as a continuum with pure services on one terminal point and pure commodity goods on the other terminal point.

In information systems engineering, the service concept is used to separate the external and internal behavior of a system (Lankhorst et al., 2005). The internal behavior can be seen as the realization of the service. A service consumer may not be really interested in the internal behavior of the system. Rather, the consumer focuses on functionality offered (what is realized considering both functional and non-functional results).

Service orientation makes a layered view of enterprise architecture models, where the service is seen as a concept that bridges different layers of an enterprise. We adopt the following classification of services by (Lankhorst et al., 2005) in the perspective of an enterprise.

- *Business Services*: These services expose business functionality to the environment. These are the services provided by the business layer of an organization to the environment.
- *Application Services*: Application services are externally visible units of application functionality, exposed through well defined interfaces.
- *Infrastructure Services*: These services are realized by infrastructure functions. These services normally include data storage services and communication services.

In this paper, we refer to the classes of Application services and Infrastructure services that are realized by software as "Software Based Services" (SBS).

Key Characteristics of Software Based Services

Software, traditionally, has been perceived as a product, requiring possession and ownership, in order to receive the desired performance. The transition from software as a product to software as a service is reflected in the distribution of software. A service is defined as a mechanism to enable access to one or more capabilities, where the access is provided using a prescribed interface and is exercised consistent with constraints and policies as specified by the service description (MacKenzie et al., 2006). Services are autonomous, platform independent, business functions that are published and described using standard description and publication languages. They are remotely invocable over different networks using standard protocols (Maximillien and Singh, 2005). A service can be accessed whenever required. However, a service remains idle until a request for invocation arrives.

SBS has the following characteristics (based on Sprott, 2006 and Wilkes, 2004) that make services different from traditional software and components, described in detail in Table 1.

These key characteristics of SBS will not directly impact the sourcing decision of services. However, these characteristics have effect over the sourcing requirements for services (functionality, time, costs, quality, ownership etc.,).

REQUIREMENTS ELICITATION FOR SOURCING SBS

In an organization, sourcing decisions are made based upon requirements with respect to functionality, quality, costs and other criteria. In this section, we will explore the service requirements (see, for example, Robison, 2007 and McCord, 2003) that impact the sourcing of SBS.

Table 1. Key characteristics of software based services

	Key characteristic	Description
1.	Discoverability	Services are discoverable and can be selected based on functional and non-functional properties by a consumer through public or private discovery processes. Services are described and published by service providers in a manner that can be discovered.
2.	Modularity	Services are designed as self-contained, independent, and modular applications. This nature makes a service to be functionally consistent across many use cases. This characteristic of service makes the service to be aligned with business.
3.	Decoupling	Services encapsulate functional component and functional interfaces, thereby making a service decoupled. The decoupled nature of services removes the dependency for a provider's specific implementation. Furthermore, as services are executed in the hosted infrastructure and a consumer sees only the result of execution, consumers are not required to install and maintain the application on their own infrastructure.
4.	Composability	The fundamental to service orientation is to design services to encourage composition. Service composition allows building coarse grained services by combining finer grained services of any level of hierarchies.
5.	Design-By-Contract	Services are specified with functional (what it does with pre and post conditions), operational (service level terms), and commercial (licensing clauses) contracts. Thus, the design by contract allows service providers and service consumers to be aware with the process and obligations of the service.
6.	Abstraction	As services are expected to support multiple contexts, services are generalized. A generalized service specification (with non project specific requirements) provides inherent business flexibility.
7.	Invocation Based Pricing	Services envisage for invocation based pricing model that requires consumers to pay only for their need and that reflects market supply and demand.

Service Functionality

An organization decides the requirement for services based on its goals (what does an organization want to achieve?) and capabilities (what should an organization be able to do?). With respect to the latter, an organization has to decide what it should be able to do itself and what it should acquire form other organizations. This determines the functional scope of services that the organization should source from external service providers.

A clear understanding of service functionality requirements make the consumers to evaluate the list of services provided by different service providers. Most service providers offer a trial version for evaluation. SBS applications, in some cases, may lack the capability to fulfill all the requirements directly. In these cases, services can be customized by the service provider (may require additional cost). Evaluating the level of customization and costs may even cause the service consumer to rethink service adoption.

During the process of sourcing, the discoverable character of services supports a service consumer to look in a repository for a service with required functionality. Services specify functional contracts describing what a service does with preconditions and post-conditions. This approach supported by the design-by-contract characteristic of services facilitates the consumer expectations.

Service Quality

A service provider specifies a list of qualities of service. Following are the prominent qualities of service (Mani & Nagarajan, 2002) that have to be considered by consumers during the sourcing process:

- *Reliability*: The ability of a service operation to be executed within the maximum expected time frame.
- *Response Time*: The time taken by a service for handling user requests (measuring

the expected delay between the moment when a service request is sent and the moment when the service is rendered).

- *Availability*: The probability for a service being accessed properly in an observation period.
- *Integrity*: The quality aspect of how the service maintains the correctness of the interaction in respect to the source.

A service consumer can discover a service specifying his expected level of qualities, in addition to a specified functionality. Furthermore, the design by contract approach of services clearly defines and describes the service level quality and terms of use of a service. This helps a service consumer understand whether the offered service meets her expected quality requirements, thereby making the sourcing decision clearer.

Security, Privacy, and Trust Aspects

As data can be either sensitive to consumers or critical to business applications, an organization needs to be highly careful in procuring services. Most organizations are skeptic in adopting services because certain data is needed to be shared with service providers that may cause data confidentiality and data integrity issues. Following are some of the important factors related to security for a service to be considered by a consumer.

- Selecting service providers using enhanced network security mechanisms for exchanging messages.
- Analyzing the access control policies and monitoring infrastructure adopted by the service provider (Coetzee & Eloff, 2007).
- Understanding the procedures adopted by service providers for intrusion prevention and vulnerability management.

As services are decoupled by hiding the service implementation, consumers are skeptic over security, privacy, and trust aspects of services. Though there is a high level of security standards offered by services, organizations hesitate to go for a service based software solution in case of an application involving highly confidential logic and sensitive data.

Service Costs

Making use of SBS comes at a cost, the price of the service, which is usually a subscription fee and often (partially) related to the actual use (Cheng et al., 2003 and Gunther et al., 2006).

In a dynamic market environment, the cost of a service depends on the perspectives of service consumers and service providers. A service consumer assesses how much she values the service and what she can afford to pay for the service. This also requires forecasting the usage level of a service. From the perspective of service providers, the estimation of cost of producing a service and the return on investment plays a critical role in determining the price.

Part of the service costs considerations may be a comparison with the costs of purchasing the software as a package. A software package has two types of costs: acquisition costs and maintenance costs. It is important not to compare service fees with both types of costs and not only the acquisition costs. An important cost advantage of services is that they are executed in hosted infrastructure at the service provider's side, so there are no maintenance costs at the consumer side.

Deployment Efforts and Resources

Sourcing SBS always requires time and resources from an organization with respect to deployment. Moreover, depending upon the gap between the required service functionality and the provided service functionality (after customization), it may also be required to adapt the service to the specific requirements of the organization.

Deployment efforts can be seen as one of the critical sourcing decision variables. Organizations may have to make a tradeoff between developing their own services and sourcing services from external providers (with or without customization) based on how quick they want the solution.

Intellectual Property Rights and Ownership of Services

Generally the intellectual property rights (IPR) of software-based services are reserved by the service provider (Gangadharan & D'Andrea, 2009). Regarding the ownership of SBS, if a particular service is delivered through software by SBS, the consumer should get the rights for reuse of the service (together with software). If a SBS is customized for a consumer, the consumer should ensure the IP rights of customizations exclusively.

The decoupled nature of services makes no ownership of (service based) software to service consumers (Bruno, 2006). As there is no possession of software at the consumer's side, the consumer is offered support from the provider and the responsibility of maintenance lies on the provider side (Han et al., 2004).

MAPPING SOURCING REQUIREMENTS OVER KEY CHARACTERISTICS OF SBS

We derive the relationship between the service requirements that impact sourcing decisions and the key characteristics of SBS. In this way, Table 2 illustrates the implications of sourcing requirements over the key characteristics of SBS. We also see that each key characteristics relate to multiple sourcing requirements.

ANALYSIS OF SOURCING APPROACHES FOR SBS

In this section, we will analyze the sourcing of SBS based on the existing literature in the field of classical purchasing, business process outsourcing, and information systems sourcing. We will evaluate the applicability of each of these sourcing models with respect to SBS.

Sourcing of SBS in Classical Purchasing Perspectives

At a high-level, the generic purchasing process for goods and the sourcing process for SBS can be expected to be quite similar. Major differences will

Table 2. Implications of sourcing requirements over key characteristics of SBS

Key characteristics of SBS	Sourcing requirements	Explanation
Discoverability	Service functionality, Service quality	Selecting a service with desired functional and non-functional properties
Modularity	Deployment efforts	Makes services self-contained with reduced dependencies, making integration and deployment easier.
Decoupling	IPR and Ownership, Security, Privacy, and Trust, Deployment efforts, Service costs	Reduces responsibility and maintainability for consumers
Composability	Deployment efforts	Allows to federate fine grained services and reduces development time
Design-by-Contract	Service functionality, Service quality	A way for consumers to know more about the service
Abstraction	Service functionality, IPR and Ownership, Deployment efforts	Supports many contexts concurrently, thereby providing flexibility
Invocation based pricing	Service costs	Reducing the cost with no upfront fees

be related to some of the strategic and tactical activities (supplier selection, contract management) while the operational activities will be more of an 'implement and use' than an order process. It can be expected that the sourcing process for SBS will also differ per purchasing situation with respect to newness (new-task situation, modified rebuy or straight rebuy) and complexity (the dominant function in the decision making unit). Because SBS are relatively new phenomena, it can be expected to be perceived as a new-task situation with a high complexity. It may involve reconsidering strategic and tactical choices and involving business, IT, financial and purchasing expertise.

The Michigan State University (MSU) model (Monczka, et al., 2005) has been well studied by researchers and is used by a large number of practitioners, amongst them some of the largest organizations. The MSU model provides a solid basis for creating a mature sourcing function with purchasing excellence, which will also be relevant for sourcing SBS. It also recognizes the need for mature enabling processes, which may be easily overlooked in a discussion about sourcing SBS from a business or technology perspective. The enabling process of developing organization and teaming strategies stresses the need for functional cooperation and integration, which will also be important for sourcing SBS where business units, the purchasing function and the IT function will all play a role.

A generic purchasing process illustrated by Van Weele (2005) starts with defining a specification followed by selecting a supplier and agreeing on a contract. Thereafter, the process continues with ordering and expediting followed by evaluation. The first three steps represent tactical purchasing functions and are primarily of a technical-commercial nature. The last three steps represent operational purchasing (or ordering) function and are primarily of a logistics-administrative nature. As these steps are closely connected, the problems in one step are often caused by deficiencies in a previous step. Hence, the Van Weele

process stresses the importance of understanding the interfaces between the different steps well by defining the output of each step clearly. Van Weele's generic purchasing process describes the procurement for products. The phases of ordering and expediting are not applicable for sourcing of SBS. The remaining phases can be applicable in sourcing SBS.

A danger of relying too much on classical purchasing insights, however, is that in general this literature is more directed towards the purchasing of goods. According to Van Weele (2005), the purchasing of services should be approached differently because the client is also involved in the production process. Furthermore, the classical purchasing literature focuses little or no attention on the IT domain.

Sourcing of SBS in Business Process Outsourcing Perspectives

Whether sourcing of SBS also involves actual 'outsourcing', which entails transferring responsibility and resources from the internal organization to an external organization, will depend upon which kind of services an organization is targeting and whether it concerns new or existing applications. For example, sourcing an electronic dictionary as a service may be more like product procurement than IT outsourcing.

With respect to the sourcing life-cycle model of Cullen et al. (2005), the phase of 'investigate' (building block 1) will be of particular importance because of the relative immaturity of the SBS market with inexperienced clients and limited service providers. 'Target' (building block 2) and 'design' (building block 4) seem critical phases because of the importance of finding suitable services to outsource and creating the right sourcing designs. Because it may be wise to start SBS with a limited scope and the need to first gain experience, 'strategize' (building block 3) seems less relevant for now. 'Negotiate' (building block 6) and 'transition' (building block 3) will mostly not be substantially different from traditional outsourcing, maybe even simpler because of the 'design-by-contract,' 'invocation based pricing' and 'decoupling' characteristics of SBS.

The eSourcing Capability Model (eSCM) (Hefley et al., 2005, Hyderr et al., 2006) covers the sourcing of services for (IT-intensive) business processes. This, however, also means that the model and practices are quite generic in nature and need to be supplemented for SBS. A major difference for SBS may be that it becomes possible to source finer grained services efficiently and effectively, increasing the number of options for selective outsourcing but also increasing its complexity. This may require more advanced portfolio management and architectural maturity. As services are opaque in nature (hiding the implementation from the interface), the service provider capabilities become less relevant from the perspectives of service consumers. However, the client will also experience the negative consequences of service failure by the service provider and contracts cannot specify everything in advance. Moreover, as the capability models show, the performance of a service provider is also determined by capabilities that are not directly related to service delivery, for example, process re-engineering and customer development. To what extend this will matter for SBS will, on the one hand, be determined by the sourcing design (for example, resource or result focused) and, on the other hand, the type of service sourced, in particular the extent to which the 'modularity' and 'and 'decoupling' characteristics of the software service applies for the business service.

In general, the sourcing decision discussions in purchasing literature and in outsourcing literature are very similar. Both address different scopes of outsourcing, such as turnkey/total or partial/selective. In line with this aspect, SBS can be sourced at different levels of granularity. Because of the 'modularity' and 'decoupling' characteristics of SBS, the options for sourcing from different suppliers will increase. Purchasing and outsourcing literature also discuss the same key criteria relate to effectiveness (core competences), efficiency, quality (capabilities), flexibility, innovation, finance, and technology.

There is a whole range of outsourcing arrangements that are more or less favorable depending upon the objectives and the conditions, such as contract-out and preferred contractor (Lacity et al., 1996). It seems that SBS literature too often extrapolates the delivery model into a sourcing design and, therefore, favors more dynamic and competitive form of sourcing. For example, a key characteristic such as 'modularity' is used to argue that services will be sourced form marketplace like service cloud. However, one could also argue that with respect to transformational outsourcing, modularity can make radical renewal easier and, therefore, results in strategic partnerships. It seems that a more ambitious SBS approach is suited for a high level of enterprise architecture maturity, from business modularity onwards.

Sourcing of SBS in Information Systems Sourcing Perspectives

The sourcing decisions from the information systems (IS) perspectives differ substantially form the purchasing and outsourcing perspective. Making a decision to buy or develop a software is rather a difficult task. As buying or developing software have their own pros and cons, the decision is prominently based upon satisfying the requirements of an organization. Some of these factors of decision making in software also impact the sourcing decision of SBS. SBS seem to some extent a continuation of the hybrid solutions with key characteristics such as 'modularity' and 'decoupling' that make a hybrid solution more feasible.

The Generic Software Acquisition Reference Process (GARP) (Getto et al., 2000) is a model based on SPRITE-S software acquisition initiatives (now renamed as Information Services Procurement Library). GARP is a hierarchical life cycle model containing the processes of acquisition initiation, the procurement process, and review of acquisition. Each process further consists of several sub-processes. These sub-processes do not have any logical sequence as the represented sub-processes possess parallel and continuous characteristics. GARP is a generic process that guides the improvement of existing software acquisition methods. Though GARP focuses on software, the fundamental principles of GARP can be applicable for services. However, in a sourcing process for services, the sub-processes are less significant. GARP does not distinguish between the different types of software that needed to be acquired. As software and SBS are significantly different in characteristics, the process of acquisition initiation for software differs significantly from that of services. Thus, GARP becomes less applicable in the field of SBS.

The Information Services Procurement Library (ISPL) (Op de Coul, 2005) provides a framework for acquiring and managing IT projects (e.g. system development) and ongoing services (e.g. managed services). According to ISPL, the acquisition process consists of three sequential process steps: acquisition initiation, procurement (one or more), and acquisition completion. The acquisition initiation process produces an acquisition plan that reflects an acquisition strategy, along with a clear understanding of systems and services requirements defining the acquisition goal. The procurement process describes obtaining

one single contract, involving tendering, contract monitoring, and contract completion. The acquisition completion is the formal completion of all the contracts of the acquisition. The ISPL framework for procuring services seems to be fit for procuring SBS. However, the acquisition initiation phase does not detail exactly the requirements for sourcing SBS. The procurement process of ISPL gives significant attention to contract monitoring and contract completion. In this way, ISPL focuses more on tactical level operations in sourcing. The definition of a service in the perspective of the ISPL is broader in scope and this is the reason that the ISPL does not focus specifically on SBS.

EVALUATION OF SOURCING APPROACHES FOR SBS

In general, the classical purchasing literature offers the widest and deepest source of sourcing knowledge. However, it may be less suited for services as it mostly focuses the purchasing of goods. This may, however, be only a limited problem for SBS because they to some extend may be more like goods than traditional services because they require no or little human involvement in service delivery. The strength of business process outsourcing approaches is that they focus on IT-intensive business services, although this can be too generic for or different for SBS (also

Table 3. Assessment of purchasing models for sourcing SBS

Perspectives	Strengths	Weaknesses
Classical Purchasing	Sourcing knowledge base Traditional way Systematic approach to the sourcing function	Focused on purchase of goods Little attention for the IS/IT domain
Business Process Outsourcing	Focused on IT-intensive services Paying attention to both business and technology issues Addresses organizational issues for IS/IT function	Sometimes too generic and/or different for SBS Sourcing SBS does not have to involve transfer of resources
Information Systems Procurement	Directed at IT (services and products) Pay attention to IT system integration and transition	Generic and/or different for SBS Limited added value when purchasing and outsourcing have been studied

includes, for example, human helpdesk for IS/IT support). However, sourcing SBS may not always involve outsourcing with respect to the transfer of internal activities and resources to external service providers. The IS procurement literature adds to the purchasing and outsourcing literature the more technical perspective where system integration and transition are important issues.

Based on the different sourcing concepts from classical purchasing, business process outsourcing, and IS procurement, we made an assessment of application of the presented approaches for sourcing SBS (Table 3). These different approaches, adapted to SBS and used in combination, can provide a suitable starting point for sourcing SBS.

CONCLUDING REMARKS

The adoption of SBS means that the business and IT functions have to deal with external service providers. This requires making sourcing decisions and the involvement of the purchasing function. While external sourcing of services and IT is not new (for example, helpdesk support), external sourcing of software services is. This raises the question to what extent existing sourcing approaches can be used for SBS and what are specific sourcing requirements for SBS. Moreover, to benefit from SBS, the sourcing should be performed in a effective and efficient manner. This requires a close cooperation between the IT function and the purchasing function. We propose that this requires, on the one hand, a thorough understanding of SBS by the purchasing function in particular the sourcing requirements for the specification. And, on the other hand, this requires a more informed IT function with respect to the different sourcing design options.

Sourcing of SBS is rather a new emerging field of research. In this paper, we have identified that the sourcing requirements for SBS have a close knit with the key characteristics of SBS. The sourcing approaches in the field of classical

purchasing, business process outsourcing, and IS sourcing can guide the sourcing process of SBS to a certain extent. However, we have explicated that the key characteristics of SBS inhibit the adoption of these classical purchasing models for SBS. The existing sourcing models need to be adapted by considering the characteristics of services. We are currently working in the direction of developing new sourcing designs for SBS, focusing on the integration of services from different vendors.

REFERENCES

Bruno, F. (2006, July). *Executing an IP Protection Strategy in a SaaS Environment. Contract Management.* Magazine, NCMA, USA.

Cheng, H. K., Demirkan, H., & Koehler, G. (2003). The Price and Capacity Competition of Application Services Duopoly. *Information Systems and e-Business Management. 1*(2).

Coetzee, M., & Eloff, J. H. P. (2007). Web services Access Control Architecture Incorporating Trust. *Internet Research, 17*(3). doi:10.1108/10662240710758939

Cullen, S., Seddon, P., & Willcocks, L. (2005). Managing IT outsourcing: The life cycle imperative. *MIS Quarterly Executive, 4*, 229–244.

Gangadharan, G. R., & D'Andrea, V. (2009). Service Orientation: Licensing Perspectives. *Journal of International Commercial Law and Technology., 4*(1).

Getto, G., Gantner, T., & Vullinghs, T. (2000). Software Acquisition: Experiences with Models and Methods. In *Proceedings of the EuroSPI*.

Grönroos, C. (2007). Service Management and Marketing: Customer Management in Service Competition (3rd ed.). Chichester, UK: John Wiley and Sons.

Gunther, O., Tamm, G., & Leymann, F. (2006). Pricing Web Services. In Dagstuhl Seminar Proceedings 06291 (The Role of Business Processes in Service Oriented Architectures).

Han, K., Kauffman, R. J., & Nault, B. R. (2004). Information Exploitation and Interorganizational Systems Ownership . *Journal of Management Information Systems, 21*(2).

Hefley, W., Loesche, E. A., Khera, P., & Siegel, J. (2005). *A Framework for Best Practices in the Sourcing Life-cycle: The Architecture of the eSourcing Capability Model for Client Organizations.* In ITsqc Working Paper Series CMU-ITSQC-WP-05-001.

Hill, T. (1977). On Goods and Services. *Review of Income and Wealth, 23*(4). doi:10.1111/j.1475-4991.1977.tb00021.x

Hyderr, E., Heston, K., & Paulk, M. (2006). The eSourcing Capability Model for Service Providers V2.01 (Tech Report), Pittsburgh, PA: Carniege Melon University.

Lacity, M. C., Willcocks, L. P., & Feeny, D. F. (1996). The value of selective IT sourcing. *Sloan Management Review, 37*, 13–25.

Lankhorst, M., et al. (2005). Enterprise Architecture at Work. New York: Springer Publications.

MacKenzie, M., Laskey, K., McCabe, F., Brown, P., & Metz, R. (2006). *Reference Model for Service Oriented Architecture.* Retrieved from http://docs.oasis-open.org/soa-rm/v1.0/soa-rm.pdf

Mani, A., & Nagarajan, A. (2002). *Understanding Quality of Service for Web Services.* Retrieved from http://www.ibm.com/developerworks/library/ws-quality.html

Maximilien, M., & Toward, S. M. (2005). Web Services Interaction Styles. In *Proceedings of IEEE Services Computing Conference (SCC).*

McCord, A. (2003) Sourcing Information Technology Services. In P. McClure (ed), EDUCAUSE Leadership Strategies Series, Volume 7 – Managing Information Resources, EDUCAUSE. New York: John Wiley and Sons.

Monczka, R., Trent, R., & Handfield, R. (2005). Purchasing & supply chain management (3rd ed.). Mason, OH: Thomson.

Op de Coul, J. (2005). IT Services Procurement based on ISPL. The Netherlands:van Haren Publishers.

Robison, L. (2007). The CIO Dilemma: Build, Buy or Borrow. Burton Group Report.

Sprott, D. (2006). Service Architecture and Engineering. *CBDI Journal. July/August.*

Van Weele, A. J. (2005). Purchasing & supply chain management: Analysis, strategy, planning and practice (4th ed.). London: Thomson.

Wilkes, L. (2004). Principles of Service Orientation. *CBDI Journal, March.*

Zeithaml, V. A., Parasuraman, A., & Berry, L. L. (1985). Problems and strategies in services marketing. *Journal of Marketing, 49*, 33–46. doi:10.2307/1251563

Chapter 12
Supplier Relationship Management in Health Care

Tobias Mettler
University of St. Gallen, Switzerland & SAP Research St. Gallen, Switzerland

Peter Rohner
University of St. Gallen, Switzerland

ABSTRACT

The structural transformation of modern societies (e.g. aging of population, mobility) as well as continuously increasing market dynamics (e.g. mergers, technological advancement) induce health care organizations, more than ever, to reduce their costs while enhancing service delivery at the same time. In other industrial sectors this was achieved by optimizing cooperation, coordination, and communication particularly with regard to the supplier base. However, as the pressure to innovate will increase extensively in the next years, similar developments are becoming relevant for the health care supply chain, too. In this chapter we therefore adapt the current findings on supplier relationship management (SRM) to the health care context. We analyze theoretical foundations of SRM and explore one particular area of application in health care, namely the ordering of pharmaceuticals by hospitals. On the basis of a case study we develop a future scenario for drugs supply management and discuss potential performance and quality improvements.

INTRODUCTION

The effects of globalization, fragmentation of markets and new technological advancement, for example in data transmission and processing, has

DOI: 10.4018/978-1-61520-603-2.ch012

an immense impact on the value chains of highly competitive industries (OECD, 2007). Despite enormous investments in innovation and the magnitude of opportunities for innovators in health care, one has not seen a fundamental change yet (Herzlinger, 2006). Nonetheless, the pressure to achieve effectiveness and efficiency is set to increase significantly as in many countries new economic principles, such as lump sums for medical treatments, are introduced in order to reduce health expenditures and enhance the competition among health care providers.

Although labor costs constitute the major share of the total costs of a medical treatment, there is still a high economic potential in improving expenditure on products and services (European Commission, 2006; The Chartered Institute of Purchasing & Supply, 2005). Supplier Relationship Management (SRM), understood as approach to systematically managing an organization's interactions with the companies that supply products and services to it, can help to reduce costs and enhance quality of service delivery (Mettler & Rohner, 2008). However, since hospital buying agents were only expected to attain the best price for the needed goods in the recent past, the trust between the buyer and the supplier is weak and the relationship is antagonistic. Therefore, and in contrast to industries with intense competition like for example the automotive or the consumer electronics industry, SRM is not paid much attention to in health care academia and practice yet. Although the adoption of electronic services saves the costs of the preparation and transmission of paper requests and invoices and eliminates costly, time-consuming errors from manual data entry by connecting ordering systems with production systems (Brynjolfsson & Yang, 1996), only 38 percent of the German hospitals implemented an electronic purchasing order and 35 percent an electronic invoice (German Association for Medical Technology, 2007). In Switzerland, the origin of this research, no such evidence exists so far, but considering the similarities between the health systems the adoption rate should be more or less at the same level. This ratio is diminutive compared to the aviation industry where 85 percent of the organizations actively use e-procurement in their daily business. Between 35 and 40 percent of hospital supply-related costs are caused by

handling and processing material and purchasing orders, while in competitive industries this amount is less than 10 percent (Grossman, 2000).

Some evidence suggests that this is going to change. To some extent hospital purchasing departments already are stipulated to contribute to revenue increases and to knowledge acquisition. Hence, the role of the supplier who formerly was considered to be an opponent (e.g. within price negotiations) will change to a business partner who contributes an added value to the hospital and therefore needs to be better involved in terms of cooperation (business relationships), coordination (processes and work practices), and communication (electronic services).

As a consequence, the concept of SRM will become more relevant for health care organizations as well as for supply chain management research. Because the hitherto existing literature is mainly focused on industrial enterprises, it is the aim of this chapter to provide a sector-specific discussion. In taking a different approach to perceive SRM, the understanding of possible impacts of SRM will be enhanced and encourage the application of these concepts and electronic services.

In order to achieve this goal, the chapter is organized as follows. First, we examine distinct definitions and theoretical foundations of SRM in order to provide an overview of the field. After this, we discuss the basic constructs of SRM such as types of business relationships, typical processes and work practices as well as exemplary electronic services supporting the implementation of SRM activities. To reference to the health care sector, we then explore the particularities of this industry and its influence on SRM. In the section that follows, we present a case study on the pharmaceuticals supply management of three Swiss hospitals in order to illustrate the potential value of SRM for health care organizations. Finally, we present some concluding remarks and offer some suggestions for future research endeavors.

DEFINITIONS AND THEORETICAL FOUNDATIONS OF SUPPLIER RELATIONSHIP MANAGEMENT

Supplier Relationship Management or Supply Management1 is a comprehensive approach to managing an organization's interactions with the firms that supply the products and services it uses. However, different definitions of the term are actually being used to comprise the concept. Some sample characterizations are:

1. *Supplier relationship management is the process that defines how a company interacts with its suppliers. As the name suggests, this is a mirror image of customer relationship management (CRM). Just as a company needs to develop relationships with its customers, it also needs to foster relationships with its suppliers [...] The desired outcome is a win-win relationship where both parties benefit* (Supply Chain Management Institute, 2008).

2. *Purchasing and Supply Management is defined as a strategic, enterprise-wide, long-term, multi-functional, dynamic approach to selecting suppliers of goods and services and managing them and the whole value network from raw materials to final customer use and disposal to continually reduce total ownership costs, manage risks, and improve performance (quality, responsiveness, reliability, and flexibility)* (Leftwich, Leftwich, Moore & Roll, 2004).

3. *SRM includes both business practices and software and is part of the information flow component of supply chain management (SCM). SRM practices create a common frame of reference to enable effective communication between an enterprise and suppliers who may use quite different business practices and terminology. As a result, SRM increases the efficiency of processes associated with acquiring goods and services, managing inventory, and processing materials* (SAP, 2003).

4. *SRM [...] refers to any supplier-facing business practices which are enabled by collaborative software and which allow companies to work with their supplier base for mutual success. Primarily, SRM tools have been developed to reduce the total cost*

Table 1. Different perceptions of SRM

	Management-oriented view	*Technology-focused view*
Conceptual foundations	• Relationship theory • Social network theory	• Process redesign • Transaction cost theory
Main focus	• Proactive development of relationship between an organization and its suppliers • Design, implementation and control of cross-organizational relationships to suppliers • Continuous advance of the 'lived' partnership to strategic suppliers • Exchange of improvement ideas between buyer and supplier	• Coordination of procurement process and monitoring of quality consistency of different suppliers • (Technically) Integration of suppliers in procurement processes • Continuous analysis and control of procurement processes and supplier performance • Automation of all procurement activities between the enterprise and supplier
Key objectives	• Enhancement of co-operation and quality of information flows • Security of supply and leverage through negotiation of better deals from suppliers (win-win situation) • Continuous improvement with suppliers by encouraging innovation • Compliance with contracts and regulations	• Better risk control through better information flows • Lean processes and consolidation of supplier base • Reduction of cycle times and process costs and better value for money (TCO) • Improvement of process quality

of ownership (TCO) for procured goods, while creating competitive advantage for an organization through deeper relationships with its suppliers (Fleming, 2004).

Looking at the above definitions, it becomes clear that differential emphasis is being placed to what exactly constitutes SRM (see Table 1). Basically, it can be differentiated between a management-oriented view (definitions 1 and 2) or a technology-focused view on SRM (definitions 3 and 4).

In the first case special interest is given to social and managerial aspects of business relationship between buyers and suppliers (e.g. this is indicated by the accentuation of the terms 'relationship' or 'value network'). Theoretical and conceptual foundations of this perception can be found in relationship theory (e.g. Anderson, Hakansson & Johanson, 1994; Dwyer, Schurr & Oh, 1987; Dyer & Singh, 1998) or social network theory (e.g. Burt, 1992; Freeman, 1979; Granovetter, 1973). Effective SRM thus means to actively design, implement, and control social relationships in order to achieve inter-organizational competitive advantage by means of mutual win-win situations.

On the other hand, the technology-focused view of SRM is rather concentrated on streamlining processes and enhancing communication in order to reduce costs and effect better value for money (e.g. this is indicated by the terms 'business practices' or 'software'). Key theories for this view are for example transaction cost theory (e.g. Bakos & Brynjolfsson, 1993; Bunduchi, 2005; Williamson, 1979) or process redesign (Curtis, Kellner & Over, 1992; Davenport & Short, 1990; Leymann & Altenhuber, 1994).

BUSINESS RELATIONSHIPS, PROCESSES, AND ELECTRONIC SERVICES

In this section we bring together the two perceptions – management-oriented and technology-focused view – in order to holistically discuss the impact of SRM on health care organizations. As opposed to the above-presented definitions, where either business or technology is in the center of concern, coherence between these extreme positions is assumed. Accordingly, we perceive SRM as a socio-technical approach to enhance cooperation (business relationships), coordination (processes and work practices), and communication (electronic services) between an organization and its suppliers to achieve a wide range of goals (e.g. process efficiency, service quality, information security, service innovation, risk avoidance). The following sub-sections thus are devoted to illustrate the three basic constructs – the 3Cs of SRM.

Types of Business Relationships (Cooperation)

The activity of an enterprise involves cooperation, both voluntary and involuntary, active and passive, of numerous and diverse constituents (Post, Preston & Sachs, 2002). In order to reduce production costs and to focus on the core competencies of the firm, enterprises are constrained to cooperate with other business units. Business units are economic units, such as e.g. corporations, divisions, national subsidiaries, profit centers or small and medium-sized enterprises, which are responsible for profits and operate within the market economy (Österle, Fleisch & Alt, 2000). Depending on the business unit, different types of relationships exist, which can be used as differentiation criteria for the diverse relationship management approaches. Five exemplary business relationship types can be differentiated:

1. *Buyer-Supplier-Relationship:* In buyer-supplier-relationships the organizational boundaries of an enterprise is pervaded by the integration of activities that are performed by suppliers. As the roles of supplier and buyer are no longer narrowly defined (Yilmaz & Hunt, 2001), a comprehensive approach to manage this relationship is needed – SRM. This is exactly the focus of this chapter.

2. *Buyer-Supplier-Pre-Supplier-Relationship:* An enlargement of SRM is the concept commonly referred to as supply network management (SNM). It not only focuses on the dyadic relationship between direct suppliers but also the entire strategic network of pre-suppliers and original equipment manufacturers (Muessigmann & Albani, 2006).

3. *Producer-Customer-Relationship:* The most important relationship, however not focus of this chapter, is the business relationship to the customer. The management of the interactions with customers is widely known as customer relationship management (CRM). CRM is often seen as a mirror image of SRM (Supply Chain Management Institute, 2008).

4. *Producer-Intermediary-Customer-Relationship:* Similar to SRM, there also exists an extension of CRM called partner relationship management (PRM), which principally concentrates on the network of intermediaries and their interaction with the enterprise (Jutla, Craig & Bodorik, 2001).

5. *Enterprise-Government-Relationship:* In the context of health care, but also in other regulated markets, the often one-way relationship with governmental authorities is important as they define the regulatory setting for the enterprise's activities and services to be rendered. However, the focus of this chapter will be exclusively on the buyer-supplier-relationship.

Processes and Work Practices for SRM (Coordination)

Processes build the basic building blocks for the implementation of an enterprise-supplier-relationship (Österle et al., 2000). *Coordination* between the processes ensures that the sourcing activities are interconnected and diaphanous. (Rüegg-Stürm, 2005) differentiates three types of processes: business processes, management processes and support processes.

Business processes in the context of procurement (see Figure 1) include all work practices and activities to guarantee the supply of goods (e.g. submission offering, contract fulfillment and shipment). On the other hand, management processes are needed for the organization, governance and development of the supplier relationships. For instance, in the short term, management processes deal with the control of every-day sourcing activities and possible irregularities (e.g. conflict management in case of non-fulfillment of a contract). In the long term, management attendance is needed to manage change and the strategic alignment of the purchasing department. Finally, support processes focus on the allocation of the purchasing department's infrastructure and on the consequent assistance of efficient and effective business process delivery (e.g. training of staff, maintenance of IT).

Reviewing the current literature in the area shows that the processes and work practices of SRM are given unequal emphasis in terms of depth and breadth. For illustrating this, four different process frameworks are discussed (see Figure 2).

The first process framework as described by (Schmid & Lindenmann, 1998) focuses on the detailed specification of work practices that are needed to initiate, arrange and complete a market transaction. As a result, processes that assist management activities (e.g. building of supply strategy) or support activities (e.g. human resources development) are completely missing.

Figure 1. Process landscape for SRM

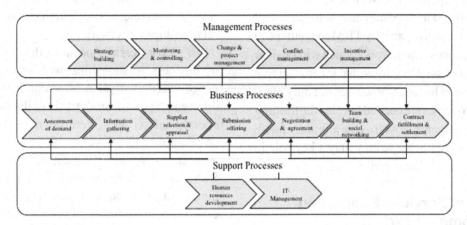

Figure 2. SRM processes and work practices

		(Schmid & Linden-mann, 1998)	(Eyholzer et al., 2002)	(Riemer & Klein, 2002)	(Appelfel ler & Buchholz, 2005)
Business processes	Assessment of demand	○	◐	◐	◐
	Information gathering	●	●	●	●
	Supplier selection and appraisal	◐	◐	●	●
	Submission offering	●	◐	◐	●
	Negotiation and agreement	●	●	●	●
	Team building and social networking	○	○	●	○
	Contract fulfillment and settlement	●	●	●	●
Management processes	Strategy building	○	◐	◐	●
	Monitoring and controlling	○	●	●	●
	Change and project management	○	○	●	◐
	Conflict management	○	○	○	◐
	Incentive management	○	○	○	◐
Support processes	Human resources development	○	○	○	●
	IT-Management	○	○	○	◐

Other frameworks such as from (Eyholzer, Kuhlmann & Münger, 2002; Riemer & Klein, 2002) complement the prior described view by integrating the management perspective. They bring forward the argument that in order to effectively control and design an enterprise-supplier-relationship, activities beyond the pure handling of market transactions are required. Nevertheless, the depth of considering management processes as part of SRM differs. For example, (Riemer & Klein, 2002) state that monitoring and controlling of the suppliers' performance as well as conjoint project and change management are crucial for enhancing the relationship between an enterprise and its suppliers. As a result, (Riemer & Klein 2002) present the only approach that explicitly integrates team building and social networking as part of their framework in order to operationalize change and project management on a business level.

At last, (Appelfeller & Buchholz, 2005) take a step forward and include human resources development and at least partially IT-Management in their SRM process framework (which we consider a support process). They argue that for an effective coordination of business processes not only management processes are needed but also the training of the buying agents as well as the alignment with the IT- personnel because they play a key role in the realization of that coordination.

Electronic Services Supporting SRM (Communication)

With the emergence of the Internet enterprises have numerous opportunities at their disposal for doing business and for communicating with business partners all over the world. Communication, as used in this chapter, is thus understood as exchange of information (Merriam-Webster Online Dictionary, 2009). In doing so, a wide range of electronic services (in the following referred to as 'service') is available these days to support the communication. In line with (Marton,

Piccinelli & Turfin, 1999), we therefore conceive *services* as the electronic virtualization of business relationships or activities.

In recent years, especially the virtualization of business relationships with customers was expedited (Parvatiyar & N. Sheth, 2001). Hence, different types of analytical, collaborative and operational services were developed for CRM (Adebanjo, 2003; Dyché, 2001; Zeng, Wen & Yen, 2003). We use the same differentiation for SRM services (and extend it with a 'supportive' dimension) in order to categorize the identified exemplary instantiations (see Table 2).

Analytical SRM (aSRM) aims at storing, analyzing, and applying knowledge about suppliers and personnel dedicated to manage the supplier's relationship. For this purpose, typical performance management and decision support tools (e.g. business intelligence, on-line analytical processing, statistics and reporting tools, data warehousing, data mining) are used.

The purpose of collaborative SRM (cSRM) is to improve the quality of supplier communication, and, as a result, increase supplier performance

Table 2. Electronic services supporting SRM

	Key objectives	Exemplary instantiations
Analytical SRM services	Enhance knowledge about suppliers to increase effectiveness of the business relationship	• Business intelligence • On-line analytical processing • Statistics and reporting tools • Data warehousing • Data mining
Collaborative SRM services	Improve quality of communication to sharpen team building and social networking	• Collaborative planning, forecasting, and replenishment (CPFR) • Contract management tools • Electronic auctions • Electronic tendering • Electronic request for information tools (E-RFI)
Operational SRM services	Raise efficiency of ordering and contract fulfillment	• Desktop purchasing • Electronic payment • Electronic product catalog (EPC) • Electronic order • Supplier self-service • Supplier portal
Supportive SRM services	Guarantee the continuity of information processing between internal and external organizational units	• Inventory control / enterprise resource planning (ERP) • Finance and controlling • Personnel administration • Enterprise content management (ECM) • Business process management (BPM)

and reliability. E-Collaboration, electronic contract management, electronic auctions, electronic tendering, and E-RFx (e.g. electronic request for information, quotation, and proposal) fall into this category.

Operational SRM (oSRM), commonly referred to as E-Procurement, includes all necessary tools for ordering and conclusion of a contract such as payment or invoice verification. Typical examples are plan-driven purchasing and desktop purchasing tools (e.g. electronic product catalog), E-Payment, E-Order, supplier self-service, and supplier portals.

Alongside analytical, collaborative, and operational SRM, other services are needed – which denominated Supportive SRM services (sSRM) –to guarantee the continuity of information processing between internal and external organizational units. For instance, search engines to retrieve all kind of information related to sourcing, inventory control systems to build the crucial bridge to the logistics department and requesters of goods, business process modeling and enterprise architecture solutions for visualizing, simulating and analyzing different structural aspects of the purchasing department, personnel administration systems for managing workforce related information, finance and controlling systems to define targets and supervise the achievement of objectives, and enterprise content management systems to dispense all kind of documentation.

BUILDING THE BRIDGE TO HEALTH CARE

Before demonstrating the practical implications of SRM services in health care organizations, we have to discuss the particularities of the health care sector compared to other commercial industries. For this purpose, the determinants of buyer-supplier-relationships are discussed first (external view) in order to explore the role of procurement in health care organizations (internal view).

Determinants of Buyer-Supplier-Relationships in Health Care: The External View

According to (Herzlinger, 2006; Porter & Olmsted Teisberg, 2004) health care is considered to be different from most other industries due to the high level of regulation, the high proportion of governmental investment, the associated low pressure in respect of effectiveness and efficiency of state-subsidized health care organizations and the lack of orientation towards customer benefit. As one consequence, the health care sector shows a relatively underdeveloped information system structure. However, in order to provide optimal health service delivery there is a long-standing practice of including information beyond the traditional boundaries of a single health care organization (Scott, 2002). Furthermore, there is an imminent obligation for cooperation in order to comply with the requirement of both, internal (e.g. doctors, pharmacists, nurses) and external stakeholders (patients, governmental agencies, suppliers). The business relationship with suppliers thus normally is subject to a variety of exogenous and endogenous factors (Mettler & Rohner, 2009b):

- Regulatory setting: The health care market is completely administered by governmental agencies, both professional (e.g. admission for pharma-related professions) and commercial (e.g. assignments to render certain services). Governmental regulations and policies constrict the freedom of action (Rainey, Backoff & Levine, 1976).
- Market structure: Health care shows, in contrast to other industries, a typical seller's market structure (Craig & Gabler, 1940). There is still a strong dependency between producers and customers (Wholey & Burns, 2003). The constitution of collaborative processes is therefore highly complex.

- Technological advancement: Like in other sectors, technology is advancing quickly. This facilitates new possibilities for cooperation (e.g. vendor managed inventories, just-in-time ordering and delivery, collaborative procurement planning). However, as health care is rather underdeveloped in terms of its IT infrastructure and health care personnel are less accustomed to work with new technologies, there is a need of acquiring not only technology but also expertise to handle it (Parente, 2000).
- Strategic positioning: Most sectors address an unambiguous and homogenous customer segment, but health care involves the variety, including clinicians, payers, government, service providers, and users (Avison & Young, 2007). The strategy of a health care organization and derived sub-strategies (e.g. supply strategy) have to be conform to the needs of every customer segment. However, to reduce complexity, variety of services and products has to be reflected critically.
- Employee behavior: Perceptions, feelings, and face-to-face contact are extremely important to the success of any change effort (Walston & Chadwick, 2003). Thus, social networking with suppliers is an important part of relationship management.
- Organizational structure: Whereas management is unified in most sectors, health care has clinical and administrative reporting lines with sometimes very different leadership philosophy and target systems (Avison & Young, 2007). This division normally has also an influence on how to do business with suppliers. As medical staff is normally more inclined to assess the supplier relationship according to the quality of the delivered products, buying agents typically are more focused on the price performance ratio.

Positioning of Procurement within a Health Care Organization: The Internal View

Health care organizations' primary assignment is to provide attendance for the healing and relief of acute illnesses, for preventive health care and for the permanent care of the chronically sick. These health services are provided alongside the patient care process (i.e. scheduling and preparation, admission, diagnosis, treatment, discharge, after-care) by means of a high division of labor between very specialized professional groups located in distinct departments or clinics (see Figure 3). Support processes like logistics thus have to be designed to serve management processes (e.g. financial planning & controlling, organizational development), medical and care processes (e.g. surgery and internal medicine) as well as for the demands on cross-disciplinary processes (e.g. the laboratory, anesthetics, or radiology). However, not only the complexity of these processes is thereby increased but also the basis for formulating company-wide procurement standards and defining commonly accepted sourcing concepts is hindered. As (Glouberman & Mintzberg, 2001) stated, operational problems of cohesion often result from differences in education, incentives, and value systems of the various professional groups, and particularly between the medical and administrative work force whereto the buying agents are counted. Hence, the distribution of power between medical and non-medical departments, organizational culture (e.g. common traditions and values) as well as the willingness for cross-disciplinary collaboration plays a major role in the implementation of SRM processes.

As a consequence of the above-mentioned dissociation of medical and non-medical functions, information about products and suppliers is largely distributed. As they build the basis of SRM services (or at least are core subject of these services), it is of particular importance to know where to find procurement relevant information.

Figure 3. Organization structure alongside the patient care process

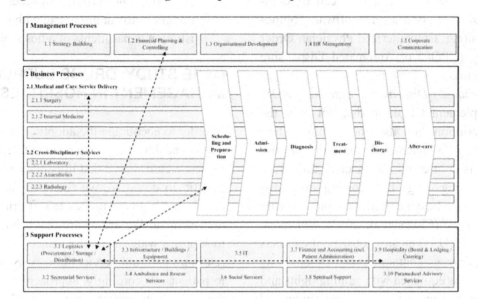

According to (Mettler & Rohner 2009a) this can be found in medical applications, which aim at storing, retrieving, processing and analyzing information for the purpose of prescribing, dispensing, and administering of pharmaceutical products, as well as in administrative applications which are used for processing business-related information such as purchasing orders or billing. Exemplary instantiations are:

- *Clinical Information Systems (CIS)* also referred to as *Hospital Information Systems (HIS)* are used to "collect, store, process, retrieve, and communicate patient care and administrative information for all hospital-affiliated activities and to satisfy the functional requirements of all authorized users" (van Bemmel & Musen, 1999). They can be composed of one or a few software components with specialty-specific extensions as well as of a large variety of sub-systems in medical specialties (e.g. Pharmacy Information System or Laboratory Information System). Typically, the Electronic Medical Record (EMR) takes

a center stage within a CIS, providing for example information on allergy, history, medications in use, diagnoses, weight, and age appropriate to the medication (Chung, Choi & Moon, 2003).

- *Pharmacy Information Systems (PIS)* are especially designed for helping pharmacists to make decisions about patient drug therapies. Their emphasis lies on reducing medical errors, improving communications between nurses and the pharmacy department, and providing integration and interoperability in closed-loop medication administration (Enrado, 2005). Key features are for example prescription management (e.g. matching of prescriptions to available pharmaceutical products), clinical screening (e.g. monitoring of drug interactions and other medication-related complications, creation of patient drug profiles), inventory management (e.g. control of stock), and reporting (e.g. generation of reports concerning the medication usage and the costs of the purchased drugs) (Biohealthmatics.com, 2006). Like in the case of a CIS, they can be composed of one or a several software components (e.g. Computerized Physician Order Entry (CPOE) or Automated Dispensing System).

- *Automated Dispensing Systems (ADS)* complement CPOE in that not only the prescription but also the administration of drugs is automated. Its main purpose is thus to "free up pharmacists' time from dispensing drugs by allowing drug dispensing to be done right at the point of care by nurses" (Chung et al., 2003). A physical part of ADS typically consists of cabinets with drawers containing medications. The cabinet is equipped with guiding lights and directs the nurse to the correct automated drawer containing the medication.
- *Unit Dose Dispensing Systems (UDDS)* are other means for automating the administration of drugs. Whereas ADS is applied at the point of care, UDDS are used for the preparation of drugs in the pharmacy department (typically for non-fluid medicines such as pills). For this purpose the required drug doses are individually prepared, packaged and labeled (Swisslog, 2008). Most significant advantages resulting from an UDDS are for example the central location of drugs (the size of the ward stock is reduced), maintained drug identity (each dose is identified according to name, strength, and the patient for which it is intended), and a reduction of the preparation time (the dose is simply removed from the medication cart, opened, and administered directly to the patient) (Murray & Shojania, 2001).
- *Administrative Information Systems (AIS)* typically are implemented for the handling of admissions, discharges and transfers of patients, scheduling of resource plans, and for the accounting of the services rendered by the procurement department (Chung et

al., 2003). They provide all necessary functionalities to communicate with the administration departments of a hospital.

CASE STUDY: DRUGS SUPPLY MANAGEMENT IN HOSPITALS

In order to encourage the adoption of SRM services in health care, it is the aim of this section to present a case study[2] that illustrates its potential benefit. In doing so, we focus on the analysis of selected business processes[3] of drugs supply management. We are aware that a hospital has to supply a wide range of products with distinct relevancy for health service delivery and proximity to patients. Accordingly, approaches to procure these products and the adoption of electronic services may differ (depending on its relevancy and proximity). However, a narrowing of the focus of the case study was needed in order to analyze SRM adoption in more detail and to further discuss possible trends. Drugs supply management is a suitable example for demonstrating the usefulness of SRM in the area.

Case Description and Data Collection

Starting from the internal view of a hospital[4], drugs supply management typically is accomplished by the pharmacy department. In order to collect the necessary information with respect to the adoption of SRM in this context, three hospitals differing in terms of organization size, complexity of assortment, and automation were analyzed during June and August 2007. Purposive sampling was chosen to select as varied cases as possible.

The first pharmacy, which was analyzed, corresponds to a public hospital with about 400 beds and a total of 55,500 patients a year. The hospital's pharmacy manages an assortment of almost 1,200 different pharmaceuticals (whereof 800 are in stock). The automation level of the hospital pharmacy is rather low compared with other industries and is mainly focused on the improvement of administrative and personnel issues of the specific organizational unit itself, thus leaving behind potential benefits of intra-organizational and inter-organizational collaboration. The second unit of analysis is a pharmacy of a regional hospital with 48,000 patients annually, 350 beds and a comparable assortment of pharmaceuticals like in the first case. However, as opposed to the first case, the automation is more focused on optimizing not only the own organizational unit but also the internal interfaces (e.g. to the logistics department). Finally, a third hospital pharmacy was analyzed, which centered their automation efforts on optimizing the whole supply chain (from supplier to the patient). Interestingly, it was the smallest hospital of these three (with 300 beds and about 31,000 patients a year). As the pharmacy department is also responsible for the procurement of medical devices, slightly more items (about 8,000) are in the assortment (whereof 1,000 are in stock).

Primary means for the collecting the data were expert interviews with the corresponding hospitals' chief pharmacists. Additionally, we used personal observational field notes (a total of more than 70 pages were generated) and secondary material (process descriptions, organizational charts, photographs) to comprise the phenomenon. To validate our observations, the field notes were sent to the pharmacists for revision, followed by further meetings for in-depth discussions.

In order to complement the internal perspective of single hospitals, an additional focus group discussion has been conducted with suppliers in September 2007. As a result of both perspectives, several consolidated process models using the Business Process Modeling Notation (BPMN)5 were derived to document our findings (also refer to Mettler & Rohner 2009a). These models are helpful to understand the perceived reality, the object system, of the surveyed organizations. As the interviewees perceive the health care system differently in accordance with their individual roles and objectives, an explicit form of representation

is needed in order to be able to understand, explain and communicate this perceived reality.

Understanding the Regular Ordering Routine for Drugs

A key activity in drugs supply management is the ordering of regular pharmaceuticals, i.e. drugs that are defined in a standard drugs list. As public hospitals have a permanent obligation for service delivery (also in case of crisis), only a marginal fault tolerance in the procurement of these drugs is admissible. Hence, sophisticated mechanisms to manage the entire supply chain are needed. However, this is currently more aspiration than reality (Burns, 2002). It becomes clear, when the flow of activities for regular ordering routines is analyzed in more detail. The regular order routine consists of ten basic activities (see Table 3).

In Hospital A the use of ICT is focused on the needs of the pharmacy staff. For this reason the activities on the part of the nursing staff have only rudimentary ICT support. As the wards repository is not standardized and not managed electronically in a PIS, there is no inventory control (i.e. the received pharmaceuticals are not managed in the pharmacy or materials management system). Feedback loops that indicate that patients are given the right drugs are missing as no automated dispensing systems are implemented. In general, ICT is only used for in-house ordering and for managing the pharmacy inventory. Additionally, due to the manual data entry of in-house orders and of master data (e.g. product and supplier information), poor data quality exists. As a further consequence of the localized use of ICT, important internal (e.g. to the logistics department) and external (e.g. to the suppliers) interfaces are lacking as well. The resulting media breaks give rise to more problems such as missing information of order and delivery status, additional labor effort for manual ordering and lengthy process cycle times.

Although Hospital B has a comparable automation level, the focus of ICT use lies more in the

Table 3. Regular order routine for drugs

Activity	Implementation			Suggested SRM Service
	Hospital A	*Hospital B*	*Hospital C*	
1. Search ward repository	Manual handling, no standardized repository	PIS with standardized repository	PIS with standardized repository	• Inventory control / ERP
2. Prepare drugs	Manual handling	Manual handling	Manual handling	-
3. Make/send internal order	Manual data entry, order by e-mail	Supported by bar code system, order by e-mail	Supported by bar code system, order by desktop purchasing tool	• Desktop purchasing • EPC
4. Check internal order	Manual handling of e-mail	Manual handling of e-mail	Automated alerts by desktop purchasing tool	• Desktop purchasing • EPC
5. Search pharmacy repository	Manual handling of search and master data entry	Automated search (PIS), but manual master data entry	Automated search (PIS); master data sourced from provider	• Inventory control / ERP
6. Deliver drugs	Manual handling	Manual handling	Manual handling	-
7. Search supplier list	Manual search in paper-based list	Manual search in paper-based list	Automated search in supplier portal	• Supplier portal • Statistics and reporting tools
8. Make/send purchase order	Fax and telephone	Fax and telephone	Supplier portal	• Supplier Portal • E-Auctions
9. Receive drugs (pharmacy)	Manual handling of invoice entry	Invoice entry supported by bar code system	Invoice entry supported by bar code system	• Supplier self-service • E-Order
10. Receive drugs (ward)	Out of control, no data entry	Controlled by bar code system	Controlled by bar code system	• Inventory control / ERP

cross-functional optimization of processes. As a result, the ward repositories are highly standardized (i.e. every repository has a defined assortment of drugs which are labeled by bar code tags) and thus can be centrally managed in the PIS. Inventory control is possible since all in-house orders have to be placed electronically by scanning the corresponding bar code (see Figure 4). However, the administration of drugs is still out of control, thus leaving behind the potential of reducing medical errors during the dispensing of drugs. Looking inside the pharmacy, problems similar to those seen in Hospital A exist here, too. Master data, purchasing orders and delivery preparation are still processed manually.

As Hospital C is rather focused on the optimization of the entire supply chain, internal and external interfaces are better developed. Internally, the realization is identical with Hospital B, hence using the bar code technology for inventory control

and in-house ordering. Externally, an electronic purchasing platform, which is connected with the internal PIS is used for the collaboration with the different suppliers. More than 80 per cent of the purchasing orders are handled through this platform. In addition, master data is obtained from a professional information provider. However, there are still areas for improvement left. For example the administration of drugs is out of control or the preparation of drugs is mainly done by hand yet. Since this is a time consuming and risky task, the use of ICT-enabled drugs management (e.g. unit dose dispensing system) should be considered.

In consideration of the three cases, it can be concluded that particularly the supportive SRM service 'Inventory control / ERP' and the operational services 'Desktop Purchasing' and 'Supplier Portal' can help pharmacists in realizing a more transparent and integrated order routine for drugs. Additionally, E-Orders or a supplier self-service

Figure 4. Use of bar code tags for inventory control

will certainly speed up the administrative activities of invoice verification. However, there are activities such as preparing or delivery of drugs, which are rather medical in nature and thus cannot be assisted by SRM services accurately.6

Understanding the Routine for Ad-hoc Requests

People are becoming increasingly mobile (e.g. cross-broder commuters, tourists, seasonal workers). As a result, hospitals are faced with new challenges to assure the continuity of clinical care of their patients. In order to guarantee a permanent service delivery, ad-hoc requests (i.e. booking appointments for pharmaceuticals, which are not in the standard-drug list of the hospital) are becoming increasingly important. Again, ten basic activities can be differentiated (see Table 4).

The situation in Hospital A, B, and C are practically identical for activities 1-4. All activities with reference to the handling of prescriptions are processed manually by filling out, sending, and processing paper-based forms. This is very time consuming for physicians, nursing staff, and pharmacists and yields to lengthy process cycle times, mispurchasing and so forth. However, much more serious in this regard are medication errors, possibly caused by illegible prescriptions (Furukawa, Raghu & Spaulding, 2008). In the United States it is assumed that medication errors provoke at least one death every day and injure approximately 1.3 million people annually (U.S. Food and Drug Administration, 2009). Hence, there is certainly room for major improvement in Switzerland, too.

For the more administrative part of the ad-hoc request routine (activities 5-8), a quite varying situation was found. When searching for an appropriate supplier, Hospital A and B spend a lot of time on the Internet as only the personal network of known suppliers is recorded in the PIS. Purchasing orders are placed by fax or by telephone. The status of orders and shipments is therefore uncontrollable. When talking to the pharmacists of Hospital A and B, they admitted that this is a major problem. As the number of ad-hoc requests is rising, it is more and more difficult for them to have an accurate overview of all pending purchasing orders.

Table 4. Order routine for ad-hoc requests

Activity	Implementation			Suggested SRM Service
	Hospital A	*Hospital B*	*Hospital C*	
1. Make/send prescription	Manual handling of paper-based form	Manual handling of paper-based form	Manual handling of paper-based form	• Desktop Purchasing
2. Check prescription	Manual handling	Manual handling	Manual handling	• Desktop Purchasing
3. Return prescription	Manual handling of paper-based form	Manual handling of paper-based form	Manual handling of paper-based form	• Desktop Purchasing
4. Analyze prescription	Manual handling	Manual handling	Manual handling	• Desktop Purchasing • Data Mining
5. Search supplier	Web search	Web search	Automated search in supplier portal	• Supplier Portal • E-RFI
6. Make/send purchase order	Fax and telephone	Fax and telephone	Supplier portal	• Supplier Portal • E-Auctions
7. Receive drugs (pharmacy)	Manual handling of invoice entry	Invoice entry supported by bar code system	Invoice entry supported by bar code system	• Supplier self-service • E-Order
8. Deliver drugs	Manual handling	Manual handling	Manual handling	-
9. Receive drugs (ward)	Out of control, no data entry	Controlled by bar code system	Controlled by bar code system	• Inventory control / ERP
10. Prepare drugs	Manual handling	Manual handling	Manual handling	-

In contrast, Hospital C uses an electronic supplier platform for searching providers and processing orders (the same as for the regular order routine). Hence, precious labor time can be saved and used for more valuable activities (e.g. for checking the prescription and for coordinating patient treatment plans with the attending physician). However, as no activity-based costing is implemented in Hospital C, no detailed information about the real efficiency increase can be given.

In order to enhance the prescription-related activities, the implementation of a desktop purchasing service (e.g. a computerized physician order entry) is suggested. Thereby readability of orders is enhanced as well as the risk of mispurchasing minimized. In addition, other services such as data mining can help to better analyze order patterns. Finally, the placement of orders can be systematized by implementing supplier portals, E-auctions, and E-orders.

CONCLUSION

The use of electronic services in health care is actually seen as an opportunity to improve not only the operating expenditure of health care organizations but also the quality of health service delivery by reducing redundancy and duplication of activities (World Health Organization, 2005). In the area of medical information systems sustainable investments are made these days by governmental authorities (Brennan, 2005) or fully private health care organizations (Suomi & Tahkapaa, 2002). As a result, the adoption and further development of administrative systems is often neglected or procrastinated. However, from the point of view of sustainable cost-savings, non-medical systems have to be implemented as well in order to realize the full range of advantages. The European Commission reported that health care organizations, which were familiar with IT-supported procurement, had sustainable cost reductions compared to others, which did not have any experiences (European Commission, 2006).

In this chapter we therefore present the concept of SRM as socio-technical approach to enhance cooperation, coordination, and communication of procurement activities within and between an organization and its suppliers. By way of a case study it was shown that hospitals are still confronted with

- paper shuffling (e.g. manual requisitions and purchasing orders, paper-based pricing information),
- multiple product handling activities (e.g. two sub-processes for regular and special drugs),
- excessive inventory carrying costs (e.g. manual entry and update of product information),
- lengthy product ordering and delivery cycle times (e.g. several process iterations when prescription is incomplete),
- data quality issues (e.g. little information on product location and product utilization),
- process quality issues (e.g. insufficient inventory control or no existing feedback loops that indicate if patients effectively received the right drugs), and
- poorly developed interfaces to suppliers (i.e. supplier is an unpredictable black box).

On the basis of the process analysis, different SRM services were suggested to (at least partially) improve de current drawbacks. However, even more benefits in drugs supply management will certainly emerge through the re-design of processes (business, management, and support) insofar that

- procurement activities are consolidated (e.g. a common approach for ordering of pharmaceuticals and other materials),
- interfaces are optimized (e.g. integrating product and supplier master data),

- laborious or precarious tasks are reduced or at least complemented by consistency checks (e.g. contraindication alert, out of stock warning, empty drip-feeding),
- effectiveness of the activities is enhanced (e.g. periodical analysis of the pharmaceutical market and monitoring of the supplier's performance),
- non-value-adding activities are outsourced to the supplier (e.g. vendor managed inventories, cross docking).

This will cause new technical and managerial challanges and will require advanced knowledge to resolve. Hence, and building on the findings of this chapter, future research and education needs to be dedicated to deliver and teach SRM models, methods and instantiations for the medical and non-medical work force in order to clarify the roles to be adopted by the different players during the implementation of supply management. Only by these means it is possible to speed up the adoption of SRM in health care organizations.

REFERENCES

Adams, M., Bates, D., Coffman, G., & Everett, W. (2008). Saving lives, saving money: The imperative for computerized physician order entry in Massachusetts Hospital. Retrieved February 27, 2009, from http://www.nehi.net/publications/8/saving_lives_saving_money_the_imperative_for_computerized_physician_order_entry_in_massachusetts_hospitals

Adebanjo, D. (2003). Classifying and selecting e-CRM applications: An analysis-based proposal. *Management Decision*, *41*(6), 570–577. doi:10.1108/00251740310491517

Anderson, J. C., Hakansson, H., & Johanson, J. (1994). Dyadic business relationships withing a business network context. *Journal of Marketing*, *58*(4), 1–15. doi:10.2307/1251912

Appelfeller, W., & Buchholz, W. (2005). *Supplier Relationship Management: Strategie, Organisation und IT des modernenen Beschaffungsmanagements*. Wiesbaden, Germany: Gabler.

Avison, D. E., & Young, T. (2007). Time to rethink health care and ICT? *Communications of the ACM, 50*(6), 69–74. doi:10.1145/1247001.1247008

Bakos, Y. J., & Brynjolfsson, E. (1993). Information technology, incentives, and the optimal number of suppliers. *Journal of Management Information Systems, 10*(2), 37–53.

Bates, D. W., Leape, L. L., Cullen, D. J., Laird, N., Petersen, L. A., & Teich, J. M. (1998). Effect of computerized physician order entry and a team intervention on prevention of serious medication errors. *Journal of the American Medical Association, 280*(15), 1311–1316. doi:10.1001/jama.280.15.1311

Benbasat, I., Goldstein, D. K., & Mead, M. (1987). The case research strategy in studies of information systems. *MIS Quarterly, 11*(3), 369–386. doi:10.2307/248684

Beuscart-Zephir, M. C., Pelayo, S., Degoulet, P., Anceaux, F., Guerlinger, S., & Meaux, J. J. (2004). A usability study of CPOE's medication administration functions: Impact on physician-nurse cooperation. *Sudies in Health Technologies and Informatics, 107*(2), 1018–1022.

Biohealthmatics.com. (2006). *Pharmacy information systems*. Retrieved February 27, 2009, from http://www.biohealthmatics.com/technologies/his/pis.aspx

Brennan, S. (2005). NHS IT project: The biggest computer programme in the world...ever! Oxford, UK: Radcliffe Medical Press.

Brynjolfsson, E., & Yang, S. (1996). Information technology and productivity: A review of the literature. *Advances in Computers, 43*, 179–214. doi:10.1016/S0065-2458(08)60644-0

Bunduchi, R. (2005). Business relationships in internet-based electronic markets: The role of goodwill trust and transaction costs. *Information Systems Journal, 15*(4), 321–341. doi:10.1111/j.1365-2575.2005.00199.x

Burns, L. R. (2002). The health care value chain: Producers, purchasers, and providers. San Francisco: Jossey-Bass.

Burt, R. S. (1992). Structural holes: the social structure of competition. Cambridge, MA: Harvard University Press.

Chung, K., Choi, Y. B., & Moon, S. (2003). Toward efficient medication error reduction: Error-reducing information management systems. *Journal of Medical Systems, 27*(6), 553–560. doi:10.1023/A:1025937916203

Craig, D. R., & Gabler, W. K. (1940). The competitive struggle for market control. *The Annals of the American Academy of Political and Social Science, 209*, 84–107. doi:10.1177/000271624020900112

Curtis, B., Kellner, M. I., & Over, J. (1992). Process modeling. *Communications of the ACM, 35*(9), 75–90. doi:10.1145/130994.130998

Davenport, T. H., & Short, J. E. (1990). The new industrial engineering: Information technology and business process redesign. *Sloan Management Review, 31*(4), 11–27.

Dwyer, F. R., Schurr, P. H., & Oh, S. (1987). Developing buyer-seller relationships. *Journal of Marketing, 51*(2), 11–27. doi:10.2307/1251126

Dyché, J. (2001). The CRM Handbook: A business guide to customer relationship management. Reading, MA: Addison-Wesley.

Dyer, J. H., & Singh, H. (1998). The relational view: Cooperative strategy and sources of interorganizational competitive advantage. *Academy of Management Review, 23*(4), 660–679. doi:10.2307/259056

Enrado, P. (2005). *Buyers guide: Pharmacy systems*. Retrieved February 27, 2009, from http://www.healthcareitnews.com/story.cms?id=3786

European Commission. (2006, October). *ICT and e-business in hospital activities: ICT adoption and e-business activity in 2006*. Bonn, Germany: eBusiness Watch.

Eyholzer, K., Kuhlmann, W., & Münger, T. (2002). Wirtschaftlichkeitsaspekte eines partnerschaftlichen Lieferantenmanagements. *HMD - Praxis . Wirtschaftsinformatik, 228*, 66–76.

Fleming, R. (2004). *Successful supplier relationship management*. Retrieved February 27, 2009, from http://www.ameinfo.com/35411.html

Freeman, L. C. (1979). Centrality in social networks: Conceptual clarification. *Social Networks, 1*, 215–239. doi:10.1016/0378-8733(78)90021-7

Furukawa, M. F., Raghu, T. S., & Spaulding, T. J. (2008). Adoption of health information technology for medication safety in U.S. hospitals. *Health Affairs, 27*(3), 865–875. doi:10.1377/hlthaff.27.3.865

German Association for Medical Technology. (2007). *Elektronisches Beschaffungswesen im Gesundheitsmarkt vor dem Durchbruch*. Retrieved February 27, 2009, from http://www.bvmed.de/themen/E-Commerce/pressemitteilung/BVMed-Umfrage_Elektronisches_Beschaffungswesen_im_Gesundheitsmarkt_vor_dem_Durchbruch.html

Glouberman, S., & Mintzberg, H. (2001). Managing the care of health and the cure of disease - Part I: Differentiation . *Health Care Management Review, 26*(1), 56–69.

Granovetter, M. (1973). The strength of weak ties. *American Journal of Sociology, 78*(6), 1360–1380. doi:10.1086/225469

Grossman, R. J. (2000). The battle to control online purchasing. *Health Forum Journal, 43*(1), 18–21.

Herzlinger, R. E. (2006). Why innovation in health care is so hard. *Harvard Business Review, 84*(5), 58–66.

Jutla, D., Craig, J., & Bodorik, P. (2001). *Enabling and measuring electronic customer relationship management readiness*. Paper presented at the 34th Annual Hawaii International Conference on System Sciences.

Koppel, R., Metlay, J. P., Cohen, A., Abaluck, B., Localio, A. R., & Kimmel, S. E. (2005). Role of computerized physician order entry systems in facilitating medication errors. *Journal of the American Medical Association, 293*(10), 1197–1203. doi:10.1001/jama.293.10.1197

Leftwich, L. M., Leftwich, J. A., Moore, N. Y., & Roll, C. R. (2004). *Organizational concepts for purchasing and supply management implementation* (No. MG-116). Santa Monica, CA: RAND Corporation.

Leymann, F., & Altenhuber, W. (1994). Managing business processes as an information resource. *IBM Systems Journal, 33*(2), 326–348.

Marton, A., Piccinelli, G., & Turfin, C. (1999). *Service provision and composition in virtual business communities*. Paper presented at the 18th IEEE Symposium on Reliable Distributed Systems.

Merriam-Webster Online Dictionary. (2009). *Communication*. Retrieved February 27, 2009, from http://www.merriam-webster.com/dictionary/communication

Mettler, T., & Rohner, P. (2008). Supplier Relationship Management im Krankenhaus. *HMD - Praxis der Wirtschaftsinformatik, 259*, 87-95.

Mettler, T., & Rohner, P. (2009a). E-Procurement in Hospital Pharmacies: An Exploratory Multi-Case Study from Switzerland. *Journal of Theoretical and Applied Electronic Commerce Research, 4*(1), 23–38.

Mettler, T., & Rohner, P. (2009b). Increasing the networkability of health service providers: The case of Switzerland. *Sprouts - Working Papers on Information Systems, 9*(1), 1-13.

Muessigmann, N., & Albani, A. (2006). *Supplier network management: evaluating and rating of strategic supply networks*. Paper presented at the 2006 ACM symposium on Applied computing.

Myers, M. D. (1997). Qualitative research in information systems. *MIS Quarterly, 21*(1), 241–242. doi:10.2307/249422

OECD. (2007). Moving up the value chain: Staying competitive in the global economy. A synthesis report on global value chains. Pariso.

Österle, H., Fleisch, E., & Alt, R. (2000). Business networking shaping collaboration between enterprises. Berlin: Springer.

Parente, S. T. (2000). Beyond the hype: A taxonomy of e-health business models. *Health Affairs, 19*(6), 89–102. doi:10.1377/hlthaff.19.6.89

Parvatiyar, A., & Sheth, N., J. (2001). Customer relationship management: Emerging practice, process, and discipline . *Journal of Economic and Social Research, 3*(2), 1–34.

Porter, M. E., & Olmsted-Teisberg, E. (2004). Redefining competition in health care. *Harvard Business Review, 82*(6), 64–76.

Post, J. E., Preston, L. E., & Sachs, S. (2002). Redefining the corporation: Stakeholder mangement and organizational wealth. Stanford, CA: Stanford University Press.

Rainey, H. G., Backoff, R. W., & Levine, C. H. (1976). Comparing public and private organizations. *Public Administration Review, 36*(2), 233–244. doi:10.2307/975145

Riemer, K., & Klein, S. (2002). Supplier Relationship Management. *HMD - Praxis . Wirtschaftsinformatik, 228*, 5–22.

Rüegg-Stürm, J. (2005). The new St. Gallen management model: Basic categories of an approach to integrated management. Basingstoke, NY: Palgrave Macmillan.

SAP. (2003). *What is supplier relationship management?* Retrieved February 27, 2009, from http://searchsap.techtarget.com/sDefinition/0,sid21_gci871756,00.html

Schmid, B. F., & Lindenmann, M. A. (1998). *Elements of a reference model for electronic markets*. Paper presented at the Thirty-First Annual Hawaii International Conference on System Sciences.

Scott, W. R. (2002). Organizations: Rational, natural, and open systems (5 ed.). Upper Saddle River, NJ: Prentice Hall.

Smith, N. (1990). The case study: A useful research method for information management. *Journal of Information Technology, 5*(3), 123–13. doi:10.1057/jit.1990.30

Suomi, R., & Tahkapaa, J. (2002). *The strategic role of ICT in the competition between public and private health care sectors in the Nordic welfare societies-case of Finland*. Paper presented at the 35th Annual Hawaii International Conference on System Sciences.

Supply Chain Management Institute. (2008). *The supply chain management processes*. Retrieved February 27, 2009, from http://www.scm-institute.org/Our-Relationship-Based-Business-Model.htm

Swisslog. (2008). *Pharmacy automation system.* Retrieved February 27, 2009, from http://www. swisslog.com/index/hcs-index/hcs-pharmacy/hcs-pharmacycomponents.htm

The Chartered Institute of Purchasing & Supply. (2005). Selling the benefits of purchasing: Learning network publication. Retrieved February 27, 2009, from www.ifpmm.org/files/LNPubsSellingBenefits.pdf

U.S. Food and Drug Administration. (2009). *Medication errors.* Retrieved February 27, 2009, from http://www.fda.gov/cder/handbook/mederror. htm van Bemmel, J. H., & Musen, M. A. (1999). *Handbook of medical informatics.* Retrieved from http://www.mieur.nl/mihandbook/r_3_3/handbook/home.htm

Walston, S. L., & Chadwick, C. (2003). Perceptions and misperceptions of major organizational changes in hospitals: Do change efforts fail because of inconsistent organizational perceptions of restructuring and reengineering? *International Journal of Public Administration, 26*(14), 1581–1605. doi:10.1081/PAD-120024412

Wholey, D. R., & Burns, L. R. (2003). Understanding health care markets: Actors, products, and relations. In S. S. Mick & M. E. Wyttenbach (Eds.), Advances in Health Care Organization Theory (pp. 99-139). San Francisco: Jossey-Bass.

Williamson, O. E. (1979). Transaction-cost economics: The governance of contractual relations. *The Journal of Law & Economics, 22*(2), 233–261. doi:10.1086/466942

World Health Organization. (2005). *eHealth: Report by the Secretariat.* Retrieved February 27, 2009, from http://www.who.int/gb/ebwha/pdf_files/WHA58/A58_21-en.pdf

Yilmaz, C., & Hunt, S. D. (2001). Salesperson cooperation: The influence of relational, task, organizational, and personal factors. *Journal of the Academy of Marketing Science, 29*(4), 335–357. doi:10.1177/03079450094207

Zeng, Y. E., Wen, H. J., & Yen, D. C. (2003). Customer relationship management (CRM) in business-to-business (B2B) e-commerce. *Information Management & Computer Security, 11*(1), 39–44. doi:10.1108/09685220310463722

ADDITIONAL READING

Banker, R. D., Kalvenes, J., & Patterson, R. A. (2000). *Information technology, contract completeness, and buyer-supplier relationships.* Paper presented at the Twenty-First International Conference on Information Systems.

Claro, D. P. (2004). Managing business networks and buyer-supplier relationships. Wageningen, The Netherlands: Wageningen University

Corbett, C. J., Blackburn, J. D., & Van Wassenhove, L. N. (1999). Partnerships to improve supply chains. *Sloan Management Review, 40*(4), 71–82.

Herrmann, J., & Hodgson, B. (2001). *SRM: Leveraging the supply base for competitive advantage.* Paper presented at the SMTA International Conference.

Macbeth, D. K. (2002). Emergent strategy in managing cooperative supply chain change. *International Journal of Operations & Production Management, 22*(7), 728–740. doi:10.1108/01443570210433517

Malone, T. W., & Crowston, K. (1994). The interdisciplinary study of coordination. *ACM Computing Surveys, 26*(1), 87–119. doi:10.1145/174666.174668

Mc Guire, G. A. (2006). Development of a supply chain management framework for health care goods provided as humanitarian assistance in complex political emergencies. Vienna, Austria: Vienna University of Economics and Business Administration.

Mettler, T., & Rohner, P. (2008). *Supplier relationship management in healthcare practice: A case study*, Paper presented at the 6th CollECTeR Iberoamerica.

Ritter, T., & Gemünden, H. G. (2003). Interorganizational relationships and networks: An overview. *Journal of Business Research*, *56*, 691–697. doi:10.1016/S0148-2963(01)00254-5

Sarpola, S. J. (2007). Information systems in buyer-supplier collaboration. Helsinki, Finland: Helsinki School of Economics.

Tang, C. S. (1999). Supplier relationship map. *International Journal of Logistics: Research & Applications*, *2*(1), 39–56. doi:10.1080/13675569908901571

Thompson, G., Frances, J., Levacic, R., & Mitchell, J. (1991). Markets, hierarchies and networks: The coordination of social life. London: Sage.

Vaidya, K., Sajeev, A. S. M., & Gao, J. *E-procurement assimilation: an assessment of e-business capabilities and supplier readiness in the Australian public sector*. Paper presented at the 7th International Conference on Electronic Commerce.

Veludo, M. L., Macbeth, D., & Purchase, S. (2006). Framework for relationships and networks. *Journal of Business and Industrial Marketing*, *21*(4), 199–207. doi:10.1108/08858620610672560

KEY TERMS AND DEFINITIONS

Analytical SRM: Electronic services aiming at storing, analyzing, and applying knowledge about suppliers and personnel dedicated to manage the supplier's relationship.

Business Networking: Management of IT-enabled relationships between internal and external business partners with the aim at making product and sales information immediately accessible to all the organizations in the supply chain.

Collaborative SRM: Electronic services aiming at improving the quality of supplier communication.

Communication: Exchange of information in order to enhance process efficiency and to improve the quality of a business relationship.

Cooperation: Forming of business relationships for common, usually economic, benefit.

Coordination: Alignment of processes and work practices in order to implement a business relationship.

E-Collaboration: Electronic services designed to effectively facilitating collaborative interactions between the buyer and the supplier such as conferencing, information sharing, project management, forecasting and planning.

E-Contract Management: Electronic services designed to systematically managing contract creating, execution, monitoring, and archiving.

E-Payment: Electronic services designed to enabling the execution of online financial transactions.

E-Procurement: Electronic services designed to facilitating purchasing and sale of supplies and services through the Internet.

E-RFx: Electronic services designed to structuring information requests between the buyer and the supplier.

Operational SRM: Electronic services aiming at raising the efficiency of ordering and contract fulfillment.

Supplier Relationship Management: Management of IT-enabled supplier relationships with the aim at enhancing the efficiency and effectiveness of cooperation, coordination, and communication between the buyer and the supplier.

Supplier self-service: Electronic services designed to helping suppliers to effectively manage replenishment through the Internet. Buyers take advantage of having real-time information of the supplier performance.

ENDNOTES

[1]   The terms Supplier Relationship Management (SRM) and Supply Management are used interchangeably in this chapter.

[2]   In information systems research the case study method is a widely accepted approach to investigate the development, implementation and use of systems and services within organizations (Benbasat, Goldstein & Mead, 1987; Myers, 1997; Smith, 1990).

[3]   See section 'Processes and Work Practices for SRM'.

[4]   See section 'Positioning of Procurement within a Health Care Organization'.

[5]   See 'Additional Materials Section'.

[6]   For this, unit dose dispensing systems or automated dispensing systems can be a solution; see section 'Positioning of Procurement within Health Care Organization'.

APPENDIX

Figure 5. BPMN process model for the regular ordering routine

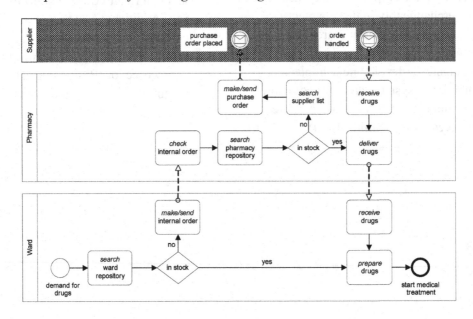

Figure 6. BPMN process model for ad-hoc requests

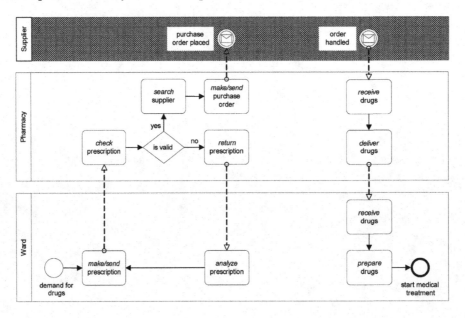

Section 5
Service Management in Industries

Chapter 13

Cargo Service Dynamics and Service–Oriented Architecture in East Asian Airports

Joyce M.W Low
National University of Singapore, Singapore

Loon Ching Tang
National University of Singapore, Singapore

Xue-Ming Yuan
Singapore Institute of Manufacturing Technology, Singapore

ABSTRACT

This chapter examines the effects of primary production and key economic factors on the cargo traffic in the East Asian airports between 1999 and 2005. Through econometric and cluster analyses, results in this chapter found a dramatic increase in the relative importance of physical capital to human capital. More specifically, adequate provisions and utilizations of physical facilities in landside operations appear to be more significant driving forces for an airport's cargo traffic performances compared to those of airside operations. In spite of the greater importance that the East Asia airport industry has attached to cost-effective operations in the recent years, airports may no longer be able to rely on size for a sustainable competitive edge with the reductions in the returns to scale. Meanwhile, there is still a close direct association between a nation's economic development and the volume of cargo traffic at its airport.

INTRODUCTION

Notwithstanding the fact that airports are traditionally established with the intention of human movements, the importance of air cargo services to businesses, the economy and the airport cannot

DOI: 10.4018/978-1-61520-603-2.ch013

be understated. According to Yung et al. (2008), increasing affordability of air cargo transport has heightened the role of airfreight in the distribution systems of many companies and put air cargo service at the foundation of international trade. Consequently, the availability of efficient air cargo services will offer a strong inducement for local and foreign companies to set up their businesses in a particular economy. The latter will benefit from additional trade gains as these companies also contribute to the growth in trade volumes by replacing part of the traditional method of local sourcing of parts, local production, local marketing and independent transportation and services with global sourcing of parts, global production, global marketing and global logistics alliances (Edger 1995). Meanwhile, Oum et al. (2003) noted that air cargo service is becoming more significant to an airport despite being a small business compared with the passenger business. Worldwide average annual cargo traffic statistics shows a growth of 7.9% in freight-tonne kilometers on international scheduled services compared to 2.1% on domestic services during the last decade (Zhang and Zhang 2002a).

Ohashi et al. (2005) anticipated that the average annual air cargo growth in Asia would lead all other international geographic markets in the next 20 years, following the recovery from the 1997 financial crisis. At the same time, liberalization of the airline industry has increased the freedom of airlines to choose where to base their domestic hubs and inter-continent gateways and which airports to use when routing their connecting traffic in a hub-and-spoke network. As airports compete with one another for airlines business, the ability to provide valued airport services such fast processing of aircraft, passengers, cargo and baggage become one of the most pertinent issues in the unending quest towards competitiveness in the regional market. Owing to the higher market concentrations[1] that exist on the cargo side than on the passenger side of the industry, the competition among airports for air cargo traffic is expected to be higher.

Several studies in the existing literature have presented a cross-sectional snapshot analysis across major Asian airports to assess and identify important factors contributing to airport competitiveness. Park (2003) looked at service, demand, managerial, facility and spatial qualities, whilst Nijkamp and Yim (2001) studied the physical,

technological, organizational, financial, ecological aspects in an airport. Ohashi et al. (2005) focused primarily on air cargo transshipment airports and examined the monetary and time cost factors. Gardiner et al. (2005) identified general factors, such as night curfews, freight forwarders and airport charges, which may exert influences on the competitiveness of the air cargo service in an airport. However, common in these studies, the discussions on how the landscapes of the air cargo service industry have evolved over time are at a minimal.

Other studies have attempted to conduct longitudinal analyses on a specific airport. For examples, Raguraman (1997), Tsai and Su (2002), Zhang (2003) and Lee and Yang (2003) traced and analyzed the air hub development strategy pursued by the government and airport authorities in Singapore, Taiwan, Hong Kong and South Korea respectively. Some of these frequently adopted strategies include the investing in physical and technological infrastructures, streamlining custom administration in their import and export licensing, upgrading the skills of the workforce and so forth to speed up air cargo processing procedures. Nonetheless, as airports are unique to one another in terms of intrinsic characteristics and operating environments, it is difficult to generalize the relative importance of the various constituents in the overall development strategies on airport performances from direct comparisons among these case studies.

Against this backdrop, the first objective of this chapter is to analyze how human and physical architectural aspects of an airport oriented towards the provision of air cargo service as well as the external environment have affected the demand for the airport cargo service in East Asia between the years 1999 and 2005. Specifically, the air cargo traffic is assumed to be related to primary production factors and macroeconomic and regulatory conditions such as physical and human capital, national income, trade volume, customs service efficiency and so forth through a Cobb-Douglas function. The selection of variables included in the analysis is justified on the basis that the presence of key production and favorable economic factors are necessary for actual traffic to materialize. That is, an airport must possess production factors in order to supply the service and favorable economic conditions allow for effective demand for the airport service. Empirical investigations (based on observational panel data of major airports in East Asia) will provide estimates for the unknown parameters in the proposed econometric model and measure the validity of the model against the behavior of the observable data. By taking a longitudinal approach, the underlying trend on the evolving influences of man-made and exogenous factors on cargo traffic can be uncovered. Such trend analysis could provide airport operators with useful foresights for sound planning of future airport operations as environmental concerns, limited land for expansion, shortage of skilled labor and high financing cost may result in the delay in obtaining the required increase in capacity.

The second objective is to assess to what extent different service strategies pursued by airports have helped to drive cargo traffic under diverse sizes and economic conditions over the study horizon. Such assessment will aid better understanding on the service and performance dynamics within the East Asia international airports industry. To accomplish this objective, airports are classified into clusters based on their relative efficiencies in the use of service-oriented architectures and their actualized traffic volumes over the study horizon. By adjusting for the varying baseline performances attributable to an airport's size and prevailing economic conditions, the cluster analysis provides a meaningful benchmarking across the airports and measures the effectiveness of distinctive service strategies adopted by major airports in the region. Particularly, cluster movements will unveil how individual airports have transformed their strategic postures or maintained their strategic positions as aggressors, challengers, defenders and passive survivors in East Asia.

In brief, findings from this chapter show that while conducive economic conditions continue to play a critical role in stimulating demand for cargo service at the airports, the importance of physical architecture has also dramatically risen relative to human factors. Particularly, adequate provisions and utilizations of physical facilities for landside operations appear to be a more significant driving force for demand of an airport's cargo service compared to those of airside operations. Despite the strong emphasis on swift and reliable services, cost savings are found to have regained their importance in the recent years. Nevertheless, the degree of scale returns has fallen so sharply over the recent years that large airports can no longer rely on size for sustainable competitive edge. Rather, airports may need to seek more creative ways to control cost. One possible means is through outsourcing

The rest of the chapter is organized as follows: Section 2 proposes a production model to explain airport cargo traffic, followed by a presentation of empirical evidences to verify the precisions of the model using ordinary least square (OLS) regressions. Section 3 benchmarks the performances of airports in terms of physical capital productivity and economic conditions and groups the airports into clusters. Section 4 discusses the findings. Section 5 points out some potential limitations and concludes the study.

THE INFLUENCES OF SERVICE-ORIENTED ARCHITECTURES AND ECONOMIC FACTORS ON AIR CARGO TRAFFIC

The Model

Airport operations are generally classified into airside and landside. Airside operations refer to the activities that facilitate the movements of aircrafts including runway services, apron services, and the loading and unloading of baggage/ freight, whereas, landside operations refer to activities associated directly with passengers and freight traffic covering the various stages of the processing of passengers' baggage and freight through the respective terminals and onto the aircraft. To maintain good service standards to airlines, an airport needs to ensure capacity adequacy at both its airside and landside. As such, the physical service-oriented architecture of an airport (also referred to as physical capital in this study) will include infrastructure and facilities (K) such as runways, gates, terminal space and so on.

Despite much use of complex sorting and conveying apparatus and automation, operations at an airport are labor-intensive. O'Conner (1995) noted that labor (L) is needed to receive goods at the loading platform, handle paper work, compute and collect the charges, provide the proper protection sort and each piece to the proper flight, and unload cargo at the destination, sort it once again and get it into the hands of the recipients. Apart from the large pool of frontline workers, an airport also employs management staffs to carry out operations and strategic planning and engineers to implement technological developments to ensure the efficiency of air cargo service in the airport as a whole. In addition, Quilty (2003) advocated that an airport should engage workforce that is highly skilled and knowledgeable with advancing technology and user demands. Recognizing that labor in different countries is characterized by different levels of productivity, the variable H_i is introduced to denote the amount of productive services supplied by workers in airport i. Here, the standard assumption that the amount of productive services each worker has depends only on the number of years of education through a function G_i, and better educated workers are more productive is applied (Romer 2001). For the purpose of the ease of mathematical tractability, the model also assumes that each worker obtains the same amount of education, denoted by E. Putting this assumption in notation, the total amount of productive labor services H_i is

$$H_i(t) = L_i(t)G_i(E) \qquad (1)$$

where $L_i(\bullet)$ is the number of workers in airport i and $G_i(\bullet)$ is a function giving human capital as a function of E at time t. Eqn. (1) also implies that of total labor productive f, $L_i(t)G_i(0)$ is raw labor and the remainder, $L[G(E)-G(0)]$ is productive services. The first derivative, $G'(\bullet) > 0$, is imposed so as to insure that the more education a worker has, the more productive services he possesses. But the second derivative, $G''(\bullet)$, is unrestricted.

In addition, there are important (exogenous) forces that drive airport traffic but are beyond the immediate control of airport operators. Particularly, Zhang and Zhang (2002b) commented that air cargo volume is strongly linked to trade volume. Macroeconomics theory postulates that trade volume is affected by economic and political factors such as GDP[2], custom service efficiency[3], political and economic stability[4], and so forth. Denoting variables X_i and $x_{i,j}$ as the aggregate and individual economic and political forces that determine throughput for a given amount of physical capital and labor services, the aggregate economic and political force (also termed as the exogenous variable) can be expressed as follows

$$X_i(t) = x_{i,1}(t)x_{i,2}(t) \ldots x_{i,n}(t) \qquad (2)$$

where $x_{i,j}(t)$ refers to the jth economic condition that is prevailing in the operating environment of airport i at time t. The multiplicative structure in (2) allows for possible interactions among the $x_{i,j}$ terms. For example, higher trade volume may result in or be a result of high GDP.

Having discussed the various possible influences of human and physical service-oriented architecture and economic conditions on demand for air cargo service, the structural equation for the determination of the volume of cargo[5] handled in airport i (denoted as Y_i) at time t takes the following mathematical form:

$$\frac{Y_i(t)}{L_i(t)} = e^{b_0} \left(\frac{K_i(t)}{L_i(t)}\right)^{b_1} \left(\frac{H_i(t)}{L_i(t)}\right)^{b_2} X_i(t)^{b_3} + \varepsilon_1$$

$\forall i = 1,2,3$ (3)

Eqn. (3) expresses the throughput per worker as a function of the physical to human infrastructure ratio, the average quality of labor and an exogenous factor. b_1 and b_2 represent the returns to scale of physical capital intensity and labor quality improvement on throughput per worker, respectively. e^{b_0} is the shift parameter. If b_1 and b_2 sum to unity, the constant returns to physical capital intensity and labor quality are implied. That is, for some given economic and political conditions, doubling the inputs doubles the amount of cargo that can be handled by each airport worker. ε_1 represents the random errors.

Taking natural logarithms on both sides of (3),

$$\ln\left(\frac{Y_i(t)}{L_i(t)}\right) = b_0 + b_1 \ln\left(\frac{K_i(t)}{L_i(t)}\right) + b_2 \ln\left(\frac{H_i(t)}{L_i(t)}\right) + b_3 \ln X_i(t) + \varepsilon_2$$

$\forall i = 1,2,3$ (4)

The use of such log functions, as in (4), allows for modeling of nonlinear relationships between input factors and estimations of parameters by means of multiple linear regressions.

Other special variations of the model are possible but with certain limitations. For example, the cargo traffic of airport i can be expressed as a Cobb-Douglas function of physical capital, labor services and economic conditions as follows:

$$Y_i(t) = e^{b_0} K_i(t)^{\alpha_1} H_i(t)^{\alpha_2} X_i(t)^{\alpha_3} + \varepsilon_3$$

$0 < a_i < 1; \forall i = 1,2,3$ (5)

A linearized model of (5) can then be obtained by taking natural logarithms that yield

$$\ln Y_i(t) = b_0 + \alpha_1 \ln K_i(t) + \alpha_2 \ln H_i(t) + \alpha_3 \ln X_i(t) + \varepsilon_4$$

(6)

This model in (6) has a potential limitation in that it allows for little or no correlation between the predictors. Correlations between predictors lead to the problem of multicollinearity, which in turn results in inflated variances and low parameters estimation precisions. Multicollinearity poses an obstacle in the context of this study since K and L are some dimensions of airport's capacity and hence expected to be correlated.

Empirical Analysis

Sample and Variables

The empirical analysis focuses on 14 major international airports across East Asia, selected on basis of data availability in the annual Airport Benchmarking Report (2002-2007 issues). Airports from the Northeast Asia region comprise Chek Lap Kok (Hong Kong), Seoul Gimpo (South Korea) Incheon (South Korea), Narita (Japan), Kansai (Japan), Beijing Capital (China), Shanghai (China), Chiang Kai Shek (Taiwan) and Macau while airports from the Southeast Asia region are Changi (Singapore), Kuala Lumpur (Malaysia), Bangkok (Thailand), Ninoy Aquino (Philippines) and Soekarno-Hatta (Indonesia).

The total capacity of physical infrastructure of airport i, K_i, is represented by the number of runways[6] in the airside operations and the total area of terminals[7] in the corresponding landside operations. As both types of operations are indispensible in the provision of air cargo service, equal weights are attached to runways and terminal areas in the computation of K_i. The amount of human service-oriented architecture in airport i is measured by the number of employees L_i who work directly for the airport operator. L_i is supplemented with information on its quality $G_i(E)$, which estimated by the average level of economic literacy[8] in the economy on the assumption that an average worker's education at the country and airport levels are the same. Although in practice it is by no means a standard assumption that human capital only depends on years of education since many studies in labor economics would suggest work experience as another important factor. Without concrete worker turnover data, the average years of education present itself as a good surrogate because it represents the general level of quality of the workforce available for hired on a national basis. Unless there is a strong evidence to suggest that there is a bias in employing worker of higher/lower education qualification in the airport industry, far short of conducting a detailed survey, using the national average level of economic literacy is not unreasonable. H_i is, hence, obtained as a product of L_i and $G_i(E)$ as in Eqn. (1).

The exogenous variable X_i is made up of five individual economic variables components, namely, GDP, trade volumes, custom service efficiency and political and economic risk ratings. These economic-related data are obtained from the World Competitiveness Yearbook (2001–2006 issues). GDP and trade volume are measured in current US dollars while custom efficiency and risk ratings are given as perceived ratings by businesses obtained through extensive surveys. For simplicity, GDP per capita is used despite the fact that the effective demand for air services in the domestic market[9] is also influenced by the income distribution in the nation and airport traffic is often affected by GDP of more than one country. The latter is partially circumvented through the incorporation of trade volume that reflects the economic conditions of international trading partners.

As variables are measured in different units, the raw data are normalized[10] before feeding them into the model of analysis. Normalizing is done such that the best performing airport in the cat-

egory is given the highest score of 10 points and the score for other airports are computed based on their performances relative to the top performing airport in the sample. When normalizing these data, some prudence needs to be exercised to maintain a meaningful scoring scheme. For airport capacity and economic measurements like GDP or trade volume, it is straightforward that airports are scored relative to the airport with the most runways or largest terminal area and nation with the highest GDP or trade volume. However, for dimensions like political and economic risk, nations with the lowest level of risk will be given the highest score of 10 and other nations are scored against the benchmark set by the best performing nation. In this way, the offsetting effects among economic variables like high GDP versus high economic risk can be prevented. Such scoring system, while retaining the original distribution of the data, also permits the modeling of relationship between cargo traffic and other performance indicators relative to the industry best practice.

Results

Separate cross-sectional multiple-regressions are run to estimate the values of parameter coefficients in (4) that will provide a best fitting model (i.e., Model 1, 2, 3 and 4) for each of the alternate years between 1999 and 2005 inclusive. That is, all the four regression models[11] take the form:

$$\ln\left(\frac{Y_i}{L_i}\right) = b_0 + b_1 \ln\left(\frac{K_i}{L_i}\right) + b_2 \ln\left(\frac{H_i}{L_i}\right) + b_3 \ln X_i + \varepsilon_2$$

The results obtained from ordinary least square (OLS) estimates are given in *Table 1* below. Apart from the constants, the coefficient estimates that are statistically significant at a 95 percent significance level are $\ln X_i$ in models 1, 2 and 4 and $\ln(K_i/L_i)$ in the models 3 and 4. Whereas at a 90 percent significance level, $\ln X_i$ is significant in all the four models, $\ln(K_i/L_i)$ is significant in models 2, 3 and

4 and $\ln(H_i/L_i)$ is significant only in model 2. It can be inferred that the physical capital intensity and nation's aggregate economic performances, but not labor quality, have a significant impact on labor productivity with physical capital intensity assuming higher importance in the more recent years. These regression models have high predictive accuracy between 83.44 to 92.26 percent.

The accompanying residual plots attached in *Figure 9,Figure 10,Figure 11and Figure 12* in Appendix A show that errors are normally distributed with constant variances and there is no apparent outlier in the sample of airports. Several tests are employed to check for multicollinearity which may lead to misleading model results. In all the four models, the signs of parameters are examined and found to turn out as expected. *t* tests confirm that the coefficients of at least one (out of the three parameters) other than the intercept are statistically significant at 95 percent confidence level and *F* test for the overall model adequacy are also significant. Noting that many data sets with significant multicollinearity may not exhibit the patterns of wrong signs and insignificant t-tests, the Tolerance and Variance Inflation

Factor (VIF) are computed. The tolerances for all variables are above 0.10, which corresponds to VIF values below 10. Additional diagnostic measures of multicollinearity are Condition Index and Variance Proportions. No multicollinearity problem is indicated since all condition indexes are less than 30 (see *Table 4* in Appendix A). As an overall check for multicollinearity, the study examines the model fits of the reduced regression models in which the non-significant parameters are removed. The absence of multi-collinearity is confirmed in *Table 2*, since all values of adjusted R-square remain very stable.

The original regression models can be rewritten to gain better insights as below.

$$\ln Y_i - \ln L_i = b_0 + b_1\left(\ln K_i - \ln L_i\right) + b_2\left(\ln H_i - \ln L_i\right) + b_3 \ln X_i + \varepsilon_2$$

which simplifies to

$$\ln Y_i = b_0 + b_1 \ln K_i + (1 - b_1 - b_2)\ln L_i + b_2 \ln H_i + b_3 \ln X_i + \varepsilon_2$$

Recalling that $H_i = L_i G_i$,

$$\ln Y_i = b_0 + b_1 \ln K_i + (1 - b_1)\ln L_i + b_2 \ln G_i + b_3 \ln X_i + \varepsilon_2$$

The coefficient estimates in the log-linear re-

Table 1. Results for original regression models, 1999 - 2005

	Model 1 (1999)	Model 2 (2001)	Model 3 (2003)	Model 4 (2005)
b_0	10.7749 (<0.001)*	11.0766 (<0.001)	11.1651 (<0.001)	11.0505 (<0.001)
b_1	0.0714 (0.8596)	0.4398 (0.0948)	0.7406 (0.0016)	0.8299 (0.0251)
b_2	0.8039 (0.1228)	0.5609 (0.0918)	0.4295 (0.1866)	0.0872 (0.9074)
b_3	1.0673 (0.0284)	0.8605 (0.0090)	0.5449 (0.0946)	0.8574 (0.0192)
Standard Error	0.3040	0.3430	0.4393	0.4341
R-Square	95.160%	93.182%	89.452%	91.453%
Adjusted R-Square	92.256%	90.909%	86.287%	88.605%
Number of observations†	9	13	14	13

*Figures in parenthesis give the p values

† Shanghai Hongqiao and Seoul Gimpo airports are taken out of the sample after 2001 and 2003 respectively, after the bulks of their traffic are channeled to Shanghai Pudong and Incheon airports.

Table 2. Results for reduced regression models, 1999 - 2005

	Model 1 (1999)	Model 2 (2001)	Model 3 (2003)	Model 4 (2005)
b_0	10.0355 (<0.001)*	11.3152 (<0.001)	10.9333 (<0.001)	11.0581 (<0.001)
b_1	N.A	N.A	0.9058 (<0.001)	0.8844 (0.0003)
b_2	N.A	0.9904 (0.0008)	N.A	N.A
b_3	1.6680 (<0.001)	0.9354 (0.0085)	0.8174 (0.0050)	0.8475 (0.0116)
Standard Error	0.3629	0.3833	0.4591	0.4121
R-Square	90.339%	90.542%	87.331%	91.440%
Adjusted R-Square	88.959%	88.650%	85.028%	89.728%
Number of observations	9	13	14	13

*Figures in parenthesis give the p values

gression function above measure the percentage change in Y_i associated with one percentage change in the respective parameters, holding the other parameters constant. Specifically, b_1, $1-b_1$, b_2 and b_3 gives the percentage change in cargo throughput for a one-percent change in K_i, L_i, G_i and X_i respectively. *Table 3* summarizes the change in the relative contributions of these various factors to cargo traffic volume.

Table 3 shows that the constant term increases from 10.7749 to 11.0505 over the six years. In other words, for an airport with one unit of physical capital, labor and economic rating, the volume of airfreight handled increases from 47806 and 62975 metric tons. The contribution of physical infrastructure to cargo traffic increases dramatically from 0.0714% increase in Y_i for a 1% increase in K_i in 1999 to 0.8299% in 2005. On the contrary, human architecture (i.e., size and skills of workforce) gives decreasing returns throughout the study horizon. The aggregate economic performance of a nation impacts the performances of

Table 3. Influences of physical and human service-oriented architectures on air cargo traffic, 1999 - 2005

Parameter	Meaning	1999	2001	2003	2005
b_0	The ln(Vol) handled by airports with one unit of K_i, L_i & G_i	10.7749	11.0766	11.1651	11.0505
b_1	The % change in throughput, Y_i, associated with 1% change in physical capital K_i	0.0714	0.4398	0.7406	0.8299
$(1-b_1)$	The % change in throughput, Y_i, associated with 1% change in labor size score L_i	0.9286	0.5602	0.2594	0.1701
b_2	The % change in throughput, Y_i, associated with 1% change in labor quality score G_i	0.8039	0.5609	0.4295	0.0872
b_3	The % change in throughput, Y_i, associated with 1% change in aggregate economic performance score X_i	1.0673	0.8605	0.5449	0.8574
$1+b_2$	Returns to scale, physical and total human capital investment	1.8039	1.5609	1.4295	1.0872

its airport most significantly, averaging 0.8325 for the six years. The overall returns to scale for the total airport development effort are derived from a summation of the rates of returns for physical facilities investment, labor force expansion and labor quality improvement.

Nonetheless, capital investment in publicly-owned airports could be positively related to the country's GDP and trade volume. In the case of private airports, political and economic risks might discourage foreign direct investment (FDI) and exert an adverse impact on capital investments in airport infrastructure since unstable political and economic situations will hamper the realization of long-term investments. The next section presents a cluster analysis to classify airports according to their airside and landside capital investments, as well as, traffic performances, in view of the differences in their political and economic conditions. A close scrutiny of airport movements among the clusters will unveil the dynamics within the airport industry and provide a better understanding on the effectiveness of the various strategies undertaken by individual airports.

CARGO SERVICE DYNAMICS IN EAST ASIAN AIRPORTS

This section explores the cargo service dynamics within the East Asia airport industry via cluster analysis. A two-step procedure is used to obtain the airport clusters. In step one, the *standard capital productivity* (for an airport of a given volume) is determined from a trend line fitted using OLS estimate in the graph with Capital Productivity[12] plotted against Cargo Volume. Similarly, the *economic volume* (that an airport is expected to achieve given her nation's economic performances) is determined from the trend line fitted in the graph with axes Cargo Volume and Nation's Economic Performances. In step two, airports are classified into clusters according to their exhibited traffic volume and capital productivity deviations

from the economic volume and standard capital productivity. Airports of particular interest will, therefore, be those airports falling into one of the four clusters:

1. Aggressor

Aggressor airports invest significantly in their physical infrastructure and facilities. To some extent, these investments have helped the airports to achieve the volume above what they could otherwise achieve given the economic and political conditions in their operating environments. The low physical capital productivity of the airports is a deliberate result from the aggressiveness of these airports to fight for more traffic volume in the near future. Other reasons for their extraordinary achievements can be accredited to their superior geographical locations, natural airport attributes, good management practices etc.

2. Defender

Defender airports are equipped with physical infrastructure and facilities above the required level for their existing volumes. While one possible rationale for keeping excess facilities is to protect market shares, it is also apparent that such investments have limited success in attracting greater volume. Relative to the competition, airports in this category may be perceived to be less attractive by users for other reasons (such as inferior geographical location, lack of supporting infrastructure, restrictive open sky policies, unfavorable service-cost ratio and so forth). As a result, defender airports suffer concurrent low capital productivity and cargo volume.

3. Challenger

Challenger airports are promising airports that have shown exceptionally good performances. At the same time, the high physical capital productivity of these airports implies good asset utilizations and return on investment. However, to answer the question on whether congestion is hindering these airports to achieve even higher volume will require additional information on aircraft turnaround time.

4. Passive Survivor

An inadequate provision of physical facilities for the existing traffic volume could be one of the causes for the high capital productivity experienced by passive survivor airports. The implied congestions reduce the attractiveness of these airports, leading to cargo traffic performances that fall below their respective economic volumes. These airports may have performed better if they have pursued a more proactive investment strategy in the capacity of airport architecture.

Airside Operations

Figure 1, Figure 2, Figure 3 and Figure 4 depicted the strategic inclination of airports for their airside operations. The balancing partition[13], represented by the dash line, suggests that low runway utilizations may be associated with high traffic above economic volume in the earlier years (i.e., 1999 and 2001). But, more recently, most airports lie close to the vertical axis. These airports achieve almost standard runway productivity for their given size but their associated deviations (in some cases, large deviations) from their respective economic volumes point to the fact that there are other deciding factors for an airport's cargo traffic.

1. North East Asia:

Figure 1. Airport Clusters – Airside Operations in 1999

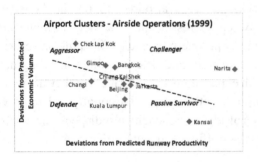

Figure 2. Airport Clusters – Airside Operations in 2001

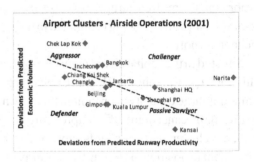

Figure 3. Airport Clusters – Airside Operations in 2003 (the balancing partition coincides with the horizontal axis)

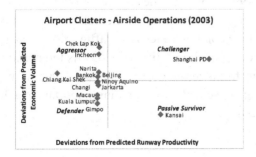

Figure 4. Airport Clusters – Airside Operations in 2005 (the balancing partition coincides with the horizontal axis)

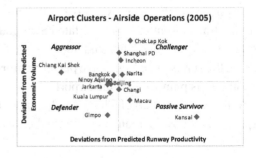

Being the major airport for the capital city of *Japan*, Narita airport is a challenger to other Asian airports in 1999 and 2001. The additional of a new runway after 2001 moves the airport into the cluster of aggressors in 2003. Perhaps, owing to lag effect of capacity investment on airlines demands, the airport returns to the status of a challenger with slight increases in traffic in 2005. The second largest Japanese airport, Kansai, is a passive survivor throughout the study horizon. With a higher runway productivity and lower cargo volume than the industry norm, this could be a sign that airside congestion is hindering further development of the airport.

Incheon airport has its beginnings as an aggressor owing to the *South Korea*'s government plan to develop the country into a regional air hub. Despite the enormous investments in capacity, the spectacular traffic growth of the airport exceeds capacity and Incheon airport becomes a challenger exhibiting relatively high runway productivity in 2005. Meanwhile, Seoul Gimpo airport transforms from an aggressor to a defender as more of its traffic is being channeled to the new Incheon airport.

Situated in the capital city of *China* in northern China, it is unsurprising that Beijing Capital airport maintains large capacity even though this may not lead to significant cargo traffic improvements. As such, the cluster analysis results show negligible movement in position of Beijing Capital airport as a defender. In recent years, eastern China experiences a soaring escalation of the manufacturing investments. Shanghai Pudong airport, in the southeast part of China, has achieved remarkable growth especially between 2001 and 2003 when the airport officially takes over most of the international traffic from under-capacitated Shanghai Hongqiao airport. Shanghai Pudong airport will take on the status of an aggressive player as more investment is pumped into the airport.

At the Southern part of China, Chek Lap Kok airport in *Hong Kong* is an aggressor in the early

2000s. By 2005, this airport has achieved an impressive traffic that gives it a runway productivity significantly above the standard productivity and hence a challenger airport status. On the other hand, defender *Macau* airport becomes a passive survivor due to the slower development of its air logistics industry relative to other parts of East Asia that places less emphasis on the airport's role as an air cargo hub. In *Taiwan*, Chiang Kai Shek airport has added a new runway after 1999. The provision of an additional runway, among other government initiatives and incentives, stimulates an obvious increase in traffic in Chiang Kai Shek airport. The airport progresses to an aggressor status rather than a mere defender in the subsequent years.

2.   Southeast Asia:

Throughout 1999 to 2005, Changi and Kuala Lumpur airports are defenders and Bangkok airport is an aggressor. Ninoy Aquino and Jarkarta Soekarno Hatta airports are on the boundary between aggressor and defender, implying low runway productivity and traffic quite on par with economic volume. These findings are congruent with expectation, considering that they are major airports for their respective country and the provision of adequate capacity is indispensable regardless of traffic or capacity utilization levels.

Landside Operations

Figure 5, Figure 6, Figure 7 and Figure 8 show that almost all airports lie near the vertical axis in 1999. However, the alignment is broken in the latter years. Particularly, the balancing partition in the capital productivity-traffic grid is a negatively sloped dash line in 2003. As the partition transforms into a positive slope in 2005, it may be inferred that cost is gaining importance in the recent years.

Figure 5. Airport Clusters – Landside Operations in 1999 (the balancing partition coincides with the horizontal axis)

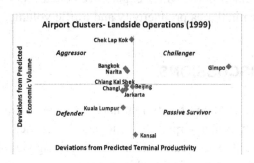

Figure 6. Airport Clusters – Landside Operations in 2001 (the balancing partition coincides with the horizontal axis)

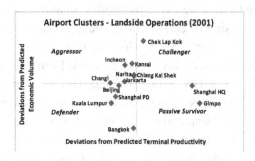

Figure 7. Airport Clusters – Landside Operations in 2003

Figure 8. Airport Clusters – Landside Operations in 2005

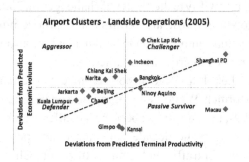

1.   Northeast Asia:

Narita airport is an unwavering aggressor that consistently performs above its economic volume. The airport provides cargo service with little landside congestion as reflected by its relatively low terminal area utilization. On the other hand, the positions of Kansai airport have been volatile over the six years. Between 1999 and 2001, the passive survivor airport joins the cluster of aggressors following a fall in terminal productivity that is accompanied by a more than proportionate increase in traffic. The perception that the potential growth of Kansai's is limited by its terminal area is further reinforced when sharp increase in terminal productivity in 2003 is met with cargo traffic reductions to a level that is below its economic volume; and the airport returns to a passive survivor status. However, this perception is later proved to be incorrect when subsequent increase in terminal area turns the airport into defender with no apparent increase in traffic. Such observation may suggest that the potential growth of Kansai airport is not hindered by landside congestion but rather by other factors. Of which, cost may be one of them.

Following the plan to convert Seoul Gimpo into a domestic airport, international traffic is being diverted to Incheon airport. As a result, Seoul Gimpo airport experiences gradual and consistent terminal productivity declines that replace the airport's initial standing as a challenger with that of a passive survivor in 2003. Meanwhile, Incheon airport progresses from an aggressor in 2001 and 2003 to a challenger in 2005 as the higher traffic utilized the airport's capacity as planned by the authorities.

Beijing Capital and Shanghai Hongqiao airports in the mainland China exhibit some signs of landside congestions. For Beijing Capital airport, a reduction of terminal area productivity in 2003 has enabled the defender airport to achieve its economic volume but an increase in terminal area productivity in 2005 gives an opposite effect. Likewise, Shanghai Hongqiao airport exhibits high terminal productivity but low traffic as a passive survivor in 2001. After the diversion of international traffic from Shanghai Hongqiao airport to the larger Shanghai Pudong airport in 2001, concurrent increases in volume and terminal productivity move the defender Shanghai Pudong airport swiftly to the cluster of challengers in 2003. Growth in traffic and terminal area productivity perpetuate into 2005 and Shanghai Pudong airport continues to grow as a challenger.

Chek Lap Kok airport is an extraordinary performer. While being an aggressor in the late 1990s, the airport has become a challenger since the turn of the decade with impressive performances in traffic and capital utilization. Chiang Kai Shek airport progresses from a defender to an aggressor to a challenger as traffic volume gradually improves over the years. The airport returns to the cluster of aggressors as additions to terminal area after 2003 ease congestion and bring along higher traffic. Macau airport also exhibits some signs of landside congestions as a passive survivor. This congestion problem is evident from the observation that an increase in terminal area productivity between 2003 and 2005 has brought along some reductions in traffic volume.

2.   Southeast Asia

Changi airport's terminal area productivity falls gradually from 1999 to 2005 while its traffic volume fluctuates around the economic volume. In Thailand, Bangkok airport experiences dramatic changes in strategic postures and performances that also show no apparent relationship to terminal area productivity. Similarly, landside congestion

is not a cause of underperformance for defender airports like Kuala Lumpur and Jarkarta Soekarno Hatta airports, which experience concurrent low terminal area productivity and traffic volume.

DISCUSSIONS

The volume of airfreight handled by an average East Asian airport has increased significantly over the six years. Alongside, the rising significance of physical architecture on airport cargo traffic is compatible with the ever-increasing airline expectations for efficient services in that an adequate provision of physical facilities relative to the cargo volume handled enables timely processing of cargo. The capacity constraints at Asian airports are well documented in the literature (for examples, Meredith 1995; Dempsy and O'Conner 1997). In particular, Hufbauer et al. (1995) witnessed the acute competitions between US and Asian carriers for slots at Narita airport due to congestions. This adverse impact of congestion on service quality to airlines becomes more severe in the late 1990s when the increase in physical infrastructure cannot keep pace with the increasing cargo and passengers traffic.

In contrast, the returns from labor show declining trends which may be attributable to the greater automations that reduce the airports' reliance on manual labor. Prior to the shift towards automation, airports like Narita and Changi that are operating under cost escalations have attempted to control their cost by hiring cheaper labor from Thailand, Philippines and India. As operating cost continues to increase, these airports resort to more extensive automations made possible through technological advancements and airport users' acceptances. Hence, the size and productivity of the workforce (i.e., human architecture) cease to play a determining role in ensuring the smooth operations of an airport and contribute less to the service quality to airport users than before. Furthermore, the diminishing returns to scale for the general effort towards rapid and reliable airport services may also indicate the increasing ease of newly developed and smaller airports to catch up with the more established and bigger ones as size of operations (leading to cost efficiency and throughput volume generation) is less of a hurdle to overcome now.

Unsurprisingly, the economic and political environment in which an airport is operating within notably affects the demand and supply of air cargo services at the airport. Higher income and quick custom clearance boost the demand for air cargo services since air cargo generally comprises high value and/or time sensitive products. Other contributing factors include shortening product lifespan, increasing JIT adoption and lowering airfreight rates that prompted shippers to move from the use of sea transport to air transport on condition that there will be greater demand for higher value and more rapidly launched new products. Furthermore, the recent development of a new airport or the upgrading of an existing airport to handle higher traffic requires airports to possess the ability to address a whole dimension of security threats identified following the 911 events and the provision of facilities so as to deliver better service and performance with the arrival of the new age of mega aircraft in the mode of the A380s and the Boeing Dream Liner. With designs relating to runway and vehicular approaches to the airport, the circulation and layouts of terminal buildings, contact gate facility and the introduction of new security and baggage handling systems and processes to be factored into the construction and development of airports, the associated enormous outlay[14] has transformed into a whole complexion of airport development financing. This leads to a surge in airport privatization programs and the use of public-private partnerships in the financing landscape of airport developments. Therefore, while it is probable for capital investment in publicly-owned airports to be related to the country's economic conditions, it is also clear that political instability might have

the capacity of attracting FDI and a relevant role in the determination of the capital investments in private airport infrastructure as unstable political situations will hamper the realization of long-term investments.

On observation of the potent effects of the physical architecture of an airport on air cargo traffic, a cluster analysis is carried out to further distinguish between the influences of airside and landside facilities. After adjusting for differences in airport size and economic conditions, it is found that high (low) runway productivity is associated with low (high) cargo traffic in 1999 and 2001. This implies that airside congestion may be hindering potential demand for air cargo service. In response, Chiang Kai Shek and Narita airports have added new runways while China and South Korea re-divert their traffic from Shanghai Hongqiao and Seoul Gimpo airports to Shanghai Pudong and Incheon airports respectively. Despite the fact that almost all airports achieved "industry standard" for runway productivity in 2003 and 2005, traffic still differ significantly among the airports. Therefore, it is reasonable to believe that other factors beyond adequate runway provision and aggregate economic circumstances play a greater role in driving demand of air cargo service. In comparison, airports' landside operations exhibited an interesting relationship between the provision of facilities and cargo traffic in years 2001 through 2005. In 2001 and 2003, airports that plan for extra capacity attract more traffic. Adequate provisions of facilities, though lowering the utilization of such facilities, ensure that cargo will be able to flow smoothly and in a more-timely manner without incurring unnecessary waiting time for loading and unloading. However, the reverse is observed in 2005. High utilization of physical landside capacity is associated with high air cargo traffic. Since high productivity (or utilization) is achieved when a large cargo volume is spread over the given capacity, it may be inferred that cost savings has become more critical under the intensifying competitive pressure and the narrowing profit margins in the downstream cargo service industry of the airlines. Hence, it may be desirable for airports like Kuala Lumpur, Jarkarta and Changi to reduce terminal capacity to lower their overheads as well as the associated variable costs.

CONCLUSION

This chapter explores the contributions of physical and human service-oriented architectures as well as the economic and political environment to the cargo traffic in airports across East Asia. Through a cluster analysis, the chapter further investigates the strategic postures exhibited by major East Asian airports and industry competition dynamics between 1999 and 2005.

In summary, findings from this chapter have shown that an average airport in the East Asia airport industry handles more traffic than before. While favorable economic condition is a major cause for the higher traffic, political stability has also become one of the critical factors following the emergence of infrastructure funds from the private sector. At the same time, the increasing returns from physical capital investment are reasonable since runway and terminal capacity shortages have negative effects on the quality of services to airport users in terms of delays and inconvenience. Between airside capacity and landside capacity, the provisions and utilizations of physical facilities for landside operations seem to be more important in driving an airport's cargo traffic in recent years. Jorge and Rus (2004) reflected these findings when they opinioned that it is the terminal capacity that determines potential output and airside capacity matters little in comparison since cargo flights can operate during off-peak periods. On the other hand, the returns from labor expansion and labor skills upgrading have fallen over the years. A possible explanation is that extensive automations of custom clearances, baggage checks procedures and so on, have reduced the reliance on manual labor.

Overall, the scale returns for the operations of air cargo services in the East Asian airport industry have fallen prominently. Two profound implications, especially for established airports, can be inferred from these results. First, smaller airports are more likely to be able achieve cost efficiency comparable to their bigger counter parts. Second, airports will need to seek more creative ways to control cost as this study also envisages that cost savings has become more critical with increasing competitive pressure. One possible means for cost control is through outsourcing of peripheral services to specialized third parties.

Admittedly, this study is not without its shortcomings. Apart from the physical and human service-oriented architectures present in an airport, it should be recognized that the quality of airport's cargo service is influenced by the availability of intermodal transfer facilities and technological infrastructure. Intermodal (or surface) accessibility that provides links to and from the airports will ensure rapid and efficient movement of goods in a door-to-door delivery (Meredith 1995; Zhang 2003; Lee and Yang 2003). Similarly, technological infrastructures such as supporting information systems simplify custom procedures by computerizing shipment information and enhance efficiency of airports by allowing pre-clearance of shipments (Ohashi et al. 2005). Furthermore, using quantity and quality of labor as the sole quantification of human architecture may be misleading due to the varying degrees of outsourcing practices at different airports, as well as, the fact that the responsibilities of airport operators and range of services provided vary greatly among the airports (Low and Tang 2006; Lam et al. 2009). With regard to the latter, future studies that consider the influences of economies of scope (services diversification strategy) on airport competitiveness and the associated implications on smaller airports would be meaningful.

REFERENCES

Air Transport Research Society. (2002–2005). *Airport Benchmarking Report: Global Standards for Airport Excellence - Part 1, 2 and 3.* Vancouver, Canada: ATRS.

Chin, T. H. A. (1997). Implications of Liberalization on Airport Development and Strategy in the Asia Pacific. *Journal of Air Transport Management, 3,* 125–131. doi:10.1016/S0969-6997(97)00020-3

Dempsey, P. S., & O'Connor, K. (1997). Air Traffic Congestion and Infrastructure Development in the Pacific Asia Region. In Findley, C., Chia L.S, and Singh, K. (Eds), Asia Pacific Air Transport – Challenges and Policy Reforms. Institute of Southeast Asian Studies.

Edgar, J. R. (1995, July 9-11). *World Air Cargo Forecast.* A paper presented at the conference on Air Transport in the Asia Pacific – Challenges, Opportunities and Options, Singapore.

Gardiner, J., Ison, S., & Humphreys, I. (2005). Factors Influencing Cargo Airlines' Choice of Airport: An International Survey. *Journal of Air Transport Management, 11,* 393–399. doi:10.1016/j.jairtraman.2005.05.004

Gillen, D., & Lall, A. (1997). Developing Measures of Airport Productivity and Performance: An Application of Data Envelopment Analysis. *Transportation Research Part E, Logistics and Transportation Review, 33,* 261–273. doi:10.1016/S1366-5545(97)00028-8

Holloway, S. (2003). Straight and Level: Practical Airline Economics, 2nd Edition. Hampshire, UK: Aldershot.

Hufbauer, G., Jaggi, G., & Findlay, C. (1995, July 9-11). Cleaning the Air-Civil Aviation Issues in the Asia Pacific. A paper presented at the conference on Air Transport in the Asia Pacific – Challenges, Opportunities and Options, Singapore.

Jorge, J. D., & de Rus, G. (2004). Cost-Benefit Analysis of Investments in Airport Infrastructure: A Practical Approach. *Journal of Air Transport Management, 10,* 311–326. doi:10.1016/j.jairtraman.2004.05.001

Kasarda, J. D., & Green, J. D. (2005). Air Cargo as an Economic Development Engine- A Note on Opportunities and Constraints. *Journal of Air Transport Management, 11,* 459–462. doi:10.1016/j.jairtraman.2005.06.002

Lam, S. W., Low, J. M. W., & Tang, L. C. (2009). Operational Efficiencies across Asia Pacific Airports. *Transportation Research Part E, Logistics and Transportation Review, 45*(4), 654–655. doi:10.1016/j.tre.2008.11.003

Lee, H., & Yang, H. M. (2003). Strategies for a Global Logistics and Economic Hub: Incheon International Airport. *Journal of Air Transport Management, 9,* 113–121. doi:10.1016/S0969-6997(02)00065-0

Low, J. M. W., & Tang, L. C. (2006). Factor Substitution and Complementarity in the Asia Airport Industry. *Journal of Air Transport Management, 12,* 261–266. doi:10.1016/j.jairtraman.2006.07.003

Meredith, J. (1995, July 9-11). *Airport Capacity Constraints in Asia Pacific.* A paper presented at the conference on Air Transport in the Asia Pacific – Challenges, Opportunities and Options, Singapore.

Nijkamp, P., & Yim, H. (2001). Critical Success Factors for Offshore Airports: A Comparative Evaluation. *Journal of Air Transport Management, 7,* 181–188. doi:10.1016/S0969-6997(01)00003-5

O'Conner, W. E. (1995). An Introduction to Airline Economics, 5th Edition. Westport CT: Praeger.

Ohashi, H., Kim, T. S., Oum, T. H., & Yu, C. (2005). Choice of Air Cargo Transshipment Airport – An Application to Air Cargo Traffic to/ from Northeast Asia. *Journal of Air Transport Management, 11,* 149–159. doi:10.1016/j.jairtraman.2004.08.004

Oum, T. H., Yu, C., & Fu, X. (2003). A Comparative Analysis of Productivity Performance of the World's Major Airports: A Summary Report of the ATRS Global Airport Benchmarking Research Report 2002. *Journal of Air Transport Management, 9,* 285–297. doi:10.1016/S0969-6997(03)00037-1

Park, Y. (2003). An Analysis for the Competitive Strength of Asian Major Airports. *Journal of Air Transport Management, 9,* 353–360. doi:10.1016/S0969-6997(03)00041-3

Quilty, S. (2003). Achieving Recognition as a World Class Airport through Education and Training. *Journal of Air Transportation, 8,* 3–14.

Raguraman, K. (1997). International Air Cargo Hubbing: The Case of Singapore. *Asia Pacific Viewpoint, 38*(1), 55–74. doi:10.1111/1467-8373.00028

Romer, D. (2001). Advanced Macroeconomics. 2nd Edition, New York: McGraw-Hill.

Taneja, N. K. (2002). Driving Airline Business Strategies through Emerging Technology, Ashgate, UK:Aldershot.

Tsai, M. C., & Su, Y. S. (2002). Political Risk Assessment on Air Logistics Hub Developments in Taiwan. *Journal of Air Transport Management, 8,* 373–380. doi:10.1016/S0969-6997(02)00016-9

World Competitiveness Yearbook (2001-2004). *World Competitiveness Yearbook.* Lausanne, Switzerland: International Institute for Management Development

Yoshida, Y., & Fujimoto, H. (2004). Japanese-Airport Benchmarking with the DEA and Endogenous-Weight TFP Methods: Testing the Criticism of Overinvestment in Japanese Regional Airports. *Transportation Research Part E, Logistics and Transportation Review, 40,* 533–546. doi:10.1016/j.tre.2004.08.003

Yung, Y. H., Chang, C. P., & Hsien, M. C. (2008). Air Cargo as an Impetus Economic Growth through the Channel of Openness: the Case of OECD Countries. *International Journal of Transport Economics, 35*(1), 31–44.

Zhang, A. M. (2002). Electronic Technology and Simplification of Customs Regulations and Procedures in Air Cargo Trade. *Journal of Air Transportation, 7,* 87–102.

Zhang, A. M. (2003). Analysis of an International Air Cargo Hub: the Case of Hong Kong. *Journal of Air Transport Management, 9,* 123–138. doi:10.1016/S0969-6997(02)00066-2

Zhang, A. M., & Zhang, Y. M. (2002a). Issues on Liberalization of Air Cargo Services in International Aviation. *Journal of Air Transport Management, 8,* 275–287. doi:10.1016/S0969-6997(02)00008-X

Zhang, A. M., & Zhang, Y. M. (2002b). A Model of Air Cargo Liberalization: Passengers vs. All-Cargo Carriers. *Transportation Research Part E, Logistics and Transportation Review, 38,* 175–191. doi:10.1016/S1366-5545(02)00004-2

ENDNOTES

[1] Taneja (2002) noted that the top ten cargo hubs account for around two-thirds of cargo movements; whereas the top ten passenger hubs account for only one-third of passengers. Holloway (2003) advocated that the growth of focused cargo alliances is likely to add further momentum to this pattern of concentration.

2   Gillen and Lall (1997) articulated that efficiency of an airport will suffer when there is a slowdown in the economy regardless of airport management ability or effort. It is reasonable that wealthier nations will enjoy higher human traffic volumes which trigger more flights to be scheduled to meet the demand. In turn, this increase in the number of flights will not only reduce connecting time for human traffic but also that of transshipment cargo due to the use of combination flights that carry both passengers and cargo. The shorter connecting time will enhance the attractiveness of an airport as an air cargo hub.

3   The trend towards more expensive aircrafts adds pressure to a terminal, making aircraft depreciations high, and aircraft utilizations and turnaround time critical. Cargo whether on a freighter or combination flight must be unloaded rapidly when a flight arrives, and outgoing traffic must be ready for quick loading. Associated with the turnaround time is the paperwork that is required. O'Conner (1995) noted that one of the greatest delays in international air cargo is the awaiting of customs clearance. Kasarda and Green (2005) highlighted that 20% of the goods transit time and 25% of costs are spent in customs clearance. Ohashi et al. (2005) added that delays in customs clearance procedure disrupt efficient logistics flows, and thus hinder the hub development in air cargo transport.

4   Tsai and Su (2002) remarked that air hub developments are closely related to government performances, and political or economic risk is important in determining the success of such developments.

5   According to Ohashi et al. (2005) and others, traffic volume is commonly used as a performance measure in the airport literature on the assumption that airports are throughput maximizers.

6   According to the Air Transport Research Society, the number of runways indicates the airside capacity of an airport. Other than the absolute number, the length and crossing of runways are other important aspects that limit flight operations. Ohashi et al. (2005) stated a minimum length of 2800 is required to accommodate the Boeing 747 – 400. Hence, the study also checks that all airports in our sample have at least one runway that is longer than 2800 meters and there is no intersection of runways.

7   Yoshida and Fujimoto (2004) advocated that the size of the terminal determines the airport's ability to load passengers and cargo into aircrafts and hence plays an important role in airport operation activity. Considering that a significant percentage of the cargo volume is transported in combination flights that carry both passengers and cargo, this study thus uses total terminal area as a proxy to the amount of physical capital used in an airport.

8   The World Competitiveness Yearbooks obtained ratings on economic literacy through extensive surveys. The ratings reflect the general perceptions of the quality and productivity of a workforce through education by businesses.

9   Chin (1997) advocated that a strong domestic market can command a certain level of air services.

10   In Sarkis (2000), normalizing is done by dividing each value of a respective airport for a given factor by the mean value of all airports for that respective input or output factor. Such mean normalization lessens the impact of large difference in data magnitude, while preserving the underlying distribution of the data.

11   An attempt to fit the parameter values, in Eqn. (6), has resulted in adjusted R-square values as low as 6 percent and wrong coefficient signs. As Yoshida (2004) observed

that labor and capital are complements, the poor model fits could probably be due to the nature of airport data that entails correlation between the predictors. For example, a large $K_i(t)$ is usually associated with large $L_i(t)$ and hence $H_i(t)$.

[12] Capital productivity is obtained by dividing volume of cargo with the total number of runway or terminal area length. High capital productivity, though signifying good asset utilization, may also imply possible congestions. In the case of runway productivity, high runway productivity may be due to bigger aircrafts or more aircrafts movements per runway. The latter may lead to longer waiting time for planes that are taking off. On the other hand, low capital productivity can be attributed to excessive investments in capital. Deliberate overinvestment may also indicate aggressiveness of airport authorities in expanding their airports.

[13] The balancing partition is constructed as a fitting dash line that minimizes extreme points of 'Deviations from Predicted Economic Volume' along the horizontal axis.

[14] Currently, the construction cost is between US$25 and US$30 million per million passengers per annum (mppa) for an international airport terminal building in the 15 to 30 mppa range. According to Changi International, this unit cost relates to the construction cost of the basic terminal building only, including support systems such as building services and baggage handling but excludes interior fit out costs and consultancy fees. Thus, a terminal building with a capacity of 25 mppa will be expected to cost between US$620 and US$750 million.

APPENDIX A

Figure 9. Residual Plots of Errors against ln (Yi/Li) of 1999

Figure 10. Residual Plots of Errors against ln (Yi/Li) of 2001

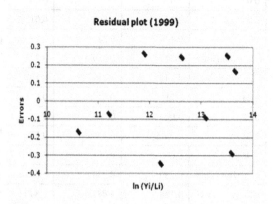

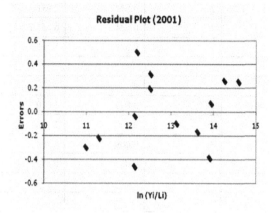

Figure 11. Residual Plots of Errors against ln (Yi/Li) of 2003

Figure 12. Residual Plots of Errors against ln (Yi/Li) of 2005

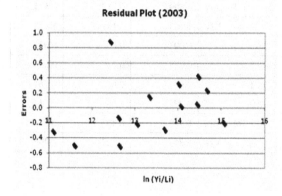

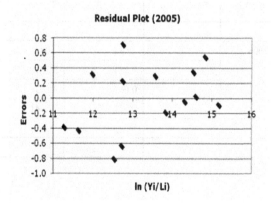

Table 4. Condition Index, Variance Proportions, Tolerance and VIF 1999-2005

Model	Dimension	Eigenvalue	Condition Index	Variance Proportions			
				(Constant)	$\ln(K_i/L_i)$	$\ln(H_i/L_i)$	$\ln(X_i)$
1999	1	3.072	1.000	0.00	0.01	0.01	0.00
	2	0.824	1.931	0.02	0.00	0.16	0.00
	3	0.084	6.051	0.07	0.84	0.59	0.01
	4	0.021	12.113	0.90	0.14	0.24	0.98
				Tolerance	0.225	0.239	0.243
				VIF	4.448	4.189	4.107
2001	1	3.093	1.000	0.01	0.01	0.01	0.01
	2	0.807	1.958	0.02	0.00	0.16	0.01
	3	0.069	6.708	0.01	0.93	0.48	0.15
	4	0.032	9.877	0.96	0.06	0.35	0.84
				Tolerance	0.239	0.223	0.544
				VIF	4.188	4.483	1.840
2003	1	3.579	1.000	0.01	0.01	0.01	0.01
	2	0.243	3.836	0.16	0.13	0.13	0.04
	3	0.142	5.023	0.06	0.50	0.24	0.09
	4	0.036	9.926	0.78	0.36	0.62	0.87
				Tolerance	0.509	0.319	0.534
				VIF	1.963	3.131	1.873
2005	1	3.647	1.000	0.01	0.00	0.00	0.00
	2	0.285	3.578	0.17	0.02	0.04	0.03
	3	0.052	8.405	0.72	0.00	0.07	0.76
	4	0.017	14.641	0.10	0.97	0.89	0.21
				Tolerance	0.147	0.133	0.557
				VIF	6.814	7.497	1.796

Chapter 14
Lifecycle Management of SLAs for Service Enterprises

Yang Li
Applications & Services, Research & Technology, British Telecom, UK

ABSTRACT

Service level agreement (SLA) is becoming an increasingly sought-after topic in recent years, as complex logistics and service chains span across geographical boundaries in the lights of globalization and new technological developments. This chapter introduces the reader to the state of the art lifecycle management of SLA for service enterprises, which covers stages of terms optimization, contract drafting and compliance tracking. In particular, the author identified deficiencies in the area of term optimization and outlines several R&D tracks that would lead to the development of industry-strength SLA optimization capabilities. An initial version of a SLA optimization toolset coded-named SLA-OASIS is reported, in the context of a telecom service, to illustrate such a concept. In addition, some out-of-box toolsets for drafting SLA contracts and tracking SLA compliance are also reviewed.

INTRODUCTION

Services are economic activities offered by one party to another, most commonly employing time-based performances to bring about desired results in recipients themselves or in objects or other assets for which purchasers have responsibility. In exchange for their money, time and effort, service customers expect to obtain value from access to goods, labor, professional skills, facilities, networks, and systems; but they do not normally take ownership of any of the physical elements involved (Lovelock, 2007).

Service level agreements (SLAs) are part of service contracts where the levels of services are formally defined. It records the common understanding about services, priorities, responsibility, guarantees and such – collectively, the level of service. For example, it may specify the level of availability, serviceability, performance, operation, or other attributes of service like billing and even penalties in the case of violation of the SLA (Encyclopedia, 2007).

DOI: 10.4018/978-1-61520-603-2.ch014

During 1980s, there were a wave of privatizations in the service sector that liberated service markets and called for regulations to protect the interests of service consumers and providers alike. Companies chose SLAs as legal means to handle relationships with their customers. In recent years, the tide of globalization further highlighted the needs of service standardization, as complex logistics and service chains emerged and spanned across country borders, which requires stricter legislation and enforcement on quality of services. European Committee, for instance, has set up initiatives on service standardization that takes effect in December 2009 (European Committee, 2007).

A full SLA management cycle consists of the following activities: terms negotiation and optimization, contract drafting, compliance tracking and reporting:

- Terms negotiation and optimization. For large service enterprises, by regulations, uniform SLAs are often provided to service customers to guarantee equivalence of services; for small and medium service providers, SLAs are often established via negotiations between service providers and service consumers.

- Contract drafting. To produce an appropriate and focused SLA requires non-trivial legal knowledge and efforts. There are some tools in the market that were designed to make the creation of SLA contracts more straightforward, which is often achieved via a collection of templates that facilitate contract drafting in a formal way (SLA-World, 2002).

- Compliance tracking and reporting. Once SLAs are created, it is important that such SLAs are kept being monitored to ensure its compliance. Industry practice showed that active monitoring of SLAs can typically save 5 to 10% of annual service contract costs. There are some commercial tools to offer the functionalities of SLA tracking and reporting (NimBUS, 2007).

Drafting SLA contracts and tracking their compliance both occur after term negotiation. During the SLA negotiations, either with regulators or service customers, it is crucial for service providers to see the direct impact of proposed SLA terms on their level of profitability, such that they can have reasoned and informed decision makings. To our knowledge, there is no commercial tool in the market that can check levels of profitability for any specified SLAs.

This chapter will walk the reader through state of the art of SLA lifecycle. To remain focused and generic, the discussions will have to be limited to a set of key SLA and operation parameters. The author will explore some work related to SLA optimization and outline some R&D tracks that help build industry-strength SLA optimization capabilities. An initial version of SLA optimization toolkit code-named SLA-OASIS, will be reported, in the context of a telecom service. Furthermore, some typical out-of-box tools that are applicable to certain activities, such as contract drafting and compliance tracking will also be reviewed.

The remaining of the chapter will be organized as follows. Section 2 defines a set of key SLA and operation parameters; Section 3 discusses SLA terms negotiation and computer-assisted optimization; Section 4 covers template-based SLA contract drafting; Section 5 reviews automated SLA compliance tracking and reporting. Finally, Section 6 concludes.

SLA AND OPERATION PARAMETERS

Generally speaking, a service enterprise can be considered as an entity that offers and fulfills a set of services. Each service is composed of the following elements: a set of service level agreements, a business process, an enterprise resource plan and a business model. In this section, we use telecom services as examples to illustrate these concepts.

Service Level Agreement

In its basic form, a service level agreement contains minimum lead time, standard lead time, pricing, delay penalty and associated customer demand.

Minimum lead time, as its name suggested, is the minimum time the customer has to wait for before receiving service; this is often determined by the nature of a service, e.g., equipments have to be put in place before a service can be started, or planning permissions for road works need to be secured before optical fibers can be laid down into ground. Standard lead time is a uniform, contractual lead time that can be offered by a service provider to its customers. It refers to the duration between order submission and order completion and is often used to characterize the capacity and competitiveness of a service enterprise.

Pricing specifies the price service customers have to pay for receiving services within standard lead time; usually the longer the standard lead time extends, the lower the price is. Delay penalty specifies penalty cost a service provider has to pay for delaying services; usually the longer the service is delayed, the higher the penalty cost is. Customer demand is the projected incoming

orders that are associated with a specific service level agreement; it tells the volumes of service order arrivals on each calendar day, which usually follows a normal distribution around an expected, average order volume.

In practice, service enterprises tend to adopt a single service level agreement that has one priced standard lead time. Alternatively, they can adopt multiple service level agreements, each having its own service lead time and price, as well as delay penalty and demand. Table 1 and Table 2 illustrate such two scenarios. Some notations are:

- MLT and SLT denote minimum lead time and standard lead time respectively.
- In "Delay Penalty" column, (1, 2) denotes that a one-day delay of service can incur a penalty cost of 2.
- In "Demand" column, (D1, 20) denotes that on a calendar day D1 the demand volume is 20.

Business Process

A business process contains a set of coordinated activities to fulfill a service function. The coordination can be represented by a set of pre-defined relationships such as "sequential" and "parallel". Each activity can be mapped to a type of resource

Table 1. A single service lead time and price

MLT	SLT	Pricing	Delay Penalty	Demand
2	5	10	(1, 2), (2, 3), (3, 4)…	(D1, 20), (D2, 10), …

Table 2. Multiple service level agreements

MLT	SLT	Pricing	Delay Penalty	Demand
2	5	10	(1, 2), (2, 3), (3, 4)…	(D1, 10), (D2, 5), …
2	4	20	(1, 5), (2, 7), (3, 9)…	(D1, 6), (D2, 3), …
2	3	30	(1, 10), (2, 15), (3, 20), …	(D1, 4), (D2, 2), …

that is required to fulfill the activity. The resource can be an internal one within the service enterprise or an external one offered by one or more service suppliers.

Even if a business process may contain multiple activities, from resourcing perspective, some of these activities can be merged together if they can be fulfilled by the same group of resource. As a result, many business processes can be simplified into single-activity processes. For multi-activity processes, their activities often require resource of different skill sets. Figure 1 and Figure 2 illustrate such two scenarios.

In Figure 1, the business process for the service contains only a single activity, called "A1", which is associated with a resource pool, named "ADSL". The resource pool is internal to the service enterprise. Intuitively, the service is to fulfill an ADSL-related function such as broadband installation, migration or cancellation.

Figure 1. A single-activity process

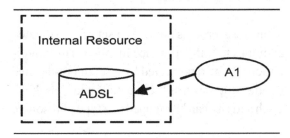

Figure 2. A multi-activity process

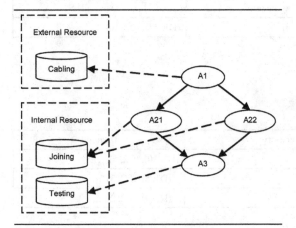

In Figure 2, the business process for the service contains four activities, called "A1", "A21", "A22" and "A3" respectively, where "A21" and "A22" are both dependent on "A1", and "A3" is dependent on both "A21" and "A22". Among them, "A1" is associated with an external resource pool, named "Cabling", "A21" and "A22" are associated with an internal resource pool, named "Joining", and "A3" is also associated with another internal resource pool, named "Testing". Intuitively, this service is to fulfill the installation of a private circuit line between two sites. It first lays a cable between Site A and Site B; it then connects the cable to the ports at both Sites; finally, it checks the quality of the line.

As indicated by Figure 2, laying a cable can be outsourced to an external supplier to fulfill the task; joining and testing the cable require expertise and authorities internal to the service enterprise. As joining the cable at Site A and Site B requires coordination with hosts at both sites, two activities are used to track these two different threads.

Enterprise Resource Plan

An enterprise resource plan covers both resourcing scheme and resource cost scheme. A resourcing scheme specifies types and volumes of resource on various calendar days. This is often contributed by both permanent and contractual resource employed by the service enterprise. A resource cost scheme specifies the cost of specific-type resource on various days; usually the costs during weekends are higher than those during weekdays. Table 3 and Table 4 give examples of resourcing schemes and resource cost scheme.

Table 3 shows resourcing scheme for "ADSL", where the resource volumes on 02/10/09 and 03/10/09 are 10 and 20 respectively. Table 4 shows resource cost scheme for "ADSL", where the costs on Sunday and Monday are 8 and 5 respectively.

Table 3. An example of resourcing scheme

Date	Resource Volume	Resource Type
02/10/09	10	"ADSL"
03/10/09	20	"ADSL"
…	…	…

Table 4. An example of resource cost scheme

Date	Resource Cost	Resource Type
Sunday	8	"ADSL"
Monday	5	"ADSL"
…	…	…

Business Model

A business model is used to determine what business value can be generated from the operational context of a service enterprise; one typical formula would look like:

- $Business\_Value = Service\_Revenue - Resource\_Cost - Delay\_Penalty$,

Where

- $Service\_Revenue = \sum_{i=1}^{Number\_of\_Orders} \Pr icing$
- $Resource\_Cost = \sum_{i=1}^{Number\_of\_Orders} \operatorname{Re} sourcing\_Cost[Completion\_Date(Order_i)]$
- $Delay\_Penalty = \sum_{i=1}^{Number\_of\_Orders} Delay\_Compensation[Completion\_Date(order_i) - Due\_Date(order_i)]$

Informally, service revenue is summed-up prices of incoming service orders; resource cost is the total costs of resources that have been consumed to fulfill the service orders; delay compensation is summed-up penalty costs for all the delayed service orders. The final business value of the service would be service revenue minus resource cost and delay penalty.

Beyond this simple formula, a number of other factors also need to be considered. For instance, by popping up service prices, or pushing down delay compensation, or increasing standard lead time, the service enterprise may dissatisfy customers and have reduced number of orders; these in turn affect business value. To what extent the changes in the service level agreements can affect the number of orders is a subtle scientific as well as business matter. Depending on the nature of the service business, a variety of functional shapes could be selected, e.g., linear, polynomial, exponential, etc; only experiments and experience can tell the most suitable ones. For illustration purpose, Figure 3 shows the interplays of these factors in a business context.

SLA NEGOTIATION AND OPTIMIZATION

The purpose of SLA Negotiation between a service provider and a service consumer is to work out an agreeable SLA policy between the two parties. As stated in the previous section, such policy often covers terms related to service lead times, pricing and delay compensation. During the negotiation process, both parties have opportunities to

Figure 3. Interplay of factors in a business model

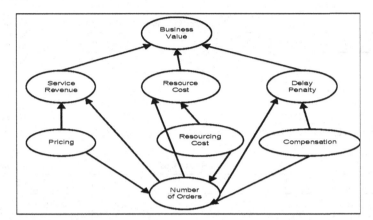

express their preferences in the SLA terms, and they also need to respect the preferences given by the other party.

From a service provider's point of view, the general objective of SLA negotiation is to achieve SLA terms that can satisfy the following criteria:

- These are constrained by the preferences of both the service provider and the service consumer,
- These can maximize the business value of the service provider.

At the core of this problem, it needs to efficiently compute an optimal business value for a given combination of SLA terms, customer demand, enterprise resource, business process and business model; once this is in place, optimizing SLA terms can be treated as fine-tuning each individual SLA parameter and selecting instances that can generate the best business values.

Technically, optimizing business value falls into the category of constraint programming and satisfaction problems and has been generally considered as NP-hard problem (Baker & Scudder, 1990). There are four typical methods applicable to this problem: Brute Force (Wikipedia, 2009), FIFO (Wikipedia, 2009), Pairwise Shift (Mannur

& Addagatla, 1993) and Tabu Search (Weng & Sedani, 2002); in this section, a brief review of these methods is provided.

As there is no out-of-box tool available to optimize SLAs for service enterprises, some desired high-level features of such toolsets are also described at the end of this section.

Problem Modeling

For simplicity purpose, the following assumptions are taken:

- There is only a single SLA associated with the service,
- The cost of resource remains the same across different days,
- There is only a single activity in the business process.

Consider a single pool of resource, R = {r_i}, $1 \leq i \leq I$, where I is the total number of days and r_i is the resource capacity (in terms of number of jobs that can be handled) on each day.

Consider a service level agreement, SLA = (MLT, SLT, P, C), where MLT is minimum lead time, SLT is standard lead time, P is price per order, C is compensation scheme for delayed orders. We assume MLT, SLT and P are single constants and

C = {c_j}, 1≤*j*≤J, where J is the total number of days and c_j is the compensation cost for *j* number of delayed days.

Consider a set of arrival orders, D = {d_k}, 1≤*k*≤K, where K is the total number of days and d_k is the number of job arrivals on each day.

For a given combination of R, SLA and D, the problem is to determine an optimal job allocation scheme that can generate best business value. As we assume that the service price and resource cost are always the same, the problem then becomes to minimize the compensation cost. That is

Min: $f(\sigma) = \sum_{h=1}^{H} c_{fin(h)-arr(h)-SLT}$, where h is

the index of an order, $H = \sum_{k=1}^{K} d_k$, and σ is an arbitrary legal job allocation sequence that satisfies the following two conditions:

$$\forall i : (\sum_{h=1}^{H} V_h) \le r_i, \text{ where } 1 \le i \le I; Vh = 1, \text{ if}$$

fin(h)=i, *Vh*=0, else   (1)

$\forall h :$ (2)

Here, we denote *arr(h)*, *sta(h)*, *fin(h)* as arrival date, start date and finish date of job *h*, respectively, and we assume *sta(h)* = *fin(h)*.

Informally, the optimal job allocation scheme is the one that has minimal total compensation cost for all the delayed orders. The job allocation scheme should also be a legal one, where the resource on each day is not over-utilized and the job can only be carried out after minimum lead time.

Brute Force

For discrete problems in which no efficient solution method is known, it might be necessary to test each possibility sequentially in order to determine if it is the solution, which is also known as *Exhaustive Search*, *Direct Search* or the *"Brute Force"* method (Wikipedia, 2009).

Figure 4 illustrates graphically such a search method, where each job is given the opportunity to try all the options applicable to it. The algorithm for calculating minimal compensation cost using *Brute Force Search* is given in Script 1. Note that UB denotes the upper bound of lead time that delays should not exceed.

Searching for all the possible solutions in an exponential space is notoriously time-consuming and operationally prohibitive. The Algorithm described in Script 1 has a computational complexity

of $O(UB-MLT)^H$, where $H = \sum_{i=1}^{K} d_i$.

Figure 4. Illustration of brute force search for optimal job allocation scheme

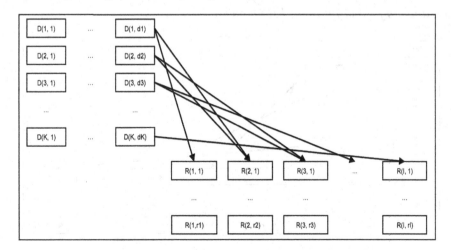

Script 1. Algorithm of brute force method to minimize compensation cost

```
Algorithm 1.1. Exhaustive_Search(Jobs[1..H], Total_
Resource[1..Q]), MLT, UB)

BEGIN
 Job_Assignment = NIL.
 Optimal_Evaluation = INF_MIN.
 Optimal_Job_Assignment = NIL.
 First_Job = Job[1].
 Rest_Jobs = Jobs[2..H].
 FOR i=Arrival_Date(First_Job)+MLT TO Arrival_Date(First_
Job)+UB DO
 Job_Assignment[First_Job] = i.
 Recursive_Exhaustive_Search (Rest_Jobs).
 IF Is-Legal_Job_Assignment(Job_Assignment, Total_
Resource[1..Q]) THEN
 Current_Evaluation = Evaluate_Compensation_Cost(Job_As-
signment).
 IF Current_Evaluation > Optimal_Evaluation THEN
 Optimal_Evaluation = Curernt_Evaluation.
 Optimal_Job_Assignment = Job_Assignment.
 ENDIF
 ENDIF
 ENDFOR
 Return Optimal_Evaluation.
END

Algorithm 1.2. Recursive_Exhaustive_Search(Jobs[1..H],
MLT, UB)

BEGIN
 First_Job = Job[1].
 Rest_Jobs = Jobs[2..H].
 FOR i=Arrival_Date(First_Job)+MLT TO Arrival_Date(First_
Job)+UB DO
 Job_Assignment[First_Job] = i.
 Exhaustive_Search (Rest_Jobs).
 ENDFOR
END
```

Assume that *MLT*=2, *UB*=8 and *H*=3000; to search exhaustively for an optimal solution will require 6^{3000} checks, which is computationally infeasible.

FIFO

In order to render some useful search results within limited timescales, people switch the objective from searching for optimal solutions to near-optimal ones, where heuristics are often used to speed up the search process or even render a near-optimal solution straight-away. *FIFO* or *First-In-First-Out* is such a heuristic, which represents an abstraction in ways of organizing and manipulation of data relative to time and prioritization; it describes the principle of a queue processing technique or servicing conflicting demands by ordering process by first-come, first-served (FCFS) behavior (Wikipedia, 2009). Figure 5 illustrates such a method, where the later jobs can only be handled after the earlier jobs have been allocated.

Script 2 provides an algorithm to use FIFO to obtain a job allocation scheme and to calculate its corresponding compensation cost.

The computational complexity of FIFO method is linear with the total number of orders, i.e., *O(H×(UB-MLT))*. However, as FIFO totally

Figure 5. Illustration of first-in-first-out (FIFO) method

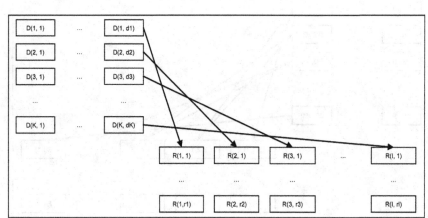

Script 2. FIFO method for job allocation

```
Algorithm 2. FIFO(Jobs[1..H], Total_Resource[1..Q], MLT,
UB)

BEGIN
Remaining_Resource = Total_Resource.
FOR i=1 TO H DO
Job = Jobs[i].
FOR j=Arrival_Date(Job)+MLT TO Arrival_Date(Job)+UB
DO
IF Remaining_Resource[j] > 0 THEN
Job_Assignment[Job] = j.
Remaining_Resource[j] = Remaining_Resource[j] – 1.
Break.
ENDIF
ENDFOR
ENDFOR
Current_Evaluation = Evaluate_Compensation_Cost(Job_As-
signment).
Return Current_Evaluation.
END
```

disregard compensation cost function, it is highly unlikely that the resulting job allocation scheme is optimal or even near-optimal.

Pairwise Shift

Pairwise shift is a constructive heuristic which determines the sequence of jobs based on their relative compensation costs (Mannur & Addagatla, 1993). It consists of the following steps:

- Step 1 – Job Ordering. This step is done by allocating all the jobs to the resource pool based on their time constraints (e.g., just before their due dates), regardless of whether or not there is enough resource to accommodate the jobs.

- Step 2 – Feasibility Checking. This step aims to eliminate the resource contentions by shifting jobs. Beginning with the first job, if the job is cleared (i.e., it does not contend resource with other jobs) it will be inserted into a partial schedule; otherwise, either delay this job or a different job to the following day. The criteria of choosing which job to delay is based on their relative compensation cost. This process continues until all the jobs are cleared and inserted into the partial schedule that eventually becomes a complete schedule.

Figure 6 illustrates such a process. The upper layer shows the result of job ordering after Step 1 and the solid black arrows indicate the elected jobs to be delayed to the following day; the lower layer shows the result of a complete schedule.

As with FIFO, Pairwise Shift method is also a linear method and has a computational complex-

Figure 6. Illustration of pairwise shift method to minimize compensation cost

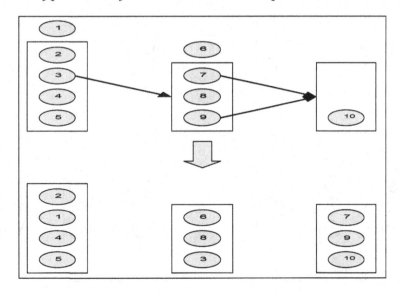

ity of $O(H \times (UB\text{-}MLT))$. Its difference from FIFO is that it considers compensation cost during job allocations, which potentially offers more optimal job allocation scheme.

However, Pairwise Shift can by no means guarantee an optimal solution. The way in which it organizes jobs and pairwise-shifts them are also very random, which represents only one of many possible job allocation schemes. In addition, Pairwise Shift has a significant limitation in that it is only capable of shifting jobs between adjacent resource pools. In more general cases, compensation cost reduction could be achieved by shifting jobs to longer distances.

Tabu Search

The job allocation schemes obtained from heuristic procedures such as FIFO and Pairwise Shift are quite random and would not normally be used directly; instead they are treated as initial solutions for *Tabu Search* (Weng & Sedani, 2002), which intelligently explores the neighborhood of the job allocation schemes to yield improved solutions if they exist.

The basic idea of Tabu Search is to slightly alter a known (current) solution and take the best obtained alternation as the new current solution. To avoid being trapped in local optima, the best neighbor that is worse than the current solution is allowed to become the new current solution. To avoid cycling, certain moves are marked as Tabu. This procedure continues till a stopping criterion is met; the stopping criterion could be a limited number of iterations or some threshold method.

A typical operation that moves the Tabu Search from current solution to its neighboring solutions is to use *Pairwise Swap* (Weng & Sedani, 2002). Figure 7 illustrates two possible neighbors from the current solution, where Neighbor 1 is obtained by swapping Job 1 and Job 9, Neighbor 2 by Job 5 and Job 7.

Figure 8 illustrates a possible path of Tabu Search from an initial solution to a final solution, where the solid arrow lines indicate the chosen path and dotted arrow lines show other possible moves at different states.

Tabu Search (Glover & Laguna, 1997) belongs to the class of Local Search (Wikipedia, 2009) algorithms that are typically incomplete algorithms,

Figure 7. Generating neighbors in Tabu Search via pairwise swap

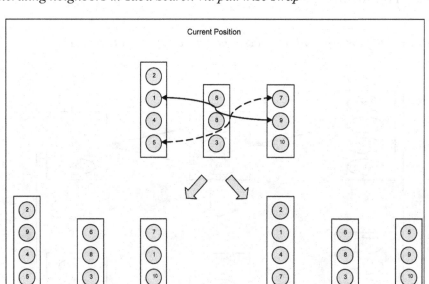

Figure 8. Search for a near-optimal solution in Tabu Search

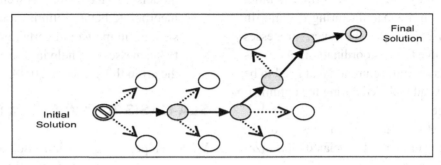

as the search may stop even if the best solution found by the algorithm is not optimal. In other words, there is no guarantee that Tabu Search can render optimal solution and the quality of final solution is highly dependent on that of the initial solution. Such a method is often opportunistic, best applicable to situations where decent initial solutions have been found and bet for chances for further improvement on those solutions. Generally speaking, the computational complexity of Tabu Search is the same as its search space, i.e., exponential or $O(UB- MLT)^H$.

Further Research Tracks and Directions

In this section, we reviewed some typical optimization methods that have been applied to the problem of minimizing delay compensation cost. In its general form, such a problem is often termed in the literature as "sequencing with earliness and tardiness penalties" (Baker & Scudder, 1990), where penalties are applied not only to tardiness but also to earliness and the durations of jobs may vary. This kind of problem has its origin from manufacturing industry where factory workshops continuously deal with mono-type of orders that arrive in volumes; both early and late completions of products would incur costs to manufacturers.

Service business resembles manufacturing business in many aspects, yet it is also typically different from the latter in that services are highly customer-interactive, time conscious and process coordinative, where service providers interact directly with customers at the front-end and coordinate timely various activities at the backend to render services. Here, the timing of services and accurate service level agreements in general are of paramount importance. Missing product delivery deadlines in manufacturing could still make products usable albeit with increased storage costs, but missing service delivery deadlines would result in total waste of service resources.

Given the state of the art in the field, to render industry-strength SLA optimization capabilities, more R&D effort yet needs to be spent in the following areas:

- More efficient and effective optimization algorithms. Existing optimization algorithms such as FIFO (Wikipedia, 2009), Pairwise Shift (Mannur & Addagatla, 1993) and Tabu Search (Weng & Sedani, 2002) often falls short to render optimal solutions and/or are too time-consuming to operate in real time. In order to facilitate service enterprises to decide optimal SLAs in real time, more efficient and effective optimization algorithms need to be devised.
- Coupling with complex business processes. Existing work in the area of sequencing with earliness and tardiness penalties (Baker & Scudder, 1990) mostly concerns with single-activity processes rather than

multi-activity ones, as the former is more common in the manufacturing domain. In the service domain, however, processes that involve timely coordination of various activities are more common that need to be modeled and included during the optimization stage.

- Incorporating elaborate business models. Existing work on SLA-related optimization such as common due date assignments and scheduling (Shabtay, 2008) often assumes a simple business model that does not consider counter-acts between business elements. As discussed in Section 2.4, there are intricate interdependencies among business elements in the context of service operation, which needs to be represented and reasoned to derive more accurate business values.

- Service chain optimization. Modern service industry accounts for between 50% and 80% of total value add in the developing and developed economies (Wolfl, 2006). There is increasing number of complex service chains that link service enterprises together via service level agreements. Existing work related to SLA optimization (Shabtay, 2008) has been limited to individual service enterprises and fail to understand the roles of sustainable SLAs in reducing volatility and number of breakdowns in the service chains.

- SLA optimization toolkit. To date, there is no out-of-box toolkit that can perform SLA optimization functions for service enterprises and service chains. Due to lack of tool support, current SLAs are derived from manual negotiations with service customers; as a result, these are often subjective and incapable of reflecting the real capabilities of service enterprises. Comprehensive toolkits that can model service level agreements, complex business processes, enterprise resource plans, elaborate business

models, service chains, as well as that can incorporate better optimization and analysis algorithms would certainly add values to businesses and help improve the state of the art in this field (Li, 2008).

SLA-OASIS Toolkit: An Example

We developed a SLA optimization and analysis toolkit for service chains, code-named SLA-OASIS, to address the deficiencies in this area. In its current version, the user can model and configure individual services and their parameters, as well as optimize SLAs to generate best business values. Figure 9 – Figure 12 show edited service parameters for PSTN provision; Figure 13 – Figure 15 show SLA optimization results.

In Figure 9 we define the minimum lead time for PSTN provision as 2 days; the standard lead time for PSTN provision as 5 days, which is priced at 10 units of local currency. For every delayed day, there is an add-up penalty of 1 unit of local currency. A forecasted seven-day demand, in term of number of PSTN orders, under these terms, arriving on each calendar day is also configured.

In Figure 10 we configure volume of planned resource that can fulfill PSTN activity across each calendar day. Also configured is the cost of each unit of resource across every day in a week.

In Figure 11 we configure business process for PSTN provision. In this case there is only a single business activity that requires resource type "PSTN". This is due to the fact that the provision of PSTN can be taken up by an individual field technician.

In Figure 12 we configure some business model parameters. In the section of *standard lead time configuration*, for instance, we define a linear, bounded function to model the impact of lead time adjustment on the change in customer demand. In the *standard lead time* dimension, the bound is given by *standard lead time lower bound* and *standard lead time upper bound*; in the *customer demand* dimension, the bound is

Figure 9. Service level agreement for PSTN provision

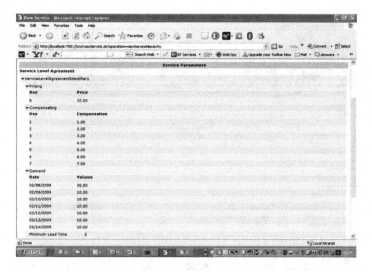

Figure 10. Enterprise resource plan for PSTN provision

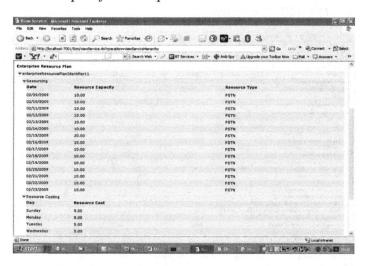

given by *maximum market boost percentage for standard lead time* and *maximum market loss percentage for standard lead time. Standard lead time increment* defines the granularity of discrete space in which search for optimal standard lead time can be conducted.

In Figure 13 we show the results of lead time optimization and analysis. In the upper section, it shows the existing configuration of standard lead time, 5 days, and calculated service revenue, resource cost, delay compensation and net busi-ness value, in this case 400.00. In the middle section, it shows the optimal standard time, which is 4 days, and associated business value, which is 497.00. Also can be seen are the projected right-first-time percentages, 28% and 100% for optimal and original scenarios respectively. The right-first-time measures indicate the likelihood of orders being delayed; in some scenarios, to delay an order may prove to be better off than to reject an order, as the income generated from the order could well offset the delay penalty.

Figure 11. Business process for PSTN provision

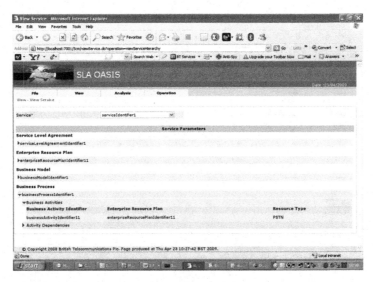

Figure 12. Business model for PSTN provision

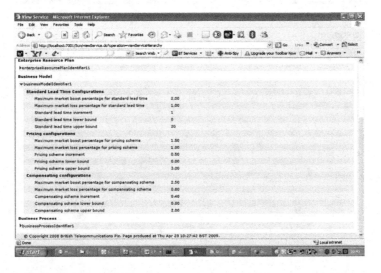

In Figure 14 we show the results of optimal pricing, 15.00, which gives a business value of 630.00. This is considerably better than the original, 10.00, which give a business value of 400.00.

In Figure 15 we show the results of optimal delay penalty scheme, which is 1.2 times higher than the original scheme. The optimal scheme gives a business value of 553.00, which is better than the original scheme that gives a business value of 400.00.

In this section we can see some use cases of SLA-OASIS toolkit in configuring enterprise service and its associated parameters, and optimizing SLA-related parameters such as lead time, pricing and delay penalty. Through such a toolkit, the user can perform what-if analysis, for instance, topping-up resources to see how it can help reduce lead time, or increasing demand to see how it can force lead time to increase, etc. In this way, the toolkit can assist service enterprises to

Figure 13. Lead time optimization

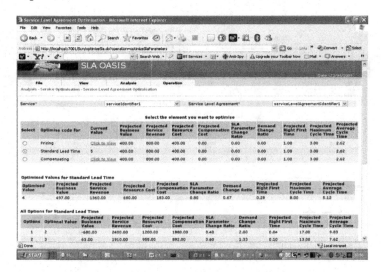

Figure 14. Pricing optimization

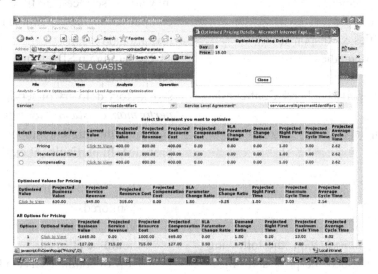

decide the most competitive yet economic service level agreements that they can set up with their customers.

SLA CONTRACT DRAFTING

Once SLA terms are decided between the service provider and service consumer, the next step is to draft a SLA contract between the two parties for legal protections. In this section, we go through typical contents related to SLA contracts and toolsets for helping draft SLA contracts.

Contents of SLA Contracts

The contents of a typical SLA contract would include the following sections:

- Introduction
- Scope of Work
- Performance, Tracking & Reporting

Figure 15. Delay penalty optimization

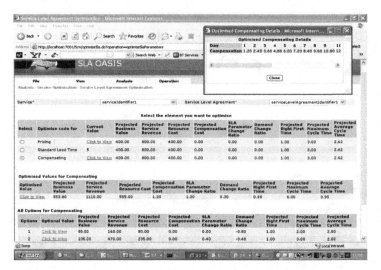

- Problem Management
- Compensation
- Customer Duties & Responsibilities
- Warranties & Remedies
- Security
- Intellectual Property Rights & Confidential Information
- Legal Compliance & Resolution of Disputes
- Termination
- General
- Signatures

In the section of *introduction*, the following aspects are often provided: purpose and objectives, parties to the agreement, commencement date, duration of the agreement and definitions. From SLA perspective, this defines to whom and for how long the SLA terms are bound.

In the section of *scope of work*, the nature of the service is specified, followed by the availability and the place of service delivery. For large service enterprises, these would normally refer to service lead times across various geographical locations. In order to provide a level of flexibility, the contract could also include terms on changes to the service, e.g., service enterprises

may adjust service lead times, pricing and delay compensation due to demand fluctuation or other operational reasons.

By setting up SLA terms such as service lead times in the contract alone would not guarantee satisfactory delivery of service. In the section of *performance, tracking & reporting*, methods of enforcing the implementation of those terms are provided. In particular, it explains

- How each individual service will be monitored,
- What benchmarks, targets and metrics should be utilized,
- How to conduct service level reporting,
- How to organize service review meetings.

There are bound to be problems occurring during the execution of services. In the section of *problem management*, types of such problems are defined; contact of service support desk is provided; route of problem escalation is given. In the events where problems are caused by service customers or they were not covered in the original specifications, compensations to service providers apply. In the section of *compensation*, it tells categories of professional fees, procedure of invoicing and payment, and interest for late payment.

As services involve direct interactions between service providers and service consumers, it is important that service customers also take responsibilities of their duties. In the section of *customer duties and responsibilities*, it states customer duties that involve clients' personnel, facilities, resources and training on specialized equipments. In the section of *security*, it would emphasize on physical and logical accesses to client facilities and resources, compliance with client security policies and measures of disaster recovery.

In the events where SLAs have been breached due to, for instance, problems cannot be resolved, remedies apply. In the section of *warranties and remedies*, it defines quality of service, indemnification of any damages by the service provider or third parties, and remedies for breaches which often involve reasonable efforts to restore service to good operating conditions on an urgent basis and payments of penalties and refunds as defined in the contract.

In addition to SLA-specific terms, a proper SLA contract also covers some other general legal aspects. In the section of *intellectual property right & confidential information*, it specifies who owns intellectual property rights generated from the work, and confidentiality policies related to data and records, etc. In the section of *legal compliance & resolution of disputes*, it outlines general aspects of governing law, export control, arbitration, and limitation of liability.

Finally, in the section of *termination*, it specifies criteria, causes and payment on termination of the contract and SLA terms. In the section of *signatures*, both parties sign off the contract to make it legally effective.

Toolset for Drafting SLA Contracts

The SLA Toolkit (SLA-World, 2002) contains a set of resources to help service providers create service level agreement contracts without specific legal expertise in this area. It contains the following resources:

- SLA Template.
- SLA Interactive Guide.
- SLA Introduction Presentation.
- SLA Audit and Review.
- Service Level Management Presentation.

Service Level Agreement Template contains a complete set of clauses for SLAs; each clause can be accepted 'as is' or edited to reflect a specific need. Each section of the template is also linked to the relevant section of the *SLA Interactive Guide* in order that the author can refer to the guidance provided before finalizing each section of his/her own specific agreement. The template is provided in MS-Word format, so that the author can edit freely and save as a separate document as wished. Figure 16 illustrates the layout of *SLA Interactive Guide* and its relationship with *SLA Template*.

SLA Introduction and *Service Level Management Presentation* contain presentation slides on SLAs and related issues. *SLA Audit and Review* provides a comprehensive checklist or questionnaire to audit and review existing SLAs. Figure 17 illustrates a fraction of SLA checklist.

SLA COMPLIANCE TRACKING AND REPORTING

After SLA terms become contractual, we move to SLA implementation stage, where SLAs are kept monitored to ensure their compliance. Nimsoft (NimBUS, 2007) is a handy toolkit for SLA monitoring and reporting. Figure 18 illustrates the architecture of Nimsoft.

The contractual SLA, in the form of either written or verbal, is fed into the *NimBUS SLA Templates*, where SLA metrics can be transposed by configuring an array of out-of-box mathematical formulas for SLA compliance calculations. Immediately after SLA metrics configuration, NimBUS automatically generates and distributes

Figure 16. SLA interactive guide and SLA template

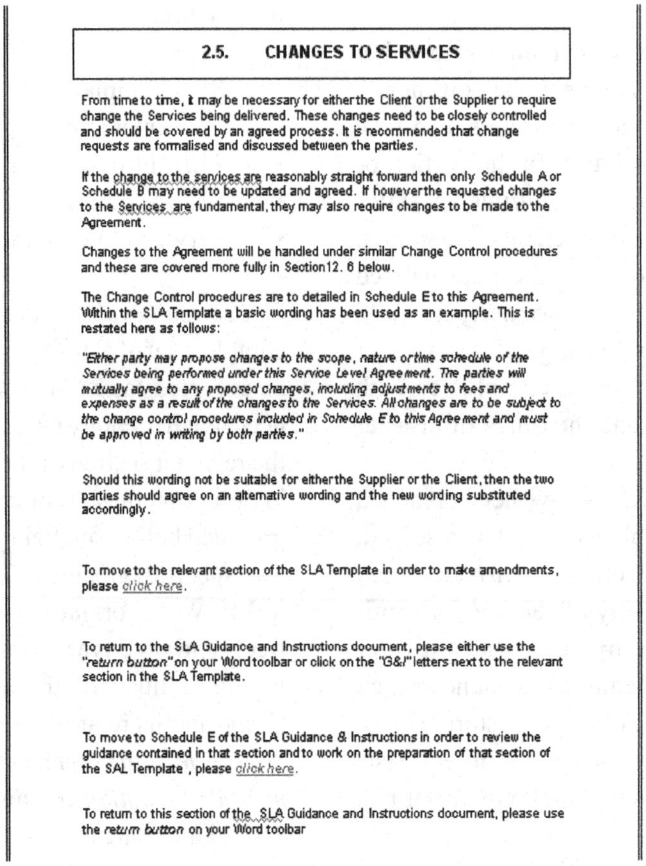

> **2.5.   CHANGES TO SERVICES**
>
> From time to time, it may be necessary for either the Client or the Supplier to require change the Services being delivered. These changes need to be closely controlled and should be covered by an agreed process. It is recommended that change requests are formalised and discussed between the parties.
>
> If the change to the services are reasonably straight forward then only Schedule A or Schedule B may need to be updated and agreed. If however the requested changes to the Services are fundamental, they may also require changes to be made to the Agreement.
>
> Changes to the Agreement will be handled under similar Change Control procedures and these are covered more fully in Section 12. 6 below.
>
> The Change Control procedures are to detailed in Schedule E to this Agreement. Within the SLA Template a basic wording has been used as an example. This is restated here as follows:
>
> *"Either party may propose changes to the scope, nature or time schedule of the Services being performed under this Service Level Agreement. The parties will mutually agree to any proposed changes, including adjustments to fees and expenses as a result of the changes to the Services. All changes are to be subject to the change control procedures included in Schedule E to this Agreement and must be approved in writing by both parties."*
>
> Should this wording not be suitable for either the Supplier or the Client, then the two parties should agree on an alternative wording and the new wording substituted accordingly.
>
> To move to the relevant section of the SLA Template in order to make amendments, please *click here*.
>
> To return to the SLA Guidance and Instructions document, please either use the *"return button"* on your Word toolbar or click on the "G&I" letters next to the relevant section in the SLA Template.
>
> To move to Schedule E of the SLA Guidance & Instructions in order to review the guidance contained in that section and to work on the preparation of that section of the SAL Template , please *click here*.
>
> To return to this section of the SLA Guidance and Instructions document, please use the *return button* on your Word toolbar

SLA compliance reports. In this section, some key features of Nimsoft are introduced.

Multi-Point Data Aggregation and Analysis

Critical to effective SLA monitoring and reporting is full access to status data representing the end-to-end service infrastructure; this also requires access to end-user quality of service metrics and service desk performance statistics. *Nimsoft Probes, Gateways, and Adapters* provide this broad data access and consolidates this information into the *Nimsoft Quality of Service (QoS) database* where the data becomes available for *Nimsoft SLA compliance calculation and reporting*.

Template-Driven SLA Definition

Nimsoft contains graphical SLA templates that facilitate SLA definitions. Examples of such configuration include *compliance period* (e.g., 1 day, 1 week, 1 month, 1 year), *operating period* (e.g., "9am to 5pm, Monday-Friday", or "7×24 except Sundays"), *compliance threshold* (e.g., 98.5%).

The *Nimsoft SLA Compliance Calculation Engine* uses mathematical formulas to analyze and summarize QoS data points according to users SLA definitions. For instance, *SLA Compliance Formulas* include: Best, Worst, Sequential, Average, Weight, AND, OR. *QoS Compliance Formulas* include: Interval, Median, and Average. All the compliance methods and formulas can be customized to create and satisfy unique SLA compliance calculation requirement.

Figure 17. SLA audit checklist

No.	Question	Yes	No
5.3	Does the SLA cover payment terms for charges?	☐	☐
5.4	Does the SLA include statements concerning the payment of taxes arising out of the agreement?	☐	☐
5.5	Does the SLA include notification of penalty interest for late payments?	☐	☐
6.0	**CUSTOMER DUTIES AND RESPONSIBILITIES**		
6.1	Does the SLA include information on the clients responsibilities for providing access, facilities and resources?	☐	☐
6.2	Does the SLA cover Client responsibilities for providing training to their personnel on operating technical or specialised equipment?	☐	☐
7.0	**WARRANTIES AND REMEDIES**		
7.1	Does the SLA include a warranty in respect of quality of service?	☐	☐
7.2	Does the SLA include a indemnification in respect of supplier negligence?	☐	☐
7.3	Does the SLA include a warranty in respect of copy rights, patents and trade secrets?	☐	☐
7.4	Does the SLA exclude responsibility for client errors contributing to such infringements to third party copy rights, patents or trade secrets?	☐	☐
7.5	Does the SLA include information in respect of remedies for breaches?	☐	☐
7.6	Does the SLA contain a Force Majeure clause?	☐	☐
8.0	**SECURITY**		
8.1	Does the SLA allow for reasonable physical access to be provided to the suppliers representative?	☐	☐

With Nimsoft, it is possible to define single or grouped SLAs, each having their own compliance thresholds defined according to different types or classes of service. Such SLA grouping features allow for organizing SLAs by branch office, customer, business unit, geography, etc.

Figure 19 illustrates an example of template-driven SLA definition.

Automated Web-Based SLA Report Generation

Nimsoft's web-based service level reports display current SLA compliance and forecasted breach. The user can

- View real-time compliance indicators for grouped SLAs;
- Drill down on individual SLA to see its service level objectives (SLOs) and SLO compliance against defined metrics;
- Drill down on individual SLO to see QoS data against defined threshold;
- View past SLA compliance performance.

Figure 20 illustrates some screenshots of these functions. The Nimsoft SLA reporting and moni-

Figure 18. Architecture of Nimsoft for SLA monitoring and reporting

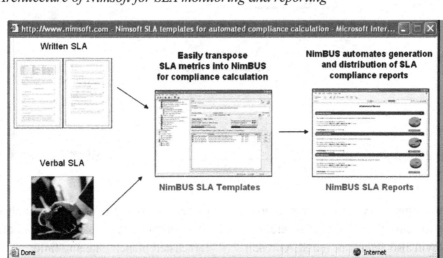

Figure 19. An Example of template-driven SLA definition in Nimsoft

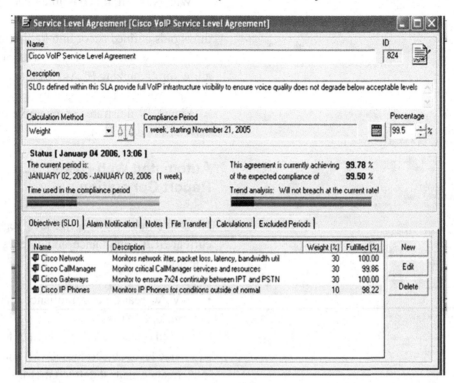

Figure 20. Some screenshot of Nimsoft SLA reporting functions

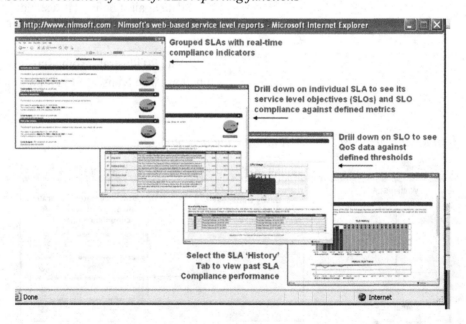

toring solution continuously perform calculations to determine if the current period SLA is safely in compliance; it will also determine if a SLA breach is imminent if a problem condition is allowed to persist. Nimsoft SLA reports include color-coded SLA compliance/breach trend indicators with forecasted breach date and time.

CONCLUSION

In this chapter, we walked the reader through the state of the art of the lifecycle management of service level agreements, which covers stages of terms optimization, contract drafting and compliance tracking.

In contrast to SLA contract drafting and compliance tracking where there are mature out-of-box toolkits available to help automate some of the most tedious tasks, there is no such tool commercially available for SLA terms optimization. To this end, the author outlined some R&D tracks that aim to produce industry-strength SLA optimization capabilities. An initial version of SLA-OASIS toolkit has also been reported to illustrate such a concept.

The author envisages that such an effort will help close the loop in the entire lifecycle of SLA management for service enterprises, where an improved level of automation can be realized across terms optimization, contract drafting and compliance tracking, thus help improve the productivity of service enterprises and maintain a less volatile, more profitable service chains.

REFERENCES

Baker, K., & Scudder, G. (1990). Sequencing with Earliness and Tardiness Penalties: A Review. *Operations Research, 38*(1), 22–36. doi:10.1287/opre.38.1.22

Encyclopedia (2007). *Service Level Agreement*. Retrieved fromhttp://www.nationmaster.com/encyclopedia/Service-Level-Agreement European Committee for Standardization (2007). *CEN Horizontal European Service Standardization Strategy (CHESS)*. Retrieved from http://www.cen.eu/cenorm/sectors/nbo/value/chesss/index.asp

Glover, F., & Laguna, M. (1997). Tabu Search, Norwell, MA: Kluwer.

Li, Y. (2008). Service Productivity Improvement and Software Technology Support. In *Proceedings of 32nd Annual IEEE Computer Software and Applications Conference*, (pp. 807-812).

Lovelock, C. (2007). Service Marketing: People, Technology, Strategy. Upper Saddle River, NJ: Prentice Hall.

Mannur, N., & Addagatla, J. (1993). Heuristic Algorithm for Solving Earliness-Tardiness Scheduling Problem with Machine Vacations. *Computers & Industrial Engineering, 25*(1-4), 255–258. doi:10.1016/0360-8352(93)90269-4

NimBUS. (2007). *NimBUS for SLA Monitoring and Reporting*. Retrieved from http://www.nimbuspartners.com/content.php?name=home.html

Shabtay, D. (2008). Due Date Assignments and Scheduling A Single Machine with A General Earliness/Tardiness Cost Function. *Computers & Operations Research, 35*(5), 1539–1545. doi:10.1016/j.cor.2006.08.017

Weng, M., & Sedani, M. (2002). Schedule One Machine to Minimize Early/Tardy Penalty by Tabu Search. Retrieved from http://fie.engrng.pitt.edu/iie2002/proceedings/ierc/papers/2208.pdf

Wikipedia (2009). *Brute Force Search*. Retrieved from http://en.wikipedia.org/wiki/Brute-force_search

Wikipedia (2009). *First In First Out*. Retrieved fromhttp://en.wikipedia.org/wiki/FIFO

Wikipedia (2009). *Local Search*. Retrieved from http://en.wikipedia.org/wiki/Local_search_(optimization)

Wolfl, A. (2006). Productivity Growth in The Services Industries – Patterns, Issues and the Role of Measurement. In Lipsey and Nakamura (eds.), Service Industries and the Knowledge Based Economy. Calgary, Canada: University of Calgary Press.

World, S. L. A. (2002). *SLA Toolkit*. Retrieved from http://www.sla-world.com/

Chapter 15
Cyber Transportation Logistics:
Architecting a Global Value-Chain for Services

Yupo Chan
University of Arkansas at Little Rock, USA

Charles-Henri Fredouët
School of Logistics, ISEL, France

Jaouad Boukachour
School of Logistics, ISEL, France

Hing-Po Lo
City University of Hong Kong, China

Chia-Chu Chiang
University of Arkansas at Little Rock, USA

Farhad Moeeni
Arkansas State University, USA

Madan Mohan Dey
University of Arkansas at Pine Bluff, USA

Albert K. Toh
University of Arkansas at Pine Bluff, USA

ABSTRACT

In today's global economy, products and services are provided across international borders. The sourcing of these products and services becomes an integral part of international businesses. Information, communication and transportation technologies (ICTT) have made this job significantly more streamlined. However, there is an advantage that big companies, such as Wal-Mart, have over small and medium size ones. While the big companies have the ICTT resources to source globally at will, small and medium enterprises (SME) are much less prepared to do so, resulting in a large competitive disadvantage. By contrasting SMEs with their more successful "big brothers," we highlight the salient ICTT features in a system architecture. This serves as a checklist for any assistance that might be rendered to SMEs and other entities in overcoming their competitive impediment. These findings are the result of numerous international workshops and conferences held in Hong Kong (the export city for a bulk of the Chinese consumer products) and in Arkansas (the headquarters of Wal-Mart).

DOI: 10.4018/978-1-61520-603-2.ch015

INTRODUCTION

In today's information and technology based global economy, the world experiences significant changes in the supply of goods and services. In the United States, call centers are not necessarily located domestically, but across the globe, including India. The biggest global retailer, Wal-Mart, imports a majority of its shelf items from China. In the last count, American Wal-Mart stores import approximately $15 billion in goods from China each year. Outside the US, Wal-Mart stores are currently located in nine countries. There is an unexpected connection between the former rice paddies in Southern China (now a major manufacturing region for consumer goods) and the remote Ozark Mountains (where Wal-Mart is headquartered). Supply chains are also critical to the public sector, as evidenced from recent experience with natural disasters such as Katrina in the US Gulf Coast and the disastrous earthquake in western China. In these instances, more can be done in delivering relief items to those dislocated in a timely and targeted fashion. The subject of *Cyber Transportation Logistics* aptly captures the interplay between e-commerce, shipments and services across the globe, robust and automatic systems of identification, and the complex worldwide supply chain for goods and services in general.

On an intellectual level, there is a mutual interest amongst selected industries in Arkansas (AR) and Hong Kong, where cyber-transportation-logistics industries are located. As mentioned, AR is the home state for Wal-Mart. Little Rock, AR is also the home for the Acxiom Corporation, a worldwide company specializing in data mining, data warehousing and consumer-market analysis. Memphis, Tennessee (TN), the international headquarters of Federal Express (FedEx), sits at the eastern border of AR. American Freightways, which provides ground operations for FedEx, is based in Harrison, AR. Among competing freight carriers—TNT, UPS—FedEx boasts the first

exclusive right to serve within China, providing a direct air link to the US. Situated at the Pearl River Delta, Hong Kong is the main export hub for Chinese consumer products. While a majority is shipped by boat, high-end items are airlifted through Hong Kong, which is the air-cargo hub of Asia, and in particular, China—the fastest growing economy in the world. We contend that a cyber-transportation-logistics case-study based on this scenario covers the salient Information, Communication, and Transportation Technology (ICTT) factors to provide some useful insights.

On an academic level, research ideas were initiated first from reciprocal faculty visits between the City University of Hong Kong (CityU) and the University of Arkansas at Little Rock (UALR), between the School of Logistics (ISEL), Le Havre, France, and the Arkansas State University. This is followed by a series of workshops and conferences. This chapter summarizes research and instructional discussions and findings resulting from these joint workshops and conferences over the last five years. These discussions include those that took place in FedEx in Memphis, TN, a Wal-Mart Distribution Center in Bentonville, AR, Acxiom Corporation in Conway, AR, the International INFORMS Conference in Hong Kong, an Identity Solutions Symposium at Arkansas State University in Jonesboro, Arkansas, and an International Conference held in the Rockefeller Conference Center on top of Petit Jean Mountain, AR. While this paper focuses on the highlights, supplemental information can be found at the website: http://syen.ualr.edu/metalab/research/.

PRIORITIES

With the advent of information/communication technology and efficient transportation, it is an understatement that the world economy is now totally interdependent between even distant lands. For example, as the U. S. and Hong Kong transition from manufacturing-based to knowledge-based service economies, there are fundamental changes in organizational structures in similar places around the globe—including operational, decision and control, and behavioral changes. Under this scenario, the authors have the unique opportunity and responsibility to reexamine the important subject of *Cyber Transportation Logistics – Architecting a Global Value Chain for Services*. The classic supply chain problem has been researched by a number of authorities (Bowersox et al. 2007, Chopra & Meindl 2007, Coyle et al. 2009, Mangan et al. 2008). However, the core problem—namely identifying a more general paradigm on the technological factors for success—has yet to be overcome.

Two major paradigms of Supply Chain Management have been proposed (Li, 2008). The first is a traditional three-stage view, involving procurement, conversion, and distribution. The second is a three-flow view, which involves financial, information, and product flows (Ding et al., 2007; Lau et al., 2007). The basic structure of today's supply-chain/logistics (SC/L) typically includes three major components: operational (information flow), decision and control (planning, sourcing and procurement decisions), and behavioral (human-system interface, relationship management). Effective integration of these components will generate the product/service value flow between SC participants such as sellers and buyers (or suppliers, logistics providers, and customers) within the SC/L network (Bowersox et al. 2007).

The core issue can be simply phrased as a cost-benefit incidence problem, i.e., the person who pays for the costs may not be the only one that obtains the benefits. To the extent that goods and services change so many hands in a supply chain before it reaches the ultimate consumer, all participants in the chain share in the costs and the benefits. In other words, it is the *values* they gain that bring the willing partners to participate in this "chain." Pick the supply-chain security problem as an example, which has gathered full attention

after the tragic event of 9/11. The participants in security assurance—whether they are the governmental bodies, the public, or the businesses—all benefit from the resulting safety and security. However, it is not so clear who should shoulder the blunt of solving this problem. It is not clear that the party that tends to the weakest point in the chain, the "Achilles heel," should be the only one responsible. A secure supply chain benefits and adds value to each party in the chain. This problem is compounded many times in a global market place involving many disparate economies, organizations, and in the lightning speed of e-commerce and supersonic travel.

Sprouting from this cost-benefit issue are many unresolved technical and technology-generated questions. For example, what are the different types of economies that participate in the supply chain (Martinez-Olvera, 2008)? Are the company's ICTT technologies robust enough to facilitate the e-commerce that results from such a supply chain? This is irrespective of whether the participant is a multinational corporation such as Wal-Mart, or a "mom-and-pop" manufacturer in Arkansas or China. In this case, technological components range from the streamlined brokerage between suppliers and consumers afforded by today's information and communication infrastructure to in-transit visibility as the shipment cross international borders. The authors contend that these questions can be answered by addressing the following research and educational thrusts. Each of these thrusts addresses a void in current research and educational activities—voids that, when filled, allow a system architecture for cyber transportation logistics (CTL) to be designed.

- E-commerce for Small and Medium Enterprises (SME),
- Seamless Enterprise Application Integration (EAI),
- In-transit visibility in the cyber space,
- Information quality and its relationship to Entity and Identity Resolution,

- Security assurance,
- Modeling and simulation technologies, and
- Educational implications (including Training and Technology Transfer).

Although the concept of Internet portals, trade exchanges, trading networks, and business-to-business (B2B) electronic marketplace is not new (Benjamin et al., 1995; Kaplan & Sawhney 2000; Pare 2003), and SC/L automation has been attempted for several years, e.g., e-SC portal (Boyson et al. 2003), electronically-enabled SCs (Yao et al. 2007), and inter-firm information systems in SCM (Karkkainen et al. 2007), concrete operational system that integrates e-marketplace with SC/L functions are still few in number (Trappey et al., 2007; Nucciarelli et al., 2008; Wang et al., 2007).

Cyber Transportation Logistics (CTL)—as envisaged here—goes beyond the traditional seller-operated or buyer-operated systems and the current generation of electronic marketplace. It integrates supply chain and logistics functions in an on-line trading infrastructure. By identifying this infrastructure, assistance can be rendered to serve SMEs to make them compete effectively in the global market place. Let us provide some examples on how this can be possible. To assist SME in their value-added competitive advantage, various automated SC/L capabilities can be incorporated into this framework, e.g., Collaborative Planning Forecasting and Replenishment, Vendor Managed Inventory, RFID, and SC Analytic software.

E-COMMERCE FOR SMALL AND MEDIUM ENTERPRISES

According to RSM McGladrey (2009), a leading national accounting, tax and business consulting firm, small- and medium-size manufacturers in the US are not enthusiastically responding to globalization. In a recent survey, only 25 percent said that globalization helped them lower cost.

A little more than 40 percent said globalization forced them to lower the prices of their products. Less than 10 percent use state incentive programs to modernize their businesses, even though there are many that are available. This is different from multi-national large corporations (such as Wal-Mart), whose businesses are built explicitly upon globalization.

Setting aside companies like Wal-Mart, 95% of the Arkansas firms have less than 100 and 87% less than 20 employees (Table 1). These firms are facing at least three obstacles: the inability to acquire the necessary capital, the lack of leverage or relationship to bring other SMEs on board for creating a coordinated supply chain, and the lack of expertise and knowledge. This is by no means limited to Arkansas. Other states in the US have similar problems. The authors further suggest that the SMEs in China are not exempt from these problems. The question is asked: How can the SMEs be better served by providing them with a potentially improved cyber-enabled capability to compete with larger companies in the global marketplace (de Haan et al., 2007; Dehning et al., 2007).

In both the Arkansas and Chinese settings (and elsewhere), one recognizes the important role a sizable number of SMEs play in their respective economies. In Arkansas, many of these SMEs provide agricultural and manufactured products to a variety of customers, including Wal-Mart. Situated in the Pearl River Delta Region, Hong Kong's important manufacturing sector is moving increasingly toward a coordinating role for less expensive products made elsewhere in China, particularly by the SMEs in the Pearl River Delta. Chinese SMEs account for the majority of the "Made in China" labels found on the shelves of Wal-Mart, as there are no such giants as General Motors and General Foods in China (Wu & Olson, 2008).

Aquaculture is an important SME industry in Arkansas. The state of Arkansas leads the nation in production of baitfish, is third in catfish production and has a long history of commercial fish farming.

Table 1. Distribution of firm sizes in Arkansas(Source: 2005 statistics of U.S. businesses data, U.S. Census Bureau)

Size	Number	Percent	Cumulative
Firms with 0 to 4 employees	30,956	58%	58%
Firms with 5 to 9 employees	9,763	18%	76%
Firms with 10 to 19 employees	5,679	11%	87%
Firms with 20 to 99 employees	4,576	9%	96%
Firms with 100 to 499 employees	1,090	2%	98%
Firms with 500 employees or more	1,550	3%	101%
Total	53,614		

About 97% of baitfish farms and 90% of catfish farms are classified as small businesses by the US Small Business Administration. Markets and marketing issues are at the forefront of the aquaculture industry in Arkansas today (Engle et al., 1990; Engle et al., 1991; Hatch et al., 1991; House et al., 2003; Kinnucan & Miao, 1999; Kinnucan et al., 1988; Kinnucan & Venkateswaran, 1990; Olowolayemo et al., 1992; Raulerson & Trotter, 1973; Rauniya et al., 1997). In order to expand markets for catfish and baitfish, it is essential to design products that match consumer preferences and to encourage consumers' recognition and acceptance of new or different products.

Today, staying ahead of the competition means making the most of limited resources and planning effectively to identify and select new opportunities. This requires better planning using a web of facilities and activities enabling the flow of goods from raw materials to finished products and finally to the customers. Solutions from the supply chain analysis can help the industry to discover and exploit the hidden opportunities in the chain by leveraging enterprise data for tactical and strategic planning. Understanding and facilitating the chain of supply from farmers to consumers (buyers) is critical.

Identification of inefficiencies in the supply chain can lead to targeted solutions that match production and demand. Customer requirements and global competition have made supply chain design more challenging and complex than ever before. The increasing pace of change is driving a need for business flexibility to develop strategies and tactics to satisfy customer demand while balancing limitations on supply and the need for operational efficiency. There is a great interest in electronic marketing of catfish and baitfish in Arkansas, to expand the market and to maintain communication between farmers and their buyers. Though some aquaculture farmers use internet for marketing activities, e-marketing of aquaculture is in its infancy.

The catfish industry in the US is facing a variety of challenges, including low-price imports and a climate of increasing regulations. Three broad strategies exist for responding to these trends. First, US catfish farmers could focus their attention on becoming a low-cost producer of catfish and compete on the basis of price. Given the higher input (feed, land, labor) costs versus other producing countries (such as China and Vietnam), this strategy is not likely be effective. Second, non-business actions could be taken by the government to increase protectionism. Such a strategy is likely to have a low probability of success given the current global trade environment that emphasizes free trade and reducing barriers to trade. Third, catfish farmers in the US can become much more consumer responsive in their marketing strategies and responsiveness in reaching the consumers. This way, they compete on the high level of consumer benefit and value delivered. Given the inherent problems with the first two options, the third strategy appears to be more appropriate for the catfish industry in the US.

Over the last several years, various studies have been conducted on catfish market and marketing (Dellenbarger et al., 2006; Drammeh et al., 2002; Quagrainie, 2006; Quagrainie & Engle, 2002a; Quagrainie & Engle, 2002b). However, the catfish industry has yet to develop pragmatic marketing strategies to meet the challenges ahead. So far, catfish marketing research has not been an integral part of catfish market development. There is a need for action research on e-marketing of catfish, where research activities will be implemented in partnership with the industry and research findings will be directly incorporated into market development efforts.

Marketing is the most important aspect of baitfish production. Retail price of baitfish is 10-15 times higher than the wholesale price. In other words, the consumer pays 10-15 times the money received by the farmer. One of the reasons is that baitfish are sold as a live product that requires extensive distribution system. The US baitfish industry has a very strong customer service orientation; the industry standard for customer service is to replace any fish losses incurred by the delivery intermediaries (Engle & Quagrainie, 2006). The live baitfish industry is also increasingly facing barriers to the interstate movement of the product. The Arkansas State Authority has recently launched a baitfish certification program to provide high quality and pathogen-free farm-raised baitfish. Based on the experience in e-marketing of other SMEs (Gilmore et al., 2007), it appears that Internet and e-marketing has a potential for marketing of Arkansas baitfish. At the same time, more can be done to streamline the distribution, delivery system.

Farm-retail price spread (calculated as the farm value share of the retail price) for farm-raised aquaculture products is around 15-20% (Engle & Quagrainie, 2006).). The marketing bill (or the difference between what the consumer pays and what the farmer receives) for US farm-raised catfish is very high. Figure 1 shows the monthly real farm-raised channel catfish prices at the producer and processor level, and the marketing bill cost for the period 1986-2003. Electronic marketing of aquaculture products and more streamlined delivery mechanism in general will help reducing intermediary cost, and thereby enhancing competitive advantage.

Figure 1 Monthly real farm-raised channel catfish prices (Source: adopted from Wiese, 2004; original data from USDA-NASS)

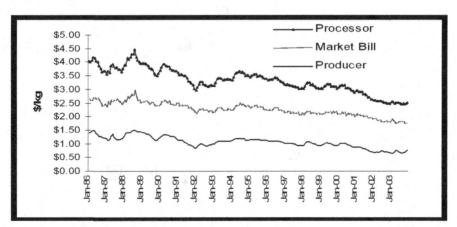

According to the University of Pennsylvania's Wharton School, Supply Chain Enterprise Systems—information, communication and management technologies that support supply chain functions—have become a central element of management strategy. Implementing these systems, however, is often a difficult undertaking with an uncertain outcome for different enterprises.

EVOLUTION OF E-COMMERCE

Here are some observations on e-commerce that is encouraging (Chu et al. 2007). The literature labels the period before 1990 as the pre-Web era. Then it was too soon to take advantage of the Internet and was a time of closed, pre-arranged, one-to-one, business-to-business commerce. In the early 1990s, e-commerce emerged with the following stages, as illustrated in Figure 2.

The initial stage is marked by the circle symbol ○: Although WWW communication had opened, a request for information was still one-way. Businesses could only react to requests. The second stage is marked by the square symbol □: Need

arose for the interactive two-way negotiation of buy–sell transactions. By tracking the footprint of a participant, cookies allowed interactivity. The third stage is marked by the triangle symbol Δ: Web sites had become both marketplaces and management platforms. It became possible to improve collaboration, strategic alliances, and one-stop business services.

To summarize

- Early 1990s was the reactive Web era
- Mid 1990s was the Interactive Web era
- Start of the 21st century launched the integrative Web era

The numerical values in Figure 2 were the count of respective core functions that had occurred in the surveyed years, expressed in terms of percentages. The symbols (circle, square, and triangle) represented core functions of reactive, interactive, and integrative nature, respectively. It can be seen that the reactive era ended around 1995, the interactive era spanned between 1996 and 1998, and the integrative era began in 1999.

Figure 2. E-commerce core functions: 1993-2001 (Chu et al. 2007)

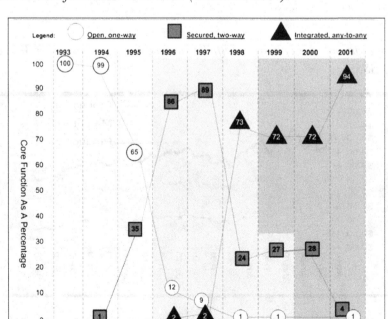

Low-cost country sourcing, outsourcing, customization and globalization are adding tremendous complexity to supply chains across the globe. Two key supply chain elements that are often taken for granted—coordination and collaboration—can mean the difference between the merely functioning and the profitable enterprises. The authors are referring to procuring goods and services from vendors around the world and delivering them to global consumers as fast and inexpensively as possible. Depending on the sourcing requirements, some responsibility for supply chain logistics may rest on the shoulder of the enterprise that places the order, not just the shippers. Our observation is that the SMEs, compared with larger enterprises, are ill prepared to take on this responsibility.

There are similarities and differences between the suppliers in the distribution of products. Again take the manufacturers from the Pearl River Delta, as well as the Arkansas suppliers. The former heavily cater for consumer products. The latter are more mixed, which includes agricultural products. According to Li (2008), low level of trust among supply-chain partners hampers information sharing in China. A win-lose perspective is prevalent between Chinese suppliers. Generally, there is a low level of visibility over inventory and demand, and a lack of process standardization and data transparency. By contrast, take the example of a cooperative industry such as Riceland in Arkansas, the largest rice-processor in the world. It is made up of many individual farmers (Ketchen & Hult, 2007), who work in a cooperative to supply the rice crop. Tyson at Springdale, AR, the largest meat processing in the world, is similarly made up of many constituent chicken farmers. These two sites—Arkansas and China—located at the opposite sides of the globe, create interesting parallels, contrasts, problems, opportunities and mutual relationships that deserve to be explored.

SEAMLESS ENTERPRISE APPLICATION INTEGRATION

To enhance the value-adding services to participating partners, the users of people-oriented e-SC/L system is a crucial factor in the efficient, effective and efficacious operation of the network. Human Factors Engineering can contribute to the design, development, and evaluation of this endeavor. Internet-based SC/L system has changed the traditional open-market negotiation in business relationship to one that facilitates dynamic coordination across the supply chain through information exchange and on-line collaboration (Barratt, 2004; Meroño-Cerdan et al., 2008). This enables not only cooperation among trading partners, information linkages can also be achieved through vendor managed inventory and EDI exchange (coordination) while supply chain integration among trading partners can be achieved through joint planning and shared gains/loss/investments (collaboration).

On-line coordination and collaboration in a distributed e-SC/L environment presents not only human factors design issues but also organizational issues of group or team interaction, and behavioral issues of cross-cultural collaborative commerce within a globally networked SC. In addition to the human elements of decision making and information processing, a significant value-chain area for the efficacious operation of the system is the relationship-based strategy of collaboration (Coyle et al., 2009). An e-SC/L platform can facilitate not only effective collaboration by enabling share use of information and mutual business benefits, it also has the potentials for establishing trusting relationship between participating trading partners in the network. Proper implementation of e-SC/L can help to remove suspicion on the part of SMEs about global commerce, and help to negate the win-lose perspective of competition among SMEs.

Going beyond human/systems interface issues, an equally important problem is Enterprise Application Integration (EAI). Enterprise applications usually consist of applications written in different programming languages, running on different platforms, and communicating to each other through different networks. In order to support daily business operations, these applications—including legacy software—need to be integrated. New applications also need to be integrated to provide efficient and reliable data exchanges among these enterprise applications. Software interoperability (Wegner, 1996) is a fundamental concern to the development of enterprise applications.

Several middleware technologies have been widely used for EAI including CORBA (CORBA, 2009), Microsoft COM/DCOM (DCOM, 2009), .NET (Microsoft .NET 2009), and Enterprise JavaBeans (Enterprise JavaBeans, 2009). The middleware technologies offer a potential solution to interoperability problems but also produce new issues such as interoperability of distinct middleware implementations (Chiang, 2001). The problems include different syntax and semantics of the interfaces. Nevertheless, the differences in the interfaces sometimes can be resolved by developing an interface adapter to convert one to another and vice versa. But very often, the fix usually leads to multiple versions of applications. Eventually, it will become difficult for software developers to maintain the consistency in the enterprise applications.

The web services technology (Webservices, 2009) has been proposed to solve the problems of EAI by connecting applications run by different companies in the supply chain. The technology provides a standard way of interfacing different applications in a seamless manner. Heterogeneous applications are exchanging messages in an XML document where a program sends a request to a Web service across the network, and receives a reply from another program. The reply is also in the form of an XML document. Thus, with Web services, companies are allowed to publish their services to their customers and suppliers and make their applications interoperable for e-commerce.

It is without a doubt that legacy applications should not be ignored when EAI is discussed. It is definitely not a good idea to suggest companies to rewrite their legacy applications for integration. One cost-effective way is to develop a wrapper around the legacy applications interfacing the Web services (Chiang, 2007). A wrapper is built to encapsulate a legacy system and provide access to the legacy system through the encapsulation layer. This layer exposes only the methods with parameter attributes to remote service requesters. In addition, the wrapper must resolve the incompatible communication issues between the legacy systems and the Web server using SOAP/XML messaging. The implementation details of the wrappers for web services integration can be found in Chiang (2007).

IN-TRANSIT VISIBILITY TECHNOLOGIES

In the first Gulf War in the early 1990's, the U.S. and her coalition partners poured an overwhelming amount of supplies to Kuwait before launching a swift war against Iraq. In spite of a lopsided technological advantage over the enemy, several lessons can be learned from the war. The most commonly known lesson is the lack of *in-transit visibility*. This refers to the unknown contents of tons and tons of supplies that were dropped off by ships, planes, and ground transport. The popular press labeled it "just in case" delivery, instead of "just in time" delivery, as supplies piled up unclaimed. Fortunately, the coalition had the luxury to begin the war at a time of its own choosing, which in effect mitigates this acute shortcoming.

In-transit visibility has progressed significantly since the first Gulf War. Prime examples are found in FedEx and UPS. Through a number of technologies, including GPS and fast communication, customers can easily find out the whereabouts of their shipment by clicking on the designated webpage. In-transit visibility is a sales advantage, highly touted by FedEx, which introduced the practice, and followed by many other just-in-time shippers (Chan & Ponder, 1979). In fact, it goes well beyond shippers, Riceland in Jonesboro AR handles its sales shipments in the same fashion.

While the global supply chain are adopting newer bar-code technologies such as two-dimensional and reduced-space codes, smart ID tags, or RFID, may gradually replace some or most bar code application for entity identification and product tracking. The process is gradual because there remain quite a few outstanding technical and non-technical issues (such as standards, security, privacy, and policy). Aside from RFID, there are quite a few competing identification-tracking technologies. UPS has watched RFID for 15 years but did not see it as an imminent solution to the problem of parcel tracking. In test runs, UPS found that RFID tags did not surpass the accuracy rate of bar code scanners. Moreover, an RFID rollout—including tags and a new technological infrastructure—would be quite costly. UPS decided that they could not simply replace optical scanners with an RFID reader and expect an improved return on investment. There have to be fundamental process changes to leverage the RFID technology, which are considerable at the present time (Ojala & Hallikas, 2006).

As a solution, 25,000 portable bar-code scanner/terminals—a competing technology to RFID—are in place at 400 UPS sites. In so doing, UPS has created one of the world's largest Wirelesses Local Area Network. Bluetooth and Wi-Fi connectivity are also being incorporated into the handheld computers carried by UPS drivers. The new electronic clipboards, first deployed in April 2005, allow a driver to receive last-minute delivery or route changes via a truck's receiver. Previously, updates came from putting the clipboard in a cradle inside the truck, which limits its portability.

When it comes to global supply chains, the potential for disruption comes in many forms, from large-scale natural disasters and terrorist attacks to plant manufacturing fires, electrical blackouts, and operational challenges such as bureaucratic requirements and red tape and shipping ports being too small to handle the flow of goods (Bogataj & Bogataj, 2007). In two representative site visits—to the Hongkong International Terminal (HIT) and the Memphis Airport operations of FedEx—it is clear that the security issue is paramount in the post-9/11 global trade. In HIT, the port capacity is also taxed to the limit, necessitating vertical stacking of container boxes.

To avoid choke points in the supply chain, containerization represents a transition in shipping technologies. Compared to the 40-ft containers, the U.S. standard of 53-foot containers is a more cost-effective way to ship freight. Sometime soon, an entrepreneur will invest billions of dollars to construct a fleet of vessels designed to handle only 53-foot equipment. China manufactures almost all of the 53-foot container units, and many are dispatched loaded with Chinese cargo. If China decides to adopt the 53-foot unit as the standard for its own internal transportation system, and to serve the commercial interests of trade between China and the US, the freight transportation map of the world will change. It appears that the days of the 40-foot container standard in international trade are coming to an end. This comes at a time that China is vying with others in the standardization of RFID technologies, often used in conjunction with containerized shipments.

One notable application of RFID in the supply chain is the tracking of assets and inventory items in real time within a facility. Such capability allows preparing efficient pick lists, efficient dispatching and routing of fork trucks and vehicles within warehouses and manufacturing facilities, efficient shelving of inventory items and much more. These solutions are known as real-time location-sensing or RTLS (Moeeni, 2008). RTLS may employ various RF tag types like passive, active, etc.

A study by Aberdeen Group (Aberdeen Group, 2009), shows that firms using RFID deliver complete and on time to 98% (against 81% for others), that traceability is made up in 2.5 hours (compared with 34 hours) and that manufacturers which use RFID make 99% in full compliance their products (compared with 86%).

However, in most of today's RFID implementations, there lacks an easy-to-use and cost-effective way to integrate a company's RFID equipment and its backend systems to enable it to enjoy the improvements in supply-chain management (SCM) that RFID technology can provide. Moreover, the cost of RFID implementation is much higher than in traditional automatic identification technology (Chen & Chen, 2007). The authors had identified three gaps:

1. An information gap exists due to the disparity of information models
2. A transaction gap exists due to the disparity in information transaction methods and
3. An authorization gap exists due to the disparity in authorization requirements.

To resolve the gaps, a middleware, RFID Application Enablement (RAE), is developed using an object-oriented approach. Object orientation enables encapsulation structured business objects that encompass RFID memberships, monitoring object conditions and defining object behaviors in terms of RFID operations and publishing RFID object information. The draft recommendation (ANEC BEUC, 2008) shows some promising measures focusing on privacy, data protection and security in the implementation of these RFID applications.

As seen in the case of Wal-Mart, SMEs may be pressured by large retailers and other players to implement RFID technology in order to comply with a prescribed information technology (IT) infrastructure and processes. Research can be employed to integrate RFID technologies with shop-floor control software for SMEs. When ex-

ecuted in conjunction with e-commerce portals, it would enable products to be tracked in real-time across the entire supply chain—all the way to the consumer (Niederman et al., 2007).

Chu et al. (2007) have proposed a "4th Party"—beyond the manufacturer, the consumer, and the regular third party broker—to use web-based e-commerce technology to coordinate activities throughout the supply chain. If the cost-benefit incidence problem is to be addressed, a "fourth" party broker can be employed for SMEs to minimize cost. This breakthrough will allow SMEs to compete effectively with larger enterprises in executing the various parts of the supply chain, which they can ill afford to do presently. In addition, a cost-benefit analysis of RFID implementation in SMEs operations may further help SMEs to gain competitive advantage in their particular markets (Leung et al., 2006).

INFORMATION QUALITY IN ENTITY AND IDENTITY RESOLUTION

Identification and tracking technologies can certainly play an important role for in-transit visibility, security assurance and storage retrieval. The real question, which is alluded to in the SME discussion above, is the respective role of the manufacturer, the shipper, the retailer, vis-à-vis the carrier in minimizing shipping "choke points" and ensuring security. This is not a simple question to answer when it comes to the incidence of costs and responsibilities. In other words, does a choke point at a port facility affect only port operations, or does it affect every party in the supply chain and, in turn, may determine the length of the queue of ships to be unloaded in Long Beach Harbor in California? Is it the sole responsibility of the port operator to address this problem, or the collective responsibility of all the parties?

HIT in Hong Kong is one of the largest transportation terminals in the world, being a terminal operated by the venerable Hutchison Port Holdings, Ltd. Strategically located in the Pearl River Delta, their shipment is destined globally from Long Beach to Rotterdam. Since 9/11, HIT has been visited numerous times by the U.S. Department of Homeland Security as part of a global war on terrorism. Since they all belong to the same company, the idea of developing a data network among the forty to fifty Hutchison terminals in the world is very appealing. Acxiom, a long established data-warehousing enterprise based in Little Rock, would definitely be able to contribute their knowledge and expertise in this area.

It is well documented that inaccurate, incomplete, inconsistent, and out-of-date information create operational errors, poor decisions, and damaged customer relations. This could cost government and industry billions of dollars a year, and transportation and logistics information is not immune from these thorny issues. For example, concerns for privacy conflict with accurate entity identification and tracking. The profusion of geographic subdivisions ranging from census tracts to traffic analysis zones often introduces inconsistencies in geo-spatial data coding, which lead toward errors in goods delivery and tracking. More precision can be achieved through geo-spatial technology based on GPS, GIS, relational database management systems and RFID principles.

The quality of information created, shared and the decisions made via the macro processes—including Internal Supply Chain Management, Customer Relationship Management and Supplier Relationship Management (Chopra & Meindl 2007)—is as good as the quality of the input data. Industry studies (GS1, 2009) show that two thirds of product information has data-quality problems. It has been long established that data entry through keyboard is extremely error prone. Bar-coding technology has substantially improved data quality. It also contributed to the efficiency of data-entry process. Bar-code standards, including the Global Trade Item Number (GTIN, a superset of the Universal Product Code or U.P.C.), Global Location Number (GLN), and several others have significantly contributed to the accurate and unique identification of various entities and objects during transaction-information exchange.

The EPCglobal organization (EPCglobal 2009) is currently overseeing various standards and protocols for the supply-chain implementation of RFID. Passive, backscatter RF tags, referred to as class 1, generation 2 (C1G2), functioning at the ultra high frequency (UHF) is currently supported by the standards. Passive tags are by far less expensive than semi-passive or active tags. UHF passive tags also offer the highest read range compared to other frequencies such as high frequency or microwave for the same level of allowable output power. The vision is to create an RFID-based network that acts as the nervous system of the supply chain for linking the physical world directly to the decision-making process. In Figure 3, Object Naming Service (ONS) is a database and look up service based on Domain Name System (DNS), which is a hierarchical naming system for computers, services, or any resource participating in the Internet. EPC Information Services (EPCIS) is an EPCglobal standard designed to enable EPC-related data sharing within and across enterprises. Together with EPC middleware, the system allows a streamline operation between manufacturers, distributors, and retailers. The automatic identification, transaction recording and tracking of trade items contributes to the quality of data and better supply-chain decisions by eliminating many intermediate agents and manual processes.

Future EPCglobal network, which encompasses ubiquitous low-powered, sensor-equipped, RFID networks that are connected through the Internet, will create new capabilities for managing the supply chain with potential strategic implications. It will provide unprecedented quality information in real time, including:

Figure 3. EPCglobal network architecture for track and trace

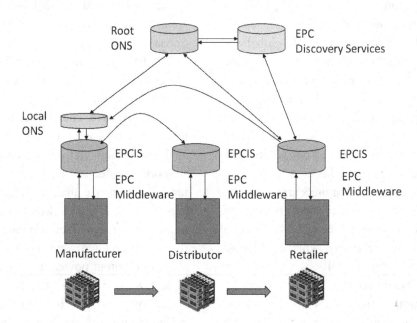

- expiration date of a given bottle of milk in the refrigerator,
- a recalled batch of hotdogs,
- the contaminated shipment of spinach,
- variation in the temperature of individual boxes of ice cream during transit
- air quality at a particular road intersection,
- traffic-flow data of an Interstate,
- the imminent failure of a pacemaker
- the location of the nearest ambulance, fire truck or police patrol vehicle.

However, current research in customer-centric information-quality management suggests that most organizations still practice "tactical data-quality management." Tactical data-quality management implies that an organization reacts to adverse data-quality events as they are discovered, in many cases by its customers. On the other hand, "strategic data-quality management" attempts to define data-quality requirements across the entire information system from data contributors and collectors, through key processes, to the delivery of the final data product. Moreover, the attainment of these requirements is assessed through periodic measurements of data quality in order to facilitate continuous quality improvement and to detect problems before data is released to customers. Data-quality/information-quality will soon be an important issue for most organizations, whether large enterprises such as Hutchison Port Holdings or SMEs. Meanwhile, interested universities could participate in this emerging topic in terms of both research and teaching (Wang, 1998).

To overcome the challenges faced by SMEs in adopting and implementing e-commerce, the CTL framework—with its on-line trading platform that includes a fourth-party logistics services—can facilitate electronic transaction by bringing together not only sellers and buyers but also shippers and carriers to collaborate on their supply chain and logistics planning. It applies information, communication and e-commerce technologies in supporting a range of SC/L activities such as e-procurement, multiple sourcing, supplier selection, collaborative planning, disruption management, and supply chain visibility (Chu et al., 2007; Pare, 2003).

The system environment not only improves connectivity among trading partners but also allows companies to communicate and collaborate in a globally networked supply chain within a single streamlined trading platform with a common user interface. By leveraging on Internet and other information and communication technologies, users of this system (e.g., logistics managers or SME owners) can access multiple sub-systems (modules) within and across the particular enterprise. This neutral and secure web-enabled trading platform adds values to the participant parties in areas such as information exchange, product visibility, and process optimization which in turn reduce inventory, decrease delivery times, and improve inventory turnarounds.

SECURITY ASSURANCE

Since the 9/11 tragedy, the supply chain security risk has been gaining fast-growing interest: global supply chain managers have started to fear that the logistics networks might be used as targets of, and/or vectors for, further terrorist attacks, leading to deep and long-lasting disruptions in the supply chains that would add to those already caused by ill-operated procurement processes, capacity constraints, and/or quality issues in factories. Therefore, global supply chain vulnerability has become a capital issue for all of the logistics networks' partners, and security is now an unavoidable high-performance factor for supply chains.

In such a context, with the growing pressure from national and international regulation bodies to enhance security, Supply Chain Management has to address an end-to-end issue: achieve a cost-effective and lead-time efficient design of

the complete SC, while at the same time including relevant security requirements, and leveraging real-world information to both assess the security level and enforce the security requirements.

A large variety and great quantity of products are in transit from diverse origins to numerous destinations. Increasingly, these products are shipped in containers, and maritime container transportation has become the premier transportation mode for the manufacturing industry. In 2002, the International Container Bureau (BIC) estimated the number of containers world-wide number as 15,000,000. Each day, those millions of containers, each carrying more than 20 tons of products, are conveyed to and from seaports on trucks, rail carriages, barges and ships. Efficient and reliable such flows may be, this huge volume of container movements, besides significantly increasing the complexity of the global maritime transportation system (Robinson 1998), poses formidable security challenges to freight and people.

Containers have for a long time been used for clandestine immigration, illegal weapons smuggling and drug smuggling. However, the associated risks (Tsai, 2006) and possible consequences are incomparable to those associated with weapons of mass destruction. A solution is to design and implement an expert system dedicated to maritime container security risk management. The approach encompasses the three core elements of (1) risk modeling, (2) risk assessment and (3) risk management (Bechini et al. 2007, GOST 2009). Risk modelling is process-based. It is an "activity-resource" model well suited for logistics systems analysis and the associated security-centric performance monitoring. The data-collection methodology followed at this stage is case-based, within a set of typical SCs involving internal (e.g., Port of Le Havre) and also external logistics actors. The processes taken into account go from the origination port to point of destination (for imports) and from point of origin to the destination port (for exports).

Risk assessment is addressed with reference to such security-dedicated standards as food industry Hazard Analysis and Critical Control Points. Associated with it is the military-born Failure Mode and Effects Analysis, which is a risk assessment of reliability widely practiced in the aerospace and automotive industries. Risk management is taken care of through the implementation of an expert-system coupling a database to a knowledge base. The database is fed with real-time and automatically collected information from the monitored logistics operations. The knowledge base is fed with the expertise of, among others, customs / police / immigration agents, lawyers, and port authorities. To optimize container transit security and facilities, the expert-system inference engine first interprets information on the incoming (from sea or from land) container and then presents a solution for dealing with each cargo, on the basis of available expert knowledge.

The expected impacts of the project at the technical and scientific levels are numerous.

- development of a service for securing the transport of cargo (better monitoring of sensitive materials and protection against malicious acts)
- Integrating sensors such as RFID, from different origins, embedded in a system of traceability and complete protection
- Development of an electronic platform with shared interfaces to the platforms of existing owners and
- Implementation of an innovative solution.

For all users, the platform offers productivity gains by optimizing the links in the transport chain. The prototype offers the potential for global service traceability and security of the transport chain. Ultimately, it offers the potential for the development of an "information system port," transferable to other port communities, either locally or globally.

As the World Customs Organization (WCO) progresses with the implementation of the WCO SAFE Framework of Standards to secure and facilitate global trade, parameters of the Authorized Economic Operator (AEO) programs are developed. Supply-chain compliance-software provides electronic collection, standardization and organization of supplier information, allowing the user to efficiently collect information required for AEO certification. Such a system may bring the cost down for SMEs who are inevitably part of the security picture.

MODELING AND SIMULATION TECHNOLOGIES

This chapter proposes IT solutions for Cyber Transportation Logistics (CTL). These include the existing IT enterprise business applications and information sharing among organizations. Enterprise Resource Planning (ERP)—broadly defined here as the science of enterprise planning, management and execution—has progressed significantly over the last two decades or so. The "curse of dimensionality" in solving these business problems has been tempered by a number of advancing techniques, including the use of asymptotic error bounds (Bramel & Simchi-Levi 1997), and a priori/robust optimization (Bertsimas & Simchi–Levi 1996, Laporte et al. 1994). Capitalizing on grid computing and the semantic web concept, today's knowledge base and E-platform allow step-by-step procedures to perform the following functions: (a) site location, (b) location-routing, (c) competitive allocation of products/services, and (d) spatial economic forecasting. They are some of the key analytic ingredients in CTL.

Chan (2005) showed that there is an emerging science in capturing most of these analysis functions. For example, many of these procedures can be captured in the judicious use of a *weight matrix* for location and allocation. Such a framework can be used to analyze *spatial equilibrium*, or the resulting trade patterns among participating enterprises. This is accomplished through competition and gaming in spatial dynamics, analyzing market share and geographic coverage. User vs. system optimization, as illustrated in the Braess' Paradox, can be generalized to other contexts, showing the results of competition vs. collaboration among SMEs. These results include Cournot–Nash equilibrium for user optimization and monopolistic-market equilibrium for system optimization respectively. Furthermore, regional and international input-output economic-development implications can be ascertained within this analytical framework. This is particularly important for venture capitalists and governments that are considering investing in a public e-trading platform. In view of the significant advances in this field, other management-science contributions toward analyzing this subject can be found in the list of references in Chan (2005).

Meanwhile, three-dimensional (3D) virtual worlds, like Second Life (SL), provide a simulation platform to investigate smart-world domains like CTL. TagCentric was first developed, which is an agent-based RFID middleware available on SourceForge. A project at the University of Arkansas (http://vw.ddns.uark.edu) is investigating ubiquitous computing, location-aware systems, virtual RFID, massive use of sensors, smart devices, workflows, ways of merging reality and virtual reality, and means of talking to devices using natural language. The potential impact of testing these technologies in a simulated world before deployment could lower costs and accelerate the pace of technological change.

EDUCATIONAL AND TRAINING IMPLICATIONS

A focus of this chapter is to show how information, communication, and transportation technologies (ICTT) play a role in global commerce. Using ICTT, we envision a CTL system architecture for global commerce. While large enterprises are well positioned to be a prominent member of CTL, SMEs are much less prepared to do so at the present time. While we paint an encouraging picture, it is clear from the above discussions that the CTL has many technical and non-technical components that discourage SME participations. One such component is education and training for the SME work force. Today's CTL work-force requires these educational and training support:

- Logistics work-force development to endow workers with familiarity and appreciation for today's ICTT
- Science, Technology, Engineering and Mathematics related enhancement for under-represented groups
- Logistics education/training on modeling-and-simulation, including virtual-reality technologies.

To show the cogency of this issue, FedEx, JB Hunt, Wal-Mart and the National Science Foundation has funded the Mid-America Transportation Center (MATC) in Arkansas to train the work force required for today's logistics industries. MATC educates and trains students in all of the three support functions for e-SCL. While the first two of the three functions are self explanatory, the third needs some explanation.

As explained, there are two major paradigms for SCM:

- Three-stage view, which consists of procurement, conversion, and distribution
- Three-flow view, consisting of financial, information, and product flows

Furthermore, it was suggested that a departure from the traditional three-stage view of supply chain management to embrace the three-flow view. Financial derivatives such as options and future contracts can help SC partners to mitigate the risk in raw materials and capacity shortage.

Furthermore, the authors provide information-based research and data-quality management best practices to the majority of CTL enterprises, including SMEs, IT-intensive industries, nonprofit and governmental bodies.

Educational institutions are starting to embrace this interpretation of SCM. Online simulation games now are used to introduce the financial-flow implications to students. For example, the Responsive.Net Simulator combines cash-flow position with lot size and lead time, with some analysis regarding the optimal ordering policy. It considers adding production capacity at different points in the simulation.

Harvard Business Publishing's SCM simulation combines cash flow with product design, vendor selection and procumbent management strategies. It also includes justification for contingency actions, such as change of contracts or an interim marketing survey.

SOME COGENT THOUGHTS

Cyber transportation logistics is a realization of the shipment of goods or the delivery of services in cyber space. It includes the IT process of planning logistics services and its subsequent integrative management. These services are implemented to facilitate the pervasive accessibility of logistic information online (Li et al., 2007). Key logistics functions such as shipping, inventory management, customer-relationship management utilize interdependent information and can be managed more effectively with integrative data service. On top of these traditional functions is the outreach to consumers who are the ultimate decision-makers that drive the entire supply chain. As mentioned, Chu et al. (2007) proposed Web-based services to replace the third party service provider, called the 4th party, that directly serving the seller and buyer in a supply chain. Another worthwhile activity may be advancing related identification-

tracking technologies to go beyond the current stalemate that surround RFID implementation. These efforts will have monumental impacts on information-based manufacturing, logistics and security assurance. While large retailers such as Wal-Mart already have this service in place, the less well-endowed SMEs do not. Apparently, the Department of Defense also needs such a service, as evidenced from the delivery of materiel and supplies during the first Gulf War.

To successfully implement a workflow in an organization, there are four fundamental elements (Karmarkar & Apte, 2007):

- Data Base Management System
- Work Flow Management System
- Administration and Monitoring (access control mechanisms, especially those that are related to other organizations)
- Applications (providing services, such as ERP)

On top of these is a partners' coordination tool, which shares the data between different administrative and monitoring elements of the organizations in a collaborative relationship. Such coordination is necessary in such partnership as Riceland, and to some extent Tyson, both of which are based in Arkansas (as mentioned). The higher the degree of coordination, the better the SC performance, which is manifested in a lessened bullwhip effect, lower inventory levels, less transportation overheads, a lower manufacturing capacity requirement, and other considerations. However, it also makes keeping the information secret more difficult, and privilege-propagation conflicts are also an issue.

In the design, development, and implementation of the CTL system, human factors research will need to be carried out to ensure human-users/CTL system equilibrium. Two areas of focused research are proposed, which are consistent with the modeling-and-simulation focus under CTL:

1. Design of Natural Human-Agent Interaction – The main goal is to evaluate appropriate forms of interaction for CTL system users. These users work closely with intelligent agents, which are used to support the delegated information processing on behalf of the human users (Nam et al., 2009; Scholtz, 2002).

2. Modeling Team Decision-Making in Multi-Cultural Contexts – Cultural background significantly influences the way humans select, interpret, process, and use information (Marks et al., 2001). Common cognitions among team members and their effective communication process are closely associated with team effectiveness (Cannon-Bowers & Salas 2001). Human Factors research can investigate the effects of cultural differences on team performance, behaviors, and team cognition (e.g., communication, shared mental model, etc.). In a global marketplace, any step to facilitate decision-making in a multi-cultural SC is mandatory.

While the state-of-the-art has progressed in the subject of CTL, SMEs have not taken advantage of the technology. This is particularly so in China (Li, 2008). SMEs in China have almost non-existing e-Commerce capability. Subpar transportation networks are prevalent, where distribution channels are inefficient, fragmented, and costly. There are no national distributors but a plethora of small and medium-sized local wholesalers. There are simply too many "nodes" in supply networks. For the Chinese labor force, there is weak professional identity among those who work in this field. There is only low awareness of the benefits of scientific SC planning and execution. Financially, the Chinese currency is not freely convertible. Department of Foreign Currency regulation encourages underground banks. Payment process hampers financial flows, eventually slowing down product flows. There is an increasing demand for better payment solutions and supplier/buyer certification agents.

Entry of international companies into Chinese markets maybe one solution. Carrefour, with 4.3 billion dollars in sales, ranked sixth among all retailers in China in 2007. Its sales were up 24% over the previous year. At a sales volume of 3.1 billion dollars, Wal-Mart has increased its store sales in China by 42% in the same period. Hong Kong, serving as the Chinese window to the developed countries, has a unique role to play in technology, business practices and manpower development for China.

LOOKING AHEAD

Globalization, technology and an ever-changing world create significant challenges and opportunities for SC management and logistics execution. To succeed, change and innovation are necessary, as painfully evident in the US "rust belt" associated with automobile manufacturing. Operating in the emerging global market, SMEs are increasingly required to effectively coordinate and cooperate with potential trading partners. E-marketplace approach can be an enabler for SC and serve to facilitate collaboration between SC partners through information, communication and transportation technologies (ICTT). Unlike a generation ago, knowledge-based technology drives today's supply and demand market. The opportunities for educating/training the work force and in advanced research are there waiting to be harnessed.

The world is converging toward the development of robust and automatic systems of in-transit visibility. Just as computers on the Internet are uniquely identified by IP addresses, objects, locations, transactions would be uniquely identified through GPS, smart cards and wireless information and other systems. The movement is stimulated by the ever-increasing need for operational streamlining, as well as accuracy, security, quality in capturing data and in the authentication process. One objective is to improve shipment efficiency, to prevent fraud, save lives, and protect properties. Another objective is found in location-based services, where telecom companies are vying to provide travelers with information ranging gas-station locations to where to eat lunch, not to say ascertaining the whereabouts of individuals or objects of interest.

With today's communication network, E-commerce has been gradually evolving into Mobile Commerce (Ngai et al., 2007). Examples include location-based services, mobile financial applications, and product locating and searching. It is clear that more research is warranted for these constituent enabling technologies: wireless network infrastructure, mobile middleware, including data stream management, database management, and wireless user infrastructure (such as mobile handheld devices). (Ngai & Gunasekaran, 2007)

As the World Customs Organization (WCO) progresses with the implementation of the WCO SAFE Framework of Standards to secure and facilitate global trade, parameters of the Authorized Economic Operator (AEO) programs are developed. Supply-chain compliance-software provides electronic collection, standardization and organization of supplier information, allowing the user to efficiently collect information required for AEO certification. Here are some issues raised by Wigand (2006):

- How to develop an AEO program for SME businesses, which do not have an advanced ERP system?
- AEO redesign process only works if legislation is changed at an international and national level.

For Chinese SMEs, for example, intellectual property protection is weak. There is a proliferation of forged brands. However, Hong Kong has restrictive laws and regulations on Intellectual Property protection. As a gateway to the outside world, again it can serve as a knowledge hub to address this problem on behalf of China, including the provision of ERP services for AEO (Pibernik & Sucky, 2007).

A large number of case studies on e-commerce in SME conducted over the last few years (e.g., Poon & Swatman, 1997; Henderson, 2001; Baourakis et al., 2002; Vlosky & Westbrook, 2002; Abate & Moser, 2003; Alexander et al. 2003; Chau, 2003; Cordeiro, 2003; Galloway et al. 2004; Grandon et al. 2004; Henderson et al., 2004; Holmes et al., 2004; Yasin et al. 2006) show that e-commerce offers SMEs significant operational and strategies opportunities. But, the implementation of effective e-commerce based business model in SMEs is not without serious organizational and technological challenges. For catfish and baitfish industries in Arkansas, various university campuses are keen to provide leadership and guidance to develop strategies for electronic marketing and physical distribution of these aquaculture products, which will keep these industries competitive and improve the welfare of the stakeholders concerned.

The rapidly evolving global SC is creating a historic demand for a technological workforce to support all components of this system. The educational and training implications of this revolution are profound. To achieve this goal requires workers who have skills not only in transportation, distribution, and logistics but also in GPS, GIS, identification technologies, Database Management Systems, and financial flow.

It is clear that sound solutions to the CTL problem require a holistic, multinational and multi-disciplinary approach that engages the talents of universities, industries and governments around the globe. The authors' goal is to marshal the interests not only of the university community, but also the industries and governmental bodies that can benefit from the results of a cooperative, entrepreneurial, educational and research activity.

ACKNOWLEDGMENT

This chapter is a combined effort of all the participating universities in the CTL consortium. We wish to acknowledge the intellectual inputs from all our colleagues across the globe. We wish to thank Radu Babiceanu, Sunny Morris, C. S. Nam, and Craig Thompson for their inputs. Hank Campbell conducted a careful editorial review of this chapter at the last stage of our writing, and provided many useful inputs. Funding sources include Grant 06-CAT-01 by the Arkansas Science and Technology Authority to the Delta Center for Identity Solutions at Arkansas State University. Much of the intellectual foundation of this chapter is based on several International Workshops on CTL; the most recent one took place at Petit Jean Mountain, AR in 2008, funded jointly by the Winthrop Rockefeller Institute and the University of Arkansas at Little Rock. The work on Security Assurance was funded by the French Research Agency and the French Region Haute-Normandie.

REFERENCES

Abate, G., & Moser, C. (2003). *E-commerce and Internet use in small businesses: Trends and issues*. (Staff paper 2003-04). Michigan State University, Department of Agricultural Economics. Retrieved June 28, 2009, from http://www.aec.msu.edu/pubs.htm

Aberdeen Group. (2009). *Aberdeen Group*. Retrieved June 28, 2009, from http://www.aberdeen.com/

Alexander, C., Pearson, J. M., & Crosby, L. (2003). The transition to e-commerce: A case study of a rural-based travel agency. *Journal of Internet Commerce*, *2*(1), 49–63. doi:10.1300/J179v02n01_05

ANEC & BEUC. (2008). *Radio frequency identification* (RFID). Retrieved June 28, 2009, from http://www.anec.eu/attachments/ANEC-ICT-2008-G-017final.pdf

Baourakis, G., Kourgiantakis, M., & Migdalas, A. (2002). The impact of e-commerce on agro-food marketing: The case of agricultural cooperatives, firms, and consumers in Crete. *British Food Journal*, *104*(8), 580–590. doi:10.1108/00070700210425976

Barratt, M. (2004). Understanding the meaning of collaboration in the supply chain. *Supply Chain Management: An International Journal*, *9*(1), 30–42. doi:10.1108/13598540410517566

Bechini, A., Cimino, M. G. C. A., Marcelloni, F., & Tomasi, A. (2007). Patterns and technologies for enabling supply chain traceability through collaborative e-business. *Information and Software Technology*, *50*(4), 342–359. doi:10.1016/j.infsof.2007.02.017

Benjamin, R., & Wigand, R. (1995). Electronic market and virtual value chains on the information superhighway. *Sloan Management Review*, *36*(2), 62–72.

Bertsimas, D. J., & Simchi–Levi, D. (1996). A new generation of vehicle routing research: Robust algorithms addressing uncertainty. *Operations Research*, *44*, 286–304. doi:10.1287/opre.44.2.286

Bogataj, D., & Bogataj, M. (2007). Measuring the supply chain risk and vulnerability in frequency space. *International Journal of Production Economics*, *108*, 291–301. doi:10.1016/j.ijpe.2006.12.017

Bowersox, D. J., Class, D. J., & Cooper, M. B. (2007). Supply chain logistics management. (2nd ed.). Boston, MA: McGraw-Hill/Irwin.

Boyson, S., Corsi, T., & Verbraeck, A. (2003). The e-supply chain portal: A core business model. *Transportation Research*, *39*, 175–192. doi:10.1016/S1366-5545(02)00046-7

Bramel, J., & Simchi-Levi, D. (1997). The logic of logistics. New York: Springer.

Cannon-Bowers, J. A., & Salas, E. (2001). Reflection on shared cognition. *Journal of Organizational Behavior*, *22*, 195–202. doi:10.1002/job.82

Chan, Y. (2005). Location, transport, and land-use: Modelling spatial-temporal information. Heidelberg, Germany: Springer.

Chan, Y., & Ponder, R. (1979). The small package air freight industry in the United States: A review of the Federal Express experience. *Transportation Research*, *13*, 221–229. doi:10.1016/0191-2607(79)90048-7

Chau, S. (2003). The use of e-commerce amongst thirty-four Australian SMEs: An experiment or a strategic business tool? *Journal of Systems and Information Technology*, *7*(1), 49–66.

Chen, S.-C., & Chen, H.-H. (2007). Implementation and application of RFID EPC information service for forward and reverse logistics. *Journal of Global Business Management*, *2*(2).

Chiang, C.-C. (2001). Encapsulating legacy systems for use in heterogeneous computing environments. *Information and Software Technology*, *43*(8), 497–507. doi:10.1016/S0950-5849(01)00160-4

Chiang, C.-C. (2007). Software modernization of legacy systems for web services interoperability. In Mario Freire and Manuela Pereira (Ed.), Encyclopedia of Internet Technologies and Applications. Hershey, PA: Idea Group Publishing.

Chopra, S., & Meindl, P. (2007). (3rd ed.). Supply chain management. Upper Saddle River, NJ Prentice Hall.

Chu, S.-C., Leung, L. C. Y., Hui, V., & Cheung, W. (2007). Evolution of e-commerce web sites: A conceptual framework and a longitudinal study. *Information & Management*, *44*, 154–164. doi:10.1016/j.im.2006.11.003

CORBA. (2009). *CORBA*. Retrieved March 9, 2009, from http://www.corba.org

Coyle, J. J. Langley, Jr., Gibson, B. J., Novack, R. A., & Bardi, E. J. (2009). (8th ed.). Supply chain management: A logistics perspective. Florence, KY: South-Western Cengage Learning.

DCOM. (2009). *DCOM*. Retrieved March 9, 2009, from http://msdn.microsoft.com/en-us/library/ms809340.aspx

de Haan, J., Kisperska-Moron, D., & Placzek, E. (2007). Logistics management and firm size: A survey among Polish small and medium enterprises. *International Journal of Production Economics*, *108*, 119–126. doi:10.1016/j.ijpe.2006.12.009

Dehning, B., Richardson, V. J., & Zmud, R. W. (2007). The financial performance effects of IT-based supply chain management systems in manufacturing firms. *Journal of Operations Management*, *25*, 806–824. doi:10.1016/j.jom.2006.09.001

Dellenbarger, L. E., Dillard, J., Schupp, A. R., Zapata, H. O., & Young, B. T. (2006). Socioeconomic factors associated with at-home and away-from home catfish consumption in the United States. *Agribusiness*, *2*, 35–46.

Ding, Q., Dong, L., & Kouvelis, P. (2007). On the integration of production and financial hedging decisions in global markets. *Operations Research*, *55*, 470–489. doi:10.1287/opre.1070.0364

Drammeh, L., House, L., Sureshwaran, S., & Selassie, H. (2002, July). Analysis of factors influencing the frequency of catfish consumption in the United States. In *Proceedings of the 2002 American Agricultural Economics Association Annual Meeting*. Long Beach, CA.

Engle, C. R., Capps, O., Dellenbarger, L., Dillard, J., Hatch, U., Kinnucan, H., & Pomeroy, R. (1990). The U. S. market for farm-raised catfish: An overview of consumer, supermarket, and restaurant surveys. Fayetteville, AR: Arkansas Agricultural Experimental Station, 925, Southern Regional Aquaculture Center 511.

Engle, C. R., Capps, O., Dellenbarger, L., Dillard, J., Hatch, U., Kinnucan, H., & Pomeroy, R. (1991). Expanding U. S. markets for farm-raised catfish. *Arkansas Farm Research, 40*(6), 5–6.

Engle, C. R., & Quagrainie, K. (2006). Aquaculture marketing handbook. Boston, MA: Blackwell Publishing.

Enterprise JavaBeans. (2009). *JavaBeans*. Retrieved March 9, 2009, from http://java.sun.com/products/ejb/

EPCglobal. (2009). *EPCglobal Standards*. Retrieved March 6, 2009, from http://www.epcglobalinc.org/standards

GS1. (2009). *GS1barcode and eCom*. Retrieved March 6, 2009, from http://barcodes.gs1us.org/dnn_bcec/Default.aspx

Galloway, L., Mochrie, R., & Deakins, D. (2004). ICT-enabled collectivity as a positive rural business strategy. *International Journal of Entrepreneurial Behavior and Research, 10*(4), 247–259. doi:10.1108/13552550410544213

Gilmore, A., Gallagher, D., & Henry, S. (2007). E-marketing and SMEs: Operational lessons for the future. *European Business Review, 19*(3), 234–247. doi:10.1108/09555340710746482

GOST. (2009). *Geolocalisation optimisation et securisation du transport de conteneurs*. Retrieved March 6, 2009, from http://projet-gost.org/

Grandon, E. E., & Pearson, J. M. (2004). Electronic commerce adoption: An empirical study of small and medium US businesses. *Science Direct, 42*(1), 197-216. Retrieved June 28, 2009, from http://www.sciencedirect.com

Hatch, U., Engle, C. R., Zidack, W., & Olowoloyemo, S. (1991). Retail grocery markets for catfish. *Alabama Agricultural Experimental Station Bulletin, 611*.

Henderson, J., Dooley, F., & Akridge, J. (2004). Internet and e-commerce adoption by agricultural input firms. *Review of Agricultural Economics, 26*(4), 505–520. doi:10.1111/j.1467-9353.2004.00196.x

Henderson, J. R. (2001). Networking with e-commerce in rural America. Retrieved June 28, 2009, from http://www.kc.frb.org/RegionalAffairs/Mainstreet/MSE_0901.pdf

Holmes, T. P., Vlosky, R. P., & Carlson, J. (2004). An exploratory comparison of Internet use by small wood products manufacturers in the north Adirondack region of New York and the State of Louisiana. *Forest Products Journal, 54*(12), 277–282.

House, L., Hanson, T., Sureshwaran, S., & Selassie, H. (2003). Opinions of U.S. consumers about farm-raised catfish: Results of a 2000-2001 survey. *Mississippi Agricultural and Forestry Experimentation Station Bulletin, 1134*.

Kaplan, S., & Sawhney, M. (2000). E-hub: the new B2B marketplaces. *Harvard Business Review, 78*(3), 97–103.

Karkkainen, M., & Laukkanen, S., Sarpola, & Kemppainen, K. (2007). Roles of interfirm information; systems in supply chain management. *International Journal of Physical Distribution & Logistics Management, 37*(4), 264–286. doi:10.1108/09600030710752505

Karmarkar, U. S., & Apte, U. M. (2007). Operations management in the information economy: Information products, processes, and chains. *Journal of Operations Management, 25*, 438–453. doi:10.1016/j.jom.2006.11.001

Ketchen, D. J., & Hult, T. M. (2007). Bridging organization theory and supply chain management: The case of best value supply chains. *Journal of Operations Management, 25*, 573–580. doi:10.1016/j.jom.2006.05.010

Kinnucan, H., Sindelar, S., Wineholt, D., & Hatch, U. (1988). Processor demand and price markup functions for catfish: A disaggregated analysis with implications for the off flavor problem. *Southern Journal of Agricultural Economics.*, *20*, 81–92.

Kinnucan, H., & Venkateswaran, M. (1990). Effects of generic advertising on perceptions and behavior: the case of catfish. *Southern Journal of Agricultural Economics*, *22*, 137–151.

Kinnucan, H. W., & Miao, Y. (1999). Media-specific returns to generic advertising: The case of catfish. *Agribusiness . International Journal (Toronto, Ont.)*, *15*, 81–99.

Laporte, G., Louveaux, F. V., & Mercure, H. (1994). A priori optimization of the probabilistic traveling salesman problem. *Operations Research*, *42*, 543–549. doi:10.1287/opre.42.3.543

Lau, A. H. L., Lau, H.-S., & Zhou, Y.-W. (2007). A stochastic and asymmetric-information framework for a dominant-manufacturer supply chain. *European Journal of Operational Research*, *176*, 295–316. doi:10.1016/j.ejor.2005.06.054

Leung, Y. T., Cheng, F., Lee, Y. M., & Hennessy, J. J. (2006). A tool set for exploring the value of RFID in a supply chain. To appear in H. Jung, F. F. Chen, & B. Jeong (Ed.), Trends in Supply Chain Design and Management: Technologies and Methodologies. Heidelberg, Germany: Springer-Verlag.

Li, E. (2008). *Supply chain management in China.* In The International Cyber Transportation Logistics Conference. Petit Jean Mountain, AR.

Li, E. Y., Du, T. C., & Wong, J. W. (2007). Access control in collaborative commerce. *Decision Support Systems*, *43*, 675–685. doi:10.1016/j.dss.2005.05.022

Martinez-Olvera, C. (2008). Methodology for realignment of supply-chain structural elements. *International Journal of Production Economics*, *114*, 714–722. doi:10.1016/j.ijpe.2008.03.008

McGladrey, R. S. M. (2009). *RSM.* Retrieved June 28, 2009, from http://www.rsmmcgladrey.com/

Meroño-Cerdan, A. L., Soto-Acosta, P., & Lopez-Nicolas, C. (2008). How do collaborative technologies affect innovation in SMEs? *International Journal of e-Collaboration*, *4*(4), 33–50.

Moeeni, F. (2008). A passive RFID location sensing. In *Proceedings of the 12th World Multi-Conference on Systemics, Cybernetics and Informatics* (pp. 84-89).

Nam, C. S., Johnson, S., Li, Y., & Seong, Y. (2009). Evaluation of human-agent user interfaces in multi-agent systems. *International Journal of Industrial Ergonomics*, *39*(1), 192–201. doi:10.1016/j.ergon.2008.08.008

Ngai, E. W. T., Cheng, T. C. E., Auc, S., & Lai, K.-H. (2007). Mobile commerce integrated with RFID technology in a container depot. *Decision Support Systems*, *43*, 62–76. doi:10.1016/j.dss.2005.05.006

Ngai, E. W. T., & Gunasekaran, A. (2007). A review for mobile commerce research and applications. *Decision Support Systems*, *43*, 3–15. doi:10.1016/j.dss.2005.05.003

Niederman, F., Mathieu, R. G., Morley, R., & Kwon, I.-W. (2007). Examining RFID applications in supply chain management. *Communications of the ACM*, *50*, 92–101. doi:10.1145/1272516.1272520

Nucciarelli, A., & Gastaldi, M. (2008). Information technology and collaboration tools within the e-supply chain management of the aviation industry. *Technology Analysis and Strategic Management*, *20*(2), 169–184. doi:10.1080/09537320801931309

Ojala, M., & Hallikas, J. (2006). Investment decision-making in supplier networks: management of risk. *International Journal of Production Economics*, *104*, 201–213. doi:10.1016/j.ijpe.2005.03.006

Olowolayemo, S. O., Hatch, U., & Zidack, W. (1992). Potential U.S. retail grocery markets for farm-raised catfish. *Journal of Applied Aquaculture, 1*, 51–71. doi:10.1300/J028v01n04_05

Pare, D. J. (2003). Does this site deliver? B2B e-commerce services for developing countries. *The Information Society, 19*, 123–134. doi:10.1080/01972240309457

Pibernik, R., & Sucky, E. (2007). An approach to inter-domain master planning in supply chain. *International Journal of Production Economics, 108*, 200–212. doi:10.1016/j.ijpe.2006.12.010

Poon, S., & Swatman, P. M. C. (1997). Small business use of the Internet: Findings from Australian case studies. *International Marketing Review, 14*(5), 385–402. doi:10.1108/02651339710184343

Quagrainie, K. (2006). IQF catfish retail pack: A study of consumers' willingness to pay. *International Food and Agribusiness Management Review, 9*(2), 16–27.

Quagrainie, K. K., & Engle, C. R. (2002a). A latent class model for analyzing preferences for catfish. *Aquaculture Economics and Management, 6*(1), 23–34.

Quagrainie, K. K., & Engle, C. R. (2002b). Analysis of catfish pricing and market dynamics: The role of imported catfish. *Journal of the World Aquaculture Society, 334*, 389–397. doi:10.1111/j.1749-7345.2002.tb00018.x

Raulerson, R., & Trotter, W. (1973). Demand for farm-raised channel catfish in supermarkets: An analysis of selected market. (Marketing Research Report No. 993). Washington DC: SDA Economic Research Service.

Rauniyar P. G., Hermann, R. O., & Hanson, G. D. (1997). Identifying frequent purchasers of seafood at home and restaurants consumption. *The Southern Business and Economic Journal*, 114-129.

Robinson, R. (1998). Asian hub/feeder nets: the dynamics of restructuring. *Maritime Policy & Management, 25*(1), 21–40. doi:10.1080/03088839800000043

Scholtz, J. (2002). Evaluation methods for human-system performance of intelligent systems. InMessina, E. R., & Meystel, A. M. (Eds.), *Proceedings of the 2002 Performance Metrics for Intelligent Systems (PerMIS) Workshop*. Retrieved June 28, 2009, from http://www.isd.mel.nist.gov/research_areas/research_engineering/Performance_Metrics/PerMIS_2002_Proceedings/Scholtz.pdf

Trappey, C. V., Trappey, A. J. C., Lin, G. Y. P., & Lee, W. T. (2007). Business and logistics hub integration to facilitate global supply chain linkage. *Proceedings of the Institute of Mechanical Engineering, Part B: J. Engineering Manufacture, 221*, 1221-1233. Retrieved June 28, 2009, from https://commerce.metapress.com/content/755k858k74706609/resource-secured/?target=fulltext.pdf&sid=4h3gmljzsnfc0q45n1ak3b55&sh=journals.pepublishing.com

Tsai, M.-C. (2006). Constructing a logistics tracking system for preventing smuggling risk of transit containers. *Transportation Research, 40*, 526–536.

Vlosky, R. P., & Westbrook, T. (2002). E-business exchange between homecenter buyers and wood products suppliers. *Forest Products Journal, 52*(1), 39–43.

Wang, R. Y. (1998). A product perspective on total data quality management. *Communications of the ACM, 41*(2), 58–65. doi:10.1145/269012.269022

Wang, Y., Potter, A., & Naim, M. (2007). Electronic marketplaces for tailored logistics. *Industrial Management & Data Systems, 107*(8), 1170–1187. doi:10.1108/02635570710822804

Webservices. (2009). *Webservices*. Retrieved March 9th, 2009, from http://www.webservices.org/

Wegner, P. (1996). Interoperability. *ACM Computing Surveys*, *28*(1), 285–287. doi:10.1145/234313.234424

Wiese, N. J. (2004). *Market characteristics of farm-raised catfish*. M.S. dissertation, University of Arkansas at Pine Bluff.

Wigand, R. (2006). Electronic value chains: supply chain management and RFID. *Proceedings of the International INFORMS Conference*. Hong Kong.

Wu, D., & Olson, D. L. (2008). Supply chain risk, simulation, and vendor selection. *International Journal of Production Economics*, *114*, 646–655. doi:10.1016/j.ijpe.2008.02.013

Yao, Y., Palmer, J., & Dresner, M. (2007). An interorganizational perspective on the use of electronically-enabled supply chain. *Decision Support Systems*, *43*, 884–896. doi:10.1016/j.dss.2007.01.002

Yasin, M. M., Czuchry, A. J., Gonzales, M., & Bayes, P. E. (2006). E-commerce implementation challenges: Small to medium sized versus large organizations. *International Journal of Business Information Systems*, *1*(3), 256–275. doi:10.1504/IJBIS.2006.008599

KEY TERMS AND DEFINITIONS

Aquaculture: Aquaculture is defined as farming of fish and other aquatic organisms under controlled condition.

Collaborative Commerce (CC): is the use of a web server hub to facilitate collaboration among suppliers, customers, and business partners in the integration of supply chain functions through information exchange, joint decision and planning across various enterprises.

Electronic Product Code (EPC): EPC is an object identification coding structure for supply chain RFID systems that currently encompasses 96 bits.

Enterprise: An enterprise is considered as a business organization.

Enterprise Application Integration (EAI): EAI is a process enables an enterprise to integrate a set of enterprise applications together.

Enterprise Resource Planning (ERP): ERP is a software application used to manage and coordinate all the information, resources, and business functions from a data store.

Fourth-Party Logistics Provider (4PL): 4PL is a provider of logistics services and solutions who operates as the sole conduit and systems integrator by managing the supply chain/logistics functions and activities of a client through the use of information technology.

Geospatial: Geospatial is used in this chapter to describe the combination of analytical and geographic attributes.

Global Location Number (GLN): GLN is a global supply chain numbering system for the identification of physical locations and legal entities.

Global Positioning System (GPS): GPS can be used to determine the geographic location.

Global Trade Item Number (GTIN): GTIN is a new 14-digit global numbering system for item class identification in the supply chain that will coexist with the 12-digit U.P.C. and 13-digit EAN codes. A serialized version of GTIN (SGTIN) allows the current bar code numbering structure be used with supply chain implementation of RFID.

Human Factors: HF is the research and systematic application of knowledge of human capabilities (e.g., sensory/perceptual, cognitive, behavioral) to the design and development of systems, services, and products to ensure effective people-systems interaction, and the safe and ease of use of technological systems.

Middleware: The software serves as the glue to connect different applications to work together.

Online Trading Platform/Infrastructure: An e-commerce model, that aside from providing information about sellers (e.g., electronic catalogs), allows multiple sellers/suppliers/vendors and buyers/customers to conduct business transactions through a web server.

Radio Frequency Identification (RFID): RFID is a technology that reads data from electronic tags to identify items.

Real Time Location Sensing (RTLS): RTLS is an RFID-based technology for asset tracking and location identification.

Section 6
Industry Service Models, Profession Development and Outlook

Chapter 16
Perceived Risk Management:
Applying the TEID Model to the Traveler Service Chain

Magali Dubosson
Haute Ecole de Gestion de Geneve (HEG), Switzerland

Emmanuel Fragnière
Haute Ecole de Gestion de Geneve (HEG), Switzerland & University of Bath, Switzerland

ABSTRACT

Purpose – To contribute to the theoretical work on service-perceived risk management of knowledge-based services (i.e. intangible and heterogeneous) and experience-based services and to suggest a framework that helps to formalize these risks and the value associated with their management, by arguing that this risk management relies on a sequence of risks (Threat, Event, Ignorance and Damage, called the TEID model) and on 3 categories of control measures (preventative, detective and protective). Design / methodology / approach – A case study research using the guidelines developed by Eisenhardt (1989) in the context of travel agency industry about how to deliver added value by selling the expertise that helps to reduce customer-perceived risks. Risk management and control process constructs were compared in order to confirm the relevance of this approach. Findings – Customers feel that travel services which are bought encompass a lot of uncertainties and annoyances (risks) about what they will be experiencing. At present customers are not willing to pay for advice that they regard as free. In order to charge and deliver more added-value, knowledge-based service providers have to make their role more tangible, aiming at reducing and managing risks. By categorizing customer-perceived risks, and by integrating control measures and assurances into their offer, providers can design new and valuable services. Service value-chains involve various providers (implicitly or otherwise) who may engender annoyance and damages as risks are a sequence of events. For their effective management risks have to be considered from the customer's point of view as this is the only way to apply an integrated approach. Originality / value – This chapter holds the potential to contribute to extending an understanding and management capacity of customer-perceived risks of knowledge-based services. It brings into play a new framework and new risk management process. It also helps with formalizing and making tangible customer added-value.

DOI: 10.4018/978-1-61520-603-2.ch016

INTRODUCTION

Knowledge-based services can be defined as services delivered by highly educated and informed employees responding to specific diagnosed customer demands by offering and delivering customized value-added solutions and relations (Debely *et al.*, 2007). Travel agents deliver this kind of expertise, and our findings can be extended to all kinds of knowledge-based services. This expertise is also a way of reducing risk along the service supply-chain.

In our attempt to develop a framework and building theory from case study research we used the guidelines developed by Eisenhardt (1989) in the context of the travel agency industry. This industry was chosen because it has to change its way of selling its expertise in order to survive. In the past most of its revenues were generated by commissions rewarding airline ticket-selling activity. These commissions were withdrawn in 2004. To compensate for the loss travel agencies, and their associations, decided to charge an overt fixed price. But customers have not been willing to pay this new fee, which represents a perceived extra cost that did not exist before. Moreover, customers see no link between this fee and a particular expertise provided by the travel agent. At the same time, travel agencies have to face a new, fierce competition as Internet players are perceived by more and more customers as an attractive alternative.

The travel industry was also chosen because it can be generalized to fit all experience-based services and "taken-on-trust" services (i.e. credence services), since customers choose their provider before experiencing and evaluating what they have actually bought. Travel is also a complex example of a service value-chain involving different providers and suppliers in various locations (airports, parking areas, shops, hotels).

From a series of 30 case studies in the travel industry context of the French-speaking part of Switzerland, we identified risks as they are perceived by customers and as they are, or are not, managed by travel agencies once they have closed the deal with their customers (Debely *et al.*, 2006). From the customers' point of view, these risks have to be handled and solutions have to be offered to them. Beforehand, these risks have to be identified and categorized according to the way that they are to be managed.

We suggest hereafter a new type of control whose design makes a distinction among the following states of "risk attributes": the threat, the event(s), the ignorance and the damage (Dubosson *et al.*, 2006). In classical approaches to control the focus is solely on the expected damage. Our control design involves 3 types of tests: whether the threat is associated with a protective system, whether the event is associated with a detection system and, finally, whether the ignorance of the problem is associated with a protection system.

Moreover, our approach focuses on the risks as they are perceived by the customers. We suggest emphasizing an ex ante treatment of risk as opposed to an ex post methodology.

The paper is organized as follows. In Section 2, we present travel services specificities as typical knowledge-based "risky" services. In Section 3, we present a brief overview of the literature on "perceived risk" in the context of services and in Section 4 the context od the Swiss travel agency industry. In Section 5, we model the "traveler service-chain" and explain its particular links with risk events. In Section 6, we present a qualitative control system that takes into account the intangible and heterogeneous nature of knowledge-based services. This control approach represents a way to improve the perception of risks in the general context of services. In section 7, we illustrate this framework of control and design by applying it to the case of the travel services industry. In conclusion, we indicate further research directions.

TRAVEL SERVICES: THEIR TYPICALITY AS KNOWLEDGE-BASED SERVICES AND AS "UNCERTAIN" EXPERIENCES

According to OFS (Swiss census data organization, www.bfs.admin.ch), travel agencies inform, counsel, organize travels and provide accommodation for, and transportation services to, the traveler. Travel services encompass the characteristics of typical service activities which are traditionally described with the help of the IHIP paradigm (Intangibility, Heterogeneity, Instantaneity and Perishability). Research has shown that intangibility is positively correlated with perceived risk (Finn, 1985; Zeithaml and Bitner, 2000). According to the literature, consumers perceive services as riskier than products (Guseman, 1981; Murray and Schlacter, 1990; Michtell and Greatorex, 1993). As stated by Mitchell and Greatorex (1993), "intangibility greatly increases the degree of perceived risk in the purchase of services by decreasing the certainty with which services can be made". Mitchell affirms that the properties of services may lower consumer confidence and increase perceived risk, mainly by augmenting the degree of uncertainty in the decision (Mitchell, 1999). As fairly intangible services, travel services need to be experienced before they can be properly assessed (Parasuraman *et al.*, 1985; Zeithaml *et al.*, 2006). They are usually sold without guarantees.

The travel agent purchases travel components on behalf of the client. Neither the customers nor the agent control most of the risks associated with the various "ingredients". The travel agent's adequate counseling may help the customer to minimize risk and "travel annoyances". For instance, the expertise of the travel agent could be crucial in the determination of the convenient connecting times or the right hotel. As the customer is participating in the design and delivery process, s/he may increase the level of risk if s/he does not behave appropriately (e.g. not being on time at the airport to catch the plane).

Nowadays, a client can "assemble" for free a tailored trip by combining offers available on the Internet, which puts price pressure on travel agencies. Actually, the assembling and the ordering steps of the process that used to be traditionally performed by the travel agents could nowadays be easily "outsourced" to the traveler. Even with such competition travel agencies can go on acting as retailers of pre-designed services but they have to deliver some more added-value as it would be difficult to compete solely on the basis of price. They have tended to develop specific niches, such as destinations that might be left over by big competitors or by the Internet, but they seem not to be sufficient. The industry fears that many small agencies might be victims of this deep crisis and its subsequent price war. To address this issue, we investigated the possibility of changing the nature of services delivered to the customer by offering a reduction of the annoyances and of the perception of risk level that are both associated with the delivery of the services. This crisis might actually be considered as an opportunity, since clients will be looking for more value-added services when consulting a travel agent.

From our findings we propose a methodology to categorize and manage operational risks and annoyances encountered all the way through the travel service-chain. Risk management could then be valued and sold to customers as a specific travel agency expertise. Our qualitative control method combines approaches borrowed from the risk management and audit professions as well as research from services marketing and service operations management.

According to the IIA glossary (Institute of Internal Auditors, www.theIIA.org), the term control means: "Any action taken by management, the board and other parties to enhance risk management and increase the likelihood that established objectives and goals will be achieved". Control is thus an important part of managerial activities. The design of controls dedicated to services is, however, extremely tedious: service intangibility and heterogeneity in particular make identification of risks difficult.

Owing to the instantaneity, heterogeneity and intangibility of services, there is little evidence of service problems. Moreover, perception of problem (quality) is subjective and the individual perception often cannot be related to what was actually delivered. The most patent clue to a service problem is a customer complaint. In order to avoid waiting for customer complaints and having to recover from a service problem, our research favors a more integrated approach. Risk management should be designed with potential problems taken into account and applied all the way down the supply-chain simultaneously with the delivery.

THE NOTION OF PERCEIVED RISK: LITERATURE REVIEW

The effect of perceived risk is believed to have a greater effect on the consumer for services (Murray and Schlacter, 1990). Perceived risk is a two-dimensional construct comprising the uncertainty involved in a purchase decision and the consequences of taking an unfavorable action (Bettman, 1972). The perception of risk has been found as totally subjective (Havelena and DeSarbo, 1990; Ross, 1975). Perceived risk was considered as a subjective expectation of loss (Peter and Ryan, 1976; Mitchell and Greatorex, 1993).

Mitchell revealed that consumers judging low probability/high consequence risks, e.g. purchasing an airline ticket, are affected more by the consequence size than by the probability, and many appear to disregard the probability altogether (Mitchell, 1998). An example often used is that car accidents kill many more people per year than airplane crashes but people tend to be more afraid of traveling by plane than by car. Slovic and Lichtenstein (1968), and Horton (1976) also found that the degree of negative consequences was much more important in determining risk than the probability of their occurrence.

Jacoby and Kaplan (1972) identified five independent types of risk: financial, performance, physical, psychological and social. Some authors later recommended combining social and psychological types of risk, as consumers found it difficult to choose between them, and using instead the psychosocial type of risk. Roselius (1971) added a sixth type of risk: time loss.

Product intangibility greatly increases the degree of perceived risk (Finn, 1985; McDougall and Snetsinger, 1990). Intangibility is composed of 3 dimensions: physical intangibility, mental intangibility, generality (Laroche *et al.*, 2001). They observed that there is a strong relationship between mental intangibility and perceived risk, an association between physical intangibility and perceived risk, but generality has either little or no direct impact on perceived risk. Laroche et al. (2003; 2004) studied the impact of intangibility on perceived risk and the moderating roles of involvement and knowledge. As they expected, involvement has a positive moderating effect and knowledge has a negative moderating effect, i.e. the more respondents were knowledgeable, the less intangibility exerted a significant impact on perceived risk. As they assumed, people perceive potential risks in the unknown.

Knowledge is recognized as a characteristic that influences how consumers evaluate the risk inherent in their purchase (Murray and Schlacter, 1990). As cited by Laroche et al., Engel et al. (1993) have defined knowledge as "the information stored within memory". Park et al. (1994) have defined knowledge assessment as a judgment process in which consumers scan memory for cues to help them evaluate their product-related experiences. Knowledge is often conceptualized with two related dimensions: experience and expertise. Expertise is potential, latent and virtually realizable by the consumer. Experience differentiates itself from expertise by the fact that it is concrete, operational and actualized by the consumer. Experience is a much less useful way of reducing risk for services than for goods because of the heterogeneity involved in producing and consuming services (Mitchell and Prince, 1993).

Tan and Cunningham et al. claim that the Internet is perceived to be riskier than the traditional service (Tan, 1999; Cunningham *et al.*, 2004). They explain this risk premium for Internet airline reservations by the high probability that users will make mistakes such as double booking, poor seating choices, failure to obtain electronic receipts or timely delivery of ticket, or paying too much for a non-transferable, non-refundable ticket. Moreover, the sole blame for the mistakes falls on the consumer, who has very limited recourse for correcting errors. For Internet shoppers information plays a key role, since information search is more effective at reducing perceived risk levels. In favour of the Internet it was revealed that Internet shopping technologies offer a reduction in the anxiety caused by judgmental service representatives (Meuter *et al.*, 2000).

"Mistakes are an unavoidable feature of all human endeavor and thus also of service delivery" (Boshoff, 1997). Nevertheless, Bitner *et al.* (1990) showed that it is not necessarily the failure itself that leads to customer dissatisfaction. What is more likely to cause dissatisfaction is an inadequate response or a lack of response from the company. Mayer *et al.* (2003) showed that the customers feel that how they were treated during the process is as important as what they actually experienced. They recognize what Grönross (1984) identified as the technical dimension (what actually happened during service delivery) and as the functional component (how the service was delivered). Failure in either dimension is likely to lead to low perceived service quality.

In this chapter we want to emphasize less "serious losses" that we will call "annoyances". In fact, we make reference to a legal term "trivial annoyance", which corresponds to an uncomfortable event that cannot justify any prosecution and thus any reparation. For "serious losses" we can assume that insurances will step in and play their role. So an annoyance risk is related to a problem of quality. In the case of travel services,

the problem is that the customer will experience and sometimes suffer from these annoyances. The customer may be able to deal with these annoyances, but sometimes s/he may not be able to solve them. In particular, the traveller may feel abandoned and lost in a foreign and distant destination. At the end of the day, even though the customer might have been able to deal with a minor problem, s/he may have experienced different kinds of risk: psychological, time loss and even financial annoyances. What if the travel agency could be helpful? How valuable would it be? Would it be considered as a perfect "after-sales" service? Would the consumer be willing to pay for it? As an upfront payment?

A CASE STUDY RESEARCH CONDUCTED IN THE CONTEXT OF THE SWISS TRAVEL AGENCY INDUSTRY

The travel agency industry in Switzerland is made up of a few big players such as Kuoni and Hotelplan and a myriad of small companies, as well as pure Internet players and brick-and-click companies. The range of activities varies depending on whether the companies consider themselves as tour operators or retailers or both. Nowadays its main activity is to retail packaged vacations or standard components that are described in brochures distributed by tour operators.

The announcement of the commission withdrawal was received by the travel agencies as an unexpected calamity. They moved from a hidden (or vague) commission to an overt outlay for the customer. As customers are not willing to pay this new fee, they buy on the Internet in order to save some money. In Switzerland, only one-third of the voyages is still booked through travel agencies (www.srv.ch, 2005).

This crisis could, however, be considered as an opportunity since clients will be looking for more value-added services when consulting a travel agent. There is an urgent need for travel agents to reconsider the offering that should be put forward to the client. Opportunities lie ahead: all the interviewed travel agents told us that clients still came to them because they recognized the value of their consulting services and the assistance they provided. They explained this trend in broad terms as they found it hard to describe more precisely the attributes of the specific value they delivered.

When starting our research we wanted to investigate through case studies the possibilities of adding and delivering more value in typical service activities. In particular, we were looking for a more precise definition of expertise and experience in knowledge-based services. As these questions should be more acute in a crisis context, we decided to focus on the travel industry. Travel agents were first interviewed with a few open-ended questions. Interviews were conducted on site in order to observe the settings and gather customer-available information such as brochures, information flyers, price lists.

Cases were selected according to the theoretical sampling approach (Glaser and Strauss, 1967). Categories were defined and added throughout the research:

- Independent travel agencies or units which were part of a multi-site group,
- Retailers, tour operators or both,
- Agencies selling tailored or standard products,
- Generalists or niche players.

Multiple cases were chosen for each category and were interviewed by two investigators. One researcher was handling the interview questions while the other recorded notes and observations. One researcher did not meet the informants and was kept out of the field in order to keep a more objective eye to the evidence (Eisenhardt, 1989).

Investigators took field notes that were then discussed in team meetings so they shared thoughts and emergent ideas and made sure that data collection and analysis overlapped (Eisenhardt,

1989). In particular, service-perceived risks and their management were added as themes in the interview protocol. We also described activities by drawing procedures and flow diagrams. Researchers analyzed within-case data and searched for cross-case patterns, i.e. open, axial and selective coding (Corbin and Strauss, 1990). We then decided to study the perceived-risks aspects from the customer point of view. Multiple cases were selected as some customers are buying mainly on the Internet or through travel agencies or both, depending on what they are buying, or because they are buying packages or various components, or both.

As the risk-management aspects were investigated, we tested whether the categorization of risk sequence as threat, event, ignorance and damage, and its associated management through preventative, detective and protective controls that were developed within a bank context, could also work in another knowledge-based service context (Dubosson *et al.*, 2006). Our transcripts recurrently show that perceiving more added value is more important than the risks that were perceived by the customer. Customers actually perceive the Internet as riskier but they prefer to buy travel services on the Internet as it is seen as more convenient, as more objective, as a broader choice at a better price. These issues were compared with the literature on service-perceived risks and service risk management. We stopped adding cases (about 30 cases) in both contexts (providers and customers) when it appeared that incremental learning was minimal (Glasser and Strauss, 1967).

THE TRAVELER SERVICE-CHAIN: CHAIN OF SERVICES AND RISK EVENTS

This descriptive part is based on in-depth interviews with fifteen consumers and fifteen travel agencies. The aim was to sketch the service-chain as experienced and felt by consumers. As suggested by Booms and Bitner (1981), in the next sections we separated process delivery from process assembly. We will first describe the buying / designing process, and then the intermediaries involved in the delivery of a travel arrangement and, finally, we explain the annoyances (i.e. risks) to be managed.

Consumer Buying Process: Designing a Trip

The biggest part of the consumer buying process could be handled by the travel agency which could help the customer to design, or could design on behalf of the customer, the delivery chain that would be experienced later by the recipient of service. When acting on behalf of the customer, the travel agency has to be assured that it has a clear understanding of the customer needs and expectations.

On the continuum of evaluation for different types of products (Zeithaml *et al.*, 2006), travel services are considered as an experience-based service whose attributes can be evaluated only after purchase and consumption. According to the definition of credence-based services, i.e. services associated with a higher degree of customization and requiring the personal intervention of the service provider (Guiltinan, 1987), travel agency activities could also, in some way, be considered as credence-based services. As cited by Mitra *et al.* (1999), the variability and the non-standardized nature of credence services lead to uncertainty about the actual cost and product performance (Murray and Schlacter, 1990) and make it difficult for the consumer to evaluate alternatives before purchase (Guiltinan, 1987). Mitra *et al.* (1999) claim that high risk credence services are associated with greater information search and greater reliance on personal information sources. This role could be partly fulfilled by a travel agent or by the Internet.

Travel agencies could therefore play a key role in reducing uncertainty and risk during the information search, alternative evaluation and purchase decision phase. Most of the interviewees acknowledged the fact that the travel agency was a good way of obtaining reliable information, getting access to a broad choice, designing complex travel arrangements, getting an expert insight about the alternatives and making professional choices (such as schedule, transfer). In most cases, as customers buy travel services without having experienced them, travel agencies could be the best way of obtaining the knowledge, experience and expertise that customers are missing.

Throughout the buying process, a travel agency can play the role of discussion partner and therefore it can make the customer more willing to accept greater risk (Woodside, 1972). This tendency to accept greater risk after discussion is called the "risky-shift" phenomenon (Pruitt, 1971). This tendency is controversial and some researchers claim that the customer accepts less risk after group discussion for high-risk products (Johnson and Andrews, 1971; Woodside, 1974).

We found, based on our transcript analysis that customers seem to appreciate travel agents' competence but do not seem willing to pay for it. For instance, some customers gather information from various travel agencies, and then they like going on the Internet and designing their own package. They feel like creating their own travel experience. They believe that most of the jobs performed by travel agencies could be handled by them with the same level of quality and efficiency. Even more, by buying on the Internet, some customers think that they can reduce the risk of not being properly understood by travel agencies. Some customers believe that travel agencies may not work in their best interest but prefer to sell the highest-margin products.

Assembling a Travel Package: Choosing Intermediaries

When organizing a journey, one has to make a series of decisions. For instance, when you book a flight, you choose an airline. By opting for an airline, you also opt for a particular route, schedule and hub, and therefore you pick an airport and all its services (parking areas, security checks, shops, customs, cafés …). so a few decisions made in the buying process imply a myriad of activities involving various companies / organizations and a lot of subcontractors (see Figure 1).

When mobilizing a unique expertise, a travel agency could design a customized offer that meets or even exceeds the customer expectations. But what if anything goes wrong? The travel package might have been designed properly: nevertheless, the customer or one of the chosen business partners (or an implicitly chosen partner, such as the airport when you choose a carrier), or some uncontrollable factors (such as a snowstorm), might cause trouble that could be experienced by the recipient of the travel package. The consumer will have to handle either what was categorized as "product-category risk" (i.e. travel services) or a "product-specific risk" (Dowling and Staelin, 1994).

Customers might be aware of the main decisions such as the airline and the hotel, but they will experience all the partners involved in the delivering of the value chain. They will have to bear the consequences of some decisions made even if they were not conscious decisions. When a travel agency recommends the use of a specific provider, or when a tour operator sells an all-inclusive package, companies involved in the value-chain are partners in a delivery process that should lead to customer satisfaction (see Figure 1).

Some of the providers might have been personally experienced by the customer or the travel agency before. Very often, they have not been. Even in the former case, as service is heterogeneous, it might be different and not as good

next time. When the travel agency advises the customer, it cannot be assured that everything will go off perfectly. Because of the partnering and all the uncontrollable factors, there is a high probability that the travel will not turn out as planned and expected. Post-purchase behavior of the travel agent is very important for services as customers will actively participate in the process and experience what was decided and designed in the earlier stages of the buying process.

Uncertainty Management

According to the US Department of Transportation (October 2005), the main complaint categories are: flight problems (cancellations, delays), oversales, mistakes made in reservations and ticketing, waiting lines, problems boarding the aircraft, fares (incorrect or incomplete information, availability, overcharges, fare increase), refunds, luggage (lost, damaged or delayed), customer service (unhelpful, inadequate meals), misleading advertising. Some events may have severe consequences; others may only cause trouble, frustration or anger. Our research confirmed these findings as the main problems experienced by customers. But they also describe less serious problems that can be considered as annoyances or at least as uncertainties (Figure 2). Most of the interviewees did not consider the travel agency as a way of reducing the risk or minimizing the negative consequences.

According to Heskett et al., perceived risks arise in large part from customer insecurity about a lack of control of the process and the absence of tangible clues to the quality of the complex

Figure 1. Examples of companies involved in a journey

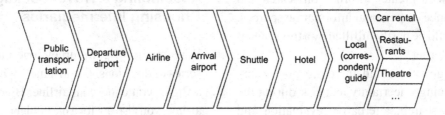

Figure 2. Activities involving customers when taking a flight

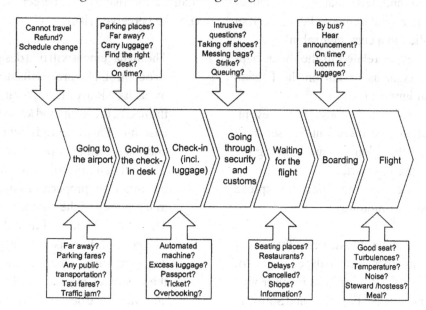

service being purchased (Heskett *et al.*, 1990). When traveling, customers may feel insecure as many questions arise as they go through the delivery process and many factors or behaviors can induce uncertainties, discomfort or even hinder customers carrying out the activities as expected (Figure 2). Moreover, the lack of information available for making service decisions and the lack of knowledge increase the risk (Bebko, 2000; Mitra *et al.*, 1999). By not having the knowledge or the correct answer, the customer feels insecure about the outcome of the process and is therefore forced to deal with uncertainty: and to the extent that the consumer realizes s/he may not attain all of her/his buying goals (i.e. fulfil her/his needs and wants), risk is perceived (Mitchell, 1998).

By developing relevant strategies to reduce perceived risks, service agents could augment purchase probabilities (Laroche *et al.*, 2003; 2004). So if service companies want to be perceived as delivering good value, they have to adopt strategies to reduce uncertainties and perceived risk at the purchase stage. To reduce consumer risk, service companies should implement initiatives that directly address the risk (or reduce the adverse consequences of the adverse outcome, e.g. giving

a refund or helping to solve a problem) or the factors that contribute to the risk (or the level of uncertainty, e.g. receiving correct information or increasing tangibility) (Laroche *et al.*, 2003; 2004; Mitchell and Boustani, 1994). Indeed, it has been found that each product has a set of risks associated with its purchase and each consumer has an individual risk tolerance which, if exceeded, means that one or more risk-reduction strategies will be employed to reduce the amount of risk perceived to a tolerable level (Mitchell, 1998). In the literature the commonest risk-reducing strategies are: sales staff knowledge, making services tangible, free trials and samples, money-back guarantee, celebrity endorsements, favorable press reports, company and brand reputation.

A CONTROL SYSTEM DESIGNED TO ADDRESS THE INTANGIBLE NATURE OF SERVICE RISKS

We tested the framework that was developed in a bank context and that suggests decomposing the risk sequence into the following steps (TEID model) (Dubosson *et al.*, 2006):

- **T**hreat (a potential risk that might endanger a bank, e.g. an inflammable Persian carpet was installed in a customer salon)
- **E**vent (an event related to the threat happens, e.g. cigar ashes fall on the Persian carpet and ignite a fire)
- **I**gnorance (or unawareness of the event, e.g. the client and the client adviser have already left the salon and are ignoring the fact that a fire has started)
- **D**amage (e.g. fire has time to spread throughout the building)

In Figure 3 we attempt to describe the importance of control in order to avoid the contagion of major risks. Very often major risks result from a sequence of minor events (Fragnière and Sullivan, 2007). The handling of trivial risks might then prevent a catastrophe occurring. Risk identification should thus be accompanied by the analysis of the dynamic linkages that exist among risks. These event-risk chains therefore constitute the framework of the risk management process.

We thus establish a relationship between a threat and its potential resulting damage. If the Internal control system (ICS) shows a lack of measures of prevention, an undesirable event might happen (e.g. lack of due diligence processes). If detection systems are defective or inexistent, the fault may spread within the company (e.g. no accurate MIS to perform the reconciliation of assets). Ultimately, if nobody is aware of the fault and if there is no protective measures (e.g. no insurance policy), the "expanding" damage could badly hurt the company which consequently won't be able to reach its objectives.

CHARTING PERCEIVED RISK MANAGEMENT: A TRAVEL AGENCY CASE

The company (i.e. the Customer Service Representative, hereafter the CSR) has to assess and manage the risk as it is perceived by the client (i.e. the perceived risk):

1. The management will first design a preventative control. This process has to be performed by each CSR in order to, for instance, define the needs, the wants and knowledge for each customer. Each client adviser must be trained and instructed to appraise customer needs. The internal control only checks that the information is properly consigned according to the policy of the company.

2. The management will then design a detective control. For instance, even if the CSR has spent time gathering information from the customer in order to define his needs and wants, the designed travel arrangement might not meet the customer needs owing to incontrollable factors (for instance, a storm). To facilitate the detective control, controllers are in charge of collecting (on a sample basis) feedbacks from clients regarding the delivery process and the experiences as felt by the customer.

3. The management will finally design a protective (or recovery) control. If the first two controls (preventative and detective) were not effective in preventing the contagion of events (e.g. bad diagnosis of customer needs), the intention is to add another control step that will mitigate the main damage occurrence (e.g. reputation risk). For instance, the performance of travel arrangements will be checked on a regular basis, for instance through customer survey, and benchmarked.

Our experience tells us that in practice auditors tend unfortunately to focus more on curative controls. From the various activities performed by the customer (cf. Figure 2), we suggest that companies disaggregate the service chains into single steps and for each of them, after having identified the potential perceived risks, define

Figure 3. Illustration of a poor ICS

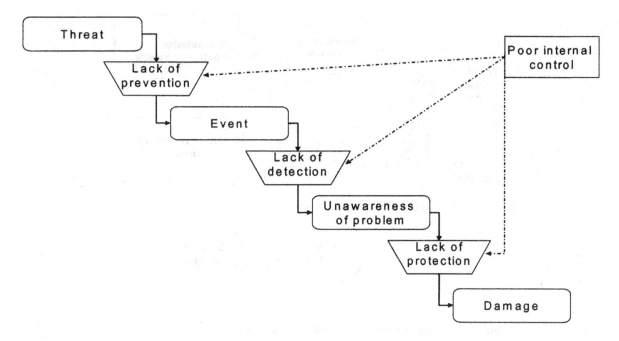

the measures which could act as preventative, detective and curative controls (Figure 4). Indeed simpler, though very effective, controls can be set up upstream and risk management could be ex ante instead of ex post.

The travel agent (Figure 4 and Figure 5) could then design new service offers based on these controls, such as a basic formula with a very cheap fee and a basic risk management with low assurance as opposed to a premium formula. The present pricing scheme adopted by the travel industry that was sometimes considered unfair, as it was charged with no link to the service provided to the client, could therefore be replaced with a new pricing scheme including different risk management levels and assurances corresponding to different fees. For instance, a premium package could include services such as calling the customer 2 hours before flying, checking and preventing overbooking and booking a new flight in case of missed connections. Using this approach, service companies could design new service offers and deliver more added-value. This value would then be recognized as such by the customers, who could be willing to pay for it.

In the bank context we already had the opportunity to recommend and monitor the implementations of such controls (involving a sequence of preventative-detective-curative controls) that were formalized with the help of tools like fault-tree analyses developed by engineers. This approach could be applied to all service activities and extended to the management of perceived risks as experienced by the customers. This approach could also help service companies to make more tangible the activities that they could perform in favor of their customers.

Having and using the right information at each step of the internal control system is critical. Controllers need to identify, analyze, evaluate and record sufficient information to perform their job. Risk-spreading might be the result of a lack of information, such as a lack of upward communication (i.e. gap one) (Zeithaml *et al.,* 2006). Poor control could also result from too much information, implying that the right information is lost somewhere within the organization. Owing to ICT tools and systems, misleading information will be forwarded as efficiently as true information (i.e. ephemeralization phenomenon) and there

Figure 4. Charting perceived risk control and management

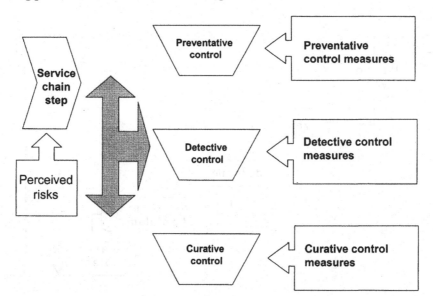

Figure 5. Travel case study: Risk management at the check-in step

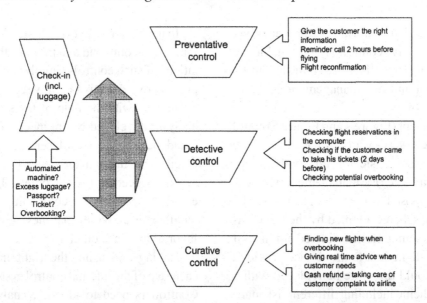

will be an increasing number of unanticipated or unintended side-effects (Heylighen, 2002). This leads to a greater difficulty in prediction and control of the overall effects of any event or process. As cited by Heylighen, the result of "data smog" is that an individual will not only miss out on potentially important information but also be aware that something is missing, while not knowing precisely what is missing, and thus feel a loss of control (Wurman, 1990).

ICS would have to be designed to deliver sufficient right information and not too much information. It also has to deliver objective (for instance, specification compliance) and subjective data (such as risks-related customer perception feedbacks).

CONCLUSION

The supply-chain in a manufacturing context corresponds to a clear sequence of events. Raw materials are transformed along the chain ultimately to become finished goods. Risk management approaches to deal with such supply-chains are thus quite well defined since product specifications can be measured through objective variables (quantity, weight, temperature, volume, material resistance ...).

In the case of knowledge-based services, "supply-chains" are not obvious to model, essentially because of their intangibility and heterogeneity. The client has a strong impact on the value-chain as delivered. The customer feeds the chain with her/his own inputs, interacts with the producer(s) in a not-so-clear sequence of events (i.e. instantaneity), and is often the subject that will be processed and transformed (e.g. more relaxed after a well-deserved vacation). The risks associated with the production of services are not visible. Most of them can only be identified and assessed by human perceptions. Our literature review indicates that the risk perception differs between people and affects their behaviors and decisions.

As indicated by Karmarkar and Pitbladdo (1995), the knowledge-based service involves a diagnosis process conducted by the producer to analyze its client's problems and provide a customized solution to address them. A good travel agent will employ its diagnostic skills to perform the risk management process for its clients: the identification, the monitoring and assessment and the mitigation of travelers' risks.

Modeling value-chain as experienced by the customer, instead of taking the point of view of a definite participating producer, enables a more complete analysis. As damage is usually the result of a cascade of different incidences, and of a lack of corresponding control, it would be useless to take only the point of view of a specific provider. Taking the standpoint of the customer might be the only way to comprehend the problem fully.

The aim of an expert risk management process would then be to intervene at the right time with the right service level for a specific customer. The added value would then be derived from the expertise of the travel agent delivered throughout the social interaction.

The control approach (i.e. TEID model and associated controls) presents the great advantage of forcing the manager to adopt a systematic and rigorous analysis of the different perceived risks. Control measures would then prevent each identified risk from becoming real and harmful. The approach would foster an upstream integrated treatment of risks. It will also make the risk manager go through a visualization process that foresees the risks as they could be experienced by the customer. Offering to the customer miscellaneous control measures makes the expert's value (i.e. travel agent) more tangible.

Research findings from the marketing discipline tell us that perception along the delivery chain is the only reality that must be acted upon. Defining and monitoring what could go wrong for a customized service in order to perform a sound risk management presumably requires adequate information. Apart from the traditional periodical customer surveys, and the treatment of customer complaints, an information system is needed when it comes to implement this approach. The right sensors should be embedded in human nature since they would reflect the situations as apprehended by customers. Not only these "human sensors" should be defined and designed, but also the resulting gathered information should be relayed to the "expert" in order to make him/her more knowledgeable in order to reach his/her diagnosis. This new breed of control system would then address the true world of services. In terms of defining the right information and making sure that it will not be lost in information overload, challenges still lie ahead.

This approach has been studied in the context of bank and travel agency contexts. These findings can be generalized to fit experience- and knowledge-based services that are not charged on a time-spent basis (for instance, a consultant day or a lawyer hour). It has now to be tested further in terms of its validity and the conditions in which it does and does not work well.

REFERENCES

Bebko, C. P. (2000). Service intangibility and its impact on consumer expectations of service quality . *Journal of Services Marketing, 14*(1), 9–26. doi:10.1108/08876040010309185

Bettman, J. R. (1973). Perceived risk and its components: A model and empirical test . *JMR, Journal of Marketing Research, 10*(May), 184–190. doi:10.2307/3149824

Bitner, M. J., Booms, B. H., & Tetreault, M. S. (1990). The service encounter: Diagnosing favorable and unfavorable incidents . *Journal of Marketing, 54*(January), 71–84. doi:10.2307/1252174

Booms, B., & Bitner, M. J. (1981). Marketing strategies and organization structures for service firms, In J. Donnelly and W. George (Eds), Marketing of Services, American Marketing Association. Chicago, Il.

Boshoff, C. R. (1997). An experimental study of service recovery options . *International Journal of Service Industry Management, 8*(2), 110–130. doi:10.1108/09564239710166245

Corbin, J., & Strauss, A. (1990). Grounded theory research: Procedures, canons, and evaluative criteria . *Qualitative Sociology, 13*(1), 3–21. doi:10.1007/BF00988593

Cunningham, L. F., Gerlach, J., & Harper, M. D. (2004). Assessing perceived risk of consumers in Internet airline reservations services . *Journal of Air Transportation, 9*(1), 21–35.

Debely, J., Dubosson, M., & Fragnière, E. (2006). The Travel Agent: Delivering More Value by Becoming an Operational Risk Manager. In*Proceedings of the Lalonde 9th International Research Seminar in Service Management,* 178-203.

Debely, J., Dubosson, M., & Fragnière, E. (2007). *The Pricing of Knowledge-based services: Insights from the Environmental Sciences,* New Delhi 2nd International Conference on Services Management. Retrieved from http://ssrn.com/abstract=951651

Dowling, G. R., & Staelin, R. (1994). A model of perceived risk and risk-handling activities . *The Journal of Consumer Research, 21*(June), 119–134. doi:10.1086/209386

Dubosson, M., Fragnière, E., & Millet, B. (2006). A Control System Designed to Address the Intangible Nature of Service Risks. In *Proceedings of the Shanghai IEEE International Conference on Service Operations and Logistics and Informatics* (June), 90-95.

Eisenhardt, K. M. (1989). Building theories from case study research. *Academy of Management Review, 14*(4), 532–550. doi:10.2307/258557

Engel, J. F., Blackwell, R. D., & Miniard, P. W. (1993). Consumer Behavior, Chicago, IL: Dryden Press.

Finn, A. (1985). A theory of the consumer evaluation process for new product concepts . *Research in Consumer Behavior, 1,* 35–65.

Fragniere, E., & Sullivan, G. (2007). Risk management. Boston, MA: Thomson, Glaser, B., & Strauss, A. (1967). The discovery of grounded theory: Strategies of qualitative research, London: Wiedenfeld and Nicholson.

Grönroos, C. (1984). A service quality model and its marketing implications . *European Journal of Marketing, 18*(4), 36–44. doi:10.1108/EUM0000000004784

Guiltinan, J. P. (1987). The price bundling of services: A normative framework . *Journal of Marketing, 51,* 74–85. doi:10.2307/1251130

Guseman, D. S. (1981). Risk perception and risk reduction in consumer services, In: J.H. Donnelly, et al. (Eds). Marketing of Services, Chicago: American Marketing Association.

Havelena, W. J., & DeSarbo, W. S. (1990). On the measurement of perceived consumer risk . *Decision Sciences, 22,* 927–939. doi:10.1111/j.1540-5915.1991.tb00372.x

Heskett, J., Sasser, W., & Hart, C. (1990). Service Breakthroughs: Changing the Rules of the Game, New York:Free Press

Heylighen, F. (2002). *Complexity and Information Overload in Society: Why increasing efficiency leads to decreasing control.* Draft paper to be submitted to Information Society, April 12.

Horton, R. L. (1976). The structure of decision risk: Some further progress . *Journal of the Academy of Marketing Science, 4*(4), 694–706. doi:10.1007/BF02729830

Jacoby, J., & Kaplan, L. (1972). *The components of perceived risk*, In: Venkatesan, M. (Ed.), *Proceedings of 3rd Annual Conference Association for Consumer Research,* Chicago, Il, (pp.382-393).

Johnson, D. L., & Andrews, I. R. (1971). Risky-shift phenomenon as tested with consumer products as stimuli . *Journal of Personality and Social Psychology, 20*(August), 328–385.

Karmarkar, U. S., & Pitbladdo, R. (1995). Service markets and competition . *Journal of Operations Management, 12*(3-4), 397–412. doi:10.1016/0272-6963(94)00014-6

Laroche, M., & Bergeron, J. & Goutaland. (2003). C. How intangibility affects perceived risk: the moderating role of knowledge and involvement . *Journal of Services Marketing, 17*(2), 122–140. doi:10.1108/08876040310467907

Laroche, M., Bergeron, J., & Goutaland, C. (2001). A three-dimensional scale of intangibility . *Journal of Service Research, 4*(1), 26–38. doi:10.1177/109467050141003

Laroche, M., McDougall, G. H. G., Bergeron, J., & Yang, Z. (2004). Exploring how intangibility affects perceived risk . *Journal of Service Research, 6*(4), 373–389. doi:10.1177/1094670503262955

Mayer, K. J., Bowen, J. T., & Moulton, M. R. (2003). A proposed model of the descriptors of service process. *Journal of Services Marketing, 17*(6), 621–639. doi:10.1108/08876040310495645

McDougall, G. H. G., & Snetsinger, D. W. (1990). The intangibility of services: measurement and competitive perspectives . *Journal of Services Marketing, 4*(4), 27–40. doi:10.1108/EUM0000000002523

Meuter, M. L., Ostorm, A. L., Roundtree, R. I., & Bitner, M. J. (2000). Self-service technologies: Understanding customer satisfaction with technology-based service encounters . *Journal of Marketing, 64*(3), 50–64. doi:10.1509/jmkg.64.3.50.18024

Mitchell, V. W. (1998). A role for consumer risk perceptions in grocery retailing . *British Food Journal, 100*(4), 171–183. doi:10.1108/00070709810207856

Mitchell, V. W. (1999). Consumer perceived risk: Conceptualizations and models . *European Journal of Marketing, 33*(1/2), 163–195. doi:10.1108/03090569910249229

Mitchell, V. W., & Boustani, P. (1994). A preliminary investigation into pre- and post-purchase risk perception and reduction . *European Journal of Marketing, 28*(1), 56–57. doi:10.1108/03090569410049181

Mitchell, V. W., & Greatorex, M. (1993). Risk perception and reduction in the purchase of consumer services . *Service Industries Journal, 13*(October), 179–200.

Mitchell, V. W., & Prince, G. S. (1993). Retailing to experienced and inexperienced consumers: A perceived risk approach . *International Journal of Retail & Distribution Management, 12*(5), 10–21.

Mitra, K., Reiss, M., & Capella, L. (1999). An examination of perceived risk, information search and behavioral intentions in search, experience and credence services . *Journal of Services Marketing, 13*(3), 208–228. doi:10.1108/08876049910273763

Murray, K. B., & Schlacter, J. L. (1990). The impact of services versus goods on consumers' assessment of perceived risk . *Journal of the Academy of Marketing Science, 18*(1), 51–65. doi:10.1007/BF02729762

Parasuraman, A., Zeithaml, V. A., & Berry, L. L. (1985). A conceptual model of service quality audits implications for future research . *Journal of Marketing, 49*, 41–50. doi:10.2307/1251430

Park, W. C., Mothersbaugh, D. L., & Feick, L. (1994). Consumer knowledge assessment . *The Journal of Consumer Research, 21*(1), 71–82. doi:10.1086/209383

Peter, J. P., & Ryan, M. J. (1976). An investigation of perceived risk at the brand level . *JMR, Journal of Marketing Research, 13*(May), 184–188. doi:10.2307/3150856

Pruitt, D. G. (1971). Conclusions: towards an understanding of choice shifts in group discussion . *Journal of Personality and Social Psychology, 20*(3), 495–510. doi:10.1037/h0031923

Roselius, T. (1971). Consumer rankings of risk reduction methods . *Journal of Marketing, 35*(January), 56–61. doi:10.2307/1250565

Ross, I. (1975). *Perceived risk and consumer behavior: A critical review*, Conference of the American Marketing Association, 19-23.

Slovic, P., & Lichtenstein, S. (1968). Relative importance of probabilities and payoff in risk taking. *Journal of Experimental Psychology Monograph, 78*(November), 1–18. doi:10.1037/h0026468

Tan, S. J. (1999). Strategies for reducing consumers' risk aversion in Internet shopping . *Journal of Consumer Marketing, 16*(2), 163–180. doi:10.1108/07363769910260515

Woodside, A. G. (1972). Informal group influences on risk taking . *JMR, Journal of Marketing Research, 9*(May), 223–225. doi:10.2307/3149962

Woodside, A. G. (1974). Is there a generalised risky shift phenomenon in consumer behaviour? *JMR, Journal of Marketing Research, 11*(May), 225–226. doi:10.2307/3150569

Wurman, R. S. (1990). Information Anxiety. New York:Bantam.

www.srv.ch (2005, September). *Swiss Issues: Le marché des voyages*: Entre globalisation et pression des coûts.

Zeithaml, V. A., & Bitner, M. J. (2000). Services Marketing: Integrating Customer Focus across the firms, 2nd ed., New York: McGraw-Hill

Zeithaml, V. A., Bitner, M. J., & Gremler, D. D. (2006). Services Marketing: Integrating Customer Focus across the firms, 4th ed., New York: McGraw-Hill

Chapter 17
Prediction Reliability of Container Terminal Simulation Models:
A Before and After Study

Armando Cartenì
University of Salerno, Italy

ABSTRACT

In this chapter attention is focused on the container terminal optimization problem, given that today most international cargo is transported through seaports and on containerized vessels. In this context, in order to manage a container terminal it is sometimes necessary to develop a Decision Support System (DSS). This chapter investigated the prediction reliability of container terminal simulation models (DSS), through a before and after analysis, taking advantage of some significant investment made by the Salerno Container Terminal (Italy) between 2003 and 2008. In particular, disaggregate and an aggregate simulation models implemented in 2003 were validated with a large set of data acquired in 2008 after some structural and functional terminal modifications. Through this analysis it was possible to study both the mathematical details required for model application and the field of application (prediction reliability) of the different simulation approaches implemented.

INTRODUCTION

The current financial crisis seems to be seriously affecting the freight transport system. In this scenario, transport terminals play a crucial role to avert the risk of recession by increasing their efficiency and automation. Only in this way is it possible both to reduce the price of the services offered (loading, unloading, dwelling, logistic services ...) and increase terminal earnings.

In this chapter attention is focused on the container terminal optimization problem, given that today most international cargo is transported through seaports and on containerized vessels. Hence the efficiency of container terminals plays a major role in transport chain economics.

A container terminal should manage in the most efficient way container vessel berths on the docks, inbound container unloading (empty or filled with cargo), outbound container loading and storage yards. This can be achieved by coordinating the

DOI: 10.4018/978-1-61520-603-2.ch017

berthing time of vessels, the resources needed for handling the workload, the waiting time of customer trucks and, at the same time, by reducing congestion on the roads, at the storage blocks and docks inside the terminal, as well as making the best use of storage space. Each of these activities significantly affects port efficiency, with consequences on the local and global economy of the freight transport system. Management of container terminal operations has thus become crucial to meet container traffic demand both effectively and efficiently.

In this context, in order to manage a container terminal it is sometimes necessary to develop a Decision Support System (DSS), i.e. a mathematical model, required both to analyze the actual system situation (to identify system inadequacies or critical points) and to verify one or more alternative projects/interventions. Indeed, a crucial element in the management process is the simulation of the effects or impacts of a project scenario. Most of these impacts can be quantitatively simulated using mathematical models, which allow us to estimate system indicators (cost-benefit indicators; multi-criteria indicators, …) without physically carrying out the hypothesized projects. Although much work has been done in this direction, the prediction reliability of such models remains uncertain.

Design and project appraisal of container terminals can be carried out through *disaggregate models* (sometimes termed microscopic models) or *aggregate models* (sometimes called macroscopic models). The main advantage of the disaggregate approach is that it allows a detailed analysis in which each activity is analysed. Of course this approach may lead to computational problems and is rather computer demanding, especially when the resulting models are to be used to support optimization. It seems better suited to operative planning or operations management. On the other hand, decisions about the container terminal configuration regarding type and amount of handling equipment, berth and yard layout, etc. are better

considered within strategic planning. In this case an aggregate approach, based on container flows rather than single container movements, could be effective.

The existing literature reports approaches to either managing a container terminal as a system and trying to simulate all elements or managing a sub-set of activities (simultaneously or sequentially following a set hierarchy). The main approaches developed are optimization and simulation. The first seeks to maximize the whole terminal efficiency or the efficiency of a specific sub-area (or activity) inside the terminal through deterministic or stochastic optimization models (for a recent review see: Steenken et al., 2004).

Examples of the former approach are in Van Hee and Wijbrands (1988), Yun et. Al. (1999), Shabayek et al. (2002) e Murty et al. (2005), where it is developed a decision support system for capacity planning of container terminals. Different approaches have regarded container storage and retrieval in the yard operations (Taleb-Ibrahimi et al.,1993), space requirement problems (Kim and Kim,1998), space requirement and crane capacity (Kim and Bae, 1998), re-marshaling strategy (Zhang et al., 2003) and storage space allocation (Zhang et al., 2002; Cheung and Lin, 2002). Regarding quay-side problems, readers can refer to Wilson (2001) and Avriel et al. (1998) for stowage of vessels, and to Chen et al. (2002), Imai et al. (1997, 2001), Lau et al. (1992) and Nishimura et al. (2001) for berth allocation. The most followed approaches are based on deterministic optimization methods. Recently a stochastic optimization model have been proposed for maximize terminal efficiency (Murty et al., 2005).

An effective, stimulating alternative approach to container terminal system analysis may lie in discrete simulation, which is the subject of this chapter. Although numerous efforts to simulate a container terminal have been made, most papers fail to adequately address model set-up, calibration and validation (see e.g. Koh et al., 1994; Yun, Choi, 1999; Shabayek, Yeung, 2002; Kia et al., 2002;

Lee, Cho, 2007), and only focus on the application and/or comparison of design scenarios. Moreover, none of them propose *before and after analysis* to simulate the model's transferability and/or reliability. Yun and Choi (1999) propose a simulation model of the container terminal system of the Pusan east container terminal. The model is developed using an object-oriented approach and estimates container terminal performances. Shabayek and Yeung (2002) propose a simulation model to analyze the performance of Hong Kong's Kwai Chung container. The approach provides good results in predicting the actual operation system of the container terminals. Recently Petering (2009) considers the block widths ranging problem in a marine container terminal by a fully-integrated discrete event simulation model.

In a simulation model, a handling equipment model (sometimes called cost function or performance function) is assigned to each activity considered in order to estimate the time required to bring one or more activities to a close (sometimes termed: activity time duration). For the author of this chapter, the definition, the estimation and the validation of the these models play a relevant and a crucial role for the implementation of a container terminal simulation model.

A handling equipment model can be assumed deterministic or stochastic. In the former case represent the average time required to bring an activity (e.g. average crane loading time); in the latter case a random variable should be calibrated in order to model the activity time duration uncertainty. From this point of view, in literature seldom this problem is investigated and few authors propose the models, deterministic or stochastic, estimated and the characteristic parameters of these models.

Classifying the container terminal activities with respect to the handling equipments that carry out the activities, we observe that the main papers report deterministic or stochastic models often referred to aggregate activities (no distinction among container typology: 20'/40', full/empty)

and seldom the model parameters (random variable characteristic parameters) are published.

With respect to the crane loading/unloading activities, the models proposed are often stochastic (except to the models proposed by Thiers (1998), Tugcu (1983), KMI (2000) and Bielli et al. (2006)) with different aggregation levels; the main random variables used are:

- crane operation time
  ○ Exponential (Yun, Choi (1999); Lee, Cho (2007));
  ○ Triangular (Lee, Cho (2007); Merkuryeva et al. (2000));
  ○ Normal (Parola, Sciomachen (2005));
  ○ Uniform (Merkuryeva et al. (2000));
- crane cycle times
  ○ Weibull (Koh et al. (1994));
- vessel cycle times
  ○ Normal (Choi (2000));
  ○ Erlang (El Sheikh (1987); Kia et al. (2002); Shabayek, Yeung (2002));

Regarding crane speed, only deterministic model are proposed (Yun, Choi (1999); Choi (2000); KMI (2000); Legato et al. (2008); Tugcu (1983); Koh et al. (1994); Thiers (1998)).

With respect to other handling equipments, Shouridis and Angelides (2002) publish the deterministic values estimated for the Straddle Carriers while Merkuryeva et al. (2000) propose to use a Tringular r.v. for estimate the Forklift loading/unloading time.

The different level of aggregation and the different activity time duration object of the estimations make difficult to compare these models.

This chapter investigates the prediction reliability of container terminal simulation models, through a *before and after analysis*. This kind of analysis is particularly suitable for model validation. In particular, the model is implemented (specified and calibrated) through a sample related to an *actual scenario*, and is validated through its capacity to reproduce the data related to an *after scenario* (after some significant system modification).

This analysis was made taking advantage of some significant investment made by the Salerno Container Terminal (Italy) between 2003 and 2008. In particular, the disaggregate and aggregate simulation models (see Cartenì et al., 2005 and de Luca et al., 2008) implemented in 2003 (*before scenario*) were validated with a large set of data acquired in 2008 after some structural and functional terminal modifications (*after scenario*). Through this analysis it was possible to study both the mathematical details required for model application and the field of application (prediction reliability) of the different simulation approaches implemented.

This chapter also reports the conclusions of a research project for container terminal analysis starting in 2003. The research project was broken down into three main steps:

1. *methodological issues*
    ○   different approach identification
    ○   model architecture identification;
    ○   model specification;
    ○   definition of decision variables;
    ○   specification of performance indicators;
2. *applications*
    ○   test-site choice;
    ○   survey to calibrate the model parameters;
    ○   actual scenario simulation;
    ○   hypothetical scenario simulation, models comparison and economic validation;
    ○   hypothetical scenario realization;
    ○   before and after analysis;
3. *conclusions*
    ○   guidelines for applications: strengths, weaknesses, fields of application for each approach, most effective indicators.

The proposed model system allows terminal performance to be measured, and two main applications may be carried out: (i) *cost analysis* in order to identify terminal critical points, and (ii) *scenario analysis* in order to simulate the feasibility, effectiveness and efficiency of hypothetical scenarios due to supply system modifications.

The chapter is divided into three sections: in the first the model architecture is described; in the second results of the model application are given; the third draws some conclusions from the study.

MODEL ARCHITECTURE

In this chapter a disaggregate simulation model was compared with an aggregate one. In general it is possible to group the simulation approaches into disaggregate and aggregate models, for each of which both advantages and disadvantages can be identified:

•   *disaggregate approach*
    advantage: allows detailed analysis in which each single activity and container movement is explicitly modeled;
    disadvantages: large simulation time and extensive data required for model parameters estimation;
•   *aggregate approach*
    advantage: low implementation costs and data; these tools allow decisions about the container terminal configuration regarding types and quantities of handling equipment, berth and yard layout, etc.
    disadvantage: works in a coarser way, where basic variables are container flows moving rather than single containers; no detailed analysis is possible.

The model parameters to be calibrated are those of the handling models (deterministic or stochastic) associated to the activities identified. Obviously the number of parameters depends on the simulation approach; disaggregate approaches generally require a larger number of parameters than the aggregate one.

Container flows moving to/from vessels, yards and gates are generally known exactly, since they are *a priori* known and independent of any variations in any characteristic of the model system (rigid demand hypothesis).

Two sample data sets are required for model application: one for model parameter estimation and another (hold-out sample) used for model validation. To validate the model many *performance indicators* (measures) can be estimated, such as:

- *global indicators,* if referring to the container terminal as a whole;
  - average crane hours per working hour;
  - average vessel time at berth;
  - average employees per vessel per shift;
  - total crane cost per crane/hour;
  - average fraction of time workers are idle;
  - …;
- *local indicators,* if referring to specific sequences of activities (or single activities);
  - vessel average load/unload time;
  - container average transfer and/or storage time;
  - … .

Both types of indicators may be expressed in different units, the most widely used being time (e.g. vessel unloading time) or number of operations per time period (e.g. number of movements per day); other units may be used such as cost per time period.

In general, a performance indicator is a function of:

- the number of containers per type: {20', 40'} × {full, empty} × {reefer, non-reefer};

- the quantity of handling equipment available per type: for example, {reach stacker, fork lift, front loader, straddle carrier ....};
- the starting system configuration, say at the initial time (any terminal activity at the initial time could influence indicator values).

Furthermore, the quantity of handling equipment available per type is a function of the starting system configuration (for example the average quantity of handling equipment per vessel is a function of the number of vessels loading/unloading).

Estimation of performance indicators are also useful for planning investments for a container terminal through a *what if* approach by comparing different project scenarios. Global indicators are generally used to assess the benefits of long-term investments; while local indicators are used to assess the benefits of medium/short-term investment and for real-time applications.

The model approaches implemented in this research project are as follows:

- a *discrete event model* as a disaggregate approach;
- a *diachronic capacitated flow network model* as an aggregate approach.

A Container Terminal (CT) can be divided into: gate, yard, and berth subsystems. Container handling equipment (sometimes called handling units) comprises storage (yard) cranes, loading/unloading (berth) cranes, yard tractors, trailers, reach stackers, shuttles … . Management of a CT consists in berth planning, yard planning, storage planning and logistics planning. Berth planning refers to planning/monitoring of the loading or unloading. Yard planning refers to optimal container allocation to the storage areas (import, export and transshipment). Storage planning concerns storage location in the vessel bay, and logistics planning regards container handling operations between the vessel's bay and the yard. After preliminary identification of all system elements (cited above), for each activity input variables, constraints and relationships are identified.

Following the general approach of transportation system analysis, a container terminal can be broken down into two main components: *supply* and *demand*. The supply sub-system is the set of facilities, services and regulations which allows containers to move inside the terminal, and the demand sub-system is represented by container flows moving to/from vessels, yards and gates. In the next sections details on supply and demand models are reported; for a full description see Cartenì et al. (2005) and de Luca et al. (2008).

Discrete Event Simulation Model: Supply Model

Discrete event simulation appears one of the most effective approaches to analyze complex systems, and the most recommendable method to analyze a container terminal system in detail. A discrete event system is a dynamic system, whose states (possibly also described by logical variables) may change each time an event (in a pre-defined set) occurs. The sequence of events describes system evolution over time (clearly in discrete a-periodic time).

The basic structure of a discrete event simulation model consists of various elements, each of which represents a container terminal activity (for all details see Cartenì et al., 2005). The connections of the whole system can be represented as an oriented graph, where *nodes* correspond to significant activities, *links* represent node connections and *paths* are a sequence of activities; in our case study, containers move along a path (see the example in figure 1).

The graph contains both origin and destination centroid nodes; an origin centroid node represents the physical point of container origin (for example: the gate-in for export macro-activity or the vessel hold for import macro-activity), while a destination centroid node represents the physical point of destination (for example: the gate-out for import macro-activity or the vessel hold for export macro-activity).

A handling equipment model is assigned to each node (activity) in order to estimate the time required to bring one or more activities to a close. The time instant at which each activity occurs is explicitly taken into account.

As said, a handling equipment model can be assumed deterministic or stochastic. In the former case represent the average time required

Figure 1. General disaggregate graph structure: export operation sub-graph

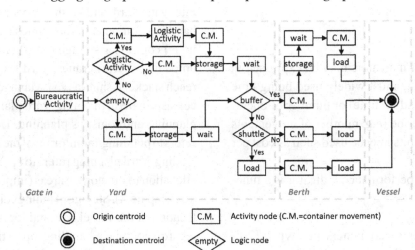

to bring an activity (e.g. average crane loading time); in the latter case a random variable should be calibrated in order to model the activity time duration uncertainty.

The model architecture proposed is able to simulate three macro-activities: *import*, *export* and *transshipment*. Through the proposed architecture it is possible to jointly simulate these macro-activities that influence each other, since they compete for common resources. Simulation of this reciprocal effect allows the sharing of infrastructures (e.g. handling equipments, yards, terminal roads) to be explicitly simulated.

Diachronic Capacitated Flow Network Model: Supply Model

With respect to the proposed aggregate approach the supply model consists of a network model (for all details see de Luca et al., 2008). The connections are represented by an oriented graph which also expresses the consistency relationships between path or link and performances or flows. The graph is used to simulate the main activities of a container terminal, each being represented by a *link*, while positions in space and/or time are represented by *nodes*. Each link generally has an associated handling equipment model relating link activity time duration to link flows (in TEUs per time unit) and a handling capacity as the maximum number of containers (per time unit) that can be handled.

Due to the discrete and dynamic nature of the system, the graph used to simulate services and their time distribution is a space-time or *diachronic* graph (see the example in figure 2). Activities regarding physical container movements (for example vessel loading by crane; shuttle transfer; container storage) may be termed *handling links* and containers waiting without any physical movement such as waiting for the next crane service may be termed *waiting links*.

Figure 2. General aggregate graph structure: export operation sub-graph

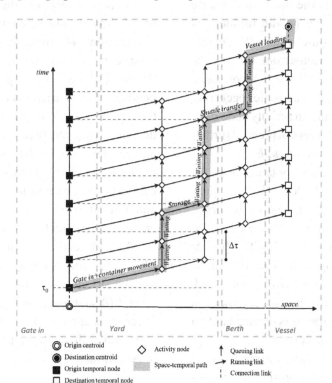

At the same time, it is possible to define various nodes: *origin centroid nodes* (defined above); *origin temporal nodes*; *activity nodes; temporal destination nodes* and *destination centroid nodes* (defined above).

An *origin temporal node* represents the first instant in which a container flow seeks to enter the system (gate in, vessel, yard) and to start its trip towards the final destination (gate out, vessel, yard). A demand flow will be associated to each temporal node. The space coordinate is the same as the corresponding *origin centroid*, while the time coordinate depends on a time interval, thus on the chosen time simulation segmentation ($\Delta\tau$). As a consequence, we will have as many temporal centroids as there are simulation segments. For instance, if the simulation lasts 6 hours (360 minutes) and the chosen time interval is $\Delta\tau = 10$ minutes, we will have 36 temporal centroids.

The connection between two successive *origin temporal* centroids is represented by a waiting link; this means that, in a current time interval, there is not enough handling capacity to allocate all demand flow towards the node. In this case the excess demand flow has to wait for the next time slot before entering the system. The *origin temporal node* is also connected to an *activity node* through a handling link. All the *activity nodes* represent the start and end of activities occurring inside a container terminal. An activity node from which a container terminal cannot proceed further is called a *temporal destination node*.

From an activity node the container flow can directly continue its transfer towards its destination, or has to wait for the next time slot to be served (handled). In the first case the activity node will be connected through a handling link with a further activity node representing the next activity; in the second case the activity node will be connected, through a waiting link, to the homologous node to the next time slot. This process is repeated until a *destination temporal node* is reached.

In such a network, a *path* is a sequence of adjacent links connecting the origin and destination nodes. Thus a path model is a sequence of activities that occurs within a specific operation. Generally, several paths connect the same origin-destination pair, and also a pair of *origin temporal* and (successive) *destination temporal* nodes.

Demand Model

The demand sub-system, as previously introduced, is represented by container flows moving to/from vessels (quay-side), yards and gates (land-side). For each macro-operation (import, export, transshipment), the demand flows may be characterized over space, time and type. As regards spatial characterization, container flow can be subdivided by zone of *origin* and *destination* and can be arranged into Origin-Destination matrices (O-D matrices). In particular, for each operation we can distinguish macro-origin and macro-destination zones (vessels, yards, gates) and for each of them different zones may exist. The O-D matrices have a number of rows and columns equal to the number of zones (represented by centroids in the graph).

In order to carry out the simulation, each demand flow should be characterized through its distribution over time, that is, over the chosen time segmentation. In general, it is assumed that the demand profiles are *a priori* known and independent of any variations in any characteristic of the supply system (rigid demand hypothesis). The demand profiles are based on empiric observations and can be assumed deterministic or stochastic. In the latter case a random variable should be calibrated in order to model the uncertainty of container flow arrivals (for example truck TEU arrivals at the gates). Finally, different O-D matrices should be estimated for each type of container (20' vs 40', full vs empty).

The origin-destination flows for each time instant (disaggregate approach) or time interval (aggregate approach) are assigned to the available paths. The flows obtained allow link flows to be estimated.

APPLICATION

In 2003, the Salerno Container Terminal commissioned the University of Salerno to develop a DSS to verify different project scenarios and improve container terminal performance. The two simulation approaches described in the previous sections were applied for the following purposes:

- to estimate Salerno Container Terminal performance;
- to pinpoint its main weaknesses;
- to simulate hypothetical scenarios in order to improve system efficiency;
- to investigate prediction reliability of the simulation models implemented through a *before and after analysis*.

The Salerno Container Terminal is a major private container terminal in southern Italy, operating 24hours/day and 7 days per week and 365 days a year. Vessels take only 20 minutes from the pilot station to the berth. The terminal operates five ship-to-shore cranes (mobile harbour crane), all equipped with twin-lift spreaders, two yard gantry cane and many reach stacker, on an area of approximately 100,000 m^2 (10 ha), used for the storage of full and empty containers.

This container terminal is both small and very efficient; it handles close to 0.4 million TEUs per year (say 40,000 TEUs/ha). These figures should be compared with terminals such as the HIT and COSCO-HIT terminals in Honk-Kong which handle 6.6 million TEUs on 122 ha of land, that is 54,000 TEUs/ha, and of the Delta Terminal in the Netherlands which handles 2.5 million TEUs, i.e. 9,000 TEUs/ha. In addition the location of Salerno's port does not allow it to expand the terminal area. Hence the Salerno Container Terminal greatly relies on an intensive rather than extensive approach to handling in order to keep pace with increasing demand.

From January 2003 to July 2005 the whole container terminal was monitored (more than 1,000 vessels were monitored). The data acquired were used for the data analysis of the vessel, gate and yard macro-areas, and particularly for estimating the berth-side/land-side demand flows (per container type and time period). Jointly with these data, an integrative survey was carried out during the first six months of 2005: all the berth macro-area activities concerning more than 3,000 containers were monitored (equal to 20% of the containers loaded/unloaded per month and equal to 1% of the containers loaded/unloaded per year). With these data the container simulation model was implemented. It was also applied to estimate different project scenarios.

In the case study at hand, the calibration phase did not present major difficulties: the subject of the simulation is a closed monitored system (the container terminal). Therefore, the amount of O-D demand flows input were exactly known, corresponding to the arrival/departure of the vessels/trucks/trains (hence the number of the TEUs is known). The only parameters to be calibrated are the parameters of the handling equipment models associated to the single activities identified, since no route choice was considered.

In 2008, after the realization of the best project scenario simulated (see before and after analysis paragraph), a new survey was made. With these data it was possible to test the prediction reliability of the model system implemented and applied.

Model Specification and Estimation

All system activities were individuated and for each activity, input variables, constraints and relationships were identified. According to the transportation system analysis approach, the Salerno container terminal was studied with respect to two main components: *demand* and *supply*. As stated above, the demand sub-system is represented by container flows moving to/from vessels, yards and gates. For container flow estimation, data analysis was used; the Origin-Destination (O-D) matrices, per type of container and time period, were estimated with respect to two levels of aggregation:

- aggregate O-D matrices per time period (undifferentiated by container type);
- disaggregate O-D matrices per time period and type of container (20', 40', 2x20', full, empty).

To specify the supply sub-system all the facilities, services and regulations which allow containers to move inside the Salerno terminal were identified. According to the model architecture introduced in section 2 both the aggregate and disaggregate graphs were implemented. For complete characterization of the supply models (aggregate and disaggregate) the handling equipment models were estimated. In particular, three handling equipment types were simulated with many activities:

- *Mobile Harbour Crane (MHC)*
  - loading time from dock to vessel
  - loading time from shuttle to vessel
  - unloading time from vessel to dock
  - unloading time from vessel to shuttle
- *Gantry Crane (GC)*
  - unloading time (to shuttle/truck)
  - loading time (from shuttle/truck)
  - unloading time (to stack)
  - loading time (from stack)
  - trolley speed (with container)
  - free trolley speed
  - crane speed
- *Reach Stacker (RS)*
  - unloading time from shuttle/truck
  - loading time to shuttle/truck
  - stacking time (to tier)

For each single activity four different handling models were estimated:

- *sample mean* as estimation of activity time duration;
  - Sample Mean Undifferentiated (**SMU**) model (undifferentiated per container type);

- Sample Mean Container Type (**SMCT**) models (20' full and/or empty; 40' full and/or empty; 2 x 20' full);
- *random variable* as representative of activity time duration
  - Random Variable Undifferentiated (**RVU***)* model (undifferentiated per container type);
  - Random Variable Container Type (**RVCT***)* models (20' full and/or empty; 40' full and/or empty; 2 x 20' full).

The analyses are divided into a preliminary descriptive analysis of experimental data and statistical analysis. In the descriptive analysis, the mean values and corresponding standard deviations are estimated. Such values are useful to develop/implement models based on sample mean variables, and allow the need for a stochastic approach to be appreciated. By contrast, statistical analysis aims to estimate the theoretical continuous cumulative distribution function $F_X(\underline{x}; \underline{\theta})$ that best fits the sample distribution function $F^{sample}(\underline{x}; n)$. Given a sample $\underline{x} = (x_1, ..., x_n)$, with mean $\bar{x}$ and variance s^2, the *Kolmogorov-Smirnov* with respect to a random variable X with parameters $\underline{\theta}$ is the statistic used to evaluate the quality of the estimation methodology and the random variable tested:

$$D_n = sup \mid F^{sample}(\underline{x}; n) - F_X(\underline{x}; \underline{\theta}) \mid = D_{n,X(}\theta_{)}(\underline{x})$$

For large values of *n*, Smirnov (1948) gives the limiting distribution of $D_n \cdot n^{1/2}$. Hence it is possible to compute the critical values $d_{n,\alpha}$ (the thresholds) for large samples (*n*>35):

$$- d_{n,\alpha} = 1.3581 / n^{1/2} \text{ for } \alpha = 0.05$$

$$- d_{n,\alpha} = 1.6276 / n^{1/2} \text{ for } \alpha = 0.01$$

For smaller sample sizes the critical values are estimated in Miller (1956).

The *Kolmogorov-Smirnov* statistic with respect to two sample distributions is the statistic used to evaluate whether two sample distributions are statistically equal. This statistic was used to evaluate whether sample distributions related to similar activities are equal (for example if the sample distribution of the 20' full container loading time is equal to that of the 20' empty container loading time).

Two estimation methods were compared: Moment estimation and Maximum Likelihood (M-L) estimation (see for example Jonson et al., 1994). Several variables (exponential, log normal ...) were tested for each activity involved and for different container types. The estimation results show differences in terms of parameter value variables between 0.5% and 12.0%. From a statistical point of view, M-L estimations show the best results. Furthermore, sometimes the Moment D_n values are greater than the corresponding thresholds $d_{n,\alpha}$. These results suggest we should prefer M-L model estimation.

Comparison among different models (random variables) showed that only Normal, Gamma and Weibull random variables were statistically sig-

nificant. The three random variables produce D_n values below the thresholds; however, D_n values related to the Gamma random variable may be observed often below the others.

We can therefore conclude while the three random variables could all be used to represent the time duration of the main container terminal handling activity, the Gamma random variable produces the best results.

In Figure 3, Figure 4 and Figure 5 estimation results are reported.

Model Validation

The model was validated in two subsequent steps. First, model outputs were compared with the data surveyed in 2003 in the container terminal in order to ascertain the suitability of the model for representing real conditions. Secondly, model outputs were compared with the data of a hold-out sample, that is a sample of data acquired in 2008 not used for model parameter estimation (see the next section). To validate the model both global and local performance indicators were estimated:

Figure 3. Mobile Harbour Crane (MHC): estimation results

Handling activity	container tipology	sample n	Moment estimation		M-L estimation (Gamma r.v. parameters)		K-S bound
			$\bar{x}$ (minutes)	s (minutes)	mean (minutes)	standard deviation (minutes)	Dn,α $\alpha = 0,05$
Loading time from dock	20F	103	1.316	0.485	1.252	0.407	0.134
Loading time from dock	40F	82	1.494	0.632	1.372	0.485	0.150
Loading time from shuttle	40E	99	1.121	0.386	1.101	0.340	0.136
Loading time from shuttle	20F	99	1.193	0.387	1.227	0.405	0.136
Loading time from shuttle	40F	242	1.272	0.389	1.244	0.375	0.087
Loading time from shuttle	2x20F	104	2.214	0.926	2.083	0.690	0.133
Unloading time to dock	20E	72	0.768	0.316	0.664	0.139	0.160
Unloading time to dock	20F	335	0.856	0.221	0.825	0.183	0.074
Unloading time to dock	40F	210	0.867	0.230	0.835	0.188	0.094
Unloading time to dock	2x20F	77	0.971	0.366	0.933	0.326	0.155

Handling activity	container tipology	sample n	Moment estimation		M-L estimation (Gamma r.v. parameters)		K-S bound
			$\bar{x}$ (minutes)	s (minutes)	mean (minutes)	standard deviation (minutes)	Dn,α $\alpha = 0,05$
Loading time	All	729	1.426	0.657	1.366	0.514	0.050
Unloading time	All	728	0.871	0.263	0.862	0.214	0.050

Figure 4. Gantry Crane (GC): estimation results

Handling activity	container tipology	sample n	Moment estimation		M-L estimation (Gamma r.v. parameters)		K-S bound
			$\bar{x}$ (minutes)	$\bar{s}$ (minutes)	mean (minutes)	standard deviation (minutes)	Dn,α $\alpha = 0,05$
Unloading time (to shuttle/truck)	all	77	1.331	0.434	1.340	0.478	0.155
Loading time (from shuttle/truck)	all	34	0.888	0.352	0.822	0.289	0.227
Unloading time (to stack)	all	109	0.760	0.309	0.766	0.352	0.130
Loading time (from stack)	all	183	0.769	0.380	0.752	0.406	0.100
Trolley speed (with container)	all	185	12.663	6.416	11.653	4.597	0.100
Free trolley speed	-	89	49.076	30.202	46.609	29.892	0.144
Crane speed	-	30	12.916	5.515	11.498	4.586	0.242

Handling activity	container tipology	sample n	Moment estimation		M-L estimation (Gamma r.v. parameters)		K-S bound
			$\bar{x}$ (minutes)	$\bar{s}$ (minutes)	mean (minutes)	standard deviation (minutes)	Dn,α $\alpha = 0,05$
Unloading time (to shuttle/truck)	20F	44	1.303	0.460	1.260	0.484	0.205
Unloading time (to shuttle/truck)	40F	33	1.367	0.402	1.410	0.461	0.231
Trolley speed (with container)	20F	39	13.243	4.142	12.740	4.275	0.217
Trolley speed (with container)	40F	146	12.508	6.902	11.203	4.530	0.112

Figure 5. Reach Stacker (RS): Estimation results

Handling activity	container tipology	sample n	Moment estimation		M-L estimation (Gamma r.v. parameters)		K-S bound
			$\bar{x}$ (minutes)	$\bar{s}$ (minutes)	mean (minutes)	standard deviation (minutes)	Dn,α $\alpha = 0,05$
Unloading time from shuttle/truck	all	173	0.215	0.114	0.186	0.074	0.103
Loading time to shuttle/truck	all	257	0.357	0.250	0.307	0.170	0.085
Stacking time (all tier)	all	152	0.288	0.157	0.260	0.146	0.110
Stacking time to tier 1	all	33	0.201	0.062	0.185	0.056	0.231
Stacking time to tier 2	all	37	0.186	0.077	0.167	0.071	0.223
Stacking time to tier 3	all	29	0.238	0.098	0.212	0.086	0.246
Stacking time to tier 4	all	29	0.355	0.148	0.334	0.118	0.246
Stacking time to tier 5	all	24	0.542	0.164	0.542	0.140	0.269

Handling activity	container tipology	sample n	Moment estimation		M-L estimation (Gamma r.v. parameters)		K-S bound
			$\bar{x}$ (minutes)	$\bar{s}$ (minutes)	mean (minutes)	standard deviation (minutes)	Dn,α $\alpha = 0,05$
Unloading time from shuttle/truck	20F	40	0.153	0.055	0.144	0.056	0.215
Unloading time from shuttle/truck	40F	21	0.236	0.119	0.200	0.087	0.287
Loading time to shuttle/truck	20E	57	0.342	0.250	0.301	0.181	0.180
Loading time to shuttle/truck	20F	67	0.344	0.205	0.304	0.155	0.166
Loading time to shuttle/truck	40F	128	0.365	0.272	0.311	0.138	0.120

- global performance indicators
  - average container dwelling time;
  - average crane hours per working hour;
  - vessel average time at berth;
  - average number of workers per vessel per shift;
  - total cost/time employed per vessel;

- ○ average fraction of time workers are idle;
- ○ total crane cost per crane/hour;
- ○ worker cost/hour per crane;
- local performance indicators
  - ○ *handling equipment indicators;*
    - ▪ vessel loading and/or unloading time;
    - ▪ quay/yard crane idle time;
    - ▪ shuttle waiting time;
    - ▪ shuttle transfer time;
    - ▪ reach stacker stacking time;
    - ▪ reach stacker idle time;
    - ▪ gate in/out waiting time;
  - ○ *container indicator;*
    - ▪ container operation time: time required to move a container with handling equipment (e.g., time spent moving a container from quay to vessel or from shuttle to stack).

The choice of these indicators was determined by the type of data measured by the terminal monitoring office. Since the output of stochastic simulation may be considered a realization of a stochastic process (the time associated to each single activity is the realization of a random variable), the values used for calibration are obtained by determining the average of 25 simulations (see Law and Kelton, 2000, about the "replication/ deletion approach" for calculating the number of simulations required to obtain an estimate of the sampling average with a fixed interval of reliability).

In table 1 the values of global indicators are reported in terms of observed data. As can be seen, for the Salerno Container Terminal we have an average container dwelling time of 7 days for export operations, 14 days for import operations and 12 days for transhipment operations. With respect to the crane global indicators we observe an average crane hours per working hour of 0.85

which points to a relatively high efficiency of crane usage. The observed vessel average time at berth is about 12 hours; for each vessel the average number of workers per vessel and per shift is about 11; the estimated fraction of time that workers are idle is about 9%.

With respect to the economic global indicators, the total worker cost per hour and per vessel is about 367 €/hour; the worker cost per hour and per crane is about 25 €/hour; while the total crane cost per crane and per hour is about 36 litres of fuel consumption.

In table 2 results in terms of absolute percentage estimation error are reported. Obviously not all the performance indicators could be estimated for all the approaches implemented; for the aggregate approaches the local indicators related to the single container cannot be estimated due to the aggregate nature of the model. However, even if the nature of the disaggregate approach allows us to simulate both disaggregate and aggregate indicators, the high costs (in terms of monetary cost, data required and simulation time) of model implementation suggested implementing a disaggregate model able to simulate the daily

Table 1. Global performance indicators

global performance indicator	observed data
average container dwelling time	7 days for export operation 14 days for import operation 12 days for transhipment operation
average crane hours per working hour	0.85
vessel average time at berth	12 hours
average number of workers per vessel per shift	11
fraction of time workers are idle	9%
total crane cost per crane / hour (liters of fuel consumption)	36 litres / hour
worker cost/hour per crane	25 € / hour
total worker cost/hour per vessel	367 € / hour

performance of the Salerno terminal. This time interval does not allow estimation of the global indicators proposed, which is why simulation of more than one day consecutively is required.

With respect to the aggregate approach, the simulation results show simulation times lower than 12 seconds. Results in terms of global indicators show an average absolute percentage error of more than 10% for the aggregate model with the Sample Mean Undifferentiated (SMU) handling model, whereas in using the Random Variable Undifferentiated (RVU) handling model the percentage estimation error is lower than 5%. With respect to the handling equipment local indicators, the SMU handling model produces an estimation error of more than 18% while the estimation error of the RVU handling model is just over 4%. Hence the aggregate approach using Sample Mean handling models can be used only for global indicator estimation while Random Variable handling models generate good results also in terms of handling equipment indicator estimations.

With respect to the disaggregate approach the use of Sample Mean handling models does not produce very good results in terms of local indicators; average percentage estimation errors are more than 11% for handling equipment indicators and about 30% for container indicators.

Results obtained using Random Variable handling models are significant; average absolute percentage errors for handling equipment indicators are more than 6% with the RVU handling model, and about 3% with Random Variable Container Type (RVCT) handling models. With respect to container indicators, when only using the RVCT handling models the absolute percentage estimation error is acceptable (>11%); in all the other cases the estimation errors are about 30%.

In conclusion, the disaggregate approach is particularly suitable for local indicator estimation. Results differ according to the handling models used; Sample Mean models could be used for estimating handling equipment indicators, with absolute percentage errors of 11%-13%; using Random Variable handling models for estimating handling equipment indicators, absolute percentage errors decrease to 3%-6%. To estimate container movement performance (container indicators) only the RVCT handling models can be used.

From the model validation results we may obtain the following application guidelines:

- due to the high implementation costs, application of the disaggregate approach is convenient (from a cost-benefit point of view) only for estimating disaggregate performance indicators (especially for the simulation of the single container movement); by contrast, due to the lower

Table 2. Absolute percentage estimation error: estimation sample

approach	handling model	simulation time (minutes)	absolute percentage estimation error		
			global indicators	local indicators	
				handling equipment	containers
aggregate	SMU	0.01	10.2%	18.4%	-
aggregate	RVU	0.20	4.8%	4.4%	-
disaggregate	SMU	0.50	n.a.	13.2%	30.8%
disaggregate	SMCT	0.60	n.a.	11.0%	29.3%
disaggregate	RVU	18.70	n.a.	6.5%	28.5%
disaggregate	RVCT	21.30	n.a.	3.0%	11.2%

implementation costs the aggregate approach should be used for all aggregate performance indicator estimation (especially for simulating global container terminal performance and at times for equipment performance estimation);

- the choice of the handling model disaggregation level and the stochastic/deterministic nature of the phenomenon play a major role in model application; if the object of the simulation is estimation of global container terminal performance, Sample Mean Undifferentiated handling models should be used; while if single container movement has to be simulated, the only suitable handling models are Random Variable Container Type models (20' full and/or empty; 40' full and/or empty; 2 x 20' full and/or empty).

To evaluate the model's sensitivity, the percentage performance indicators variations with respect to the input variables percentage variations (e.g., percentage variation of equipment numbers or of equipment performances) were estimated. In figure 6 some representative results obtained with the discrete event simulation model implemented are

reported (results related to the other performance indicators and referred to the diachronic capacitated flow network model are analogous).

With respect to the gate-in activity, the truck waiting time (queue waiting time plus service time) percentage variation was estimated with respect to the service time percentage variation; the simulation results show an expected decrease benefit effect; in particular, -10% of service time produce about -35% of truck waiting time; -20% of service time produce about -55% of waiting time while -30% of service time produce more than -70% of waiting time.

With respect to the vessel loading time, one of the main critical point of the Salerno terminal is the low arrival frequency of the shuttles near the vessels; for this reason, a crane number increase not produce great reduction in term of vessel loading time (see figure 6); instead, a shuttle leg time reduction produce significant vessel loading time variation (e.g., -30% of shuttle lag time produce about -30% of vessel loading time). This phenomena is verified till the crane capacity is reached; then only a combined increase of crane number with the shuttle lag time could further increase the performance of the loading activity.

Figure 6. An example of model's sensitivity: vessel loading time and gate in waiting time variation (results of discrete event simulation model)

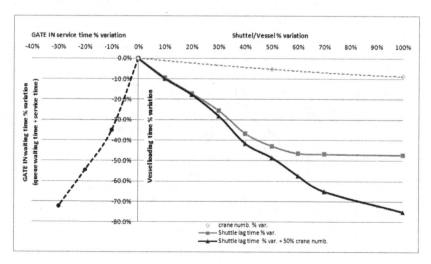

Before and After Analysis

As said, this chapter investigates the prediction reliability of container terminal simulation models, through a *before and after analysis*.

This kind of analysis is particularly suitable for model validation; in particular, the disaggregate and aggregate simulation models implemented in 2003 (*before scenario*) were validated with a large set of data acquired in 2008 after some structural and functional terminal modifications (*after scenario*).

Through a *what if* approach, the model system implemented was used to identify a sample of project scenarios which improve the performance of the Salerno terminal (with respect to the 2003 scenario). A project scenario has some system modifications (e.g., variation in number of cranes per vessel; yard layout changes; shuttle lag time variation). To identify the choice set some constraints were taken into account, such as budget availability, terminal layout and handling equipment availability.

The choice of which project scenario to improve was made through economic evaluation (see figure 7). For all the project scenarios, variations in performance indicators with respect to the 2003 scenario were estimated. In particular, both the aggregate model (with Sample Mean Undifferentiated handling models) and the disaggregate one (with Random Variable Container Type models) were used. The first model was used to evaluate global indicators while the second was used to estimate the local indicators introduced above. These indicator variations were converted into economic profit (in Euros); for example an hour of vessel loading saved was converted into Euros saved per vessel hour saved. This profit includes all the costs economized such as vessel time at berth, container dwelling time, number of workers per vessel per shift and number of shifts per vessel.

The choice of the best project to improve was made by comparing profits with the costs (in euro) required to modify the system (e.g., the cost of a new crane or changing the yard layout).

Figure 7. Methodology for project scenario identification: economic evaluation

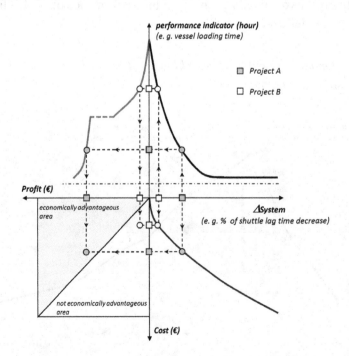

Such economic comparisons showed that some scenarios, in spite of transport benefits, were not economically advantageous since profits were lower than realization costs (see Figure 7).

The main characteristics of the project scenario chosen are:

- a new automated gate in/out with two new gates (4 gates in all);
- a new yard layout: new location inside the terminal and increase in size;
- a new yard crane (3 in total);
- new shuttle paths from gate to yard and from yard to berth.

The data acquired in 2008 related to this improved project scenario (as said, not used for model estimation) were compared with the estimated ones to test the prediction reliability of the model system implemented.

Judging from the average percentage prediction error (table 3), the model system implemented has a good capacity to reproduce the data acquired in 2008; the aggregate model with SC handling has an average prediction error of more than 7% in terms of global indicators; while the disaggregate model with SCT handling models produces an average prediction error of about 4% with respect to equipment indicators and about 10% with respect to container indicators. In conclusion the model system applied has a good capacity to reproduce the project scenario implemented, confirming the validation results reported in table 2.

The validation results suggest the fields of applications of the model approaches implemented:

- the aggregate approach is useful for aggregate performance indicator estimations (global indicators), both aggregate and disaggregate handling models could be used; this approach, through a *what if* approach, could be used to assess the benefits of long-term investments (e.g., a new berth or a new automated control system) or to assess the benefits of medium-term investment (for example a new yard layout or a new gate in/out);
- the disaggregate approach is useful for estimating disaggregate performance indicators related to handling equipment, with possible use of both aggregate and disaggregate handling models; this approach could be used to assess the benefits of short-term investments (e.g., a new handling equipment or new shuttle paths for traffic congestion reduction);
- the disaggregate approach with Random Variable models handling models differentiated by container type is the only approach useful for estimating single container movement; this approach is particularly suitable for real-time applications (e.g., real-time container flow control or emergency control).

CONCLUSION

This chapter investigated the prediction reliability of container terminal simulation models, through a *before and after analysis*, taking advantage of some significant investment made by the Salerno

Table 3. Absolute percentage prediction error: hold-out sample

approach	handling model	simulation time (minutes)	absolute percentage prediction error		
			global indicators	local indicators	
				handling equipment	containers
aggregate	RVU	0.22	7.4%	-	-
disaggregate	RVCT	22.09	-	3.9%	9.7%

Container Terminal (Italy) between 2003 and 2008. In particular, the disaggregate and aggregate simulation models implemented in 2003 (see Cartenì et al., 2005 and de Luca et al., 2008) were validated with a large set of data acquired in 2008 after some structural and functional terminal modifications. Through this analysis it was possible to study both the mathematical details required for model application and the field of application (prediction reliability) of the different simulation approaches implemented.

The validation results suggested several guidelines for applications. Due to the high implementation costs, the disaggregate approach application is convenient (from a cost-benefit point of view) only for disaggregate performance indicator estimations (especially for simulating single container movements). By contrast, due to lower implementation costs the aggregate approach is more suitable for all aggregate performance indicator estimations (especially to simulate global container terminal performance and, at times, equipment performance estimation). Furthermore, choice of the handling model disaggregation level and the stochastic/deterministic nature of the phenomenon play a major role in the model application; if the object of the simulation is to estimate all performance in the container terminal, Sample Mean Undifferentiated handling models could be used; while if simulation of single container movements is required, the only suitable handling models are the Random Variable models disaggregated by container type (20' full and/or empty; 40' full and/or empty; 2 x 20' full and/or empty).

The results of this research show that under some specific hypotheses a terminal simulation model could be used to reproduce a hypothetic project scenario. The proposed model system allows terminal performance to be measured, and two main applications may be carried out: (i) *cost analysis* in order to identify terminal critical points, and (ii) *scenario analysis* in order to simulate the feasibility, effectiveness and efficiency of project scenarios due to supply system modifications.

With respect to the field of application, the aggregate approach was shown to be useful for predictions in terms of aggregate performance indicators (global indicators); this approach, through a *what if* approach, could be used to assess the benefits of long-term investments or to assess the benefits of medium-term investment. The disaggregate approach was found useful to predict the effects of project scenarios in terms of disaggregate performance indicators related to handling equipments and single container movements; this approach could be used to assess the benefits of short-term investments and is particularly suitable for real-time applications.

This kind of Decision Support System (DSS) could be used by a terminal operator seeking to choose the best project to develop and wishing to maximize firm benefits.

ACKNOWLEDGMENT

Salerno Container Terminal through Antonio Barbara provided most of data and supported the *ad hoc* surveys. All the results reported in this chapter are the author's estimations; Salerno terminal is not responsible for the values published. The author is grateful to G.E. Cantarella and S. de Luca as partners of the research project, and Pasquale Modica for his assistance in data collection.

REFERENCES

Avriel, M., Penn, M., Shpirer, N., & Witteboon, S. (1998). Stowage planning for container ships to reduce the number of shifts. *Annals of Operations Research, 76*, 55–71. doi:10.1023/A:1018956823693

Bielli, M., Boulmakoul, A., & Rida, M. (2006). Object oriented model for container terminal distributed simulation. *European Journal of Operational Research, 175*, 1731–1751. doi:10.1016/j.ejor.2005.02.037

Cartenì, A., Cantarella, G. E., & de Luca, S. (2005). A simulation model for a container terminal. In *Proceeding of the European Transport Conference (ETC) 2005*, Strasbourg, France.

Chen, C.-Y., & Hsieh, T.-W. (2002, July). A time–space network model for the berth allocation problem. *19th IFIP TC7 Conference on System Modeling and Optimization*, Cambridge, UK, 1999.

Cheung, R. K., Li, C.-L., & Lin, W. (2002). Inter-block crane deployment in container terminals. *Transportation Science, 36*(1), 79–83. doi:10.1287/trsc.36.1.79.568

Choi, Y. S. (2000). *Simulator for Port Container Terminal Using An Object-Oriented Approach.* PhD thesis, Quality System Analysis Lab., Industrial Engineering, Pusan National University.

de Luca, S., Cantarella, G. E., & Cartenì, A. (2008). A macroscopic model of a container terminal based on diachronic networks. Schedule-Based Modeling of Transportation Networks. Wilson, Nuzzolo (Ed.). Springer.

El Sheikh, A. A. R., Paul, R. J., Harding, A. S., & Balmer, D. W. (1987). A microcomputer-based simulation study of a port. *The Journal of the Operational Research Society, 38*(8), 673–681.

Imai, A., Nagaiwa, K., & Tat, C. W. (1997). Efficient planning of berth allocation for container terminals in Asia. *Journal of Advanced Transportation, 31*(1), 75–94. doi:10.1002/atr.5670310107

Imai, A., & Nishimurra, E. (2001). Papadimitriou S. The dynamic berth allocation problem for a container port. *Transportation Research Part B: Methodological, 35*, 401–417. doi:10.1016/S0191-2615(99)00057-0

Kia, M., Shayan, E., & Ghotb, F. (2002). Investigation of port capacity under a new approach by computer simulation. *Computers & Industrial Engineering, 42*, 533–540. doi:10.1016/S0360-8352(02)00051-7

Kim, K. H., & Bae, J. W. (1998). Re-marshaling export containers in port container terminals. *Computers & Industrial Engineering, 35*(3–4), 655–658. doi:10.1016/S0360-8352(98)00182-X

Kim, K. H., & Kim, H. B. (1998). The optimal determination of the space requirement and the number of transfer cranes for import containers. *Computers & Industrial Engineering 35*(3– 4), 427–430.

KMI – Korea Maritime Istitute (2000). A Study on the System Design and Operations of Automated Container Terminal. *Internal report.*

Koh, P. H., Goh, J. L. K., Ng, H. S., & Ng, H. C. (1994). Using simulation to preview plans of a container port operations. *Proceedings of the 1994 Winter Simulation.* Tew, Manivannan, Sadowski, Seila (Ed.).

Lai, K. K., & Shih, K. (1992). A study of container berth allocation. *Journal of Advanced Transportation, 26*(1), 45–60. doi:10.1002/atr.5670260105

Lee, S. Y., & Cho, G. S. (2007). A Simulation Study for the Operations Analysis of Dynamic Planning in Container Terminals Considering RTLS. *IEEE Xplore® digital library.*

Legato, P., Gullì, D., Trunfio, R., & Simino, R. (2008). Simulation at a Maritime Container Terminal: Models and Computational Frameworks. In *Proceedings of the 22th European Conference on Modelling and Simulation* (ECMS 2008), Nicosia (Cyprus), 261-269.

Merkuryeva, G., Merkuryev, Y., & Tolujev, J. (2000). Computer simulation and Metamodelling of logistics processes at a container terminal. *Studies in Informatics and Control, 9*(1), 1–10.

Murty, K. G., Liu, J., Wan, Y., & Linn, R. (2005). A decision support system for operations in a container terminal. *Decision Support Systems, 39*(3), 309–332. doi:10.1016/j.dss.2003.11.002

Nishimura, E., Imai, A., & Papadimitriou, S. (2001). Berth allocation in the public berth system by genetic algorithms. *European Journal of Operational Research, 131*, 282–292. doi:10.1016/S0377-2217(00)00128-4

Parola, F., & Sciomachen, A. (2005). Intermodal container flows in a port system network: Analysis of possible growths via simulation models. *International Journal of Production Economics, 97*, 75–88. doi:10.1016/j.ijpe.2004.06.051

Petering, M. E. H. (2009). Effect of block width and storage yard layout on marine container terminal performance. *Transportation Research Part E, Logistics and Transportation Review, 45*, 591–610. doi:10.1016/j.tre.2008.11.004

Shabayek, A. A., & Yeung, W. W. (2002). A simulation model for the Kwai Chung container terminals in Hong Kong. *European Journal of Operational Research, 140*, 1–11. doi:10.1016/S0377-2217(01)00216-8

Steenken, D., Voss, S., & Stahlbock, R. (2004). Container terminal operation and operations research - a classification and literature review. *OR-Spektrum, 26*, 3–49. doi:10.1007/s00291-003-0157-z

Taleb-Ibrahimi, M., Castilho, B. D., & Daganzo, C. F. (1993). Storage space vs. handling work in container terminals. *Transportation Research Part B: Methodological, 27*(1), 13–32. doi:10.1016/0191-2615(93)90009-Y

Thiers, G., & Janssens, G. (1998). A Port Simulation Model as a Permanent Decision Instrument. *Simulation, 71*, 117–125. doi:10.1177/003754979807100206

Tugcu, S. (1983). A simulation study on the determination of the best investment plan for Istanbul seaport. *The Journal of the Operational Research Society, 34*(6), 479–487.

Van Hee, K. M., & Wijbrands, R. J. (1988). Decision support system for container terminal planning. *European Journal of Operational Research, 34*, 262–272. doi:10.1016/0377-2217(88)90147-6

Wilson, I. D., Roach, P. A., & Ware, J. A. (2001). Container stowage preplanning: using search to generate solution, a case study. *Knowledge-Based Systems, 14*, 137–145. doi:10.1016/S0950-7051(01)00090-9

Yun, W. Y., & Choi, Y. S. (1999). A simulation model for container-terminal operation analysis using an object-oriented approach. *International Journal of Production Economics, 59*, 221–230. doi:10.1016/S0925-5273(98)00213-8

Zhang, C., Liu, J., Wan, Y.-W., Murty, K. G., & Linn, R. J. (2003). Storage space allocation in container terminals. *Transportation Research Part B: Methodological, 37*, 883–903. doi:10.1016/S0191-2615(02)00089-9

Zhang, C., Wan, Y.-W., Liu, J., & Linn, R. (2002). Dynamic crane deployment in container storage yards. *Transportation Research Part B: Methodological, 36*(6), 537–555. doi:10.1016/S0191-2615(01)00017-0

KEY TERMS AND DEFINITIONS

Before and After Analysis: This kind of analysis is particularly suitable for model validation. In particular, the model is implemented (specified and calibrated) through a data sample related to an *actual scenario* (actual system configuration), and is validated through its capacity to reproduce the data related to an *after scenario* (after some significant system modification) and not used for model's estimation.

Decision Support System (DSS): In the transportation system analysis, a DSS is a mathematical model, usefull both to analyze the actual system situation (to identify system inadequacies or critical points) and to verify one or more alternative projects/interventions. Indeed, a crucial element in the management process is the simulation of the effects or impacts of a project scenario. Most of these impacts can be quantitatively simulated using mathematical models, which allow us to estimate system indicators (cost-benefit indicators; multi-criteria indicators, …) without physically carrying out the hypothesized projects.

Handling Equipment Model: (sometimes called cost function or performance function) is a model assigned to each container terminal activity in order to estimate the time required to bring one or more activities to a close (sometimes termed: activity time duration). A handling equipment model can be assumed deterministic or stochastic. In the former case represent the average time required to bring an activity (e.g. average crane loading time); in the latter case a random variable should be calibrated in order to model the activity time duration uncertainty.

Chapter 18
New Profession Development:
The Case for the Business Process Engineer

Ying Tat Leung
IBM Almaden Research Center, USA

Nathan S. Caswell
Janus Consulting, USA

Manjunath Kamath
Oklahoma State University, USA

ABSTRACT

Adding engineering discipline to defining and managing the operation of business processes has become a truism although results of practical application have been mixed. This chapter argues that an obstacle to business process (re)engineering is the lack of a business process engineer role with an associated professional education, tools, and community. The main argument derives from an analysis of the domain structure for system design and comparison with existing practices in manufacturing engineering. We observe that: (1) At present there does not exist a profession of business process engineers. Their role in a firm is filled, on an ad-hoc basis, by business line personnel, information technology analysts or architects, and/or management consultants; (2) There is an increasingly critical need to master the subject of business process engineering for an individual firm as well as the general U.S. industry; (3) Other professionals, while having their own specialized skills valuable to a firm, do not necessarily have the optimal skill set for business process engineering. We therefore conclude that there is an urgent need for a professional business process engineer. We discuss the skills required of this profession and briefly describe a first course offered at a university on this subject. We propose that academic institutions should seriously consider such a new program today.

DOI: 10.4018/978-1-61520-603-2.ch018

INTRODUCTION AND PRELIMINARIES

It would be reasonable to assume that business transformation, process redesign or reengineering, an area much talked about by industry and academia, and practiced by a wide gamut of industries for more than a decade, is a fairly well defined academic and/or professional discipline. Our careful examination of this area indicates that this is not the case. In this paper, we argue for the need of such a discipline, which should be practised by a business process engineer (BPE). The success of the profession and ultimately, the business enterprises it serves depends on associated professional community, education, and standards.

Historical Background

The goal of every enterprise is profitable, efficient, and effective delivery of valuable products and services to a customer. Since the industrial revolution, the complexity of accomplishing this goal has increased through regular cycles of technological innovation followed by adaptive business restructuring to effectively capture new value. Enterprises have moved from basic production, to transporting goods to remote markets, to managing corporations of a national or international scale [Perez, 2002]. In the present "information age" cycle, information processing, communication and storage technologies shift the focus of innovation from task-oriented productivity to system responsiveness. Recognition of time as a competitive differentiator (see e.g., Blackburn [1990]) and the more recent focus on globalization are driving a dramatic increase in coordination and coherence across worldwide systems. Finding means to cope with the increased complexity is essential to the core enterprise goal.

Simple automation of existing coordination structures is not sufficient. In manufacturing, digital processing has recapitulated the technologi-cal evolution since the industrial revolution. In manufacturing, the first wave of computerization focused on factory automation but often failed to deliver the expected cost saving. Postmortem studies revealed that even locally effective automation addressed only about 5% of factory cost structure. Addressing the remaining 95% drove a new engineering discipline focused on coordinating manufacturing processes and supply chain management utilizing the basic, physical production steps. Recognizing cross-functional business processes (see, e.g., Davenport and Short [1990]), we came to realize that a set of related tasks in different functional areas - say, sales, purchasing, design, manufacturing, and distribution - had to be treated collectively. The focus again was placed on automating activities, but this time across functional areas, within large "turn-key" enterprise resource planning (ERP) systems.

The pattern of business automation is not dissimilar to that of the first wave of factory automation with a focus on automated tools for individual activities. Results similar to that of factory automation occurred for similar reasons [Davenport, 1998]. However, we cannot expect information technology (IT) to compensate for the inadequacies of a business process design. Automating an unproductive task will consume unnecessary resources even faster. On the other hand, automating a well designed process could provide additional yet critical benefits of time reduction for the overall process. When time delays cannot be eliminated or reduced through process design (such as in a step of physically transforming materials), automation is our last resort.

In this chapter we observe that the sequence of activities in business process design and engineering is analogous to that of a manufacturing process design. We elaborate this comparison in Section 2. Such similarity leads us to argue the need for a business process engineer as a more general version of the more familiar manufacturing systems engineer or process planner. This new role does not replace the typical multi-disciplinary team that is assigned the responsibility of designing a business process, but rather adds critical skills to the team so that the resulting process design is technically sound. We describe the role of the business process engineer in more detail in Section 3 and propose in Section 4 propose a core skill set a BPE ought to possess. Section 5 discusses our experience in an initial step towards business process engineering education. In our concluding remarks in Section 6, we explain why it is important to recognize the need for the role of BPE and devote adequate resources for the creation of such at the present time. The time to act is now.

A preliminary version of the material contained in this chapter was presented at the IEEE International Conference on Service Operations and Logistics, and Informatics in 2006 [Leung et al. 2006].

Definitions and Related Literature

There are several definitions and interpretations of terms related to business processes. We establish working definitions that we will use in this chapter. Similar definitions can be found in the literature; the Appendix provides a brief comparison.

We use variations of the definitions used in Davenport and Short [1990] and Towill [1997a], but are more specific to exclude manufacturing activities for this discussion (in general, business processes include manufacturing processes):

Business Process. A set of logically related activities in the day-to-day operation of a business, including planning activities (e.g., resource planning), business transactional activities (e.g., purchasing raw materials and selling products), customer service and support activities (e.g., handling warranty issues).

Business Process Engineering. We adopt the definition of Business Systems Engineering (BSE) suggested in Towill [1997a] as our definition for business process engineering: "BSE is a systems approach to designing new business processes and redesigning existing business processes. It

provides a structured way of maximizing both customer value and the performance of the individual business." [Towill 1997a]

Business Process Engineer (BPE). We argue in this paper that there is a need for a professional role in the framework of BSE as defined in Towill [1997a, b]. This professional role, whom we call a Business Process Engineer, would be a key contributor in the multi-disciplinary team that Towill advocated. The job of a BPE is design and development of business processes that provide efficient and effective composition and coordination of individual skilled activities to bridge the strategic needs of the business.

Since the influential work by Hammer and Champy [1997], many authors have discussed the importance of business process engineering. More recently, Karmarkar [2004] proposes several key competencies for a business enterprise to compete in the services based economy, one of which is business process design. In Chesbrough [2004], the author puts forth an agenda for services innovation research and argues, "Any useful understanding of the opportunities and risks that are unique to services innovation will invariably involve business process modeling, business models, systems integration and design." As we shall see later, these activities constitute a key set of components of business process engineering. Rouse [2004] proposes that industrial engineers need to expand their focus to the entire business enterprise and even external entities that interact with it, including its suppliers, distributors, customers, and competitors. The author points out a number of potential education and research topics, a crucial one of which is understanding the relationships between these entities and the entire value stream that flows within and between these entities. These relationships are manifested on a day-to-day basis in intra- and inter-enterprise business processes that need to be designed and controlled in an optimal way. Our chapter contributes along the same line of thought as these works, but we show in detail why there is a need for business process engineering and specify what role a business process engineer would play in the overall design and operation of an enterprise.

A related work is Tien and Berg [2003], in which the authors propose a set of engineering methods and principles for service systems. These methods span the entire life cycle of a service transaction, from planning to execution to measurement. Our proposed role of the business process engineer would be a practitioner of some of these methods to design and engineer a business process. In particular, all of the four major characteristics of a service system (information driven, customer centric, e-oriented, and productivity focused) would be key foci of the business process engineer. Business process engineering would be a part of service systems engineering, but is not limited to service enterprises. It is applicable and useful for traditional manufacturing industries as well as government institutions.

In the last several years there has been a fairly wide recognition in academia of the need of a transformation in business related academic programs to reflect the needs of the changing environment. Most notable are proposals in Industrial Engineering [Askin et al., 2004; Kamath and Mize, 2003; McGinnis, 2002; Rouse, 2004; Settles, 2003] and Business (e.g. Smith and Fingar [2002: Appendix E]). This chapter is a contribution to defining the requirements for these new programs.

Obviously, business processes have been in existence as long as businesses themselves. They are a necessity for a business to operate and deliver its output, be it a physical product or a service. It is only relatively recently (about two decades ago) that we have used the term "business processes" and have focused on studying them. The reason is that up until then business processes were relatively simple and to a large extent manual. There was only one or two ways of doing things. Manufacturing processes, on the other hand, were already quite complex and required several engineering disciplines to set up production (most often including electrical engineering, mechanical

engineering, and industrial or production engineering)[1]. Today, business processes have also become quite complicated due to several reasons. First, as physical products become increasingly complex, the complexity of processes that support and coordinate all the manufacturing related functions has also grown accordingly. Second, logistics (and hence all its associated processes), be it material supply, distribution of products, or even logistics of information from suppliers, distributors, and end users have become a round-the-clock, global operation. Third, new technology has raised new possibilities and alternatives. For example, a customer can now place an order through different means: phone, email, fax, electronic data interchange, or the world-wide web. An order management process has to handle all of these alternatives. Finally, the combination of the above three factors has increased the complexity and alternative possibilities of business processes that they now rival manufacturing processes. Coupled with the tremendous growth of the service industries where business processes are the "manufacturing" processes, it is natural to seriously consider the subject of business process engineering now.

A Framework for System Design

For the exposition of the proposed BPE role, we start from an articulation of the general problem of system design shown in Figure 1. This framework forms the basis for analysis of existing roles in business design and comparison with analogous domains. Referring to Figure 1, three horizontal layers appear in business design, corresponding to the design of the system as a whole, design of a configuration of components, and design of the components themselves. Such a three-layered framework has its roots from general systems theory (see, e.g., Bertalanffy (1976)).

The "system definition" layer (i.e., the top layer) defines the intent of the system, its positioning within a known external environment,

Figure 1. A framework for business system design

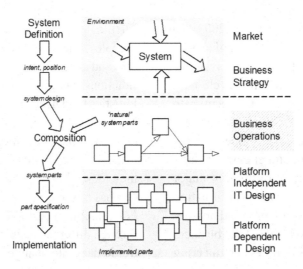

and external behavior of the system in interacting with its environment. The outcome of a system definition activity is a description of the external interactions of the system defining its relationships with the environment from the perspective of the environment (such as a customer). The external environment involved is generally very different in nature from the internals of the business system. Engineering this top layer obviously requires strategic considerations of the environment that are only possible with distinct training, skills, and knowledge.

The "implementation" or component layer (i.e., the bottom layer) focuses on the design of each of a set of parts from which the system is assembled. The design takes place from the perspective of an execution infrastructure for the business. Each component ultimately will represent a physical entity (such as a human operator trained in some specific tasks, a machine for producing physical parts, or a database engine), since a business will deliver some physical entity or activity to a customer.

In a typical business process engineering exercise, the top layer is likely to be outside the scope of the design effort. The top layer is the job of senior executives or entrepreneurs whose

approaches or "algorithms" are an entire research subject. The outcome of the top layer is usually given at the outset of the business process engineering project.

In a way, one can also view that the bottom layer is often outside the scope of a business process engineering exercise. Unlike the top layer, the bottom layer is usually not explicitly given, but it is practically constrained to a finite set of choices, such as machine types, software packages, or traditional job descriptions or functional positions (for humans). It is entirely possible that new machines or software packages can be custom built from scratch, but such cases are not very common. It would be technically easier to create new job descriptions, but would still be nontrivial to gain acceptance and success of the new position.

On the right side of Figure 1, we map our system design framework onto the specific case of designing a business system. To this end, we chose to use the four layer framework proposed by Kumaran [2004]. The system definition layer corresponds to the market definition and business strategy stages, the system composition to the business operations and platform independent

IT design stages, the implementation layer to the platform independent IT design and platform dependent IT design stages. The business operations stage is the logical design of the business operations required to satisfy the overall or strategic objectives as defined by the top layer of business strategy and design. Commonly the case nowadays, the business operations are supported by information technology. The platform independent IT design stage is where the logical design of the supporting IT system takes place. This design is usually different from the business operations design because very rarely one can completely automate the entire business. (At least so far we have not seen a completely automated business.) The logical design is independent of the software or hardware platforms that might be used for its actual implementation. The platform dependent design is the detailed specification of the supporting IT system that can be built or purchased (or partially purchased and partially built) without knowledge of any of the layers above it. It is a blue-print of the system that can be given to, say, a third party system development vendor to build.

DESIGN AND DEVELOPMENT OF A BUSINESS PROCESS AND A MANUFACTURING PROCESS

In this section we present the adaptations of the above system design framework for the design of a business process and a manufacturing process. As we will see, the framework adapted for manufacturing process design is commonly found and is relatively well understood. By comparing the business process design version with the manufacturing one, we can identify gaps in business process design that is practiced today, in particular the missing role of the business process engineer.

To examine the separate cases of designing a business process and a manufacturing process, we assume that the external characteristics of the system, the strategy layer, are given. For the manufacturing process this includes the material input and product produced. Following Nigam and Caswell [2003] we take purpose of a process to be the attainment of some operational goal, such as a sales transaction, and the product to be a *business artifact*. A business artifact is a representation of the information required to know the current state of progress toward the goal.

Referring to Figure 1, the first step in the system composition band is identification of the parts that will perform the activities to produce the business artifact in question. Figure 2 is a more detailed version of the right side of Figure 1, including the typical roles that are responsible for the different design stages. For a manufacturing process, the manufacturing strategy includes specifications such as make or buy, or the extent to which we make the product, the type of production facility – existing or new, job shop or highly automated flow line, etc. Similarly, for a business process, the business strategy will include considerations such as what part of the process is done in house or outsourced and the location and nature of the facility - existing or new. Clearly, the exact factors to be considered depend on the nature of the business artifacts, the existing business environment and long-term strategy of the firm, the expected volume, profit, and life expectancy of the business artifacts and their possible follow-on relatives, etc. At the same time, high level strategic goals are set, such as target lead times, customer order lead times, target work-in-process inventory levels, and finished goods inventory levels.

For the exposition of this chapter, we purposely chose to assume that a cellular manufacturing approach will be used in the example of manufacturing process design. The design of many business processes has much in common with the design of manufacturing cells, as observed independently by MacIntosh [1997]. Further, we assume that we will use product oriented manufacturing cells, i.e. one or few dedicated cells will be designed for the product line in question.

Figure 2. A framework for business process and manufacturing process design

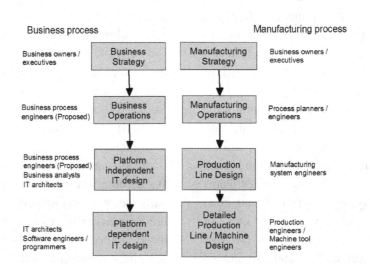

Design and Development of a Manufacturing Process

Based on the manufacturing strategy, overall planning of the manufacturing operation begins. Figure 3 depicts the sequence of activities after setting the manufacturing strategy. Besides following the systems design approach discussed above, this procedure is consistent with the typical manufacturing systems design practice of going from "rough-cut" to detailed design, as advocated by Browne et al. [1985], Nyman [1992], Suri [1985], among others. The first task in the manufacturing operation activity is to determine a manufacturing process plan for the products to be built, i.e. the processing steps required to transform the raw material to the final product. For example, a metal part may go through the steps of cutting, turning, milling, and final polishing steps. Complex parts may involve subassemblies which can either be purchased or made in-house. So make-vs.-buy decisions for subassemblies or components may be required at this stage. Once the process plan is developed, it will have to be executed by a physical manufacturing facility. Likely the firm already has certain existing manufacturing operation (which may be cellular or otherwise, or a mixture), so the

current task is to plan how the new cells fit into the existing facility and what impact they have on the existing operation. At this point only the key input and output of the new cells need to be known – raw materials and end products from the corresponding cells, or any work-in-process which have to be sent outside of the cells for processing, such as to a central paint shop or an electroplating line. In order to ascertain the input and output of the new cells, a very high level concept of the cells has to be developed, such as a preliminary grouping of products into families and assigning families to cells, the type and a rough number of the cells needed. In particular, product grouping is not a trivial task; many approaches and algorithms have been proposed in the literature for product or machine grouping to form manufacturing cells. Chapter 5 in Nyman [1992] proposed an approach for macro facility planning, assuming that the process plans are given and with an emphasis on planning for an entire facility from scratch.

Besides the direct production activities, the requirements of the new cells and new products on planning and control functions (such as production and inventory planning, shop floor order scheduling, and materials planning), and other indirect support functions (such as equipment maintenance and shipping) have to be considered. Using the lead time and inventory targets set by the manufacturing strategy, an approach to master production and inventory planning for the new products is devised. Existing planning methods for other products are very useful starting points. The production order release mechanism and intra-cell or department level shop floor scheduling are also designed, taking into account the corresponding processes for other, existing portions of the factory.

Once we have laid out what cells we will have, what goes in and comes out of those cells, and how those cells are controlled (in the production control sense) in the previous "manufacturing operation" activity, we can start to design the innards of each cell. This is the production line design activity in Figure 3. In this activity, the conceptual flow of material within the cell is developed, rough sizing of equipment is performed, and a high level layout of the cell is developed. Alternative designs are considered and evaluated using suitable analysis tools, such as modeling and simulation. Representative products (such as the

Figure 3. Manufacturing cell design framework (numbers in parentheses refer to chapter numbers in Nyman [1992])

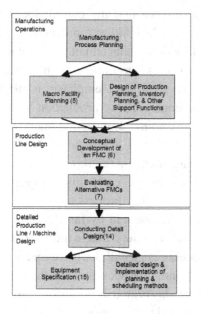

basic product in a family) or aggregated products (such as an "average" product in a family) can be used for most of the work here. As well, qualitative evaluation such as flexibility, future expansion capability, ease of maintenance, level of human skills required, and environmental considerations have to be performed. Chapters 6 and 7 in Nyman [1992] contain a practical approach to the production line design activity.

At the end of the production line design activity, we have a chosen cell design that represents the best cost benefit trade-off with reference to our strategic goals. This chosen cell design will have to be fully developed into an implementable plan, with all details such as the full specification of material handling and production equipment, as well as that of planning and control software and hardware. Sizing of all equipment (i.e., number of machines and their production rates) has to be determined. For decisions such as how many buffer spaces should be allowed for the input and output of each machine, or what the algorithm for loading jobs onto each machine should be, detailed analysis using simulation modeling is often necessary. Contrary to earlier activities, all parts that are planned to be produced by the new cells may have to be modeled. Besides performance issues, other aspects such as the handling of deadlocks (if it is a fully automated system) or the handling of reworks have to be considered. Chapter 14 in Nyman [1992] gives a comprehensive account of detailed design with an emphasis on the design of the physical cells. It also touches upon a control aspect – cell scheduling. Other facets of control, such as methods for production planning or inventory management of components and raw materials need to be considered as well. Chapter 15 in Nyman [1992] provides guidelines to equipment specification and request for proposals. Although these guidelines were apparently written with a focus on physical equipment, they also apply to software that is used for planning and control.

Design and Development of a Business Process

In business process design, we find it useful to follow the general approach used in manufacturing process design described above. Our proposed framework of business process design, as shown in Figure 4, thus follows a similar hierarchy of design/development activities. Nevertheless, some of the design considerations in a business process are different from those of a manufacturing process, since there are some fundamental differences in the nature of the two types of processes. Some of the key differences are as follows.

1. Because the processing of the business artifact in a business process is often information related and will mostly be supported by information technology, the emphasis will be on the logical rather than physical transformation of the business artifact. Physical facility planning will be simplified. For example, the input and output of the process can often be handled physically by a computer or communication network.

Figure 4. Business process design framework

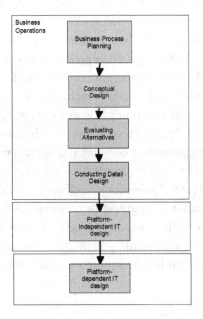

In other cases where physical transformation is needed, such as an equipment repair, the physical part is typically of small effort relative to the entire service process which includes handling a service call, traveling to the equipment site or the customer shipping the equipment, and getting the required service parts. The coordination of all these activities becomes more important than the physical repair operation.

2. The nature of an individual operation spans two extremes, from a manual operation carried out by a human operator with possibly large processing times with a high variance, to completely automated operation performed by a computer algorithm with very short and relatively deterministic processing times. Most automated processing steps can in fact be considered to be instantaneous at the logical design stage.

3. In many cases, information technology is the only "machine" available for automating business processes. At this point in time for most businesses, software is the major issue. Consequently, there is a much more pronounced emphasis on software in the first level process design activities, as can be seen from Figure 2.

4. We observe that the current focus of the software design/development is more on the transaction management aspect (e.g., work flow). This is as opposed to manufacturing where significant emphasis is placed on planning, such as production and inventory planning. Transaction management in manufacturing would be production order management, materials order management, and the like. Clearly this is important to a manufacturing process as well, but is not quite the one and by far the most focused upon. We believe that in the future business process design will also place equal emphasis on planning aspects and that they are not as such today primarily because manufacturing process design is more mature.

5. Because a business process usually involves human decisions and interventions, the number of possible paths is large and it is more important to provide exception handling capabilities in the process. This is especially true in service industries where the business artifact is co-produced with the customer [Vargo and Lusch 2004] and the customer is actively influencing how the process will proceed. Since the customer experiences the process first hand, in a way the business process itself is a business artifact seen by the customer. Hence we see the rise of the topic "experience engineering." [Carbone and Haeckel, 1994].

In business process design, given an overall business strategy (discussed above), the next step is to design the business operations. This is composed of several activities, as shown in Figure 4. Business process planning is analogous to developing a manufacturing process plan, where each operation step and the sequence of steps is specified logically. This differs from a manufacturing process plan in that the focus is on the requirements of the process, i.e., what the process needs to do, rather than the exact detailed steps ("the how"). For example, the operations may include a phone call being received, being routed to the appropriate operator, operator conversing with the caller, and so on. One of these operations may indeed be "manufacturing the product" but only a high level specification will be considered (e.g. system input and output).

Conceptual design will be focused on developing to some detail the necessary steps and their sequence, the logical interaction and impact of the process at hand on existing processes, and physical locations of human operators when intensive interaction between people is expected. As well, high level ideas are developed on how business artifacts are grouped such that a group is handled by a corresponding set of operators or a particular version of the process. Different logi-

cal alternatives are explored, such as combining certain operations, reducing checks and controls, centralized vs. decentralized operations [Hammer and Champy, 1993; Buzacott, 1996]. The level of detail in the conceptual design should be adequate to provide a meaningful comparison of different alternatives in terms of cost, response times, or other measures. Evaluating alternative designs is similar to the analogous step in manufacturing process design. Suitable analysis tools, including quantitative ones such as mathematical modeling and simulation and qualitative ones such as expert ranking, can be used to estimate the performance of the different alternatives.

One design is then chosen and full fledged details will be developed for that design. For example, a detailed specification of each activity in the business process, the exact sequences of the activities, the level of resources (human and machine) required to deliver the expected volume of work are drawn. The specification of each activity includes the input, output, and how the input is transformed to obtain the output. The machine requirements are most likely IT requirements, and at this point in the design process these are specified in terms of functional (e.g., what data need to be provided by the system) and non-functional (e.g., response time or volume of storage) requirements. With the detailed design, the process should be executable with the appropriate human operators, albeit completely manually.

The platform-independent IT design describes the processes and information flows that the user has chosen to implement in an IT system to support the overall business process. It does not assume a particular implementation (such as hardware and software platforms), allowing iterative performance improvement that are consistent with the requirements set by the previous detailed design step.

The platform-specific IT design defines the actual IT processes in a specific realization of the platform-independent IT design. Here hardware and software specifications are drawn. Today, many software tools can be used to help assemble or generate the actual code that is run during the operation of the business process. For example, modern enterprise resource planning (ERP) systems are becoming highly configurable. Once a specific ERP system is selected, the designer uses appropriate tools to assemble modules found in the system to develop a specific realization.

Note that in Figure 3 we have depicted the activities as sequential with one way arrows. However, this is not true in practice; feedback between two activities in sequence exists and the first activity may be revisited after the second activity is partially performed. For example, in the detailed production line design block, we may find that the chosen design may not be able to achieve our objectives (such as production lead time) and we may have to go back to the production line design block to explore other alternative designs that were proposed but not chosen. In fact, the entire manufacturing design block may feed back to the product design block (not shown in Figure 3) such that a product design may be modified to make it more manufacturing friendly. Such is the presently well-known principle of design for manufacture.

THE ROLE OF A BUSINESS PROCESS ENGINEER

To date, virtually all business process engineering work (including both one-time re-engineering efforts and continuous process improvement activities) has proceeded under the key assumption that facilitated interactions of subject matter experts (SME) is sufficient to re-engineer complex systems. Business process design work is canonically performed by a multi-disciplinary team selected from organizations currently operating the business. (See e.g., Hammer and Champy [1993], Towill [1997a, b]). More often than not, such design or redesign work is commenced when the business is facing a crisis, such as when it is

under intense financial pressure or when it is under severe attacks by new or very strong competitors. Typical teams include the following roles:

1. A business or executive sponsor. This is usually filled by a senior executive of the enterprise, whose role is to ensure that the process design effort will be a success, including the allocation of adequate resources to the effort.

2. A process owner who is responsible for the results produced by the process. This role ensures that the process produces the required output at a performance level that is satisfactory to the business.

3. Workers who carry out parts of the process on a daily basis. They are the subject matter experts (SMEs). They provide requirements to the design and also act as experts in how a necessary output can be achieved independent of any specific tool or system used.

4. IT architects whose primary purpose is to develop a high level design of the IT system to support the business processes and establish a design framework for all sub-systems to follow. They focus on the IT infrastructure such as computing networks and platforms, and technical aspects of applications such as availability, scalability, reliability, maintainability, and cost. They take user requirements (including functional requirements) from the SMEs and even though they may make suggestions to the process design, their rationale is IT based. IT architects also serve as the SME in the IT area, providing expertise on what is or is not possible from the technology point of view. The chief architect is typically the single point of contact for all matters related to IT, and may have overall responsibility for all such matters.

5. IT analysts who primarily act as the bridge between the users (the process workers or the SMEs) and the IT system developers or vendor. They take user requirements from

the SMEs, document them and translate them into technical specifications of IT applications, and help develop a new application, or help choose and implement a commercially available one to support the processes.

6. Human resources (HR) or organizational change experts to provide expertise on matters related to job description, human performance incentives, organizational design that accompanies the process design, or work culture.

7. The customer of the process is sometimes part of the team to ensure a smooth process handoff during production.

Such experts drawn from the existing business generally have a stake in the status quo. The assumption is that such a team has all the knowledge and skill required to design an integrated system: the only thing they lack is the ability to work together, so facilitation and structuring the reengineering activity is required. This often leads to the hiring of management consultants who bring a structured methodology or approach that they have used in the past.

The above approach results in "design by committee" solution[2]. Characteristics of such solutions, such as local optimization and a lack of overall cohesion or accountability, often occur in descriptions of reengineering efforts. Accountability for the design, as opposed to the project accountability (i.e., for meeting project completion dates and budgets), may appear to rest with the process owner role, but this may not be the case in practice. The process owner is generally an executive role, responsible for the execution of the process and accountable for the results produced by the process, but not for the design of the process itself. Changes to the process design are therefore often left to natural adaptation with details determined by the local workers.

Further, many types of changes to an existing process are inelastic due to the time that it takes to change such things as culture, incentives, commu-

nication patterns, and infrastructure. The speed of an organic adaptation process is diffusion limited, with the rate determined by the gradient between the old and the new, which is typically rather slow for smallish differences. A new equilibrium may take long to establish, or may even be unstable, e.g., oscillating. Instability may occur as a result of changes starting at different places, meeting and modulating each other in some way, and then re-propagating again. It is interesting to note that at times there can be many changes happening to no eventual productive purpose.

What is lacking in this common scenario is a role that takes an active process design function focused on the consistency, completeness, and optimization of the system as a whole rather than on its parts. We believe that this role should be filled by a professionally trained business process engineer. The business process engineer possesses skills of process engineering at the general or abstract level and applies them to the process design at hand. He/she provides expert guidance to the team, leads the team through a structured process of process design and engineering, performs the necessary technical analysis, helps interpret the results of the analysis, and brings in knowledge of what information and other technologies can provide to support or enable the process. (Today, some management consultants provide some of these capabilities, most notably a structured process or "methodology" to perform business process engineering.) With this role, the new design will not be blindly or overly dependent on what is being done today or what the SME's have seen in their own experience. (However, the existing design is always available as a starting point of a new design.)

Figure 5 conceptually compares the present state of design by committee and the future state of having a business process engineer as the professional designer in the team. The existing team members are still very much needed in the future, but we also need the input and effort of a professional process designer.

As Figure 2 depicts, the business process engineer in many aspects plays the analogous role of the manufacturing process planner or engineer, as follows.

1. Just as manufacturing process planners or engineers design and optimize a production process plan for a physical product, business process engineers design and optimize a business process to produce the required output, be it an information based business artifact or a customer experience encountered in a service.
2. Similar to the make-vs.-buy decision in manufacturing, the business process engineer determines what, if any, portion of the process or business artifact is outsourced or purchased from a supplier. This decision is based on an analysis of strategic considerations, cost, response time, ease of managing the process interfaces, as well as the availability of outsourcing providers.
3. Just as manufacturing process engineers work with manufacturing systems engineers and machine engineers, business process engineers work with IT architects, analysts, and software engineers for detailed design and development.

Because of the fundamental differences between a manufacturing process and a business process noted earlier, the business process engineer has a slightly different responsibility in the business operations task (see Figure 1) from that of the manufacturing process engineer in the manufacturing operations task. The following represent the respective implications of the differences in the processes as discussed in Section 2.

1. There is no separate physical production line design task in business process design. Capacity planning of human operators is performed in the business operations task. The business process engineer effectively represents a combination of the manufacturing process engineer and the manufacturing systems engineer.
2. The supporting IT system is usually not a bottleneck in interactive usage mode and is hence ignored in the capacity planning of human operators. In cases where IT system is used intensively and where the computation time is significant, the IT system is usually used in batch mode without human intervention.
3. IT hardware and base operating systems are limited to a few standard choices. Software, either purchased as-is, custom built, or most

Figure 5. Business system designers: The present and the future

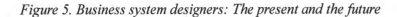
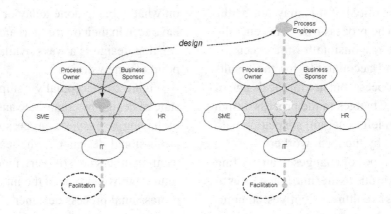

likely custom configured, is a major focus of business process design. Further, the software applications supporting a business process are often of an interactive, real time nature. (In manufacturing systems, there are also real time software applications, such as those in machine control. Such are usually outside the scope of the manufacturing process engineer.)

As discussed earlier, today's emphasis is on transaction management software in business process design. On the other hand, the nature of a business process (as we defined it) usually entails substantial human involvement. The business process engineer therefore would have a stronger focus on human-human or human-computer interaction, group dynamics, negotiation, and real-time decision making. (In manufacturing systems, there is obviously an important human element to them and past human factors studies have focused on a most directly relevant aspect - humans performing physical tasks.)

It is interesting to note that few industries have existing or emerging roles that are close to a BPE. In hospitals, the role of industrial engineers is filled by management engineers, a well accepted professional job in the field [HIMSS 2009]. Hospitals have notoriously complex and potentially inefficient processes, even though they do not make a traditional, physical product. We would like to generalize this role to all other industries.

THE SKILL SET OF A BUSINESS PROCESS ENGINEER

In this section we discuss the skill set required to perform the role of a business process engineer explained in the previous section. While an extensive discussion of skills needed by the BPE and their justification are outside the scope of this chapter, we present our preliminary work on

identifying the key skills for a successful BPE. We note that many of these technical areas are not new in themselves. Some specific techniques and methods have already been proposed in the literature [Biemans et al. 2001; Buzacott, 1996; Chadha, 1995; Osmundson et al., 2004; Park and Park, 1999; Rouse, 2005; Sousa et al., 2002; Tait, 1999; Towill, 1997a, b]. Others have grown out of other disciplines but have wide applicability in business process engineering. Just like when computer science started more than half a century ago, many topics then were part of other fields such as mathematics and electrical engineering.

Critical Skills of a BPE

We assume that basic scientific thinking, engineering fundamentals, and mathematics, such as those provided by an undergraduate engineering degree program, are already covered. We use an outcome-based approach to describe the skill set of a BPE. We group the skills according to the focus areas within a BPE's job scope, as shown in Figure 6. For each focus area of a BPE shown in Figure 6, we list, in Table 2, Table 3, and Table 4, the key educational outcomes relevant to that area and the corresponding topics that need to be taught in order to achieve the educational outcomes. In addition, Table 1 contains the educational outcomes and the respective topics for a basic set of skills of a BPE.

AN INITIAL STEP IN BUSINESS PROCESS ENGINEERING EDUCATION

College Level Education in Business Process Engineering

The two logical home departments for business process engineering education at the undergraduate and graduate level are Industrial Engineering (IE) and the Business School. The former may present the greatest opportunity to develop and offer such a program because of the current status of IE education and practice, its unique mix of human-technology-business tradition, and the applicability of many of its existing courses. The IE community is beginning to realize that modernizing the curriculum is critical to the future of the IE discipline. Several efforts have been underway to define the IE of the future [Askin et al., 2004; Kamath and Mize, 2003; Kuo and Deuermeyer, 1998; McGinnis, 2002; Rouse, 2004; Settles, 2003]. Today's IEs do much more than task-oriented efficiency studies. The scope of IE has gone beyond the design of the physical work place and production processes to the design of systems involving knowledge/information work [Kamath and Mize, 2003]. BPE is a natural extension of the traditional, physical production space into the non-production space. We submit that BPE should be part of the core program of the "new" industrial engineer.

Programs offered by Business Schools have been undergoing rapid changes driven by relatively recent technology advancements. They have taken the lead role in offering programs and options that focus on information systems, e-commerce, and supply chains. However, these programs produce mainly business analysts or information system analysts, a primary role of whom is to act as a liaison between the business users and the software developers and vendors. These programs emphasize business and IS/IT concepts and are somewhat weak in system design content. Nevertheless, much knowledge offered by business schools today, such as business strategy, financial planning, business performance measurement, is fundamental to a BPE (as evidenced by our discussion throughout Sections 3 and 4 in this chapter). This is similar to the existing relationship between business schools and industrial engineering departments today.

Pilot Offering of a BPE Course

A senior-level elective course titled "Engineering Business Processes" was designed and approved as part of the Bachelor of Science curriculum in Industrial Engineering and Management (BSIE&M) at Oklahoma State University, Stillwater, OK, US. The course format included traditional lectures by the instructor and several presentations by the students. Due to the limited hours in a single undergraduate course, only a key subset of the all the skills discussed in Section 4 was included in the course. The topics were grouped into three modules (i) Overview of business concepts and introduction to BPE, (ii) Modern enterprise concepts, and (iii) Modeling, analysis, design and implementation of business processes.

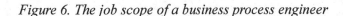

Figure 6. The job scope of a business process engineer

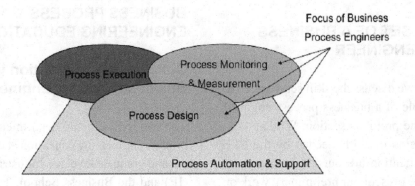

Table 1. BPE skill set – basics

Educational Outcome	Relevant Topics
Basic understanding of management, organization, corporate structure Understanding of contemporary business/enterprise concepts Understanding of production system concepts applicable to business processes Understanding of service systems concepts Ability to apply systems engineering principles and approaches to solve a business problem	How businesses are organized and managed. Economics of organization. Functional silos and cross-functional processes. JIT, Lean, Six Sigma, etc. Virtual enterprises/integration, supply chains, business ecosystems, and e-business. Enterprise ontology and business architecture. Manufacturing system organization (process/product/cell). Quality assurance and process control. Manufacturing vs. service operations and physical vs. knowledge work environments. Current topics in service sector domains such as retail, healthcare, entertainment, IT services, and professional services. Service quality concepts. System engineering fundamentals. Engineering problem solving and design approaches. Structured and object-oriented approaches for information system design and development

Table 2. BPE skill set – process design

Educational Outcome	Relevant Topics
An ability to develop descriptive process models An ability to (re)design a business process An understanding of human behavior in the workplace	Process modeling techniques such as IDEF0/IDEF3, Event-driven Process Chains (EPC), and Petri nets. Process and value stream mapping. Design principles (e.g. modularity, postponement, and impact of process variance on design); service orientation (e.g., service oriented modeling). Analysis techniques of a qualitative (e.g., control-flow verification) and a quantitative (e.g. response times using simulation and analytical techniques) nature. Design methodology that covers identification of tasks (what), development of control flow (how), and assignment of tasks to resources (who). Impact of technology on human performance including human interface issues, human-centered design and user-friendliness. Impact of people behavior on work system's success. Application of anthropological techniques. Employee satisfaction and customer satisfaction. Ethical and privacy issues.

Feedback from the students indicated that they believed that the course was value-adding to their program. One of students who is currently employed by a global oil and gas company has seen distinct benefits in the following three areas – in understanding how to model data and data relationships, in identifying 'how-to' automate business processes with long-term maintenance in mind, and in looking beyond the process 'step' level and evaluating how business processes span across the organization (impact and touch points).

While the above represents the experience of only one university, it should be noted that the BSIE&M program has a structure that is very similar many such programs in the US. Hence, it is quite plausible that a course such as the one above could be offered at least as an optional course in other similarly structured IE programs in the US.

CONCLUDING REMARKS

Business process re-engineering, some ten years after its widely publicized inception as a mainstream tool to improve business performance, is still somewhat controversial. Many organizations have varying degrees of success with it. While the concept of BPR is more commonly accepted as a valid approach for a business to stay competitive in today's fast changing environment, how and by whom should a BPR exercise be carried out remains debatable. The issue we explore in this article, namely the non-existence of a professional business process engineer today, is one probable contributing factor to the uncertain results of BPR projects.

Table 3. BPE skill set – process monitoring and measurement

Educational Outcome	Relevant Topics
An understanding of the need for process monitoring and measurement An ability to support the design a measurement system	Common measures of success. Linking business strategy and measurement, e.g., balanced score card. Measurement as a process management tool. Measurement as an incentive tool. Measurement as a feature of the service, e.g., service level agreements and contractual terms. Defining and selecting measures, including the use of modeling techniques. Determining how measurements are calculated utilizing existing techniques such as statistical process control, statistical sampling, on-line analytical processing (OLAP), and real-time performance dashboards. Application of measurement instruments for human subjects, e.g. surveys and panels.

Table 4. BPE skill set – process automation and support

Educational Outcome	Relevant Topics
Basic understanding of knowledge management concepts Basic understanding of enterprise applications and general technology capability Basic understanding of business process automation technologies	Knowledge representation, document engineering, agents, ontologies, and unified modeling language (UML). Introduction to ERP, customer relationship management (CRM), supply chain management, financial/accounting systems, IT management systems, and IT infrastructure technologies. Information exchange and integration, using data warehousing, extensible markup language (XML), and related technologies. Process choreography using workflow management systems and service oriented computing. Using commercial applications to implement common business processes.

Many factors contribute to today's fast changing business environment: unprecedented changes in political landscapes globally, explosion of technological inventions, man-made trends from the fashion and entertainment industries, global competition aided by enhanced communication and the dismantling of trade and political barriers. Undeniably a major factor is the advancement and proliferation of information technology such as the personal computer or the cellular phone, the world-wide web which can be reached from a multitude of devices, and software technologies

Figure 7. U.S. non-farm employment profile 1959-2008[3]

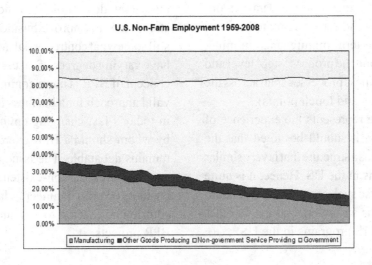

that have made IT a much friendlier tool when compared to that of the past. Such IT tools have and will enable the automation and transformation of many business processes and in some cases entire industries. Well-known examples: Rental car check-out and check-in, on-line auctions or reverse auctions in the B2B and B2C space, or even the process of collecting information for and filing individual income tax. Many of these important transformations have been invented by individual entrepreneurs who relied on their keen observations on certain inefficiencies of a familiar business process. In order to exploit, on a broad scale in all industries, the use of technology in transforming (i.e., beyond automating) business processes into more effective ones, we need more resources than the gifted entrepreneurs who, by definition, are only interested in opportunities that are extremely profitable to them.

As is widely known in the U.S., the continued shift of the economy from manufacturing to services has underscored the importance of non-production processes (see Figure 7). It has been estimated that two-thirds of the U.S. non-farm labor force belongs to the category of service providing (rather than goods-producing) workers. While our know-how in manufacturing process design and management had propelled U.S. manufacturing to the top in the past, we need to do the same for service industries for the U.S. economy to survive and continue to grow in this changing, global environment. Business process engineering to service industries is the equivalent of manufacturing engineering to manufacturing industries.

It is also essential to note that the government in the U.S., while employing about the same fraction of non-farm people as the total of manufacturing and other goods producing sectors since 2003, is largely engaged in non-production activities (see Figure 7). It can be argued that business process engineering is therefore as crucial as manufacturing engineering, based on the needs of the government sector alone. In this age of emphasis on

lean and efficient governments, business process engineering is a crucial subject for the U.S. and other governments in developed countries.

Further, because IT is almost the sole, and certainly the predominant, technology available for a business process, the success of the IT industry will have an intimate relationship with the success of business process engineering. For one, many requirements of IT will come from the needs of engineering a business process. The days of IT as a pure automation tool are numbered in developed countries. Significant new developments in IT will go hand in hand with new, innovative ways of transforming an existing business process. Major IT vendors (such as IBM) have already recognized this trend, as can be seen by their emphasis on the business transformation business in the last several years. The continued success of the IT industry, especially in developed economies, will to a significant extent depend on our success in business process engineering.

REFERENCES

Askin, R., Goldberg, J., Goetschalckx, M., Kuo, W., Rardin, R., & Wysk, R. (2004). IE curriculum renovation. Panel discussion, *Industrial Engineering Research Conference*, Houston, TX.

Bertalanffy, L. V. (1976). General system theory: Foundations, development, applications. Revised edition, New York: George Braziller Inc.

Biemans, F. P. M., Lankhorst, M. M., Teeuw, W. B., & van de Wetering, R. G. (2001). Dealing with the complexity of business systems architecting. *Systems Engineering, 4*(2), 118–133. doi:10.1002/sys.1010

Blackburn, J. D. (1990). Time-based competition: the next battleground in American manufacturing. New York: McGraw-Hill.

Browne, J., Chan, W. W., & Rathmill, K. (1985). An integrated FMS design procedure. In Annals of Operations Research, 3, K.E. Stecke & R. Suri (Eds.), Basel-Switzerland: J.C. Baltzer, 207-238.

Buzacott, J. A. (1996). Commonalities in re-engineered business processes: Models and issues. *Management Science, 42*(5), 768–782. doi:10.1287/mnsc.42.5.768

Carbone, L. P., & Haeckel, S. H. (1994). Engineering customer experiences. *Marketing Management, 3*(3), 8–19.

Chadha, B. (1995). A model driven methodology for business process engineering. In *Proceedings of the ASME Computers in Engineering Conference*.

Chesbrough, H. W. (2004). A failing grade for the innovation academy. *Financial Times (North American Edition)*, (September): 25.

Chesbrough, H. W. (2005). Towards a new science of services. In Breakthrough ideas for 2005. *Harvard Business Review, 83*(1), 16–17.

Curtis, B., Kellner, M. I., & Over, J. (1992). Process modeling. *Communications of the ACM, 35*(9), 75–90. doi:10.1145/130994.130998

Davenport, T. H. (1998). Putting the enterprise into the enterprise system. *Harvard Business Review, 76*(4), 121–131.

Davenport, T. H., & Short, J. E. (1990). The new industrial engineering: Information technology and business process design. *Sloan Management Review, 31*(4), 11–27.

Hammer, M., & Champy, J. (1993). Reengineering the corporation. New York: Harper Business.

Healthcare Information and Management Systems Society (HIMSS). (2009). What is a management engineer or process improvement professional? Retrieved April 2009, from www.himss.org.

Kamath, M., & Mize, J. H. (2003). Impact of major driving forces on IE education and practice. In *Proceedings of 2003 Industrial Engineering Research Conference*, Portland, OR.

Karmarkar, U. (2004). Will you survive the services revolution. *Harvard Business Review, 82*(6), 100–107.

Kumaran, S. (2004). Model driven enterprise. In *Proceedings of the Global EAI Summit*, Banff, Canada, 166-180.

Kuo, W., & Deuermeyer, B. (1998). IE2-the IE curriculum revisited: Developing a new undergraduate program at Texas A&M University. *IIE Solutions, 30*(6), 16–22.

Leung, Y. T., Caswell, N., & Kamath, M. (2006). The case for the business process engineer. In *Proceedings of the IEEE International Conference on Service Operations and Logistics, and Informatics*, Shanghai, China, 1119-1124.

MacIntosh, R. (1997). Business process re-engineering: New applications for techniques of production engineering. *International Journal of Production Economics, 50*(1), 43–49. doi:10.1016/S0925-5273(97)89132-3

McGinnis, L. (2002). A brave new education. *IIE Solutions, 34*(12), 27–31.

Nigam, A., & Caswell, N. (2003). Business artifacts: An approach to operational specification. *IBM Systems Journal, 42*(3), 428–445.

Nyman, L. R. (1992). Making manufacturing cells work. Drabber, MI: Society of Manufacturing Engineers.

Osmundson, J. S., Gottfried, R., Chee, Y. K., Lau, H. B., Lim, W. L., Poh, S. W. P., & Tan, C. T. (2004). Process modeling: A systems engineering tool for analyzing complex systems. *Systems Engineering, 7*(4), 320–337. doi:10.1002/sys.20012

Park, J. Y., & Park, S. J. (1999). IBPM: An integrated systems model for business process reengineering. *Systems Engineering*, *1*(3), 159–175. doi:10.1002/(SICI)1520-6858(1998)1:3<159::AID-SYS2>3.0.CO;2-H

Perez, C. (2002). Technological revolutions and financial capital: The dynamics of bubbles and golden ages. Northampton, MA: Edward Elgar.

Rouse, W. B. (2004). Embracing the enterprise. *Industrial Engineer*, *36*(3), 31–35.

Rouse, W. B. (2005). Enterprises as systems: Essential challenges and approaches to transformation. *Systems Engineering*, *8*(2), 138–150. doi:10.1002/sys.20029

Settles, S. F. (2003). Information systems engineering emphasis. In *Proceedings of 2003 Industrial Engineering Research Conference*, Portland, OR.

Smith, H., & Fingar, P. (2002). Business process management: The third wave. Tampa, FL: Meghan-Kiffer Press.

Sousa, G. W. L., Van Aken, E. M., & Groesbeck, R. L. (2002). Applying an enterprise engineering approach to engineering work: A focus on business process modeling. *Engineering Management Journal*, *14*(3), 15–24.

Suri, R. (1985). Quantitative techniques for robotic systems analysis. In Handbook of Industrial Robotics, S.Y. Nof (Ed.), Chapter 31. New York: Wiley.

Tait, F. (1999). Enterprise process engineering: A template tailored for higher education. *CAUSE/EFFECT Journal*, *22*(1), 40-43, 57.

Tien, J. M., & Berg, D. (2003). A case for service systems engineering. *Journal of Systems Science and Systems Engineering*, *12*(1), 13–38. doi:10.1007/s11518-006-0118-6

Towill, D. R. (1997a). Successful business systems engineering. Part 1: The systems approach to business processes. *Engineering Management Journal*, *7*(1), 55–64. doi:10.1049/em:19970109

Towill, D. R. (1997b). Successful business systems engineering. Part 2: The time compression paradigm and how simulation supports good BSE. *Engineering Management Journal*, *7*(2), 89–96. doi:10.1049/em:19970209

Vargo, S. L., & Lusch, R. F. (2004). Evolving to a new dominant logic of marketing. *Journal of Marketing*, *68*(1), 1–17. doi:10.1509/jmkg.68.1.1.24036

ENDNOTES

[1]   There are many obvious examples of fairly complicated products that have been in large-scale production since World War II. They include consumer products such as automobiles and televisions, not to mention commercial aircraft and shipbuilding.

[2]   Perhaps the comparison point to make here is that the factory level design isn't going to be performed by a production line workers' committee. They are a clear source of input as to what works, what is problematic but do not have the overall, integrating viewpoint.

[3]   Other goods producing sector includes mining & logging, construction. Non-government service providing sector includes trade, transportation, & utilities; information; financial services; professional & business services; education & health services; leisure & hospitality; other services. Data source: U.S. Bureau of Labor Statistics, Annual Average Employment, retrieved from ftp://ftp.bls.gov/pub/suppl/empsit.ceseeb1.txt, April 2009.

APPENDIX

Comparison of Definitions Related to Business Processes in the Research Literature

In the research literature, there are several definitions and interpretations of terms related to business processes. We provide a brief comparison of those definitions with that used in this chapter.

Process

Any activity or group of activities that takes an input, adds value to it and provides an output to an internal or external customer. Processes use an organization's resources to provide definitive results on behalf of the business [Towill, 1997a].

Our definition of a process agrees in principle with the above. However, we wish to emphasize the ordering present within a group of activities by qualifying "activities" above with "activities arranged or linked in a specified order." The activities of a process are not just a set, but a set with very specific relations between the elements. We also note the often neglected role of resources in defining both the structure of a process and interactions between processes. The value of processes is not just in aggregating the functional activities but in coordinating actions and resources.

Business process

A linked or natural group of skills and competencies which start from a set of customer requirements and deliver a total product or service [Towill, 1997a].

A set of logically related tasks performed to achieve a defined business outcome [Davenport and Short, 1990].

In general, we use a variation of the above definitions and add examples of the groups of activities, which allows us to use a narrower definition for this article:

A set of logically related activities in the day-to-day operation of a business, including planning activities (e.g., resource planning), manufacturing activities (e.g., building a gadget), business transactional activities (e.g., purchasing raw materials and selling products), and customer support activities (e.g., handling warranty issues).

However, in this chapter, we use the term business process to mean non-manufacturing activities, to distinguish from manufacturing activities for convenience of comparison. We also use "activities" instead of "tasks". As is customary, an activity is defined as a collection of closely related tasks and is therefore a level above a task in the process hierarchy.

Business Process Redesign/Reengineering (BPR)

The means by which an organization can achieve radical change in performance as measured by cost, delivery time, service and quality via the application of the systems approach which focuses on a business as a set of customer-related core business processes rather than as a set of organizational functions [Towill, 1997a].

The analysis and design of work flows and processes within and between organizations [Davenport and Short, 1990].

... the fundamental rethinking and radical redesign of business processes to achieve dramatic improvements in critical, contemporary measures of performance, such as cost, quality, service and speed (Hammer's definition from [MacIntosh, 1997]).

... the redesign of an organization's business processes to make them more efficient [Curtis et al., 1992].

BPR is seen by some as a tool or technique that has transformed organizations to the "degree that Taylorism once did [Davenport and Short, 1990]." BPR has been differentiated from the constant tweaking of process details (a.k.a. continuous process improvement or CPI) by the "radical" or step changes that it causes in an enterprise's processes. In addition, cross-functional processes and the advancements in IT are often associated with BPR activities.

Our focus in this chapter is on business process design/engineering and we believe that our definition and approach can easily be adapted to redesign/reengineering situations by making the obvious changes. Like Towill [1997a, b] we also advocate a systems approach, wherein the focus is on the behavior and performance of the total enterprise.

Business Systems Engineering (BSE)

BSE is a systems approach to designing new business processes and redesigning existing business processes. It provides a structured way of maximizing both customer value and the performance of the individual business [Towill,1997a].

Business Process Engineer (BPE)

Towill's [1997a, b] work certainly help lay a foundation for our thesis here. We argue in this paper that there is a need for a professional role in the framework of BSE as defined by Towill [1997a, b]. This professional role, whom we call a Business Process Engineer, would be a key contributor in the multi-disciplinary team that Towill advocated. As we will see in the later sections of this paper, the BPE draws on the principles of systems thinking with skills from a set of different yet related disciplines of business, industrial engineering, operations research, computer science, and information systems and technology. It is a professional discipline whose purpose is the design and development of business processes.

Chapter 19
Logistics Services in the 21st Century:
Supply Chain Integration and Service Architecture

Marcus Thiell
Universidad de los Andes, Colombia

Sergio Hernandez
Universidad de los Andes, Colombia

ABSTRACT

Due the cross-functional character of logistics tasks and the cross-organizational structure of most logistics chains, the logistics service industry is strongly affected by business dynamics. Since the 1950s, this industry has experienced a variety of changes; While logistics was traditionally concerned with the fulfilment of functions like transportation and warehousing, modern logistics service offerings also encompass services like network design and carbon footprint assessment. But not just the scope of logistics services has changed. Additionally logistics business models developed from 1PL to 4PL, indicating a shift from the provision of execution tasks to tactical tasks and from fragmented logistics solutions to integrative logistics solutions for complete logistics chains. As a consequence, logistics service providers at the beginning of the 21st century have many options to configure their service offerings. But which options exist to comply with the requirements in a modern competition being fought supply chain versus supply chain rather than firm versus firm? After analyzing the dynamics in the logistics service industry and the importance of logistics for an effective and efficient supply chain management, this chapter will focus on options how logistics service providers can construct single logistics services (service architecture), their logistics service program (service program architecture) and their appearance on the market (service provider architecture) in order to fulfil their role within today's supply chains and to improve supply chain performance.

DOI: 10.4018/978-1-61520-603-2.ch019

INTRODUCTION: DYNAMICS IN THE LOGISTICS SERVICES INDUSTRY

The logistics service industry – in charge of managing the flows of products (goods as well as services) and the related information involved in the creation, transformation and delivery of value between the point of origin to the point of consumption – receives an increasing recognition as contributor to achieve competitive advantages in today's business environment. Whenever companies decide to extend, to reduce, to outsource or to integrate their operations, also logistics operations are affected. Each type of decision mentioned changes the structure of an internal value chain and/or external supply chain and consequently also the requirements on the logistics services which are responsible for the effective and efficient management of flows within chains.

Nowadays statements can increasingly be found which stress that modern competition is being fought chain versus chain rather than company versus company, and that these chains need to provide competitive total value across a balanced set of cost, quality, speed, responsiveness and also environmental as well as social aspects (Loren 2005, Ketchen & Hult 2007, Heizer & Render 2008) – these two latter aspects influence the logistics service industry at large.

In this chapter we will provide insights into options for the logistics service industry to fulfill their role within today's supply chains and to improve supply chain performance by focusing on the architecture of the services, the service programs and the organizational forms of logistics service providers.

Logistics Services: Definition, Scope and Characteristics

Services are intangible economic goods in form of offered promises, which concretization require the integration of external factors into the provision process and leads to tangible and/or intangible results (Thiell 2008). Linking this general definition of services with the content of logistics tasks, the logistics service provision process consists of all activities concerned with the effective and efficient management of the flows of products and related information between the point of origin and the point of consumption in order to meet or exceed customers' requirements.

These activities are provided in-house (e.g. production logistics), by governmental institutions (e.g. customs, security) and to a large extent by specialized services companies to consumers as

Table 1. Logistics business services

Service Category (functional service groups)		Services, e.g.
Traditional Categories	Transportation	• Inbound and Outbound Transportation of Products • Reverse Transportation
	Storage	• Stock Keeping • Load and Unload
	Handling	• Cross Docking • Break Bulking
	Order Processing	• Tracking & Tracing • Customs Clearance
Non-traditional Categories	Order Finishing	• Labeling • Manufacturing Postponement
	Consulting	• Network Design • Process Re-engineering

well as to organizations. In this chapter we will primarily focus on business-to-business transactions.

As demonstrated in Table 1, the scope of logistics services is very wide as the term 'logistics' is not supported by a single verb but covers several functions in the context of bridging spatiotemporal disparities in value networks (Wegner 1993, Gebhardt 2006).

Figure 1. Services classification (Maister & Lovelock 1982)

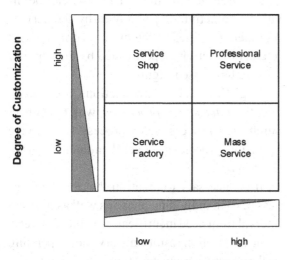

While transportation, order processing, storage and handling are denoted as basic or traditional logistics services, modern logistics service offerings also contain order finishing and consulting services, as these services are sometimes necessary to solve customer specific logistics problems in today's competitive environment (Klaas 2002).

Due to their heterogeneity it is difficult to position logistics services as a whole into existing service classifications (see Figure 1), as the following two examples demonstrate: Goods transportation services on the one hand would probably be classified as 'service factory' as their degree of customization as well as their degree of interaction can be described as 'low'. Logistics consulting services on the other hand could in general be denoted as 'professional service' due to their high degree of interaction and also customization.

Despite of the difficulties to position logistics services into existing schemes, they have certain characteristics in common, which are deduced from the above mentioned service definition (see Table 2).

These characteristics are important issues for the logistics services transaction because they lead

Table 2. Characteristics of logistics services (based on Thiell 2008)

Criteria	Logistics Services Characteristics
Result of the provision process	Intangible/Tangible
Offering	Intangible
Storage	Cannot be stored
Transport	Cannot be transported
Participants in the production process	Production requires an interaction between customer and the service provider
Moment of agreement between supplier and customer	Agreement before end-combination of production factors
Transfer of ownership	Utilization; transfer of service ownership impossible. (Transfer of goods and rights within the service process is possible.)
Degree of homogenization	Heterogeneous
Proportion of fixed costs	Heterogeneous
Pricing	Often not transparent
Quality evaluation	High proportion of experience-qualities (quality in general is evaluated after the contract was signed)

to asymmetric information and cause a special structure of the transaction processes.

Based on findings of the International/Industrial Purchasing and Marketing Group (IMP-Group), the transaction processes of logistics services can be described as a combination of *actors*, *resources* and *activities* (Axelsson & Wynstra 2002). Originally developed as an approach to describe and to analyze dyadic structures, this approach was decentrally further developed towards several network models (Håkansson 1982; Håkansson & Johanson 1992; Håkansson & Snehota 1995).

Essential relations between the above mentioned basic elements can be described as following (Calaminus 1994): Actors use and control resources; actors perform activities; actors connect resources via activities. The relevance of this basic model – also denoted as ARA-model – in the context of the topic treated in this chapter becomes clear as the description and analysis of interactions are explicitly considered. Thus, the model corresponds to a substantial characteristic of logistics services transactions, the interaction between service provider and client in the service transaction process.

Actors can be differentiated into inter-organizational actors (e.g. buying center, selling center, intermediaries) and intra-organizational actors (e.g. user department, sales department), which in general pursue different goals in the transaction process.

Resources are the tangible and intangible production factors involved in the transaction process controlled by different members of an organization. Different characteristics of resources between transaction partners finally constitute a business relationship (e.g. the capabilities of the service provider to solve the buyer's problem) (Calaminus 1994).

Activities are executed by actors as a sequence of target-oriented operations (Håkansson & Snehota 1995). In the context of logistics service transactions these activities can be divided into activities performed by the service provider, activities of the buying company and interaction-activities performed by the supplier *and* the buyer (see Figure 2).

Logistics service transactions are consequently *interaction processes* which connect purchasing process, sales process and service provision process at several moments during the transaction.

It is necessary to mention that the detailedness of each individual phase as well as the time interval from need identification to the 'delivery' of the transaction result can vary a lot depending on the transaction constellation, which itself is determined by type and importance of the logistics service as well as by the buy-class – the degree of repetition of the transaction process from the buyers point of view (Robinson et al. 1967).

Figure 2. Logistics services transactions as interaction processes (based on Thiell 2008)

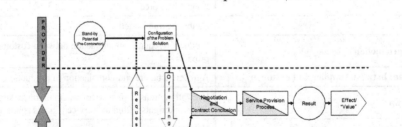

As demonstrated above, the transaction process of logistics services in its generic structure is already complex. An important driver of its actual complexity is the amount of single services necessary to solve the customer's problem, as the number of elements of the transaction in terms of actors, resources and activities increases with an extended scope of services required.

Evolution of Logistics Service Offerings

In 1955, while logistics were already established in military systems for centuries, MORGENSTERN in his article 'Note on the Formulation of the Theory of Logistics' introduced the term 'logistics' in the context of business problems (Morgenstern 1955). This publication serves as a fixed point for the description of the evolution of logistics services. BALLOU for example separates the early stages of business logistics into the phases 'the dormant years' (before 1950) and 'the developmental years' (1950-1970), followed by a third stage, 'the takeoff years', which began in the 1970s (Ballou 1985).

We will describe the evolution of logistics services starting from the second stage, when market dynamics led to a continuous integration of logistics services with an impact on the architecture of logistics service offerings, and, consequently also on the business models of logistics services providers (see Figure 3). While all business models (1PL, 2PL, 3PL, and 4PL) still exist in today's logistics service industry, they developed sequentially in the course of time and suit as a basis to describe the evolution of logistics services offerings in terms of changes of the service architecture:

- *First Party Logistics (1PL)*: Until the 1970s logistics services were primarily performed in-house by manufacturing companies. These companies belong to the group of 1PL-providers, which own logistics assets (e.g. trucks and warehouses) and have the capabilities to execute the logistics tasks of warehousing and transport services on behalf of procurement, production and sales requirements. Mainly international logistics operations were outsourced to freight forwarding specialists (Engel et al. 2003).

- *Second Party Logistics (2PL)*: Influenced by an increasing internationalization of operations and the emergence of new management concepts like 'lean management' and management principles like the 'concentration on core competences' in the 1980s, companies began to intensify the

Figure 3. Evolution of logistics service business models (Kuehne + Nagel 2008)

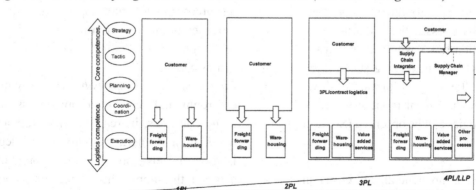

outsourcing of logistics services. Logistics service providers which assume the basic logistics tasks of their clients and operate on the execution level are denoted as 2PL-providers (e.g. freight forwarders, shipping companies, consolidators).

- *Third Party Logistics (3PL)*: In the 1990s a logistics concept called 3PL or 'contract logistics' developed from 2PL. By extending the management functions to planning and coordination of logistics tasks and also offering value-added services (see 3.1), 3PL-providers are able to provide complete logistics service packages (in general) on the basis of longer-term relationships (Marasco 2008).
- *Fourth Party Logistics (4PL)*: Already in the middle of the 1990s the next type of logistics service business models formed, denoted as 4PL (also described as 'lead logistics' [LL]). While 3PL-providers *can* also reach the tactical level of the customer's management system within long-term strategic partnerships, 4PL includes two core tasks of tactical nature: supply chain integration and supply chain management. This integration and management of several actors in the supply chain includes logistics services and passes the company borders of the customer as it also ideally integrates upstream (e.g. suppliers) and downstream (e.g. distributors) actors of the chain. The objective to integrate complete supply chains stresses the importance of the information flows within them. In the concept of 4PL an increasing substitution of material flows by information flows supported by the use of modern information technologies can be observed (Schmitt 2006).

Although there is no general consensus in literature regarding the definition and scope of tasks covered by each logistics business model

described above, it becomes clear that logistics tasks performed by service providers on the one hand developed from execution tasks to tactical tasks. Starting before the 1950s on a 'fragmentary basis' (Bowersox et al. 1986), the evolution of logistics business models on the other hand also demonstrates the tendency towards the offering of integrative logistics solutions for complete logistics chains.

Logistics Trends at the Beginning of the 21st Century

Due to the cross-functional character of tasks and the cross-organizational structure of most logistics chains, logistics are strongly affected by business dynamics. Reducing the wide range of current business trends to perhaps the most relevant ones, this section will refer to the impact of 'globalization', 'environmental responsibility', 'visibility', and the trend towards 'supply chain integration' on logistics systems:

- *Globalization*: Already long-lasting, the globalization trend influences logistics operations still to a large extent. Globalization efforts of clients result in increasing demand for global coverage of logistics service offerings. But the expansion of procurement, production and/or distribution networks also creates a higher complexity of logistics systems because new actors, resources and activities operating in heterogeneous market environments need to be integrated in existing structures of logistics chains.
- *Environmental Responsibility*: Growing environmental consumer awareness in many countries, increasing prices for raw materials and energy, environmental legislation and also pressure from dominant actors in the supply chain force companies around the world these days to implement reverse logistics systems and closed-loop

supply chains (Voigt & Thiell 2004). The tendency to implement 'environmental responsibility' into the target systems of clients affects the logistics service industry concerning three relevant aspects: (1) Environmental friendliness becomes a criterion in the selection process of logistics service providers, often resulting in necessary investments of the providers to improve e.g. their 'carbon footprint'. (2) Furthermore, this trend offers (new) business opportunities for logistics service providers in terms of options to expand their service program. (3) Closed-loop supply chains also add actors, resources and activities to existing logistics systems and consequently increase their complexity. Nonetheless, it is widely recognized that 'closing the chain' creates higher customer satisfaction and consequently value to the companies who implement reverse logistics systems (Kumar & Malegeant 2006).

- *Visibility*: Driven by performance improvements of information technologies (e.g. Internet-Technologies, Radio Frequency Identification [RFID]) and the reduction of their cost, the trend towards end-to-end supply chain visibility affects today's (global) logistics chains to a large extent. Striving for an effective coordination of all chain activities requires visibility which in turn depends on the optimized use of information technologies. In a chain with high visibility, emerging opportunities and risks can rapidly be identified, reported and anticipated – a substitution of material flows by information flows becomes possible. But if visibility is missing or information flows are interrupted, excess inventory, late delivery, high expediting cost, production downtime, etc. are often the consequence. In this sense, visibility along the chain becomes an important issue for logistics clients. Logistics services providers can,

for example, respond to this need with the offering of services like tracking & tracing, automated shelf replenishment using RFID, and locate-to-order strategies in the distribution channel. Nevertheless, critically concerning the realization of end-to-end supply chain visibility are still the necessary investments and the operating costs of the technologies, which in particular cause problems for small and medium sized logistics service providers.

- *Supply Chain Integration*: Companies nowadays strive for the management of complete supply chains, from raw material suppliers to end customers, in which the 'relevant business system' fighting for competitive advantages on the markets is no longer determined by the legal independency of companies, but by the economic dependency between the actors of a chain (Loren 2005, Ketchen & Hult 2007). Supply chain integration asks for integrated logistics chains managed in the ideal case by one focal organization as multiple suppliers would fragment the chain. For example, 4PL is a concept supposed to fulfill these market requirements but it also provides a challenge for the logistics industry in terms of need for a *culture of collaboration*.

These mentioned trends finally demonstrate that business dynamics determine the current status of logistics systems and provide permanent challenges for their management.

LOGISTICS SERVICES AND SUPPLY CHAIN MANAGEMENT

Roles of Logistics Services Providers along the Supply Chain

Within the structure of a supply chain – a connected series of resources and actors involved in

Figure 4. Position of logistics in the supply chain

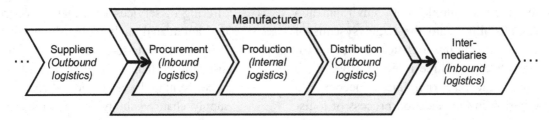

the creation, transformation and delivery of value to end customers – logistics services are the 'vital link', because a chain's internal and external elements need to be managed in a way that 'value' flows frictionless through the complete chain to the end customers (see Figure 4).

As a practical example, Figure 5 presents a typical supply chain of the semiconductor industry, indicating activities performed by logistics service providers at each interface between the actors in the chain.

Due to the above described relation, logistics management is *part* of supply chain management responsible for all tasks concerning the management of *flows* of products and the related information within this connected series. The roles assigned to logistics service providers refer to four aspects:

- Logistics service providers manage the *intra-organizational flows* of products and related information between the functional areas of procurement, production, and manufacturing as well as the *cross-organizational flows* between legally independent actors of a supply chain.

- Logistics service providers are *'information providers'* for supply chain management. Because of their position at every interface of a supply chain, the sum of information available in the complete logistics system is of high value for supply chain management. Managing the information of the logistics system in an effective and efficient way can serve as a 'radar system' to identify supply chain risks and opportunities, it can help to reduce the 'bullwhip effect' (Lee et al. 1997), and in

Figure 5. Position of logistics service providers in the semiconductor industry (based on U.S. International Trade Commission 2005)

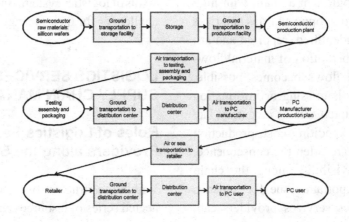

general it can improve the quality of strategic, tactic and operational planning. But such achievements can only be realized if the logistics system is managed centralized or if information within the chain is shared in a collaborative way.

- Logistics service providers may also play the role as '*neutral agents*' within a supply chain. For example, in a case where at least two supply chain actors decide to transfer the responsibility for the optimization of the logistics performance level between them to a logistics service provider, this provider may be able to balance the interests of the co-contractors by subordinating individual interests under the objective to reach the optimal performance level of the defined system. But depending on the number of actors involved, the existence of different power-positions and the level of collaboration between them, such arrangements can result in very complex contracts.
- Logistics service providers are '*value-adding partners*' of the clients in terms of contributors to the achievement of the clients' objectives.

The latter role of logistics service providers is the subject of the next section.

The Impact of Logistics Services on Supply Chain Performance

Defining 'Supply Chain Performance' as the capability of a supply chain to create, to transform and to deliver value to customers; the following describes the multi-dimensional impact of logistics services on supply chain performance in terms of influencing cost, effectiveness, efficiency, and also the creation of intangible assets:

- *Cost*: The direct profit impact of logistics services is generally measured by the percentage of logistics costs on the product price or the sales volume. According to The Latin America Logistic Center, logistics cost as a percent of the product price in the United States account for 9%, while in Latin America this percentage rises up to 20% (Latin America Logistics Center 2005). A reduction of this amount should be a main concern of management as it has an important impact on the competitiveness of companies and chains, especially in global competition. Given the increasing environmental awareness in many countries around the world, the integration of the external/environmental costs in the calculation of the logistics costs (e.g. based on carbon assessments) will be reality in the future and the logistics cost will, ceteris paribus, increase. Logistics service providers already develop the capabilities to support their clients in taking actions to reduce these types of costs associated with the provision of logistics services.

- *Effectiveness*: Strategic decisions such as those in the context of the globalization of the sales markets and the supply markets are often made under the participation of external service providers – typically consulting companies. As described above, logistics service providers – particularly 3PL and 4PL – nowadays also offer this type of service. Although the final decisions are made by the management of the clients, logistics service providers influence the decision making processes and consequently the effectiveness of the client's business system. Without getting into detail, it is important to mention that several types of logistics services (e.g. network engineering) can initiate future costs but also can avoid future cost (e.g. restructuring of the logistics network). By influencing the effectiveness of the client's business, logistics services can have a significant impact on a company's policy and future development due to their often strategic character.

- *Efficiency*: Logistics services which are part of the primary value-adding activities like those described in the value chain of PORTER (Porter 1987) directly contribute to the efficiency of the client's value/supply chain. By influencing the efficiency, logistics services can contribute to avoid *costs* (e.g. avoidance of production downtime and reduction of inventory), to ensure the *quality* of the processes and products (e.g. avoidance of product obsolescence and deterioration, improvement of order fill-rates), to influence time-related objectives in a positive way (e.g. reduction of throughput, storage, and lead time), and also to improve the environmental performance of the client, e.g. by minimizing the carbon emission via optimized route planning or by selecting sustainable carriers.

- *Creation of Intangible Assets*: Logistics services with a direct contact to the end customer (the customer of the logistics service customer) can support the creation of intangible assets in terms of 'customer satisfaction' and 'customer loyalty'. Based on their execution performance and their capabilities, logistics service providers consequently can directly contribute to the creation of competitive advantages for their customers. Another way how logistics services support the client in creating intangible assets is the transfer of the image or reputation of the service provider to the client. The perceived competences of a logistics service provider can consequently be used as a surrogate for the client's capabilities and improve his image on the markets. This is closely related to findings of KRALJIC who stresses logistics performance as an important criterion to evaluate the *power*-relation between buyer and seller (Kraljic 1988).

With an increasing recognition of the importance of logistics services for the company and chain performance also an enhanced value proposition of logistics service providers is observable. Customers expect balanced total value across cost, quality, speed, and responsiveness, but increasingly also environmental aspects. As logistics services affect all these competitive parameters, they can contribute to secure and to strengthen the competitive position of their clients. Due to this, not just cost – even when the total cost of ownership are taken into consideration – should be the focus in evaluating the supply chain performance of logistics services (Stock & Zinszer 1987; West 1997).

The modality of how logistics service providers can improve supply chain performance depends to a large extent on the architecture of the service offerings – this subject will be addressed in the next section.

THE ARCHITECTURE OF LOGISTICS SERVICE OFFERINGS

Using three different levels of system aggregation, the following part addresses how today's logistics service providers deliver value to supply chains by developing single logistics services (*service architecture*), their logistics service program (*service program architecture*) and finally, their organizational form on the market (*service provider architecture*).

The Service Architecture: Primary Services and Secondary Services

The view of the *service architecture* refers to the market appearance of the logistics service offering and provides information about its components in the case of demand. Depending on their degree of independence, logistics services offerings can be differentiated in 'primary services' and 'secondary or value-added services'.

Primary services are independently marketable sales offerings, which are the core part of the contract between logistics service provider and client. *Secondary services* on the other hand are offered in linkage with primary services and are directed to them. On the basis of KOTLER, Figure 6 visualizes the relation between primary and secondary services in form of a shell model.

If the offering of secondary services is a legal requirement or market standard (order qualifier) they are denoted as *obligatory* secondary services which are by definition an integral part of the service architecture. If their offering is not compulsory; these services are called *facultative* secondary services. Not being a market standard, logistics services providers can differentiate themselves and realize competitive advantages based on them (order winner).

Figure 7 demonstrates in a simplified way a logistics services bundle consisting of a primary service and two secondary services. But as typically also materials and rights become part of a market offering, logistics service providers finally offer in many cases '*product bundles*' with tangible and intangible components. Despite this fact, the following explanations will focus on pure logistics service offerings.

The Service Program Architecture: Homogeneous and Heterogeneous Bundles

In addition to the above described relation between primary and secondary services, logistics service offerings can also differ based on the number of primary services a company is offering – based on this criterion providers exist who offer just one primary service (*single-service program*) while others provide several primary services (*service bundles*).

The term *homogeneous service bundles* indicates that a logistics service provider offers several services around one functional task of logistics (*service group*) as described in Table 1. In the case of the service group 'transportation' it could for example mean that the service program of a provider contains air, land, sea, and rail transport. This example demonstrates a typical way to diversify the service program of a logistics service provider – a function (here transportation) is kept as the nucleus of the program, being expanded by the transport mode. Another option is to extend the service program by diversifying the type of goods being transported (e.g. reefer cargo, heavy cargo, bulk cargo, etc.).

But given the nature of logistics projects initiated by specific problem statements of the customers, the service program architecture often represents *heterogeneous service bundles* containing for example a combination of the functions of transportation, cargo handling, storage, and consulting. This phenomenon is in accordance with the current market offerings of 3PL- and 4PL-providers and indicates again that the general scope of modern logistics tasks is not based on a single function but represents a cross-functional approach in the context of the management of material and information flows, from which range heterogeneous bundles are frequently required.

Figure 6. The extended service offering (based on Kotler 1988)

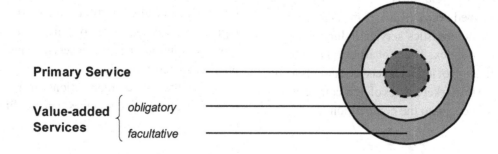

Primary Service

Value-added Services { *obligatory* / *facultative* }

Figure 7. Logistics as a product bundle (based on Freiling 1995)

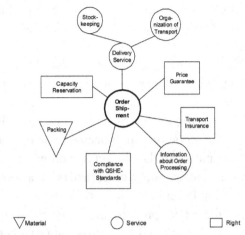

The Service Provider Architecture: Specialists, Full-Service Providers and Service Networks

The next aggregation level concerning the architecture of logistics service offerings refers to the organizational form chosen to provide services and service programs. In accordance with the terms used within the network-models of the IMP-Group (Håkansson 1982; Håkansson & Johanson 1992; Håkansson & Snehota 1995), organizational forms can be described as different types of structural arrangements of actors, resources and activities.

The establishment of organizational forms for marketable products can be interpreted as a reaction to changed competitive conditions in the course of time (Siebert 1999), which are in general determined by the horizontal market relations on the sales markets (*competitive situation*) and the vertical market relations towards the customer segments (*power relations*).

As described above (see 1.3) the *competitive situation* in the logistics service industry is dynamic and complex. The globalization and also the liberalization of logistics service markets lead furthermore to market entries of new competitors which add intensity to the competition.

In addition to the competitive situation, it is also important for service providers to consider the *power relations* between them and their customers. Notwithstanding the importance of logistics services for the value provision of their customers (see 2.2); power-relations are not necessarily 'seller-dominant'. Likewise it would not be adequate to conclude that the competitive situation on the sales markets leads across the board to 'buyer-dominant' power constellations. Here it is important to mention that logistics service providers need to understand how they can provide value to their customers (see 3.1.and 3.2), and they also need to anticipate the market strategies used in the supply departments of their clients. Two types of market strategies can be perceived as supply management trends, which have an impact on the topic addressed in this chapter: the reduction of the supply base (Gadde & Jellbo 2002; Hagberg-Andersson et al. 2000) and the complementary tendency to cover the service requirements in a 'one-stop-shopping'-manner.

Depending on the type of power-relation between supplier and client, logistics service providers can be directly exposed to requests concerning their organizational form; as such requirements can be an integral part of the supplier selection process or be used as criterion for programs aimed to reduce the supply base.

The objective to protect and/or to strengthen the competition position in a complex and dynamic business environment can therefore – apart from measures to improve efficiency by process and resources optimization – also be fostered by means of the adjustment of the service provider architecture. Such a re-arrangement of actors, resources and activities can consequently result in a modification of the so far existing organizational form, which ideally constitutes the platform for a logistics service provider to deliver competitive problem solutions in terms of services and service programs to customers.

Three alternative organizational forms for the provision of logistics services can be differentiated:

- *Logistics Specialists*: autonomous logistics service providers offering of a single-service program (e.g. truck transportation company);
- *Logistics Full-Service Providers*: autonomous logistics service providers offering homogeneous or heterogeneous service bundles (e.g. freight forwarding company);
- *Logistics Service Networks*: cooperative (inter-organizational) logistics service offerings managed by a focal organization (e.g. cooperation of SME, 4PL).

Led by the question 'Which are the pros and cons of each alternative?' and focusing on the potential value for the customers, these alternatives will be described and evaluated below.

Logistics Specialists

Logistics Specialists are autonomous logistics service providers who offer a single-service program within a functional service group. In the ideal case, the service offering is a result of a 'concentration on core competencies' which results in a reduced but high-quality product range. The service offering in general is limited by the marketability of the service, which represents an economic limitation of the degree of specialization.

In the context of logistics service interaction processes, two transaction types can be distinguished (see Figure 8): *single service transactions* ('Case 1') and *service bundle transactions* ('Case 2').

Single service transactions describe a transaction type in which a customer requires exactly one specific service (resource, capability; r_1) to solve a problem (P). As demonstrated in Figure 8, this does not exclude that the service provider possesses this problem-solving capability in an almost identical specification (e.g. skills, equipment). The evaluation of this case leads to the following results:

- The buying company just acquires resources it actually needs ('lean purchasing').
- Bureaucratic restraints with negative impact on the transaction times are rare.
- Uncertainty regarding the competence of the service provider is limited due to the service provider's degree of specialization.
- High costs due to the quality of the service can be expected. This effect can be compensated by economies of scale.
- The degree of utilization of the service provider can cause problems, resulting in higher supply risks in terms of potential bottlenecks and/or more complexity for the supply function of the client due to a necessary expansion of the supply base.

Figure 8. Logistics specialists (based on Voigt & Thiell 2003)

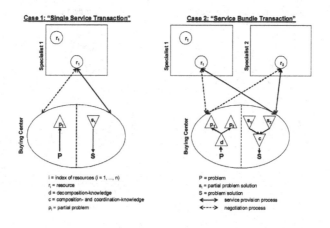

The second transaction type refers to a situation in which a comprehensive problem shall be solved through the purchase of several – autonomously provided – services (r_1 and r_2) which consequently form a homogenous or heterogeneous service bundle. To successfully realize such a transaction, the customer needs to hold two internal resources: 'decomposition-knowledge (d)' to de-compose a comprehensive problem into several (marketable) partial problems, as well as 'composition- and coordination-knowledge (c)' to integrate partial problem solutions to a problem-solution. This 'Case 2' is characterized by the following pros and cons:

- Receipt of a high-quality service bundle with positive impact on several competitive parameters is probable as competitive service offerings are combined.
- Highly educated purchasing professionals are necessary to manage the transaction complexity. A non-availability of this in-house resource of the client can lead to poor performance.
- Increasing (de-)composition and coordination effort with an increasing size of a problem, probably resulting in higher coordination effort at the interfaces, costly and time-consuming care of many bilateral

supplier relationships, and increasing process costs as well as longer process times. Advantages regarding the quality can be compensated by these negative effects.

The use of *Logistics Specialist* for service bundle transactions consequently seems only recommendable for problems characterized by a sequential structure (e.g. logistics services along a chain) or in situations when the required services are unconnected concerning temporal aspects and content. But, based on the above mentioned reasons, the strengths of Logistics Specialists are single service transactions.

Logistics Full-Service Providers

A *Logistics Full Service-Provider* is an autonomous logistics service provider being able to offer homogeneous or heterogeneous service bundles (see 3.2), as several resources ($r_1, r_2, \ldots r_n$) can be integrated within an intra-organizational network to satisfy the needs of a customer in case of a specific demand (see Figure 9). The buying company is consequently confronted with a logistics service provider whose service offering architecture is in accordance with the buying companies' objectives to reduce the number of direct suppliers and transaction-interfaces.

Figure 9. Logistics full-service providers (based on Voigt & Thiell 2003)

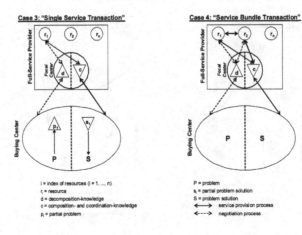

Using the two transaction types described above, 'Case 3' demonstrates that the term 'Full-Service Provider' does not necessarily mean that the full-service is always provided; the term corresponds to the resources which in their combination determine the range of capabilities to solve comprehensive problems.

A single service transaction between service provider and customer as demonstrated in 'Case 3' differs from 'Case 1 – Single Service Transaction with a Logistics Specialists' due to the 'Focal Center', a *broker* who centralizes the resources 'decomposition-knowledge of problems (d)' and 'composition- and coordination-knowledge of partial problem solutions (c)'. As a consequence, this center encompasses two additional capabilities: it provides the front-office processes in interaction with the customer and also coordinates the service provision.

Zooming into the resource-structure of the focal center in the case of demand for a service bundle, Figure 10 shows the linkage between the focal center and the used resources (service components) in terms of an *active intra-organizational network*. The 'network-knowledge (x)', another capability necessary to be provided by the focal center, shall ensure the internal coordination. Evaluating 'Case 3' leads to this conclusion:

- The perceived supply risk of the buying company can subjectively be lower, if the buyer had prior experience with the Full-Service Provider (modified rebuy).
- The use of further resources of the Full-Service Provider – particularly the focal center – in general leads to higher costs.
- The Full-Service Provider's size and the degree of utilization of *all* resources can also lead to higher costs.

The assessment of 'Case 4' comes to the following result:

- In comparison with 'Case 2 – Service Bundle Transaction with a Logistics Specialist', it is not necessary that the buying company provides resources for the (de-)composition and coordination. Therefore the use of a Full-Service Provider can lead to a reduction of interfaces and less coordination effort for the client, to a decrease of complexity and uncertainty within the buying company and finally to a positive impact on costs and duration of the transaction.
- But diametrical effects can occur, if the Full-Service Provider's company size results in bureaucratic company structures, which in turn can lead to an increase in transaction time and higher costs.

The strength of Full-Service Providers is finally the offering of service bundle transac-

Figure 10. 'Focal center' and the 'active intra-organizational network'

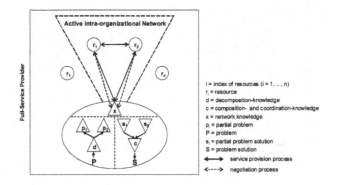

tions. To cover competences at the 'border of the Full-Service Provider', sometimes independent specialists are hired (e.g. consultants). Temporarily, these actors become integral parts of the Full-Service Provider as sub-contractors. This phenomenon shows a smooth transition to inter-organizational networks

Logistics Service Networks

While Service Specialists as well as Full-Service Providers can be regarded as established organizational forms in the provision of logistics service offerings, *Logistics Service Networks* are a comparably new form. Such inter-organizational networks allow on the one hand a specialization of the network members based on the principles of division of work and on the other hand an integration of single services to service bundles. Typically, Logistics Service Networks consist of legally independent actors and are managed by a focal organization.

To classify networks, management literature uses the criterion 'stability of the configuration' with the main characteristics 'stable' and 'unstable' (Sydow 1999.; Hess 1998). The use of this criterion seems also to be suitable in the context of Logistics Service Networks: The

network platform presenting the potential of the network on the market should be highly stable to provide a concrete point of reference for the supplier-identification. The transaction-network responsible for the service provision in the specific case of demand and often just temporarily formed is consequently less stable.

In deference to the service offering of Full-Service Providers, the legal independence between the actors in a Logistics Service Network can be highlighted, even if the economic dependency can be high. As demonstrated in Figure 11, the transaction structures of 'Case 5' and 'Case 6' are similar to the corresponding ones of Full-Service Providers. But, as the network consists of legally independent actors, each resource can be a selling center itself; hence the functions of the focal center in the Full-Service Provider architecture are performed by a *focal organization*.

Compared with 'Case 1 – Single Service Transaction with a Logistics Service Specialist', so far the preferable organizational form when single service transactions are to be performed, Logistics Service Networks have the advantage that multiple resources of the same type reduce the supply risk of the customer. But on the other hand, potential disadvantages result from comparable longer process times and increased costs.

Figure 11. Logistics service networks (based on Voigt & Thiell 2003)

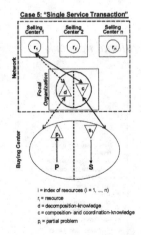 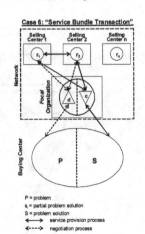

The service bundle transaction, so far advantageous in 'Case 4 – Service Bundle Transaction with a Full Service Provider', shows nearly identical (dis-)advantages when provided by service networks. Possible advantages of Logistics Service Networks may arise if the network has a higher flexibility concerning the availability of resources and when it causes lower overhead-cost. On the contrary, disadvantages could occur if the coordination effort in the network leads to inefficiencies. However, these differences are not based on the service offering architecture but on the management processes of the providers and can hence turn into the opposite.

The requirements of buying companies based on the above mentioned trends and the characteristics of logistics services seem to be achieved by Service Networks, as they fulfill the request for specialization of each network actor and are capable to satisfy the need for service bundles. Despite the stability of the network platform, an expansion of the network at its borders is possible. The existence of a focal organization additionally reduces the number of interfaces, while a multiple existences of resources within the network can significantly reduce supply risks.

To sum it up: Advantages and disadvantages of logistics service providers architectures can be identified using the basic structure of the ARA-model. But as transaction constellations for logistics services and their determinants may vary to a large extent, theoretically deduced conclusions have just the character of tendencies. Logistics Service Networks still wait for a wider diffusion on the markets. But if these networks are able to provide high-quality products, to establish brands, and to receive reputation, joining them can be a suitable alternative for logistics service providers – especially in service segments dominated by a large percentage of Small and Medium-Sized Companies (SME).

CONCLUSION

Given the title of this chapter, 'Logistics Services in the 21st Century – Supply Chain Integration and Service Architecture', it can finally be concluded that logistics service providers have many options to configure their service offerings nowadays as logistics services per se are not a commodity good anymore. The potential of logistics as a cross-functional service to provide value to supply chains in a multi-dimensional way might shift logistics into the position of an important contributor to achieve competitive advantages for companies and complete chains. Realizing this potential in the modern business environment, the presented findings are supposed to support logistics service providers in the process of rethinking and restructuring their current architectures of services, of service programs and also of their organizational forms.

REFERENCES

Axelsson, B., & Wynstra, F. (2002). Buying Business Services. Chichester, UK: Wiley-Blackwell.

Ballou, R. H. (1985). Business Logistics – Management Planning and Control. Englewood Cliffs, NJ: Bauer.

Bowersox, D. J., Closs, D. J., & Helferich, O. K. (1986). Logistical Management – A Systems Integration of Physical Distribution, Manufacturing Support, and Materials Procurement, 3rd Ed., New York: MacMillan.

Calaminus, G. (1994). Netzwerkansätze im Investitionsgütermarketing – Eine Weiterentwicklung multi-organisationaler Interaktionsansätze? (in English: Network Approaches in Industrial Marketing – A Further Development of Multi-organizational Interaction Approaches?). In: Kleinaltenkamp, M., & Schubert, K. (Eds.), Netzwerkansätze im Business-to-Business-Marketing – Beschaffung, Absatz und Implementierung neuer Technologien, Wiesbaden, pp. 93-124.

Engel, A., Schmidt, K. A., & Geraedts, S. (2003). Fourth Party Logistics Service Provider (4PL) – Osnabrück, Germany: Ein Neues Logistikkonzept (in English: Fourth Party Logistics Service Provider – A new Logistics Concept).

Freiling, J. (1995). *Die Abhängigkeit der Zulieferer.* Wiesbaden, Germany: Ein strategisches Problem (in English: The Dependency of Suppliers – A Strategic Problem).

Gadde, L.-E., & Jellbo, O. (2002). System Sourcing – Opportunities and Problems. *European Journal of Purchasing and Supply Management, 8*(1), 43–51. doi:10.1016/S0969-7012(01)00013-2

Gebhardt, A. (2006). Entscheidung zum Outsourcing von Logistikleistungen – Rationalitätsanforderungen und Realität in mittelständischen Unternehmen (in English: The Outsourcing Decision of Logistics Services – Rational Requirements and the Reality in Medium-sized Companies), Wiesbaden, Germany: Springer/Verlag

Hagberg-Andersson, Å., Kock, S., & Åhman, S. (2000). Managing Buyer-Supplier Relationships in a Supply Network – The Buyer's Perspective. In: *Proceedings of the 2000 International Marketing and Purchasing Conference,* Bath, The Netherlands.

Håkansson, H. (1982). International Marketing and Purchasing of Industrial Goods – An Interaction Approach. Chichester, UK: Håkansson, H., & Johanson, J. (1992). A Model of Industrial Networks. In Axelsson, B., & Easton, G. (Ed.). Industrial Networks – A New View of Reality, London, (pp. 28-34).

Håkansson, H., & Snehota, I. (1995). Developing Relationships in Business Networks. London: Routledge.

Heizer, J., & Render, B. (2008). Operations Management, 9th Ed., Upper Saddle River, NJ: Prentice Hall.

Hess, T. (1998): Unternehmensnetzwerke – Abgrenzung, Ausprägung und Entstehung (in English: Business Networks – Classification, Characteristics, and Development). In: Arbeitspapiere der Abt. Wirtschaftsinformatik II der Universität Göttingen, Nr. 4/1998, Göttingen.

Ketchen, D. J., & Hult, T. M. (2007). Bridging Organization Theory and Supply Chain Management – The Case of Best Value Supply Chains. *Journal of Operations Management, 25,* 573–580. doi:10.1016/j.jom.2006.05.010

Klaas, T. (2002). Logistik-Organisation: Ein konfigurationstheoretischer Ansatz zur logistikorientierten Organisationsgestaltung (in English: Organisation of Logistics – A Configuration-theoretic Approach for the Logistics-oriented Design of Organizations), Wiesbaden, Germany: Springer/Verlag.

Kotler, P. (1988). Marketing-Management – Analyse, Planung und Kontrolle (in English: Marketing Management – Analyzing, Planning, and Controlling), 4th Ed., Stuttgart, Germany: Verlag.

Kraljic, P. (1988). Zukunftsorientierte Beschaffungs- und Versorgungsstrategie als Element der Unternehmensstrategie (in English: Future-oriented Procurement- and Supply-Strategy as Element of the Corporate Strategy). In: Henzler, H.A. (Ed.), Handbuch Strategische Führung, Wiesbaden, Germany, (pp. 477-497).

Kuehne & Nagel (2008, February 27). *Kuehne-Nagel Lead Logistics Solutions – Supply Chain Management & Sustainable Development.* Presentation of A. Quillaud in Luxemburg.

Kumar, S., & Malegeant, P. (2006). Strategic Alliance in a Closed-loop Supply Chain – A Case of Manufacturer and Eco-non-profit Organization. *Technovation, 26*(10), 1127–1135. doi:10.1016/j.technovation.2005.08.002

Latin America Logistics Center. (2005): Análisis de Costo total de Logística en Empresas Colombianas 2004-2005 (in English: Analysis of the Total Cost of Logistics in Colombian Companies 2004-2005), Bogotá, Columbia.

Lee, H. L., Padmanabhan, V., & Whang, S. (1997). The Bullwhip Effect in Supply Chains. *Sloan Management Review, 38*(3), 93–102.

Loren, G. (2005). Network vs. Network – The New Arena of Competition. InHarvard Business Review 'Supply Chain Strategy', Reprint No. P0503D.

Maister, D. H., & Lovelock, C. H. (1982). Managing Facilitator Services. *Sloan Management Review, 23*(4), 9–20.

Marasco, A. (2008). Third-party Logistics – A Literature Review. *International Journal of Production Economics, 113*(1), 127–147. doi:10.1016/j.ijpe.2007.05.017

Morgenstern, O. (1955). Note on the Formulation of the Theory of Logistics. *Naval Research Logistics Quarterly Review, 2*, 129–136. doi:10.1002/nav.3800020303

Porter, M. E. (1987). Wettbewerbsstrategie – Methoden zur Analyse von Branchen und Konkurrenten (in English: Competitive Strategy – Methods to Analyze Industries and Competitors), 4th Ed., Frankfurt/New York: Robinson, P. J., Faris, C. W., & Wind, Y. (1967). Industrial Buying and Creative Marketing, Boston: Schmitt, A. (2006). 4PL-providing als strategische Option für Kontraktlogistikdienstleister – Eine konzeptionell-empirische Betrachtung (in English: 4PL-provision as Strategic Option for Contract Logistics Providers – A Conceptual-empirical View). Wiesbaden, Siebert, H. (1999). Ökonomische Analyse von Unternehmensnetzwerken (in English: Economic Analysis of Business Networks). In: Sydow, J. (Ed.): Management von Netzwerkorganisationen. Wiesbaden, Germany (pp. 7-27).

Stock, J. R., & Zinszer, P. H. (1987). The Industrial Purchase Decision for Professional Services. *Journal of Business Research, 15*(1), 1–16. doi:10.1016/0148-2963(87)90014-2

Sydow, J. (1999). Management von Netzwerkorganisationen – Zum Stand der Forschung (in English: Management of Network Organisations – State of the Art). In: Sydow, J. (Ed.): Management von Netzwerkorganisationen, Wiesbaden, Germany (pp. 279-314).

Thiell, M. (2008). *Strategische Beschaffung von Dienstleistungen* (in English: Strategic Supply Management of Services), Saarbrücken, U.S. International Trade Commission (2005). *Logistic Services – An Overview of the Global Market and Potential Effects of Removing Trade Impediments.* Investigation No. 332-463. Washington, DC.

Voigt, K.-I., & Thiell, M. (2003). Beschaffung wissensintensiver Dienstleistungen – Net Sourcing als alternative Bezugsform (in English: Procurement of Knowledge-based Services – Net Sourcing as Alternative Approach). In: Bruhn, M./Stauss, B. (Ed.): Dienstleistungsnetzwerke, Wiesbaden, Germany (pp. 287-318).

Voigt, K.-I., & Thiell, M. (2004). Industrielle Rücknahme- und Entsorgungssysteme – Eine modellgestützte Analyse alternativer Organisationsformen am Beispiel der Automobilindustrie (in English: Industrial Reverse Logistics Systems – A Model-based Analysis of Alternative Organizational Forms Using the Example of the Automotive Industry). In: Prockl, G./Bauer, A./Pflaum, A./Müller-Steinfahrt, U. (Ed.): Entwicklungspfade und Meilensteine moderner Logistik – Skizzen einer Roadmap, Wiesbaden, Germany (pp. 389-418).

Wegner, U. (1993). Organisation der Logistik – Prozess- und Strukturgestaltung mit neuer Informations- und Kommunikationstechnik (in English: Organization of Logistics – Process- and Structure-design with Modern Information and Communcation Technology), Berlin, Germany.

West, D. C. (1997). Purchasing Professional
Services – The Case of Advertising Agencies. In .
*International Journal of Purchasing and Materials
Management, 33*(3), 2–9.

Compilation of References

Abate, G., & Moser, C. (2003). *E-commerce and Internet use in small businesses: Trends and issues.* (Staff paper 2003-04). Michigan State University, Department of Agricultural Economics. Retrieved June 28, 2009, from http://www.aec.msu.edu/pubs.htm

Aberdeen Group. (2009). *Aberdeen Group.* Retrieved June 28, 2009, from http://www.aberdeen.com/

Abramson, N. (1970). The ALOHA System - Another alternative for computer communications. In *Proceedings of AFIPS Fall Joint Computation Conference, 37,* 281-285. Retrieved from http://doi.acm.org/10.1145/1478462.1478502

Ackoff, R. L. (1974). Redesigning the Future: a systems approach to societal problems. New York: John Wiley & Sons.

Ackoff, R. L., & Sasieni, M. W. (1968). Fundamentals of Operations Research. New York: John Wiley & Sons.

Adams, G. (2007). Pharmaceutical manufacturing: RFID-reducing errors and effort. *Filtration & Separation, 44*(6), 17–19. doi:10.1016/S0015-1882(07)70179-9

Adams, M., Bates, D., Coffman, G., & Everett, W. (2008). Saving lives, saving money: The imperative for computerized physician order entry in Massachusetts Hospital. Retrieved February 27, 2009, from http://www.nehi.net/publications/8/saving_lives_saving_money_the_imperative_for_computerized_physician_order_entry_in_massachusetts_hospitals

Adebanjo, D. (2003). Classifying and selecting e-CRM applications: An analysis-based proposal. *Management Decision, 41*(6), 570–577. doi:10.1108/00251740310491517

Agarkar, A. (2007). *Warehouse Voice Picking.* Retrieved May 5, 2007, from http://blogs.oracle.com/logistics/2007/05/warehouse_voice_picking.html

Agarwal, R., & Sambamurthy, V. (2002). Principles and models for organizing the information technology function. *MIS Quarterly Executive, 1*(1), 1–16.

Agrawal, G. K., & Berg, D. (2007). Technology in the service development process: A missing dimension. *International Journal of Services Technology and Management, 8*(2/3), 107–122. doi:10.1504/IJSTM.2007.012863

Air Transport Research Society. (2002–2005). *Airport Benchmarking Report: Global Standards for Airport Excellence - Part 1, 2 and 3.* Vancouver, Canada: ATRS.

Airos, E., Korhonen, R., & Pulkkinen, T. (2007). *Satelliittipaikannusjärjestelmät (Satellite navigation systems).* The Finnish Defence Forces. Riihimäki. Retrieved June 5, 2009 from http://www.mil.fi/laitokset/pvtt/satelliittipaikannus.pdf

Akkaya, K., & Younis, M. (2005). A survey on routing protocols for wireless sensor networks. *Ad Hoc Networks, 3*(3), 325–349. doi:10.1016/j.adhoc.2003.09.010

Akyildiz, I. F., Su, W., Sankarasubramaniam, Y., & Cayirci, E. (2002). A survey on sensor networks. *Communications Magazine, IEEE, 40*(8), 102–114. doi:10.1109/MCOM.2002.1024422

Alberts, D. S., Garska, J. J., & Stein, F. P. (1999). Network Centric Warfare: Developing and Leveraging Information Superiority. Retrieved April 2, 2009, from http://www.nps.edu/Academics/Centers/CEP/docs/Alberts_NCW.pdf

Albrecht, K. (1998). *La Revolución del servicio*. 3R Editores LTDA.

Albrecht, K., & Zemke, R. (1985). Service America. New York:Mc.Graw Hill.

Alex, J., & Jumar, U. (2005). Simulation zum integrierten Prozessentwurf von Abwassersystemen, *GWF Wasser/Abwasser, 145*(2005), Nr.10. http://simba.ifak.eu/simba/

Alexander, C., Pearson, J. M., & Crosby, L. (2003). The transition to e-commerce: A case study of a rural-based travel agency. *Journal of Internet Commerce, 2*(1), 49–63. doi:10.1300/J179v02n01_05

Aligning CoBiT 4.1. (2008). *Aligning CoBiT 4.1., ITIL V3 and ISO/IEC 27002 for Business Benefit, A Management Briefing From ITGI and OGC*. Rolling Meadows, IL: IT Governance Institute. Retrieved March 8, 2009, from http://www.isaca.org

Àlvarez, C., et al. (2004). Efficient and reliable high level communication in randomly deployed wireless sensor networks. In *Proceedings of the second international workshop on Mobility management & wireless access protocols* (pp. 10information and communication technologies (ICTs)Information technologyOperating system (OS)6-110).

Ambler, T., (2004). Why Financial Managers Need To Think About Marketing, Corporate Finance Review. Jul/Aug, 9(1), 14-21

Anastasi, G., Conti, M., Francesco, M., & Passarella, A. (2009). Energy conservation in wireless sensor networks: A survey. *Ad Hoc Networks, 7*(3), 537–568. doi:10.1016/j.adhoc.2008.06.003

Andal-Ancion, A., Cartwright, P. A., & Yip, G. S. (2003). The digital transformation of traditional businesses. Sloan Management Review, (Summer): 34–41.

Anderson, J. C., Hakansson, H., & Johanson, J. (1994). Dyadic business relationships withing a business network context. *Journal of Marketing, 58*(4), 1–15. doi:10.2307/1251912

Anderson, M., Banker, R., & Ravindran, S. (2006). Value Implications of Investments in Information Technology. Management Science, 52(9), 1359–11367. doi:10.1287/mnsc.1060.0542

ANEC & BEUC. (2008). *Radio frequency identification (RFID)*. Retrieved June 28, 2009, from http://www.anec.eu/attachments/ANEC-ICT-2008-G-017final.pdf

Angeles, R. (2005). RFID technologies: supply-chain applications and implementation issues. *Information Systems Management, 22*(1), 51–65. doi:10.1201/1078/44912.22.1.20051201/85739.7

Anonymous,. (2003). 10 emerging technologies that will change the world. *MIT's Technology Review, 106*(1), 33–49.

Appelfeller, W., & Buchholz, W. (2005). *Supplier Relationship Management: Strategie, Organisation und IT des modernenen Beschaffungsmanagements*. Wiesbaden, Germany: Gabler.

Appiah, A., & Agyemang, F. (2004). Electronic Retail Payment Systems: User Acceptability and Payment Problems in Ghana, School of Management, Business Administration, Blekinge Institute of technology. Blekinge, Sweeden.

Artemis (2008). *European Technology Platform, Embedded Intelligence and Systems*, Retrieved from http://www.artemis.eu/

Arumugam, D., & Ambravaneswaran, V. (2008). 2D localization using SAW-based RFID systems: a single antenna approach. Int. J. RFID Technology and Applications., 1(4), 417–438.

Askin, R., Goldberg, J., Goetschalckx, M., Kuo, W., Rardin, R., & Wysk, R. (2004). IE curriculum renovation. Panel discussion, *Industrial Engineering Research Conference*, Houston, TX.

Avison, D. E., & Young, T. (2007). Time to rethink health care and ICT? *Communications of the ACM, 50*(6), 69–74. doi:10.1145/1247001.1247008

Avriel, M., Penn, M., Shpirer, N., & Witteboon, S. (1998). Stowage planning for container ships to reduce the number of shifts. *Annals of Operations Research,* *76,* 55–71. doi:10.1023/A:1018956823693

Axelsson, B., & Wynstra, F. (2002). Buying Business Services. Chichester, UK: Wiley-Blackwell.

Ayers, J., (2003, July). Don't get buried in customer data-use it. Harvard Business School Working Knowledge, July 21st.

Aznar, J. (2006) Jerónimo Aznar Bellver-Dialnet, [en línea], Retrieved July 30, 2066, http://dialnet.uniroja.es/servlet/extaut?codigo=336[07.30.2006]

Baker, C. R., et al. (2007). Wireless sensor networks for home health care. In *Proceedings of the 21st International Conference on Advanced Information Networking and Applications Workshops, 2,* 832-837.

Baker, K., & Scudder, G. (1990). Sequencing with Earliness and Tardiness Penalties: A Review. *Operations Research, 38*(1), 22–36. doi:10.1287/opre.38.1.22

Bakos, Y. J., & Brynjolfsson, E. (1993). Information technology, incentives, and the optimal number of suppliers. *Journal of Management Information Systems, 10*(2), 37–53.

Ballou, R. H. (1985). Business Logistics – Management Planning and Control. Englewood Cliffs, NJ: Bauer.

Ballou, R. H. (2004). Business Logistics/Supply Chain Management – Planning, Organizing, and Controlling the Supply Chain.Upper Saddle River, New Jersey: Prentice Hall.

Banerjee, S., & Basu, A. (1993). Model type selection in an integrated DSS environment. *Decision Support Systems, 9*(1), 75–89. doi:10.1016/0167-9236(93)90024-W

Banker, R. D., Kalvenes, J., & Patterson, R. A. (2000). *Information technology, contract completeness, and buyer-supplier relationships*. Paper presented at the Twenty-First International Conference on Information Systems.

Baourakis, G., Kourgiantakis, M., & Migdalas, A. (2002). The impact of e-commerce on agro-food marketing: The case of agricultural cooperatives, firms, and consum-

ers in Crete. *British Food Journal, 104*(8), 580–590. doi:10.1108/00070700210425976

Barras, R. (1990). Interactive Innovation in Financial and Business Service: The vanguard of the service revolution. *Research Policy, 19,* 215–237. doi:10.1016/0048-7333(90)90037-7

Barratt, M. (2004). Understanding the meaning of collaboration in the supply chain. *Supply Chain Management: An International Journal, 9*(1), 30–42. doi:10.1108/13598540410517566

Bartens, S. (2008). *China setzt auf Ausbau,* Logistik auf den Punkt, Heft 6.

Bates, D. W., Leape, L. L., Cullen, D. J., Laird, N., Petersen, L. A., & Teich, J. M. (1998). Effect of computerized physician order entry and a team intervention on prevention of serious medication errors. *Journal of the American Medical Association, 280*(15), 1311–1316. doi:10.1001/jama.280.15.1311

Bazuin, B. J., Atashbar, M. Z., & Kirishnamurthy, S. (2004, January 4-7). A prototype burst transceiver for SAW sensors interrogation, International Conference on Intelligent Sensing and Information Processing (pp. 190-195), Chennai, India.

Beamon, B. (1998). Supply Chain Design and Analysis: Models and Methods. *International Journal of Production Economics, 55*(3), 281–294. doi:10.1016/S0925-5273(98)00079-6

Beamon, B. (1999). Measuring supply Chain Performance. *International Journal of Operations & Production Management, 19*(3), 275–292. doi:10.1108/01443579910249714

Bebko, C. P. (2000). Service intangibility and its impact on consumer expectations of service quality. *Journal of Services Marketing, 14*(1), 9–26. doi:10.1108/08876040010309185

Bechini, A., Cimino, M. G. C. A., Marcelloni, F., & Tomasi, A. (2007). Patterns and technologies for enabling supply chain traceability through collaborative e-business. *Information and Software Technology, 50*(4), 342–359. doi:10.1016/j.infsof.2007.02.017

Bechteler, T. F., & Yenigün, H. (2003). 2-D Localization and Identification Based on SAW ID-Tags at 2.5 GHz. IEEE Trans, MTT, 51(5), 1584–1590. doi:10.1109/TMTT.2003.810142

Bednarz, A. (2001) Gartner: CRM deployment plans holding steady, Computer World, September, http://www.computerworld.com/action/article.do?command=viewArticleBasic&articleId=64179

Beesley, A. (1996). Time compression in supply chain. *Industrial Management & Data Systems, 96*(2), 12–16. doi:10.1108/02635579610112606

Bellido, L. (2004). Metodología para la Evaluación de Servicios de Telecomunicaciones desde la perspectiva del usuario. Dpto. de Ingeniería de Sistemas Telemáticos, Universidad Politécnica de Madrid.

Belton, V., & Gear, T. (1983). On a Short-Coming of Saaty's Method of Analytic Hierarchies. *Omega, 11*(3), 228–230. doi:10.1016/0305-0483(83)90047-6

Benbasat, I., Goldstein, D. K., & Mead, M. (1987). The case research strategy in studies of information systems. *MIS Quarterly, 11*(3), 369–386. doi:10.2307/248684

Benedetto, J., & Ferreira, P. (2000). Modern Sampling Theory: Mathematics and Applications. Boston: Birkhauser.

Benjamin, R., & Wigand, R. (1995). Electronic market and virtual value chains on the information superhighway. *Sloan Management Review, 36*(2), 62–72.

Bensky, A. (2004), Short-range wireless Communication: Fundamentals of RF system design and application (second edition), New York: Elsevier

Berkowitz, B. (2001, April 20). Technology catches up to runners. *Washington Post, sec. E*, pg.1.

Berry, L. L., & Parasuraman, A. (1991). Marketing Services: Competing through Quality. New York: Free Press.

Berry, L. L., Shankar, V., Parish, J. T., Cadwallader, S., & Dotzel, T. (2006). Creating new markets through service innovation. *Sloan Management Review, 47*(2), 56–63.

Bertalanffy, L. V. (1976). General system theory: Foundations, development, applications. Revised edition, New York: George Braziller Inc.

Bertsimas, D. J., & Simchi–Levi, D. (1996). A new generation of vehicle routing research: Robust algorithms addressing uncertainty. *Operations Research, 44*, 286–304. doi:10.1287/opre.44.2.286

Bettman, J. R. (1973). Perceived risk and its components: A model and empirical test. *JMR, Journal of Marketing Research, 10*(May), 184–190. doi:10.2307/3149824

Beuscart-Zephir, M. C., Pelayo, S., Degoulet, P., Anceaux, F., Guerlinger, S., & Meaux, J. J. (2004). A usability study of CPOE's medication administration functions: Impact on physician-nurse cooperation. *Sudies in Health Technologies and Informatics, 107*(2), 1018–1022.

Bhatt, G., & Grover, V. (2005). Types of information technology capabilities and their role in competitive advantage: an empirical study. *Journal of Management Information Systems, 22*(2), 253–277.

Bielli, M., Boulmakoul, A., & Rida, M. (2006). Object oriented model for container terminal distributed simulation. *European Journal of Operational Research, 175*, 1731–1751. doi:10.1016/j.ejor.2005.02.037

Biemans, F. P. M., Lankhorst, M. M., Teeuw, W. B., & van de Wetering, R. G. (2001). Dealing with the complexity of business systems architecting. *Systems Engineering, 4*(2), 118–133. doi:10.1002/sys.1010

Bilderbeek, Hertog, P. D., & Marklund, G. (1998). Service innovation: knowledge intensive business service as cooproducers of innovation .*The Result of SIS Synthesis Paper 3*, 1.

Biohealthmatics.com. (2006). *Pharmacy information systems*. Retrieved February 27, 2009, from http://www.biohealthmatics.com/technologies/his/pis.aspx

Bitner, M. J. (2001). Self-service technologies: What do customers expect? Marketing Management., 10(1), 10–12.

Bitner, M. J., Booms, B. H., & Tetreault, M. S. (1990). The service encounter: Diagnosing favorable and unfavorable incidents. *Journal of Marketing, 54*(January), 71–84. doi:10.2307/1252174

Bitner, M., J., Brown, S., Meuter, M. (2000). Technology infusion in service encounters. Academy of Marketing Science Journal., 28(1), 138–150. doi:10.1177/0092070300281013

Blackburn, J. D. (1990). Time-based competition: the next battleground in American manufacturing. New York: McGraw-Hill.

BMBF - Bundesministerium für Bildung und Forschung. (2007). *IKT 2020 - Forschung für Innovationen.* Retrieved from http://www.bmbf.de/de/9069.php

BMVBS - Bundesministerium für Verkehr. Bau und Stadtentwicklung (2009). *Masterplan - Güterverkehr und Logistik.* Retrieved from http://www.bmvbs.de/Verkehr/Gueterverkehr-Logistik-,2829/Masterplan.htm

Bogataj, D., & Bogataj, M. (2007). Measuring the supply chain risk and vulnerability in frequency space. *International Journal of Production Economics, 108,* 291–301. doi:10.1016/j.ijpe.2006.12.017

Booms, B., & Bitner, M. J. (1981). Marketing strategies and organization structures for service firms, In J. Donnelly and W. George (Eds), Marketing of Services, American Marketing Association. Chicago, Il.

Bose, I., & Pal, R. (2005). Auto-id: managing anything, anywhere, anytime in the supply chain. *Communications of the ACM, 48*(8), 100–106. doi:10.1145/1076211.1076212

Boshoff, C. R. (1997). An experimental study of service recovery options. *International Journal of Service Industry Management, 8*(2), 110–130. doi:10.1108/09564239710166245

Boukerche, A. (2008). Algorithms and protocols for wireless sensor networks. New York: John Wiley & Sons.

Bowersox, D. J., & Daugherty, P. J. (1995). Logistics paradigms: the impact of information technology. *Journal of Business Logistics, 16*(1), 65–80.

Bowersox, D. J., Class, D. J., & Cooper, M. B. (2007). Supply chain logistics management. (2nd ed.). Boston, MA: McGraw-Hill/Irwin.

Bowersox, D. J., Closs, D. J., & Helferich, O. K. (1986). Logistical Management – A Systems Integration of Physical Distribution, Manufacturing Support, and Materials Procurement, 3rd Ed., New York: MacMillan.

Boyson, S., Corsi, T., & Verbraeck, A. (2003). The e-supply chain portal: A core business model. *Transportation Research, 39,* 175–192. doi:10.1016/S1366-5545(02)00046-7

Brady, M. (2005, September). The role of information technology in marketing: Crucial but overlooked and underexploited. In Proceedings of the Irish Academy of Management Conference, Galway, CD Rom.

Brady, M. K., & Cronin, J. J. (2001). Some New Thougths on Conceptualizing Perceived Service Quality: A Hierarchical Approach. *Journal of Marketing, 65*(3), 34–49. doi:10.1509/jmkg.65.3.34.18334

Brady, M., & Fellenz, M. R. (2007, August), The Service Paradox: Supporting Service Supply Chains with Product-Orientated ICT', IEEE/Informs Soli International Conference on Service Operations, Logistics and Informatics, Philadelphia.

Brady, M., Fellenz, M. R., & Brookes, R. (2008). The history of Information and Communication Technologies (ICT) with the marketing domain: Reframing the ICT dimension within the CMP framework. Journal of Business and Industrial Marketing, 23(2), 108–114. doi:10.1108/08858620810850227

Brady, M., O'Connor, M., & Saren, M. (2006, July). Marketers for the 21st Century Need ICT Education, In Academy of Marketing Conference, University of Middlesex, Brady, M., Saren, M., & Tzokas, N., (2002). Integrating Information Technology into Marketing Practice: The IT Reality of Contemporary Marketing Practice. Journal of Marketing Management, 18(5-6), 555–578.

Bramel, J., & Simchi-Levi, D. (1997). The logic of logistics. New York: Springer.

Brandl, M., Schuster, S., Scheiblhofer, S., & Stelzer, A. A new Anti-Collision Method for SAW tags using Linear Block Codes, 2008 IEEE International Frequency Control Symposium, 284-289

Brennan, S. (2005). NHS IT project: The biggest computer programme in the world...ever! Oxford, UK: Radcliffe Medical Press.

Brethon, P., MacHulbert, J., & Pitt, L. (2005). Consuming technology: Why marketers sometimes get it wrong. California Management Review, 48(1), 110–128.

Brown, P., Hartmann, C., et al. (2007). Asset Tracking on the International Space Station Using Global SAW Tag RFID Technology, 2007 IEEE Ultrasonics Symposium, New York, (pp. 72 – 75).

Browne, J., Chan, W. W., & Rathmill, K. (1985). An integrated FMS design procedure. In Annals of Operations Research, 3, K.E. Stecke & R. Suri (Eds.), Basel-Switzerland: J.C. Baltzer, 207-238.

Bruno, F. (2006, July). *Executing an IP Protection Strategy in a SaaS Environment. Contract Management.* Magazine, NCMA, USA.

Brynjolfsson, E., & Yang, S. (1996). Information technology and productivity: A review of the literature. *Advances in Computers, 43*, 179–214. doi:10.1016/S0065-2458(08)60644-0

Bulst, W.-E., Fischerauer, G., & Reindl, L., choll, G., et al. (2001). State of the art in wireless sensing with surface acoustic waves. IEEE Transactions on Industrial Electronics, 48(2), 265–271. doi:10.1109/41.915404

Bunduchi, R. (2005). Business relationships in internet-based electronic markets: The role of goodwill trust and transaction costs. *Information Systems Journal, 15*(4), 321–341. doi:10.1111/j.1365-2575.2005.00199.x

Burgess, R. (1998). Avoiding supply chain management failure: lessons from business process re-engineering. *International Journal of Logistics Management, 9*(1), 15–23. doi:10.1108/09574099810805717

Burns, L. R. (2002). The health care value chain: Producers, purchasers, and providers. San Francisco: Jossey-Bass.

Burt, R. S. (1992). Structural holes: the social structure of competition. Cambridge, MA: Harvard University Press.

Business Week. (1999, August 30). 21 ideas for the 21st century. Retrieved April 1, from http://www.business-week.com/1999/99_35/2121_content.htm

Buzacott, J. A. (1996). Commonalities in reengineered business processes: Models and issues. *Management Science, 42*(5), 768–782. doi:10.1287/mnsc.42.5.768

Cahnson, S. (1998), Electronic Payment Systems Handbook of Cyberspace Center, *Hong Kong University of Science & Technology,* Retrieved from http://www.cyber.ust.hk/handbook7/hb7main.html

Calaminus, G. (1994). Netzwerkansätze im Investitionsgütermarketing – Eine Weiterentwicklung multi-organisationaler Interaktionsansätze? (in English: Network Approaches in Industrial Marketing – A Further Development of Multi-organizational Interaction Approaches?). In: Kleinaltenkamp, M., & Schubert, K. (Eds.), Netzwerkansätze im Business-to-Business-Marketing – Beschaffung, Absatz und Implementierung neuer Technologien, Wiesbaden, pp. 93-124.

Calder, A., & Watkins, S. (2006). International IT Governance [London: Kogan Page.]. *An Executive Guide to ISO, 17799*(I), SO27001.

Callaway, E. H. (2004). Wireless sensor networks: architectures and protocols. New York: CRC Press.

Callaway, E., Hsu, S., & Shankar, R. (2002). JAN: A communications model for wireless sensor networks, Technical Report, TR-CSE-02-12, Boca Raton, FL: Department of Computer Science and Engineering, Florida Atlantic University.

Cannon-Bowers, J. A., & Salas, E. (2001). Reflection on shared cognition. *Journal of Organizational Behavior, 22*, 195–202. doi:10.1002/job.82

Cantú, H. (2001). Desarrollo de una Cultura de Calidad. New York: McGraw Hill.

Cao, X., Chen, J., Zhang, Y., & Sun, Y. (2008). Development of an integrated wireless sensor network micro-environmental monitoring system. *ISA Transactions*, *47*(3), 247–255. doi:10.1016/j.isatra.2008.02.001

Carbone, L. P., & Haeckel, S. H. (1994). Engineering customer experiences. *Marketing Management*, *3*(3), 8–19.

Carlzon, J. (1987). Moments of Truth. Cambridge, MA: Ballinger Publishing Co.

Cartenì, A., Cantarella, G. E., & de Luca, S. (2005). A simulation model for a container terminal. In *Proceeding of the European Transport Conference (ETC) 2005*, Strasbourg, France.

Cascarino, R. E. (2007). Auditor's Guide to Information Systems Auditing, Hoboken, NJ: J.Wiley & Sons.

Cassel, P., Eddy, C., & Price, J. (2002). Aprendiendo Microsoft Access. Pearson Educación.

Cedillo, M., Sanchez, J., & Sanchez, C. (2006). The new relational schemas of inter-firms cooperation: the case of the Coahuila automobile cluster in Mexico. *International Journal of Automotive Technology and Management*, *6*(4), 406–418. doi:10.1504/IJATM.2006.012233

Ceken, C. (2008). An energy efficient and delay sensitive centralized Mac protocol for wireless sensor networks. *Computer Standards & Interfaces*, *30*(1-2), 20–31. doi:10.1016/j.csi.2007.06.001

Chadha, B. (1995). A model driven methodology for business process engineering. In *Proceedings of the ASME Computers in Engineering Conference*.

Chakravorty, R. (2006). A programmable service architecture for mobile medical care. In *Proceedings of the 4th Annual IEEE International Conference on Pervasive Computing and Communications Workshops (PerCom '06)*, pages 532-536.

Chan, Y. (2005). Location, transport, and land-use: Modelling spatial-temporal information. Heidelberg, Germany: Springer.

Chan, Y., & Ponder, R. (1979). The small package air freight industry in the United States: A review of the Federal Express experience. *Transportation Research*, *13*, 221–229. doi:10.1016/0191-2607(79)90048-7

Chapman, R. L., Soosay, C., & Kandampully, J. (2002). Innovation in logistics and the new business model: a conceptual framework. *Managing Service Quality*, *12*(6), 358–371. doi:10.1108/09604520210451849

Chase, A. Jacobs. (1998). Production and Operations Management. Eighth edition, New York: McGraw Hill.

Chau, S. (2003). The use of e-commerce amongst thirty-four Australian SMEs: An experiment or a strategic business tool? *Journal of Systems and Information Technology*, *7*(1), 49–66.

Chen, C.-Y., & Hsieh, T.-W. (2002, July). A time–space network model for the berth allocation problem. *19th IFIP TC7 Conference on System Modeling and Optimization*, Cambridge, UK, 1999.

Chen, F. (2005). Explanation of the new concept of modern logistics services. *Journal of Storage Transportation & Preservation of Commodities*, *1*, 10–12.

Chen, J. S., & Tsou, H. T. (2007). Information technology adoption for service innovation practices and competitive advantage: the case of financial firms. *Information research: an international electronic journal*, *12(3)*, 314. Retrieved April 3, 2009, from http://InformationR.net/ir/12-3/paper314.html

Chen, R., Sun, C., Helms, M., & Kennyjih, W. (2008). Aligning information technology and business strategy with a dynamic capabilities perspective: A longitudinal study of a Taiwanese semiconductor company. *International Journal of Information Management*, *28*(5), 366–378. doi:10.1016/j.ijinfomgt.2008.01.015

Chen, S. J., & Hwang, C. L. (1991) Fuzzy Multiple Atribute Decision Making: Methods and Applications. Lecture Notes in Economics and Mathematical Systems, No. 375. Berlin, Germany.

Chen, S.-C., & Chen, H.-H. (2007). Implementation and application of RFID EPC information service for forward and reverse logistics. *Journal of Global Business Management*, *2*(2).

Cheng, H. K., Demirkan, H., & Koehler, G. (2003). The Price and Capacity Competition of Application Services Duopoly. *Information Systems and e-Business Management. 1*(2).

Chesbrough, H. W. (2004). A failing grade for the innovation academy. *Financial Times (North American Edition)*, (September): 25.

Chesbrough, H. W. (2005). Towards a new science of services. In Breakthrough ideas for 2005. *Harvard Business Review, 83*(1), 16–17.

Cheung, R. K., Li, C.-L., & Lin, W. (2002). Interblock crane deployment in container terminals. *Transportation Science, 36*(1), 79–83. doi:10.1287/trsc.36.1.79.568

Chiang, C.-C. (2001). Encapsulating legacy systems for use in heterogeneous computing environments. *Information and Software Technology, 43*(8), 497–507. doi:10.1016/S0950-5849(01)00160-4

Chiang, C.-C. (2007). Software modernization of legacy systems for web services interoperability. In Mario Freire and Manuela Pereira (Ed.), Encyclopedia of Internet Technologies and Applications. Hershey, PA: Idea Group Publishing.

Chiasserini, C. F., & Rao, R. R. (2000). Routing protocols to maximize battery efficiency. In *Proceedings of MILCOM: 21st Century Military Communications Conference*, 1, 496-500.

Chin, T. H. A. (1997). Implications of Liberalization on Airport Development and Strategy in the Asia Pacific. *Journal of Air Transport Management, 3*, 125–131. doi:10.1016/S0969-6997(97)00020-3

Choi, Y. S. (2000). *Simulator for Port Container Terminal Using An Object-Oriented Approach*. PhD thesis, Quality System Analysis Lab., Industrial Engineering, Pusan National University.

Chong, C. Y., & Kumar, S. P. (2003). Sensor Networks: Evolution, Opportunities, and Challenges. *Proceedings of the IEEE, 91*(8), 1247–1256. doi:10.1109/JPROC.2003.814918

Choobineh, J. (1991). A diagramming technique for representation of linear models. *OMEGA International Journal of Management Science, 19*(1), 43–51. doi:10.1016/0305-0483(91)90033-P

Chopra, S., & Meindl, P. (2007). (3rd ed.). Supply chain management. Upper Saddle River, NJPrentice Hall.

Choy, K. L., So, S. C. K., Lau, H. C. W., Kwok, S. K., & Chan, F. T. S. (2006). Development of an integrated logistics information system for third party logistics facilitators. *International Journal of Business Performance Management, 8*(2/3), 170–193. doi:10.1504/IJBPM.2006.009035

Chr, P. H. (2004). Logistiksysteme – Betriebswirtschaftliche Grundlagen. Berlin Heidelberg: Springer-Verlag

Chris, K., Naveen, S., & David, W. (2004). TinySec: a link layer security architecture for wireless sensor networks. In *Proceedings of the 2nd International Conference on Embedded Networked Sensor Systems*, New York: ACM Press.

Christopher, M. (1992). Logistics and supply chain management: Strategies for reducing costs and improving services. London: Pitman Publishing

Chu, S.-C., Leung, L. C. Y., Hui, V., & Cheung, W. (2007). Evolution of e-commerce web sites: A conceptual framework and a longitudinal study. *Information & Management, 44*, 154–164. doi:10.1016/j.im.2006.11.003

Chung, K., Choi, Y. B., & Moon, S. (2003). Toward efficient medication error reduction: Error-reducing information management systems. *Journal of Medical Systems, 27*(6), 553–560. doi:10.1023/A:1025937916203

Clarke, R. (1998). *Electronic Data Interchange (EDI): An Introduction*. Retrieved from http://www.rogerclarke.com/EC/EDIIntro.html

Claro, D. P. (2004). Managing business networks and buyer-supplier relationships. Wageningen, The Netherlands:Wageningen University

Cobi, T. 4.1. Executive Summary Framework (2007) *ISACA*. Rolling Meadows, IL. Retrieved March from http://www.isaca.org

Coetzee, M., & Eloff, J. H. P. (2007). Web services Access Control Architecture Incorporating Trust. *Internet Research, 17*(3). doi:10.1108/10662240710758939

Cohen, W. M., & Levinthal, D. A. (1990). Absorptive Capacity: A New Perspective on Learning and Innovation. Administrative Science Quarterly, 35(1), 128–152. doi:10.2307/2393553

CORBA. (2009). *CORBA*. Retrieved March 9, 2009, from http://www.corba.org

Corbett, C. J., Blackburn, J. D., & Van Wassenhove, L. N. (1999). Partnerships to improve supply chains. *Sloan Management Review, 40*(4), 71–82.

Corbin, J., & Strauss, A. (1990). Grounded theory research: Procedures, canons, and evaluative criteria. *Qualitative Sociology, 13*(1), 3–21. doi:10.1007/BF00988593

Cornell Database Group. (2009). *Cougar: The Network Is the Database*. Retrieved April 2, 2009, from http://www.cs.cornell.edu/bigreddata/cougar/index.php

Council on Competitiveness. (2004, December). *Innovate America: thriving in a world of challenge and change*. Presented at Global Innvation Ecosystem 2007 Symposium.

Coyle, J. J. Langley, Jr., Gibson, B. J., Novack, R. A., & Bardi, E. J. (2009). (8th ed.). Supply chain management: A logistics perspective. Florence, KY: South-Western Cengage Learning.

Craig, D. R., & Gabler, W. K. (1940). The competitive struggle for market control. *The Annals of the American Academy of Political and Social Science, 209*, 84–107. doi:10.1177/000271624020900112

Cronin, J. J., & Taylor, S. (1992). Measuring Service Quality: A Reexamination and Extension. *Journal of Marketing, 56*(July), 55–68. doi:10.2307/1252296

Cronin, J. J., & Taylor, S. a. (1994). SERVPERF versus SERVQUAL: Reconciling performance based and perceptions-minus-excpectations measurement of service quality. *Journal of Marketing, 58*, 125. doi:10.2307/1252256

Crosby, P. (1984). Quality Without Tears. New York: McGraw Hill.

Cullen, S., Seddon, P., & Willcocks, L. (2005). Managing IT outsourcing: The life cycle imperative. *MIS Quarterly Executive, 4*, 229–244.

Cunningham, L. F., Gerlach, J., & Harper, M. D. (2004). Assessing perceived risk of consumers in Internet airline reservations services. *Journal of Air Transportation, 9*(1), 21–35.

Curran, J., & Meuter, M. (2005). Self-service technology adoption: comparing three technologies. Journal of Services Marketing, 19(2), 103–114. doi:10.1108/08876040510591411

Currie, W. (1996). Organizational structure and the use of information technology: Preliminary findings of a survey in the private and public sector. *International Journal of Information Management, 16*(1), 51–64. doi:10.1016/0268-4012(95)00061-5

Curtis, B., Kellner, M. I., & Over, J. (1992). Process modeling. *Communications of the ACM, 35*(9), 75–90. doi:10.1145/130994.130998

Daft, R. L., & Lengel, R. H. (1984). Information richness: A new approach to managerial behafviour and organization design. In B.M. Staw & L.L. Cummings (eds.), Research in organizational behaviour, 6, 191-233. JAI Press.

Daft, R. L., & Macintosh, N. B. (1981). A tentative explanation into the amount and equivocality of information processing in organizational work units. Administrative Science Quarterly, 26, 207–224. doi:10.2307/2392469

Daft, R. L., Lengel, R. H., & Trevino, L. K. (1987, September). Message equivocality, media selection, and manager performance: Implications for information systems. MIS Quarterly, •••, 355–366. doi:10.2307/248682

Dağtaş, S., Pekhteryev, G., Şahinoğlu, Z., Çam, H., & Challa, N. (2008). Real-Time and Secure Wireless Health Monitoring. International Journal of Telemedicine and Applications, 2008, Article ID 135808, 10 pages

Davenport, T. (2006). Competing on Analytics. Harvard Business Review, (January): 99–107.

Davenport, T. H. (1993). Process Innovation: Reengineering Work Through Information Technology. Cambridge, MA: Harvard Business School Press.

Davenport, T. H. (1998). Putting the enterprise into the enterprise system. *Harvard Business Review, 76*(4), 121–131.

Davenport, T. H., & Grover, V. (2001). 'Special issue; Knowledge management. Journal of Management Information Systems, 18(1), 3–4.

Davenport, T. H., & Harris, J. G. (2005). Automated decision making comes of age. Sloan Management Review, 46(4), 83–89.

Davenport, T. H., & Short, J. E. (1990). The new industrial engineering: Information technology and business process redesign. *Sloan Management Review, 31*(4), 11–27.

Davenport, T. H., Harris, J. G., & Kohli, A. K. (2001). 'How do they know their customers so well? Sloan Management Review, (Winter): 63–73.

Davenport, T., Hammer, M., & Metsisto, T. (1989). How executives can shape their companies' information systems. *Harvard Business Review, 67*(5), 130–134.

Day, G. S. (2006). Aligning the organization with the market. Sloan Management Review, 48(1), 41–49.

DCOM. (2009). *DCOM*. Retrieved March 9, 2009, from http://msdn.microsoft.com/en-us/library/ms809340.aspx

de Haan, J., Kisperska-Moron, D., & Placzek, E. (2007). Logistics management and firm size: A survey among Polish small and medium enterprises. *International Journal of Production Economics, 108*, 119–126. doi:10.1016/j.ijpe.2006.12.009

de Luca, S., Cantarella, G. E., & Cartenì, A. (2008). A macroscopic model of a container terminal based on diachronic networks. Schedule-Based Modeling of Transportation Networks. Wilson, Nuzzolo (Ed.). Springer.

Debely, J., Dubosson, M., & Fragnière, E. (2006). The Travel Agent: Delivering More Value by Becoming an Operational Risk Manager. In *Proceedings of the Lalonde 9th International Research Seminar in Service Management*, 178-203.

Debely, J., Dubosson, M., & Fragnière, E. (2007). *The Pricing of Knowledge-based services: Insights from the Environmental Sciences*, New Delhi 2nd International Conference on Services Management. Retrieved from http://ssrn.com/abstract=951651

Dehning, B., Richardson, V. J., & Zmud, R. W. (2007). The financial performance effects of IT-based supply chain management systems in manufacturing firms. *Journal of Operations Management, 25*, 806–824. doi:10.1016/j.jom.2006.09.001

Dellenbarger, L. E., Dillard, J., Schupp, A. R., Zapata, H. O., & Young, B. T. (2006). Socioeconomic factors associated with at-home and away-from home catfish consumption in the United States. *Agribusiness, 2*, 35–46.

Demirhan, D., Jacob, V., & Raghunathan, S. (2006). Information technology investment strategies under declining technology cost. *Journal of Management Information Systems, 22*(3), 321–350. doi:10.2753/MIS0742-1222220311

Dempsey, P. S., & O'Connor, K. (1997). Air Traffic Congestion and Infrastructure Development in the Pacific Asia Region. In Findley, C., Chia L.S, and Singh, K. (Eds), Asia Pacific Air Transport – Challenges and Policy Reforms. Institute of Southeast Asian Studies.

DHL. (n.d.). *Logbook in cooperation with Technische Universtat Darmstadt*.Retrieved from http://www.dhl-discoverlogistics.com/cms/en/course/technologies/connection/edi.jsp

Ding, Q., Dong, L., & Kouvelis, P. (2007). On the integration of production and financial hedging decisions in global markets. *Operations Research, 55*, 470–489. doi:10.1287/opre.1070.0364

Dodgson, M., Gann, D., & Salter, A. (2008) The Management of Technological Innovation, Strategy and Practice. Oxford, UK: Oxford University Press.

Dominick, C. (2008). *Supplier Partnerships: Your End of the Deal.* Retrieved from http://www.nextlevelpurchasing.com/articles/supplier-partnership.html

Dowling, G. R., & Staelin, R. (1994). A model of perceived risk and risk-handling activities. *The Journal of Consumer Research, 21*(June), 119–134. doi:10.1086/209386

Drammeh, L., House, L., Sureshwaran, S., & Selassie, H. (2002, July). Analysis of factors influencing the frequency of catfish consumption in the United States. In *Proceedings of the 2002 American Agricultural Economics Association Annual Meeting.* Long Beach, CA.

Drucker, P. (1954). The Practice of Management, New York and Evanston: Harper & Row

Drucker, P. F. (1985). Innovation and entrepreneurship: practice and principles, New York: Harper & Row.

Du, W. (2005). A pairwise key predistribution scheme for wireless sensor networks. *ACM Transactions on Information and System Security, 8*(2), 228–258. doi:10.1145/1065545.1065548

Dubosson, M., Fragnière, E., & Millet, B. (2006). A Control System Designed to Address the Intangible Nature of Service Risks. In *Proceedings of the Shanghai IEEE International Conference on Service Operations and Logistics and Informatics* (June), 90-95.

Duclos, L., Vokurka, R., & Lummus, R. (2003). Conceptual Model of Supply Chain Flexibility. Industrial Management Data Systems, 103(6), 446-456.Eiglier, P. & Langeard, E. (1991). El marketing de servicios. New York: McGraw Hill.

Dutertre, B., Cheung, S., & Levy, J. (2004). Lightweight key management in wireless sensor networks by leveraging initial trust. *Technical Report SRI-SDL-04-02.* Retrieved April 3, 2009, from http://www.csl.sri.com/users/bruno/publis/sri-sdl-04-02.pdf

Dwyer, F. R., Schurr, P. H., & Oh, S. (1987). Developing buyer-seller relationships. *Journal of Marketing, 51*(2), 11–27. doi:10.2307/1251126

Dyché, J. (2001). The CRM Handbook: A business guide to customer relationship management. Reading, MA: Addison-Wesley.

Dyer, J. H., & Singh, H. (1998). The relational view: Cooperative strategy and sources of interorganizational competitive advantage. *Academy of Management Review, 23*(4), 660–679. doi:10.2307/259056

Edgar, J. R. (1995, July 9-11). *World Air Cargo Forecast.* A paper presented at the conference on Air Transport in the Asia Pacific – Challenges, Opportunities and Options, Singapore.

Edmonson P. J., & Campbell C. K. (2004). Encoded SAW RFID tags and sensors for multi-user detection using IDT finger phase modulation US6827281

Eisenhardt, K. M. (1989). Building theories from case study research. *Academy of Management Review, 14*(4), 532–550. doi:10.2307/258557

El Sheikh, A. A. R., Paul, R. J., Harding, A. S., & Balmer, D. W. (1987). A microcomputer-based simulation study of a port. *The Journal of the Operational Research Society, 38*(8), 673–681.

Elson, J., Girod, L., & Estrin, D. (2002). Fine-grained network time synchronization using reference broadcasts. ACM SIGOPS Operating Systems Review, 36(SI), 147-163.

Encyclopedia (2007). *Service Level Agreement.* Retrieved from http://www.nationmaster.com/encyclopedia/Service-Level-Agreement European Committee for Standardization (2007). *CEN Horizontal European Service Standardization Strategy (CHESS).* Retrieved from http://www.cen.eu/cenorm/sectors/nbo/value/chesss/index.asp

Engel, A., Schmidt, K. A., & Geraedts, S. (2003). Fourth Party Logistics Service Provider (4PL) – Osnabrück, Germany: Ein Neues Logistikkonzept (in English: Fourth Party Logistics Service Provider – A new Logistics Concept).

Engel, J. F., Blackwell, R. D., & Miniard, P. W. (1993). Consumer Behavior, Chicago, IL: Dryden Press.

Engle, C. R., & Quagrainie, K. (2006). Aquaculture marketing handbook. Boston, MA: Blackwell Publishing.

Engle, C. R., Capps, O., Dellenbarger, L., Dillard, J., Hatch, U., Kinnucan, H., & Pomeroy, R. (1990). The U. S. market for farm-raised catfish: An overview of consumer, supermarket, and restaurant surveys. Fayetteville, AR: Arkansas Agricultural Experimental Station, 925, Southern Regional Aquaculture Center 511.

Engle, C. R., Capps, O., Dellenbarger, L., Dillard, J., Hatch, U., Kinnucan, H., & Pomeroy, R. (1991). Expanding U. S. markets for farm-raised catfish. *Arkansas Farm Research*, *40*(6), 5–6.

Enrado, P. (2005). *Buyers guide: Pharmacy systems*. Retrieved February 27, 2009, from http://www.healthcareitnews.com/story.cms?id=3786

Enterprise JavaBeans. (2009). *JavaBeans*. Retrieved March 9, 2009, from http://java.sun.com/products/ejb/

Enterprise Value. *Governance of IT Investments*. (2006). *Enterprise Value: Governance of IT Investments, The Val IT Framework*. Rolling Meadows, IL: IT Governance Institute. Retrieved March 8, 2009, from http://www.isaca.org

ENV 12313 Traffic and Traveller Information (TTI). (May 1996-June 1997). *TTI Messages via Traffic Message*.

EPCglobal. (2009). *EPCglobal Standards*. Retrieved March 6, 2009, from http://www.epcglobalinc.org/standards

European Commission (2006). *Sustainable Surface Transport – Research Technological Development and Integration*, Luxemburg: Office for Official Publications of the European Communities.

European Commission. (2006, October). *ICT and e-business in hospital activities: ICT adoption and e-business activity in 2006*. Bonn, Germany: eBusiness Watch.

Evans, J., & Lindsay, W. (2001). The management and control of quality. Quinta edición, South-Western College Pub.

Eyholzer, K., Kuhlmann, W., & Münger, T. (2002). Wirtschaftlichkeitsaspekte eines partnerschaftlichen Lieferantenmanagements. *HMD - Praxis. Wirtschaftsinformatik*, *228*, 66–76.

Fabbe-Costes, N., & Jahre, M. (2008). Supply chain integration and performance: a review of the evidence. *The International Journal of Logistics Management*, *19*(2), 130–154. doi:10.1108/09574090810895933

Fachberger, R., & Bruckner, G. (2004). Applicability of LiNbO3, Langasite and GaPO4 in high temperature SAW sensors operating at radio frequencies, IEEE. Trans. UFFC, 51(11), 1427–1431.

Fagerberk, J., Mowery, D., & Nelson, R. (2004). The Oxford Handbook of Innovation, New York: Oxford University Press.

Fellenz, M. R., Augustenborg, C., Brady, M., & Greene, J. (2009). Requirements for an evolving model of supply chain finance: A technology and service providers perspective. In K.S. Soliman (ed.), Proceedings of the International Business Information Management Conference: 1171-1179. Cairo, Egypt.

Fellenz, M., & Brady, M. (2008). Managing the Innovative Deployment of Information and Communication Technologies (ICTs) for Global Service Organizations. International Journal of Technology Marketing, 3(1), 39–55. doi:10.1504/IJTMKT.2008.017339

Fenn, J., & Linden, A. (2005). Gartner's Hype Cycle Special Report for 2005. Stamfort, CT: Gartner, Inc. Retrieved February 14, 2008, from http://www.gartner.com/resources/130100/130115/gartners_hype_c.pdf

Fernández, M. (1996). Como medir la calidad en los servicios. Información Comercial Española ICE: *Revista de economía, 755*,113-125.

Fichman, R. G. (2001). The role of aggregation in the measurement of information technology-related organizational innovation. *MIS Quarterly*, *25*(4), 427–455. doi:10.2307/3250990

Fink, L., & Neumann, S. (2009). Exploring the perceived business value of the flexibility enabled by information technology infrastructure. *Information & Management*, *46*(2), 90–99. doi:10.1016/j.im.2008.11.007

Finn, A. (1985). A theory of the consumer evaluation process for new product concepts. *Research in Consumer Behavior*, *1*, 35–65.

Fisher, M., Raman, A., & McClelland, A. (2000). Rocket science retailing is almost here - are you ready? Harvard Business Review, 78(4), 115–124.

Fleming, R. (2004). *Successful supplier relationship management.* Retrieved February 27, 2009, from http://www.ameinfo.com/35411.html

Flores, A. (2004), Medición de la efectividad de la cadena de suministro. Primera edición, Panorama Editorial.

Fragniere, E., & Sullivan, G. (2007). Risk management. Boston, MA: Thomson, Glaser, B., & Strauss, A. (1967). The discovery of grounded theory: Strategies of qualitative research, London: Wiedenfeld and Nicholson.

Främling, K. (2002). *Tavaravirran seuranta osana Internet-pohjaista tuotetiedon hallintaa. (Tracking of deliveries as a part of Internet based product data management).* Retrieved April 15, 2009 from http://dialog.hut.fi/publications/TiekeArtikkeli.pdf

Franceschini, F., & Cignetti, M. (1998). Comparing tools for service quality evaluation. *International Journal of Quality, 3*(4).

Freeman, L. C. (1979). Centrality in social networks: Conceptual clarification. *Social Networks, 1,* 215–239. doi:10.1016/0378-8733(78)90021-7

Freiling, J. (1995). *Die Abhängigkeit der Zulieferer.* Wiesbaden, Germany: Ein strategisches Problem (in English: The Dependency of Suppliers – A Strategic Problem).

Friend, S. C., & Walker, P. H. (2001). Welcome to the new world of merchandising. Harvard Business Review, 79(11), 5–11.

Frohlich, M. (2002). E-integration in the supply chain: Barriers and performance. Decision Sciences, 33(4), 537–557. doi:10.1111/j.1540-5915.2002.tb01655.x

Furukawa, M. F., Raghu, T. S., & Spaulding, T. J. (2008). Adoption of health information technology for medication safety in U.S. hospitals. *Health Affairs, 27*(3), 865–875. doi:10.1377/hlthaff.27.3.865

Gadde, L.-E., & Jellbo, O. (2002). System Sourcing – Opportunities and Problems. *European Journal of Purchasing and Supply Management, 8*(1), 43–51. doi:10.1016/S0969-7012(01)00013-2

Galbraith, J., R (2005) "Designing the Customer-Centric Organization: A Guide to Strategy, Structure, and Process, Jossey Bass Business and Management Series

Gallouj, F., & Weinstein, O. (1997). Innovation in Service. *Research Policy, 26,* 537–556. doi:10.1016/S0048-7333(97)00030-9

Galloway, L., Mochrie, R., & Deakins, D. (2004). ICT-enabled collectivity as a positive rural business strategy. *International Journal of Entrepreneurial Behavior and Research, 10*(4), 247–259. doi:10.1108/13552550410544213

Gangadharan, G. R., & D'Andrea, V. (2009). Service Orientation: Licensing Perspectives. *Journal of International Commercial Law and Technology., 4*(1).

Gardiner, J., Ison, S., & Humphreys, I. (2005). Factors Influencing Cargo Airlines' Choice of Airport: An International Survey. *Journal of Air Transport Management, 11,* 393–399. doi:10.1016/j.jairtraman.2005.05.004

Gaynor, M., Moulton, S., Welsh, M., Rowan, A., LaCombe, E., & Wynne, J. (2004). Integrating Wireless Sensor Networks with the Grid. *IEEE Internet Computing, 8*(4), 32–39. doi:10.1109/MIC.2004.18

Gebhardt, A. (2006). Entscheidung zum Outsourcing von Logistikleistungen – Rationalitätsanforderungen und Realität in mittelständischen Unternehmen (in English: The Outsourcing Decision of Logistics Services – Rational Requirements and the Reality in Medium-sized Companies), Wiesbaden, Germany: Springer/Verlag

Geoffrion, A. M. (1987). An Introduction to Structured Modeling. *Management Science, 33*(5), 547–588. doi:10.1287/mnsc.33.5.547

German Association for Medical Technology. (2007). *Elektronisches Beschaffungswesen im Gesundheitsmarkt vor dem Durchbruch.* Retrieved February 27, 2009, from http://www.bvmed.de/themen/E-Commerce/pressemitteilung/BVMed-Umfrage_Elektronisches_Beschaffungswesen_im_Gesundheitsmarkt_vor_dem_Durchbruch.html

Gerrits, J. W. M. (1995). Towards Information Logistics, An Exploratory Study of Logistics in Information Production. Amsterdam, The Netherlands: Vrije University.

Getto, G., Gantner, T., & Vullinghs, T. (2000). Software Acquisition: Experiences with Models and Methods. In *Proceedings of the EuroSPI*.

Ghiani, G., Laporte, G., & Musmanno, R. (2004) Introduction to Logistics Systems Planning and Control. Chichester: J.Wiley & Sons.

Ghosh, A., & Das, S. (2008). Coverage and connectivity issues in wireless sensor networks: A survey. *Pervasive and Mobile Computing, 4*(3), 303–334. doi:10.1016/j.pmcj.2008.02.001

Gillen, D., & Lall, A. (1997). Developing Measures of Airport Productivity and Performance: An Application of Data Envelopment Analysis. *Transportation Research Part E, Logistics and Transportation Review, 33*, 261–273. doi:10.1016/S1366-5545(97)00028-8

Gilmore, A., Gallagher, D., & Henry, S. (2007). E-marketing and SMEs: Operational lessons for the future. *European Business Review, 19*(3), 234–247. doi:10.1108/09555340710746482

Glazer, R. (1991). Marketing in an information-intensive environment: Strategic implications of knowledge as an asset. Journal of Marketing, 55(4), 1–19. doi:10.2307/1251953

Glouberman, S., & Mintzberg, H. (2001). Managing the care of health and the cure of disease - Part I: Differentiation. *Health Care Management Review, 26*(1), 56–69.

Glover, F., & Laguna, M. (1997). Tabu Search, Norwell, MA: Kluwer.

Gopal, C., & Cypress, H. (1993). Integrated Distribution Management: Competing on customer service, time and cost. The Business One Irwin.

GOST. (2009). *Geolocalisation optimisation et securisation du transport de conteneurs.* Retrieved March 6, 2009, from http://projet-gost.org/

Govindan, R. (2004). Datacentric routing and storage in sensor networks. In Znati, T., Sivalingam, K., & Raghavendra, C.S. (eds.), Wireless sensor networks (pp.185-205). Boston: Kluwer Academic Publishers.

Grandon, E. E., & Pearson, J. M. (2004). Electronic commerce adoption: An empirical study of small and medium US businesses. *Science Direct, 42*(1), 197-216. Retrieved June28, 2009, from http://www.sciencedirect.com

Granovetter, M. (1973). The strength of weak ties. *American Journal of Sociology, 78*(6), 1360–1380. doi:10.1086/225469

Greenyer, A. (2006). Back from the grave: The return of modelled consumer information. International Journal of Retail & Distribution Management, 34(3), 212–219. doi:10.1108/09590550610654375

Gronroos, C. (1982). *Strategic Management and Marketing in the Service Sector.* Helsingfors: Swedish School of Economics and Racine.

Grönroos, C. (1984). A service quality model and its marketing implications. *European Journal of Marketing, 18*(4), 36–44. doi:10.1108/EUM0000000004784

Gronroos, C. (1984). *Strategic Management and Marketing in the Services Sector.* Helsingfors: Swedish School of Economics and Business Administration.

Grönroos, C. (1994). From Marketing Mix to Relationship Marketing: Towards a Paradigm Shift in Marketing. *Management Decision, 32*(2), 4–20. doi:10.1108/00251749410054774

Gronroos, C. (2006). On defining marketing: Finding a new roadmap for marketing. Marketing Theory, 6, 395–417. doi:10.1177/1470593106069930

Grönroos, C. (2007). Service Management and Marketing: Customer Management in Service Competition (3rd ed.). Chichester, UK: John Wiley and Sons.

Grossman, R. J. (2000). The battle to control online purchasing. *Health Forum Journal, 43*(1), 18–21.

Grover, V., Fiedler, K. D., & Teng, J. T. C. (1999). The role of organizational and information technology antecedents in reengineering initiation behavior. *Decision*

Sciences, 30(3), 749–781. doi:10.1111/j.1540-5915.1999.tb00905.x

GS1. (2009). *GS1barcode and eCom*. Retrieved March 6, 2009, from http://barcodes.gs1us.org/dnn_bcec/Default.aspx

Guiltinan, J. P. (1987). The price bundling of services: A normative framework. *Journal of Marketing, 51*, 74–85. doi:10.2307/1251130

Gulati, R. (2007). Silo busting: How to execute on the promise of customer focus. Harvard Business Review, 85(5), 98–106.

Gulati, R., & Oldroyd, J. B. (2005). The quest for customer focus. Harvard Business Review, 83(4), 92–101.

Gummesson, E. (2007). Exit services marketing – enter service marketing. Journal of Consumer Behaviour, 6(2), 113–142.

Gunther, O., Tamm, G., & Leymann, F. (2006). Pricing Web Services. In Dagstuhl Seminar Proceedings 06291 (The Role of Business Processes in Service Oriented Architectures).

Guseman, D. S. (1981). Risk perception and risk reduction in consumer services, In: J.H. Donnelly, et al. (Eds). Marketing of Services, Chicago: American Marketing Association.

Haartsen, J. C. (2000). The Bluetooth radio system. *IEEE Personal Communications, 7*(1), 28–36. doi:10.1109/98.824570

Habermann, A. W. (1978). Dynamically Modifiable Distributed Systems. In *Proceedings of a Workshop on Distributed Sensor Nets* (pp. 111-114). Pittsburgh, PA: Carnegie Mellon University.

Haefner, J. (n.d.). Web-based POS? *10 Benefits of Web-Based Point of Sale Software*. Retrieved from http://www.merchantos.com/web_based_pos_benefits/

Haenselmann, T. (2006). Sensornetworks. *GFDL Wireless Sensor Network textbook*. Retrieved April 2, 2009, from http://www.informatik.uni-mannheim.de/~haensel/sn_book

Hagberg-Andersson, Å., Kock, S., & Åhman, S. (2000). Managing Buyer-Supplier Relationships in a Supply Network – The Buyer's Perspective. In: *Proceedings of the 2000 International Marketing and Purchasing Conference,* Bath, The Netherlands.

Haiyin, L., Xiangdang, W., Yunkai, Z., & Yanling, N. (2006). Analysis on the Impetus of 3PL service innovation. *Journal of Logistic Technology, 5*, 15–17.

Håkansson, H. (1982). International Marketing and Purchasing of Industrial Goods – An Interaction Approach. Chichester, UK: Håkansson, H., & Johanson, J. (1992). A Model of Industrial Networks. In Axelsson, B., & Easton, G. (Ed.). Industrial Networks – A New View of Reality, London, (pp. 28-34).

Håkansson, H., & Snehota, I. (1995). Developing Relationships in Business Networks. London: Routledge.

Hammer, M., & Champy, J. (1993). Reengineering the corporation. New York: Harper Business.

Han, K., Kauffman, R. J., & Nault, B. R. (2004). Information Exploitation and Interorganizational Systems Ownership. *Journal of Management Information Systems, 21*(2).

Han, Q. (2006). Service Innovation of 3PL Company: financial logistics. Beijing, China: University of International Business and Economics.

Han, T., Lin, W., Lin, J. M., Wang, W. B., Wu, H. D., Shui, Y. A., et al. (2008).Errors of Phase and Group Delays in SAW RFID with Phase Modulation. IEEE Ultrasonics Symposium.

Han, T., Shi, W., & Lu, W. (2003). Reflection of impedance-loaded SAW IDT and its application in wireless information. Chin. J. Electron., 12(2), 185–188.

Han, T., Wang, W. B., Lin, J. M., Wu, H. D., Wang, H., & Shui, Y. (2007). Phases of Carrier Wave in a SAW Identification Tags. IEEE Ultrasonics Symposium,(pp. 1669-1672)

Han, T., Wang, W. B., Wu, H. D., & Shui, Y. A. (2008). Reflection and Scattering Characteristics of Reflectors in SAW Tags. IEEE Transactions on Ultrasonics, Ferroelectrics, and Frequency Control, 55(6), 1387–1390. doi:10.1109/TUFFC.2008.802

Hao, Y., & Foster, R. (2008). Wireless body sensor networks for health-monitoring applications. *Physiological Measurement, 29*, 27–56. doi:10.1088/0967-3334/29/11/R01

Harrop, P., & Das, R. (2009). *Wireless Sensor Networks 2009-2019: The new market for ubiquitous sensor networks (USN).* Retrieved April 3, 2009, from ID http://www.idtechex.com/research/reports/wireless_sensor_networks_2009_2019_000212.asp

Hartmann, C. S. (2002). A global SAW ID tag with large data capacity. In. Proceedings of the IEEE Ultrasonics Symposium, 1, 65–69.

Hartmann, C. S. (2004, March 15-19). Design of global SAW RFID tag devices. In Proceedings of Second Int. Symp. on Acoustic Wave Devices for Future Mobile Communication Systems., Chiba.

Hartmann, C. S., & Claiborne, L. T. (March 26-28). Fundamental Limitations on Reading Range of Passive IC-Based RFID and SAW-Based RFID, 2007. In Proceedings of IEEE International Conference on RFID, (pp.41 – 48).

Hartmann, C. S., et al. (2004). Anti-collision methods for global SAW RFID tag systems, IEEE Ultrasonics Symposium,(pp. 805-808).

Hatch, U., Engle, C. R., Zidack, W., & Olowoloyemo, S. (1991). Retail grocery markets for catfish. *Alabama Agricultural Experimental Station Bulletin, 611.*

Havelena, W. J., & DeSarbo, W. S. (1990). On the measurement of perceived consumer risk. *Decision Sciences, 22*, 927–939. doi:10.1111/j.1540-5915.1991.tb00372.x

Healthcare Information and Management Systems Society (HIMSS). (2009). What is a management engineer or process improvement professional? Retrieved April 2009, from www.himss.org.

Hefley, W., Loesche, E. A., Khera, P., & Siegel, J. (2005). *A Framework for Best Practices in the Sourcing Life-cycle: The Architecture of the eSourcing Capability Model for Client Organizations.* In ITsqc Working Paper Series CMU-ITSQC-WP-05-001.

Heinzelman, W., Chandrakasan, A., & Balakrishnan, H. (2000). Energy-efficient communication protocol for wireless sensor networks. In *Proceeding of the 33rd Hawaii International Conference on System Science, 8*, 8020.

Heizer, J., & Render, B. (2008). Operations Management, 9th Ed., Upper Saddle River, NJ:Prentice Hall.

Helo, P., & Szekely, B. (2005). Logistics information systems – An analysis of software solutions for supply chain co-ordination. *Industrial Management & Data Systems, 105*(1), 5–18. doi:10.1108/02635570510575153

Henderson, J. R. (2001). Networking with e-commerce in rural America. Retrieved June 28, 2009, from http://www.kc.frb.org/RegionalAffairs/Mainstreet/MSE_0901.pdf

Henderson, J., Dooley, F., & Akridge, J. (2004). Internet and e-commerce adoption by agricultural input firms. *Review of Agricultural Economics, 26*(4), 505–520. doi:10.1111/j.1467-9353.2004.00196.x

Herrmann, J., & Hodgson, B. (2001). *SRM: Leveraging the supply base for competitive advantage.* Paper presented at the SMTA International Conference.

Herzlinger, R. E. (2006). Why innovation in health care is so hard. *Harvard Business Review, 84*(5), 58–66.

Heskett, J., Sasser, W., & Hart, C. (1990). Service Breakthroughs: Changing the Rules of the Game, New York:Free Press

Hess, T. (1998): Unternehmensnetzwerke – Abgrenzung, Ausprägung und Entstehung (in English: Business Networks – Classification, Characteristics, and Development). In: Arbeitspapiere der Abt. Wirtschaftsinformatik II der Universität Göttingen, Nr. 4/1998, Göttingen.

Heung, V., Wong, M., & Qu, H. (2000). Airport-restaurant service quality in Hong Kong. *The Cornell Hotel and Restaurant Administration Quarterly, 41*(3), 86–96.

Heylighen, F. (2002). *Complexity and Information Overload in Society: Why increasing efficiency leads to decreasing control*. Draft paper to be submitted to Information Society, April 12.

Hidaka, K. (2006, April). Trends in Services Sciences in Japan and Abroad. *Science & Technology Trends Quarterly Review, 19*, 35–47.

Hill, J. (2000). System architecture directions for networked sensors. *SIGOPS Operating Systems Review, 34*(5), 93–104. doi:10.1145/384264.379006

Hill, T. (1977). On Goods and Services. *Review of Income and Wealth, 23*(4). doi:10.1111/j.1475-4991.1977.tb00021.x

Holland, C. P., & Naude, P. (2004). The metamorphosis of marketing into an information-handling problem. Journal of Business and Industrial Marketing, 19(3), 167–177. doi:10.1108/08858620410531306

Holloway, S. (2003). Straight and Level: Practical Airline Economics, 2nd Edition. Hampshire, UK: Aldershot.

Holmes, T. P., Vlosky, R. P., & Carlson, J. (2004). An exploratory comparison of Internet use by small wood products manufacturers in the north Adirondack region of New York and the State of Louisiana. *Forest Products Journal, 54*(12), 277–282.

Horton, M. A. (2002). Deployment ready multimode micropower wireless sensor networks for intrusion detection, classification, and tracking. *Proceedings of the Society for Photo-Instrumentation Engineers, 4708*, 290–295.

Horton, R. L. (1976). The structure of decision risk: Some further progress. *Journal of the Academy of Marketing Science, 4*(4), 694–706. doi:10.1007/BF02729830

Hossein, M. (2002). Supply Chain: Crisp and Fuzzy Aspects. *International Journal Appl. Math. Computer Science, 12*(3), 423–435.

House, L., Hanson, T., Sureshwaran, S., & Selassie, H. (2003). Opinions of U.S. consumers about farm-raised catfish: Results of a 2000-2001 survey. *Mississippi Agricultural and Forestry Experimentation Station Bulletin, 1134.*

Howard, M., & Worboys, C. (2003). Self-service - a contradiction in terms or customer-led choice? Journal of Consumer Behaviour, 2(4), 382–392. doi:10.1002/cb.115

Hoyt, J., & Huq, F. (2000). From arms-length to collaborative relationships in the supply chain: an evolutionary process. *International Journal of Physical Distribution & Logistics Management, 30*(9), 750–764. doi:10.1108/09600030010351453

Huang, T. C., Lai, H. R., & Ku, C. H. (2006). A deployment procedure for wireless sensor networks. Retrieved April 5, 2009, from: http://acnlab.csie.ncu.edu.tw/wasn06/CR2/p19.pdf

Hubaux, J. P. (2001). Toward self-organized mobile ad hoc networks: the Terminodes project. *IEEE Communications, 39*(1), 118–124. doi:10.1109/35.894385

Huber, G. P., & Daft, R. L. (1987). The information environment of organizations. In F. M. Jablin, L. L. Putnam, K. H. Roberts, & L. W. Porter (eds.), Handbook of organizational communication (pp. 130-164). Newbury Park, CA: Sage.

Hufbauer, G., Jaggi, G., & Findlay, C. (1995, July 9-11). Cleaning the Air-Civil Aviation Issues in the Asia Pacific. A paper presented at the conference on Air Transport in the Asia Pacific – Challenges, Opportunities and Options, Singapore.

Huiming, L. (2006). Logistic service and integrated innovation. *China Ocean Shipping Monthly, 6*, 71–73.

Humby, C., Hunt, T., & Philips, T. (2008). Scoring points: How Tesco continues to win customer loyalty (2nd ed.). London, Kogan Page.

Hyderr, E., Heston, K., & Paulk, M. (2006). The eSourcing Capability Model for Service Providers V2.01 (Tech Report), Pittsburgh, PA: Carniege Melon University.

IBM. (n.d.). *IBM Research*. Retrieved from http://www.research.ibm.com/ssme/

Imai, A., & Nishimurra, E. (2001). Papadimitriou S. The dynamic berth allocation problem for a container port. *Transportation Research Part B: Methodological, 35*, 401–417. doi:10.1016/S0191-2615(99)00057-0

Imai, A., Nagaiwa, K., & Tat, C. W. (1997). Efficient planning of berth allocation for container terminals in Asia. *Journal of Advanced Transportation, 31*(1), 75–94. doi:10.1002/atr.5670310107

Inmon, W. H. (2002). Building the Data Warehouse. New York: Wiley Computer Publishing.

ITAA. (n.d.). *Information technology definition aggregation.*Retrieved April 3, 2009, from itaa Web site: http://www.itaa.org/es/docs/Information%20Technology%20Definitions.pdf

ITAF. *A Professional Practices Framework for IT Assurance* (2008) *ISACA*, Rolling Meadows, IL, Retrieved March 8, 2009, from http://www.isaca.org

Iyengar, S. S., & Brooks, R. R. (2004). Distributed sensor networks. Boca Raton, FL: Chapman & HalVCRC.

Jablonski, S., & Bussler, C. (1998). Workflow Management, Modeling Concepts, Architecture and Implementation. London: International Thompson Computer Press, ITP.

Jacoby, J., & Kaplan, L. (1972). *The components of perceived risk*, In: Venkatesan, M. (Ed.), *Proceedings of 3rd Annual Conference Association for Consumer Research*, Chicago, Il, (pp.382-393).

Jankowicz, A. (1991). Business Research Projects. London: Chapman and Hall.

Jea, D., & Srivastava, M. B. (2006). A remote medical monitoring and interaction system. In *Proceedings of the 4th International Conference on Mobile Systems, Applications, and Services (MobiSys '06)*, Uppsala, Sweden.

Johnson, D. L., & Andrews, I. R. (1971). Risky-shift phenomenon as tested with consumer products as stimuli. *Journal of Personality and Social Psychology, 20*(August), 328–385.

Jones, P., Clarke-Hill, C., Shears, P., Comfort, D., & Hillier, D. (2004). 'Radio frequency identification in the UK: Opportunities and challenges. International Journal of Retail & Distribution Management, 32(3), 164–171. doi:10.1108/09590550410524957

Jorge, J. D., & de Rus, G. (2004). Cost-Benefit Analysis of Investments in Airport Infrastructure: A Practical Approach. *Journal of Air Transport Management, 10*, 311–326. doi:10.1016/j.jairtraman.2004.05.001

Jun, L., & Wang, Y. (2007). How to Select the Way and Strategy of logistics enterprise service iInnovation. *Journal of Logistic Technology, 26*(1), 14–16.

Juran, J. (2001). Manual de Calidad. New York: McGraw Hill.

Jutla, D., Craig, J., & Bodorik, P. (2001). *Enabling and measuring electronic customer relationship management readiness*. Paper presented at the 34th Annual Hawaii International Conference on System Sciences.

Kalakota, R., & Robinson, M. (2000). E-Business 2.0 Roadmap for Success. Reading, MA: Addison-Wesley.

Kamath, M., & Mize, J. H. (2003). Impact of major driving forces on IE education and practice. In *Proceedings of 2003 Industrial Engineering Research Conference*, Portland, OR.

Kameoka, A. (2006). Saabisu, seihin, gijyutu inobesyon wo yuugou, sousyutu, hukan suru tougougata senryaku roodo mappingu [An integrated strategic road mapping that fuses, creates and surveys service, product and technical]. *Operations research as a management science research, 51*(9), 573-578.

Kandampully, J. (2002). Innovation as the core competency of a service organization: the role of technology, knowledge and networks. *European Journal of Innovation Management, 5*(1), 18–26. doi:10.1108/14601060210415144

Kaplan, S., & Sawhney, M. (2000). E-hub: the new B2B marketplaces. *Harvard Business Review, 78*(3), 97–103.

Karkkainen, M., & Laukkanen, S., Sarpola, & Kemppainen, K. (2007). Roles of interfirm information; systems in supply chain management. *International Journal of Physical Distribution & Logistics Management, 37*(4), 264–286. doi:10.1108/09600030710752505

Karl, H., & Willig, A. (2003). A short survey of wireless sensor networks, TKN technical report TKN-03-018.

Retrieved April 3, 2009, from http://www.tkn.tu-berlin.de/publications/papers/TechReport_03_018.pdf

Karlof, C., & Wagner, D. (2003). Secure routing in wireless sensor networks: attacks and countermeasures. In *Sensor Network Protocols and Applications, 2003. Proceedings of the First IEEE. 2003 IEEE International Workshop on*, (pp. 113-127).

Karmarkar, U. (2004). Will you survive the services revolution. *Harvard Business Review, 82*(6), 100–107.

Karmarkar, U. S., & Apte, U. M. (2007). Operations management in the information economy: Information products, processes, and chains. *Journal of Operations Management, 25*, 438–453. doi:10.1016/j.jom.2006.11.001

Karmarkar, U. S., & Pitbladdo, R. (1995). Service markets and competition. *Journal of Operations Management, 12*(3-4), 397–412. doi:10.1016/0272-6963(94)00014-6

Karn, P. (1990). MACA - A new channel access method for packet radio. *ARRL/CRRL Amateur Radio 9th Computer Networking Conference appears in* (pp. 134-140). London: ARRL.

Kasarda, J. D., & Green, J. D. (2005). Air Cargo as an Economic Development Engine- A Note on Opportunities and Constraints. *Journal of Air Transport Management, 11*, 459–462. doi:10.1016/j.jairtraman.2005.06.002

Kauniskangas, M. (2007). *Asiakkaasta partneri (From customer to partner)*. Logistiikka – The magazine of Finnish Association of Purchasing and Logistics, Iss. 5.

Kauremaa, J., & Auramo, J. (2004). Logistiikan sähköisten tieto- ja viestintäteknologioiden hyödyntäminen – Kokemuksia suomalaisista yrityksistä (Utilization of electronic information and communication technologies in logistics – Experiences from Finnish companies). Technology Review 154/2004. Tekes.

Kekäläinen, H. (2006). Logistics technology roadmap for e-business. Technology Review 189/2006. Tekes.

Ketchen, D. J., & Hult, T. M. (2007). Bridging organization theory and supply chain management: The case of best

value supply chains. *Journal of Operations Management, 25*, 573–580. doi:10.1016/j.jom.2006.05.010

Khurrum, S., & Bhutta y Faizul, H. (2002). Supplier selection problem: a comparison of the total cost of ownership and analytic hierarchy process approaches. *Supply Chain Management: An International Journal, 7*(3), 126–135. doi:10.1108/13598540210436586

Kia, M., Shayan, E., & Ghotb, F. (2002). Investigation of port capacity under a new approach by computer simulation. *Computers & Industrial Engineering, 42*, 533–540. doi:10.1016/S0360-8352(02)00051-7

Kim, J., & Park, K. H. (2009). An energy-efficient, transport-controlled Mac protocol for wireless sensor networks. *Computer Networks, 53*(11), 1879–1902. doi:10.1016/j.comnet.2009.03.002

Kim, K. H., & Bae, J. W. (1998). Re-marshaling export containers in port container terminals. *Computers & Industrial Engineering, 35*(3–4), 655–658. doi:10.1016/S0360-8352(98)00182-X

Kim, K. H., & Kim, H. B. (1998). The optimal determination of the space requirement and the number of transfer cranes for import containers. *Computers & Industrial Engineering 35*(3–4), 427–430.

Kinnucan, H. W., & Miao, Y. (1999). Media-specific returns to generic advertising: The case of catfish. *Agribusiness. International Journal (Toronto, Ont.), 15*, 81–99.

Kinnucan, H., & Venkateswaran, M. (1990). Effects of generic advertising on perceptions and behavior: the case of catfish. *Southern Journal of Agricultural Economics, 22*, 137–151.

Kinnucan, H., Sindelar, S., Wineholt, D., & Hatch, U. (1988). Processor demand and price markup functions for catfish: A disaggregated analysis with implications for the off flavor problem. *Southern Journal of Agricultural Economics., 20*, 81–92.

Klaas, T. (2002). Logistik-Organisation: Ein konfigurationstheoretischer Ansatz zur logistikorientierten Organisationsgestaltung (in English: Organisation of

Logistics – A Configuration-theoretic Approach for the Logistics-oriented Design of Organizations), Wiesbaden, Germany: Springer/Verlag.

KMI – Korea Maritime Istitute (2000). A Study on the System Design and Operations of Automated Container Terminal. *Internal report.*

Koh, P. H., Goh, J. L. K., Ng, H. S., & Ng, H. C. (1994). Using simulation to preview plans of a container port operations. *Proceedings of the 1994 Winter Simulation.* Tew, Manivannan, Sadowski, Seila (Ed.).

Konstantas, D., Jones, V., & Herzog, R. (2002). Mobihealth - innovative 2.5 / 3g mobile services and applications for healthcare. Retrieved April 5, 2009, from http://aps.ewi.utwente.nl/public/bibliografie/Thessaloniki.pdf

Koppel, R., Metlay, J. P., Cohen, A., Abaluck, B., Localio, A. R., & Kimmel, S. E. (2005). Role of computerized physician order entry systems in facilitating medication errors. *Journal of the American Medical Association, 293*(10), 1197–1203. doi:10.1001/jama.293.10.1197

Kotler, P. (1988). Marketing-Management – Analyse, Planung und Kontrolle (in English: Marketing Management – Analyzing, Planning, and Controlling), 4th Ed., Stuttgart, Germany: Verlag.

Kotler, P., Wong, S., & Armstrong, G. (2007). Principles of Marketing, 12th International Edition, London: Pearson.

Kraljic, P. (1988). Zukunftsorientierte Beschaffungs- und Versorgungsstrategie als Element der Unternehmensstrategie (in English: Future-oriented Procurement- and Supply-Strategy as Element of the Corporate Strategy). In: Henzler, H.A. (Ed.), Handbuch Strategische Führung, Wiesbaden, Germany, (pp. 477-497).

Kuehne & Nagel (2008, February 27). *Kuehne-Nagel Lead Logistics Solutions – Supply Chain Management & Sustainable Development.* Presentation of A. Quillaud in Luxemburg.

Kumar, S., & Malegeant, P. (2006). Strategic Alliance in a Closed-loop Supply Chain – A Case of Manufacturer and Eco-non-profit Organization. *Technovation, 26*(10), 1127–1135. doi:10.1016/j.technovation.2005.08.002

Kumaran, S. (2004). Model driven enterprise. In *Proceedings of the Global EAI Summit*, Banff, Canada, 166-180.

Kuo, W., & Deuermeyer, B. (1998). IE2-the IE curriculum revisited: Developing a new undergraduate program at Texas A&M University. *IIE Solutions, 30*(6), 16–22.

Kuypers, J. H., Reindl, L. M., Tanaka, S., & Esashi, M. (2008). Maximum Accuracy Evaluation Scheme for Wireless SAW Delay-Lin Sensors. IEEE Transactions on Ultrasonics Perforlctrics, and Frequency Control, 55(7), 1640–1651. doi:10.1109/TUFFC.2008.840

Laaksonen, P., Nelimarkka, P., & Nyman, M. (2004). *Logistiikan tulevaisuus Itämeren alueella. Yhteenveto asiantuntijoiden kirjoituksista ja keskustelutilaisuudesta 16.8.2004 (The future of logistics in the Baltic Sea area. The summary of the articles and discussion by experts Aug 16, 2004).* Retrieved May 4, 2009, from http://www.tedim.com/default.asp?file=819

Lacity, M. C., Willcocks, L. P., & Feeny, D. F. (1996). The value of selective IT sourcing. *Sloan Management Review, 37*, 13–25.

Lacoss, R., & Walton, R. (1978). Strawman design for a DSN to detect and track low flying aircraft. In *Proceedings of 1978 Distributed Sensor Nets Conference on*, (pp. 41-52).

LaFollette, R. M. (1995). Design and performance of high specific power, pulsed discharge, bipolar lead acid batteries. In *Proceedings of the 10th Annual Battery Conference on Applications and Advances*, 43-47.

Lai, K. K., & Shih, K. (1992). A study of container berth allocation. *Journal of Advanced Transportation, 26*(1), 45–60. doi:10.1002/atr.5670260105

Lai, K.-H., Wong, C. W., & Cheng, E. T. C. (2006). Institutional isomorphism and the adoption of information technology for supply chain management. *Computers in Industry, 57*(1), 93–98. doi:10.1016/j.compind.2005.05.002

Lam, S. W., Low, J. M. W., & Tang, L. C. (2009). Operational Efficiencies across Asia Pacific Airports. *Transportation Research Part E, Logistics and Transportation Review, 45*(4), 654–655. doi:10.1016/j.tre.2008.11.003

Lankhorst, M., et al. (2005). Enterprise Architecture at Work. New York: Springer Publications.

Lansford, J., & Bahl, P. (2000). The design and implementation of HomeRF: a radio frequency wireless networking standard for the connected home. *Proceedings of the IEEE, 88*(10), 1662–1676. doi:10.1109/5.889006

Laporte, G., Louveaux, F. V., & Mercure, H. (1994). A priori optimization of the probabilistic traveling salesman problem. *Operations Research, 42,* 543–549. doi:10.1287/opre.42.3.543

Laroche, M., & Bergeron, J. & Goutaland. (2003). C. How intangibility affects perceived risk: the moderating role of knowledge and involvement. *Journal of Services Marketing, 17*(2), 122–140. doi:10.1108/08876040310467907

Laroche, M., Bergeron, J., & Goutaland, C. (2001). A three-dimensional scale of intangibility. *Journal of Service Research, 4*(1), 26–38. doi:10.1177/109467050141003

Laroche, M., McDougall, G. H. G., Bergeron, J., & Yang, Z. (2004). Exploring How Intangibility Affects Perceived Risk. *Journal of Service Research, 6*(4), 373–389. doi:10.1177/1094670503262955

Latin America Logistics Center. (2005): Análisis de Costo total de Logística en Empresas Colombianas 2004-2005 (in English: Analysis of the Total Cost of Logistics in Colombian Companies 2004-2005), Bogotá, Columbia.

Lau, A. H. L., Lau, H.-S., & Zhou, Y.-W. (2007). A stochastic and asymmetric-information framework for a dominant-manufacturer supply chain. *European Journal of Operational Research, 176,* 295–316. doi:10.1016/j.ejor.2005.06.054

Lee, H. L., Padmanabhan, V., & Whang, S. (1997). The Bullwhip Effect in Supply Chains. *Sloan Management Review, 38*(3), 93–102.

Lee, H., & Yang, H. M. (2003). Strategies for a Global Logistics and Economic Hub: Incheon International Airport. *Journal of Air Transport Management, 9,* 113–121. doi:10.1016/S0969-6997(02)00065-0

Lee, S. Y., & Cho, G. S. (2007). A Simulation Study for the Operations Analysis of Dynamic Planning in Container Terminals Considering RTLS. *IEEE Xplore® digital library.*

Lee, Y.-D., & Chung, W.-Y. (2009). Wireless sensor network based wearable smart shirt for ubiquitous health and activity monitoring. *Sensors and Actuators. B, Chemical, 140*(2), 390–395. doi:10.1016/j.snb.2009.04.040

Leftwich, L. M., Leftwich, J. A., Moore, N. Y., & Roll, C. R. (2004). *Organizational concepts for purchasing and supply management implementation* (No. MG-116). Santa Monica, CA: RAND Corporation.

Legato, P., Gullì, D., Trunfio, R., & Simino, R. (2008). Simulation at a Maritime Container Terminal: Models and Computational Frameworks. In *Proceedings of the 22th European Conference on Modelling and Simulation* (ECMS 2008), Nicosia (Cyprus), 261-269.

Lehtonen, S., & Plessky, V. (2000). Unidirectional SAW Transducer for Gigahertz Frequencies. IEEE Trans. UFFC, 50(11), 1404–1406.

Lei, L., & Guisheng, W. (2003). Service innovation. Tsinghua University Press.

Leung, Y. T., Caswell, N., & Kamath, M. (2006). The case for the business process engineer. In *Proceedings of the IEEE International Conference on Service Operations and Logistics, and Informatics*, Shanghai, China, 1119-1124.

Leung, Y. T., Cheng, F., Lee, Y. M., & Hennessy, J. J. (2006). A tool set for exploring the value of RFID in a supply chain. To appear in H. Jung, F. F. Chen, & B. Jeong (Ed.), Trends in Supply Chain Design and Management: Technologies and Methodologies. Heidelberg, Germany: Springer-Verlag.

Levasseur, R. E. (2007). People Skill: Marketing OR/MS - A People Problem. *Interfaces, 37*(4), 383–384. doi:10.1287/inte.1060.0254

Levinson, M., (2003, December 1-12). The RFID Imperative. CIO Magazine.

Levy, M., Powell, P., & Tetton, P. (2001). SMEs: Aligning IS and the strategic context. Journal of Information Technology, 16, 133–144. doi:10.1080/02683960110063672

Leymann, F., & Altenhuber, W. (1994). Managing business processes as an information resource. *IBM Systems Journal, 33*(2), 326–348.

Li, E. (2008). *Supply chain management in China*. In The International Cyber Transportation Logistics Conference. Petit Jean Mountain, AR.

Li, E. Y., Du, T. C., & Wong, J. W. (2007). Access control in collaborative commerce. *Decision Support Systems, 43,* 675–685. doi:10.1016/j.dss.2005.05.022

Li, G., Yang, H., Sun, L., & Sohal, A. S. (2009). The impact of IT implementation on supply chain integration and performance. *International Journal of Production Economics, 120*(1), 125–138. doi:10.1016/j.ijpe.2008.07.017

Li, Q., Ji., X., Shi, W. & Han.- T. (2009). Walsh Matched-Threshold Filtering in SAW Tag Applications to Provide Multiple-Access Capability. Journal of Shanghai Jiaotong University, 14(6), 681–685. doi:10.1007/s12204-009-0681-3

Li, Y. (2008). Service Productivity Improvement and Software Technology Support. In *Proceedings of 32nd Annual IEEE Computer Software and Applications Conference*, (pp. 807-812).

Li, Yanfong, & Pu, Guoan. (2003). Research on the value of third-party logistics. *Journal of Commercial Research.* (17), 166-168.

Liao, S., Chem, Y., Liu, F., & Liao, W. (2004). Information technology and relationship management: a case study of Taiwan's small manufacturing firm. *Technovation, 24*(2), 97–108. doi:10.1016/S0166-4972(02)00037-8

Liao, W., & Wang, H. (2008). An asynchronous Mac protocol for wireless sensor networks. *Journal of Network and Computer Applications, 31*(4), 807–820. doi:10.1016/j.jnca.2007.07.001

Lin, C., & Ho, Y. (2007). Technological Innovation for China's Logistics Industry. *Journal of Technology Management and Innovation, 2*(4).

Lin, J. S., & Hsieh, P. (2006). The role of technology readiness in customers' perception and adoption of self-service technologies. International Journal of Service Industry Management, 17(5), 497. doi:10.1108/09564230610689795

Lin, L. C. (2009). An integrated framework for the development of radio frequency identification technology in the logistics and supply chain management. *Computers & Industrial Engineering, 57*(3), 832–842. doi:10.1016/j.cie.2009.02.010

Little, J. D. C. (2004). Model and Managers: The Concept of a Decision Calculus. *Management Science, 50*(12), 1841-1853 (a reprint of a paper originally published in *Management Science*, 1970, *16*(8), 75-89).

Liu, D., Ning, P., & Du, W. (2005). Group-based key pre-distribution in wireless sensor networks. *ACM Transactions on Sensor Networks, 4*(2), 11.

Liu, J., Zhao, F., Cheung, P., & Guibas, L. (2004). Apply geometric duality to energy-efficient non-local phenomenon awareness using sensor networks. *Wireless Communications, IEEE, 11*(6), 62–68. doi:10.1109/MWC.2004.1368898

Liu, L., & Li, H. (2006). How to achieve service innovation by logistic enterprise. *Logistics Infor Monthly, 9,* 67–69.

Logistiikka (2001). Paikannuksen merkitys tavaraliikenteessä (The meaning of positioning in cargo transport). *Logistiikka – The Magazine of Finnish Association of Purchasing and Logistic, 6,* 36–38.

Loren, G. (2005). Network vs. Network – The New Arena of Competition. InHarvard Business Review 'Supply Chain Strategy', Reprint No. P0503D.

Lorincz, K. (2004). Sensor networks for emergency response: challenges and opportunities. *Pervasive Computing, IEEE, 3*(4), 16–23. doi:10.1109/MPRV.2004.18

Lovelock, C. (2007). Service Marketing: People, Technology, Strategy. Upper Saddle River, NJ: Prentice Hall.

Lovelock, C. H. (1983). Classifying Services to Gain Strategic Marketing Insights. *Journal of Marketing, 47*(3), 9–20. doi:10.2307/1251193

Lovelock, C. H. (1994). Product Plus: How Product + Service = Competitive Advantage. New York: McGraw-Hill.

Loveman, G. (2003). Diamonds in the data mine. Harvard Business Review, 81(5), 109–113.

Low, J. M. W., & Tang, L. C. (2006). Factor Substitution and Complementarity in the Asia Airport Industry. *Journal of Air Transport Management, 12*, 261–266. doi:10.1016/j.jairtraman.2006.07.003

Lu, G. (2005). The analysis of situation and question about the third party logistics in our country. *Journal of Logistic Science Technology, 28*(6), 50–51.

Lubecke, O. B., & Lubecke, V. M. (2002). Wireless house calls: using communications technology for health care monitoring. *IEEE Micro, 3*(3), 43–48. doi:10.1109/MMW.2002.1028361

Lui, T.-W., & Piccoli, G. (2007). Degrees of Agility: Implications for Information Systems Design and Firm Strategy. In Desouza K.C. (Ed.) Agile Information Systems (pp.112-134), Amsterdam: Elsevier, Butterworth-Heinemann.

Lurie, N., & Mason, C. (2007). Visual Representation: Implications for Decision Making. Journal of Marketing, 71, 160–177. doi:10.1509/jmkg.71.1.160

Lysons, K., & Farrington, B. (2006). Purchasing and supply chain management. Pearson Education Limited.

Mabert, V. A., & Venkataramanan, M. A. (1998). Special research focus on supply chain linkages: Challenges for design and management in the 21st century. *Decision Sciences, 29*(3), 537–552. doi:10.1111/j.1540-5915.1998.tb01353.x

Macbeth, D. K. (2002). Emergent strategy in managing cooperative supply chain change. *International Journal of Operations & Production Management, 22*(7), 728–740. doi:10.1108/01443570210433517

MacIntosh, R. (1997). Business process re-engineering: New applications for techniques of production engineering. *International Journal of Production Economics, 50*(1), 43–49. doi:10.1016/S0925-5273(97)89132-3

MacKenzie, M., Laskey, K., McCabe, F., Brown, P., & Metz, R. (2006). *Reference Model for Service Oriented Architecture.* Retrieved from http://docs.oasis-open.org/soa-rm/v1.0/soa-rm.pdf

Maister, D. H., & Lovelock, C. H. (1982). Managing Facilitator Services. *Sloan Management Review, 23*(4), 9–20.

Mäkinen, T., Mäntynen, J., & Vanhatalo, J. (2005). *Logistiikka ja kuljetusjärjestelmät (Logistics and transport systems* (Tech Report 38.) The Tampere University of Technology, Faculty for transport technologies.

Malone, T. W., & Crowston, K. (1994). The interdisciplinary study of coordination. *ACM Computing Surveys, 26*(1), 87–119. doi:10.1145/174666.174668

Mani, A., & Nagarajan, A. (2002). *Understanding Quality of Service for Web Services.* Retrieved from http://www.ibm.com/developerworks/library/ws-quality.html

Mannur, N., & Addagatla, J. (1993). Heuristic Algorithm for Solving Earliness-Tardiness Scheduling Problem with Machine Vacations. *Computers & Industrial Engineering, 25*(1-4), 255–258. doi:10.1016/0360-8352(93)90269-4

Marasco, A. (2008). Third-party Logistics – A Literature Review. *International Journal of Production Economics, 113*(1), 127–147. doi:10.1016/j.ijpe.2007.05.017

Marchand, D. (2000). Why information is the responsibility of every managers? In Marchand D. (Ed.) Competing with Information (pp. 3-17), Chichester, UK: John Wiley and Sons, Ltd.

Marchand, D. A., Kettinger, W. J., & Rollins, J. D. (2000). Information orientation: People, technology and the bottom line. Sloan Management Review, (Summer): 69–79.

Mardia, K. V., Kent, J. T., & Bibby, J. M. (1979). Multivariate Analysis. New York: Academic Press.

Martínez, A., Cantú, M., Cedillo, G., & Arriaga, J. (2006) *Medición del desempeño de proveedores de servicio y su importancia en la cadena de suministro.* XXVIII Congreso Internacional Calzatecnia, León Guanajuato.

Martínez, E., & Escudey, M. (1998). Evaluación y decisión multicriterio. UNESCO-Editorial Universidad de Santiago, Chile.

Martinez-Olvera, C. (2008). Methodology for realignment of supply-chain structural elements. *International Journal of Production Economics, 114*, 714–722. doi:10.1016/j.ijpe.2008.03.008

Marton, A., Piccinelli, G., & Turfin, C. (1999). *Service provision and composition in virtual business communities.* Paper presented at the 18th IEEE Symposium on Reliable Distributed Systems.

Matthing, J., Kristensson, P., Gustafsson, A., & Parasuraman, A. (2006). Developing successful technology-based services: the issue of identifying and involving innovative users. Journal of Services Marketing, 20(5), 288–297. doi:10.1108/08876040610679909

Maximilien, M., & Toward, S. M. (2005). Web Services Interaction Styles. In *Proceedings of IEEE Services Computing Conference (SCC).*

Mayer, K. J., Bowen, J. T., & Moulton, M. R. (2003). A proposed model of the descriptors of service process. *Journal of Services Marketing, 17*(6), 621–639. doi:10.1108/08876040310495645

Mc Guire, G. A. (2006). Development of a supply chain management framework for health care goods provided as humanitarian assistance in complex political emergencies. Vienna, Austria: Vienna University of Economics and Business Administration.

McAfee, A. (2006). Mastering the Three Worlds of Information Technology. Harvard Business Review, 84(11), 141–149.

McClune, J. (2003) Contentious Debate? It Works at Philips: A technology powerhouse masters the "strategic

conversation", Interview Series, Mercer Management Journal, 16. Retrieved from http://www.oliverwyman.com/ow/pdf_files/MMJ16_Interview_Contentious_Debate.pdf

McCord, A. (2003) Sourcing Information Technology Services. In P. McClure (ed), EDUCAUSE Leadership Strategies Series, Volume 7 – Managing Information Resources, EDUCAUSE. New York: John Wiley and Sons.

McDonald, M., & Wilson, H. (1999). Improving marketing effectiveness through IT. Cranfield Management Research Series - working paper, (pp. 30-45).

McDougall, G. H. G., & Snetsinger, D. W. (1990). The Intangibility of Services: Measurement and Competitive Perspectives. *Journal of Services Marketing, 4*(4), 27–40. doi:10.1108/EUM0000000002523

McGinnis, L. (2002). A brave new education. *IIE Solutions, 34*(12), 27–31.

McGladrey, R. S. M. (2009). *RSM.* Retrieved June 28, 2009, from http://www.rsmmcgladrey.com/

McGovern, G. (2000). Managing information in the digital age: How the reader is king. Irish Marketing Review, 13(2), 55–61.

McGovern, G., & Moon, Y.,(2007, June 2-7). Companies and the Customers Who Hate Them, Harvard Business Review.

McHugh, G., Fahy, J., & Butler, P. (1998). Accountant behaving badly: A marketing perspective. Irish Marketing Review, 11(1), 19–26.

McLaughlin, S., Paton, R. A., & Macbeth, D. K. (2006). Managing change within IBM's complex supply chain. *Management Decision, 44*(8), 1002–1019. doi:10.1108/00251740610690586

Meredith, J. (1995, July 9-11). *Airport Capacity Constraints in Asia Pacific.* A paper presented at the conference on Air Transport in the Asia Pacific – Challenges, Opportunities and Options, Singapore.

Merkuryeva, G., Merkuryev, Y., & Tolujev, J. (2000). Computer simulation and Metamodelling of logistics processes at a container terminal. *Studies in Informatics and Control, 9*(1), 1–10.

Meroño-Cerdan, A. L., Soto-Acosta, P., & Lopez-Nicolas, C. (2008). How do collaborative technologies affect innovation in SMEs? *International Journal of e-Collaboration, 4*(4), 33–50.

Merriam-Webster Online Dictionary. (2009). *Communication.* Retrieved February 27, 2009, from http://www.merriam-webster.com/dictionary/communication

Mettler, T., & Rohner, P. (2008). *Supplier relationship management in healthcare practice: A case study,* Paper presented at the 6th CollECTeR Iberoamerica.

Mettler, T., & Rohner, P. (2009a). E-Procurement in Hospital Pharmacies: An Exploratory Multi-Case Study from Switzerland. *Journal of Theoretical and Applied Electronic Commerce Research, 4*(1), 23–38.

Mettler, T., & Rohner, P. (2009b). Increasing the networkability of health service providers: The case of Switzerland. *Sprouts - Working Papers on Information Systems, 9*(1), 1-13.

Meuter, M. L., Ostorm, A. L., Roundtree, R. I., & Bitner, M. J. (2000). Self-service technologies: Understanding customer satisfaction with technology-based service encounters. *Journal of Marketing, 64*(3), 50–64. doi:10.1509/jmkg.64.3.50.18024

Meyronin, B. (2004). ICT: the creation of value and differentiation in services. Managing Service Quality, 14(2/3), 216–225. doi:10.1108/09604520410528635

Milenkovic, A., Otto, C., & Jovanov, E. (2006). Wireless sensor networks for personal health monitoring: Issues and an implementation. *Computer Communications, 29*(13-14), 2521–2533. doi:10.1016/j.comcom.2006.02.011

Miller, A. (2004). Order Picking for the 21st Century Voice vs. Scanning Technology A White Paper, *Principal Tompkins Associates,* Retrieved from http://www.baxtek.com/products/vocollect/Voice_v_Scan_White_Paper.pdf

Min, L., & Zhiqi, F. (2002). The logistics model selection. *Outlook Weekly, 32,* 39–40.

Minoli, D. (2002). Hotspot networks: Wi-Fi for public access locations. New York: McGraw-Hill.

Mishra, R. K. (2006). Role of information technology in supply chain management. Retrieved April 1, 2009, from www.indianmba.com/Faculty_Column/FC461/fc461.html.

Mitchell, A. (2001). Radical Innovation. BT Technology Journal, 19(4), 60–64. doi:10.1023/A:1013730529933

Mitchell, V. W. (1998). A role for consumer risk perceptions in grocery retailing. *British Food Journal, 100*(4), 171–183. doi:10.1108/00070709810207856

Mitchell, V. W. (1999). Consumer perceived risk: Conceptualizations and models. *European Journal of Marketing, 33*(1/2), 163–195. doi:10.1108/03090569910249229

Mitchell, V. W., & Boustani, P. (1994). A preliminary investigation into pre- and post-purchase risk perception and reduction. *European Journal of Marketing, 28*(1), 56–57. doi:10.1108/03090569410049181

Mitchell, V. W., & Greatorex, M. (1993). Risk perception and reduction in the purchase of consumer services. *Service Industries Journal, 13*(October), 179–200.

Mitchell, V. W., & Prince, G. S. (1993). Retailing to experienced and inexperienced consumers: A perceived risk approach. *International Journal of Retail & Distribution Management, 12*(5), 10–21.

Mitra, K., Reiss, M., & Capella, L. (1999). An examination of perceived risk, information search and behavioral intentions in search, experience and credence services. *Journal of Services Marketing, 13*(3), 208–228. doi:10.1108/08876049910273763

Miyazaki, M. (1990). Atarasii sisutemuzu apuroochi to taiwagata OR: taiwagata OR no houhouronteki haikei wo nagamete [New Systems Approach and Interactive OR: Looking at methodological background of interactive OR]. *Operations research as a management science research, 35*(8), 454-456.

Moe, R. L. (1988). Networking and Ship-To-Shore Ship-To-Ship Communication, CH2585-8/88/00005-3, IEEE. http://ieeexplore.ieee.org/iel5/738/906/00023558.pdf?arnumber=23558

Moeeni, F. (2008). A passive RFID location sensing. In *Proceedings of the 12ᵗʰ World Multi-Conference on Systemics, Cybernetics and Informatics* (pp. 84-89).

Moeller, R. A. (2001) Distributed data warehousing using Web technology, how to build a more cost-effective and flexible warehouse, New York: Amacom.

Moeller, R. R. (2008) Sarbanes-Oxley Internal Controls, Effective Auditing with AS5, CobitT, and ITIL. Hoboken, NJ: J.Wiley & Sons.

Monczka, R., Trent, R., & Handfield, R. (2005). Purchasing & supply chain management (3rd ed.). Mason, OH: Thomson.

Morgenstern, O. (1955). Note on the Formulation of the Theory of Logistics. *Naval Research Logistics Quarterly Review, 2*, 129–136. doi:10.1002/nav.3800020303

Morimoto, N., & Sawatani, Y. (2005, November). Saabisu saiensu no kanousei [The Potential of Service Science]. *Diamond Harvard Business Review*, 109-124.

Muessigmann, N., & Albani, A. (2006). *Supplier network management: evaluating and rating of strategic supply networks*. Paper presented at the 2006 ACM symposium on Applied computing.

Mukohara, T., & Sekiguchi, Y. (2002). The DSS architecture based on problems specification and model/solver independence. In E. Kozan, & A. Ohuch (Ed.), Operations Research/Management Science at work: Applying Theory in the Area Pacific Region (pp.281-298). The Netherlands: Kluwer Academic Publishers.

Mukohara, T., Sekiguchi, Y., & Bao, J. (2005). Jittaikanren gainen no kakutyou niyoru sukejyuuring mondai kijyutu no tokutyou to ouyou [Scheduling Problems Specification by Extending Entity-Relationship Concept: Characteristics and Applications]. *Transactions of the Operations Research Society of Japan, 48*, 66–84.

Murphy, F. H. (2005). ASP, The Art and Science of Practice; Elements of a Theory of the Practice of Operations Research: A Framework. *Interfaces, 35*(2), 154–163. doi:10.1287/inte.1050.0126

Murray, K. B., & Schlacter, J. L. (1990). The impact of services versus goods on consumers' assessment of perceived risk. *Journal of the Academy of Marketing Science, 18*(1), 51–65. doi:10.1007/BF02729762

Murty, K. G., Liu, J., Wan, Y., & Linn, R. (2005). A decision support system for operations in a container terminal. *Decision Support Systems, 39*(3), 309–332. doi:10.1016/j.dss.2003.11.002

Myburgh, S. (2000). The convergence of information technology and information management. Information Management Journal, 34(2), 4–16.

Myers, M. D. (1997). Qualitative research in information systems. *MIS Quarterly, 21*(1), 241–242. doi:10.2307/249422

Nadeem, M. (2007). Emergence of Customer-Centric Branding: From Boardroom Leadership to Self-Broadcasting. Journal of American Academy of Business, 12(1), 44–49.

Nam, C. S., Johnson, S., Li, Y., & Seong, Y. (2009). Evaluation of human-agent user interfaces in multi-agent systems. *International Journal of Industrial Ergonomics, 39*(1), 192–201. doi:10.1016/j.ergon.2008.08.008

Naxtor Technologies. (2008). *Naxtor Technologies discuss positive effects of IT on warehouse operations.* Retrieved from http://www.ferret.com.au/c/Naxtor-Technologies/Naxtor-Technologies-discuss-positive-effects-of-IT-on-warehouse-operations-n817737/tags

Nelly, A., Gregory, M., & Platts, K. (1995). Performance Measurement System Design. *International Journal of Operations & Production Management, 16*(4), 19–34.

Nevalainen, E. (2006). *Kuljetusriskien hallinta (Management of transportation risks).* Pohjola Insurance Ltd. Retrieved January 7, 2009 from http://www.finva.fi/eoppiminen/materiaalit/Materiaali2006/Nevalainen_luento_2006.pdf

New South Wales Government. (2009). *Department of State and Regional Development.* Retrieved from http://www.business.nsw.gov.au/innovation/sectors/logistics.htm

Ng, H. S., Sim, M. L., & Tan, C. M. (2006). Security issues of wireless sensor networks in healthcare applications. *BT Technology Journal*, 24(2), 138–144. doi:10.1007/s10550-006-0051-8

Ng, J. W. P., et al. (2004). Ubiquitous monitoring environment for wearable and implantable sensors (UbiMon). In *Proceedings of the 6th International Conference on Ubiquitous Computing (UBICOMP '04)*, Nottingham, UK.

Ngai, E. W. T., & Gunasekaran, A. (2007). A review for mobile commerce research and applications. *Decision Support Systems*, 43, 3–15. doi:10.1016/j.dss.2005.05.003

Ngai, E. W. T., Cheng, T. C. E., Au, S., & Lai, K. (2007). Mobile commerce integrated with RFID technology in a container depot. *Decision Support Systems*, 43(1), 62–76. doi:10.1016/j.dss.2005.05.006

Niederman, F., Mathieu, R. G., Morley, R., & Kwon, I.-W. (2007). Examining RFID applications in supply chain management. *Communications of the ACM*, 50, 92–101. doi:10.1145/1272516.1272520

Nigam, A., & Caswell, N. (2003). Business artifacts: An approach to operational specification. *IBM Systems Journal*, 42(3), 428–445.

Nijkamp, P., & Yim, H. (2001). Critical Success Factors for Offshore Airports: A Comparative Evaluation. *Journal of Air Transport Management*, 7, 181–188. doi:10.1016/S0969-6997(01)00003-5

NimBUS. (2007). *NimBUS for SLA Monitoring and Reporting*. Retrieved from http://www.nimbuspartners.com/content.php?name=home.html

Nishimura, E., Imai, A., & Papadimitriou, S. (2001). Berth allocation in the public berth system by genetic algorithms. *European Journal of Operational Research*, 131, 282–292. doi:10.1016/S0377-2217(00)00128-4

Nolan, R. (1973). Computer data bases: The future is now. Harvard Business Review, 51(5), 98–114.

Nolan, R. (1998, July-August 3-14). Connectivity and control in the year 2000 and beyond. Harvard Business Review.

Nonaka, I., & Takeuchi, H. (1995). The knowledge-creating company: How Japanese companies create the dynamics of innovation. New York: Oxford University Press.

Normann, R. (1991). Service Management: Strategy and Leadership in Service Business. Second Edition, pp. 16-17. New York: John Wiley & Sons Ltd.

Nucciarelli, A., & Gastaldi, M. (2008). Information technology and collaboration tools within the e-supply chain management of the aviation industry. *Technology Analysis and Strategic Management*, 20(2), 169–184. doi:10.1080/09537320801931309

Nyman, L. R. (1992). Making manufacturing cells work. Drabber, MI: Society of Manufacturing Engineers.

Nysveen, H., Pedersen, P., & Thorbjørnsen, H. (2005). Explaining intention to use mobile chat services: moderating effects of gender. Journal of Consumer Marketing, 22(5), 247–257. doi:10.1108/07363760510611671

O'Brien, T. V., Schoenbachler, D. D., & Gordon, G. L. (1995). Marketing information systems for consumer products companies: A management overview. Journal of Consumer Marketing, 12(5), 16–36. doi:10.1108/07363769510147777

O'Conner, W. E. (1995). An Introduction to Airline Economics, 5th Edition. Westport CT: Praeger.

O'Connor, M., & Brady, M. (2006, September). The Hotel Sector In Ireland–Technology-Based Marketing Enterprises? Irish Academy of Management Conference, University of Cork, Ireland.

O'Hara, B., & Petrick, A. (1999). The IEEE 802.11 Handbook: A Designer's Companion. New York: IEEE Press.

OECD. (2007). Moving up the value chain: Staying competitive in the global economy. A synthesis report on global value chains. Pariso.

Ohashi, H., Kim, T. S., Oum, T. H., & Yu, C. (2005). Choice of Air Cargo Transshipment Airport – An Application to Air Cargo Traffic to/ from Northeast Asia. *Journal of Air Transport Management*, 11, 149–159. doi:10.1016/j.jairtraman.2004.08.004

Ojala, M., & Hallikas, J. (2006). Investment decision-making in supplier networks: management of risk. *International Journal of Production Economics, 104,* 201–213. doi:10.1016/j.ijpe.2005.03.006

Olowolayemo, S. O., Hatch, U., & Zidack, W. (1992). Potential U.S. retail grocery markets for farm-raised catfish. *Journal of Applied Aquaculture, 1,* 51–71. doi:10.1300/J028v01n04_05

Op de Coul, J. (2005). IT Services Procurement based on ISPL. The Netherlands:van Haren Publishers.

Osmundson, J. S., Gottfried, R., Chee, Y. K., Lau, H. B., Lim, W. L., Poh, S. W. P., & Tan, C. T. (2004). Process modeling: A systems engineering tool for analyzing complex systems. *Systems Engineering, 7*(4), 320–337. doi:10.1002/sys.20012

Österle, H., Fleisch, E., & Alt, R. (2000). Business networking shaping collaboration between enterprises. Berlin: Springer.

Ostermayer, G., Pohl, A., Hausleitner, C., Reindl, L., & Seifert, F. (1996). CDMA for wireless SAW sensor applications. In Proc. IEEE Int.Spread-Spectrum Tech. Applicat. Symp., (pp. 795–799).

Oum, T. H., Yu, C., & Fu, X. (2003). A Comparative Analysis of Productivity Performance of the World's Major Airports: A Summary Report of the ATRS Global Airport Benchmarking Research Report 2002. *Journal of Air Transport Management, 9,* 285–297. doi:10.1016/S0969-6997(03)00037-1

Palmer, J. W., & Markus, L. M. (2000). The performance impacts of quick response and strategic alignment in specialty retailing. *Information Systems Research, 11*(3), 241–259. doi:10.1287/isre.11.3.241.12203

Panayides, P. M., & So, M. (2005). Logistics service provider-client relationships. *Transportation Research Part E, Logistics and Transportation Review, 41*(3), 179–200. doi:10.1016/j.tre.2004.05.001

Pantazis, N. A., & Vergados, D. D. (2007). A survey on power control issues in wireless sensor networks. *Communications Surveys & Tutorials, IEEE, 9*(4), 86–107. doi:10.1109/COMST.2007.4444752

Pantazis, N. A., Vergados, D. J., Vergados, D. D., & Douligeris, C. (2009). Energy efficiency in wireless sensor networks using sleep mode TDMA scheduling. *Ad Hoc Networks, 7*(2), 322–343. doi:10.1016/j.adhoc.2008.03.006

Parasuraman, A., & Zeithaml., V. A. (2004). *Service Quality.* Marketing Science Institute.

Parasuraman, A., Berry, L. L., & Zeithaml, V. A. (1991). Understanding customer expetations of service. Sloan Management Review. Cambridge, MA: Harvard Business Press.

Parasuraman, A., Zeithaml, V. A., & Berry, L. L. (1985). A Conceptual Model of Service Quality and Its Implications for Future Research. *Journal of Marketing, 49*(Fall), 41–50. doi:10.2307/1251430

Parasuraman, A., Zeithaml, V. A., & Berry, L. L. (1988). SERVQUAL: A Multiple Item Scale for Measuring Consumer Perceptions of Service Quality. *Journal of Retailing, 64*(1), 12–40.

Pare, D. J. (2003). Does this site deliver? B2B e-commerce services for developing countries. *The Information Society, 19,* 123–134. doi:10.1080/01972240309457

Parente, S. T. (2000). Beyond the hype: A taxonomy of e-health business models. *Health Affairs, 19*(6), 89–102. doi:10.1377/hlthaff.19.6.89

Park, J. Y., & Park, S. J. (1999). IBPM: An integrated systems model for business process reengineering. *Systems Engineering, 1*(3), 159–175. doi:10.1002/(SICI)1520-6858(1998)1:3<159::AID-SYS2>3.0.CO;2-H

Park, W. C., Mothersbaugh, D. L., & Feick, L. (1994). Consumer knowledge assessment. *The Journal of Consumer Research, 21*(1), 71–82. doi:10.1086/209383

Park, Y. (2003). An Analysis for the Competitive Strength of Asian Major Airports. *Journal of Air Transport Management, 9,* 353–360. doi:10.1016/S0969-6997(03)00041-3

Pärkkä, J., et al. (2002). A wireless wellness monitor for personal weight management. In *Proceedings of*

IEEE EMBS International Conference on Information Technology Applications on, (pp. 83-88).

Parola, F., & Sciomachen, A. (2005). Intermodal container flows in a port system network: Analysis of possible growths via simulation models. *International Journal of Production Economics, 97,* 75–88. doi:10.1016/j.ijpe.2004.06.051

Parvatiyar, A., & Sheth, N., J. (2001). Customer relationship management: Emerging practice, process, and discipline. *Journal of Economic and Social Research, 3*(2), 1–34.

Paton, R. A., & Mclaughlin, S. (2008). Services innovation: Knowledge transfer and the supply chain. *European Management Journal, 26,* 77–83. doi:10.1016/j.emj.2008.01.004

Payne, A. (2006) Handbook of CRM, Oxford, UK: Butterworth-Heinemann

Peng, H. (2007). Research of customer services of third party logistics business. Beijing, China: Beijing Jiaotong University.

Perez, C. (2002). Technological revolutions and financial capital: The dynamics of bubbles and golden ages. Northampton, MA: Edward Elgar.

Perkins, C. E. (2001). Ad hoc networking, Reading, MA: Addison-Wesley.

Perrig, A., Szewczyk, R., Tygar, J. D., Wen, V., & Culler, D. E. (2002). Spins: security protocols for sensor networks. *Wireless Networks, 8*(5), 521–534. doi:10.1023/A:1016598314198

Peter, J. P., & Ryan, M. J. (1976). An investigation of perceived risk at the brand level. *JMR, Journal of Marketing Research, 13*(May), 184–188. doi:10.2307/3150856

Petering, M. E. H. (2009). Effect of block width and storage yard layout on marine container terminal performance. *Transportation Research Part E, Logistics and Transportation Review, 45,* 591–610. doi:10.1016/j.tre.2008.11.004

Piasecki, D. (2001). Order Picking: Methods and Equipment for Piece Pick, Case Pick, and Pallet Pick Operations, *Inventory Operations Consulting L.L.C.* Retrieved from http://www.logprojects.lt/uploads/Order_picking_methods.pdf

Pibernik, R., & Sucky, E. (2007). An approach to inter-domain master planning in supply chain. *International Journal of Production Economics, 108,* 200–212. doi:10.1016/j.ijpe.2006.12.010

Piercy, N., (1981) Marketing Information bridging the quicksand between technology and decision-making, The Quarterly Review of Marketing, Fall, 1-15.

Pohl, A. (2000). Review of wireless SAW sensors. IEEE Trans. UFFC, 47(2), 317–332.

Pohto, P., Sihvola, I., & Kallio, J. (2005). Logistiikan sähköisten tieto- ja viestintäteknologioiden hyödyntäminen – Kokemuksia Euroopasta (Utilization of electronic information and communication technologies in logistics – Experiences from Europe). Technology review 173/2005. Tekes.

Poon, S., & Swatman, P. M. C. (1997). Small business use of the Internet: Findings from Australian case studies. *International Marketing Review, 14*(5), 385–402. doi:10.1108/02651339710184343

Porter, M. E. (1985). Competitive Advantage. New York: Free Press.

Porter, M. E. (1987). Wettbewerbsstrategie – Methoden zur Analyse von Branchen und Konkurrenten (in English: Competitive Strategy – Methods to Analyze Industries and Competitors), 4th Ed., Frankfurt/New York

Porter, M. E., & Olmsted-Teisberg, E. (2004). Redefining competition in health care. *Harvard Business Review, 82*(6), 64–76.

Post, J. E., Preston, L. E., & Sachs, S. (2002). Redefining the corporation: Stakeholder mamangement and organizational wealth. Stanford, CA: Stanford University Press.

Prahalad, C. K., & Ramaswamy, V. (2003). The new frontier of experience innovation, MIT. Sloan Management Review, 44(4), 12–18.

Prahalad, C. K., & Ramaswamy, V. (2004). Co-creation experiences: The next practice in value creation. Journal of Interactive Marketing, 18(3), 5–14. doi:10.1002/dir.20015

prEN 50067: (1997, July) *Specification of the radio data system* (RDS).

Prestwood, D. C. L., & Schumann, P. A. Jr. (1997, July 15). *Innovate! Applying Innovation to the Business of Peru* A Summary of the Talk Given at the III Summit on Competitiveness in Lima, Peru.

Prestwood, D. C. L., & Schumann, P. A., Jr. (1994). Innovate! New York:McGraw-Hill.

Pruitt, D. G. (1971). Conclusions: towards an understanding of choice shifts in group discussion. *Journal of Personality and Social Psychology, 20*(3), 495–510. doi:10.1037/h0031923

Pulli, H., Kajander, S., & Tapaninen, U. (2007). Satamasidonnaisten yritysten tietotarpeet. (Information needs of port related companies). Research report of University of Turku, Centre of Maritime Studies, B:149, Turku

Punakivi, M., Aminoff, A., Auramo, J., Pajunen-Muhonen, H., Lehtinen, J., & Yrjölä, H. (2001). *Karkelo – Kartoitus elektronisen liiketoiminnan logistiikasta (Survey of the logistics of electronic business)*. Retrieved February 3, 2009, from http://www.tuta.hut.fi/logistics/publications/Karkelo.pdf

Quagrainie, K. (2006). IQF catfish retail pack: A study of consumers' willingness to pay. *International Food and Agribusiness Management Review, 9*(2), 16–27.

Quagrainie, K. K., & Engle, C. R. (2002a). A latent class model for analyzing preferences for catfish. *Aquaculture Economics and Management, 6*(1), 23–34.

Quagrainie, K. K., & Engle, C. R. (2002b). Analysis of catfish pricing and market dynamics: The role of imported catfish. *Journal of the World Aquaculture Society, 334*, 389–397. doi:10.1111/j.1749-7345.2002.tb00018.x

Quilty, S. (2003). Achieving Recognition as a World Class Airport through Education and Training. *Journal of Air Transportation, 8*, 3–14.

Radjou, N. (2003). U.S. manufacturers' *supply chain* mandate. *World Trade, 16*(12), 42–46.

Raguraman, K. (1997). International Air Cargo Hubbing: The Case of Singapore. *Asia Pacific Viewpoint, 38*(1), 55–74. doi:10.1111/1467-8373.00028

Raines, R. R. (1996). Getting the Message Through: A Branch History of the U.S. Army Signal Corps, CMH Pub 30-17. (pp. 224). Washington, DC: Center of Military History, United States Army.

Rainey, H. G., Backoff, R. W., & Levine, C. H. (1976). Comparing public and private organizations. *Public Administration Review, 36*(2), 233–244. doi:10.2307/975145

Ramaswamy, V. (2008). Co-creating value through customers' experiences: The Nike case. Strategy and Leadership, 36(5), 9–14. doi:10.1108/10878570810902068

Ramirez, R. (1999). Value co-production: Intellectual origins and implications for practice and research. Strategic Management Journal, 20(1), 49–65. doi:10.1002/(SICI)1097-0266(199901)20:1<49::AID-SMJ20>3.0.CO;2-2

Ranchhod, A. (2004). The changing nature of cyber-marketing strategies. Business Process Management Journal, 10(3), 262–276. doi:10.1108/14637150410539678

Rao, A., Papadimitriou, C., Shenker, S., & Stoica, I. (2003). Geographic routing without location information. In *Proceedings of the 9th Annual International Conference on Mobile Computing and Networking on*, (pp.96-108).

Ratliff, H. D., & Nulty, W. G. (1997). Logistics composite modelling, In The planning and scheduling of production systems–Edited by Artiba, A. & Elmaghraby, S.E. Chapman & Hall (eds.), Methodologies and applications.

Raulerson, R., & Trotter, W. (1973). Demand for farm-raised channel catfish in supermarkets: An analysis of selected market. (Marketing Research Report No. 993). Washington DC: SDA Economic Research Service.

Rauniyar P. G., Hermann, R. O., & Hanson, G. D. (1997). Identifying frequent purchasers of seafood at home and restaurants consumption. *The Southern Business and Economic Journal*, 114-129.

Reichheld, F. F., & Schefter, P. (2000). E-loyalty. Harvard Business Review, 78(4), 105–113.

Reinikainen, P., Mäntynen, J., & Rantala, J. (1997). *Logistiikan perusteet (The basics of logistics)*. Tampere, Finland: Tampere University of Technology, The Faculty for Transport Technologies. *RE:view*, 27.

Riemer, K., & Klein, S. (2002). Supplier Relationship Management. *HMD - Praxis. Wirtschaftsinformatik, 228*, 5–22.

Ritter, T., & Gemünden, H. G. (2003). Interorganizational relationships and networks: An overview. *Journal of Business Research, 56*, 691–697. doi:10.1016/S0148-2963(01)00254-5

Robinson, P. J., Faris, C. W., & Wind, Y. (1967). Industrial Buying and Creative Marketing, Boston

Robinson, R. (1998). Asian hub/feeder nets: the dynamics of restructuring. *Maritime Policy & Management, 25*(1), 21–40. doi:10.1080/03088839800000043

Robison, L. (2007). The CIO Dilemma: Build, Buy or Borrow. Burton Group Report.

Rodero, J. A., & Piattini, M. (2000). Auditing Data Warehouses. In Piattini M.(Ed.) Auditing Information Systems (pp.109-148), Hershey, PA: Idea Group Publishing.

Romer, D. (2001). Advanced Macroeconomics. 2nd Edition, New York: McGraw-Hill.

Römer, K., & Mattern, F. (2004). The design space of wireless sensor networks. *IEEE Wireless Communications, 11*(6), 54–61. doi:10.1109/MWC.2004.1368897

Roselius, T. (1971). Consumer rankings of risk reduction methods. *Journal of Marketing, 35*(January), 56–61. doi:10.2307/1250565

Ross, I. (1975). *Perceived risk and consumer behavior: A critical review*, Conference of the American Marketing Association, 19-23.

Rouse, W. B. (2004). Embracing the enterprise. *Industrial Engineer, 36*(3), 31–35.

Rouse, W. B. (2005). Enterprises as systems: Essential challenges and approaches to transformation. *Systems Engineering, 8*(2), 138–150. doi:10.1002/sys.20029

Rubery, J., Earnshaw, J., Marchington, M., Cooke, F. L., & Vincent, S. (2002). Changing organizational forms and the employment relationship. *Journal of Management Studies, 39*(5), 645–672. doi:10.1111/1467-6486.00306

Rüegg-Stürm, J. (2005). The new St. Gallen management model: Basic categories of an approach to integrated management. Basingstoke, NY: Palgrave Macmillan.

Ruizmercader, J., Meronocerdan, A., & Sabatersanchez, R. (2006). Information technology and learning: Their relationship and impact on organizational performance in small businesses. *International Journal of Information Management, 26*(1), 16–29. doi:10.1016/j.ijinfomgt.2005.10.003

Ruiz-Olalla, C. (2001). Gestión de la calidad del servicio, [en línea] *5campus.com, Control de Gestión*. Retrieved May 24, 2009, from http://www.5campus.com/leccion/calidadserv

Rytsy, A. (2007). *RFID veti väkeä Logistics 2007 -tapahtumassa (RFID raised interest in Logistics 2007 event)*. Logistiikka – The Magazine of Finnish Association of Purchasing and Logistics, 5, 38–39.

Saaty, T. (1980). The Analytic Hierarchy Process. New York: McGraw Hill International.

Sabogal, J., & Tholke, J. (2004). Compliant manufacturing with SAP in the pharmaceutical industry. *Die Pharmazeutische Industrie, 66*(11), 1405–1412.

Sadler, I. (2007), Logistics and Supply Chain Integration, Los Angeles: Sage Publications.

Salmela, E., Nieminen, L., & Lukka, A. (2006). *Prosessien kehitys ja ICT:n hyödyntäminen hankintatoimin-*

nassa, logistiikassa ja toimitus- ja kysyntäketjun hallin-nassa (Development of processes and utilization of ICT in purchasing, logistics and supply chain management.). Retrieved February 17, 2009, from http://partnet.vtt.fi/serviisi/tiedostot/serviisi_loppuraportti.pdf

Salmela, H., & Jahnukainen, M. (2003). IT enabled global customer service: findings and conclusions from six case studies, In Reponen, T, (ed.), Information Technology-Enabled Global Customer Service. Hershey, PA:Idea Group Publishing.

Salvador, F., Forza, C., & Claes, B. (2007). Effectiveness of the Product Configuration Task: Theory Formalization and Test, *POMS 18th Annual Conference,* Dallas, TX.

Sambamurthy, V., Bharadwaj, A., & Grover, V. (2003). Shaping agility through digital options: reconceptualizing the role of information technology in contemporary firms. *MIS Quarterly, 27*(2), 237–263.

SAP. (2003). *What is supplier relationship management?* Retrieved February 27, 2009, from http://searchsap.techtarget.com/sDefinition/0,sid21_gci871756,00.html

Sarpola, S. J. (2007). Information systems in buyer-supplier collaboration. Helsinki, Finland: Helsinki School of Economics.

Satty, T. (2000). Fundamentals Of Decision Making and Priority Theory. Pittsburgh, PA: RWS Publications.

Schelp, J., & Winter, R. (2007) Integration Management for Heterogeneous Information Systems. In Desouza K. C. (Ed.) Agile Information Systems (pp.134-150), Amsterdam: Elsevier, Butterworth-Heinemann.

Schmid, B. F., & Lindenmann, M. A. (1998). *Elements of a reference model for electronic markets.* Paper presented at the Thirty-First Annual Hawaii International Conference on System Sciences.

Schmitt, A. (2006). 4PL-providing als strategische Option für Kontraktlogistikdienstleister – Eine konzeptionell-empirische Betrachtung (in English: 4PL-provision as Strategic Option for Contract Logistics Providers – A Conceptual-empirical View).

Schoeneman, J. L., & Sorokowski, D. (1998). Authenticated tracking and monitoring system (ATMS) tracking shipments from an Australian uranium mine. In *Proceedings of the 31st Annual 1997 International Carnahan Conference on Security Technology on*, (pp. 231-240).

Scholl, G. (2003). SAW-based radio sensor systems for short-range applications. IEEE Microwave Magazine, 4(4), 68–76. doi:10.1109/MMW.2003.1266068

Scholtz, J. (2002). Evaluation methods for human-system performance of intelligent systems. In Messina, E. R., & Meystel, A. M. (Eds.), *Proceedings of the 2002 Performance Metrics for Intelligent Systems (PerMIS) Workshop.* Retrieved June 28, 2009, from http://www.isd.mel.nist.gov/research_areas/research_engineering/Performance_Metrics/PerMIS_2002_Proceedings/Scholtz.pdf

Schultze, U., & Orlikowski, W. J. (2004). A Practice Perspective on Technology-Mediated Network Relations: The Use of Internet-Based Self-Serve Technologies. Information Systems Research, 15(1), 87–106. doi:10.1287/isre.1030.0016

Schweidel, D. A., Fader, P. S., & Bradlow, E. T. (2008). Understanding Service Retention Within and Across Cohorts Using Limited Information. Journal of Marketing, 72(1), 82–94. doi:10.1509/jmkg.72.1.82

Scott, W. R. (2002). Organizations: Rational, natural, and open systems (5 ed.). Upper Saddle River, NJ: Prentice Hall.

Seth, N., Deshmukh, G., & Vrat, P. (2005). Service quality models: a review. *International Journal of Quality & Reliability Management, 22*(9), 913–949. doi:10.1108/02656710510625211

Seth, N., Deshmukh, G., & Vrat, P. (2006a). A framework for measurement of quality of service in supply chains. *Supply Chain Management: An International Journal, 11*(1), 82–94. doi:10.1108/13598540610642501

Seth, N., Deshmukh, G., & Vrat, P. (2006b). SSQSC: a tool to mesure supplier service quality in supply chain. *Production Planning and Control, 17*(5), 448–463. doi:10.1080/09537280600741764

Settles, S. F. (2003). Information systems engineering emphasis. In *Proceedings of 2003 Industrial Engineering Research Conference*, Portland, OR.

Shabayek, A. A., & Yeung, W. W. (2002). A simulation model for the Kwai Chung container terminals in Hong Kong. *European Journal of Operational Research, 140,* 1–11. doi:10.1016/S0377-2217(01)00216-8

Shabtay, D. (2008). Due Date Assignments and Scheduling A Single Machine with A General Earliness/Tardiness Cost Function. *Computers & Operations Research, 35*(5), 1539–1545. doi:10.1016/j.cor.2006.08.017

Shah, D., Rust, R., Parasumam, A., Stalin, R., & Day, G. (2006). The path to customer centricity. Journal of Service Research, 9(2), 113–124. doi:10.1177/1094670506294666

Shih, E., et al. (2001). Physical layer driven protocol and algorithm design for energy-efficient wireless sensor networks. In *MobiCom '01: Proceedings of the 7th annual international conference on Mobile computing and networking,* (pp. 272-287). New York: ACM.

Siltala, T. (2007). *RFID ei vielä tartu (RFID does not spread yet).* Retrieved December 20, 2009, from http://www.tietoviikko.fi/taustat/kaikki_jutut/article136836.ece

Singh, J. (1996). The importance of information flow within the supply chain. *Logistics Information Management, 9*(4), 28–30. doi:10.1108/09576059610123132

Singleton, T. W. (2009). What Every IT Auditor Should Know About IT audits and data. *ISACA Journal, 2,* 12–13.

Sisodia, R. S. (1992). Marketing information and decision support systems for services. Journal of Services Marketing, 6(1), 51–64. doi:10.1108/08876049210035773

Slack, N., Chambers, S., & Johnston, R. (2001). Operation Management. Essex, UK: Pearson Education Limited.

Slovic, P., & Lichtenstein, S. (1968). Relative importance of probabilities and payoff in risk taking. *Journal of Experimental Psychology Monograph, 78*(November), 1–18. doi:10.1037/h0026468

Smirnov, A., & Chandra, C. (2001). *Information Technologies for Supply Chain Management,* (pp. 437-460)

Smith, H., & Fingar, P. (2002). Business process management: The third wave. Tampa, FL: Meghan-Kiffer Press.

Smith, N. (1990). The case study: A useful research method for information management. *Journal of Information Technology, 5*(3), 123–13. doi:10.1057/jit.1990.30

Sohraby, K., Minoli, D., & Znati, T. (2007). Wireless sensor networks: Technology, protocols, and application. New York: John Wiley & Sons, Inc.

Sousa, G. W. L., Van Aken, E. M., & Groesbeck, R. L. (2002). Applying an enterprise engineering approach to engineering work: A focus on business process modeling. *Engineering Management Journal, 14*(3), 15–24.

Spekman, R. E., Kamauff, J. W., & Myhr, N. (1998). An empirical investigation into supply chain management: a perspective on partnership. *International Journal of Physical Distribution & Logistics Management, 28*(8), 630–650. doi:10.1108/09600039810247542

Spekman, R., & Sweeney, P. (2006). RFID: From concept to implementation. International Journal of Physical Distribution and Logistics Management, 36(10), 736–754. doi:10.1108/09600030610714571

Sprott, D. (2006). Service Architecture and Engineering. *CBDI Journal. July/August.*

Srivastava, L. (2005, July). RFID and the internet of things. Presented at ICT Trends and Challenges in the Global Era. International Telecommunication Union, Twist, D. C., (2005). The impact of radio frequency identification on supply chain facilities. Journal of Facilities Management, 3(3), 226–236. doi:10.1108/14725960510808491

Statistics Finland. (2008). Use of information technology in enterprises 2008. Statistics Finland, Helsinki.

Steenken, D., Voss, S., & Stahlbock, R. (2004). Container terminal operation and operations research - a classification and literature review. *OR-Spektrum, 26,* 3–49. doi:10.1007/s00291-003-0157-z

Stelzer, A. (2004). Identification of SAW ID-Tags Using an FSCW Interrogation Unit and Model-Based Evaluation. IEEE Trans. UFFC, 51(11), 1412–142.

Stelzer, A., Schuster, S., & Scheiblhofer, S. (2004). Readout Unit for Wireless SAW Sensors and ID-Tags, in 2nd International Symposium on Acoustic Wave Devices for Future Mobile Communications (pp. 37–44), Chiba, Japan.

Stock, J. R., & Zinszer, P. H. (1987). The Industrial Purchase Decision for Professional Services. *Journal of Business Research*, *15*(1), 1–16. doi:10.1016/0148-2963(87)90014-2

Straubhaar T. (2008). *Drei Vorteile der Krise*, Logistik auf den Punkt, Heft 6.

Stuart, I., McCutcheon, D., Handfield, R., McLachlin, R., & Samson, D. (2002). Effective case research in operations management: a process perspective. *Journal of Operations Management*, *20*(5), 419–433. doi:10.1016/S0272-6963(02)00022-0

Studman, C. J. (2001). Computers and electronics in postharvest technology – A review. *Computers and Electronics in Agriculture*, *30*(1-3), 109–124. doi:10.1016/S0168-1699(00)00160-5

Su, W., et al. (2004). Communication Protocols for Sensor Networks. In Raghavendra, C.S., Sivalingam, K., & Znati, T. (Eds.). Wireless Sensor Networks, New York: Kluwer Academic.

Sundbo, J., & Gallouj, F. (2000). Innovation as a loosely coupled system in services. *International Journal of Service Technologies and Management*, *1*(1), 15–36. doi:10.1504/IJSTM.2000.001565

Suomi, R., & Tahkapaa, J. (2002). *The strategic role of ICT in the competition between public and private health care sectors in the Nordic welfare societies-case of Finland.* Paper presented at the 35th Annual Hawaii International Conference on System Sciences.

Supply Chain Management Institute. (2008). *The supply chain management processes.* Retrieved February 27, 2009, from http://www.scm-institute.org/Our-Relationship-Based-Business-Model.htm

Suri, R. (1985). Quantitative techniques for robotic systems analysis. In Handbook of Industrial Robotics, S.Y. Nof (Ed.), Chapter 31. New York: Wiley.

Sussman, J. M. (2005). *An Introduction to Intelligent Transportation Systems, SPRING 1.212, Lectures 2, 3.* Retrieved from ocw.mit.edu/NR/rdonlyres/Civil-and-Environmental-Engineering/1-212JSpring-2005/5B253ABF-EC98-4E53-BA43 4F78500628EA/0/lec3.pdf

Swatman, P. M. C., & Swatman, P. A. (1991, February). Electronic data interchange: organizational opportunity, not technical problem. In *Proceedings of the Conference of the DBIS '91 – 2nd Australian Conference on Information Systems and Database* (pp. 290-307). University of New South, Wales, Sydney. Tompkins Associates Monograph Series, (n.d.). *Warehouse Management Systems Technologies, Transforming Customer Satisfaction Through Better Inventory Management.* Retrieved from http://www.idii.com/wp/tompkins_wms.pdf

Swisslog. (2008). *Pharmacy automation system.* Retrieved February 27, 2009, from http://www.swisslog.com/index/hcs-index/hcs-pharmacy/hcs-pharmacy-components.htm

Sydow, J. (1999). Management von Netzwerkorganisationen – Zum Stand der Forschung (in English: Management of Network Organisations – State of the Art). In: Sydow, J. (Ed.): Management von Netzwerkorganisationen, Wiesbaden, Germany (pp. 279-314).

Tait, F. (1999). Enterprise process engineering: A template tailored for higher education. *CAUSE/EFFECT Journal*, *22*(1), 40-43, 57.

Taleb-Ibrahimi, M., Castilho, B. D., & Daganzo, C. F. (1993). Storage space vs. handling work in container terminals. *Transportation Research Part B: Methodological*, *27*(1), 13–32. doi:10.1016/0191-2615(93)90009-Y

Talvela, J. (2006). Lyhyen kantaman langattomat tekniikat (Short range wireless techniques). Kotka, Finland: Kymenlaakso University of Applied Sciences. (Research Article 2007).

Tan, S. J. (1999). Strategies for reducing consumers' risk aversion in Internet shopping. *Journal of Consumer Marketing*, *16*(2), 163–180. doi:10.1108/07363769910260515

Taneja, N. K. (2002). Driving Airline Business Strategies through Emerging Technology, Ashgate, UK:Aldershot.

Tang, C. S. (1999). Supplier relationship map. *International Journal of Logistics: Research & Applications*, *2*(1), 39–56. doi:10.1080/13675569908901571

Terzi, S., & Cavalieri, S. (2004). Simulation in the supply chain context: a survey. *Computers in Industry*, *53*, 3–16. doi:10.1016/S0166-3615(03)00104-0

The Chartered Institute of Purchasing & Supply. (2005). Selling the benefits of purchasing: Learning network publication. Retrieved February 27, 2009, from www. ifpmm.org/files/LNPubsSellingBenefits.pdf

Thiell, M. (2008). *Strategische Beschaffung von Dienstleistungen* (in English: Strategic Supply Management of Services), Saarbrücken, U.S. International Trade Commission (2005). *Logistic Services – An Overview of the Global Market and Potential Effects of Removing Trade Impediments*. Investigation No. 332-463. Washington, DC.

Thiers, G., & Janssens, G. (1998). A Port Simulation Model as a Permanent Decision Instrument. *Simulation*, *71*, 117–125. doi:10.1177/003754979807100206

Thompson, G., Frances, J., Levacic, R., & Mitchell, J. (1991). Markets, hierarchies and networks: The coordination of social life. London: Sage.

Tian, X. (2008). *Research on the innovative model and guarantee system of the third party logistics service in household appliance industry.* Tianjing: Tianjin Polytechnic University.

Tien, J. M., & Berg, D. (2003). A case for service systems engineering. *Journal of Systems Science and Systems Engineering*, *12*(1), 13–38. doi:10.1007/s11518-006-0118-6

Towill, D. R. (1997a). Successful business systems engineering. Part 1: The systems approach to business processes. *Engineering Management Journal*, *7*(1), 55–64. doi:10.1049/em:19970109

Towill, D. R. (1997b). Successful business systems engineering. Part 2: The time compression paradigm and how

simulation supports good BSE. *Engineering Management Journal*, *7*(2), 89–96. doi:10.1049/em:19970209

Tradenet Services srl, (2008). *A Closer Look at Third Party Shipping Arrangements*. Retrieved from http://www.blogsharp.com/news_9626.html

Trappey, C. V., Trappey, A. J. C., Lin, G. Y. P., & Lee, W. T. (2007). Business and logistics hub integration to facilitate global supply chain linkage. *Proceedings of the Institute of Mechanical Engineering, Part B: J. Engineering Manufacture, 221*, 1221-1233. Retrieved June 28, 2009, from https://commerce.metapress.com/content/755k858k74706609/resource-secured/?target=fulltext.pdf&sid=4h3gmljzsnfc0q45n1ak3b55&sh=journals.pepublishing.com

Triantaphyllou, E. (2000). Multi-criteria decision making methods: a comparative study. The Netherlands: Kluwer Academic Publishers.

Tsai, M. C., & Su, Y. S. (2002). Political Risk Assessment on Air Logistics Hub Developments in Taiwan. *Journal of Air Transport Management*, *8*, 373–380. doi:10.1016/S0969-6997(02)00016-9

Tsai, M.-C. (2006). Constructing a logistics tracking system for preventing smuggling risk of transit containers. *Transportation Research*, *40*, 526–536.

Tugcu, S. (1983). A simulation study on the determination of the best investment plan for Istanbul seaport. *The Journal of the Operational Research Society*, *34*(6), 479–487.

Turner, C. (2000). The information e-conomy, Business strategies for competing in the digital age. London: Kogan Page.

U.S. Food and Drug Administration. (2009). *Medication errors*. Retrieved February 27, 2009, from http://www.fda.gov/cder/handbook/mederror.htm van Bemmel, J. H., & Musen, M. A. (1999). *Handbook of medical informatics*. Retrieved from http://www.mieur.nl/mihandbook/r_3_3/handbook/home.htm

Ueda, M., & Sekiguchi, Y. (2005). Mondaiteigi wo katuyou suru APS sofutouea sentaku tejyun no yuukousei nikansuru kenkyuu [Effectiveness of a Procedure for

ASP Software Selection Based on Problem Specification]. *Journal of the Japan Society for Production Management, 11*(2), 57–66.

Vaidya, K., Sajeev, A. S. M., & Gao, J. *E-procurement assimilation: an assessment of e-business capabilities and supplier readiness in the Australian public sector.* Paper presented at the 7th International Conference on Electronic Commerce.

Van Ark, B., Broersma, L., & Den Hertog, P. (2003). Services innovation, performance and policy: a review. Retrieved April 30, 2009, from http://www.ez.nl/dsresource?objectid=143412&type=PDF

van Dam, T., & Langendoen, K. (2003). An adaptive energy-efficient Mac protocol for wireless sensor networks. In *SenSys '03: Proceedings of the 1st international conference on Embedded networked sensor systems,* (pp. 171-180). New York: ACM Press.

Van Hee, K. M., & Wijbrands, R. J. (1988). Decision support system for container terminal planning. *European Journal of Operational Research, 34,* 262–272. doi:10.1016/0377-2217(88)90147-6

Van Riel, A. C. R., Lemmink, J., & Ouwersloot, H. (2004). High-technology service innovation success: a decision-making perspective. *Journal of Product Innovation Management, 21*(5), 348–359. doi:10.1111/j.0737-6782.2004.00087.x

Van Weele, A. J. (2005). Purchasing & supply chain management: Analysis, strategy, planning and practice (4th ed.). London: Thomson.

Vandaele, D., & Gemmel, P. (2007). Purchased business services influence downstream supply chain members. *International Journal of Service Industry Management, 18,* 307–321. doi:10.1108/09564230710751505

Vargo, S. L., & Lusch, R. F. (2004). Evolving to a new dominant logic for marketing. Journal of Marketing, 68(1), 1–17. doi:10.1509/jmkg.68.1.1.24036

Vargo, S. L., & Lusch, R. F. (2008). Services Dominant Logic, Continuing the evolution. Journal of the Academy of Marketing Science, 36(1), 1–10. doi:10.1007/s11747-007-0069-6

Veludo, M. L., Macbeth, D., & Purchase, S. (2006). Framework for relationships and networks. *Journal of Business and Industrial Marketing, 21*(4), 199–207. doi:10.1108/08858620610672560

Venkataramanan, M. V. (1998). Special Research Focus on Supply Chain Linkages: Challenges for Design and Management in the 21st Century. *Decision Sciences, 29*(3).

Venkatesh, V., Davis, F., & Morris, M. (2007). Dead Or Alive? The Development, Trajectory And Future Of Technology Adoption Research. Journal of the Association for Information Systems., 8(4), 267–287.

Verdone, R., Dardari, D., Mazzini, G., et al. (2008). Wireless sensor and actuator networks Technologies. London: Academic Press.

Vlosky, R. P., & Westbrook, T. (2002). E-business exchange between homecenter buyers and wood products suppliers. *Forest Products Journal, 52*(1), 39–43.

Voigt, K.-I., & Thiell, M. (2003). Beschaffung wissensintensiver Dienstleistungen – Net Sourcing als alternative Bezugsform (in English: Procurement of Knowledge-based Services – Net Sourcing as Alternative Approach). In: Bruhn, M./Stauss, B. (Ed.): Dienstleistungsnetzwerke, Wiesbaden, Germany (pp. 287-318).

Voigt, K.-I., & Thiell, M. (2004). Industrielle Rücknahme- und Entsorgungssysteme – Eine modellgestützte Analyse alternativer Organisationsformen am Beispiel der Automobilindustrie (in English: Industrial Reverse Logistics Systems – A Model-based Analysis of Alternative Organizational Forms Using the Example of the Automotive Industry). In: Prockl, G./Bauer, A./Pflaum, A./Müller-Steinfahrt, U. (Ed.): Entwicklungspfade und Meilensteine moderner Logistik – Skizzen einer Roadmap, Wiesbaden, Germany (pp. 389-418).

Wagner, S. M., & Boutellier, R. (2002, November-December). Capabilities for managing a portfolio of supplier relationships. *Business Horizons, 45*(6), 79–88. doi:10.1016/S0007-6813(02)00263-X

Walker, W. E. (2000). Policy Analysis: A Systematic Approach to Supporting Policymaking in the Public Sector. *Journal of Multi-criteria Decision Analysis*, 9(1-3), 11–27. doi:10.1002/1099-1360(200001/05)9:1/3<11::AID-MCDA264>3.0.CO;2-3

Walston, S. L., & Chadwick, C. (2003). Perceptions and misperceptions of major organizational changes in hospitals: Do change efforts fail because of inconsistent organizational perceptions of restructuring and reengineering? *International Journal of Public Administration*, 26(14), 1581–1605. doi:10.1081/PAD-120024412

Wang, G. (2004). Manufacturing Supply Chain Design and Evaluation. *International Journal of Advanced Manufacturing Technology*, 25, 93–100. doi:10.1007/s00170-003-1791-y

Wang, N., Zhang, N., & Wang, M. (2006). Wireless sensors in agriculture and food industry - Recent developments and future perspective. *Computers and Electronics in Agriculture*, 50(1), 1–14. doi:10.1016/j.compag.2005.09.003

Wang, R. Y. (1998). A product perspective on total data quality management. *Communications of the ACM*, 41(2), 58–65. doi:10.1145/269012.269022

Wang, W. B., Han, T., Zhang, X. D., Wu, H. D., & Shui, Y. A. (2007). Rayleigh wave reflection and scattering calculation by source regeneration method. *IEEE Transactions on Ultrasonics, Ferroelectrics, and Frequency Control*, 54(7), 1445–1453. doi:10.1109/TUFFC.2007.405

Wang, X., & Chen, G. 2007). The services innovative research on third-party logistics enterprise. *Journal of Modern management science*, 2, 5-7.

Wang, Y., Potter, A., & Naim, M. (2007). Electronic marketplaces for tailored logistics. *Industrial Management & Data Systems*, 107(8), 1170–1187. doi:10.1108/02635570710822804

Want, R., Farkas, K. I., & Narayanaswami, C. (2005). Guest editors' introduction: Energy harvesting and conservation. *Pervasive Computing, IEEE*, 4(1), 14–17. doi:10.1109/MPRV.2005.12

Waterman, J., et al. (2005). Demonstration of SMART (Scalable Medical Alert Response Technology). *Proceedings of AMIA 2005 Annual Symposium*, pages 1182-1183.

Waters, D. (2003). *Logistics An Introduction to Supply Chain Management*. London: Palgrave Macmillan.

Webservices. (2009). *Webservices*. Retrieved March 9th, 2009, from http://www.webservices.org/

Webster, F., & Malter, A., & Shankar Ganesan. (2005). The Decline and Dispersion of the Marketing Competence, MIT. Sloan Management Review, 46(4), 35–43.

WEF. (2008). *The Global Competitiveness Report 2008–2009*. London: Palgrave Macmillan.

Wegner, P. (1996). Interoperability. *ACM Computing Surveys*, 28(1), 285–287. doi:10.1145/234313.234424

Wegner, U. (1993). Organisation der Logistik – Prozess- und Strukturgestaltung mit neuer Informations- und Kommunikationstechnik (in English: Organization of Logistics – Process- and Structure-design with Modern Information and Communcation Technology), Berlin, Germany.

Weick, K. E. (1995). Sensemaking in organizations. Thousand Oaks, CA, Sage.

Wei-Ning, P., & Chinyao, L. (2005). Supplier evaluation and selection via Taguchi loss functions and an AHP. *International Journal of Advanced Manufacturing Technology*, 27(5-6).

Weng, M., & Sedani, M. (2002). Schedule One Machine to Minimize Early/Tardy Penalty by Tabu Search. Retrieved from http://fie.engrng.pitt.edu/iie2002/proceedings/ierc/papers/2208.pdf

West, D. C. (1997). Purchasing Professional Services – The Case of Advertising Agencies. In. *International Journal of Purchasing and Materials Management*, 33(3), 2–9.

White, A. (2005). RFID: Why reusable asset tracking is the best place to start. San Jose, CA: BEA White Paper, BEA Systems Inc.

White, R. M., & Voltmer, F. W. (1965). (n.d.). "Direct piezoelectric coupling to surface elastic waves. Applied Physics Letters, 7, 314–316. doi:10.1063/1.1754276

Wholey, D. R., & Burns, L. R. (2003). Understanding health care markets: Actors, products, and relations. In S. S. Mick & M. E. Wyttenbach (Eds.), Advances in Health Care Organization Theory (pp. 99-139). San Francisco: Jossey-Bass.

Wiesbaden, Siebert, H. (1999). Ökonomische Analyse von Unternehmensnetzwerken (in English: Economic Analysis of Business Networks). In: Sydow, J. (Ed.): Management von Netzwerkorganisationen.Wiesbaden, Germany (pp. 7-27).

Wiese, N. J. (2004). *Market characteristics of farm-raised catfish*. M.S. dissertation, University of Arkansas at Pine Bluff.

Wigand, R. (2006). Electronic value chains: supply chain management and RFID. *Proceedings of the International INFORMS Conference*. Hong Kong.

Wikipedia (2009). *Brute Force Search*. Retrieved from http://en.wikipedia.org/wiki/Brute-force_search

Wikipedia (2009). *First In First Out*. Retrieved from http://en.wikipedia.org/wiki/FIFO

Wikipedia (2009). *Local Search*. Retrieved from http://en.wikipedia.org/wiki/Local_search_(optimization)

Wilding, R., & Delgado, T. (2004). RFID – Applications within the Supply Chain. *Supply Chain Practice*, 6(2), 36–49.

Wilkes, L. (2004). Principles of Service Orientation. *CBDI Journal, March.*

Williamson, O. E. (1979). Transaction-cost economics: The governance of contractual relations. *The Journal of Law & Economics*, 22(2), 233–261. doi:10.1086/466942

Wilson, I. D., Roach, P. A., & Ware, J. A. (2001). Container stowage preplanning: using search to generate solution, a case study. *Knowledge-Based Systems*, 14, 137–145. doi:10.1016/S0950-7051(01)00090-9

Wind, Y. (2008). A plan to invent the Marketing we need today. MIT Sloan Management Review, 49(4), 21–28.

Wolfl, A. (2006). Productivity Growth in The Services Industries – Patterns, Issues and the Role of Measure-ment. In Lipsey and Nakamura (eds.), Service Industries and the Knowledge Based Economy. Calgary, Canada: University of Calgary Press.

Womack, J. P., & Jones, D. T. (2005, March). Lean Consumption. Harvard Business Review, 58–68.

Woo, A., & Culler, D. E. (2001). A transmission control scheme for media access in sensor networks. In *MobiCom '01: Proceedings of the 7th annual international conference on Mobile computing and networking,* (pp. 221-235). New York: ACM Press.

Wood, A. D., & Stankovic, J. A. (2002). Denial of service in sensor networks. *Computer, 35*(10), 54–62. doi:10.1109/MC.2002.1039518

Woodside, A. G. (1972). Informal group influences on risk taking. *JMR, Journal of Marketing Research, 9*(May), 223–225. doi:10.2307/3149962

Woodside, A. G. (1974). Is there a generalised risky shift phenomenon in consumer behaviour? *JMR, Journal of Marketing Research, 11*(May), 225–226. doi:10.2307/3150569

World Competitiveness Yearbook (2001-2004).*World Competitiveness Yearbook.* Lausanne, Switzerland: International Institute for Management Development

World Health Organization. (2005). *eHealth: Report by the Secretariat.*Retrieved February 27, 2009, from http://www.who.int/gb/ebwha/pdf_files/WHA58/A58_21-en.pdf

World, S. L. A. (2002). *SLA Toolkit*. Retrieved from http://www.sla-world.com/

Wu, D., & Olson, D. L. (2008). Supply chain risk, simulation, and vendor selection. *International Journal of Production Economics, 114*, 646–655. doi:10.1016/j.ijpe.2008.02.013

Wurman, R. S. (1990). Information Anxiety. New York:Bantam.

www.srv.ch (2005, September). *Swiss Issues: Le marché des voyages*: Entre globalisation et pression des coûts.

X-Change Corporation Delivers Surface Acoustic Wave (SAW) Tag Technology for the Oil and Gas Industry. Retrieved from http://www.thefreelibrary.com/X-Change+Corporation+Delivers+Surface+Acoustic+Wave+(SAW)+Tag... -a0176649458

Xianwei, S., & Zhang, Z. (2001). The Service model and development research of modern Logistics. *Science of Science and Management of S. & T, 12*, 46–50.

Xu, H., Sharma, S. K., & Hackney, R. (2005). Web services innovation research: towards a dual-core model. *International Journal of Information Management, 25*(4), 321–334. doi:10.1016/j.ijinfomgt.2005.04.004

Yamada, Y. (1984). Manegiment sisutemu to OR: tokushuu ni attate [Management system and OR: In planning for this special topic]. *Operations research as a management science research, 29*(11), 632.

Yao, Y., Palmer, J., & Dresner, M. (2007). An interorganizational perspective on the use of electronically-enabled supply chain. *Decision Support Systems, 43*, 884–896. doi:10.1016/j.dss.2007.01.002

Yasin, M. M., Czuchry, A. J., Gonzales, M., & Bayes, P. E. (2006). E-commerce implementation challenges: Small to medium sized versus large organizations. *International Journal of Business Information Systems, 1*(3), 256–275. doi:10.1504/IJBIS.2006.008599

Ye, W., Heidemann, J., & Estrin, D. (2001). An energy-efficient MAC protocol for wireless sensor networks. *Proceedings of Twenty-First Annual Joint Conference of the IEEE Computer and Communications Societies, 3*, 1567-1576.

Yilmaz, C., & Hunt, S. D. (2001). Salesperson cooperation: The influence of relational, task, organizational, and personal factors. *Journal of the Academy of Marketing Science, 29*(4), 335–357. doi:10.1177/03079450094207

Yin, R. (1989). Case Study Research: Design and Methods. 2nd Edition, Newbury Park, CA: Sage

Yoshida, Y., & Fujimoto, H. (2004). Japanese-Airport Benchmarking with the DEA and Endogenous-Weight

TFP Methods: Testing the Criticism of Overinvestment in Japanese Regional Airports. *Transportation Research Part E, Logistics and Transportation Review, 40*, 533–546. doi:10.1016/j.tre.2004.08.003

Younis, M., Youssef, M., & Arisha, K. (2002). Energy-aware routing in cluster-based sensor networks. *Proceedings of the 10th IEEE/ACM International Symposium on Modeling, Analysis and Simulation of Computer and Telecommunications Systems on*, (p.129).

Yun, S., Lee, J., Chung, W., Kim, E., & Kim, S. (2008). A soft computing approach to localization in wireless sensor networks. *Expert Systems with Applications, 36*(4), 7552–7561. doi:10.1016/j.eswa.2008.09.064

Yun, W. Y., & Choi, Y. S. (1999). A simulation model for container-terminal operation analysis using an object-oriented approach. *International Journal of Production Economics, 59*, 221–230. doi:10.1016/S0925-5273(98)00213-8

Yung, Y. H., Chang, C. P., & Hsien, M. C. (2008). Air Cargo as an Impetus Economic Growth through the Channel of Openness: the Case of OECD Countries. *International Journal of Transport Economics, 35*(1), 31–44.

Zanping, L. (2005). Service science-an emerging science in 21st century. *China Information Review, 5*11-13.

Zeithaml, V. A., Bitner, M. J., & Gremler, D. D. (2006). Services Marketing: Integrating Customer Focus across the firms, 4th ed., New York: McGraw-Hill

Zeithaml, V. A., Parasuraman, A., & Berry, L. L. (1985). Problems and strategies in services marketing. *Journal of Marketing, 49*, 33–46. doi:10.2307/1251563

Zeithaml, V., Berry, L., & Parasuraman, A. (1988). Communication and control processes in the delivery of service quality. *Journal of Marketing, 52*, 35–48. doi:10.2307/1251263

Zeithaml, V., Berry, L., & Parasuraman, A. (2004). Service Quality. Marketing Science Institute.

Zeng, Y. E., Wen, H. J., & Yen, D. C. (2003). Customer relationship management (CRM) in business-to-business (B2B) e-commerce. *Information Management & Computer Security, 11*(1), 39–44. doi:10.1108/09685220310463722

Zhang, A. M. (2002). Electronic Technology and Simplification of Customs Regulations and Procedures in Air Cargo Trade. *Journal of Air Transportation, 7,* 87–102.

Zhang, A. M. (2003). Analysis of an International Air Cargo Hub: the Case of Hong Kong. *Journal of Air Transport Management, 9,* 123–138. doi:10.1016/S0969-6997(02)00066-2

Zhang, A. M., & Zhang, Y. M. (2002a). Issues on Liberalization of Air Cargo Services in International Aviation. *Journal of Air Transport Management, 8,* 275–287. doi:10.1016/S0969-6997(02)00008-X

Zhang, A. M., & Zhang, Y. M. (2002b). A Model of Air Cargo Liberalization: Passengers vs. All- Cargo Carriers. *Transportation Research Part E, Logistics and Transportation Review, 38,* 175–191. doi:10.1016/S1366-5545(02)00004-2

Zhang, C., Liu, J., Wan, Y.-W., Murty, K. G., & Linn, R. J. (2003). Storage space allocation in container terminals. *Transportation Research Part B: Methodological, 37,* 883–903. doi:10.1016/S0191-2615(02)00089-9

Zhang, C., Wan, Y.-W., Liu, J., & Linn, R. (2002). Dynamic crane deployment in container storage yards. *Transportation Research Part B: Methodological, 36*(6), 537–555. doi:10.1016/S0191-2615(01)00017-0

Zhang, Z., Cheng, T., & Yan, B. (2006). A Portal of Logistics Service Provider to Integrate Supply Chain. In *Proceedings of the 2006 IEEE Asia-Pacific conference on Services Computing (APSCC'06).*

Zhen, L. (2007). Study on the logistics industry disparity between China and developed country. *Journal of Fuiian Radio & TV University, 3,* 35–37.

ZVEI - Institut für Zukunftsstudien und Technologiebewertung. (2007). *Integrierte Technologie-Roadmap.* Retrieved from http://www.ttn-hessen.de/npkpublish/filestore/77/zvei.pdf

About the Contributors

Zongwei Luo is a senior researcher at the E-business Technology Institute, The University of Hong Kong (China). Before that, he was working at the IBM TJ Watson Research Center in Yorktown Height (NY, USA). He also served as the Affiliate Senior Consultant to ETI Consulting Limited. His research has been supported by various funding sources, including China NSF, HKU seed funding, HK RGC, and HK ITF. His research results have appeared in major international journals and leading conferences. He is the founding Editor-in-Chief of the International Journal of Applied Logistics and serves as an associate editor and editorial advisory board member in many international journals. Dr. Luo's recent interests include applied research and development in the area of service science and computing, innovation management and sustainable development, technology adoption and risk management, and e-business model and practices, especially for logistics and supply chain management.

* * *

Alp Ariburnu is a graduate student in Marmara University. He is studying in Industrial Engineering Department. His undergraduate study was Industrial Engineering too. He graduated with honor degree with 3.18 / 4 GPA. His graduation project was on inventory management and he created a stock management program for a retailer company using Visual Basic programming tool. Alp is working on parallel machines scheduling with robotics aspect for his thesis. He is experienced in business life as well. He worked in Turkish Airlines which is one of the biggest companies in Europe. Currently, he is working on academic subjects to be beneficial for the literature.

Jaouad Boukachour is an Associate Professor of Computer Sciences at Le Havre University, France. His research interests include: Scheduling Problems, Operational Research, and Supply Chain Management. He has supervised a number of PhD researchers in areas such as logistics and scheduling aircraft landings. Currently, he is supervising six PhD students working on traceability, modelling road traffic, job shop scheduling, scheduling aircraft landings and vehicle routing. He has published more than 30 referred research papers. Within the French CPER 2006 (State-Region Project Contract), he was responsible for Modelling Optimisation and Simulation of physical and information flows in an industrial logistics project. Currently, he heads two projects about tracking container shipments, funded by French National Research Agency (ANR) and CPER 2008.

Mairead Brady is a Lecturer in Marketing at the School of Business, Trinity College Dublin lecturing at undergraduate, masters and to experienced managers. She is a co-author on the 1st European edition of the classic Kotler text: Kotler, Keller, Brady, Goodman and Hansen,(2009) Marketing Management, European Edition.. Her research focuses on the assimilation of information and communication technologies (ICT) into contemporary marketing practice (CMP), service organisations and along global supply networks (GSN). She is the author of many journal articles including the Journal of Marketing Management, the Journal of Business and Industrial Marketing, International Journal of Technology Marketing, and Management Decision along with many conference publications including the European, British and Irish Academy of Management and Marketing conferences.

Armando Cartenì, Civil Engineering degree on Transportation at the University of Naples "Federico II" and PhD in Transportation System Analysis since 2004, is research assistant at the University of Salerno. Research activity has been focused on the development of models and methods for transportation system both for passenger and for freight, main topics are: demand flow direct and indirect estimation; freight demand models (trip and tour based); aggregate and disaggregate models for transportation terminal analysis. Results of research activity, carried out within national and international research projects. He has published over thirty papers on his research in national and international journals and proceedings.

Nathan S. Caswell is a Sr. Consultant with Janus Consulting focused on enabling businesses to improve strategic effectiveness, adaptability, manageability, and efficiency by aligning strategic, operational, and IT systems. Over a 27 year career at the IBM Thomas J. Watson Research Center he developed methods for engineering business management and operational systems while leading several projects in the HealthCare, Retail, Food Service, Manufacturing, and Business Transformation areas. Recent work has involved developing analysis models for networks of mutually outsourced businesses. He has received project related awards, holds several patents and authored over 25 professional publications.

Miguel Gaston Cedillo-Campos is a Professor of Supply Chain Management and Director of the Supply Chain Research and Development Center in the Tecnológico de Monterrey. He is also a Research Associate for the Logistics Systems Research Unit at COMIMSA. In 2004, he received with honors a PhD degree in Logistics Systems Dynamics from the University of Paris, France. He has worked for logistics businesses in Mexico and as a consultant on supply chain management for companies like Daimler-Chrysler, Caterpillar, Mabe, WTC Confianza, IBM, Met-Mex Peñoles, and several Mexican State Governments. His current research interests include service operations in supply chains, supply chain security, urban distribution, and design of supply chains oriented to emerging markets. He is co-author of book "Dynamic Analysis of Industrial Systems" published by Editorial Trillas.

Yupo Chan is Professor & Founding Chair of the Systems Engineering Department at the University of Arkansas at Little Rock. He received his BS degree in civil engineering, MS degree in transportation systems/economics and Ph.D. degree in operations research, all from the Massachusetts Institute of Technology. Dr. Chan has written numerous journal articles and books. The most recent ones include: Location, Transport and Land-use: Modeling Spatial-Temporal Information, Springer-Verlag, Forthcoming, 750 pages (with Web-based software) and Location Theory and Decision Analysis, ITP/South-Western, 2000, 533 pages. (with Computer Software disk) His research interests include telecommunication systems, transportation systems, networks and combinatorial optimization, multi-criteria decision-making, spatial-temporal information, econometrics and technology assessment. He has previously held faculty positions at the Air Force Institute of Technology, Washington State University, State University of New York, Stony Brook and Pennsylvania State University. Dr. Chan is a Fellow of the American Society of Civil Engineers and has won numerous awards for his work, including the Harland Bartholomew Award of the American Society of Civil Engineers, the Koopman Prize of the Operations Research Society of America and a Congressional Fellowship with the Office of Technology Assessment.

Wu Chengjuan is a undergraduate student of the Shenzhen Tourism College of Jinan University, and her major is ecommerce. Recently she has participated in some research and development projects such as the development of recommender systems in eCommerce and scientific and technological innovation projects and she also interested in analyzing the problems and the future development about logistics industry in China.

Chia-Chu Chiang is an associate professor at the Computer Science department of the University of Arkansas at Little Rock (UALR). Prior to joining UALR, he worked for VIASOFT, a software development company, in Phoenix. Dr. Chiang obtained his Ph.D in Computer Science from Arizona State University in 1995. For many years, he has worked on several projects sponsored by NSF, DOD, and industrial companies including Syntell and Acxiom. His research results have been published in journals, conferences, and book chapters. He is a member of ACM, IEEE, and ABET. Also, he often volunteers to work for conference chairs, reviewers, committee members, and journal editors.

Ren Congying is an undergraduate student of Shenzhen Tourism College of Jinan University. In view of the significance and the developmental trend of eCommerce in future, she selected eCommerce as her main research fields. She has participated in some research and development projects such as the Intangible Cultural Heritage research activity, 'Nan Feng Chuang' research activity and scientific and technological innovation projects.

Madan Mohan Dey is a Professor of Aquaculture Economics and Marketing, University of Arkansas at Pine Bluff (UAPB), USA. He is an agricultural economist with twenty years of post PhD experience in multi-disciplinary agricultural research and development activities. His main areas of expertise include aquaculture economics and marketing, international trade policy analysis, food sector modeling, impact assessment, economics of development and diffusion of agricultural technologies, and project planning and management. Before joining UAPB, he worked for various institutes (The WorldFish Center, International Rice Research Institute, and International Food Policy Research Institute) of the Consultative Group of International agricultural Research (CGIAR) system for more than 15 years. He served the Government of Bangladesh for 10 years in different capacities (teaching, research and policy planning), and have conducted collaborative research with other advanced research institutes including the Yale University (USA).

Martin R. Fellenz received his Ph.D. from the Kenan-Flagler Business School at The University of North Carolina at Chapel Hill. He is Senior Lecturer in Organisational Behaviour and Director of Postgraduate Teaching & Learning at the School of Business, University of Dublin, Trinity College. He regularly consults with leading domestic and international firms. Much of this work is located at management board level and focuses on enabling client organizations to adapt to environmental, strategic and technological change, and on developing management capabilities to successfully lead and manage such changes. His research focuses on behavioural aspects of organisational change and transformation, in particular the implications of environmental and technological change for individuals, organisational design, and management processes and practices. In addition, he studies organisational justice and fairness; managerial and organisational aspects of evolving global business systems (with a particular focus on service industries); and issues in higher education and management development.

Erwin Fielt is currently a member of the Business Process Management Group of the School of Information Technology at the Queensland University of Technology. In his research, he focuses on the intersection between business and ICT where new ICT applications have to result in net benefits for individuals and organizations. Erwin Fielt works as Postdoctoral Research Fellow in the Business Service Management project of the Smart Services CRC. Within this project, he is responsible for coordinating the involvement of the different academic and industry partners and he conducts research on Service Oriented Business Models, Service Portfolio Management and Service Quality Management. Erwin Fielt has a PhD from the Delft University of Technology and a MSc from the University of Twente, both in the Netherlands.

Emmanuel Fragnière is Service Operations Management and Risk Management Professor at the Geneva School of Business Administration (HEG). He is head of LEM-HEG, an institute specialized in market researches. He is a Lecturer in Management Science at the School of Management of the University of Bath (United Kingdom). He previously occupied senior positions in risk management (Banque Cantonale Vaudoise, the fourth largest bank of Switzerland and Cargill). His research interests are primarily in risk management and knowledge-based services design and control. His previous research appears in European Journal of Operations Research, Management Science, Interfaces and Environmental Modeling and Assessment.

Charles H. Fredouet, MBA, Ph.D, is a professor of supply-chain and sea-port management at Le Havre University (LHU)'s School of Logistics. After 20 years of research in the field of information and decision-support systems, Prof. Fredouet turned to global logistics management (network and process modeling, strategic and operational decision support, local and global performance measurement), with a specific interest to maritime ports (interfacing supply-chain management and sea-port management). He is a member of the Supply Chain Council and reviewing for TRB's International Trade and Transportation Committee. A former vice-president of Le Havre University, Prof. Fredouet heads LHU's School of Logistics research center; he has also acted as president of the SEFACIL Research Institute, dedicated to global supply-chain securization and facilitation issues.

G.R. Gangadharan is a research scientist at Novay (formerly Telematica Institute), Enschede, The Netherlands. His research interests are mainly located on the interface between technological and business perspectives. His research interests include service oriented computing, Internet software engineering, intellectual property rights, free and open source systems, and business models for software and services. Dr. Gangadharan has published several research papers in international journals, conference proceedings, and book chapters. He is codesigner of ODRL-S, a language for describing service licenses. He has a PhD in information and communication technology from the University of Trento, Trento, Italy, an MS in information technology from the Scuola Superiore Sant'Anna, Pisa, Italy, and an MSc in computer science from Manonmaniam Sundaranar University, Thirunelveli, India. Dr. Gangadharan is a member of the IEEE society. He can be reached at gr@novay.nl

Roman Gumzej, born 1970 in Maribor, Slovenia, received a doctorate in computer science and informatics from University of Maribor in 1999. He worked both in industry (Institute of Information Science, IZUM Maribor) and academia (University of Maribor), before he was elected assistant professor at the Faculty of electrical engineering and computer science at University of Maribor in 2004. He was a visiting researcher at ifak e.V. Magdeburg, Germany in 2002 and at the Chair of Computer Engineering at Fernuniversität in Hagen, Germany in 2007. Currently he is assistant professor at the Faculty of logistics at the same university. His research interests comprise all major areas of hard real-time computing with special emphasis on operating systems, co-design and quality-of-service in embedded and logistics applications. He has conducted a national and co-operated in several national and international research projects. He has authored or co-authored several refereed book chapters, and about 40 journal publications and conference contributions, and is involved in international professional organizations and program committees of several conferences.

Tao Han was born in Shandong Province, China, in 1973. He received his master's degree in automatic control engineering from Shandong University of Technology, Jinan, China, in 1999. In 2002, he received the Ph.D. degree in instrument science and technology from Shanghai Jiaotong University, Shanghai,China. His Ph.D. dissertation was on the wireless SAW sensors and identification tags. He currently works in Shanghai Jiaotong University as an associate professor. His research interests are in the field of acoustic sensors and signal processing in measurement. Dr. Han is a member of IEEE, and a senior member of China Instrument and Control Society.

Albalicia Martínez-Hernández is a Professor of Service Operations at the Universidad Tecnológica de Torreón and a Research Associate for the Logistics Systems Research Unit at COMIMSA, an Engineering Consulting Firm and Research Center that belongs to the National Council of Science and Technology of Mexico. In 1998, she graduated from Instituto Tecnológico de la Laguna, as an Industrial Engineer. In 2007, she got her Master in Science Degree in Industrial Engineering and Manufacturing Systems, from COMIMSA (National Council of Science and Technology) in Saltillo, Coahuila. She worked in the private sector for industrial businesses in Mexico. Currently, she is a member of the board of the Strategic Center for Company Development (CEIDEM).

Sergio Hernandez is a Ph.D. candidate in Industrial and Systems Engineering at Florida International University, Miami, and holds a MBA from Universidad de los Andes, Bogotá. Since 2003 he works as Assistant Professor at the Universidad de los Andes School of Management, Bogotá, teaching Modeling in the undergraduate program and Value Network Management in the graduate program. He also works as consultant at the Center for Strategy and Competitiveness (CEC) of UniAndes School of Management. Formerly he was a Manager and Senior Consultant at Deloitte and Arthur Andersen.

Luo Jing earned her Master of Art majoring in English in Northwestern Polytechnic University of China, with an emphasis in applied linguistics, translation and cross-cultural communication. Now she works as a teacher in Shenzhen Tourism College of Jinan University. Her research focuses on tourism English, business English and culture.

Manjunath Kamath is Professor and Graduate Program Director of Industrial Engineering and Management, Oklahoma State University, Stillwater, OK. He is also the Director of the Center for Computer Integrated Manufacturing Enterprises and Associate Site Director of the Center for Engineering Logistics and Distribution (CELDi), a multi-university NSF-I/UCRC. He has an extensive research background in enterprise modeling, discrete-event systems modeling and performance evaluation using queuing theory, discrete-event simulation, and Petri nets. His current research focuses on the development of freight movement modeling methodologies, development of a process-modeling framework for next-generation enterprises, modeling supply chain networks, and modeling knowledge work environments.

Ying Tat Leung is a Research Staff Member in the Services Research Department at the IBM Almaden Research Center in California. His current research interests are on the modeling of different aspects of service enterprises, including their business strategy, business performance, and the value of their business transformation. Before moving to Almaden in 2004, he spent almost 10 years at the IBM Thomas J. Watson Research Center in New York, working on various subjects spanning the entire supply chain. Prior to IBM, he was a Senior Member of Research Staff at Philips Laboratories, the research arm of Philips Electronics, in New York. Ying Tat holds a B.Sc. from the University of Hong Kong, M.S. and Ph.D. degrees from the University of Wisconsin – Madison, all in Industrial Engineering.

Gong Li, presently a PhD student majoring in Industrial Engineering at North Dakota State University. He obtained his B.E. degree of Mechanical Engineering and M.E. degree of Mechatronic Engineering in 1996 and 2003, respectively, from China University of Mining and Technology, China. Having accumulated more than ten years' research experience, Mr. Li's research interests include green supply chain management, advanced manufacturing technology, electromechanical integration technology, process simulation and optimization. Mr. Li is a member of IIE and ASME.

Yang Li is a principal research scientist from British Telecom (BT). He received BSc, MSc and PhD degrees in computer science and has applied intelligent technology to the areas of service creation, marketing, delivery and management. Yang is an inventor of 17 granted and filed patents, and founded IEEE international workshop series on "Barriers towards Internet-Driven Information Services". He published extensively in the leading journals and conferences, winning accolades such as "top accessed article in IJSEKE" and "BT Gordon Radley papers premium". Beyond his thought leadership, Yang has also successfully led the downstream of his research innovations to BT Lines of Business, such as automated service reservation tool, saving millions of pounds for the company. He is a frequent industrial supervisor for MSc, PhD students and graduates from top UK universities and also serves as an editorial member for a number of international journals, conferences and workshops.

Martin Lipičnik, born 1947 in Celje, received a doctorate from the Faculty for Architecture, Civil engineering and Geodesy at the University of Ljubljana in 1984. After graduation he started to work on projects for a construction company in Celje in 1970 where he held the position of the head of the construction sector. After that he pursued his academic career by continuing his studies at the Faculty of civil engineering in Zagreb from which he obtained the Master of Science degree in 1979. He was a co-founder of the Roads and road-traffic department at the Faculty of Technical sciences at the University of Maribor. After the foundation of the Faculty of Civil Engineering at the same university he was one of the initiators of the study-program Traffic Engineering at this faculty and successfully led the program-research group Traffic and Logistics for a number of years. He founded the Institute of Traffic Sciences to examine the harmonized function of the uniform traffic system and led the Traffic management project team after the foundation of the Centre for Interdisciplinary and Multidisciplinary research and Studies of the University of Maribor in 2001. At about the same time when the project team grew into the Institute of logistics CIMRS UM, he was empowered the manager of the newly-founded Faculty of logistics at the University of Maribor and since then holds the position of the dean. He is involved in numerous national and international professional organizations and conference boards as president or member. Among other he is president of the annual traditional International scientific and professional congress named Transport, Traffic, Logistics and member of the Committee for international relations at the University of Maribor. He also led the project council for the Optimization of the public bus traffic in the Republic of Slovenia at the Ministry of Transport, and has been a member of the project council for the preparation of the traffic policy of the Republic of Slovenia. He is a national coordinator of the international COST project (COST C6 - "Towns and infrastructure planning for safety and urban quality for pedestrian") and national coordinator of the bilateral scientific cooperation with the Republic of Hungary and with the Republic of Croatia. He also led the projects of the Slovenian distribution centers for the Slovenian Logistics Cluster (TLG). He is author of six books, two patents and many articles published in magazines, congresses and symposiums.

Hing-Po Lo is a Professor in Statistics in the Department of Management Sciences, City University of Hong Kong. He is also the Director of the Statistical Consulting Unit at the University. As an applied statistician, Dr. Lo has been promoting the application of statistics through teaching, research, and consultancy for many years. Dr Lo's research interest is in discrete choice modeling, competitive bidding and statistical modeling in marketing research and transportation. He has published articles in Biometrics, Ecology, Transportation Research, Transportmetrica, Canadian Journal of Statistics, European Journal of Marketing, Journal of the Operational Research Society, Journal of Urban Planning and Development, ASCE, Construction Management and Economics, and Journal of Construction Engineering and Management.

Joyce M.W. Low is a Research Fellow in the National University of Singapore. She received her Bachelor's and Master's degrees from the Business School before obtaining her PhD degree in 2009 from the same university. Parts of her doctoral dissertation have been published in respectable journals such as Journal of Air Transport Management, Transportation Research Parts A and E, Networks and Spatial Economics and International Journal of Production Economics. She is also an active reviewer for a number of international journals in the disciplines of transportation, logistics and economics.

Tobias Mettler at present, after working several years in the consulting business, is employed as researcher at the Competence Center Health Network Engineering, Institute of Information Management at the University of St. Gallen (http://ehealth.iwi.unisg.ch). He holds a master's degree in information systems of the University of St. Gallen and is currently working on his PhD in the field of organizational change engineering of health service providers.

Farhad Moeeni is professor of Computer and Information Technology and the Founding Director of the Automatic Identification Laboratory at Arkansas State University. He holds a M.S. degree in industrial engineering and a Ph.D. in operations management and information systems, both from the University of Arizona. His articles have been published in various scholarly outlets including Decision Sciences Journal, International journal of Production Economics, International Journal of Production Research, International Transactions in Operational Research and several others. He is a frequent guest lecturer on the subject of information systems at the "Centre Franco Americain", University of Caen, France. Current research interests are primarily in the design, analysis and implementation of automatic identification for data efficiency and quality. Methodological interests include design of experiments, simulation and operations research techniques. He is one of the pioneers in designing and teaching the subject of automatic identification within MIS programs. Dr. Moeeni is currently the principle investigator of a multi-university research project funded by Arkansas Science and Technology Authority, Co-founder of Consortium for Identity Systems Research and Education (CISRE), and on the Editorial Board of the International Journal of RF Technologies: Research and Applications.

Zhang Mu is a professor and Chief of the GIS & Tourism Laboratory at the Shenzhen Tourism College of Jinan University, China. He earned his Bachelor and Master degree both major in Geography and later received a diploma and a Ph. D degree in Geography from Fujian Normal University of China, mainly focus on the GIS application in resources development and environment protection. In his postdoctoral research, he also engaged in GIS technology applications and the projects researches have involved agriculture, land use and tourism planning. Since 1985, he has been working as a teacher in college and university for more than 23 years and involved in several national and local government R&D projects. His research interests include geography, e-commerce in tourism, tourist resources development & planning, and the GIS application in tourism. He has more than 70 publications to his credit in Chinese and international journals or conferences in these areas.

Malgorzata Pankowska is an Assistant Professor of the Department of Informatics at the Karol Adamiecki University of Economics in Katowice, Poland. She received the qualification in econometrics and statistics from the Karol Adamiecki University of Economics in Katowice in 1981, the Ph.D. degree in 1988 and the Doctor Habilitatus degree in 2009, both from the Karol Adamiecki University of Economics in Katowice. She participated in EU Leonardo da Vinci Programme projects as well as gave lectures within the Socrates Program Teaching Staff Exchange in Braganca, Portugal, Trier, Germany, Brussels, Belgium, and in Vilnius, Lithuania. She is a member of ISACA and the Secretary in the Board of the Polish Scientific Society of Business Informatics. Her research interests include Virtual Organization development, ICT project management, IT outsourcing, information governance, and business information systems design and implementation.

Antti Posti (26) graduated as a Master of Science in Department of Industrial Engineering and Management, majoring in Logistics and Supply Chain Management at Lappeenranta University of Technology in 2009. Posti did his Master's Thesis at University of Turku in the Centre for Maritime Studies in the research project, which examined Finnish transit traffic and value-added services related to it. He has also completed a Bachelor's Degree in Electronics and Telecommunications Engineering at Kymenlaakso University of Applied Sciences in 2006. Posti has worked in different types of jobs mainly in the fields of logistics and information technology. Currently, Posti works at University of Turku in the Centre for Maritime Studies as a researcher in the project, which studies the role of tracking and tracing of cargo deliveries in seaport related supply chain. The main purpose of the project is to clarify, in which ways the companies in the supply chain track and trace the transportations.

Hennariina Pulli (28) graduated as a Master of Science in Department of Industrial Engineering and Management, majoring in Knowledge Management at Lappeenranta University of Technology in

2005. Pulli did her Master's Thesis in the research project, which studied electronic invoicing and the factors that affect the adoption of electronic invoicing in companies. Pulli has worked, among others, as a production planner at a telecommunication industry company Tellabs. Currently, Pulli works at University of Turku in the Centre for Maritime Studies as a researcher in the project, which studies the role of tracking and tracing of cargo deliveries in seaport related supply chain. The main purpose of the project is to clarify, in which ways the companies in the supply chain track and trace the transportations.

Peter Rohner is managing the Competence Center Health Network Engineering which is concerned with e-government and e-health issues, at the Institute of Information Management at the University of St. Gallen (http://ehealth.iwi.unisg.ch). He earned a master's degree in information systems and a doctorate degree with a work on architecture and integration of distributed systems. He is currently working on his postdoctoral lecture qualification in the areas of e-government and e-health. He is a member of several Swiss national expert panels in these two interconnected fields and managing partner of BEG & Partners, a consultancy specialized in management of hospitals and public administrations (http://www.begpartners.com).

Jing Shi received his Ph.D. in industrial engineering from Purdue University, West Lafayette, IN, USA in 2004. He is currently an Assistant Professor in the Department of Industrial Engineering at North Dakota State University, Fargo, ND, USA. His research interests include wireless sensor network/RFID, computer vision, structure health monitoring, and mathematical modeling for renewable energy and health care systems. He has authored more than 40 papers on these topics, which have been published in referred journals and conference proceedings. Dr. Shi is also a member of IEEE, IIE, and ASME.

Yongan Shui graduated from the physics Department of Beijing University, Beijing, China in 1953. Since 1978, he has been an associate professor and professor with the Institute of Acoustics at Nanjing University, Nanjing, China. He was a visiting scientist at Ginzton Laboratory of Stanford University, Stanford, CA, from 1982 to 1983; a research professor at the Polytechnik Institute of New York in 1983; an invited professor at 'Ecole Sup'erieure de Physique et de Chimie Industrielles de la Ville de Paris (ESPCI), Paris, France, from 1987 to 1988; a visiting professor at the Material Research Laboratory, Pennsylvania State University, University Park, PA, from 1983 to 1984. He now is retired from Nanjing University and works as adjunct professor of Shanghai Jiaotong University, Shanghai, China. Professor Shui is a fellow of the Acoustic Society of China. His research interests include surface acoustic wave (SAW), SAW devices, ultrasonic transducers, and nonlinear acoustics. He has published more than 80 papers and received many awards from the State Education Ministry, Jiangsu Province, and the Ministry of Electronics of China.

Mario Cantú Sifuentes is a Professor of Industrial Statistics and a Research Associate for the Logistics Systems Research Unit at COMIMSA. He got the Industrial Engineering degree at the Saltillo Institute of Technology. He received a PhD degree in Statistics from the University of Chapingo, Mexico. Dr. Cantú-Sifuentes has a Master in Science Degree in Nuclear Engineering from the National Polytechnic Institute of Mexico and a Master in Science Degree in Statistics from the Universidad Autónoma Antonio Narro. From 1977 to 1983 he worked in projects for private and public sectors. His research work in statistics has been published in several leading academic journals and international conferences.

Loon Ching Tan is an Associate Professor and Head of the Department of Industrial and Systems Engineering in the National University of Singapore. He obtained a PhD degree in 1992 from Cornell University in the field of Operations Research. He is on the editorial review board of the Journal of Quality Technology and has been an active reviewer for a number of international journals. He has been consulted on problems demanding innovative applications of probability, statistics and other operations research techniques; and is also a well-known trainer in Six Sigma.

Ulla Tapaninen (39) graduated as a Doctor of Technology at Helsinki University of Technology in 1997. Professor Tapaninen has also completed a degree of Master of Philosophy at Cranfield University in 1996. Previously, Tapaninen has worked, among others, in various tasks of an expert in a Finnish shipping company Finnlines Oy (1996–2006) and as a researcher in the field of logistics at Helsinki University of Technology (1992–1996). In 2006, Tapaninen started as a professor at University of Turku in the Centre for Maritime Studies. She has a long experience in public (national and EU) funded research projects since 1992 as a Researcher, Project Director and Board member in the areas of logistics, maritime and cross-border transportation, logistics information handling and maritime safety.

Albert K. Toh is an associate professor of psychology in the Departments of Social & Behavioral Sciences, University of Arkansas at Pine Bluff (UAPB). He received his MSc. Degree in applied psychology from Aston University, UK, and Ph.D. in Human Factors/Psychology from University of South Dakota (1983). He was a visiting scientist at the Cognitive Science Lab of Catholic University of America, and has held academic positions in Nebraska and Ohio. Prior to the academia, he has previously worked as a Human Factors professional in the US Department of Transportation and various consulting companies in the areas of traffic safety and applied cognitive research. His current research interests include Human Factors in supply chain/logistics, collaborative e-commerce, and risk perception and analysis.

Magali Dubosson Torbay is Marketing Professor and Director of the Geneva School of Business Administration (HEG) where she teaches Services marketing and Marketing Strategy. She is also a Lecturer at Ecole Polytechnique Fédérale de Lausanne (EPFL, Switzerland) and Essec Management Education (Paris, France). How to price and distribute knowledge-based services are her core research areas. She is also working on the following academic topics: services marketing, internet business models, web 2.0 marketing, e-services, netnography, service risk management, and wealth management. Her previous research appears in Journal of Services Research (IIMT), Journal of Wealth Management and Thunderbird International Management Review.

Marcus Thiell holds a Ph.D. in Business Administration (Dr. rer. pol.) from Friedrich-Alexander-University in Erlangen-Nuremberg, and a MBA (Diplom-Kaufmann) from Hamburg University. He has worked as Research Associate at the Department of Industrial Management at the Friedrich-Alexander University in Nuremberg, and as lecturer in Economics at the Akademie des Handwerks in Hamburg. Since 2007 he is Assistant Professor at the Universidad de los Andes School of Management, Bogotá, teaching Operations, Logistics, Supply Management and Value Network Management in undergraduate, graduate, and executive programs. He also works as consultant at the Center for Strategy and Competitiveness (CEC) of UniAndes School of Management.

Bikem Turkeli is a graduate student in Marmara University, Industrial Engineering Department. She is graduated from Işık University, Industrial Engineering Department with full scholarship. She completed the Minor Program in Computing Systems offered by the Department of Computer Engineering. She is graduated with Honor degree with 3.10 / 4.00 GPA. Her graduation project was about order picking and during her study; she used Visual Basic programming language. She is now working on solving bi-criteria open shop scheduling problem with Genetic algorithm and Tabu Search algorithm. In her thesis study, she will develop JAVA programming language for Genetic algorithm and Tabu search algorithm and will use this structure in open shop scheduling problem program. She did her practical trainings in FORTIS Bank and in BSH (Bosch and Siemens Home Appliances Group) Washing Machine factory.

Masayuki Ueda was born in Sendai City (Miyagi Prefecture), Japan in 1975. He earned a bachelor's degree in commerce from Otaru University of commerce in 1999. And, he earned a master's degree (2002) and a doctor's degree (2006) in business administration from Hokkaido University. He belonged to the Venture Business Laboratory of Hokkaido University, where he was a part-time researcher from 2006 to 2009. He has been a part-time instructor at Sapporo University and Sapporo Gakuin University since 2007. His current research interests are focused primarily on decision support with non-mathematical problem description. He is a member of JSPM (The Japan Society for Production Management).

Özalp Vayvay, Ph.D., is working of Industrial Engineering Department at Marmara University. He is currently the Chairman of the Engineering Management Department at Marmara University. His current research interests include technology & innovation management, business process reengineering, total quality management, operations management, supply chain management. Dr. Vayvay has been involved in R&D projects and education programs for a over the past 10 years.

Li Wenli earned her Ph. D. degree from the University of Hong Kong with an emphasis in supply chain management. Now she works as an associate professor in Shenzhen Tourism College of Jinan University. Her research interests cover supply chain management, revenue management, service management and service marketing.

Ye Xiang is an undergraduate student of the Shenzhen Tourism College of Jinan University. He has participated in some R & D projects such as "'Nan Feng Chuang" research activity, Challenge Cup in Jinan University and Scientific and technological innovation projects. He also interested in analyses of the present situation and the problems about logistics enterprise in China. And the eComerce is his main research fields.

Xue-Ming Yuan is a Research Scientist of Singapore Institute of Manufacturing Technology (SIMTech) and Adjunct Associate Professor of the Department of Industrial and Systems Engineering, National University of Singapore. He has held various academic positions in China, France, Hong Kong and Singapore. He has published a number of scientific papers in the leading academic journals which include IEEE Transactions, IIE Transactions, Operations Research, European Journal of Operations Research, Journal of Applied Probability, etc. He has been leading many research and industry projects in the areas of Demand Forecasting, Inventory Network Optimisation, Global Supply Chain Optimisation and Management, Stochastic Models and Algorithms, and E-Commerce Fulfillment. His academic and industrial contributions and achievements have been included in Marquis Who's Who in the World, Marquis Who's Who in Science and Engineering.

Index